The

World

Encyclopedia

of

SOCCER

The

World

Encyclopedia

of

SOCCER

MICHAEL L. LaBLANC

and RICHARD HENSHAW

Gale Research Inc.

DETROIT • WASHINGTON D.C. • LONDON

∞™ This book is printed on acid-free paper that meets the minimum requirements of American National Standard for Information Sciences— Permanence Paper for Printed Library Materials, ANSI Z39.48-1984.

Printed in the United States of America
Published simultaneously in the United Kingdom
by Gale Research International Limited
(An Affiliated company of Gale Research Inc.)

ISBN 0-8103-8995-9

10 9 8 7 6 5 4 3 2 1

I(T)P™

The trademark **ITP** is used under license.

STAFF

Michael L. LaBlanc and Richard Henshaw, *Editors*
L. Mpho Mabunda, *Associate Editor*
Marilyn Allen, *Editorial Associate*
Michael J. Tyrkus, *Assistant Editor*

Sonia Benson, Suzanne M. Bourgoin, Nicolet V. Elert, Kevin Hile, Michelle Kaufman, L. Mpho Mabunda, Mary Ruby, Les Stone, Jerrold B. Trecker, Brian Trusdell, *Contributing Editors*

Peter M. Gareffa, *Senior Editor, Contemporary Biographies*
David E. Salamie, *Senior Editor, New Product Development*
Don Wellman, *Senior Copywriter*

Jeanne Gough, *Permissions Manager*
Margaret A. Chamberlain, *Permissions Supervisor (Pictures)*
Pamela A. Hayes, Keith Reed, *Permissions Associates*
Susan Brohman, Arlene Johnson, Barbara A. Wallace, *Permissions Assistants*

Mary Beth Trimper, *Production Director*
Shanna Philpott Heilveil, *Production Assistant*
Cynthia Baldwin, *Art Director*
Mark C. Howell, *Cover Designer*
Kathleen Hourdakis, *Page Designer*

Cover photo by arrangement with The Bettmann Archives

Advisory Board

Paul Kennedy

Paul Kennedy is Managing Editor of *Soccer America* Magazine and is one of the most knowledgeable observers of the sport in the United States.

Les Stone

Les Stone is a free-lance writer on a variety of subjects from classical music to sports, and is an avid soccer fan.

Jerrold B. Trecker

Jerry Trecker, a sports columnist for the *Hartford Courant,* has covered soccer since 1957. He has also done play-by-play and analysis for ESPN and will serve as that network's backgrounder for the 1994 World Cup.

Brian Trusdell

Brian Trusdell has reported on international sports for the Associated Press since 1984, covering the Barcelona Summer Olympics and the World Cup qualifying draw. He has also contributed articles to *Soccer Digest* and its parent publication, *Inside Sports.*

This book is dedicated to the memory of Richard Henshaw

1945-1990

CONTENTS

Copyright by Pressebild Baumann

FOREWORD

NOT A DREAM

November 30, 1991, 7:00 p.m. was the beginning of the best four hours of my life. I remember it all vividly: filled with a patriotism I had never felt before I held my hand over my heart and sang our national anthem with all my strength. I revelled in how much this particular game meant to me and to so many American soccer enthusiasts. It meant more than who was the best team in the world. It meant something to every American even if they never knew. It was a first step for women, then for Americans, then for soccer, and, finally, for eighteen young women, their coaches, parents, and thousands of admiring and devoted fans.

This was the World Cup Final—the first ever Women's Championship! The scene was Tiahne Stadium in Guangzhou, China, where over 60,000 fans, including about 1,000 Americans, witnessed us narrowly defeat Norway 2-1. The game was filled with emotion and passion, with beautiful and sloppy play, with hard play and sportsmanship. But when it was all over, we, the United States, were World Champions!

I'll never forget the exhilaration of standing on the stage immediately following the game. As the medals were placed over our heads I felt both relief and utter disbelief. The pride overwhelmed me and tears fell endlessly down my face. My love for my teammates, my coaches, and my country could not ever be greater. And then a strange thing happened. As I was leaving the stadium I thought to myself, "Is this just a dream?" So I glanced over my shoulder one last time at the scoreboard, hoping it had not changed. It was not a dream.

Nor is it a dream that the 1994 World Cup is coming to the United States. I can't contain my excitement! I'll be the first in line for tickets, outfitted in my soccer attire and on the edge of my seat for all 52 games. For all the pageantry and beauty of the Women's World Cup, it lacked one major ingredient: the rich history and heritage of previous championships.

I grew up following the last several World Cups and found myself idolizing many of its stars: Pelé, Beckenbauer, Platini, Maradona, and Matthaus. I also remember seeing some of them and others in person during the glory years of the North American Soccer League. As an avid Seattle Sounders follower during the 1970s and early 1980s I had the privilege to grow up with and around this beautiful game. I learned about its history, its personalities, and its passion.

Now, you too can learn about the beauty, the art, and the science of soccer. Let *The World Encyclopedia of Soccer* enlighten you about this, the most beautiful game in the world. Whether you are a beginner or a seasoned soccer person, there is no doubt in my mind you'll enjoy reading this treasure of soccer information and insight. Indeed, it is must reading and a great source of reference into the world's game.

Shannon Higgins

Shannon Higgins, chosen as Soccer America's *National Player of the Year in 1988 and 1989, culminated her five-year career with the U.S. Women's National Team with the World Championship victory. She is currently head coach of the George Washington University women's soccer team.*

INTRODUCTION

The sum of any popular sport is more than the game itself. Over time, as simple games played on rough fields or bumpy city streets evolve into professional sports, they develop traditions that celebrate the human drama that gives the game its life: stories of heroic plays, last-minute victories and defeats, disputed calls, humorous and touching anecdotes. The game and its shared traditions symbolize and evoke the best, and the worst, of the human competitive spirit in each of us.

Soccer is unquestionably the world's most popular sport (over 1.5 *billion* viewers tuned in for the 1990 World Cup) and the most colorful, particularly in the level of emotional intensity it evokes in its fans. In 1968 an 18-year-old fan in El Salvador fatally shot herself following a Salvadoran loss to rival Honduras, reportedly because she "could not bear to see [her] fatherland brought to its knees." The Salvadoran president, his ministers, and the national team attended her nationally televised funeral.

Soccer has been banned by kings, decried from the pulpit, blamed for riots, suicides, and heart attacks, and even precipitated a recent full-scale military conflict within the last quarter-century. And yet, with the exception of a few celebrity names—Pelé, Maradona, Beckenbauer—most Americans remain oblivious to the sport on the international level.

Are You Ready for the World?

All that is about to change. When World Cup competition hits America's shores in 1994 the United States will become the focus of worldwide sports attention on a scale most Americans have never imagined. The World Cup is a truly international event, one that has been compared to the Super Bowl, World Series, NBA Finals, and Stanley Cup playoffs all rolled into one and then some. Unfortunately, even many knowledgeable U.S. sports fans will find themselves caught in this global spotlight without a clue.

The World Encyclopedia of Soccer is your key to the Cup and to exciting soccer tournaments worldwide. The *Encyclopedia* opens with a spectator's guide to the 1994 World Cup competition that provides essential background information on the sport and the significance of the World Cup as well as a preview of the competition's scheduled events. Subsequent sections provide detailed narratives on all aspects of the sport, including:

- **A history of the game**
- **The complete rules of the game**
- **An overview of the various strategies and tactics**
- **Informative biographies of the sport's greatest players**
- **Profiles of teams from around the world**
- **Accounts of the great soccer tragedies and disasters**
- **Coverage of international and U.S. soccer associations, leagues, and teams**
- **An exploration of the status of women's soccer**
- **A look at Olympic competition**
- **A glossary of terms *and* concepts**
- **Charts, statistics, photographs, drawings, and diagrams**
- **A reader-friendly index**

And much more, including a sprinkling of informative and entertaining trivia throughout the book, covering topics from ancient Aztec ball games to modern soccer witch doctors. *The World Encyclopedia of Soccer* puts a human face on the sport and provides a wealth of detailed information that will meet the demands of even the most avid fan.

Special Thanks

The publishers wish to acknowledge the special contribution of the late Richard Henshaw, who passed away while revising his ground-breaking 1979 classic, *The Encyclopedia of World Soccer*. Much of the information he prepared, as well as his unique insight and enthusiasm for the sport, has been incorporated into *The World Encyclopedia of Soccer*. We would also like to express our gratitude to his widow, Grace Wong Henshaw, for her cooperation and assistance in the preparation of this book, and to Lauren Fedorko and Diane Schadoff of Book Builders Incorporated.

The

World

Encyclopedia

of

SOCCER

THE WORLD CUP

A SPECTATOR'S GUIDE TO THE 1994 GAMES

Allsport

The World Cup

THE WORLD CUP

When the International Soccer Federation (FIFA) announced that the 1994 World Cup would be played in the United States, a competition that began on a limited basis in 1930 came full circle.

The award of the competition to the U.S.A.— made in Zurich on the Fourth of July 1988— confirmed that the world's most popular game would make a serious attempt to extend its range to the one major world nation which has not made soccer its chief sporting interest.

In a very real sense, the decision to send the 1994 World Cup competition to the United States also signified another major change in the sport's championship. Once a competition limited to the elite soccer-playing nations of the globe, the World Cup has grown steadily during the stewardship of FIFA President Joao Havelange.

A Brazilian, Havelange had won election to the sport's top post in 1974 vowing to take the game worldwide, especially into Africa, Asia, and the sections of America which were still growing in soccer interest.

A World Cup in the United States, following the expansion of the field from 16 to 24 teams and the creation of similar world tournaments for players 17-Under, 20-Under, and 23-Under (the Olympics), confirmed Havelange's desire to make the World Cup a tool for selling his sport as well as determining its champion.

The 1994 tournament in America, although the 15th since the Jules Rimet Trophy was first offered in 1930, will be only the fourth played by a 24-nation field.

It will include the largest ever representation from Africa, which will qualify three countries, and could for the first time showcase three teams from the CONCACAF (Central-North America and the Caribbean) region. The one-time European dominance of the qualifying field is shrinking, as the number of nations playing at a high level increases.

The World Cup itself can take credit for inspiring that leap in participation. Not only does the quadrennial tournament focus the eyes of the world on the competing countries, it also generates massive revenues which can be plowed back into the development of the sport.

In the United States, Cup competition will be staged at nine different sites, with some format changes that promise to take the game to a wide audience. The tournament will open June 17, 1994 in Soldier Field, Chicago and conclude a month later at Pasadena's Rose Bowl.

There will also be matches played in some of the great stadiums of the country: greater Boston's Foxboro Stadium, the Cotton Bowl in Dallas, Giants Stadium in East Rutherford, NJ, the Citrus Bowl in Orlando, Stanford Stadium in

Palo Alto, CA, and Washington's Robert F. Kennedy Stadium. The tournament will also attract worldwide attention because the Pontiac Silverdome (which serves the greater Detroit area) will stage the first-ever indoor World Cup games.

FIFA is hoping that the exposure by the U.S. media, including the fact that the tournament will, for the first time, be completely covered by English language American television, will boost the game's image and secure its future in North America. That is one aim of the 1994 championship, but only one.

Source of National Pride

There is also the matter of the national pride and satisfaction that this world event generates. When Cameroon reached the 1990 World Cup quarterfinals, all of Black Africa rejoiced in the achievement. Victories by Costa Rica over European powers Scotland and Sweden set off spontaneous celebrations in the streets of San Jose.

And workers have reported bleary-eyed to their jobs all over Asia since the tournament became a worldwide television spectacular. For sports-mad Australians, Chinese, Japanese and Koreans, that has meant World Cup games in the wee-hours of the morning, something that might change in the next century when the Asians are expected to host their first finals.

How has this event managed to gain its grip on the world imagination? Quite simply, soccer's World Cup is the ultimate world championship event, combining the elements which define all successful sports promotions: It is a tournament for the best players in the world; it matches nation against nation, continent against continent over a five-week competition; it contains the sudden-death element of all knockout tournaments with upsets always possible; and, it

features a simple game, one easily understood and passionately followed by most of the people of the globe.

It wasn't always that way, of course. When the World Cup began in 1930 only 13 nations took part. There was no lengthy qualifying process and many of the players were amateurs. Today, more nations chase a place in the World Cup finals than belong to the United Nations, and all of the top players are fully professional.

The World Cup has become the pinnacle for players and national teams. Even those athletes whose club salaries are calculated in the millions of dollars and whose achievements include every major club trophy are lured by the challenge and rewards for the competition.

The World Cup Format

To understand what the World Cup is, we have to understand the way it is structured and organized. Start with the competitors themselves. The World Cup brings together 24 national teams, each made up of 22 players.

Players are eligible to play for the country of their birth or naturalization or their parents' birth. Play is arduous. Qualifying for the World Cup finals may mean surviving a series of elimination matches stretching over 18 months, with high-pressure games fitted into an already-jammed calendar of important club matches.

It would be like asking an American football player to play an additional, vitally important game every fourth Wednesday throughout the National Football League season. While concentrating on taking his own club to the Super Bowl, this player would also have to fit into another team pursuing qualifying competition for another, nationally significant event. It is easy to see the magnitude of the physical and psychological demands on the players.

The national teams that compete for the World Cup have full-time managers, men whose jobs may be the most difficult in all of sport. Not only does the national team boss have the responsibility of selecting his players, he also has the job of creating a team. That can often lead to decisions which provoke the barbs of journalists and the anger of fans.

The kinds of arguments that fuel our "hot-stove leagues" are common in world soccer where a national team manager must decide whether to pick one great player over another or, in some cases, elect to play two stars with similar attributes together on the same team.

A True World Event

Add in the fact that national teams reflect the personality and style of their nations and you have the second element that makes a World Cup special. There is no one way to play soccer. Instead, the game has taken on different characteristics in different climates.

The European game tends to be played at a higher speed than the Equatorial game; the Latins are often more adept at individual ball skills developed on dry, hard fields than are their northern counterparts who regularly play half a season in windy, rain-lashed conditions.

Similarly, each region's spectators create their own atmosphere. A typical European spectator appreciates the hard-running, fully-committed attitude beloved by Americans. African or Latin American fans are more apt to applaud a subtle bit of individualism than all-out effort.

The World Cup, naturally, offers that contrast in styles. Can the individualistic Brazilians, with their backs who play like wingers and their midfielders who sometimes spend as much time in front of goal as European strikers, defeat the tightly-organized defenses woven together by

the managers of Germany and Italy? Can the quicksilver dribbling skills of a Cameroon winger be negated by the zone tactics of European defenses? What rewards for artistry? What price organization?

Today, those issues are not just hotly-debated for the five-week period when the World Cup is played but throughout the two-year period when qualifying takes place. The road to the finals costs managers jobs and players their reputations and may even lead nations to reassess the way they coach and teach the game.

Victory is often seen as reaffirmation of national ideas, while defeat may be the spur to major change. League schedules may be realigned and competitions deferred in order to prepare the national team for its ultimate challenge.

It is hard to imagine that the originators of that 1930 competition could have foreseen today's global giant. Granted, international soccer was already more than a half-century old when those 13 teams gathered in Montevideo to play for the first World Cup, but the most important soccer-playing nations, including Austria, England, Germany, Italy, and Scotland, didn't even bother to attend.

The British had been competing against each other since 1872 and perceived the newly-created World Cup as something less than a major event. There was also a dispute within FIFA about part-time payments to amateur players who took part in the Olympics.

Internationalizing the Sport

Indeed, the creation of the World Cup was a deliberate attempt on the part of FIFA, backed by the growing power of continental Europe's soccer-playing nations, to wrest world control of the game from British grasp. The Britons not only had begun the game and spread it worldwide during the heyday of their Empire, they had also retained control over the playing rules and the standard of international play. It was widely conceded that England was the best at playing the game—although it could by no means claim an older pedigree than neighboring Scotland—and visiting European sides routinely met defeat when they played in London or at other British sites.

Nevertheless, there was a rapidly-growing constituency that viewed the matter quite differently. South America, still geographically isolated from Europe in the days before rapid travel, was developing its own breed of players. This was particularly true of Argentina, Brazil, and Uruguay. The World Cup would serve as the stage for these new—and stylistically different—giants of the game.

On the European Continent, Austria, Germany, and Italy were also taking soccer seriously. The passion with which Italians approach the sport today may have been nurtured in the 1930s, when Benito Mussolini spared no expense to help Italy win two World Cups, including the 1938 event on Italian soil. Obviously there were political gains to be made from supporting a nationalistic game that could serve to validate policies of revolutionary governments.

This was a lesson well-learned by the Communists a generation later. They would also see achievement in world sport as a means of generating support for their own regimes, although Olympic soccer success, rather than World Cup wins, became their avenue.

Early Italian Dominance

The first three World Cups produced two winners, Uruguay and Italy, and established some precedents for later tournaments. The public response to the event in Uruguay (1930), Italy (1934), and France (1938), proved that soccer could capture the imagination with a well-presented international event.

The Olympics continued to be regarded as a major soccer championship during this period, but FIFA's new championship was steadily making inroads. British teams still stayed away, but the world was introduced to new stars and several legends were created.

The Italians revered Silvio Piola, still thought by many to be the greatest center forward ever produced by his country, and coach Vittorio Pozzo rivalled the Austrian Hugo Meisl, who had built a great national team, as the master coach of Europe.

The first questions about defining nationality also arose, as Italy used three Argentines of Italian parentage, but the back-to-back victories by the *Azzurri* convinced most observers that they were, indeed, kings of the sport on the eve of World War II.

South America was also now seen as a producer of great individuals, the Brazilian forward Leônidas, nicknamed the Black Diamond, emerging from a 6-5 victory over Poland as a hero of the 1938 tournament in France.

But there were also clashes in styles that turned physical in nature and raised the first questions about the problems of international games matching teams from different continents. That is a debating point still alive today.

The Second Era

After the interruption caused by World War II, the World Cup returned to center stage in 1950 to begin its second era. It featured a remarkable result in the 1950 final and the first truly unbelievable upset in soccer history.

Brazil was the scene of that World Cup, the giant Maracana Stadium readied to host crowds of 200,000 for the greatest sporting spectacular in history. The host country was widely expected to win the trophy but fell to Uruguay, 2-1 in the final.

England, too, emerged from its isolation and entered the championship. This was the era of great individual English players like Stanley Matthews, later knighted for his services to the sport, and some in the soccer world eagerly anticipated an English march through the opposition.

Instead, a stunned global soccer populace learned that the great England team had been beaten 1-0 by the United States in remote Belo Horizonte. It is reported that the scoreline was so unbelievable that many journalists waited for the corrected version that never came.

What both Brazil and England had learned was to become a part of World Cup lore: nothing was guaranteed in a game where playing conditions, the role of the crowd, and the vagaries of fortune all come into play. The competitors were taking the World Cup seriously; it was simply not possible just to show up and win.

For America that triumph meant nothing at all. This was an era in the United States when sports fans were absorbed in the New York Yankees-Brooklyn Dodgers rivalry, when college football was becoming a national sport, and new professional games like basketball were starting to gain a foothold.

The U.S. win on a goal scored by the Haitian Larry Gaetjens passed without comment, and soccer gained no benefit as a U.S. sport. Indeed, it would be 40 years before another American team even qualified for a World Cup finals, 40 years during which the tournament itself would undergo a remarkable transformation.

The Magic Magyars

The 1954 competition was staged in Switzerland, home of FIFA, and the tournament once again produced an upset of incredible proportions. The games began with the expectation of Hungarian victory by the Magic Magyars, the team that had captured the world's imagination with a pair of stunning victories over England.

Hungary had been the first team ever to defeat the English on British soil, scoring a 6-3 triumph in 1953, a match that shocked the English out of their complacency and gave renewed credence to the notion that the World Cup, not the British Home International Championship (a tournament involving England, Northern Ireland, Scotland, and Wales) was the real prize.

When Hungary repeated that triumph in Budapest five months later (by the score 7-1) there was a widespread belief that nothing could deny them the Jules Rimet trophy, a concept furthered by their march through the opening phase of the tournament.

Led by Ferenc Puskas, Nandor Hidegkuti, and Sandor Kocsis the Hungarians hammered opponents like South Korea, 9-0, and even West Germany, 8-3.

All that hope caved in on the day of the final when West Germany took the trophy on a goal by Helmut Rahn, manager Sepp Herberger having won the psychological battle of wits. The Germans had fielded reserves in the earlier rounds and seemed more rested by the final.

Germany, a nation devastated by war and now divided in two, had pulled off the impossible and established itself as the new power of European soccer. Since that triumph, the Germans have been the most consistent of all European entries, winning the trophy twice more and appearing in three other finals.

Hungary, for its part, never again attained such acclaim. The great team was broken up by revolution and fate. Its top players were out of the country when Soviet tanks rolled into Budapest to crush a popular uprising in 1956 and many of the Hungarian stars chose political asylum in Spain rather than return to their Communist homeland. Puskas achieved European Cup greatness with Real Madrid, and Hungarian soccer had to be content with occasional Olympic achievement.

If 1954 was a case of one set of stars eclipsed by the unexpected, the next World Cup, held in Sweden, would be the making of the modern game. It served to introduce the man whose face and physique became synonymous with the game he played: Pelé.

The Reign of Pelé

Pelé burst onto the world consciousness in Stockholm as a 17-year-old, scoring twice in a final that saw Brazil defeat the host nation 5-2, ushering in an era of Brazilian dominance.

Pelé would play in four different World Cup finals and lift the trophy three times as Brazil not only captured the imagination of fans the world over but also retired the original Jules Rimet Trophy after their 1970 victory in Mexico. But for injuries to key players, including Pelé, Brazil might also have been a finalist in 1966, the only interruption in their marvelous spell atop the world game.

It was not just Pelé, whose radiant smile communicated his obvious joy in the game, but the manner in which the Brazilians won that endeared them to the fans and helped turn soccer from a sport to an entertainment. The promise seen in Leônidas a quarter-century before was now revealed as distinctly Brazilian, a commitment to artistry and invention.

Pelé scored more than one thousand goals during his grand career, not only because he had the ability to finish his chances but because he thought of plays that others could not imagine. Like Wayne Gretzky in ice hockey, he saw the options available on every play. Like Gretzky, too, Pelé was the supreme passer as well as goal-scorer, a player who lifted his teammates to superb performance. And, again like Gretzky, he proved a perfect ambassador for his sport.

While Pelé and his Brazilians won in 1958 and again in Chile in 1962, it was not until 1970 that the full impact of the Brazilian influence was felt worldwide. That was because the 1966 finals held in England, and won by the host country, were the first of the modern technological age.

Transformed by Television

When Brazil won in Stockholm and Santiago the world could not watch on live television; radio descriptions and the written word were soccer's ambassadors. In 1966, however, the satellite revolution had begun. England's controversial extra time victory over West Germany was seen live by a world audience and even watched the same day in the United States.

The advent of big-time television coverage was to change FIFA and the World Cup profoundly. While much of the world still followed that English World Cup through radio or their news

papers and magazines, the massive audience for the finals was so impressive that even the United States took notice.

Immediately after the conclusion of Cup competition two professional leagues were formed and the game at last achieved a foothold, however tenuous, on American soil. What was to evolve into the North American Soccer League was a direct result of that Wembley crowd in

1966, its enthusiasm and emotion at the final transmitted through the small screen.

Mexico 1970

By 1970, television linked the world to the Mexican World Cup, a tournament marketed for television with European prime-time viewers in mind. Games were scheduled so as to attract the maximum audience and even Americans were lured to the matches on closed-circuit television.

And because Brazil, England, Italy, and West Germany all were near the peak of their powers, the tournament produced exquisite games, some of the classics of the modern age. Because they were seen around the world, they pushed the sport and its great championship tournament to an extraordinary level.

Three games stand out from that event. The first round Guadalajara clash between Brazil and England, old champions and new, star-studded and star-crossed, will be remembered for Gordon Banks' miraculous save of a Pelé header and the Jairzinho goal that decided the game in Brazil's favor.

It is also worth noting that New York City's Madison Square Garden, then still fresh from its reopening on 33rd Street, was sold out, a 20,000-plus audience watching the television pictures from Mexico and a delirious Brazilian crowd spilling onto the neighboring streets to celebrate victory that Sunday afternoon. It was something New Yorkers and other Americans had never seen.

Then there was the tournament's apex, a pulsating overtime game between Italy and West Germany that saw five goals scored in the extra 30 minutes as the Italians prevailed 4-3 in the huge Aztec Stadium. Brazil, meanwhile, had marched unbeaten through the tournament, its attack fueled by Pelé, Jairzinho, Tostao, Rivelino,

and Gerson, its defense anchored by Carlos Alberto, and the whole orchestrated by Mario Zagalo, who would become the first man to win a World Cup as both player and manager.

The final in Mexico City was Pelé's last triumph on the World Cup stage, a 4-1 victory that made Brazil the undisputed masters of the game and gave the sport an image that still persists.

Pelé's opening goal that afternoon, celebrated by the great man's leap into the arms of a teammate, fist raised high in triumph, is the single most recognizable soccer image for Americans because it became the signature of ABC-TV's *Wide World of Sports* opening.

For two decades Pelé's soaring joy was seen in millions of households; Pelé finished his club career with the New York Cosmos and went on to become a persuasive spokesman for a greater American presence in the game.

Sven Simon

Pelé celebrates his goal against Italy in the 1970 World Cup final with teammate Jairzinho.

But there were other heroes as the game evolved between 1958 and 1970. Pelé's great teammate, Garrincha, the little winger who captivated audiences with his penetrating dribbles and who inspired the 1962 triumph in Chile when Pelé was injured, was another of the super Brazilians.

So was the calm, efficient Carlos Alberto, whose upright, visionary style of defensive play would help to define the game at the back. There was the midfielder Gerson, spraying passes in all directions, and the speedy, powerful Jairzinho who scored in every game in Mexico to establish an unbeatable record.

The Pride of Britain

Set against those Brazilians—all pace, invention, and ideas—were the qualities that England's 1966 champions brought to the game. Managed by Alf Ramsey, who decided that old-time playing styles were no longer relevant in the changing game, England built its side around the elegance of Bobby Charlton and the sagacity of Bobby Moore. Both players exuded what the world had come to define as "English gentlemanly behavior" in an era when the Beatles were redefining pop music and British fashion was sweeping the pop world.

Charlton, whose devastating shots were already legendary at Manchester United, had survived the Munich disaster of 1958, in which many of that great United team were killed in an air crash. His ability to hold together the United side and carry his own skills to the highest level for club and country made him a figure loved throughout the British Isles. He did it all with a kind of common man's touch, too.

Moore, elegant and cool in his defender's role, was the antithesis of the flashy players, almost the archetypal Englishman-with-the-umbrella at a time when such stereotypes were viewed favorably in Britain.

F.Y.I.

Broadcasting

The first radio broadcast of a soccer game was of a first division match between Arsenal and Sheffield United on January 22, 1927, from Highbury, London.

The first television transmission was an extract of the 1937 F.A. Cup Final between Preston North End and Sunderland from Wembley Stadium, London.

To date, some national leagues, including those of Great Britain, do not permit complete, live coverage of league or cup matches, since league administrators fear that a loss of box office receipts would result. The British Broadcasting Corporation, for example, can only transmit edited 57-minute versions of a given match at some time after the match is completed.

In contrast, in the United States, the leagues have vigorously sought to gain air time in an effort to gather revenues from lucrative contracts. Latin American leagues have vacillated despite the central position radio and television broadcasts have played in the lives of supporters.

What made Moore special was that element all great players possess, the ability to set the action to his own pace and always to have the time necessary to complete his ideas. He inspired his team as captain and won the world's admiration for his ability to rise to the very top of his profession without the slightest bit of ostentation.

Moore's counterpart was Franz Beckenbauer, a young West German who came into the 1966 World Cup and emerged in 1974 as captain of the winning nation from a position he himself defined, that of *libero* or free-back. Beckenbauer play was influenced by the style created by Moore and Carlos Alberto, a defender-leader of both style and substance.

Not only did Beckenbauer captain the team,, he also played the role of attack leader when the opportunity appeared; he was skillful enough to play as a front-runner, secure enough to know exactly when to leave his position as central defender and blend into the attack. By such moves, Beckenbauer added the extra man that unbalanced opposing defenses and helped to alter the game.

"Total Football"

The 1974 tournament was won by West Germany, but it was equally notable for the emergence of Holland and for a new concept of play that was to dominate the next 20 years. The press dubbed it "Total Football," and its architects were Stefan Kovacs and Rinus Michels, who had created Europe's top club side of the day, Ajax Amsterdam.

One of the world's great players, Johan Cruyff, had a host of talented teammates to make it all work. Holland finished as runner-up in both 1974 and 1978, once with Cruyff at the controls, once without him, but their influence on the game was greater than the performance on the field.

Total Football, simply put, was a redefinition of the individual player's role. Where he once was strictly an attacker if a forward, a playmaker-defender if in midfield, and a defender if a back, under the new direction, every player became an interchangeable part of a machine that changed continuously.

The nickname "Clockwork Orange" (after Anthony Burgess's novel of the day and the bright Dutch shirts) was applied to patterns that saw Dutch fullbacks turning into wingers, midfielders into center backs, and even strikers into *liberos*.

Initially, teams were overcome by the versatility of the Dutch and the sides that copied their style of play. The memorable way in which Holland disposed of Uruguay in the first round, then Argentina and Brazil in the second phase, seemed to argue for the Europeans' greater physical strength and overall speed.

What it demonstrated was the fact that Holland—and those who imitated them—had managed to combine their physical abilities with a quickly-sprung offside trap to catch the more leisurely, ball-control oriented Latin sides unawares.

The response was quick enough. Argentina actually beat Holland at its own game in the 1978 final, although their 3-1 overtime victory was not a totally accurate reflection of the day's play. Even the Brazilians discovered that it was necessary to add more muscle to their style.

At the same time that the game was changing on the field-players becoming quicker, fitter, and more adaptable—the World Cup was also changing in another arena. Because of growing interest around the world, spurred by the Havelange-led desire to take the game to new areas, there was pressure to enlarge the World Cup format.

Resistance, of course, came from the old-line nations who argued that it didn't make sense to add "outsiders" to a tournament until they had proved themselves on the field. Havelange and FIFA won the day in time for the 1982 event, when the action on the field proved the reformers correct.

Cup Format Expanded

The Spanish World Cup was the first to encompass 24 teams. It was bulky, to be sure, and the format required alterations in time for 1986, but the addition of African nations certainly caused an immediate stir. Cameroon played three matches, drew them all, including one against eventual champion Italy, and went home with honor.

Algeria did even better, defeating West Germany in a memorable upset and then claiming that its elimination was "engineered" by collusion between the Germans and their Austrian neighbors in the final game of the first round. Algeria had played the day before, so both Austria and Germany knew exactly what was required to get themselves into the next phase. When those countries played out a sterile draw while angry Algerians waved money in the stands, FIFA decreed that in future all decisive group matches would kick off at the same time.

The expansion of the tournament wasn't an unqualified success, however. Hungary smashed a hapless El Salvador side 10-1 in the first round, and the Kuwaitis caused a stir when a team representative tried to order his players off the field in a controversial game against France.

The expanded Cup format, with more games and a longer schedule, threatened to become too bulky to handle, with the second round, like the first, based on group competition rather than a straight knockout.

What the tournament lost in early round drama was regained by the theatrical conclusion. A talented Brazilian team, widely expected to win the trophy based on its first round performance, was upset by Italy in the second stage, as a "morality play" developed on the field.

Not only were the Italians staging a boycott of their own sometimes hyper-critical press corps, but their ace player, Paolo Rossi, had just resumed playing after serving a suspension for a home-based scandal that had scarred the national game.

Veteran goalkeeper Dino Zoff, too, was struggling for personal redemption, having been roundly criticized for allowing the Dutch to hit long-range shots past him in the 1978 competition. Zoff proved not only that he was still in his prime, but he had the ultimate pleasure of accepting the World Cup trophy after Italy beat West Germany in the Madrid final.

Rossi had come through to lead the tournament in scoring after he'd personally eliminated Brazil with a three-goal performance. And there was poetic justice in the West German defeat, many said, after their performance against the Austrians and their defeat at the hands of Algeria.

The next World Cup had been scheduled for Colombia, but the increase in size to 24 teams, coupled with the ever-increasing cost of staging the tournament, led that country to return the rights to FIFA.

The United States made a bid to host the 1986 event, with Beckenbauer, Pelé, and former U.S. Secretary of State Henry Kissinger advancing the American cause, but FIFA turned to Mexico, a previous host and a country with both the stadia and the soccer tradition to stage the tournament. It proved an inspired selection.

Not only did Mexico put on a brilliant tournament, the 1986 event proved the occasion for another world star to emerge from the shadow of promise into the full glare of the spotlight. The 1986 World Cup belonged ultimately to Diego Maradona.

Maradona

Few players had arrived on the international scene with the burden of expectations that accompanied Maradona. He had gone from a poverty-stricken background to instant fame in his home country, first as a youth player, then as a bona fide star with one of the nation's revered clubs, Boca Juniors.

Maradona, however, was not picked for the 1978 World Cup. Argentine boss Cesar Luis Menotti thought the pressure of playing at home would be too much for the 17-year old. Although Maradona was included in the 40-man pre-finals roster, Menotti elected to leave him out of the 22-man squad that won the trophy in Buenos Aires.

Maradona thus began his World Cup career in Spain in 1982, a situation made even more difficult because he had just concluded a big-money transfer with Barcelona. Argentina was playing its games in the city where Maradona was expected to lead his new club to European glory, a prospect that had the Catalonians anticipating triumphs over the hated rivals, Real Madrid.

Allsport

Maradona scores his world-famous "Hand of God" goal in the 1986 Mexico City World Cup.

The storybook tale never happened. Maradona's Argentina did not find the blend and was beaten in the opening game of the 1982 tournament. Argentina eventually crashed out in the second round with losses to both Brazil and Italy. Maradona was ejected from his final 1982 World Cup match. His tenure at Barcelona was also truncated. Before his great 1986 tournament he had already been sold to Napoli of the Italian League in another big-money deal.

"The Hand of God"

In Mexico, Argentina seized the initiative as Maradona struck top form. He also achieved international notoriety when he fisted in a goal against England in the quarterfinal and produced the famous "hand of God" explanation for the score.

In that same game Maradona also produced one of the great goals of all World Cups, weaving past defenders on a 50-meter dash before tucking the ball into the net.

There was magic, too, in the semifinal win over Belgium and, although Maradona was closely marked in the final by West Germany, it was one of his passes that released Jorge Burruchaga on the run for the winning goal. At the finish everyone saluted Argentina and its star. The Aztec Stadium had a real hero to cheer.

By now the World Cup was also getting greater attention in America. Both the 1982 and 1986 tournaments had been televised in the United States. All of the games were telecast on the Spanish-language television network, and many were carried by PBS or the networks.

ABC televised the Madrid final live and NBC shared coverage from Mexico with the growing sports programming cable network, ESPN.

Newspaper coverage of the event was increasing, too, so the feats of Maradona received attention even in a nation which still thought that football meant the NFL.

Italia '90

The 1990 tournament took on added significance for both FIFA and the Americans after the decision to award the 1994 Cup to the United States was made. Now it became important that the U.S. team qualified for the finals, not only because of the added publicity that would accrue to the Italia '90 competition, but also because the International Federation was under pressure to demonstrate that Americans took the sport seriously.

Fortunately, because of the brief success enjoyed by the NASL, there was emerging talent in the United States that could, finally, make it to the final stages.

The Americans had been attempting qualification all along, but most efforts had foundered against the Mexicans. When it seemed that the United States might have the players capable of qualification for the 1986 event, a defeat against Costa Rica brought an abrupt end to the adventure. In the 1990 qualifying round, the agony was prolonged until the final game, when a Paul Caligiuri goal in Port of Spain, Trinidad, finally earned the Americans a passport to the finals.

The results in Italy were less than glorious, both for the United States and the World Cup. The American team lost all three of its first round matches, but did get some praise for a 1-0 defeat against the host nation in Rome's Olympic Stadium.

Overall though, the tournament failed to come to life because the changes in the game that had begun with Total Football now seemed to stifle creativity in favor of a heavily physical approach.

An unsatisfactory tournament ended with a 1-0 West German win over Argentina in a repeat of the 1986 final, but spectators and administrators alike left Italy with the sense that changes had to come for 1994.

Those changes are already underway. FIFA initiated several rules modifications to return the attacking balance to a sport where the ever-better defenders had gained too much an edge. Deliberate fouls are now punished with automatic ejection; offside is now harder to manipulate by defensive teams; and goalkeepers' movements outside the goal area have been limited.

The result has been an increase in the use of a more offense-oriented strategy in leagues around the world and the prospect of a more wide-open style of play, which should make the 1994 tournament more entertaining, action-packed, and appealing to American TV audiences.

Questions Remain

There are other questions about 1994, however. Foremost is whether the Europeans can win the world's top soccer trophy somewhere other than on their own soil.

Although Europe and South America have evenly split the 14 previous competitions, only Brazil has ever won outside its own hemisphere, with that 1958 Swedish triumph that first revolutionized interest in the tournament.

There are also the very real questions about America's ability to stage and support the event. On the positive side is the fact that no country has as many ethnic groups as the United States. Almost every visiting nation can expect a warm welcome, and the fact that every team will have its own coterie of "home fans" will make this World Cup unique.

But the negative side is that the American sports fans are not soccer followers or soccer knowledgeable. Neither is the U.S. sports media. No one can expect that soccer will push baseball off the front of the sports page in June and July of 1994. Indeed, the early games in the 1994 competition will be more important than ever, for they may well establish both the tone of the tournament and the response of the American media and its public.

What isn't in question is the fact that the World Cup has grown into a mega-event with sponsorship, television and national prestige all wrapped into one package. There is more pressure on players and teams than ever before, but that also translates into greater opportunity.

The World Cup now creates reputations and future salaries as the rich soccer clubs line up to sign the emerging stars from Africa and Asia as well as the established nations of the soccer world.

In 1930 the World Cup challenged the old order in the form of Britain's control of the game. In the era immediately after the Second World War, the same competition became the vehicle for Brazil to prove its mastery of the game. Next came the great European age as the game evolved into a physically demanding spectacular that could be packaged for billions.

What 1994 could offer is the preview of a new age, one that brings America into the soccer fold and extends the range of the game and its championship. The 1998 event is already set for France, but the first World Cup of the 21st Century will likely take place in Asia, as the FIFA soccer revolution continues full steam into the next age.

1994 WORLD CUP SCHEDULE

CITY	LOCATION	DATES
BOSTON	FOXBORO STADIUM	JUNE 21, 23, 25, 30, JULY 5
CHICAGO	SOLDIER FIELD	JUNE 17, 21, 26, 27, JULY 2
DALLAS	COTTON BOWL	JUNE 17, 21, 27, 30, JULY 3
DETROIT	PONTIAC SILVERDOME	JUNE 18, 22, 24, 28
LOS ANGELES	ROSE BOWL	JUNE 18, 19, 22, 26, JULY 3
NEW YORK/NEW JERSEY	GIANTS STADIUM	JUNE 18, 23, 25, 28, JULY 5
ORLANDO	CITRUS BOWL	JUNE 19, 24, 25, 29, JULY 4
SAN FRANCISCO	STANFORD STADIUM	JUNE 20, 24, 26, 28, JULY 4
WASHINGTON, D.C.	RFK STADIUM	JUNE 19, 20, 28, 29, JULY 2

F.Y.I.

When the World Cup comes to Detroit's Pontiac Silverdome on June 18, 1994, it will mark the first time that Cup competition will be played in an indoor stadium. Since soccer on the international level is played on natural turf, Silverdome officials were faced with the dilemma of making grass grow indoors. Previous attemps dating back to the Houston Astrodome in the 1960s had been unsuccessful. The problem: indoor stadiums, even those equipped with translucent domes, don't allow enough light in to support the growth of healthy grass. The solution: researchers at Michigan State University devised a system of interlocking hexagonal trays, each seven and a half feet wide and filled with six inches of topsoil, to serve as a portable, living playing surface. The grass is grown outdoors, treated with special nutrients to strengthen it, and then the 3,500-pound trays are marked and reassembled inside the stadium. Each tray (1988 in all) rests three inches above the Silverdome's cement floor to allow drainage and requires only watering and mowing for the two-week duration of competition. The system proved successful during the 1993 U.S. Cup games, with players reporting that they didn't encounter any problems with the movable turf. Following the completion of the U.S. Cup, the trays were moved into the Silverdome's parking lot, where they were reassembled to await the 1994 World Cup showdown.

WORLD CUP RESULTS

YEAR	SITE	WINNER	RUNNER-UP
1930	URUGUAY	URUGUAY	ARGENTINA
1934	ITALY	ITALY	CZECHOSLOVAKIA
1938	FRANCE	ITALY	HUNGARY
1950	BRAZIL	URUGUAY	BRAZIL
1954	SWITZERLAND	WEST GERMANY	HUNGARY
1958	SWEDEN	BRAZIL	SWEDEN
1962	CHILE	BRAZIL	CZECHOSLOVAKIA
1966	ENGLAND	ENGLAND	WEST GERMANY
1970	MEXICO	BRAZIL	ITALY
1974	WEST GERMANY	WEST GERMANY	THE NETHERLANDS
1978	ARGENTINA	ARGENTINA	THE NETHERLANDS
1982	SPAIN	ITALY	WEST GERMANY
1986	MEXICO	ARGENTINA	WEST GERMANY
1990	ITALY	WEST GERMANY	ARGENTINA

Note: No competition was held in 1942 or 1946 due to World War II.

1: THE HISTORY OF SOCCER

Tracing the history of basketball is easy. Go back to Springfield, Massachusetts, with Dr. James Naismith in 1891 and you'll find him nailing his memorable janitor-provided peach baskets to the walls of the local YMCA.

To find out when or where baseball began is a little more muddled. Credit usually goes to either Alexander Cartwright in 1845 and/or the more famous Abner Doubleday in 1839. And then there's the New Yorkers and New Jerseyans who argue where the first game was played, Cooperstown, New York, or Hoboken, New Jersey.

But for real muddle, you can't beat the game of soccer. The Chinese, Japanese, Greeks, Romans, Egyptians and the Anglos and Saxons, kicking about the head of a Danish Viking conqueror, all have laid a claim to the ancient origins of the game.

With names from *tsu chu* to *kemari* to *harpastum* to *espiskyros* (or *espikiros)* to "mob football," all bear some resemblance to the game we know today—if by the mere use of the foot to propel a round object at some time during the "contest."

However, the sport hundreds of millions of people around the world play and even its name of "soccer" is generally accepted to have begun in England. Despite all the various forms of its predecessors, soccer has changed little since those days in the mid-19th century.

Roots of the Game

The earliest recorded form of the game dates back as far 1697 B.C. in ancient China, where an emperor named Huang-Ti is said to have invented *tsu chu* (or *tsu-chu), tsu* referring to kicking, and *chu* referring to a ball of animal hide that was stuffed with cork and animal hair. Pictures from the era show a strong resemblance to today's game, with participants apparently trying to kick the ball through two bamboo posts.

Military manuals dating from the Han Dynasty include a physical education regimen specifying the playing of *tsu chu,* but a version that was described as a game played with a leather ball filled with hair and feathers. The object, according to the manual, was to kick the ball through a goal 30-40 centimeters (approximately 2-3 feet) wide, consisting of a net affixed to long bamboo poles.

Another version of the game appeared a bit rougher, with the player using his feet, chest, back and shoulders while warding off opponents. One report dated to 80 B.C. tells of a game where the bamboo poles were 30 or more feet high with players alternating attempts to kick the ball through the posts.

Japanese *Kemari*

The Japanese played a similar game called *kemari* at about the same time, although there are those who pinpoint the date to around 500-600 B.C. (what's a thousand years or so?) The rules of *tsu chu* and *kemari* were apparently similar enough that teams from the two areas were able to play against one another.

But *kemari,* played in a circle, supposedly was a more ceremonial game, not as competitive as *tsu chu.* Historical reports say there was no sign of a struggle for the ball, as in the Chinese game, but one where the players had to pass it to one another in a small space without it touching the ground.

Another soccer-type game that pre-dates Christ is *koura,* played by the Moslem Berbers in the seventh century B.C. in northern Africa. The game apparently revolved around a fertility rite that was played as a way of inducing better crop yields.

The problem linking these games to the modern version is that they have appeared to have died out, with little if any evidence showing them to have been exported to Europe, and particularly England, where the game was codified.

Balls found in the tombs of Egyptian pharaohs along with drawings on the walls of the tombs suggest that they also had a hand in the game.

A woodcut depicting the ancient Japanese game Kemari, which resembled modern soccer.

Greek Connection

Whether the game was transferred across the Mediterranean is unknown. But the ancient Greeks, known for athletic competitions such as the Olympics, might be considered the originators of the game we know today. A game they called *espiskyros* was played on a ground marked by boundary lines and included both kicking and throwing elements.

It is believed that game was adopted, or stolen, by the Romans, who added their own special twist. Two games were said to have developed, one being *follis,* which used a large ball filled with hair tossed into the air and where the object was to keep it aloft by using the hands.

Another, *harpastum,* used a smaller ball that was tossed back and forth among participants, and opponents tried to intercept it or tackle (in the NFL sense of the word) the person with it. Also marked by boundary lines and a center line, the object of *harpastum* was to get the ball over the opponents' line.

In essence, it was a much rougher version than the Greeks preferred. Apparently though, in neither game was the objective to kick the ball into a goal.

Game Moved North

In ancient Florence (you can see the game moving north), residents there played a game called *calcio,* employing 27 players on a side and one ball where the objective was to throw, kick or carry the ball over the goal, that is get it there any way you could. Similar versions of this later would reappear in England under the title of mob football, which was something like a semi-organized riot.

Whether known as *calcio* or *harpastum,* the game was apparently very popular among the

Roman legionnaires, who, it is assumed, took their recreational activity with them when occupying the empire, including the British Isles.

Here is where one can choose on which path he or she likes to take this little tale. One account says the English observed their Roman invaders kicking about a head severed from one of their conquered foes. From this, they inflated the bladder of an animal and, using the streets for a playing field, football (soccer) was born.

Then, of course, there is the story that in 217 A.D., residents of Derby, England, used the skulls of their Roman conquerors as a ball to kick around. Because of a rivalry at one form of the game or another between two church parishes in Derby—St. Peter's and All Saints—the town's name (pronounced Darby) would become synonymous with any regional rivalry in soccer.

The Internazionale-AC Milan derby, for instance, is at least a twice-annual affair in the city of Milan, Italy, that pits two of the Italian first division's most famous and perennial powerhouse clubs at each others throats.

Used Human Heads

But there are even more legends about the use of a human head for a ball. One has it that in the 10th century at Kingston-on-Thames, near London, residents who were celebrating victory over a band of Danish marauders decapitated the Viking captain and used his head for their game.

Another, from 1050, says a group of workmen digging in a battlefield came across the skull of a Dane, and, since Scandinavians weren't very popular in England at the time, began to kick it around and aim it at targets.

While evidence suggests the Romans may have brought the game to the British Isles, some believe the early forms of the sport were present before the Romans appeared.

Similar to the Berber game of *koura,* the British were playing a game associated with Shrove Tuesday—the day before the start of Lent on the Christian calendar—to bring about a bountiful harvest. The ball, the head of a sacrificed animal and representing the sun, was ceremoniously kicked about in a game between competing villages with the victor winning the right to bury the poor beast's noggin in their own fields.

Other accounts say the head had to be kicked about the field to fertilize the field and, thus, had to be protected from anyone who would take it away.

In 1175, a monk by the name of William Fitzstephen described a game played by youths on Shrove Tuesday outside London called, in Latin, *ludus pilae:* a game of ball. His description indicates a well-ordered event, absent of violence, but no details of the game's rules.

Mob Football

But somewhere over the next couple of centuries, the game lost its orderly way. By the 1300s, mayhem was more indigenous than kicking a ball. Having moved into the streets, the game regularly produced injuries and destroyed property, most notably homes and storefronts. Played on an ad hoc field, i.e. the streets, the object was to get the ball into the goal by *any* means possible.

Things got so bad that in 1314, King Edward II decreed imprisonment for anyone playing the game. Edward II's proclamation made special note of the "great noise in the city caused by the hustling over large balls."

The royal harrumph seemed to do little to diminish the game's popularity. By 1331, Edward III

declared similar measures to try to quell the game. At the same time the authorities in France were attempting to suppress what has now become known as the period of mob football.

Part of Edward III's problem was not only the mayhem but the fact that his soldiers had grown so fond of the game it was taking time away from their practice of archery, the state-of-the-art military technology and a requirement for the Hundred Years War against France from 1338 to 1453. King Edward declared: "It is forbidden, on pain of imprisonment, to indulge in football, stonethrowing, catapulting wood and iron objects and all such frivolous games without gain."

A 17th-century English print depicts a mob football game sprawling through city streets.

Richard II, Henry IV, Henry V, and Henry VIII also made decrees banning the game so as to get their armies back to practicing military stuff. In the 15th century, the Scottish parliament convened by James I proclaimed in 1424 "That na man play at the Fute-ball."

Sport Domesticated

With the end of the Middle Ages, the game began to calm itself, albeit slowly. It was confined to pre-established field, much to the delight of townspeople, and by 1580 had been introduced as an intramural sport on Britain's college campuses. Each school developed its own set of rules, the first sign of standardization, and within 40 years a form of intercollegiate play had developed. Furthering to quiet the game was the spread of Puritanism, which squelched play on Sundays, although Oliver Cromwell is said to have enjoyed the game in his days at Cambridge in the early 1600s.

This, however, did not mean the game was completely, or even mostly, gone from the streets. In 1716 John Gay wrote about walking the streets of London and spying "the furies of the foot-ball war" and musing: "whither shall I run?"

Richard Mulcaster, headmaster of the Merchant Taylors Schools and St. Paul's, provided the justification for legitimizing the sport. While headmaster at Merchant Taylors from 1561 to 1586, he argued that the game, with a much stronger set of rules, could be made used as an educational tool to teach discipline and, at the same time, help foster physical fitness.

The Americas were not without some input. Fourteen years after the arrival of the Pilgrims at Plymouth Rock, William Wood described a game played with a ball of some sort by the native New England Indian population. The game was played on a broad sandy beach with anywhere from 30-40 men or as many as 1,000.

Development Stalled

Back in England, the game appeared to be emerging from its official banishment when in 1681 King Charles II gave permission for a special game between his serfs and those of the Earl of Albermarle. He even came to watch, but it's unlikely he went so far as to participate in a wave.

But Charles died in 1685, and the game—with all the attempts by governments to quell it because of its violent nature in the public streets—appeared to hibernate, at least in its development, for approximately the next 150 years.

The mob game was still played, in its rather violent format, as one illustration from 18th century London shows a gang of men playing with a ball, one man on the ground another holding his shin writhing in pain.

With rowing, cricket, and boxing having far more public acceptance, it wouldn't be until the early 1800s that soccer would show significant improvement in its development. That development, and acceptance, came with its introduction to the public schools.

Rules Varied

Education officials, whether by design or not, saw the wisdom of Mulcaster's argument and encouraged play at both the public-school and collegiate level.

But with no established rule-making body, each school developed its own rules based on its own peculiarities, lending themselves to what was available.

If a school had wide open grounds, like at Rugby School, a rougher version was more common. The more confined by walls, a game which relied more on dribbling skills developed. It became known as the dribbling game.

Regardless, handling the ball was fairly common in both versions that were developing, although the idea of picking it up and carrying it was supposedly unknown until the now legendary William Webb Ellis supposedly did so out of frustration during a game at Rugby School in 1823. Or so goes the story. It became loosely known as "the handling game."

The truly first attempt to standardize any rules for any of these games was in 1846 when Dr. Thomas Arnold, headmaster at Rugby School, set down regulations which allowed for kicking and tripping, known in the lexicon of the day as hacking, and for carrying the ball.

Standardization

Two years later, at Cambridge, former pupils of the various schools that played the games met to find some common ground among the two major versions. But the majority at the meeting having come from the more confined atmospheres of Eton, Harrow, and Winchester, preferred the dribbling game.

They expressed their dislike for carrying the ball. Those that had adopted Arnold's rules were not so much against giving up the carrying of the ball, although they weren't wild about it, their biggest complaint was the abolition of hacking, an ingredient thought necessarily manly but one they eventually would outlaw themselves later.

In 1862 J.C. Thring published a shortened version of 10 rules for what he called "The Simplest Game," the second rule of which allowed for essentially a fair catch—allowing the ball to be caught by the hands and placed at a player's feet to be kicked.

In 1863, a further attempt was made to clarify the rules. In a series of meetings, the first of which was held in Freemason's Tavern in London, 11 leading London clubs and schools created the English Football Association.

The creation of the Football Association, and thus the game it generated—association football

as opposed to rugby football—was also the creation of the term soccer.

It apparently was common slang among college students of the day to take the root of a word and ad "ers" to it, i.e. brekkers for breakfast. Rugby was called ruggers and the dribbling game was dubbed "soccers," apparently from the "soc" in association. Soccer, however, is still more popularly known simply as football throughout the world.

The Modern Era

England and Scotland played the first international match on November 30, 1872, at the West of Scotland Cricket club in Glasgow. The game ended—fittingly, as some of the sport's detractors would say—in a 0-0 draw. Since the Scots did not have a national association yet, they were represented by Queens Park, the oldest Scottish club team at the time.

The English team was, as are national teams today, essentially an all-star squad selected by the Football Association (FA). In 1886 the English FA would award those selected for the team—and at the time that meant only the 11 starters because substitutions were not allowed (for injury or otherwise)—a velvet cap complete with tassel.

It is an honor that is continued today and has led to the term of "being capped" or having x-number of caps represent the number of times an individual has played for his country in full international matches—those against other national teams.

The Scottish Football Association was founded in 1873, with the Welsh association three years later and the Irish equivalent in 1880. But the explosion in the popularity of the sport is most linked with the English FA's introduction of a single-elimination tournament simply called the Football Association Cup.

Decided upon in 1872 and first staged a year later, the cup—literally, a 20-pound sterling trophy inscribed with the words "The Football Association Challenge Cup"—was to be the reward for winning the tournament, which any club could enter.

The FA Cup is still staged in that manner, with amateur clubs comprised of every-day laymen drawn and competing against first-division, internationally-known powerhouses such as Liverpool, Arsenal, and Manchester United in the annual event.

The first tournament, with 15 entrants, drew a modest crowd of fewer than 2,000 for the final on March 16, 1873, at Kennington Oval between the Wanderers and Royal Engineers. Coincidentally or not, the Wanderers, who were captained by FA President C.W. Alcock—a driving force to initiate the tournament—won 1-0.

Popularity Spread Globally

Throughout this period, the game was played mostly by former collegians and public school graduates; exclusively upper-class and strictly on an amateur basis. But with the Industrial Revolution, people flocked to the major population centers like London. Since the game was primarily played in London, the lower classes became more exposed to it. Unlike cricket, the simplicity of soccer was an attractive element.

By 1882, there were 73 teams entered in the FA Cup and about 7,000 were on hand for the final where the Old Etonians beat Blackburn Olympic, now Blackburn Rovers, 1-0. By 1900, 242 teams had entered and in 1901 a crowd of 110,000 attended the final.

Britain was at its zenith as a global power and just like the Roman legionnaires, businessman from England stationed in New Zealand and Australia to India and South America took their games with them. Again the simplicity and lack of equipment needed was a feature that made soccer easily exportable and accepted.

The British employees of the Argentine railroads, which were British owned, formed all the local clubs and the Argentine Football Association was founded by a Briton, Alexander Hutton.

Similarly, in Uruguay employees of the Central Uruguayan Railroad formed the Central Uruguayan Railroad Cricket Club in 1891. That would lead to the formation of the Uruguayan FA in 1900 and the club would change its name in 1913 to Penarol, one of the most famous clubs in the world.

In much the same manner the game was adopted on the European mainland. In 1892, a group of Englishmen formed the Genoa Cricket and Football Club in Italy but because there were few opponents the competitions were few. That was until 1896, when a ship's doctor and goalkeeper, James Spensley, proposed allowing the local population, all 50 of them, as members.

The following year, the citizens of Turin formed their own club, the infamous Juventus, and the immediate mushrooming in popularity led to the formation of the Italian Football Federation.

Rise of Professionalism

Along with the rise in popularity came the arrival of professionalism. The English FA fiercely opposed any professional players in their game, expelling the club Accrington in 1883 for "offering inducements" to players—mainly Scottish imports.

But by 1885 the FA had to relent as professionals were becoming too numerous. In 1888, under the urging of Aston Villa chairman William McGregor, the Football League was born, still allowing the FA to control the rules of the game, but establishing a schedule and championship for professional clubs.

However, like the game between the Sheffield football organization and the London-based FA illustrated, rules were still not generally accepted "everywhere." In the myopia of the day that meant the British Isles.

So in 1882, the football associations of England, Scotland, Wales, and Ireland met to form the International Board to standardize rules throughout. This explains why in the official "laws" of the game dimensions are noted in yards instead of meters.

The four nations began to compete for the British championship in 1884. They were the original four national associations, but soon would be joined by the federations in Holland and Denmark (1889); New Zealand (1891); Hutton's Argentina (1893); Chile, Switzerland and Belgium (1895); Italy (1898); the aforementioned Uruguay and Germany (1900); Hungary (1901); and Finland (1907). The United States would get into the act in 1913.

FIFA Formed

But the biggest date in the development of soccer, besides 1863 and 1872 would be 1904—the year FIFA was formed. With several countries already having formed national associations, international play among nations on the European continent was well underway.

Following a match between Belgium and France in Brussels on May 1, 1904, the secretaries of the two respective country's teams, Louis Muhlinghaus of Belgium and Robert Guerin of France, discussed the formation of an international soccer organization on the European continent.

Twenty days later, Guerin convened a meeting in Paris along with delegates from France, Belgium, Denmark, the Netherlands, Spain, Sweden, and Switzerland to create the Fédération Internationale de Football Association—which translates into the International Federation of Association Football.

Guerin had invited the British, particularly members of the English FA. But the English, filled with themselves over regularly thrashing their opponents in internationals, declined. After all, they had the International Board. What was to be gained by joining this gang?

FIFA was not created to usurp the International Board. Quite the contrary. In its adoption of its articles of foundation, it included the rules of the FA and the International Board.

The English would realize their mistake and join a year later, in 1905. It would respond in kind by adding members of FIFA to the International Board, which still governs the sport's rules.

Rules Codified

The International Board's work was significant in the early days. It approved the penalty kick in 1891, the penalty area in 1902, and the corner kick in 1914. The biggest change came in 1925 when the offside rule was changed from three defenders to two.

But after sanctioning such major changes its work would slow. By 1937 the kind of revisions being implemented included the penalty arc, which is the small arc at the top of the penalty area which players must remain outside of, in addition to the penalty area, when a penalty kick is being taken.

But since the 1990 World Cup, rule changes have been more dramatic. At least in soccer terms. Because the 1990 World Cup in Italy was the lowest scoring ever—a paltry 2.21 goals per game—FIFA realized the game had become too defensive.

Within two years FIFA proposed and the Board outlawed goalkeepers from handling any ball last touched by one of his own players—in other words, a backpass.

International play would continue to grow in the years following FIFA's formation. After two stints as a demonstration sport at the 1896 and 1900 Olympics, including representation of some nations by club teams, soccer became a medal event at the 1904 Games in St. Louis.

The World Cup

After several attempts to organize a championship on its own, FIFA finally established one in 1930, the beginning of the World Cup. With the World Cup the game would grow phenomenally. The quest for soccer's holy grail would make legends of men named Pelé, Bobby Charlton, Dino Zoff, Franz Beckenbauer, and Diego Maradona.

The simplicity and appeal to the common man and woman would make soccer grow throughout the 20th century to become the world's most popular sport.

Thirteen nations participated in the first World Cup in 1930 with an average attendance of 24,139 for the 18 games. By 1950 in Brazil, an average of 60,000 saw the 22 games involving 13 teams, including a record 199,854 for the final at Rio de Janeiro's famed Marcana Stadium.

In 1958 FIFA increased the field to 16 teams, and by 1982 that was further hiked to its present-day 24. In 1990 in Italy, 2.5 million attended the

52-game championship with another 1.5 billion watching at some point on television.

Regional Competition

While the World Cup was growing, so was play on a national level. There are professional leagues throughout the world, and even where one doesn't exist, nearly all 178 FIFA-affiliated countries stage a national championship called a cup—thank the drunkards in Freemason's Tavern and Mr. Alcock.

Even if a country has a professional championship, it also stages a single-elimination cup tournament that additionally includes the amateur teams.

Furthermore, in the drive to determine the best club team, regional arms of FIFA, like the Union of European Football Associations (UEFA)—which governs the game in Europe—have devised annual championships among the best clubs from their member countries.

UEFA began staging its Champions Cup, which takes the professional league champions of all of the European countries and plays them off in a single-elimination tournament, in 1956. It added the Cup Winners Cup, the winners of all those national cup tournaments, in another tournament in 1961.

There is also the UEFA Cup, originally called the Inter-Cities Fairs Cup, which includes the best teams from throughout Europe that didn't qualify for one of the other two competitions.

Similarly, South America has its annual international club championship called the Libertadores Cup. The winners of the European Champions and Libertadores Cups meet annually in the Toyota Cup (formerly the Intercontinental Cup)

in Tokyo for an informal world club champion-ship.

The Artemio Franchi Trophy is the equivalent for the national teams, pitting the South American, or Copa America, champion against the European champion. The Copa America, or America Cup, is the oldest of the continental championships, begun in 1916 when Argentina won.

The Europeans wouldn't get around to the idea until 1960, and the region the United States belongs to, CONCACAF—which stands for the Confederation of North, Central American and Caribbean Football—didn't start its championship, the Gold Cup, until 1991.

FIFA would add the Under-20, or World Youth Championship, in 1977; the Under-17 Championship in 1985 and a Women's World Championship in 1991—won by the United States.

This growth in popularity created a passion unrivaled in other sports. But with that passion, one shared throughout the world like none other, have come problems—and tragedy.

Disasters and Tragedies

Four of the most notorious airplane crashes involving sports teams were soccer clubs. One occurred on May 4, 1949, when 22 died, including the entire Turin team, in a crash in their hometown of Torino, Italy.

Many others can recall the seven players and officials of England's Manchester United who died on February 6, 1958, on a runway in Munich, West Germany, when the club was returning from a European Champions Cup match.

On December 8, 1987, a Fokker F-27 turboprop crashed while trying to land at Lima, Peru, in foggy weather, claiming the lives of 17 players,

six officials, four trainers, three referees, eight fans, and five crew members. The crash essentially wiped out the Peruvian first-division club Alianza. And most recently, on April 28, 1993, the Zambian national team died in a crash off Gabon.

But even more so, soccer has become associated with violence and death; some disasters created by fans, other incidents blamed on government officials, and some well beyond any control.

The most notorious of the latter was the so-called "Fútbol War." By providing the spark but not the cause, soccer and war will forever be intertwined.

The Fútbol War

The July 1969 armed conflict between Honduras and El Salvador killed 3,000, wounded another 12,000, and left an additional 150,000 homeless. The war lasted fewer than five days, thus giving it the name it is better known by in Latin America: "The 100 Hour War".

Starting with a simmering 130-year border dispute, relations between Honduras and El Salvador deteriorated in the 1960s due to the enactment of the Central American Common Market Agreement at the beginning of the decade. The pact favored the more industrialized El Salvador over the predominantly agrarian Honduras.

Tensions were high in 1968 when Honduras began expelling 300,000 migrant Salvadorans. On May 3, 1969, 57 Salvadoran families were ordered to leave a site in Guacamaya. On June 4th, 54 families were removed by force.

Four days later, the Salvadoran national team lost a World Cup qualifying game to Honduras 1-0 in the Honduran capital of Tegucigalpa after a sleepless night resulting from the Latin American practice of banging tin cans, honking car horns, and making noise anyway possible outside of the hotel of the visiting team to prevent it from resting.

At the game, riots broke out in the stands among the fans. In El Salvador, 18-year-old Amelia Bolanios was watching the game on television and, after seeing Robert Cordona of Honduras score to win the game in the final minute, took her father's gun and shot herself dead. The following day Salvadoran newspaper *El Nacional* wrote that the girl "could not bear to see her fatherland brought to its knees."

The Salvadoran president, his ministers, and the national team attended her nationally televised funeral. On June 14, Honduras travelled to San Salvador for what is called the "return leg." Like their Honduran counterparts, Salvadoran fans broke the windows where the Honduran team was staying, throwing in, among other things, dead rats.

With Salvadoran soldiers surrounding the stadium, the Honduran flag was burned and a dish rag was sent up the pole instead—to a large cheer. Honduras lost 3-0 and was escorted to the airport in armored personnel carriers.

But two Honduran fans weren't so lucky; they were killed. Several others were injured and more than 150 cars of Hondurans were burned. Since both sides had won one game, a third was necessary to break the tie.

On June 27 in neutral Mexico City, El Salvador won 3-2, eventually going on to represent CONCACAF in the 1970 World Cup.

After accusations by both sides of airspace infringement, and fueled by the nationalism generated in the World Cup qualifiers, on July 14, Salvadoran planes bombed four Honduran cities and its army pushed 25 miles into Honduras. Salvador justified their actions by claiming their right to "defend the human rights of their countrymen" and end what it called Honduran "genocide."

With the intervention of the Organization of American States and several Latin American countries, a cease-fire was arranged on July 18. But true peace would take longer to cement.

More commonly, soccer has been association with passion-of-the-moment, or random violence, absent of any historical genesis. Nearly 300 were killed and another 500 injured in riots in Lima on May 24, 1964, after Argentina beat Peru on a last-minute goal.

The most notorious in recent memory, one that provoked some to claim the sport was returning to mob football, took place on May 29, 1985, at Brussels, Belgium, in what has become known as the Heysel Stadium riots.

The Heysel Riots

Heysel was the site for the championship game of the 1984-85 European Champions Cup tournament, pitting England's Liverpool against Italy's Juventus. A thug element had been growing in England for several years, and it reached its climax in the stands before kickoff.

Supporters of Liverpool, some obviously drunk, began arguing and then fighting with Juventus fans. The fight developed into a full-scale riot, and eventually a cement wall separating the two groups collapsed, killing 39 people, mostly Juventus fans.

Captured on television, the sight of fans beating one another sent shockwaves through the world, not only the soccer community. Belgian courts would blame local police and UEFA for poor security arrangements. But they would also blame Liverpool fans for causing the riots.

UEFA would ban all English clubs, although not the national team, from any European competition for five years. With the violence still occurring in England at domestic league games, government officials there contemplated an identification-card system to quell the thugs.

At the 1990 World Cup, FIFA arranged for England and the Netherlands, a nation whose fans have an equally bad reputation, to play their first round match on the island of Sardinia to better control the fans and limit damage.

Other Disasters

Besides the violence of fans, people have died in other disasters at stadiums ill equipped to handle the massive crowds that soccer games have attracted.

One of the earliest known disasters of this type occurred in Buenos Aires, Argentina on June 24, 1968. Seventy-two people were killed after a regular season first-division match between River Plate and Boca Juniors when fans trying to leave the stadium mistakenly headed for a closed exit and were crushed.

In 1988, 93 people died and another 100 were injured in Katmandu, Nepal, when fans fleeing a hailstorm again found locked exits and were crushed. In 1985, only 18 days before the Heysel riots, a cigarette ignited a wooden grandstand in Bradford, England and killed 56.

The Hillsborough Tragedy

But the most famous of these incidents, which led to changes in stadium requirements by local authorities and FIFA, was the one the killed 95 in Sheffield, England, on April 15, 1989, at an English FA Cup semifinal game between Liverpool and Nottingham Forest.

Until this time, terrace or standing sections were very common. The "real" fans would buy an inexpensive ticket for an unreserved place—usually behind the goals—to stand and watch the game.

At Hillsborough Stadium in Sheffield, the terrace section already was filled to capacity. But a great throng of fans was outside the stadium, clamoring and pushing to get in. In an attempt to avoid what police thought would turn into another riot, authorities opened the gates to allow in the fans.

But they sent them down a corridor onto the already filled terrace section. The onrushing mass trapped those near the riot fences that surrounded the field to prevent people from invading the playing surface. Unable to climb over, they were crushed.

Reforms Initiated

The Hillsborough tragedy led to the abolition of terrace sections and most crowd-control fences, and the requirement by FIFA that all stadiums that host its sanctioned matches provide a seat for all fans.

To prevent further tragedies, FIFA and other soccer officials have taken steps such as the banning of temporary seating structures, like the one that collapsed at a 1991 French Cup semifinal game on the island of Corsica and killed 10 and injured 800.

Soccer's detractors point to the thug element and the disasters that have plagued the sport as a way of criticizing it. Soccer officials counter by saying violence has accompanied other sports, such as the riots following the Detroit Pistons 1989 championship or the mayhem that occurred during the parade to celebrate the Dallas Cowboys 1993 Super Bowl victory.

F.Y.I.

Wins and Defeats

The longest undefeated run in international competition was achieved by Hungary—a stretch of 29 matches between May 14, 1950 (3-5 vs. Austria) and the World Cup final, July 4, 1954 (2-3 vs. Germany FR). This run included only four draws.

Excluding war years, Hungary was undefeated at home for 17 consecutive years between June 8, 1939 (1-3 vs. Italy) and May 20, 1956 (2-4 vs. Czechoslovakia). If unofficial wartime internationals are included, this run extends only from 1943 (2-7 vs. Sweden) to 1956. Both are records.

Brazil has been undefeated in its national stadium, the Maracan, for 22 consecutive years: from July 7, 1957 (1-2 vs. Argentina) to the present.

Real Madrid was undefeated at home for eight consecutive years between February 1957 (2-3 vs. Atletico Madrid) and March 1965 (0-1 vs. Atletico Madrid). This run included 114 wins and 8 draws.

Fiorentina was undefeated for 33 consecutive Italian first division matches in 1955-56, and compiled the following record: 34-20-13-1-59-20-53.

Longest undefeated run in the World Cup: 13 matches by Brazil between 1954 (2-4 vs. Hungary) and 1966 (1-3 vs. Hungary).

Most wins in the World Cup: 33 (Brazil)

Most defeats in the World Cup: 17 (Mexico)

2: Rules

How the Game is Played

The rules of soccer have remained remarkably uniform for nearly 150 years, but their evolution from English public school games to international competitions required nearly a century of adaptations until the game played today took its definite shape.

In the second half of the 20th Century, rule makers have continued to tinker with items like offside, substitution, and methods of match management, but the major playing concepts were well-established by mid-century.

Laws of the Game

The Laws of the Game, which govern all aspects of soccer the world over, are the responsibility of the International Football Association Board (IFAB), which meets every June to consider proposed changes, clarifications, and instructions to national associations and referees.

The Laws have been reviewed on an ongoing basis since their original drafting in 1863, first by The Football Association in London, and by the IFAB since 1882. Changes are still taking place, the most recent in effect for the 1992-93 international season.

The first Laws, formulated at the inaugural meetings of The Football Association from October to December 1863, were based on the Harrow School Rules and Cambridge University Rules of 1848, 1854-58, and 1863, and to a lesser extent by the Eton College Rules of 1862. They were also anticipated by the Sheffield Rules of 1857 and The Rules of The Simplest Game (Uppingham School) of 1860.

Prior to 1863, there were as many differing sets of rules as there were schools, universities, and clubs. The Football Association Laws were an experiment by which teams from different locales could play under a uniform code for the first time.

The acrimonious discussion that ensued for two months while the Laws were being drawn up ultimately produced a split that led to the birth of association football (soccer), as distinct from rugby football, ending the era of two different English ball games known collectively as "football."

The original version of the Laws of the Game contained some elements of rugby (e.g., the fair catch), but the major proposals as set forth by rugby adherents were voted down.

The Laws of the Game were drafted originally

for members of the F.A. only, all of which were based in the London area. In the north, the Sheffield Rules had existed since 1857, and though
they were similar in many ways to the Football Association Laws, it was not until 1877 that the Football Association and the Sheffield Association agreed on a set of rules, unifying England under the London association.

The various indigenous schools rules, meanwhile, continued to be used on school grounds, but as of 1863, club level and all first class soccer followed the dictates of the Football Association Laws of the Game. They came to accepted as the world's rules as the game spread in the 20th Century.

The exact text of the original Laws is as follows:

1. The maximum length of the ground shall be 200 yards, the maximum breadth shall be 100 yards, the length and breadth shall be marked off with flags; and the goal shall be defined by two upright posts, 8 yards apart, without any tape or bar across them.

2. A toss for goals shall take place and the game shall be commenced by a place kick from the centre of the ground by the side losing the toss for goals; the other side shall not approach within 10 yards of the ball until it is kicked off.

3. After a goal is won, the losing side shall be entitled to kick off, and the two sides shall change goals after each goal is won.

4. A goal shall be won when the ball passes between the goal posts or over the space between the goal-posts (at whatever height), not being thrown, knocked on, or carried.

5. When the ball is in touch, the first player who touches it shall throw it from the point on the boundary line where it left the ground, in a direction at right angles with the boundary line, and the ball shall not be in play until it has touched the ground.

6. When a player has kicked the ball, any one of the same side who is nearer to the opponent's goal line is out of play, and may not touch the ball himself, nor in any way whatever prevent any other player from doing so, until he is in play; but no player is out of play when the ball is kicked off from behind the goal line.

7. In case the ball goes behind the goal line, if a player on the side to whom the goal belongs first touches the ball, one of his side shall be entitled to a free kick from the goal line at the point opposite the place where the ball shall be touched. If a player of the opposite side first touches the ball, one of his side shall be entitled to a free kick at the goal only from a point 15 yards outside the goal line, opposite the place where the ball is touched, the opposing side standing within their goal line until he has had his kick.

8. If a player makes a fair catch, he shall be entitled to a free kick, providing he claims it by making a mark with his heel at once; and in order to take such a kick he may go back as far as he pleases, and no player on the opposite side shall advance beyond his mark until he has kicked.

9. No player shall run with the ball.

10. Neither tripping nor hacking shall be allowed, and no player shall use his hands to hold or push his adversary.

11. A player shall not be allowed to throw the ball or pass it to another with his hands.

12. No player shall be allowed to take the ball from the ground with his hands under any pretext whatever while it is in play.

13. A player shall be allowed to throw the ball or pass it to another if he made a fair catch or

catches the ball on the first bounce.

14. No player shall be allowed to wear projecting nails, iron plates, or gutta percha on the sole or heels of his boots.

CHANGES TO THE LAWS

None of the original Laws has remained intact down to the present time. During their first few years of existence, major changes appeared in rapid succession, as befitting their experimental nature.

1863-1870

The following 1863 Laws were amended as described:

Law I: Tapes added between goal posts.

Law II: Change goals at halftime if game is scoreless.

Law IV: Goals must be scored under the tape.

Law V: Player making throw-in may not play ball twice.

Law VI: Player is offside when fewer than three opponents are between him and the opponent's goal line when the ball is played to him, if he himself is between his teammate with the ball and the opponent's goal line, replacing the old rule by which a player was offside merely by being between his teammate with the ball and the opponent's goal line when the ball was played to him.

Law VII: Goal kick replaces kick out.

Law VIII: Fair catch and all handling eliminated.

Law X: Charging from behind forbidden.

1871-1878

a) Players of either side were required to line up in their own half of the field before each kick off.

b) Change of goals was required only at half-time.

c) The side that did not kick off at start of first half does so at start of second.

d) A player of the opposite side who last touched the ball before going into touch makes the resulting throw-in.

e) A ball from a throw-in may travel in any direction and is required to travel six yards, being in play when it crosses the touch line.

f) The corner kick was introduced in 1872.

g) Goalkeepers defined; punching or throwing the ball, though not carrying, is authorized.

h) Charging of a player who is facing his own goal authorized.

i) Cleats were allowed.

j) A free kick was introduced as punishment for offside, handling, tripping, hacking, and charging.

k) Kick-offs, corner kicks, and all free kicks were defined as "indirect." That meant a goal could not be scored unless another player touched the ball.

l) The umpire's authority broadened as the idea of "advantage" began to come into the game: ball could remain in play after possible offside, handling, tripping, hacking, or charging until

the umpire himself decided the foul has occurred.

1880-1900:

a) An attacking player cannot be offside if the ball was last played by an opponent.

b) Referees are introduced with limited authority.

c) A goal is awarded against a team whose player prevents a goal from being scored by handling.

d) Corner kicks are exempted from the offside rule.

e) The old handling rule was rescinded.

f) The two-hand throw-in was introduced.

g) A penalty kick was introduced for tripping, holding, or handling committed within 12 yards of the offending player's own goal line.

h) A goalkeeper facing a penalty kick was permitted to advance not more than six yards from his own goal.

i) The weight of ball was fixed at 13-15 oz.

j) Referees were brought onto the field and given authority, including timekeeping; two linesmen were authorized to assist the referee; umpires were abolished.

k) Cleats were restricted to specified studs or bars.

l) A penalty kicker was prohibited from playing the ball twice in succession.

m) Extra time at the end of a match was authorized for a penalty kick to be taken.

n) A player was permitted to charge a goal-
keeper fairly if goalkeeper is playing the ball or obstructing an opponent.

o) The referee's absolute authority and the linesmen's neutrality was established.

p) The ball must pass wholly over the goal line or touch line to be a goal or out of play.

q) A standing throw-in replaced the running throw-in.

r) The number of players on a team was limited to eleven.

s) The length of a game was fixed at 90 minutes.

t) The goalkeeper was restricted to handling in his own half of the field.

u) Handling was added to list of infringements requiring a penalty kick.

v) The goalkeeper was limited to two paces while carrying ball.

w) The concept of "intentionality" was introduced in the Laws, adapted from an 1893 in-
struction to referees.

1900-1950

a) The direct free kick was introduced for major infringements in 1903 and the advantage clause was formally introduced.

b) The linesman's role as assistant to the referee was clarified.

c) The drop ball was introduced.

d) Leather was required for outer casing of balls.

e) Fair charging (shoulder charging) was expressly authorized.

f) The goalkeeper was limited to lateral movements on his goal line during penalty kick.

g) The offside law was limited to the attacking half of the field (1907).

h) The goalkeeper was limited to handling within his own penalty area and the distance of opposing players from the position of a free kick was increased to 10 yards (1913).

i) The 10 yard rule was applied to corner kicks and striking an opponent was mentioned as a major infringement (1914).

j) Throw-ins were exempted from the offside rule and goalkeepers were required to wear yellow jerseys. Subsequently keepers were required to wear shirts "distinguished" from the others on the field (1921).

k) The offside rule was altered to require only two opponents between an attacking player and the goal line (1925).

l) A player taking throw-in was required to have both feet on the touch line (1925).

m) The corner kick was changed from an indirect to a direct free kick and a direct free kick replaced the indirect free kick as punishment for holding, hacking, charging, striking, handling, and other serious infringements (1927).

n) The goalkeeper was required to stand still on his goal line until a penalty kick is taken (1929).

o) The goalkeeper was permitted to take four paces while carrying the ball. Subsequently a keeper was allowed to bounce the ball to gain additional steps, but the 4-step rule is once again in force (1931).

p) Unlawful throw-ins became punishable by a throw-in for the opposing side rather than a free kick.

q) The ball from a goal kick was required to travel outside the penalty area.

r) The weight of ball was increased to 14-16 oz.

s) The goalkeeper was required to stand on his goal line between the posts for a penalty kick.

In 1938 the Laws of the Game were completely remodeled and rewritten by Sir Stanley Rous, who later served as President of FIFA from 1961 to 1974; the only substantive changes were the addition of certain infringements punishable by an indirect free kick. These remain the basic format for the laws today.

In 1950 the referee for an international match was required to be a citizen of a neutral country, unless otherwise agreed upon by both sides.

1950-Present

a) Obstruction made was punishable offense by an indirect free kick, even in the penalty area.

b) Referees for international matches had to be chosen from an official list of international referees.

c) A decision by the referee became irreversible if the game had been restarted.

d) The application of the advantage clause was irreversible, even though the expected advantage did not materialize.

e) A fourth official was introduced to work on the sidelines at major matches, coordinating substitutions and assisting the referee as instructed.

f) The number and method of substitution was defined and revised (see below, Substitutions).

g) The deliberate foul became punishable by an automatic expulsion from play, including goal-keepers even if the foul resulted in a penalty kick.

h) Deliberate handling to prevent a goal or a goal-scoring chance became punishable by an automatic expulsion.

i) Beginning in 1992-93 the backpass to the goalkeeper was limited in an effort to prevent time-wasting. A goalkeeper was not allowed to play the ball with his hands if it was deliberately kicked to him by a teammate.

FIELD OF PLAY

Defining the Field

Along with the changing nature of the rules of the game, the playing field itself was gradually defined over the first century of the game's history. However there is still no universally required field size and even the 1994 World Cup may include some fields of varying widths.

The evolution of the present field of play was in the making for many decades, as shown by the following chronology of major changes and developments:

1863-1900

1863: Maximum length of 200 yards and maximum width of 100 yards was specified, corner flags were required and goals were defined as two upright posts eight yards apart without any tape or crossbar between them.

1865: Tapes were stretched between either goal post eight feet above the ground.

1875: A minimum length of 100 yards and minimum width of 50 yards was specified.

1883: Crossbars replaced tapes and touch lines were added to all sides of the field.

1891: The center spot and center circle were added as well as semi-circular lines six yards from either goal post to designate the goal area.

A 12-yard line at either end of the field was marked off to designate the penalty area and a theoretical 18-yard line introduced to indicate the position of a penalty kick. Goal nets were also allowed.

1894: The maximum width of goal posts and crossbars was fixed at five inches.

1896: The minimum height of corner flags was fixed at five feet.

1900-1950

1901: A broken line 18 yards from the goal line was added to determine the position of penalty kicks.

1902: The halfway line, the present rectangular goal area and the penalty area were introduced. The penalty spot was added 12 yards from the goal line.

1937: The penalty arc was added.

1939: The maximum width of touch line and goal line was fixed at five inches.

1950-Present

1966: The minimum width and depth of cross-bar and goal post was fixed at four inches.

Playing Surfaces

The International Board has been reluctant to act on the composition of playing surfaces, but with sophisticated technologies emerging and expanded international competition in differing climates, this has become increasingly important factor in modern soccer.

Grass surfaces are still required for most major competitions—especially the World Cup. The advance of artificial surfaces presented a new set of problems.

The first soccer match ever played on an artificial surface was an exhibition match between Real Madrid and West Ham United at the Astrodome, Houston, Texas, in 1966.

The first World Cup qualification match to be played on artificial surface was Syria vs. Iraq in 1976 at the Malaz Ground, Riyadh, Saudi Arabia, and it was followed some weeks later by a second match between the same teams.

FIFA subsequently banned qualifying or finals matches on such surfaces, but several countries, Russia in particular, use such surfaces to combat extreme weather.

The 1994 World Cup in the United States will make history when the first indoor World Cup match is played in the Pontiac Silverdome, although real grass will be laid in the Silverdome for those matches.

Substitution Rules

Limits on Substitutions

Substitutions in soccer have traditionally been a highly restrictive undertaking. One of the early axioms of football games in the nineteenth century was that if a team suffered the loss of an injured player, it was just bad luck and had to be endured. The notion of substituting one player for another as a tactical maneuver was thought to be unfair.

The present rule, as delineated by a decision of the International Football Association Board and governing all levels of competition throughout the world, allows five eligible substitutes per game, providing the names of prospective substitutes are made known to the referee before the kickoff.

The actual Laws of the Game, however, restrict the number of substitutions per game to two. The five-substitution decision is meant to give local authorities a parameter within which to formulate their own policies regarding substitutions. The two-substitute rule is enforced in all competitions that come under the direct supervision of FIFA.

Most of the world's leading soccer nations have retained the two-substitution rule, and it is this rule most commonly observed in first-class competition. In U.S. school and youth soccer unlimited substitution is usually allowed.
American collegiate rules place some limits on substitutions, but college rules still remain different from the FIFA laws of the game.

Laws permitting substitution are a recent development. A decision of the International Board in 1932 first mentioned allowing limited substitution in international matches if mutually agreed upon by both teams.

In 1956 the International Board authorized incapacitated goalkeepers to be replaced at any time during the game and one other incapacitated player at any time before the end of the first half, but this rule was restricted exclusively to youth tournaments under FIFA auspices.

Two years later, the 1956 rule was extended to include all levels of competition and thus for the first time substitution was not specifically forbidden in the upper reaches of the game.

In 1965, the number of nominated players was increased to five, but actual substitutions remained at two. A major change occurred in 1967, when FIFA authorized two substitutes per game for any reason, injury or otherwise, but the ruling was restricted to friendlies and qualification rounds for the 1968 Olympic Games and the 1970 World Cup.

When the rule was eventually adopted for the final rounds of these competitions, the two-substitution rule came into common use as an integral part of the Laws.

In the 1994 World Cup, all eligible members of the team may be nominated as substitutes, but only two may still actually be used. It is thought that the next change in substitution rules may involve the direct substitution of one specialist goalkeeper for another, but no decision has yet been made.

There are additional rules that govern the substitution of players: 1) A player who is sent off may not be replaced; 2) a substitute may not enter the field of play except at stoppages and after the referee has beckoned him to do so, nor may he enter the field of play until the player he is replacing has left the field of play.

BREAKING TIES

Penalty Kick Contests

In 1970 the International Football Association Board accepted a proposal that provided for a penalty kick contest to replace the practice of choosing lots to decide the result of a drawn game. The penalty kick contest is put into effect only if extra time has not produced a winner, and is restricted exclusively to knockout competitions, such as national cups and international championships.

The rules and conditions of the procedure, whose official name is "taking of kicks from the penalty mark," are as follows:

1. The goal at which all the kicks are taken is chosen by the referee.

2. A coin toss by the referee determines which team kicks first.

3. Each team is entitled to at least five kicks, which are taken alternately, first by one team then the other.

4. If, before five kicks are completed, one player fails to score and his opposite number scores, the taking of kicks is ended by the referee.

5. If, after five kicks are completed, both teams have scored the same number of goals, the procedure continues until one team has scored more than the other after both have taken an equal number of kicks.

6. The team that scores the greater number of goals is declared the winner of the contest, but the game is recorded as a draw with an additional notation that the winner was decided on penalty kicks.

7. If the goalkeeper is injured during the contest, he may be replaced by a teammate who is already on the field or by a substitute, the latter provided his team has not already made use of the maximum number of substitutes permitted by the rules.

8. Only players who are on the field at the end of the match may qualify to take kicks.

9. No player may take a second kick until all eligible teammates have had their turn.

10. Other than the kicker and goalkeeper, all players must remain within the center circle while the kick is in progress.

11. The goalkeeper who is waiting for his turn to defend must remain in the field of play but outside the penalty area at least 10 yards from the penalty spot and further than 18 yards from the goal line.

12. Unless superseded expressly by the rules above, all Laws of the Game apply throughout the contest.

Recently the penalty-kick tie-breaker system has come under close scrutiny. FIFA was concerned about the number of such games in the 1990 World Cup finals and has directed that sudden death overtime periods be experimented with to encourage teams to try to win in the extra 30 minutes rather than play for the penalty kicks. The first experiment with sudden death took place at the FIFA World Youth Cup held in March 1993 in Australia.

GAME OFFICIALS

Referees

A soccer referee is a most powerful sports official, in charge of all aspects of the match. His decisions are final. He is supported in his effort by two linesmen, whose task is to assist in administering the Laws.

Referees have nine basic duties to perform, as specified by the Laws:

1. Enforce the Laws.

2. Administer the advantage rule.

3. Keep score and act as timekeeper.

4. Suspend or terminate the game if necessary, submitting a detailed report of the decision to the proper authority.

5. Caution, and if necessary, send off players guilty of fouls or misconducts, submitting a detailed report of the decision to the proper authority.

6. Prevent all persons other than authorized players and linesmen from entering the field of play without permission.

7. Stop the game to allow a seriously injured player to be attended.

8. Restart the game after a stoppage.

9. Decide that the game ball meets all specified requirements.

A referee's authority begins as soon as he enters the field and extends to offenses committed during a stoppage or when the ball is out of play. He may choose to reverse a decision of his own if he wishes, provided he has not already restarted play.

Application of the advantage rule is irreversible, even if the expected advantage does not materialize. He should take care that his stoppages are wholly necessary and do not unduly impede the progress of the game: the Laws are written to penalize deliberate fouls or misconducts.

Although the referee is empowered to terminate a game in the event of "grave disorder," he may not determine the results of the game; this is left to proper authorities upon receipt of the referee's detailed report.

When a player commits two separate offenses at the same time, the referee should address the more serious offense. Referees must clearly indicate player cautions by showing a yellow card to the player and the spectators. Expulsions are indicated by displaying a red card.

Linesmen

Although the linesmen are merely his assistants on the field, the referee is obliged to accept their information regarding an action that he was not in a position to see clearly. On the other hand, if the referee determines that he was, in fact, well positioned to see a given action, such contrary opinions as may be expressed by a linesman should be ignored.

If a linesman is guilty of improper conduct, the linesman should be relieved of his duties by the referee and replaced with a suitable substitute.

As the name indicates, linesmen are positioned on the sidelines, one on each side of the field. Each is supplied a brightly colored flag by the host team, preferably one of red or yellow. A linesman's specific duties are to indicate when the ball is out of play, and to assist in determining which team is entitled to a corner kick, goal kick, or throw-in.

Linesmen also indicate offside positions, although the referee actually makes the offside ruling. In addition, when it is apparent that the referee did not see an offense being committed, the linesman must signal the referee immediately, but he may not determine and administer penalties for fouls or misconducts. If, however, in the opinion of the referee, a foul or misconduct was observed clearly by the referee, the linesman should refrain from assisting him unless called upon by him to do so.

All international matches, other than those in the amateur or youth categories, must be officiated by referees and linesmen from the official list of International Referees as supplied by FIFA. International referees and linesmen must be selected from a neutral country or countries, unless otherwise agreed upon by both teams. They are required to wear the authorized FIFA badge on their shirt or blazer and should take care that the color of their uniform is distinct from the colors of players' uniforms. Black is recommended.

Numerous attempts have been made over the decades to increase the number of referees to two, but the International Football Association Board has consistently rejected such a proposal. The decision that referees at international matches should come from neutral countries was made by the International Board in 1950. Lately there has been talk of increasing the power of the linesmen and even of incorporating television replays, but no decisions have been made on either subject.

3: Tactics

Tactics and Strategy

Soccer is primarily an intuitive exercise; this has been one of it great appeals to potential players the world over. To confine it to "patterns," such as those of American football and basketball, would undermine its attraction to viewers and practitioners alike.

The game's rules themselves are indicators of this characteristic, since they leave an inordinate amount of discretion to the referee, more so than in almost any other ball game.

The desire to carry on these traditions and to refrain from the adoption of quasi-military maneuvers has been reaffirmed in recent years by the game's sharp reaction to the entrenched atmosphere of *catenaccio,* a product of Italy, in favor of the free and fluid "Total Football" of Holland and Germany in the 1970s.

The biggest conflict in the tactical evolution of the game has been that of orientation: attack vs. defense. Weaker teams at all levels of every game are prone to resort to defense-oriented approaches; highly skilled teams tend to have the confidence to attack. If there is an identifiable historical trend it is probably the general transformation of soccer from a purely attacking strategy to a more defensive one.

The gentlemen players of Victorian England were hardly inclined to let the game come to them. Indeed, goalkeepers of the mid-nineteenth century took turns in that role, because it was duly regarded as the least honorable position to play. Sam Hardy, Americo Tesoriero, and other pioneer goalkeepers changed all that, and, conversely, in the twentieth century many of the world's leading offensive players have been fullbacks, center halfbacks, and sweepers.

In the end, nostalgic worries over the loss of attacking soccer in the modern game are easy to come by but of little use; all these trends are cyclical.

Alcock's Dribbling Game

(Figure 1): The earliest soccer "formation" emerged in the 1860s when football teams were gradually splitting into two camps—association football and rugby football. Until the 1860s, most codes prohibited forward passing altogether, necessitating forward movement of the ball by dribbling only.

C. W. Alcock and his club, Wanderers F.C., the chief proponents of the dribbling game, argued that it represented pure soccer, as distinct from rugby where passing the ball (albeit by hand) was a distinctive trait. In the dribbling game there were seven (or eight) forwards, each a dribbling expert, one or two halfbacks in support of the attack, and one fullback to challenge the opposing dribbler.

Scottish Passing Game

(Figure 2): Queen's Park Glasgow, the Scottish national team, and the London club Royal Engineers created the first tactical revolution during the 1870s when they introduced the concept of passing among their players. The soccer-rugby split had occurred by this time, and the passing game was the first sign that soccer was maturing.

To accommodate the increased goalscoring potential, another fullback was added on defense, thus reducing the forward line to six players. The Scottish method was eventually perfected by the English amateur club Corinthians during the 1880s, and became commonplace. Ultimately, it signaled the birth of modern soccer.

The Classic Formation, 2-3-5

(Figure 3): The development of passing techniques spelled the need for tighter, more sophisticated defenses, and in the late 1870s a third halfback was seen on some teams (Cambridge University, 1877, and Wrexham F.C., 1878). England's national team first employed three halfbacks in 1884, followed by Scotland in 1887, by which time the practice was widely adopted.

Preston North End was the first really successful club to use the 2-3-5, winning the first two English championships in 1889 and 1890. The 2-3-5 remained the standard formation in soccer for 40 years, and was used in Central Europe until the post-World War II era, modified by a lower intensity and a more fluid expression, yielding the so-called "Danubian" style.

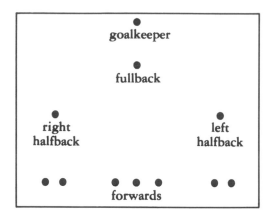

Figure 1

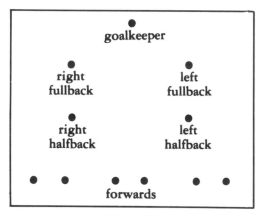

Figure 2

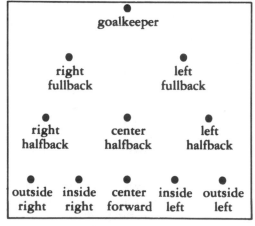

Figure 3

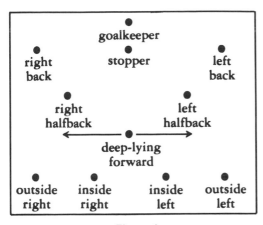

Figure 4

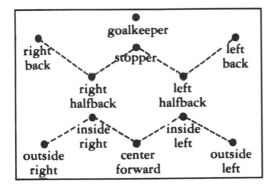

Figure 5

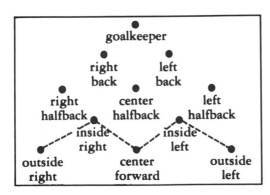

Figure 6

Charlie Buchan's Third Back Game

(Figure 4): After the offside law change of 1925, goalscoring in English soccer increased immediately by 33 percent. Arsenal's inside forward Charlie Buchan, an exceptionally bright player with excellent goalscoring skills in his own right, suggested to his manager Herbert Chapman that the center half be pulled back to a purely defensive position to mark the opposing center forward (hence his designation as stopper). In addition, an inside forward who was more adept at distribution than goalscoring was pulled back to a deep-lying forward position. Chapman's Arsenal adopted this with great success in the late 1920s.

W-M Formation

(Figure 5): This became an immediate extension of Buchan's third-back back plan, in which both inside forwards, rather than just one, were drawn back, creating the geometric appearance of a W-shaped defense and M-shaped offense.

Herbert Chapman's Arsenal of the 1930s, which dominated English soccer for a decade, made it world famous, and it remained the standard formation in England and assorted anglophile right strongholds until the 1950s.

Metodo, or "Method"

(Figure 6): Vittorio Pozzo, manager of Italy's national team during its decade of world domination in the 1930s, adapted the highly successful attacking center right half concept of Manchester United's 1907-11 team—which he had observed closely while living in England—and combined it with the attacking M of Arsenal's W-M formation. In the 1940s, Pozzo reluctantly transformed his attacking center half into a stopper, a revised plan he called *sistema* ("system").

Verrou, or Swiss Bolt

(Figures 7 & 8): Developed by Karl Rappan, Austrian manager of Servette Geneva and Grasshoppers Zurich during the 1930s, the "Swiss Bolt" called for separate attack and defensive formations.

In the attack mode (figure 7), a 3-3-4 pattern emerged in which the center back and two wing backs advanced all the way to the midfield line; the three halfbacks supported the forward line of two wings and two insides, the center half serving as a virtual deep-lying center forward.

In the defensive formation (figure 8), all 11 players retreated deep into their own half; the center half became a center back, and the center back became a deep center back who roved from one side to the other (hence the "bolt" designation), much as the libero, or sweeper did in later years.

The purpose of the plan was to create the illusion that an opposing attack or defense was in turn, outmanned, but it required great stamina from its players. Verrou was important in anticipating the more garrisoned Italian bolt system, *catenaccio.*

Hungarian W Attack

(Figure 9): Hungary lost one match in six years between 1950-56 (the World Cup final in 1954) playing its own 4-2-4, a system unknown in Europe up to that time, and more accurately called the Hungarian W attack. It called for three center forwards, one deep-lying (Hidegkuti) and two well-advanced (Kocsis on the right and Puskás on the left), flanked by two slightly receding wings.

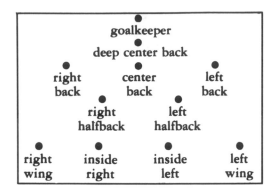

Figure 7

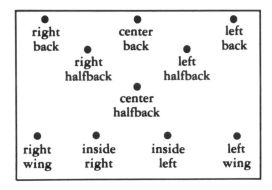

Figure 8

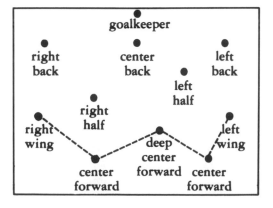

Figure 9

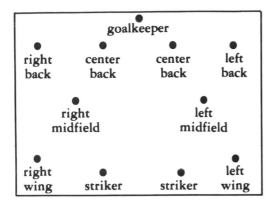

Figure 10

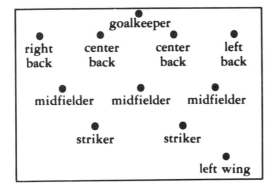

Figure 11

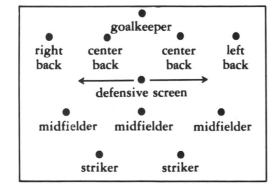

Figure 12

The two midfielders were staggered: Bozsik on the right supporting the attack, Zakarias on the left acting as the first line of defense. Three backs brought up the rear, but they too advanced to the opponent's half of the field on attacks.

The 4-2-4 System

(Figure 10): This was introduced by the Paraguayan national team under coach Fleitas Solich in the 1953 South American Championship, but it was made famous by the scintillating Brazilian World Cup-winning team of 1958. Brazil's two center backs in the middle of the defense were flanked by two wing backs who were expected to initiate attacks along the touch lines (resulting in an astonishing 2-4-4).

The two midfield players were offense-minded as well, and the forward line consisted of two central strikers (Vava and Pelé), and two wings (Garrincha and Zagalo), the former an attacking right side winger, the latter a supportive winger who dropped back on the left side.

The 4-3-3 System

(Figure 11): This system, still widely used, was seen in its most entertaining form when Brazil employed two central strikers and a wing on the forward line. The former left wing of the 4-2-4 (Zagalo) had by now dropped back to an authentic left midfield role. Right and left backs were free to advance at will as they had in the 4-2-4. A modified form of the 4-3-3 has one center forward and two wings evenly displaced.

Wingless 4-4-2

(Figure 12): England won the World Cup of 1966 with this formation, but eventually entered a long period of mediocrity with it as well. There were four backs at the rear; a roving "defensive screen (Stiles) in the sweeper tradition (but in

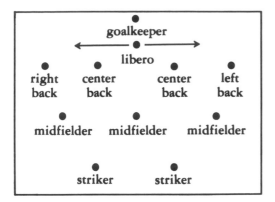

Figure 13

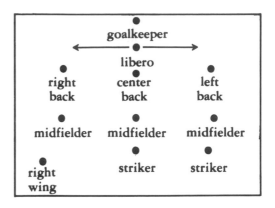

Figure 14

front of his other defenders); three midfielders, the central one of these (Charlton) a virtual deep-lying center forward; and two central strikers.

The wing positions were in effect erased from the field. This was one of the weakest attacking systems yet devised, but it provided an effective defense.

Catenaccio

(Figures 13 & 14): The roots of this pervasive defense plan go back to the northeast of Italy in the late 1930s, probably as a result of exposure to the *verrou*. In 1948, Triestina employed it successfully against the big clubs of the Italian league that had recently been inundated with high-scoring foreign players. Other small clubs adopted some form of catenaccio, and by the early 1950s even the giant Milan and Turin clubs had adopted it.

Catenaccio ("great bolt" or "chain") involved three or four defenders who were supported in the rear by a *libero* (sweeper) who roamed from side-to-side plugging up the slightest hole left by a defender. In front of the defense, three

midfielders more often defended than attacked, and there were two or three strikers on the forward line.

In *catenaccio,* the offensive thrust usually took the form of a counterattack rather than a slow build-up. Its most garrisoned form involved a back line of four plus the sweeper, and a forward line of only two (figure 13).

A second form included three backs and three forwards (figure 14). *Catenaccio* eventually engulfed Italy and helped its well-rehearsed practitioners to dominate European club tournaments during the 1960s.

The Italian national team however, was unsuccessful with this system, and it was eventually unable to disassociate the system itself from the defensive attitude it created.

Beckenbauer's All-Purpose Sweeper Plan

The various systems were so interlocked by the late 1960s that diagrammatic patterns began to lose their significance altogether. In West Germany, the ex-midfielder Franz Beckenbauer, one of the most complete players in the history of the game, transformed the sweeper position into an attacking as well as defensive role.

Beckenbauer roamed from side to side both in front of and behind the defensive line, and occasionally launched an attack, sometimes advancing into the opponent's penalty area to score goals.

Though Beckenbauer's sweeper role could be adapted to almost any existing system, it has most often been incorporated into a 4-3-3.

The genius of Beckenbauer's concept, however, was that it virtually obviated all traditional systems, and anticipated the less restrictive marking that gave rise to "total football."

Total Football

"Total football," as practiced first by the superbly gifted Dutch club Ajax and eventually by Holland and West Germany, is less a system than an attitude, in which intuitive playmaking and individual initiative allow all players to adopt attacking or defensive postures as the situation warrants.

It combines very high levels of skill with thoughtful, deliberate passing, yet without rigid patterns. It is a constant movement and refocusing of pivotal points on the field, wholly dependent on the action that has immediately preceded it. Players of enormously wide-ranging talent, such as Franz Beckenbauer and Johan Cruyff, are particularly well suited to it.

4: Who's Who in Soccer

A Roster of Soccer's Greatest Players

ADEMIR
(1924—)

Full name: Ademir Marques de Meneses. The complete center forward, Ademir emerged as a world famous star in the 1950 World Cup and led Brazil's astounding forward line, one of the greatest ever seen in the game, with the gifted Jair at inside left and Zizinho at inside right. Ademir was a perfectly balanced player who shot with either foot effectively, dribbled in mazes around his defenders, and had blinding speed.

He was also among the most versatile of players, and, while his worldwide fame was derived from those amazing performances at center forward, he was equally well known in Brazil as an outside left.

He began his career with Esporte Recife, and at age 19 was chosen for the Pernambuco selection to play in the Brazilian championship for state teams. Rio's Vasco da Gama signed him in 1944, and the following year he and Jair helped Vasco to a memorable Rio league title.

In 1946, he moved to Fluminense, guiding his new club to its own championship, but in 1947 he returned to Vasco and became synonymous with that club's domination of the Rio soccer until the early 1950s. Vasco and Ademir won

further league titles in 1947,1949,1950, and 1952. In the 1950 World Cup, he led all scorers, and in his 37 international appearances for Brazil he converted 32 times. He finally retired from Vasco in 1956 and went into broadcasting. Ademir's father was the incomparable Domingos da Guia, defender extraordinaire for Brazil in the 1930s.

ALCOCK, CHARLES WILLIAM
(1842-1907)

The outstanding figure to emerge from the earliest years of modern soccer, Alcock influenced nearly every aspect of the game. He and other Old Harrovians (Harrow graduates), including his brother, J.F. Alcock, founded the Forest Football Club, the first organization devoted exclusively to playing the "dribbling game" (the precursor of soccer as we know it).

As captain of Wanderers, the greatest club of its day, Alcock became the prime mover of soccer's first tactical plan: the adoption of dribbling as the most effective way to advance the ball.

Alcock was one of the founding members of The Football Association in 1863, and helped to draft the first Laws of the Game. He was elected to the Executive Committee of The Football

Association in 1866, and four years later became its honorary secretary.

In that post Alcock served as the chief instigator of The Football Association Challenge Cup (F.A. Cup), which was launched in 1871 and was the world's first organized competition. He also initiated the first internationals between England and Scotland in 1870—hence his designation as "the father of international football."

By 1870, Alcock had become the game's most important historian and commentator. His famous *Football Annual* was first published in 1869, and he continued to write important books and articles on soccer until his death.

ANDRADE, JOSE LEANDRO
(1901-1957)

The famous right half of Uruguay during its golden era of the 1920s, Andrade had the ball juggling skills of the greatest center forwards. He was an idol with his fellow countrymen, and commanded universal respect among both South American and European players.

Andrade started with Bella Vista, the small Montevideo club, but soon moved to mighty Nacional, and when the 1924 Olympic Games opened in Paris, he was already a star with his national team. He was instrumental in Uruguay's winning of the gold medal, and in 1925 he was one of the standouts in the Nacional team that toured Europe so successfully.

Andrade starred in Uruguay's South American Championship triumphs of 1923, 1924, and 1926, and Uruguay's second gold medal win at the 1928 Olympic Games.

After retiring from the national team he was recalled for the first World Cup in 1930, and he

dazzled his opponents again, renewing his international stardom with his agility and keen sense of positioning. He finally retired from the game in 1933, but his nephew, Victor Rodriguez Andrade, carried on the famous name as a star for Uruguay in the 1950 World Cup.

BAGGIO, ROBERTO
(1967—)

Perhaps no player better typifies the big-money, high-profile life of modern soccer players than Italian idol Roberto Baggio. Fans of his Fiorentina-Florence club rioted when their star was sold to Juventus-Turin on the eve of the 1990 World Cup and his exploits are detailed in almost soap opera fashion by the aggressive Italian media.

Coming into big-time soccer in the age of widespread television and marketing, Baggio's remarkable on field skills, coupled with his good looks and personality off the pitch combined to make him a superstar.

After breaking into Italian soccer with Lanerossi Vicenza in 1982, Baggio moved to Fiorentina in 1985 to spend five seasons that saw him rise to star status. Utilizing a powerful right foot, a knack for making free kicks bend and dip and the pace to beat defenders in foot races, Baggio established himself as a player able to score goals in the ultra-tough Italian First Division.

He attracted the attention of all the top clubs, eventually agreeing to a then-record $15 million transfer to Juventus in 1990.

Baggio was under intense pressure to produce goals at both club and international level. In the 1990 World Cup he was eclipsed by Salvatore (Toto) Schillaci's six-goal performance; in his early days at Juventus he also heard the critics when he didn't immediately set goal-scoring records.

Baggio showed the resilience necessary for a great player, fighting his way back to prominence for both club and country. He adopted a pony-tail for his curly, dark hair, a flamboyant gesture which seemed to say "pay attention," rather than attempting to duck the spotlight.

BANKS, GORDON
(1937—)

Banks was the finest English goalkeeper of all time and an inspiration to a whole generation of European keepers. His level-headedness and

Allsport

Gordon Banks

ceaseless drive to improve on past performance earned him immense popularity among players and fans alike. Banks had natural acrobatic

abilities from the beginning, and he became an exceptionally astute student of the geometry of goalkeeping, as evidenced by the brinkmanship he displayed in the penalty area so consistently throughout his career.

Signed by third division Chesterfield at age 18, Banks was snapped up immediately after military duty in 1959 by first-division Leicester City.

Three years after his international debut in 1963, he excelled for England in its 1966 World Cup triumph, and drew world acclaim. Widely thought to be the best keeper in the world—"as safe as the Banks of England"—he was transferred to Stoke City in 1967.

In 1970, Banks was awarded an O.B.E., and at the World Cup in Mexico topped all goalkeeping performances in recent memory with saves that left Pelé and others shaking their heads in disbelief. He reached his peak in 1972 when he led Stoke to a League Cup victory at Wembley, the first title in the club's history.

Seven months later, in a sudden turn of fate, he was the victim of a tragic car accident in which he lost the use of one eye.

An attempted comeback following his long recuperation was generally unsatisfactory although he played for a time with the Ft. Lauderdale Strikers in the NASL before retiring.

BARESI, FRANCO
(1960—)

Playing in a country where defense has always been dominant helped Franco Baresi hone his techniques, but the sweeper of AC Milan and the Italian national team did more than follow in the traditional path.

During his professional career with AC Milan, Baresi helped to liberate the Italian sweeper from the purely defensive role of the 1960s and 1970s, redesigning the position by leading carefully planned counterattacks and coming forcefully into the play at free kicks.

A compact, powerfully built man, Baresi used speed, anticipation, and jumping ability more than for his pure pure power. Although no one can question his competitive nature, it is not for hard tackling, but correctly-timed moves that Baresi will be remembered.

He played at the heart of the Milan side during the era when one of Europe's great club teams was assembled and led Italy to revival of fortune after the dip following the 1982 World Cup victory.

Baresi made his debut with Milan in 1977-78, and for Italy (against Romania) in 1982. Although a member of the Cup-winning team in 1982, Baresi did not play in the final. He was captain of his country when Italy hosted the World Cup in 1990, finishing third after a dramatic penalty kick shoot-out loss to Argentina in the semifinals.

BECKENBAUER, FRANZ
(1945—)

Franz Beckenbauer would have been certain of his place in soccer history well before July 1990, but when he coached West Germany to the World Cup title he simply added to an extraordinary career. That triumph over Argentina on a humid Rome night allowed Beckenbauer to join Brazil's Mario Zagalo as one of just two men to have both played for and coached World Cup champions.

Beckenbauer's World Cup title as a player came when he captained the 1974 West German side

Allsport

Franz Beckenbauer

to victory at the Munich Olympic Stadium in a stirring final victory over Holland.

It was a suitable conclusion to a career in international soccer that had already seen him play in the 1966 World Cup Final and take part in the memorable 1970 semifinal against Italy when he played the 30-minute overtime period with a broken collarbone. Few soccer fans disputed his right to reign as captain of a world championship side four years later.

Nicknamed Kaiser Franz because of his elegant, upright, commanding style of play, Beckenbauer not only dominated European soccer during his playing career, he helped to create a new position.

Playing center back, a spot which had become increasingly defensive during the 1960s when Italian soccer's *catenaccio* was the operative style, Beckenbauer changed the nature of the last man's role to that of *libero,* or free-back.

Choosing when to back up his defenders as a traditional sweeper and when to venture into midfield to lead the attack, he made the West German team a world power by injecting a new direction to the offense with his remarkable vision for the game and with his accurate passing skills.

Beckenbauer played most of his career for Bayern Munich and accumulated 100 international selections by the 1976 European Championship final before concluding his career in the United States as a member of the New York Cosmos.

Although he was no longer in his prime, his ability to draw upon experience and his reading of the game defined his contributions to the North American Soccer League and the sport in the United States.

BERGKAMP, DENNIS
(1969—)

A tall, penetrating striker, Bergkamp is the latest in a line of great attackers from the Amsterdam club, Ajax. Like his predecessors Johan Cruyff and Marco van Basten, he is headed for an international career that will include playing his club soccer outside the Netherlands.

After scoring 49 goals in two seasons with Ajax and leading the Dutch attack in the 1992 European Championship on a team that included the more experienced van Basten, Bergkamp was pursued and signed by Inter of Milan for delivery to the Italian League at the start of the 1993-94 season.

Bergkamp began his Dutch League career with Ajax in the 1986-87 season and has already played on a UEFA Cup winning side as Ajax became the third European club to win all of the continent's major club trophies.

Bergkamp scored six goals as Ajax swept to the title, teaming with his Swedish international strike partner Stefan Pettersson. Bergkamp has also played for a Dutch Cup winner (1986-87) and a Dutch championship side (1989-90) in his first five years with Ajax.

Effective in the air in the traditional North European manner, Bergkamp is also quick off the mark and skilled with the ball at his feet.

BEST, GEORGE
(1946—)

This Irish phenomenon from the slums of Belfast captured the imagination of the soccer world and the press for 10 turbulent years during his stay with Manchester United, but ultimately he buckled under the intense pressure of publicity and lost his form before receding into the lower echelons.

Popperfoto

George Best

Best's mastery of ball control skills was complete, and he was equally brilliant with either foot or his head, gaining lasting fame as a dazzling and theatrical dribbler.

A child prodigy, Best was discovered and signed by a Manchester United scout at age 15 in 1961, and two years later made his debut for United at right wing. Best won his first cap for Northern Ireland against Wales at age 17, and scored three goals in his first seven internationals. In over 350 appearances for United, he scored 135 goals.

Playing on the same team as Bobby Charlton and Denis Law, heroes of England and Scotland respectively, Best won the English Footballer of the Year award in 1967 and 1968, and joined Law and Charlton in becoming European Footballer of the Year (1968) after starring in United's win in the European Cup.

All of Best's peak years were spent as a central striker, but he was also a schemer and often came dribbling out of the midfield to place a dangerous ball or take a shot.

Outspoken in his disdain for tactics, Best brought the art of improvisation to its highest level. He once taunted a Chelsea defender by taking off his own red jersey, and, with his foot on the ball, held it in front of his opponent like a bullfighter.

Best has sat on the ball in an F.A. Cup final, scored a goal from a headstand with a volley, dribbled the ball down half the length of the field with his thighs, and on numerous occasions trapped the ball with his backside.

In 1972, exhausted by the demands he placed on himself, Best walked away from United. He eventually played with the Los Angeles Aztecs for two seasons.

A one-year stint at second-division Fulham in 1976-77 resulted in an unresolved contract dispute and a worldwide FIFA ban, despite his signing with the Ft. Lauderdale Strikers the following season.

With 31 international appearances behind him before his first retirement in 1972, Best was given another chance with Northern Ireland in 1976 and 1977, and he added three more caps to his total. But, like his club-level performances after leaving United, he showed only glimpses of his earlier genius.

BICAN, JOSEF (1913—)

Born of Czech parents in Vienna, "Pepi" Bican played for the national teams of both Czechoslovakia and Austria, and was probably the most accomplished goalscorer ever to play for either country. He was a crowd-pleasing ball artist who scored and created goals with equal agility, though his preference was always to keep the ball on the ground rather than volley or head it.

His shooting and passing skills were based on accuracy and were invariably linked to uncanny ball juggling movements that frustrated his defenders and brought his fans to their feet.

In 1923, two years after his father had died of an injury received while playing for Hertha Vienna, Bican was signed by the same club, though he was only 10 at the time. It was not merely a sentimental gesture because his skills were already apparent.

Rapid Vienna, one of Austria's greatest clubs, secured his transfer while he was still in his mid-teens, and he was soon selected to play on Austria's great national team under Hugo Meisl.

At age 21, he was one of the few bright stars in the sagging Austrian team at the 1934 World Cup, and after playing at Admira Vienna, he moved to Slavia Prague in 1937.

Having played for Austria 19 times before his move to Prague, Czechoslovakia was delighted to include him on its national team from 1937 until the outbreak of World War II. During his tenure with the Czech team, Bican scored 17 goals in 14 international appearances. He retired in 1952.

BLANCHFLOWER, DANNY
(1926—)

Full name: Robert Blanchflower. Blanchflower was a world-class right halfback from Northern Ireland whose tactical brilliance was a highlight of British soccer for over a decade.

As captain of Tottenham Hotspur between 1959-64, he was the brains behind the most sophisticated team in postwar Britain—a team that also won the first English league and cup double in this century (1960-61).

In addition to his extraordinary skills, Blanchflower's rebelliousness against the traditional British emphasis on physical conditioning at the expense of ball control skills and his inspiring leadership abilities, especially in directing tactical maneuvers on the field, catapulted him into national prominence.

Similar characteristics were seen in his captaincy of Northern Ireland, a team he led through its greatest era in the late 1950s when it qualified for the World Cup and advanced to the second round over Czechoslovakia and Argentina.

Originally signed by Glentoran of Belfast in 1945, Blanchflower moved to Barnsley of the English second division in 1949, and from there he went on to the venerable Aston Villa, moving to Tottenham in 1954. He made his international

debut against Scotland in 1949 and, making 56 appearances, continued to play for his national team until 1963.

In 1964, after well over 600 club appearances and two Footballer of the Year awards (1958 and 1961), he was advised by his Spurs manager, Bill Nicholson, that he was about to be dropped from the first team, and retired.

BLOKHIN, OLEG
(1952—)

Perhaps the finest field player ever produced by the Soviet Union, Oleg Blokhin ranks alongside the giant goalkeeper Lev Yashin as a national hero. An ashen-faced blond with a willowy build, Blokhin was a true winger in an era when the game was almost completely devoid of such traditional wide-lying craftsmen, but he also combined a lethal goal-scoring touch with his ability to turn defenses inside out.

The son of a track-and-field star, Blokhin was blessed with near-Olympic speed. Indeed, at one time he was rated along with the Soviet Olympic sprint champion Valery Borzov for potential, but his first love was soccer and he never pursued a possible Olympic future.

Instead he won his bronze medal as a member of the 1976 Dynamo Kiev side (which also doubled as the Soviet Olympic soccer team in Montreal) and created a list of club and national records that will never be broken in light of the recent dissolution of the old Soviet government.

Blokhin came to prominence as a member of the Dynamo Kiev team that dominated Soviet soccer in the 1970s and early 1980s. They won the European Cup Winners Cup with a stunning display of attacking soccer in 1974-75. Blokhin played 427 times for Dynamo and was a Ukrainian national hero as he piled up the medals. His career with the Soviet Union included 107 selections and 39 goals before his retirement from international play following the 1986 World Cup.

Blokhin continued to make history when he was one of the first Soviet players to leave the U.S.S.R. for a career in Western Europe. At the end of his playing days he took over the managerial job at Olympiakos, one of the traditional Greek First-Division powers.

BONIEK, ZBIGNIEW
(1956—)

One of the first great Eastern European players to leave a Communist-governed country and make a major name in the West, Zbigniew Boniek overcame all odds and achieved.

After spending 11 years in his native Poland with Zawisza Bydgoszcz, Boniek moved to the Italian First Division as a member of the great Juventus sides 1982-85, playing alongside French hero Michel Platini in a side which won a European Cup (1985), a European Cup Winners Cup (1984) and an Italian League title (1984). He moved to AS Roma after the 1984-85 season, then continued his career in the sport as a coach and television commentator.

A rangy player, Boniek was one of several Polish stars to come through the successful program which produced Olympic champions and World Cup challengers through the 1970s and early 1980s.

Boniek was the driving force behind the 1982 Polish team that reached the World Cup semifinal, but had the misfortune to be suspended for the game against Italy because he had accumulated two yellow card cautions throughout the tournament. His absence cost Poland much of its attacking power.

At Juventus, Boniek teamed effectively with the gifted Platini. He was often the recipient of telling passes from his French midfield teammate and the two seemed to have a sixth sense that allowed Boniek to know exactly when to start his run; Platini, precisely when to release the pass.

Boniek often looked fragile, but that was misleading as defenders found to their misfortune. He had the turn of speed needed to create space and his endurance was such that he was usually most dangerous in the closing stages of play.

BOZSIK, JOSZEF
(1925-1978)

Bozsik was the finest attacking wing half in Europe during the 1950s, and the playmaker of mighty Honvéd and Hungary during their golden eras. He was the greatest halfback Hungary has ever produced, and became a model for hundreds of others in Europe after the glorious international successes of his national team.

Bozsik was an immaculate passer at both long and short distances, and delighted in anticipating the moves of his forward line, which happened to include the incomparable Ferenc Puskás, his best friend since childhood; Sandor Kocsis; Nandor Hidegkuti; and Zoltan Czibor.

Bozsik made his international debut for Hungary in 1947 against Bulgaria, and for the next nine years won a host of domestic and international honors.

As midfield general he played on five Hungarian championship teams with Honvéd and the legendary Hungarian national team that won the

1952 Olympic gold medal. His only major embarrassment occurred in the semifinals of the 1954 World Cup-in the so-called "Battle of Berne"—when he and Brazil's Nilton Santos were sent off for fighting.

After the Hungarian uprising in 1956, Bozsik returned to Budapest with the touring Honvéd team rather than join Puskás and others in the West, and was elected to the national House of Deputies. Always a family man and loyal member of the Honvéd organization, Bozsik remaineded with his fallen club until his retirement in 1962.

Bozsik was selected to play for Hungary in the 1958 World Cup—at center forward and inside forward—and returned to the national team before the 1962 World Cup to help his country qualify, though he did not play in the 1962 finals.

In his farewell match in 1962 against Uruguay, he gained his 100th cap, and he celebrated the occasion by scoring his eleventh international goal, a testament to his tendencies as an attacking halfback.

BUTRAGUENO, EMILIO
(1963—)

Nicknamed *El Buitre* (The Vulture), a Spanish play on words that tied the scavenging nature of the vulture to Butragueno's name, the Real Madrid star defied the odds of smallish size and suffocating expectations to create a lasting club and country career.

Butragueno's best day came in the 1986 World Cup in Mexico City when he scored four times in a stunning Spanish victory over fancied Denmark, personally executing the favored side in a 5-1 rout.

Butragueno's light build and lack of height would seem to have worked against him, but his ability in ghost into unexpected positions and his penchant for snapping up loose balls, rebounds, and tight-angled chances earned him The Vulture appellation and inspired a great era of Real Madrid success.

Although the European Cup eluded Real in the 1980s, Butragueno played on two UEFA Cup winners and five consccutive league champions (1986-1990) after joining the famous side in 1983. Still a leader of the attack in the 1990 World Cup, Butragueno maintained a regular place in the Spanish national team from his debut in 1984 through the Italia 90 tournament.

CANTONA, ERIC
(1966—)

Sometimes labeled the "bad boy of French soccer," Cantona emerged in the late 1980s as a quicksilver talent with a flair for the dramatic and the controversial. Not only does he score crucial goals for France, he has also proved his ability to succeed in English soccer, a league with a completely different style from the French First Division. A dark-haired, ruggedly handsome forward, Cantona also attracted a wide following of fans who appreciated his style on and off the field.

Cantona broke into French soccer in 1983-84 with Auxerre. After scoring 13 goals in the 1986-87 season he was snapped up by the more famous Olympique Marseille, where he spent two spells but never completely settled into the side.

In between, Cantona had a season with Montpellier and tours of duty with Bordeaux and Nimes. His stay in France included run-ins with officials, but also saw him establish himself as an international striker of great power. He scored goals at the rate of nearly one every two games he played for France as Michel Platini regularly included him in the selection.

In 1991-92 Cantona joined Leeds United in a surprise transfer and quickly established himself as a vital part of the championship English First Division team. Just as unexpectedly he was transferred in the fall of the following season, this time joining Manchester United. Once again he quickly was among the goals as United aimed at a title.

Noted for wonderful ball control and a sense of seizing the improbable opportunity, Cantona teams effectively with Jean-Pierre Papin in the French national team and has also proved capable of adjusting his sometimes individualistic attack approach to fit into the more rigorous English style.

CHARLES, WILLIAM JOHN (1931—)

The unique career of John Charles, the greatest Welsh player since Billy Meredith, peaked in the unlikely milieu of Italy. With his muscular six-foot, two-inch frame, Charles was an uncommon center forward whose skills with the ball belied his size. He was revered as much for his temperament as for his gifts as a player, and he also possessed the priceless ability to play well at all positions on the field.

Charles was signed by second division Leeds United at age 16 while working on the grounds staff of Swansea, his home-town club, and started by playing at center half. In 1950 he became the youngest Welsh international in history and three years later won a regular place in the Wales lineup after his Leeds manager switched him to center forward.

Charles's rare combination of assets drew the attention of Juventus in Italy, where during his five seasons (1957-62) he was a key element in the winning of three Italian championships and two Italian league cups. John Charles, the "gentle giant," scored over 260 goals in his career, and made 543 league appearances. His 15 goals for Wales were scored in 38 games.

CHARLTON, BOBBY (1937—)

Charlton was the premier English forward of the postwar era and the most admired player in England since Sir Stanley Matthews. He was equally respected by foreign observers, who saw him as a ball artist with panache and elusive skills in the Latin style, though in fact he was the son of a Northumberland miner.

His left foot produced a powerful and accurate shot as well as hairsplitting passes and pin

pointed flicks, and he was equally adept at all positions on the forward line except right wing.

Charlton scored 198 goals in 606 appearances with Manchester United. Between 1958-70, he appeared for England 106 times, a world record until it was broken by Bobby Moore in the early 1970s, and scored 49 goals, still the English record.

Bobby Charlton was truly the archetype of a national idol. He survived the 1958 Munich air disaster, and together with his famous manager, Matt Busby, represented the transition between the two phenomenal teams that United produced before and after that shattering tragedy. He was a model of decorum and sportsmanship and rarely, if ever, fouled an opposing player.

Teamed with his brother Jackie (the England and Leeds United center half), Charlton was the

Allsport

Bobby Charlton

spearhead of England's World Cup triumph of 1966, and in that same year was chosen both European and English Footballer of the Year.

Two years later he and Busby, whose relationship with him had grown into one of great friendship, remembered with bitter tears the nightmare of 1958, as United won the European Cup after a 10-year climb back to the top of international club competition.

COMBI, GIAMPIERO
(1902-1956)

Combi was generally regarded as Italy's greatest goalkeeper, and one of the three or four finest anywhere between the world wars. More than any other player, Combi represented the transition from Italy's building years during the 1920s and its golden era of the World Cup triumphs in 1934 and 1938.

His entire career was spent with Juventus, whom he inspired to championships in 1926 and 1931-34 playing behind some of the greatest backfields of his day.

Combi's international career, however, was tenuous at first. He made his debut for Italy in 1924 against Hungary, but after seven goals were scored against him, he was not selected again until the following year, and not regularly until the 1928 Olympic Games in Amsterdam.

As the automatic choice in goal from 1928 on, he accumulated enough caps to captain the 1934 World Cup team (by Italian tradition that role automatically goes to the player with the most international appearances), and retired from active play altogether immediately afterwards.

Combi's 47 international appearances was a record for an Italian goalkeeper until it was broken in the 1970s by Dino Zoff, who is sometimes mentioned as Combi's equal.

CRUYFF, JOHAN
(1947—)

The most exciting player in Europe during the 1970s, Cruyff's most important asset was his ability to excel at any function on the field. Perhaps the greatest Dutch player of all time, he was the driving force behind Holland's rise to the top of world soccer after 1970.

Cruyff led his original club, Ajax Amsterdam, tthree successive European Cup triumphs and his national team to a worldwide reputation as the leading exponent of "total football," though he and Holland failed the ultimate test in the 1974 World Cup final. On the field, he was at once an awesome striker and orchestrator *par excellence,* pushing his forward line while drawing the defense out to help the attack.

Johan Cruyff

Cruyff joined Ajax in his native Amsterdam at the age of 10. Seven years later he was a starting player, and at age 18 he made his international debut for Holland against Hungary, scoring a goal from the midfield.

Though he twice led the Dutch league in scoring (1967 and 1972), he set up many more goals than he converted, and his unique skills led Ajax to the Dutch championship six times.

Accorded the Dutch Footballer of the Year award in 1968 and 1969, he was voted European Footballer of the Year three times (1971, 1973, and 1974), the last coming after his controversial transfer to Barcelona in 1973 for $1.53 million.

Shortly before the 1978 World Cup, Cruyff retired from the Dutch national team, and in the 1978 close-season, he left Barcelona having scored 42 goals in his four seasons there. He

turned successfully to coaching at the end of his playing days, winning a European Cup at Barcelona in 1992.

CUBILLAS, TEOFILO
(1949—)

Without question the most stunning player Peru produced in the mid-1970s, Cubillas ranked at or near the top of great South American stars. Cubillas made his first team debut for Alianza Lima in 1968 at age 18, and one year later he was picked to play for Peru in the World Cup qualifying round. At the 1970 World Cup, he burst onto the world scene with five goals in four games and contributed much to Peru's fluid attack and unexpected success.

After the World Cup of 1970, Cubillas received offers from several dozen clubs in Europe and South America, but the Peruvian government blocked his transfer until 1973, when he joined Switzerland's FC Basel.

This association was short-lived, however, and he moved to FC Porto in Portugal, remaining there for four years and delighting Portuguese fans. While at Porto he adopted an attacking midfield role, which he used very effectively with his powerful shot.

Urged home to help Peru qualify for the 1978 World Cup, he returned to Alianza in 1977, helping his famous old club win a first division title by scoring 22 goals in 35 games, and he produced one of the few genuine world-class performances in the final rounds in Argentina.

Having completed his international commitment to Peru's 1978 World Cup venture, he accepted a lucrative offer from the Ft. Lauderdale Strikers and played in the United States until the end of his career.

DEAN, WILLIAM "DIXIE"
(1907—)

England's greatest goalscoring center forward, Dean was a classic English center forward—strong, aggressive, and, above all, powerful in the air—who scored not so much with nimbleness of feet as with determination and a sense of authority. In 1927-28, he scored 60 goals in league competition for Everton, an English record that still stands and is not far off from the world record for 42 games in top-level competition. This total, in fact, was achieved in only 39 games due to injury. His total of 349 goals for one club, however, remains unbeaten.

In international competition, Dean scored an incredible 18 goals in 16 appearances for England, including 12 in his first five games, which were all played before the age of 21. His 37 career hat tricks are also an English record.

Syndication Intl.

Dixie Dean

Each of these figures would be higher were it not for Dean's endless battle with injuries. A marked player from his earliest days, his life once hung in the balance after an abdominal injury.

In 1925 he broke his skull in an automobile accident. It apparently had little or no effect on his play, as Dean went on to score more goals with his head than any player in English soccer history.

At age 16, Dean was signed by Tranmere Rovers, across the river from Liverpool, and two years later, in 1925, he moved to Everton, where he achieved lasting fame and popularity. His appearances for England were made from 1927-33, and would have been doubled or tripled had it not been for his injuries. He also lost as many as 100 league appearances through injury.

DE VECCHI, RENZO
(1894-1967)

De Vecchi stands as Italy's first great idol of the amateur era and the greatest name in Italian soccer before the golden era of the 1930s. De Vecchi was a left back of great skill, and his level of expertise compared favorably with his counterparts in the more developed European soccer countries of that period. Though De Vecchi antedated Italy's rise to the front ranks of international competition, his following was so loyal that he became known as *il figlio di dio* ("The Son of God").

De Vecchi was signed by Milan while still in his early teens, and in 1910, at age 16, made his international debut as a substitute against Hungary. His place in Italy's first team was established against Hungary the following year—Italy's third international—and he went on to make a record 43 appearances before his retirement in 1925, twenty-six of those (1920-25) as captain.

Photograph by Sven Simon

Didi

DIDI
(1928—)

Full name: Valdir Pereira. The master of the midfield strategy, Didi probably knew more about the role of orchestrator and linkman than any South American player before or since. Didi was also world famous as a dead ball artist, especially for his astonishing *folha seca* ("dry leaf"), or banana kick. It was in his former capacity, however, that he achieved lasting fame.

Didi led the Brazilian team to its stunning World Cup triumph in 1958, a tribute eagerly acknowledged by the players and press alike, and he emerged from this campaign with the tag "world's greatest player." In 1950 he entered the record books as part of a Rio selection by scoring the first goal ever converted in the new Maracanaaa Stadium.

In 1952 Didi made his international debut for Brazil against Mexico, and eventually accumulated a total of 73 appearances. He played in the 1954 World Cup in Switzerland, and in 1956 moved to Botafogo where he was to play out his career, except for one brief interlude.

After his extraordinary impact on the 1958 World Cup, he was signed by Real Madrid, but his star billing raised the ire of Alfredo Di Stefano, who considered himself to be the world's greatest player.

Di Stefano made Didi's life in Madrid uncomfortable and Real loaned him to Valencia. Disappointed, Didi asked to be returned to Botafogo in 1960, and he led his old club to two Rio titles in 1961 and 1962 before retiring.

Didi ultimately embarked on a second highly successful career as a coach, first with Sporting Cristal in Lima, Peru, and in 1970 with the talented Peruvian national team that performed so well in the World Cup of that year.

DI STEFANO LAUTHE, ALFREDO
(1926—)

Next to Pelé, Di Stefano's name is most often mentioned as the greatest player of all time. Di Stefano's ability to perform all tasks on the field elevated him above the stature of other great players.

His ball control and shooting skills were peerless, and he invariably determined the style and pace of the game, and organized and supported the defense as well as the attack. He was powerfully built, showed endless stamina, stayed at peak condition throughout his career, and rarely, if ever, was caught motionless on the field.

Deutsche Presse-Agentur

Alfredo Di Stefano

Born of Italian parents in Argentina, Di Stefano joined Ríver Plate in 1942 and won a place on its first team two years later. After a one-year loan to Huracan in 1945 (scoring 50 goals in 66 games), he returned to Ríver Plate and in 1947 replaced the legendary Adolfo Pedernera at center forward, topped the Argentine goalscoring list, and made the first of seven appearances for Argentina.

In 1949, he joined the mass movement of South American players to the breakaway Colombian League, and until 1953 was the hero of Millonarios de Bogota, guiding it to two championships during his five-year tenure while collecting four caps from Colombia along the way. In 292 appearances for Millonarios, he scored 259 goals.

Santiago Bernabeu, the owner of Real Madrid, signed him in 1953, transforming European soccer with one stroke of the pen. "The Blond Arrow of Ríver Plate" remained with Real until 1964 and achieved everything that could possibly be asked of a player.

As a deep-lying center forward and orchestrator for the greatest club-level team ever seen, he scored 405 goals in 624 appearances, raising his cumulative goalscoring figure to over 800 (fourth highest ranking in history).

Di Stefano played on a record six European Cup-winning teams, was twice European Footballer of the Year (1957 and 1959), and led the Spanish league in scoring five times. Perhaps his most unique accomplishment was scoring 49 goals in European Cup competition alone.

He became a naturalized Spaniard and made 31 international appearances for Spain, scoring 23 goals, and finally rounded out his career with a two-year stint at Espanol (1964-66), scoring 19 goals in 81 games as he approached his fortieth year.

EUSEBIO
(1942—)

Full name: Eusebio da Silva Ferreira. This extraordinary native of Mozambique led Benfica and Portugal to the heights of world soccer and became the most lethal goal scorer in Europe during the 1960s.

His rare combination of lightening speed and the ability to pivot and dribble through a phalanx of defenders made him one of the most explosive and entertaining players of the postwar era.

Eusebio was the leading scorer in Portugal for nine seasons between 1964-73. He twice scored the most goals of any European player in one season (1968 and 1973), made a record 77 international appearances for Portugal, and was voted European Footballer of the Year in 1965.

Wide World Photos

Eusebio

All told, Eusebio led his club to ten Portuguese championships and five cup victories in 14 seasons. Serious knee operations in 1967 and 1969 initiated his slow decline, but it was not until 1974 that he showed serious signs of weakening.

FACCHETTI, GIACINTO (1942—)

The nonpareil of European attacking fullbacks, Facchetti is one of the unique players in the history of the game. Standing over six-feet, two-inches tall and weighing 185 pounds, he developed a keen sense for the goal while playing center forward as a boy.

Throughout his professional career, he was never content with being a mere overlapping back—a role that alone would have made him an international star by virtue of his commanding presence—but his deft ball control skills and exceptionally powerful right foot shot often led him into face-to-face challenges with opposing goalkeepers.

His 42 league goals in 1967-68 were scored in 26 matches. In the 1966 World Cup, with Portugal losing to North Korea by 3-0, he scored four goals in succession and set up a fifth to take Portugal to an astounding 5-3 victory.

A child prodigy in the African shantytown section of Lourenco Marques, Eusebio was signed at age 15 by the leading local club, Sporting. Before his eighteenth birthday he had scored 55 league goals. His first appearance for Benfica was made in the 1961 Tournoi de Paris, during which he and Pelé alternately outdazzled each other in a series of unforgettable displays.

Three months later he made his international debut for Portugal while still aged 19. The following season he was the spearhead in Benfica's second European Cup win in a row.

In his 18 years with Inter Milan, Facchetti scored nearly 60 goals, all coming forward from the left back or sweeper position. In international competition he scored three goals for Italy. Moreover, these tallies were often in open field situations, and in 1965, his goal against Liverpool in the European Cup semifinals was the winner that eventually led Inter to its second consecutive European club championship.

Facchetti first appeared as a center forward for his fourth division home town club, Trevigliese, while still in his mid-teens, and in 1960 was transferred to nearby Inter Milan, where he was converted into a left back. He remained at Inter for the duration of his career, and gained a first team place in 1962-63, scoring four goals in 31 appearances that season.

Facchetti's hard tackling, gazelle-like control in the air, and his accurate reading of attacks, in addition to his striking instincts, soon brought him national fame, and in 1963 he made his international debut against Turkey in Istanbul. Under manager Helenio Herrera, he and Inter won three Italian championships, two European Cups, and two Intercontinental Cups between 1963-66. He reached the 90 mark in 1977, and captained the team 65 times.

FAUSTO
(1905-1939)

Full name: Fausto dos Santos. This world-class center half was one of the first Brazilian players to enjoy an international reputation, largely through his superb performance in the 1930 World Cup. He began his career in 1926 as an amateur with his hometown club, Bangu AC, in the Rio suburb of that name, and two years later, having achieved much respect as an inside forward, he moved to Vasco da Gama as a center half.

Fausto's highly intelligent tactics as a linkman and his superb ball control were the main factor in Vasco's winning the 1929 Rio league championship, and that same year he made his international debut for Brazil in a friendly with Yugoslavia. In the 1930 World Cup, he combined masterfully with inside forward Preguinho, and soon acquired the nickname *Maravilha Negra* ("Black Wonder").

On Vasco's 1931 tour of Europe, Fausto captured the attention of Barcelona, and he returned to play for the giant Catalan club until 1933, when his health began to decline and he was transferred to Young Fellows Berne. In 1934, he returned to Vasco, helping his old club to win another Rio title, but he was left out of the 1934 World Cup squad because of his professional status (a controversial issue in Brazil at the time).

In 1936 Fausto moved to Flamengo, where poor health continued to plague him. He was unable to compete in the 1938 World Cup because of one of his numerous bouts with influenza. In 1939 he developed tuberculosis and was admitted to a sanitorium in Minas Gerais, where he died later that year at age 34.

FINNEY, THOMAS
(1922—)

Inevitably compared to his contemporary at outside right, Stanley Matthews, Finney was perhaps the most complete No. 7 in English soccer history. He was a master ball artist, and, unlike Matthews, he was equally adept with either foot and could finish with great authority on a consistent basis. He scored a record 30 goals for England in 76 appearances.

The most troubling controversy in the postwar English game was whom to select on the right wing—Matthews or Finney—and it was often settled by playing both, Finney on the left, and Matthews on the right. Ultimately, Finney played 40 times for England on the right, and 33 on the left.

Finney's 12-year international career began in 1947, one month after he joined the first team of Preston North End. Preston was the only club Finney ever played for; he signed with them as an amateur in 1937, and, despite turning professional in 1940, his official debut was put off until 1946 because of the war.

In 1960, at age 38, Finney was prematurely forced to retire from Preston with a sustained groin injury while still the top scorer for his club. For 23 years he almost single-handedly kept Preston in the top flight of league competition, but failed to gain a single league or cup honor.

FRIEDENREICH, ARTUR
(1892-1969)

The first idol of Brazilian soccer, Friedenreich was a center forward of dazzling skills and untold popularity. Pelé notwithstanding, he is still considered by many to be the best player Brazil has ever produced, and he is the greatest goalscorer in world soccer history, his 1329 career goals in senior competition having officially been acknowledged by FIFA.

Friedenreich was the phenomenon of his age, showing imagination, an unprecedented under-

AP/Wide World Photos

Artur Friedenreich

standing of the game, total mastery of his skills, and an improvisational style. The legends that sprang up around him were legion.

There were myths concerning his exotic name, his powerful kick, and other superhuman movements, and in 1930 the country nearly came to a standstill when it was rumored that he had been killed during the revolution of that year. In addition, he paved the way for blacks and mestizos to play with top flight Brazilian clubs: he himself was one of the first mestizos to do so.

The son of a German father and black Brazilian mother of humble origins, "Fried" started his career in 1909 with Germania FC, the club of the German immigrant colony in his native Sao Paulo.

His longest and most important association, however, was with CA Paulistano of Sao Paulo. He led this great team to championships in 1917, 1918, 1919, and 1921, and his fame spread across the ocean when he dominated Paulistano's triumphant tour of Europe in 1925, scoring bewildering goals wherever he went.

In 1930 he became one of the original members of the new Sao Paulo FC, which, after only one year in existence, won the Paulista title on the heels of his incredible goalscoring artistry. Friedenreich closed his career in 1935 with Flamengo, the only Rio de Janeiro club he ever consented to join.

Friedenreich made 22 appearances for Brazil, a high number in that era of limited international competition, and his debut coincided with Brazil's very first international contest—against Exeter City F.C. in 1914.

By virtue of his great success and popularity, he was responsible not only for the admission of racially mixed players in the upper levels of Brazilian competition but also for black and mestizo fans embracing the game as their own.

GALLACHER, HUGH
(1903-1957)

Gallacher was Scotland's greatest center forward ever and one of Europe's most opportunistic goal scorers during the period between the wars. From 1921-39, Hughie Gallacher scored 387 league goals in 541 appearances, the vast majority with English clubs, and in a mere 20 international appearances tallied for 22 goals, including five in one match against Northern Ireland in 1929. His five-foot, five-inch frame was massively built and gave him extraordinary balance as he weaved his way through defenders with uncanny control.

While playing for his home town amateur club, Bellshill Athletic, in 1920, Gallacher was selected for Scotland's Junior team, and in that same year was signed by the Scottish second division club Queen of the South. Scottish first division Airdrieonians lured him away after one season, and he led little Airdrie to a Scottish cup in 1924, and three successive second place finishes behind Rangers in the Scottish league.

Gallacher's inevitable transfer to one of the well-heeled clubs of England came in 1925—to Newcastle United—and there he became an instant favorite. He was made captain of the club at age 24, and in his first year as captain (1926-27) led Newcastle to a championship. He moved to Chelsea and played at peak or near peak form for four more years before his transfer to Derby County in 1934 signaled the start of his decline.

GARRINCHA
(1933—)

Full name: Manuel Francisco dos Santos. *Garrincha* is a Portuguese expression meaning "little bird," and it was given to this astonishing Brazilian player because the polio he had suffered from as a child made one of his legs look

Syndication International Ltd.

Hugh Gallacher

Metelmann

Garrincha

slightly distorted—an unlikely beginning for the player some would call the greatest dribbler the game has ever seen. Garrincha was a right wing phenomenon who glided to the heights of world soccer with Brazil in the World Cups of 1958 and 1962. In 51 appearances for Brazil, he was on the losing side only once.

At age 14, he joined his local club, Pau Grande, as an inside left, and in 1953 tried out for the big Rio club Botafogo, winning a place on the team from the start. The following year he was chosen to play on a Rio selection. In 1957, he made his debut for Brazil in the South American Championship but was dropped until a World Cup qualifying match some months later, his reinstatement having been demanded by the other players.

Garrincha burst onto the world scene in Brazil's third game in the 1958 World Cup against the U.S.S.R., and in the final against Sweden he set up the first two goals by dribbling around his defenders to the gasps of the Stockholm crowd.

He helped Botafogo win three Rio championships from 1957-62, and in the 1962 World Cup reached his peak of dazzling artistry, scoring two goals against England in the quarter-finals and two against Chile in the semi-finals, each more incredible than the other.

Garrincha made one more memorable performance, against Bulgaria in the 1966 World Cup, at a time when his career was in its twilight.

GASCOIGNE, PAUL
(1967—)

At a time when England was seeking a gifted, creative player to lend some variety to the national team, Paul Gascoigne took on the larger-than-life role of midfield genius, emotional upstart, and tabloid hero. A left-sided player whose chunky physique belies his quick starts and sprinting ability, Gascoigne moved from Newcastle to Tottenham to World Cup 1990 hero status without missing a beat.

Unlike several other England players whose creative flair never seemed to quite fit the hard-working, hard-running players who surround them in the league and national team, Gascoigne has proved able to stand the pace and still add something special.

His free kicks have a South American flair to them, his weaving, dribbling runs look more like those which characterize the Continental game, while his competitiveness and fire are all English in their manner.

After playing four seasons with Newcastle United, in 1988 Gascoigne moved to Tottenham Hotspur, where he scored a classic FA Cup semifinal goal against Arsenal at Wembley Stadium and picked up a horrific injury in the subsequent final against Nottingham Forest.

That damaged cruciate ligament almost cost Gascoigne and Spurs a $10 million deal with Lazio, but the player came back from the blow to join the Rome club in Italy for the 1992-93 season.

Gascoigne's most famous night, however, came in Turin. As the motor of a surprising England World Cup team he drove his side through a 1-1 semifinal draw with Germany, but burst into tears when he received a yellow card that meant automatic suspension from his team's next game.

Those tears, caught on international television, showed the human side of a player whose exploits often made tabloid newspaper headlines of the most conventional type.

Francisco Gento

GENTO LOPEZ, FRANCISCO
(1933—)

The speediest left winger of his time, "Paco" started as a boy with Nueva Montana, Astillero Santander, and Real Santander before Real Madrid signed him and Di Stefano at the same time in 1953.

His 18 years with Real bridged the gap between three generations of Real teams, and his longevity helped to create a set of unique records. He was the only player to participate in all eight of Real's European Cup finals, and he stands alone by scoring in 11 consecutive European Cup competitions (1956-66).

When Di Stefano retired in 1964, Gento became captain, and led Real to its sixth European title two years later.

He made 43 international appearances for Spain, though unfortunately, he was not selected for Spain's 1964 European Nations' Cup winning team, which would have been his only chance to collect an honor at the national level.

In his later years, he was Spain's captain. In 1971, at the age of 38, he played in the European Cup Winners' Cup final against Chelsea, completing a remarkable career that saw him win 12 league championship and six European Cup medals.

GOYCOCHEA, SERGIO
(1963—)

In many ways the 1990 World Cup tournament in Italy belonged to Sergio Goycochea. When Argentina lost regular keeper Nery Pumpido to a broken leg in the opening quarter of their second match in Italy, Goycochea stepped in as his replacement and resurrected his career.

His penalty kick saves carried Argentina to shoot-out victories over Yugoslavia and Italy, earning the defending champions a place in the final and Goycochea the reputation as the greatest penalty kick saver in the world.

It is a reputation his subsequent play has done nothing to diminish: in 1993 he saved the spot kicks that gave Argentina victory over Denmark in the match between South American and European champions for the Artemio Franchi Trophy.

Goycochea, a tall, athletic keeper with long arms and a wonderful sense of anticipation, made his debut in top class Argentine soccer with Ríver Plate in 1982. He remained with the club through the 1989 when he was transferred to the Colombian club, Millonarios.

Unfortunately, his move to Colombia coincided with the suspension of that country's championship, hence he arrived in Italy for the 1990 World Cup without having played a competitive match for almost a season. That served to make his performance in Italy all the more remarkable.

After the World Cup, Goycochea played for a brief spell in France, but returned to South America to play for the top Paraguayan clubs, Cerro Porteno and Olimpia. He was named Argentina's Footballer of the Year after his 1990 exploits and remained the country's top-choice goalkeeper heading into the 1994 qualifying competition.

GULLIT, RUUD
(1962—)

Although injuries slowed the career of Holland's great midfielder-attacker, the impression of powerful, dreadlocked Ruud Gullit will always remain a part of soccer in the 1980s. It was his long-striding runs and whiplash shots, his collection of sharply angled headers and an unerring sense of when to produce the unexpected which helped boost Holland to the 1988 European Championship and helped to transform AC Milan from a good Italian League side to the scourge of European club soccer.

After playing three years with Haarlem, Gullit broke into the Dutch big time with Feyenoord in 1982, where he played three seasons. It was at PSV Eindhoven, from 1985-87 when he produced 46 goals in 68 games, that his star truly rose to international level, attracting the attention of Milan, whom he joined in 1987.

Gullit's impact in Italian soccer was immediate as he teamed with Frank Rijkaard and Marco van Basten, two other imports from Holland, to create the all-action Milan style coached by

Arrigo Sacchi. Back-to-back European Cups in 1989 and 1990 were coupled with world club titles in the same two years.

A troublesome knee injury that required more than one surgical intervention slowed Gullit in the 1989-90 season, when he made only three first-team appearances for Milan and caused him to enter the 1990 World Cup at less than full strength. His inability to play at top form was blamed by some for Holland's failure to reach expectations.

HIDEGKUTI, NANDOR
(1922—)

The vital element of Hungary's revolutionary "W" attack during the early 1950s, Hidegkuti was one of the only players on this national team who was not a member of Honvéd at one time or another.

As Hungary's deep-lying center forward, his function was primarily to feed the ball to Ferenc Puskás and Sandor Kocsis, but he himself scored 39 goals in his 68 international appearances, and he was so skilled a player that he turned his role into a multi-purpose midfielder as well as center forward.

Hidegkuti learned the game in the streets of a poor section of Budapest, and in 1943 signed with lowly Elektromos. In 1947, two years after his international debut, he moved to MTK, one of Budapest's great sporting institutions, and soon became one of the league's leading scorers. He was not a regular choice for the national team, however, until 1952, when he participated with great success in Hungary's gold medal-winning effort in the Olympic Games.

Hidegkuti figured prominently in Hungary's 6-3 thrashing of England in 1953 and in the 1954 World Cup, where he scored one of his most famous goals with a diving header against Uruguay. He continued to play for MTK—at inside right rather than center forward—until his retirement, and also played for Hungary in the 1958 World Cup, though with little of his old flair. His relatively late start as an international put him well into his thirties by this time, and he finally retired in 1958, with the nickname "Old Man."

JAMES, ALEXANDER
(1902-1953)

The outstanding character in British soccer between the wars, James was a soccer genius whose scheming for the legendary Arsenal team of the 1930s was the central factor in that club's success. As a deep-lying inside forward, it was James who often initiated counterattacks in the midfield and, through his deft and imaginative distribution of the ball, gave life to a tactical theory that eventually altered the way soccer was played everywhere for decades.

Above all, James was known for the knee-length baggy shorts he wore throughout his career, prompting a continuous stream of cartoons about the short Scot who seemed to have no torso.

James started playing in his native Scotland with the amateur clubs Belshill Athletic and Ashfield before moving to Raith Rovers in 1922. By the time Preston North End had signed him three years later, he had developed into a goalscoring inside forward, and with Preston scored 53 goals in 147 appearances between 1925-29.

His new assignment at Arsenal (playmaker) required a complete change of roles, but since this was a condition for his signing with Arsenal in the first place, he accepted it grudgingly. Arsenal's success during James tenure there—four league championships and two F.A. Cup wins—justified his personal sacrifice.

Alexander James

JENNINGS, PAT
(1945—)

Pat Jennings wound up his playing career in the giant Guadalajara Stadium as little Northern Ireland took on mighty Brazil in the 1986 World Cup. It was a fitting stage for one of the great soccer players to conclude a lifetime between the goalposts, his 119th cap allowing him to finish at the very top of the game.

No one ever doubted Jennings' courageous, aggressive goalkeeping style, a style that made him one of the leading figures in the English League throughout a career that included stops at Watford, Tottenham Hotspur, and Arsenal.

His personality was such that he was one of the few players able to move from one great North

London club to the other and not make enemies. The Spurs fans who had cheered him through 472 matches did not lose respect for their hero when he crossed the city to play 237 times for Arsenal.

That international success came late in Jennings' career was no fault of his, but rather a consequence of playing for one of Europe's smallest soccer nations. Often he had stood between under-strength Northern Irish sides and heavy defeats so it was poetic justice when things turned around for manager Billy Bingham's team.

The 1982 team qualified for the World Cup second round and included a win over host Spain in its bag. The 1986 team did well to qualify, allowing Jennings to wrap up his career in the world spotlight.

KOCSIS, SANDOR
(1929—)

Perhaps the greatest header of the ball in the history of the game, Sandor Kocsis was the prolific goalscoring inside right of the Hungarian "Magic Magyars" in the early 1950s. He was, above all, known for his acrobatics on the field, and for his specialty he acquired the nickname "Golden Head," but he could also perform all the other functions of a forward with alarming agility.

In 1948, at age 19, he entered the first team of Ferencváros, and, after helping this great "Fradi" team win a championship, he made his first appearance for Hungary in 1949.

After a one-year stint at EDOSZ, Honvéd snapped him up in 1950, and he remained there in the company with so many great Hungarian stars of the period. He was the Hungarian scor-

ing leader in 1951 (30), 1952 (36), and 1954 (33), and during this period scored 75 goals for Hungary, including 11 in the 1954 World Cup.

When the 1956 Hungarian uprising broke out, Honvéd was on tour, and, like Puskás and Czibor, Kocsis decided to flee to the West. For several months, he was a player-coach at Young Fellows in Switzerland.

Barcelona signed him in 1957, but he was used sparingly because of a FIFA ban he received after leaving Honvéd. In 1958-59 with Barcelona, Kocsis began a long run of high-scoring seasons reminiscent of his great days in Budapest.

KOEMAN, RONALD
(1963—)

Known for thundering free kicks and an uncompromising style of defensive play, Ronald Koeman helped to put Holland and FC Barcelona on top of the European soccer world. A sturdy, stolid-faced blond, Koeman's forays out of defense and his deadly long-range shots were his trademark for both club and country.

One of those free kicks brought Barcelona the 1992 European Cup in extra time at Wembley Stadium, while his dominant role in defense helped Holland to win its only major soccer honor, the 1988 European Championship.

Koeman, whose older brother Erwin also played for Holland, made his soccer debut with the Dutch League club FC Groningen in 1980-81 before moving on to Ajax Amsterdam in 1983.

Unlike so many of the Dutch stars of his era, he did not remain long in Amsterdam. Instead, he signed with PSV Eindhoven in 1986 and was a member of the European Cup winning side of 1987-88.

Koeman joined Barcelona in 1989-90 at a cost of nearly $6.5 million and immediately helped the Catalonian club to eclipse its arch rival Real Madrid in the fierce battle for honors in Spain and Europe.

Koeman's trademark free kicks are the result of a powerful right foot. His drives from as far away as 40 yards can deceive goalkeepers both with their pure speed and their late swerves. He is especially dangerous when striking free kicks around the penalty area because he can literally drive the ball through the defensive wall of players when he gets the trajectory just right.

In addition, Koeman developed into one of the steadiest penalty kick takers in the game, his policy simply to shoot the ball as hard as possible from the 12-yard spot.

Deutsche Presse-Agentur GmbH

Raymond Kopa

KOPA, RAYMOND
(1931—)

One of the most versatile forwards of the post-war era, originally an outside right, Kopa eventually became a roaming center forward whose chief asset among many was a gift for dribbling. During his peak years in the late 1950s, he was often mentioned with Di Stefano and Puskás as one of the world's top players.

Having started his career with SCO Angers, Kopa was signed by Albert Batteux's Stade de Reims in 1951, and made his first appearance for France "B" in 1952. With Reims, he adopted the role of orchestrating center forward, and helped his club win the French championship in 1955.

In the 1955-56 European Cup, Kopa played so superbly against Real Madrid in the final that the Spanish champions lured him away, and he proceeded to play in the next three European Cup finals for them.

In 1958, he combined with inside forward Just Fontaine to lead France to a third-place finish in the World Cup. Elected European Footballer of the Year that same year, Kopa returned to Reims in 1958 and took up where he left off, playing happily with his old club until 1964.

His last international appearance was in 1962 against Hungary, his 45th, and he retired with 17 international goals.

KROL, RUUD
(1949—)

In an age when attackers and midfielders grabbed most of the headlines, Rudolf (Ruud) Krol made a name for himself as a defender, but it would be incorrect to say that the great Dutchman played strictly a defensive game. Tall, lanky, feathery in his movements and strong in his surging runs, Krol was a defender-cum-midfielder, one of the many players around whom Rinus Michels built the great Dutch national team of the 1970s, revolutionizing soccer in the process.

Krol began his lengthy career at Ajax Amsterdam in 1968, arriving at a time when the club was collecting together some of the finest talent in Europe. He remained at Ajax for 12 years, playing for seven Dutch championship teams and four Dutch Cup winners while enjoying a hat trick of European Cup wins (1971-73) and one world club championship. He was at the heart of the defense which so quickly created attacks in a side that utilized all 10 field players interchangeably.

Although Krol did not play on a World Cup winner, his 83 caps included appearances in both the 1974 and 1978 finals. He also spent a year in the North American Soccer League with the Vancouver Whitecaps before wrapping up his playing days in Italy. He joined Napoli in 1980-81 after his brief stop in Canada.

LAW, DENIS
(1940—)

Law was one of Europe's most clever and exciting inside forwards of the postwar era and the finest British player in that position since his fellow Scot, Alex James; though, unlike James, Law functioned as a goalscorer rather than a playmaker.

Law's skills were completely developed both in the air and on the ground. A measure of his magnetic qualities was his great popularity and selection as European Footballer of the Year (1964) while playing with two other soccer legends, Bobby Charlton and George Best, at Manchester United.

Law was signed at age 15 by an English club (Huddersfield) directly from his schoolplaying days in Aberdeen, and in 1959 he became the youngest Scottish international in this century.

One year later, he went to Manchester City for the British record transfer fee of £55,000, but stayed for only one season after Italy's Torino paid £100,000 for him.

Law returned to England the following year with Manchester United, where he had always hoped to play, and there appeared a record 55 times for Scotland, the last being his World Cup debut against Zaire in 1974.

After scoring over 210 league and 29 international goals, he finally left active play and embarked on a successful career in sports broadcasting.

LAWTON, THOMAS
(1919—)

England's legendary center forward of the 1940s, Lawton succeeded Dixie Dean in that position at Everton and successfully challenged Dean's reputation as the greatest center forward in his country's history. He was the most commanding header of the ball ever seen in Britain, and ranks with Sandor Kocsis as perhaps the premier header of all time.

Lawton was a teenage prodigy with Burnley from 1935, and in 1937, at age 17, he joined Everton, establishing a precedent for hard bargaining with club managements. Before his career was over in 1956, he had played officially for six clubs.

His first great season was in 1937-38 with Everton, and during the war Lawton played for several clubs around the country while in uniform, reaching his peak of skill and goalscoring

Thomas Lawton

power. It was estimated that during the war he scored almost 300 goals in over 250 club and 22 international appearances—all unofficial—and, with Stanley Matthews, shone brightly as England's greatest diversion from wartime's bleakness.

LEÔNIDAS
(1913—)

Full name: Leônidas da Silva. A small, rubbery Brazilian center forward, Leônidas made the bicycle kick famous in the late 1930s. He was so agile that he could take bicycle kicks with both feet, sometimes controlling the ball with one foot and kicking it with the other.

Leônidas stole the show at the 1938 World Cup and helped Brazil to win its first big interna-

tional success: third place in the world championship. In addition, his speed and exceptional ability to read the field elevated him to the top rank of all-time great center forwards.

Leônidas was probably the most complete player in that position Brazil has ever had. Furthermore, he drew the world's attention to Brazil as a potential international power, and in a sense was the last bridge between the chaotic years of Brazilian amateurism and Brazil's rise to world prominence after World War II.

His nicknames were *O Diamante Negro* ("The Black Diamond") and *O Homen Borracha* ("The Rubber Man"). In his international debut for Brazil, against Uruguay in 1932 at age 18, he scored two goals.

Nacional Montevideo signed him immediately thereafter, and one year later, having played a major part in Nacional's winning the Uruguayan championship in 1933, he returned to Brazil and helped Vasco da Gama win a Rio championship.

Leônidas played in the 1934 World Cup, returned to spearhead Botafogo's Rio title in 1935, and finally settled at Flamengo from 1936-42, his most productive period. He rounded out his career with a long stay at Sao Paulo before finally retiring in 1950.

LINEKER, GARY
(1960—)

Gary Lineker's career will be remembered for his second-leading goal tally in an England international shirt and for all of the crucial goals he produced in top-level soccer for clubs in England and Spain. Lineker will be recalled as one of the ambassadors of his sport, a player who won as many friends for his approach to the game and the world as he did by scoring goals.

A star almost from the time that he broke into top level soccer with Leicester City in 1978, Lineker always was among the top goalscorers despite the fact that he was neither exceptionally big, fast, or skilled in the air. Instead, he used the thinking-man's approach to scoring, always testing the defenders to their very limit, pushing that one extra step forward, making the unexpected late run to touch in a cross that seemed out of reach.

Those qualities were never better illustrated than in the 1986 Mexican World Cup when Lineker personally powered England from a slow start to the quarterfinals, leading the tournament in scoring with six goals. After a season with Everton just prior to that World Cup success, Lineker moved to FC Barcelona where he spent 1986-89 as the leader of the Catalonians' attack. He scored regularly in Spain but also gained positive notice for learning his new country's language and fitting neatly into the culture.

Lineker returned to England to play with Tottenham Hotspur in 1989-90, again led the attack in the 1990 World Cup, and wound up scoring 28 goals in his final season with Spurs (1991-92).

He continued to confound the establishment, however, when he announced that he would leave English soccer to play in the newly-created J-League, signing a lucrative contract with the Japanese club Grampus Eight of Nagoya, starting Japanese language lessons and saying that he wanted to help the sport's professional growth in Asia.

One of the most polished of spokesmen for the game, Lineker contributed both in the way he played and in what he said. He never was shown a yellow card throughout his career at the top level in Europe and his work as a television commentator for major British networks helped to define his style and attitude toward the sport.

MAIER, JOSEF "SEPP" (1944—)

Maier was widely regarded as the successor to Gordon Banks as the world's greatest goalkeeper of the 1970s. After a shaky start in international competition, Maier became an important element in West Germany's rise to the top after the 1970 World Cup. A devotee of physical fitness programs, Maier was fundamentally an acrobat with a clowning personality.

Pfeil Photo

Josef Maier

Maier started with the youth team of TSV Haar, but at age 14 he was signed by Bayern and placed in its youth team with the young Franz Beckenbauer. Maier made 11 West German Youth international appearances, as well as four for West Germany "Amateur," and entered Bayern's first team at age 18.

Maier's extraordinary career has included winning the World Cup, European Football Championship, European Cup (three times), European Cup Winners' Cup, Intercontinental Cup, West German league championship and the West German cup, accumulating 95 international appearances.

MALDINI, PAOLO
(1968—)

Paolo Maldini was born to play at AC Milan, but unlike so many others burdened with a great potential, the Italian national team defender never missed a beat in living up to a predetermined role in life.

The son of Cesare Maldini, who captained AC Milan to the 1963 European Cup, Paolo stepped into the same team at the age of 16 in 1984 and immediately proved a remarkable player. He was an international by age 20 and the mainstay of both club and country by the turn of the calendar into the 1990s.

Dark-haired, with wide, sparkling eyes, Maldini could have been a matinee idol in another era. Instead, as an uncompromising defender he first made his name for his solid play at the back, then developed into a free-ranging attacker-defender as the game opened up and players were expected to fit into multiple roles.

Partnering veteran Franco Baresi in the heart of both the Milan and Italy defense, Maldini developed the technique of attacking down the left flank, perfecting his ball control and crossing abilities so that he took on the style of a secondary winger without losing his defensive capabilities.

As the Milan style of play evolved from the overly defensive to a balanced, attack-oriented game under Arrigo Sacchi, Maldini proved one of the most adept at changing his game to take advantage of the newfound freedom.

When Sacchi moved on to take charge of the Italian World Cup team, Maldini quickly became the linchpin of the national side's ability to convert defense into attack. He also took a more active role at set plays, coming forward to utilize his height to head corners.

Maldini has the ability to strike the ball through a crowd of players, so much so that he was as dangerous when meeting a defensive clearance as he was when rising to the available headers.

MARADONA, DIEGO ARMANDO
(1960—)

The enduring pictures of Diego Maradona's career serve to define the controversial, sometimes enigmatic man: his weaving run past what looked like the entire England defense en route to a remarkable goal in the 1986 World Cup finals is contrasted with his fisted score in the same game at the same tournament.

His million-dollar smile as he lofted the World Cup high above his head in the Aztec Stadium is matched by the tearful, contentious response to defeat in 1990 in the Rome Olympic Stadium; his bending free kicks and pinpoint passes call up one image, his penchant for making the most an opponent's foul presents another.

For Maradona nothing ever seemed straightforward. That may have been because few players in any sport ever came into international prominence with such fanfare. Maradona emerged from the poverty of Argentina's back streets to win a place in the country's First Division at 16.

Maradona was already a major star with Argentinos Juniors when the 1978 World Cup was staged in his homeland, but national team

Allsport

Maradona

boss Cesar Luis Menotti thought the pressure would be too great and left the teenager off the side, which eventually won.

That didn't diminish Maradona's appeal or potential. In 1980 he scored 43 goals for Argentinos Juniors and was snapped up by Boca Juniors, one of the most popular clubs in the land. He immediately led them to a national title and was expected to help Argentina successfully defend its World Cup in 1982 in Spain.

To add more pressure, he was also sold to FC Barcelona before that championship, so arrived in Spain under the most intense of spotlights. The 1982 World Cup and the career at Barcelona, lasting just two seasons, were rare low points for the tiny, powerful midfielder with legs capable of producing cannon-like shots or imparting the delicate spins and dips which bedevil defenders.

Maradona moved to Napoli of the Italian League in 1984-85, helping that club to two titles in a seven-season stay. He also was the main focus of the 1986 Argentina World Cup winners in Mexico, his career at its peak as he married the individualistic artistry which characterized his playmaking and passes to a collection of teammates who could anticipate the sudden decisions which made Maradona a special orchestrator of an attack.

That high point was followed by a gradual decline, the 1990 World Cup generally unsuccessful for the player, although Argentina did quite unexpectedly reach the final. Shortly thereafter a positive drugs test led to a 15-month suspension from world soccer.

Maradona showed his resilience at that point, training and awaiting his return to the top level which came in the fall, 1992 when he signed with Spanish First Division club Seville to play with his former Argentina national team manager Carlos Bilardo. His rehabilitation included a return to the Argentine national team in 1993, when he led the side against Brazil in a 100th anniversary match.

MATTHAUS, LOTTHAR (1961—)

European and World player of the year in 1990, World Cup captain of the 1990 champions, a star in both the German Bundesliga and the Italian Serie A, Lotthar Matthaus ranks as one of the finest midfield players of his era, one he helped to shape and define. The lithe owner of a thunderous shot and a deceptive change of pace, Matthaus became a midfielder of consummate skill.

He spent his early years with Borussia Moenchengladbach, then stepped onto the stage as the leading player at Bayern Munich, Inter Milan and, ultimately, the world in the 1990 World Cup. A serious knee injury sidelined the German star for the 1992 European Championships and kept him out of major soccer action until the fall of 1992, but his return to Bayern Munich and the highest level of play suggests that he may still have a part to play in Germany's 1994 World Cup defense in the United States.

Matthaus debuted in German amateur soccer in 1978 but quickly joined Gladbach for the 1979-80 Bundesliga season, remaining with the club until Bayern signed him in 1984-5. The Bavarian team paid the record fee (in Germany) of over $1 million for his contract.

He later left the home league for Italy when he signed with Inter Milan at a lofty cost of nearly $5 million in 1988-89, a price which proved a bargain when he led Inter to the Italian League title in 1989. A UEFA Cup (1991) is also among his trophies.

MATTHEWS, STANLEY (1915—)

Matthews is the greatest name in English soccer. As with the others in his pantheonic ranking, Matthews's greatness was multifaceted rather than limited to a single attribute. Before the age of 20 he was already regarded as the finest dribbler ever produced in England, a reputation he carried with him until he was well into his forties. Though he was more valuable in feeding halfbacks or other forwards, he scored 71 goals in 698 official league appearances and converted for 11 goals in 54 appearances for England. Had it not been for the interruption of World War II and the presence of Tom Finney during the immediate postwar years, he would certainly have been England's choice at outside right for 20 years or more.

P.A. Reuter Features Ltd., London

Sir Stanley Matthews

A measure of his esteem in the national life of his country is the knighthood bestowed upon him in 1965—when he was still playing in the first division 34 years after his league debut—an honor not accorded to any other player in British soccer.

Matthews was signed as an amateur with second division Stoke City at age 15, playing on its Central League team until his first team debut in 1932, and he made his international debut against Wales in 1935. His move to Blackpool in 1947—after helping Stoke to stay in the first division throughout his stay there—was a severe blow to Stoke fans.

In 1953 Matthews scored Blackpool's winning goal with only moments left in the F.A. Cup final against Bolton, a legendary match in English annals known affectionately as the "Matthews Final." This proved to be the only cup medal of his career. He was accorded the honor of being selected first European Footballer of the Year; when he retired two years later, he had already turned 50 years old and had been knighted.

Mazzola, Alessandro
(1942—)

One of Europe's most talented strikers during the 1960s, Mazzola provided the goalscoring punch for Inter Milan during its great period of domination in Europe, and later achieved further acclaim as the midfield leader in Italy's return to form in 1968 and 1970. He was, by all accounts, the equal of his extraordinary father, Valentino, who died in the Torino air disaster in 1949.

Their touching father-and-son story, combining the careers of two immensely popular public figures, is quite unique in Italian sports. Sandro was six years old and already interested in the game when the Torino tragedy occurred, and while still a boy he was brought into the Inter youth program with his younger brother, Ferruccio.

In 1961, Mazzola graduated to the senior team—his brother eventually moving elsewhere to a fine career with other clubs—and in 1962 he gained a regular place at center forward in the first team, scoring 10 goals in 23 games.

He made his international debut in Italy's 1963 defeat of Brazil, scoring once from a penalty kick, and in 1964 he became Italy's first Footballer of the Year. His dazzling footwork and close ball control spearheaded Inter's three Italian championships and two European Cup triumphs between 1963 and 1966.

In the final of the 1968 European Championship, he emerged as an attacking midfielder, replacing the injured Gianni Rivera, and turned the tide for Italy in its win over Yugoslavia. His new role was to cause much controversy over the next two years as he and Rivera, two of Italy's greatest stars and the opposing captains in Milan's bitter archrivalry, competed for Italy's attacking midfield role.

The matter was finally settled by the president of the Italian Football Federation before the 1970 World Cup; Mazzola was to play the first half and Rivera in the second half of each game. This plan was carried out until the final against Brazil, when Mazzola's superb work in the first half precluded any possibility of substitution. Rivera later came on as the replacement center forward.

In 1971, Mazzola led Inter to another league championship, and three years later he was the only one of Italy's many aging stars who performed with distinction in the World Cup. He bowed out of international competition immediately afterwards, having accumulated 70 caps and 22 goals, and in 1977 he retired from Inter after 405 appearances and 115 goals, most of them scored before 1968.

Mazzola, Valentino
(1919-1949)

Mazzola was the legendary captain and chief goalscorer of the Torino side that won five Italian championships in a row during the 1940s, and the captain of the postwar Italian team. He was quite possibly the most gifted inside left ever produced by his country, though his son Sandro's arch rival, Gianni Rivera, would have to be rated his equal.

Strong and possessing great stamina, he was a brilliant tactician. Tragically, Mazzola died at the peak of his career in the Torino air disaster of 1949 that decimated his club and national team for years to come.

Valentino Mazzola

Publifoto

While in his teens, Mazzola joined Tresoldi in his native Cassano d'Adda. After playing for the Alfa Romeo company team in Milan, he was signed by Venezia in 1939 and formed an effective partnership with his inside right, Ezio Loik.

Valentino Mazzola made his international debut in 1942 against Croatia, and with Leik nearly always at his side, he appeared in Italy's next 12 consecutive internationals, taking over as captain in his eighth appearance in 1947.

Nine of these 12 internationals resulted in victories. In 1942, he and Loik were lured to Torino, and in 1943 he won his first league championship medal. Three more followed—in 1946, 1947, and 1948—and in 1947 Mazzola was the league's leading scorer.

In 1948-49, he was leading his club to another sure championship, when, five weeks away from the end of the season, the Superga disaster ended the lives of the entire team. Mazzola's loss to Italian soccer was uniquely penetrating. He had scored four goals for Italy, and in little more than 220 club appearances, converted 109 times.

MEAZZA, GIUSEPPE (1910-1979)

The premier goalscorer during much of Italy's golden era in the 1930s, Meazza's 355 goals in senior-level competition was an Italian record until it was broken by Silvio Piola. Meazza placed among the top four scorers in each of the first seven seasons of the national league (1930-36), finishing at the head of the list on three occasions.

He was one of only two players to participate in both of Italy's World Cup winning endeavors—1934 and 1938—and he was captain of the team in the latter. His 33 goals in 53 appearances for Italy was also a long-held record.

Meazza was a center forward-turned-inside right whose skills included nearly every trick at a player's disposal. He was a master dribbler and had such a feel for the ball that he was equally dangerous on a fast run or with a delicate flick and pivot.

"Peppino" first appeared in 1927 for Inter Milan (renamed Ambrosiana-Inter in 1928) at age 17, and in his first season scored 12 goals. In 1928-29, the final year of the old regional league system, he scored a career-high 33 goals, and the following season, at age 20, he led the league for the first time. It was also in 1930 that he made his international debut against Switzerland, scoring two goals, and for the next nine years was rarely left out of the national team.

In 1933, Italian manager Vittorio Pozzo moved Meazza to inside right, and, with Schiavio and later Piola at center forward, Italy's was the most gifted forward line in prewar Europe. Though

Meazza occasionally played at center forward again, both the 1934 and 1938 World Cups were won with him at inside right.

MEREDITH, WILLIAM
(1874-1958)

The first and greatest of all Welsh soccer idols and perhaps the most important European right wing of all time, Billy Meredith was a pioneer of great intelligence who perfected the winger's art by working endlessly on timing and ball control.

Meredith ultimately became the master of crosses on-the-run and other wing skills that are now taken for granted. Meredith's career, nearly all of which was played in the first division, was phenomenally long, encompassing 30 years, from 1894-24, and his 51 international appearances set a record for Wales that was not broken for many decades.

Syndication International Ltd.

Billy Meredith

Though he scored over 300 goals, his main function was to assist others in scoring, and it is estimated that he made over 1,000 appearances at club level.

MOORE, ROBERT
(1941-1993)

Moore was a world-class defender whose 10-year captaincy of England drew universal respect and led to an unflinching reputation for consistency and natural leadership abilities. He joined the cockney-based West Ham United in his native East London as a youth, turning professional in 1958, and immediately became an England youth international. Selected for England "Under-23" before he had even reached his club's first team, he went on to make a record 18 "Under-23" appearances.

Moore's full international debut was made in 1962 against Peru, and one year later he became England's youngest captain at age 22. As a brilliant reader of the game, he led England to its World Cup victory in 1966 and was voted the outstanding player in the tournament by the journalists present.

At the World Cup in 1970—his third—he topped his performance of four years earlier, and was named the best defender in the world by many of his opponents, Pelé among them. During the 1970s Moore continued to be unsurpassed in his ability to out-position opponents, a skill he acquired early in his career to make up for his moderate speed off the mark.

Moore remained at West Ham, a previously undistinguished club until 1975, guiding it to an unexpected F.A. Cup win in 1964, and an even more surprising European Cup Winners' Cup triumph the following year. In 1974, he retired from the national team with 108 appearances, a world record that stood until 1978.

Sven Simon

Gerhard Müller

MÜLLER, GERHARD
(1945—)

Der Bomber, Müller's nickname, speaks well of his attributes. The extraordinary goalscoring center forward for Bayern München and West Germany holds more records than any other player in history—other than Pelé. Among other unprecedented feats, he became his country's authentic national hero in 1974 when he scored the goal that won the World Cup for the West German team.

Müller was European Footballer of the Year in 1970; top scorer in the West German league in 1967, 1969, 1970, 1972, 1973, and 1975; leading scorer in three successive European Cups (1973-75) and one European Cup Winners' Cup (1967); top scorer in the 1970 World Cup; the only player in history to score two hat tricks in the final rounds of the World Cup (1970); West German Footballer of the Year in 1967 and 1969.

He started his career as a youth player with the small Bavarian club TSV Nördlingen, and in 1964 he was signed by the Bayern club (after training as a weaver), starting for the first team in 1965-66. Müller made only one youth appearance for West Germany before he entered full international competition in 1966 against Turkey.

By the early 1970s, Müller had surpassed Uwe Seeler's West German scoring record, and when he retired from the national team after the 1974 World Cup (after a total of 63 World Cup appearances), Müller had amassed a total of 68 goals. Müller's success was due to his explosive shot and his uncanny sense of positioning and anticipation.

A competent if unspectacular dribbler and tackler, Müller specialized in quietly preying on the ball as if lying in wait, and then once he gained control of the ball his deadly accuracy and cannon-like power took over, a technique entirely appropriate for his short, muscular form and massive legs.

NEESKENS, JOHAN
(1951—)

A quicksilver midfielder as equally good in the tackle as he was on attack, Johan Neeskens was one of the world's top players and helped to define the Holland era in the world's game.

An adherent of the Dutch philosophy of "total soccer," his ability to cover huge spaces at full speed without sacrificing either skill or creativity made him the archetypal midfielder. At the same time, he was among the first of the Dutch stars to translate his fame into big money contracts, moving first to FC Barcelona, then on to the New York Cosmos.

Neeskens made his international debut in 1970 while still a teenager, having broken into the strong Ajax side that was on the verge of dominating European soccer. Working alongside Johan Cruyff, he proved the perfect foil to Cruyff's more silky skills. The pair inspired Holland to the 1974 World Cup finals, where Neeskens scored the only goal in a heartbreaking 2-1 defeat.

The years at Barcelona and in New York saw Neeskens' game gain international appreciation. He was still a vital part of the Holland side that finished second again in the 1978 World Cup and continued to play for his country until 1981. He finished with 49 caps.

Photograph by Herbert Mehrens

Ernst Ocwirk

OCWIRK, ERNST
(1926—)

The last and perhaps greatest of the old-fashioned attacking center halfbacks, Ocwirk was both the inspiration and backbone of Austria's superb national team in their glory years during the early 1950s.

His classic midfield role was played flawlessly as he guided his team, whether national or club, through their deliberate motions. He passed the ball impeccably and possessed excellent ball control skills, especially for a man of his height (over six feet).

Ocwirk was picked as captain of FIFA World XIs twice during his career, a distinct honor, and he led Austria to many great victories up to and including the 1954 World Cup. By this time, however, Austria's outmoded short passing game

was discarded and he switched to an orthodox wing half. While the tactical machinery no longer revolved around him as the hub, his commanding presence naturally preserved his long standing-function as the team dynamo.

His career started with Stadlau and Floridsdorfer AC during World War II, but in 1947 he moved to the venerable FK Austria, where he remained for nine years and established his reputation. He also made his international debut in 1947, and in 62 international appearances he managed to score six goals.

In 1956, by now a deep-lying inside forward, he was released to play as a professional at Sampdoria in Genoa, where he remained until the year 1961.

PAPIN, JEAN-PIERRE
(1963—)

His blond, curly hair and aquiline features not-withstanding, Jean-Pierre Papin is no typical forward. Although possessed of some of the individual flair and temperament which sometimes is defined as the Gallic style, Papin emerged from the shadow of Michel Platini as a modern forward, equally at home when beating defenders with a turn of speed or flick of skill or by simply overpowering the defenders through sheer physical willingness in the penalty area.

His was a style and combination that helped lift France back into the international arena and helped to make two clubs, Marseille and AC Milan, the most feared of Europe in the last years of the 20th Century.

Papin began his career in the amateur Vichy side in 1981 but needed to leave his homeland to catch the attention of the biggest clubs. Although he had a brief tour with Second Division Valenciennes in 1984, it wasn't until he spent the 1985-86 season with FC Bruges in Belgium, where he scored 20 goals, that Marseille came calling.

His signing in 1986-87 touched off the greatest era in Olympique history, a run of French championships, a place in the European Cup final in 1991, and ranking as one of Europe's finest sides.

Papin's appearance just as Platini was retiring helped France to remain in the top echelons, especially since his strike rate as the French attack leader was remarkable in an era of tight defenses. Through his first 37 matches in the Tricolor shirt, Papin had scored 21 goals, averaging better than one every other match. Named European Player of the Year in 1991, Papin left Marseille for Milan after the 1991-92 season.

PASSARELLA, DANIEL
(1953—)

A sturdy, dark-haired man with an untiring work rate and the willingness to go hard into the tackle, Daniel Passarella dominated the Argentine defense for a decade, played on a 1978 World Cup winner and went on to translate his on-field knowledge into a coaching career that took him back to the famous Buenos Aires club where he had earned most of his playing fame. Passarella broke into Argentine soccer with lower division Sarmiento in 1971 but quickly moved to Ríver Plate in 1973 to begin a ten-year stay with that great club.

He played on seven different championship sides with River and was part of that great moment in the club's Estadio Monumental where Argentina defeated Holland in the 1978 World Cup final.

A solid, reliable defender who was capable of shooting accurately when he came forward, Passarella took his skills to the Italian League at the end of the 1982 World Cup, playing with Fiorentina of Florence.

At the end of his playing days, Passarella returned to Ríver Plate as coach of the club he had played on for ten years.

PEDERNERA, ADOLFO
(1918—)

Pedernera, *el maestro,* was quite possibly the greatest Argentine forward of all time, though he is challenged by several others for this honor in a country that has produced many great stars. He was, nevertheless, a true genius in his favorite position of center forward, though he was so versatile that Argentina used him in all five forward positions.

Pedernera was the leader of the most famous Argentine forward line in history, *la maquina,* which took Ríver Plate to great heights in the early 1940s. Flanked by two other Argentine greats, José Moreno and Angel Labruna, he was a supreme strategist and precision shooter, and left a legacy for the Argentine game in perfecting the role of deep-lying center forward.

PELÉ
(1940—)

Full name: Edson Arantes do Nascimento. Pelé is most celebrated player of all time and is probably the best, though some Brazilians still believe Artur Friedenreich has never been surpassed, and some Europeans would rank Alfredo Di Stefano as his equal. Pelé's statistical record is staggering, but anyone who has ever seen him play will think first of his genius as a stylist on the field.

It is probably true, as Brazilian observers have often pointed out, that Pelé would have become the world's most accomplished player at any position, but it was at inside left that he received all the accolades a player could possibly muster.

The perfection of his physical attributes, moreover, has been miraculously paralleled by a gracious and engaging personality, as well as a strong desire to teach and lead, which have brought him universal recognition as a genuine world idol.

Memories focus on flashes of movement: body feints, dribbles in which his feet are an unnecessary luxury, headers taken over towering defenders, and widely arched shots around walls of players. In his first goal against Sweden in 1958, he pushed the ball over his shoulder with his thigh, pivoted, and fired a shot past the hapless goalkeeper.

In 1961, against Fluminense at the Maracanaa, he dribbled from his own penalty area past six oncoming defenders and the goalkeeper—into the opponent's net. (This famous goal became immortalized as the *Gol de Placa,* or, Commemorative Silver Plate Goal.)

Among his haunting, yet prophetic, near-misses was that quick shot in his World Cup debut against the U.S.S.R. that hit the post and left the great Yashin beaten.

Some have tried to explain Pelé's magical qualities in physiological terms: his well-placed center of gravity for the particular skills needed in the game, or his uncommon peripheral vision. Pelé himself, however, simply pointed to God-given gifts.

Born in the small village of Três Coraçóes in the state of Minas Gerais, he was the son of Dondinho, a lowly paid professional center forward with second division Bauru, the local club. While playing on the "barefoot team Sete de Sétembro in 1952, he acquired the name Pelé, the meaning of which is unknown even to him.

He appeared briefly with Ameriquinha, the youth team whose inspiration was the big Rio club América FC, and at age 13 he was discovered by former World Cup star Waldemar de Brito, manager of Bauru. After two and one half years on the Bauru junior team, Baquinho, Pelé was brought by Waldemar de Brito to Santos FC in the port city of the same name, and there he played on its junior team for the summer.

In 1956, Pelé made his first team debut for Santos against AIK Stockholm in an international friendly. At age 16, he became a regular first team member, and before he turned 17 made his international debut for Brazil against Argentina. Coming on as a substitute, he scored Brazil's lone goal, and three days later he started for Brazil against the same Argentine team.

Pelé

In the 1958 World Cup, he appeared in Brazil's third game against the U.S.S.R., and played in each game thereafter, scoring six goals, including a hat trick against France and two against Sweden in the final that won Brazil's first world championship.

These performances in Sweden captured the imagination of the soccer world, and elevated him immediately to the heights of international acclaim. Every wealthy club in Europe offered record transfer fees for his services, but the Congress of Brazil declared him an official national treasure and forbade his sale or trade. In 1960, he signed a second contract with Santos.

Pelé's Santos became the dominant force in Brazilian soccer. It won four Sao Paulo championships between 1958-62, two more in 1964 and 1965, and three in a row between 1967-69.

Throughout this period, Pelé achieved legendary feats: 127 goals in 1959, 110 goals in 1961, 101 goals in 1965, and in the intervening years an average of over 70 goals each season.

In 1962 and 1963, he led Santos to win both the Copa Libertadores and the Intercontinental Cup, the latter before appreciative crowds in Lisbon and Milan. Santos' tours of Europe became the talk of the continent.

Unfortunately, an injury in Brazil's opening game of the 1962 World Cup prevented Pelé from participating in his country's second world championship win, and in the years that followed additional injuries became a serious problem.

Invariably, less talented opponents resorted to triple-teaming and fouling him. After Brazil was knocked out of the 1966 World Cup in England, Pelé complained bitterly of permissive referees, and vowed not to play in a World Cup again, but four years later he shone more brightly than ever before in helping Brazil to win an unprecedented third world championship. His stunning header against Italy put Brazil ahead in the final, and he assisted on each of Brazil's additional goals in an unforgettable display.

In 1969 he became the third player in history to score 1,000 goals, though his were undoubtedly achieved with stiffer opposition than those of Friedenreich and Franz Binder before him. In 1971, before 130,000 impassioned fans at the Maracanaa, he retired from the national team, and in 1974 he played his last game with Santos.

In that sad farewell to his club of 18 years, Pelé trotted around the stadium before leaving the field at halftime. With tears running down his face he listened to the sounds of chanting fans pleading with him to: "Stay! Stay!" His retirement was thought to be permanent.

In 1975, he stunned the soccer world by signing a $3.5 million contract with Warner Communications, owners of the New York Cosmos. The contract called for him not only to play for Cosmos but also to promote the game throughout the United States in an effort to turn soccer into a major commercial sport.

After two and one-half seasons, Pelé made a second farewell appearance at Giants Stadium in 1977 and turned his attention to a host of business obligations. He also began touring the world in highly selective efforts to promote the skills and sportsmanship in soccer that he himself faithfully practiced.

Biographies of Pelé have been written in or translated into over 100 languages, and the giant stadium Maceió Estadio Rei Pelé is named for him. He is thought to hold the world record for number of appearances in any category (1,362), though his total number of goals scored (1,280) remains second in ranking behind that of Friedenreich.

Pelé holds the world record for number of career hat tricks (92), number of goals scored at full international level (97), including a record seven international hat tricks), and he was the scoring leader in Sao Paulo league competition from 1957 to 1965, 1969, and again in 1973. He was also the scoring leader in the South American Championship in 1959 and the Copa Libertadores in 1965, and was selected Latin American Footballer of the Year in 1973.

PIOLA, SILVIO
(1913—)

A strong, tall center forward, Piola is perhaps the greatest Italy has ever produced and was possibly the best in Europe during the 1940s. Piola's style was aggressive rather than delicate, and he was especially good in the air. He was the star of Italy's World Cup triumph of 1938, providing a

AP/Wide World Photos

Silvio Piola

marked contrast to the more subtle Meazza. Eventually Piola broke Meazza's Italian record of 355 league goals, and in 34 international appearances he scored 30 times. Though his number of international appearances was cut short by the war, his career was nonetheless very long and transcended at least two generations of Italian players.

Piola was the spearhead of Italy's superb attack in the 1938 World Cup, scoring five goals and helping Meazza and others with most of their goals.

PLATINI, MICHEL
(1955—)

The essence of the French soccer revival in the decades of the 1970s and 1980s, Michel Platini became more than just a soccer player; by the time France had won a European championship in 1984 and come agonizingly close to the

World Cup itself in both 1982 and 1986, Platini was a national treasure.

Platini's promise was so extraordinary that the French Football Federation maintained Platini's amateur status so that he would be eligible for the 1976 Olympics even though he was already a First Division star in France. He duly represented his country at the Montreal Games before turning professional and by the time he joined St. Etienne—then the most successful team in France—he was the acknowledged star of the French game.

The three years at St. Etienne brought 58 goals and a major contract with Italian League power Juventus, a deal which began after that heartbreaking 1982 World Cup in Spain. Spurred on by Platini and the rest of a midfield that also contained Jean Tigana and Alain Giresse, France reached the semifinals and actually led West Germany 3-1 in the first period of overtime before losing a penalty kick shoot-out at the end of a 3-3 tie.

Platini was the architect of the crisp passes, dangerous free kicks and penetrating runs that made that exciting French team so difficult to defend. Platini not only maintained his superstar status with Juventus, he actually increased it, stepping into the tough Italian League and continuing to score regularly. He netted 20 goals in the championship season of 1983-84 and became so famous that he even hosted a television show while still an active player.

Along the way he helped the French win the 1984 European Championship which they hosted, but the long-awaited World Cup in 1986 brought further disappointment, not the ultimate reward.

After winning one of the great World Cup matches of all time, a quarterfinal penalty kick decider against Brazil in the heat of Guadalajara, the French again lost in the semifinals, again to West Germany, denying Platini the chance to end his playing career with a World Cup victory.

After a brief time as coach of the national team, during which time France qualified for the 1992 European Championships without losing a match, Platini retired from an active role on the field, saying that he was not happy with the pressures of being a national team boss. He is currently actively helping the FFF prepare to host the 1998 World Cup and continues in his role of soccer commentator.

PUSKÁS, FERENC (1926—)

Puskás, the stocky "Galloping Major of Hungary," was one of the leading figures in postwar European soccer. As an inside left with Honvéd and the legendary Hungarian national team of the early 1950s, he possessed one of the most

AP/Wide World Photos

Ferenc Puskás

powerful left-foot shots ever seen, and his abilities were little diminished when he began a second career with Real Madrid after the 1956 Hungarian uprising. Puskás scored 83 goals in 84 appearances for Hungary, and he made a habit of leading the league in scoring both in Hungary and his adopted Spain.

Puskás defied all the commonly accepted traits of a great player. He was short, squat, paunchy, and seldom used his right foot or his head, but ultimately all he needed was his exceptional knowledge of the game and his left foot.

Puskás's playing career began in 1943 with Kispest in the Budapest suburb of that name, and in 1945, at age 18, he made his international debut against Austria in his country's first post-war international match. In 1948, his club was incorporated into the new army club, Honvéd, and with his long-time friend and teammate Jószef Bozsik, he became the nucleus of Honvéd's great success.

Puskás was the Hungarian scoring leader in 1948 (50 goals), 1949-50 (31), 1950 (25), and 1953 (27), and with the title of major in the Hungarian army, he was captain of the national team that became a legend in its own time.

Led by Puskás's scoring prowess, Hungary was undefeated from 1950-54, won the Olympic gold medal in 1952, and advanced to the final of the 1954 World Cup.

While he was in South America on a tour with Honvéd in 1956, the Hungarian uprising took place, and Puskás decided not to return home. In 1958 he was signed by Real Madrid, home of the legendary Alfredo Di Stefano and a string of European Cup medals, and his career was reborn.

Puskás resumed his role at inside left, snugly positioned between center forward Di Stefano and the flying outside left Francisco Gento, resulting in one of the greatest forward lines in history.

Real was elevated to new heights, including a fifth consecutive European Cup triumph, and a sixth several years down the road. Puskás was the Spanish scoring leader in 1960 (26), 1961 (27), 1963 (26), and 1964 (10), and he eventually made four international appearances for Spain. When he finally retired from Real in 1966 at age 39, he had amassed 324 goals in 372 games.

Perhaps his two most memorable feats were the four goals he scored against Eintracht Frankfurt in the 1960 European Cup final and his hat trick at the hands of Benfica in the 1962 final, both for Real Madrid.

RIVELINO, ROBERTO
(1947—)

A cunning left-foot shot, a shoulder-dipping, ambling run and a lethal arsenal of free kick ploys made Roberto Rivelino the hero of both club and country. A member of the 1970 World Cup winners, leader of the great Corinthians of Sao Paulo sides during the 1965-1975 era, Rivelino followed in the tradition of marvelous attacking Brazilians, adding a midfielder's vision to his skills as a nonimal winger.

Despite the fact that Rivelino was already a national attraction in Brazil by the time the 1970 World Cup kicked off in Mexico, his play for what many observers still call the finest championship team brought him international acclaim.

He lined up alongside Pelé, Tostao and Jairzinho in as fine a four-man attack as was ever assembled, his particular left-side skills a perfect complement to the danger Jairzinho posed on the right.

Sven Simon

Roberto Rivelino

Although he did not wear his favorite uniform number (10) in the national team until after Pelé's retirement, Rivelino walked the difficult line in the shadow of a legend, defining his own game and establishing his own reputation.

His memorable free kicks, which often seemed able to bend around or dip through the defensive walls, bedeviled goalkeepers across the globe and earned him the admiration of fans.

Rivelino's international career continued through the 1974 and 1978 World Cups, but an injury in the first match of the 1978 event kept him out of most of his final World Cup competition.

RIVERA, GIANNI
(1943—)

Rivera was perhaps the cleverest inside forward in Italian soccer history. His bumpy career was crowned in 1969 when he was chosen European Footballer of the Year and became the only one of Italy's half dozen major international stars of the period to be so honored.

A prodigy in his teens, Rivera gained a first team place with his second division hometown club, Alessandria, at age 15, and he made eight appearances with Italy's youth team before having his option purchased by AC Milan in 1960 for $182,000. At the time, he was still only 16 years old.

Rivera immediately won a first-team place with Milan, and in 1962 he made his full international debut against Belgium. One year later, at age 19, he was the runner-up to Lev Yashin in European Footballer of the Year balloting, based largely on his extraordinary contribution to Milan's European Cup triumph.

Though most of the Italian team was to blame for their lamentable showing in the 1966 World Cup, Rivera received more blame than most, and his career fluctuated from then on.

Through his magical footwork and inventive playmaking, he continued to excel for his club, and as captain in 1968 he led Milan to another league championship by a gaping nine-point margin, followed the next year by a second European Cup win and the European Footballer of the Year Award.

Between 1968-70, he was embroiled in a sharp controversy with Sandro Mazzola, his opposite number and captain at Inter Milan, over who should adopt which role on the national team.

When it was decided by the president of the Italian Football Federation that in the 1970 World Cup both would play in their newly found attacking midfield roles—with Rivera substituting for Mazzola at half time—it was Rivera who appeared to be the recipient of the short end of the bargain.

During the 1970s Rivera regained his composure after his troubles with the national team and resumed his scheming inside forward role to lead Milan to a European Cup Winners' Cup title in 1973. He bowed out of international competition after the 1974 World Cup with 60 caps and 14 goals.

ROSSI, PAOLO
(1956—)

Paolo Rossi will be forever remembered for one tournament, the 1982 World Cup in Spain, but even his brilliant performance in that championship should not be allowed to completely define his career.

A natural goalscorer, Rossi had already compiled a brilliant record before leading Italy to the World Cup victory, but the manner of his comeback from suspension to the star role in Spain served to elevate the event to level of high drama.

Rossi spent the early days of his career in the Juventus youth program but made his first great impression on the game at Lanerossi Vicenza. During three seasons (1976-79) he rattled in 60 goals to become the acknowledged leader of the Italian strike force.

His play in the 1978 World Cup in Argentina earned him recognition as the second-best player in the tournament in the prestigious journal *France Football's* voting.

Suspended just prior to the tournament, Rossi came into the 1982 World Cup well short of match practice. In the end, it made no difference for the slight, dark-haired attacker with an instinct for goals and a willingness to put his head or body into tight places among defenders.

After Italy struggled in the opening phase, Rossi took personal charge. He scored all three goals against Brazil as Italy upset the favorites, 3-2, then grabbed both in the 2-0 semifinal victory over Poland.

He added the opening goal in the 3-1 final win over Germany to finish as the top scorer in the championship and instantly became a national hero.

RUMMENIGGE, KARL-HEINZ
(1955—)

Karl-Heinz Rummenigge was the dominant player on a West German national team which came close to, but did not win major world honors during his era. A blond, stocky forward possessed of both a strong shot and an excellent heading ability, Rummenigge rattled in the goals during a 10-season career at Bayern Munich and also produced in the biggest matches, but had the misfortune to play in two losing World Cup finals, each time hampered by a nagging injury.

Rummenigge had much better fortune in club play and also wore the West German national shirt in a 1980 European Championship side. During his decade at Bayern Munich (1974-1984) the club won three Bundesliga titles, two German Cups, three European Cups and one world club championship. Rummenigge contributed 162 goals in those 10 seasons, including 29 in the 1980-81 campaign, his personal high tally.

Playing in an age when the German sides were noted for both their power and technical efficiency, Rummenigge carved out his reputation by scoring crucial goals that turned matches. He grabbed the German goal in extra time that cut a France lead to 3-2, starting a comeback that resulted in an eventual German win on penalty kicks and a place in the 1982 final.

In the 1986 final he came off the substitute's bench to score the goal which sparked a German revival from a 2-0 deficit, although Argentina ultimately scored again and captured the trophy.

SANTOS, DJALMA
(1929—)

Perhaps the greatest right back in the history of the game, Djalma Santos's longevity became a Brazilian legend. He played in four World Cups (1954-66), having made his international debut in 1952, and retired in 1968 at age 39 after he had made his 100th international appearance in a Copa Rio Branco match against Uruguay.

But longevity was far from his only attribute. He was a master tackler who remained cool and unperturbed no matter what the opposition. His style was to jockey rather than charge, and when the moment was ripe he moved in for the kill, rarely if ever overcommitting himself.

The success of his strategy was seen throughout his entire career. In addition, he was Brazil's deadly accurate penalty taker, and, in consort with his frequent partner in the backfield, Nilton Santos (no relation), he never hesitated to overlap and go on the attack.

Djalma Santos spent his lengthy career entirely in his home town of Sao Paulo. He entered senior-level competition in 1948 with Portuguesa de Desportos, and stayed there until 1959, when he was transferred to the much larger Palmeiras.

His coolness and leadership led directly to Palmeiras's splendid run to the final of the Copa Libertadores in 1961, and, to Portuguesa's dismay, the 34-year-old Djalma Santos was se-

lected for the 1962 World Cup-winning team in Chile after his former club had decided he was finished.

SANTOS, NILTON
(1926—)

Full name: Nilton dos Santos. With Djalma Santos (no relation), he formed half of the greatest attacking fullback combination in history. Nilton played on the left side for both his club, Botafogo, and Brazil. In international competition he and Djalma Santos perfected a tandem that was based on good communication and an understanding of each other's abilities.

When one would attack, the other would stay behind, and vice versa. Though they never played together at the club level, they starred together for Brazil over 70 times, Nilton accumulating a total of 83 caps.

Kurt Schmidtpeter

Nilton Santos

Nilton's career was extraordinarily long, and almost all of it was spent with Botafogo. He started as a goalscoring forward with Flecheiras, located on the Ilha do Governador in Rio, but in 1948 Botafogo took him on as a center half. He made his first team debut, however, as a left half, and never abandoned that position throughout his career.

Santos's first appearance for Brazil was in 1949 at the South American Championship, but he did not participate in the 1950 World Cup. Nilton's low point, unfortunately, was the infamous "Battle of Berne" against Hungary in the 1954 World Cup.

During that competition he was sent off, but he went on to serve the Brazilian national team with distinction in its World cup triumphs of 1958 and 1962, the latter at age 37. In 1964, having won practically every trophy available to a Brazilian player, he retired.

SCARONE, HECTOR
(1898-1968)

Of all the great Uruguayan stars of the 1924-30 period, Scarone stands out as a prototype of the traditional Uruguayan forward. His mastery of all the skills associated with a classic inside right was developed to its limit.

Scarone was an exceptionally hard worker and very tough competitor, but the genius of old-fashioned Uruguayan scoring artists was that they could switch instantly from their role as effective team player to that of individual ball artist.
No one was more successful at this than Hector Scarone. He scored regularly for both club and country, schemed with great sophistication when he was off the ball, and shot with pinpoint accuracy.

Scarone's career began in 1912 when, at age 14, he joined the third division Montevideo club Sportsman, and he was quickly snapped up by Nacional the following year. Nicknamed *El Magico* ("The Magician"), he made his international debut in 1919 in the South American Championship.

He played an important role in the winning of Uruguay's gold medal at the 1924 Olympics, and two years later he accepted an offer to play for Barcelona in Spain. He returned after only six months and was high scorer in the South American Championship of 1927.

At the 1928 Olympics, he scored the winning goal for Uruguay in the final, elevating his status as a national hero still further, and he was one of only two players in Uruguay's 1930 World Cup-winning team that had played in both the 1924 and 1928 Olympics finals.

In all, he appeared 64 times for Uruguay, an exceptionally high total in the golden era of amateur soccer in South America.

SCHIAFFINO, JUAN
(1925—)

The extraordinary inside forward of Penarol and Uruguay, Schiaffino possessed opportunistic instincts and a fighting spirit that enabled him to carry on the great tradition of Uruguayan players in that position. Not large in size, he defied predictions that he could not last in international class competition against bruising defenders, and he proved to be one of the great players of the 1950s.

In 1943, at age 17, he was brought into Penarol's youth team, and one year later he started on the first team at inside left. The following year, he was selected for Uruguay in the South American

Championship, and he eventually became the star of two World Cups and two of the most famous games in World Cup history.

In the final match of the 1950 World Cup against Brazil, Schiaffino scored Uruguay's first goal and set up the second by Ghiggia, creating the 2-1 win that gave his country its second world championship. In the 1954 World Cup, having increased his usefulness by becoming a wing half with playmaking responsibilities, he became a world star.

In the famous semi-final against Hungary, sometimes called the greatest game ever played, Uruguay held on until well into overtime and it was only after Schiaffino's injury that Hungary was able to win 4-2. In all he made 22 appearances for his native country.

After the 1954 World Cup, he was signed by AC Milan for a world record transfer fee of $200,000, and he immediately spurred the giant Italian club to a league title. He led Milan to two more championships, and only six months after the 1954 World Cup played the first of four internationals for Italy, his parents having been Italian-born.

In 1958 he took Milan to the European Cup final, but two years later he was released to AS Roma. Having slowed down considerably, he played in a variety of positions for two years and retired in 1962.

SCHILLACI, SALVATORE
(1964—)

For six glorious weeks in 1990 Salvatore Schillaci was the hero of his country and the talk of the world. He led Italy's World Cup bid with a six-goal performance that had a fairy tale-like qual-

ity, elevating Schillaci to a star status that proved to be both a blessing and a curse.

A native of Sicily, Schillaci played his early career in the relative obscurity of Messina, spending four undistinguished seasons in the Third Division, three more in the Second.

That final campaign at Messina, when he scored 23 times in 35 games, caught the attention of Juventus, which signed him for the 1989-90 season.

After a 15-goal debut in 30 games for the Turin club, Schillachi was a fringe member of the Italian team that would host the 1990 World Cup.

He did not start the opening game against Austria but came on as a substitute with 15 minutes to play. Four minutes later his header gave Italy a 1-0 triumph and the Schillaci World Cup saga had begun.

Schillachi went on to score against Czechoslovakia, Uruguay, Ireland and Argentina in the march to the semifinals, adding a final goal in the third place game against England to finish as the tournament's top marksman.

But those statistics don't capture the story. Schillaci, nicknamed "Toto" after a popular Italian comic strip character, had touched a nerve among the populace. Flags and posters bearing his likeness sprouted across the land; he was the common man's player, the hero who had come from simple origins to hold a nation's attention.

But just as his star rose, it descended. Unable to live up to such unrealistic expectations, Schillaci struggled the next two seasons at Juventus. He had scored more times in the World Cup than he did in all of the next campaign when 29 matches produced just five goals. By 1992-93 he had been transferred to Inter and was attempting to rebuild his international career.

SCHLOSSER, IMRE
(1888-1968)

Hungary's first idol and goalscoring legend, Schlosser made 68 international appearances between 1906-27, a runaway world record until it was broken by Czechoslovakia's Frantisek Planicka and Switzerland's Severino Minelli in the late 1930s.

His record of 59 goals for Hungary was not broken until Puskás and Kocsis surpassed it in the early 1950s, and in Hungarian league competition he was the leading scorer for seven consecutive seasons from 1909.

Schlosser scored six goals against Switzerland in 1911 and five more against Czarist Russia in 1912, but his most famous international goals were the two he made in Hungary's 6-1 romp over Italy in 1910. His league goalscoring high mark was 42 in 1910-11 and 1912-13.

A bow-legged inside left, he was most closely associated with the great Budapest club Ferencvaros, and when he was transferred to arch rival MTK in the late 1910s fans were incredulous.

He led both clubs to many successive league championships, and in the 1920s returned to his first love, Ferencvaros, to finish his career.

Schlosser later became a leading referee, and in 1955, wearing his old international jersey, he ceremoniously kicked off the ball in Hungary's one-hundredth meeting with Austria, a unique honor accorded by the Hungarian F.A.

SEELER, UWE
(1936—)

The most popular player in German soccer and a symbol of German gallantry on the field, Seeler was greeted with chants of "Uwe! Uwe!" by German crowds throughout his entire career.

He was an acrobatic and thoroughly courageous center forward whose physical prowess belied his short and stocky frame, best exemplified, perhaps, by his famous flying headers and over-head kicks.

Seeler played in four World Cups for West Germany (1958-70) and spent his entire career with one club, Hamburger SV. Indeed, his father had been a player with HSV, and Uwe himself signed on at age 10.

As a youth player, he scored approximately 600 goals for HSV teams, and in 1954, at age 17, he made his full international debut for West Germany against France. In 72 appearances for his country, he scored 43 goals, a record since broken by Gerd Müller.

His career with HSV's first team lasted from 1954-72, during which time he scored 551 senior-level goals, another record broken by Müller, and made upwards of 700 appearances. Seeler was the leading goalscorer in West Germany in 1956 (32), 1959 (29), 1960 (36), 1961 (30), and 1964 (30), and was West German Footballer of the Year three times.

He made his first real impact on the national team in the 1958 World Cup and probably reached his peak at the 1962 World Cup in Chile.

Seeler captained the West German squad in the 1966 and 1970 assemblages, and, having successfully adopted a new role as attacking midfielder, finally retired from the national team after a friendly against Hungary in 1970.

Uwe Seeler displays his acrobatic goalscoring abilities with one of his famous bicycle kicks.

Seeler led HSV to three championship play-offs in 1957, 1958, and 1960, gaining the title itself in the last of these, and in 1968 he scored eight goals in HSV's highly successful European Cup Winners' Cup campaign.

Seeler's career almost ended with an Achilles tendon injury in 1965, but it was saved by a delicate tendon transplant operation, and he only missed six months of active play. He retired in 1972.

SHILTON, PETER
(1949—)

By the time Peter Shilton finished his England international career against Italy in the 1990 World Cup third-place match he had written a new definition of consistency. Never flashy, but always secure, Shilton demonstrated that never-ending work, positional acumen, and a willingness to anticipate, then react, was the formula for the modern goalkeeper.

All told he played 125 times for his country in an international career that spanned 19 years. Many felt that he was just as good, if not better, at age 41 as when he made his start in professional soccer.

Shilton probably would have established unreachable records for international team selections had he not shared a good portion of his career with Ray Clemence. For a time in the 1970s Clemence was the preferred "number one among equals" with Shilton not completely establishing himself as the unquestioned England selection until the 1980s. He then played for his country in three World Cups and earned the admiration of everyone in the game.

Shilton played more than 100 matches with five different English League teams: Derby County, Leicester City, Nottingham Forest, Southampton, and Stoke City. His work habits became legendary as he crafted his position with daily practice sessions and theoretical work which helped to change the way goalkeeping was viewed.

SINDELAR, MATTHIAS
(1903-1939)

Generally regarded as the finest player Austria has ever produced, Sindelar was an extraordinary center forward with skills so subtle that he became famous for dribbling the ball into the net rather than shooting. His nickname was *der Papierene* ("the Man of Paper"), because he was extremely thin and his agile movements often gave the appearance of a piece of paper floating through the air.

His inventiveness was truly amazing, and defenders never knew what he would pull out of his bag of tricks next. Sindelar, or "Motzl," as his friends called him, first played for Hertha Vienna in his late teens, and in 1923 he was signed by Amateure (later renamed FK Austria).

His international debut for Austria, in which he scored a goal, was made in 1926 against Czechoslovakia. His rise to fame corresponded exactly with that of the famous Wunderteam that came to dominate European soccer during the early 1930s.

Sindelar was not a prolific goalscorer, but he sometimes converted several times in one game, as in Austria's famous 2-1 defeat of Italy in 1932, and its still more memorable 8-2 burial of Hungary later that same year. In that game, Sindelar scored three goals and created the other five with selfless cunning.

His last international for Austria—against Switzerland in 1937—was marked by another goal, his 27th in 43 appearances. His movements, even at this time, defied description, and were sorely missed when he finally retired to realize his dream of opening a Viennese coffee house he named Cafe Annahof, for his wife.

Sindelar, a Jew, became the target of harassment by Nazi authorities. He grew increasingly depressed and in 1939 he disappeared from sight. Although some observers believe he committed suicide, this was a period when many Jews living under Nazi rule are known disappeared. After his disappearance, the small street in which his cafe was located was renamed Sindelargasse.

SIVORI, ENRIQUE OMAR
(1935—)

The *enfant terrible* of Argentina, Sivori was a gifted inside left—with subtle and complete ball control skills—who first made his mark in his native Argentina and later took Italy by storm. While he was a ball artist supreme, Sivori was also hot-tempered and was cautioned by referees constantly.

This caused him much notoriety, and he was thrown out of at least 20 senior-level games during his career. Yet, he was elected European Footballer of the Year in 1961, and every wealthy club in Europe sought his services.

Sivori was raised in the ranks of Ríver Plate, the great Buenos Aires club, and made 12 appearances for Argentina, including its 1957 South American Championship victory, all before the age of 22. In 1957, Italy's Juventus paid Ríver Plate a world record 190 million lire for him, and placed him next to the Welsh center forward John Charles.

Sivori and Charles led Juventus to Italian championships in 1958, 1960, and 1961, and in 1960, Sivori led the Italian league in scoring with 27 goals. He went on to play for Italy nine times, scoring eight goals, and became proficient at several positions in the midfield as well as on the forward line.

He scored 135 goals for Juventus before he was transferred to Napoli in 1965, and four years later he retired after a slow and steady decline.

He returned to Argentina a millionaire and was eventually asked to coach Rosario and Estudiantes before taking over Argentina's junior team in 1972 and Ríver Plate in 1974. After another brief stint with the Argentine F.A. in 1976, he returned to coach in Naples, and in 1978 he became coach of Velez Sarsfield in Buenos Aires.

STOICHKOV, HRISTO
(1966—)

Perhaps the finest player to emerge from Eastern Europe in the modern era, Hristo Stoichkov has learned to control both his fiery competitive nature and his collection of skills. A member of the FC Barcelona European Cup winners of 1992, Stoichkov is a rangy, fast forward who combines a hard shot, a willingness to work in the tight spaces, and a fearless attitude in front of goal.

The most expensive player ever developed in Bulgaria, he probably is among the five most valuable players in the game today.

Stoichkov began his career with Maritza Plovdiv in 1983-84 but was quickly snapped up by CSKA, the army club, during the era of Communist rule in Bulgaria. Although he missed one complete season with an injury, he developed into a feared striker, scoring 38 goals in the 1989-90 season, his last one with CSKA.

That performance caught the eye of the Western European clubs, Barcelona winning the race with a $3.75 million bid for his services. The three-time Bulgarian player of the year (1989, 1990, 1991) did not begin with immediate success in Spain.

An altercation with a referee led to a lengthy suspension during Stoichkov's initial season in Barcelona, but he returned to first team duty a better disciplined, but still a full-speed ahead competitor.

As a result of defenders' concentrating on him, Stoichkov has been limited in his goals at the national team level, but he still had helped to lift the Bulgars into contention for a 1994 finals place.

SUAREZ MIRAMONTE, LUIS
(1935—)

Spain's legendary inside left, Suarez's lengthy career spanned over 20 years and brought him many honors both in Spain and Italy. He was a player of many skills, being equally accomplished in passing, shooting, and scheming; and he ranks as perhaps the finest talent ever produced in his native country.

He was signed at age 18 (in 1953) by one of his hometown clubs, RCD La Coruna, and after a showstopping debut against Barcelona in a first division match, he was secured by the same Barcelona as quickly as possible.

In 1955-56, while still a second-team member, he scored 10 goals in 21 appearances, and made his international debut for Spain in 1957 before he had even secured a first-string place on the star-studded Barcelona team.

In the late 1950s, Suarez was an important member of the extraordinary Spanish forward line that included Kubala, Di Stefano, and Gento, and at Barcelona his combinations with Kubala and Kocsis made theirs the only forward line in Europe that could challenge the fame and success of Real Madrid's front five.

He was chosen European Footballer of the Year in 1960, and after 216 appearances and 112 goals, was brought to Inter Milan in 1961 by his former Barcelona manager, Helenio Herrera, for a world record fee of $420,000.

Under Herrera's *catenaccio* system, Suarez became a deep-lying inside forward who actually served as the midfield schemer, and he carried out his role with the utmost success.

He was the major factor behind Inter's domination of European club competitions in the mid-1960s, and his leadership and all-around abilities led Spain to its European Nations' Cup triumph of 1964.

In 1970 Suarez was suddenly transferred to Sampdoria, and in 1972, after 30 international appearances and 13 goals, he was selected by his old teammate Ladislav Kubala to make another appearance for his country against Greece, resulting in his most memorable performance. After retiring, he became a coach leading Spain to the 1990 World Cup finals.

TESORIERO, AMERICO MIGUEL
(1899-1977)

Tesoriero is Argentina's greatest goalkeeper of all time. Intuitive, daring, and tenacious, he played during the "romantic era" of South American soccer and was known for his keen sense of positioning around the goalmouth. Tactically, Tesoriero was ahead of his time in that he regularly came out to intercept attacking forwards.

Tesoriero's career (1916-27) was spent almost entirely at Boca Juniors—he played briefly for Deportivo del Norte in 1922—and he made 41 international appearances for Argentina, an exceptionally high figure in view of the fewer number of internationals played in those early years. His international debut for Argentina was made in 1919 against Paraguay.

Always the most magnetic player on the field, Tesoriero was instantly recognizable by his slender physique and his ever-present grey woolen sweater.

TOSTAO
(1947—)

Full name: Eduardo Goncalves de Andrade. The selfless center forward and decoy of Brazil's 1970 World Cup team, Tostao penetrated defenses mercilessly.

He was that rare center forward who was as useful with his back to the goal as he was facing it. Tostao's strength was his exceptional intelligence and knowledge of the game, though his skills were highly refined as well, especially those involving his left foot.

His function as a decoy for Pelé and others was a natural outgrowth of his keen awareness of all that occurred around the penalty area. Penetrating with the ball or taking a through pass, he would often attract the attention of his defenders and in an instant pass with perfect accuracy to an oncoming teammate who himself would score the goal. Just as often, he would have his back to the goal and pivot on a dime to score.

His rare blend of skills and selflessness was a key element in the astounding performance of Brazil in the 1970 World Cup. At age 19, he made his international debut for Brazil against Chile, and a few short weeks later he began scoring goals for his national team, in particular against Hungary in the 1966 World Cup.

By 1969, many thought Tostao's career as a world-class player had ended when he was hit in the left eye by a ball in a league match against

Allsport/Pressens Bild

Tostao

Corinthians Paulista. The medical diagnosis pointed to a detached retina, and with the World Cup pending, he decided to have surgery performed at an eye hospital in Houston, Texas. The operation was successful but the press and fans worried about his every move.

During the World Cup he directed vital passes to Pelé, Jairzinho, and Rivelino, playing in every game and setting up numerous goals. He became a national hero and received worldwide fame.

The following year, he was elected the first Latin American Footballer of the Year. In 1972, he was transferred to Vasco da Gama for a record $520,000, but one year later the eye injury became aggravated again, and he was forced to retire.

VAN BASTEN, MARCO
(1964—)

Marco van Basten burst onto the scene at the Youth World Cup in Mexico in 1983. Nearly a decade after that debut van Basten had exceeded all expectations to earn the right to be linked with the greatest Dutchman of them all, Johan Cruyff.

Like Cruyff, van Basten was initially a product of the Ajax Amsterdam club, starting his career as a professional in 1981. In his six seasons with Ajax, van Basten sharpened his goal-scoring touch to such an extent that he led all of Europe's marksmen with 37 in 1985-86.

He moved to Milan in 1987 and has subsequently become one of the most consistently productive imports in Italian soccer history. Along the way, van Basten has collected a bevy of personal honors and built an international career topped off with a remarkable goal in the 1988 European Championship final when Holland defeated the Soviet Union, 2-0 to win its first major soccer title.

Van Basten has been named European Footballer of the Year three times, most recently in 1992; he has played in every major competition open to a soccer star, including the world club championship, the European Champions League and the World Cup.

Van Basten's goal-scoring ability is a combination of planning and an almost elastic-like ability to stretch his frame to connect with crosses. Especially good on the ground and in tight spaces, he has developed the skill of turning and shooting around defenders who attempt to shut down the space behind him. He is also an accurate, powerful header of the ball and, as that 1988 Euro finals goal showed, he can volley balls with an instinctive sense of coordination.

WALTER, FRITZ
(1920—)

This energetic inside forward was the first great figure in postwar German soccer, and he did more than any player to elevate West Germany to the front ranks of world competition. He was primarily an inside left, but throughout much of his career he fell back into the midfield, pushing his other forwards toward the goal and distributing accurate through balls, many of which eventually found their way into the net.

Walter was first and foremost the on-field emissary of German national team manager Sepp Herberger, with whom he developed an extraordinary 18-year relationship, and, as captain, he led the West German team that won the 1954 World Cup.

A tactical wizard and inspirational leader, Walter led that surprising team to one of the greatest upsets in the history of the game, the 3-2 victory over Hungary in the final, and paved the way for the eras of Seeler and Beckenbauer.

Already a goalscoring inside left for FC Kaiserslautern, the only club he ever played for, he was selected by Herberger for the national team in 1940 against Rumania, and scored twice in that debut. Hat tricks followed in the next two matches, but the war intervened and Walter was drafted as a paratrooper.

His experiences in the war were so painful that for the rest of his career he never flew to away games. After the war he reunited with Herberger and led West Germany back into international competition following its reinstatement with FIFA in 1950. Walter and his brother Otmar led Kaiserslautern to national championships in 1951 and 1953, and in the 1954 World Cup in Switzerland he finally achieved international recognition.

WRIGHT, WILLIAM
(1924—)

Wright is best known as a world-class halfback whose skills in the middle part of the field were overshadowed by his staggering statistics as an English international. His club-level career, spent entirely at Wolverhampton, was impressive. After his debut against Belgium in 1947, he played in all but three of England's next 107 games, including 70 in a row after October 1951, a world record.

During this time, he captained England 90 times, another world record, finally bowing out of international competition in 1959 with 105 appearances, yet another world record that has since been broken. His first 51 internationals were played at right half, but he later switched to center half, where he appeared 46 consecutive times.

Though his teams fared poorly in three World Cups, he himself was always exempt from criticism. His leadership both on and off the field was unquestioned, but he suffered at times from the public's skepticism of his "perfect" image.

YASHIN, LEV
(1929-1990)

The greatest and most famous Russian player of all time, Yashin was also the most admired goalkeeper of his or any other era. His acrobatics and reliability were obvious to all, but a further measure of his greatness was his ability to instill confidence in his entire team and spread his good sportsmanship over the whole field.

Yashin controlled not only his goalmouth during a game but the entire penalty area—and to a greater extent than most keepers dared to contemplate.

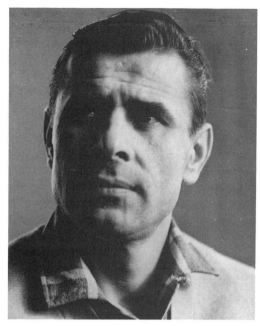

Lev Yashin

Always dressed in his black jersey or sweater, he led his club, Dinamo Moscow, and especially the U.S.S.R., to fame and success during the 1950s and 1960s.

After playing for a factory team called Tushino near his native Moscow in 1945, he joined Dinamo as an ice-hockey player, but the great Dinamo goalkeeper Alexei Khomich discovered him in 1950 and trained him to be his successor.

Yashin made his club debut for Dinamo in 1953 and his international debut against Bulgaria in 1954, achieving instant international recognition with the Soviet national team at the 1956 Olympic Games.

Yashin was the inspiration of the Soviet teams that reached the quarterfinals of three World Cups (1958-66) and won the first European

Nations' Cup in 1960. For his services he was awarded his government's Red Banner of Labor and Order of Lenin medals as early as 1957 and 1960, respectively.

Yashin made a record 600 appearances for Dinamo, including 291 in league competition, another record, and finally bowed out of international competition with 78 caps. In 1971, a commemorative game was played in his honor in Moscow between Dinamo and a FIFA World XI before 100,000 spectators, and the next day he became general manager of the only club he had ever played for.

ZAMORA MARTINEZ, RICARDO (1901-1978)

The greatest of all Spanish idols, Zamora was Europe's most spectacular goalkeeper during the 1920s and 1930s, and, unlike his equally great Czech counterpart and contemporary, Frantisek Planicka, the object of an unprecedented cult in his native country.

Zamora was an acrobatic and flashy keeper in the Latin style, and in a record 47 international appearances spanning 16 years, he conceded only 40 goals, seven of them at the hands of England in one match in 1931.

In that famous international at Arsenal Stadium, played while he was at the height of his powers, he was reduced to tears at the whistle in one of the most memorable scenes in international soccer annals.

At age 15 he signed with the lesser of Barcelona's two big clubs, Espanol, but in 1919 he moved across town to CF Barcelona. After three seasons, he returned to his beloved Espanol and remained there until 1930.

AP/Wide World Photo

Ricardo Zamora Martinez

Zamora made his international debut in the 1920 Olympic Games, leading Spain to a silver medal, and starred for his country 14 years later against Italy in the second World Cup.

In 1930, Real Madrid paid Espanol a world record transfer fee for a goalkeeper of 150,000 pesetas. Zamora finally retired from active play in 1936 after making a total of 473 club appearances.

He served as the manager of the newly reconstituted Atletico Aviacion de Madrid (Atletico Madrid) in 1939, and after World War II managed several clubs, including Espanol, before taking over the national team briefly in 1952. In 1967, Zamora was honored with a FIFA testimonial match, Spain vs. Rest of the World, and in retirement remained the most popular sports figure in Spanish history.

ZICO
(1953—)

Full name: Artur Antunes Coimbra. Like so many Brazilian players of the post-Pelé era, Zico suffered by comparison to the great man but managed to escape from the glare of publicity to make his own personal career one of high success. Although he did not play on a World Cup winning side, Zico was part of arguably one of the best teams never to win the tournament, the 1982 Brazil entry.

Zico first came to attention as a star with the popular Rio giants, Flamengo. He scored 34 goals during the 1979 season when Flamengo was in the midst of a run which saw them capture three Rio championships in four years as well as the South American Liberators Cup and the world club championship.

He moved to Udinese in the Italian League in 1983-84 and immediately demonstrated the same remarkable scoring touch, collecting 19 goals in 24 matches in a league noted for tough defense. At an age (41) when many players have retired, Zico showed that his enjoyment of the game was undiminished, signing with the Kashima Antlers in a new Japanese professional league scheduled to begin play in 1993. He said that he wanted to help establish the sport in a new country as his career-ending contribution to the game.

ZOFF, DINO
(1942—)

When Italy won the 1982 World Cup they beat all the odds, as did goalkeeper Dino Zoff, who

Copyright by Horst Müller

Dino Zoff

rebounded from a disastrous 1978 tournament to star in Spain at the age of 40 and win the admiration of the soccer public.

One of the most consistent goalkeepers of all time, Zoff's club career spanned more than 20 years in Italian soccer, many of those campaigns with powerful Juventus where he made his reputation as a big match player. Zoff's mastery of the position was so great that defenders felt especially secure in front of him.

Nevertheless, Zoff heard the critics in 1978 when a long-range drive by Arie Haan flew past him, allowing Holland to go on to the final and condemned Italy to a third-place appearance.

It would have been no surprise had his international career ended then, but the man who made his gray keeper's shirt famous refused to accept that scenario.

Instead, he remained in the game and emerged from the 1982 tournament to hold the World Cup aloft as captain of the world champions. He finished his international career with 112 caps.

Zoff's career began in 1961 with Udinese and he spent time with Mantova and Napoli before moving to Juventus in 1972. Over the next decade he was part of a side that won six Italian championships, an Italian Cup and the UEFA Cup.

At the end of his playing career, Zoff stepped successfully into management, first as the leader of the 1988 Italian Olympic team, then as boss of Juventus.

He led his former side to an Italian Cup-UEFA Cup double in 1989-90 before leaving to take the head coach's job at Lazio of Rome in 1990-91.

TRANSFERS

Transfers in Europe and South America have traditionally involved straight cash transactions. The trading of one player for another, or trades combined with a sum of cash, is uncommon and confined mainly to North America.

The transfer system, which was developed in England near the end of the last century, is currently undergoing a major upheaval, because the amounts of players' signing-on fees, i.e., the percentage of a transfer fee to which a player is entitled, are increasing rapidly, sometimes reaching vast six-figure sums. While historically limited to 5 percent, signing-on fees have recently taken on the appearance of bonuses, as practiced in major American sports.

In Western Europe, where the rights of players are generally more respected than elsewhere, the transfer system is based on a traditional procedure. When, for strategic or personal reasons, a club decides to dispense with a player's services, it notifies the player of its intention, and puts him on a transfer list. A value price, or proposed transfer fee, is established, and other clubs are invited to meet that price.

In some cases, a player is offered as a free transfer, in which case his market value is zero. After an agreement has been reached by two clubs, the fee is paid by the purchasing club, usually in installments over a period of time.

An agreement cannot be completed unless the player consents to move to the new club. Certain countries in which player associations have little power do not require a player's consent. Uruguay, in particular, has suffered a number of player strikes in recent years over this issue.

In some cases, a player may request to be transferred to a specific club, but he will probably waive his right to a percentage of the transfer fee if he does so.

A transfer may involve other kinds of reciprocation, especially in the case of international transfers. If the purchasing club is especially popular or successful, a friendly may be arranged with the selling club in order to gain box-office revenues. In Eastern Europe, except for Yugoslavia, money and gifts sometimes change hands, as in the West, but many transfers are determined by sports officials, who, for one reason or another, wish to elevate the stature of a given club, or to punish a given player.

Various national associations have, for specified periods of time, prohibited their players from being transferred abroad, or vice versa. Such restrictions are usually made in an effort to minimize the impact of transfers on gate receipts, the quality of play at home, or a national team manager's ability to organize and prepare his squad properly.

Spain allows two foreign players per club. Austria prohibits the transfer abroad of any player under 26 years of age. In preparation for the 1978 World Cup, both Argentina and Uruguay blocked all transfers abroad of selected internationals.

Eastern European countries, with the exception of Yugoslavia, have stringent international transfer regulations, although Poland made some exceptions after its high placement in the 1974 World Cup. There are no restrictions on transfers between any two British countries or between them and the Republic of Ireland.

Transfers existed in England even before the legalization of professionalism in 1885, although all transactions were made under the table. Aston Villa was the first big spender in the marketplace. As early as 1892, Villa paid £100 to West Bromwich Albion for Scottish star Willie Groves, and an additional £40 for John Reynolds, the great right halfback. Any fees or bonuses given to players during this period were informally decided.

One of the earliest records of a signing-on fee has been traced to an unknown forward, formerly of Celtic, who in 1892 asked "£8 down; £3 a week and 25s. during the close season" to sign with the little Liverpool club Bootle F.C. But to trade athletes in a commodities market like so many pounds of beef was reprehensible to the opponents of professionalism.

Indeed, the subject of transfer fees became the most rankling issue within the larger debate over professionalism in both soccer and rugby. A Captain Philip Trevor, writing in *Badminton Magazine* (April 1897), had this to say for misguided ideals:

"Transfer papers have been prepared with all the detailed care and accuracy of the title deeds of a property and his leasehold services have been acquired in accordance with the fluctuating conditions of the market and the then value of the article bartered. The old gladiator system lacked the completeness of the recognized procedure under which prominent football players are now bought, sold and manipulated, but the balance of sportsmanship probably lies with the Romans."

Nevertheless, the practice of transferring players to help a club improve the quality of its team became increasingly common. In 1899, an attempt was made to place a ceiling on the amount that could be requested in a transfer fee, but in 1908 the last effort to set ceilings was abandoned as impracticable.

Finally, in 1912, the legality of the transfer system was upheld in the English courts in the famous test case, *L.J. Kingaby v. Aston Villa.* Kingaby, a Villa player whose desire to be transferred had been thwarted by the excessive transfer fee his club was asking, lost his suit to be released from the club, but, in so doing, established the legality of the existence of Villa's transfer fee in the first place.

Transfer systems adopted by other countries in subsequent decades were modeled on the English idea, whether inadvertently or by design, and remain unchanged to this day, with the exception of appropriate legal variations.

Some countries have now formulated free agent clauses, whereby a player cannot be retained against his will after his contract has expired. England was one of the first countries to enact such a rule in 1963.

5: NATIONAL PROFILES

AFGHANISTAN

Address: Football Federation of the National Olympic Committee, Kabul. *Founded:* 1933. *FIFA:* 1948. *National stadium:* National Stadium, Kabul (25,000); *largest stadium:* National Stadium. *Colors:* Red jerseys, white shorts.

While the level of play in Afghanistan is not advanced, an organizing body was founded as early as 1922 as an adjunct of the amateur sports committee that was to become the National Olympic Federation in 1933.

An actual football association was created in the early 1950s. To date, the Football Association of Afghanistan remains an affiliate of the Olympic committee, the controlling body of all sports in the country.

A league centered in Kabul was inaugurated during the 1930s and now numbers 30 participants. It is uncertain when an Afghan selection first engaged in international competition, but the earliest official recording of a full international was a 6-0 loss to Luxembourg during the 1948 Olympic Games in London.

This match is the only occasion on which Afghanistan played in a competition of intercontinental caliber.

ALBANIA

Address: Albanian Football Federation, Rruga Dervish Hima NR 31, Tirana. *Founded:* 1930. *FIFA:* 1932. *UEFA:* 1954. *National stadium:* Qemal Stafa, Tirana (24,000); *largest stadium:* Qemal Stafa. *Colors:* Red jerseys, black shorts. *Season:* September to June.

Soccer was introduced in Albania at the turn of the century by a variety of foreign residents, but Albanians themselves played the game very little before World War I. As in other parts of the Ottoman Empire, their Turkish rulers discouraged it for political reasons, and it was left to foreign residents in Tirana to form the first league around 1909.

During the 1920s the game spread rapidly. With the accession to power of King Zog in the coup of 1928, organized sport became a facet of government policy, and the Djelmenija Shqiptare (Albanian Football Section) was founded. The local leagues that had sprung up during the 1920s were structured into a national league, and a leading club, SC Tirana, emerged to dominate the next decade.

Plans were made to enter the qualifying rounds of the 1938 World Cup, and for a while it seemed Albanian soccer was on the verge of entering the mainstream of Europe. Administrative difficulties, however, beset the league after 1936, and all hope of progress was ended by the Italian occupation in 1939.

The People's Democracy, established in 1946, immediately set out to put the game on a firm footing, and had as its motivating force a new community of neighbors in the Balkan region.

As host of the 1946 Balkan Cup, the Albanian national team finished on top of the standings, despite a 3-2 loss to Yugoslavia, with wins over Bulgaria (3-1) and Rumania (1-0). This was Albania's first foray into international competition, and it remains to date its only high placing in an international tournament.

Between 1947 and 1953, Albania regularly played against all the nations of Eastern Europe other than the U.S.S.R., gaining victories over Rumania, Bulgaria, Poland, and Czechoslovakia twice, while drawing five and losing nine during the same period.

From 1954 to the early 1960s, Albania remained almost totally isolated from international competition, although there was one game with the German Democratic Republic in 1958 at Tirana (1-1), and a selection from the People's Republic of China visited Tirana as early as 1961.

In 1965, Albania made its first attempt to qualify for the World Cup, but the country remains largely unsuccessful in international play. A surprising breakthrough, however, occurred in 1962 when the national association entered its champion club, Partizan Tirana, in the European Cup, and its national team in the European Championship. Here, also, wins have been few.

The first division of 16 clubs is the country's top level of play. By far the most successful postwar clubs have been Dinamo, the team of the Ministry of Internal Affairs (police, security, etc.) with 15 titles, and Partizan, the army team with

14. A cup competition for all affiliated clubs of the upper and lower divisions was introduced in 1968. Dinamo and Partizan each had 12 Cup wins through 1992.

ALGERIA

Address: Federation Algerienne de Football, Route Ahmed Ouaked, PO Box 39, Alger—Dely Ibrahim. *Founded:* 1962. *FIFA:* 1963. *CAF:* 1964. *National stadium:* Algerian Olympic Stadium, Cheraga (80,000); *largest stadium:* Stade Olympique d'Alger. *Colors:* Green jerseys, white shorts. *Season:* September to June. *Honors:* 1990 African Nations Cup.

Algeria made the breakthrough to international attention in 1982, defeating West Germany in their first World Cup finals appearance. They also qualified for the 1986 finals in Mexico to solidify their position as the leading North African country in the 1980s but in neither championship did they progress beyond the opening round.

French colonists and workers introduced the game in Algiers and Oran at least as far back as the 1890s, while the Ligue d'Alger was founded in 1918, and a championship of the Algiers district was introduced in 1920.

A league was also founded at Oran in the western part of present-day Algeria in 1920, and its championship was introduced the same year, while the game in the eastern part of present-day Algeria was centered in Constantine.

In addition to these local competitions, an annual series of Inter-League matches developed between Constantine and Tunis (1931), Algiers and Tunis (1932), and Constantine and Algiers (1949). During the late 1930s and 1940s, Algiers participated in the Constantine-Tunis series, and in its own series with Tunis it was victorious on all but a few occasions. These were precursors to international competition.

The national Federation Algerienne de Football was founded in 1962, the year of Algeria's independence, and joined FIFA and the African Football Confederation almost immediately. The association is also a member of the North African Maghreb Confederation.

Shortly after independence an Algerian national league was established. The First Division of 16 members includes clubs from Algiers, Oran, Constantine, Setif, Batna, Guelma, and the Algiers suburb El Harrach. Club soccer has grown in popularity with the African Champions Cup sparking interest.

Algeria's first real international breakthrough was on the club level. In 1976, Mouloudia Chalia, the first Algerian club to enter either of the African club cups, won the African Champions' Cup by defeating the defending champions, Hafia of Guinea.

After splitting home and away legs by scores of 0-3 and 3-0, the winner was decided on penalty kicks. Among Mouloudia's difficult opposition in the earlier rounds was the famous Nigerian club Rangers, runner-up to Hafia the previous year. Since then, JE Tizi-Ouzon (1981), Entente Setif (1988) and JS Kabylie (1990) have won the top African prize.

ANGOLA

Address: Angolan FF, P.O. Box 3449, Luanda. *Colors:* Red shirts, black shorts, red socks.

Angola entered the 1994 World Cup but was eliminated in the first round in a group won by Zimbabwe. League soccer existed under Portuguese colonization for many years. The Liga de Football de Luanda was founded in 1922 and became affiliated with Portugal in 1932, a relationship that lasted until civil war intensified in 1974. Now independent, Angola supports 276 clubs.

ANTIGUA

Address: Antigua Football Association, P.O. Box 773, St. John's. *Founded:* 1967. *FIFA:* 1970. *National stadium:* Antigua Recreation Ground, St. John's (30,000); *largest stadium:* Antigua Recreation Ground. *Colors:* Gold jerseys, black shorts. *Season:* August to December.

The Antigua Amateur Football Association became affiliated with The Football Association in London before World War II, and in 1967 sought and gained permission from FIFA to reconstitute its national association as an independent body.

The island's population tends to favor cricket, but soccer interest is growing. In 1992, the national team reached the second round of CONCACAF World Cup qualifying. The Antigua Football Association sponsors a national championship and a national cup competition.

ARGENTINA

Address: Asociación del Fútbol Argentino, Viamonte 1366/76, 1053 Buenos Aires. *Founded:* 1893. *FIFA:* 1912. *CONMEBOL:* 1916. *Largest stadium:* Estadio Monumental, River Plate, Buenos Aires (78,000). *Colors:* Sky blue jerseys with white stripes, black shorts. *Season:* March to December. *Honors:* World Cup winner (1978, 1986), runner-up (1930, 1990); Olympic runner-up (1928); South American Championship winner (1921, 1925, 1927,

1929, 1937, 1941, 1945, 1946, 1947, 1955, 1957, 1959, 1991), runner-up (1916, 1917, 1920, 1923, 1924, 1926, 1935, 1942, 1959, 1967). World Under 20 Champion, 1979.

Argentina is the birthplace of soccer in South America and has long been one of the world's leading soccer powers. South America's first club, first league competition, and first national governing body were all Argentine. The first international matches played in South America, both at the club and national levels, involved Argentine teams.

Argentina, in fact, was the first independent nation outside Europe to fully develop the game. With its long and proud soccer playing heritage, it has consistently produced superbly skilled players since the 1910s, and though many of these have been lost to wealthy clubs abroad, a flood of excellent players has always seemed to take their place.

The national teams of Argentina have dominated South American competition since the beginning, even at the expense of mighty Brazil, and Argentine clubs have stood out decisively in the Copa Libertadores.

Yet, Argentina failed to live up to its potential and win the highest honors in world competition until it finally captured the World Cup in 1978 before its own fans in Buenos Aires. It repeated in 1986 and was losing finalist in 1990.

Between its amateur golden era during the 1920s and that emotionally charged triumph in 1978, Argentina was often a disappointment, and its reputation for intimidating behavior on the field overshadowed the genuine skill of so many of its players.

Soccer was first played in Argentina (and South America generally) along the Rio de la Plata by British sailors and maritime workers in the early 1860s. In 1867, the Buenos Aires Football Club, the first of its kind in Latin America, was founded by members of the five-year-old Buenos Aires Cricket Club, most of whom were British railroad workers.

By 1880, an active League of British teams was under way in Buenos Aires. British railroad workers, who also played a leading role in spreading the game, founded Quilmes F.C. in the Buenos Aires suburb of the same name in 1887 and Rosario Central F.C. in the big Rio Parana city of Rosario in 1889. These two are now the oldest clubs in Argentina.

The cultural homogeneity of Argentine life during this period helped to speed up the assimilation of soccer into the activities of working class people, nearly all of whom had European backgrounds. This was in marked contrast to Brazil's multiracial society, in which Afro-Brazilians confronted racial impediments on the playing field until the 1920s.

In Argentina, soccer was relatively free to make its way through all strata of a racially unified society. This process was well under way by the 1880s, despite the domination of organized competition by the British, and accounts for Argentina's early rise to the top of South American soccer. The situation in Uruguay was quite similar.

The presence of the British was central to Argentina's rapid development on the playing fields. In 1891, Alexander Hutton founded the forerunner of Argentina's present first division, the Campeonato Metropolitano, and the first official league competition in South America. It was dominated for 20 years by British Clubs: Lomas Academicals won the first six titles in a row and Alumni F.C., the team of former English High School players and the most popular club of its day, won nine titles beginning in 1901.

Dozens of important clubs were founded in the 1890s and immediately after 1900, including Buenos Aires' "big five": Ríver Plate (1901), Rácing Club (1903), Boca Juniors (19050, Independiente (1905), and San Lorenzo.

Ríver Plate and Independiente were formed by British players, and Rácing Club was founded by French residents and "portenos" (Argentine-born but of European extraction). Boca Juniors was founded in the main by Italians, and its formation stands out as an important harbinger in the history of Argentine soccer.

After the turn of the century, British players and officials in the front ranks were gradually replaced by European immigrants who poured into Argentina by the millions. The Italians became especially prominent, and it was largely through the Italian community that Argentine soccer advanced so rapidly between 1900 and 1930.

In 1902, the English baron Sir Thomas Lipton donated a trophy to the Argentine Football Association, and this prompted the introduction in 1905 of the Lipton Cup (Argentina vs. Uruguay), the first regularly scheduled international competition outside the British Isles.

The first match in Buenos Aires—resulting in a scoreless draw—was also the international debut of both countries and the beginning of international competition in South America.

In 1906, Argentina and Uruguay started a second international series, the Newton Cup, and for almost 25 years these two competitions were played on an annual basis. In 1912, the governing body cast off its anglicized name and became known as the Asociación Argentina de Football (AAF); earlier in the year it had become the first South American association to join FIFA.

In 1931, professionalism was adopted with the formation of a new outlaw league, the Liga Argentina de Football (LAF); the amateur Asociación Argentina de Football, meanwhile, continued to operate for four years. In 1934, the Consejo Nacional del Football Argentino was formed as an interim body, and in the early months of that year the AAF transferred its rights of international recognition to the new Consejo Nacional, with the blessing of the LAF.

Before the end of the year, the AAF agreed to merge with the LAF under the name Asociación del Football Argentino (AFA), and the Consejo Nacional quickly lost its rights to the AFA, where it has remained ever since.

In 1916, Argentina invited the governing bodies of Brazil, Uruguay, and Chile to participate in the first annual South American Championship in Buenos Aires, during which the four announced the formation of the Confederacion Sudamericana de Football (CONMEBOL), the world's first continental confederation.

In the first, second, and fourth editions of the South American Championship, Argentina placed second to up-and-coming Uruguay, and in the third edition placed a distant third.

In the 1921 edition at Buenos Aires, Argentina finally won the title and did so with an undefeated record against Brazil, Uruguay, and Paraguay. This was its first major international honor. The South American Championship has remained Argentina's premier success story through the decades.

In 35 editions since 1916, Argentina has won 13 times. Seven of these came during the 20-year stretch between 1927 and 1947, during which some of Argentina's greatest teams and players were seen. The most recent in 1991 ended a 32-year drought for the proud nation.

The great romantic period in Argentine soccer began before World War I with the fall of the British clubs and the rise of Italian and other European influences. Rácing, known affectionately as "the academy," was the greatest club of this era. Indeed, no club has ever dominated the Argentine game as did Rácing with its seven consecutive championships between 1913 and 1919, followed by two more in the early 1920s.

During the 1920s, when two leagues were in competition, the other four big Buenos Aires clubs came to the forefront, though none dominated either league consistently, except perhaps for Boca Juniors, which won the regular league's title five times.

Honors in the "outlaw" league were shared by Rácing, Independiente, Ríver Plate, and San Lorenzo. In 1925, Boca became the first Argentine club to make a tour of Europe, its degree of success was reflected in the results: 15 won, one drawn, and three lost.

After the introduction of professionalism in 1931, Buenos Aires' greatest rivalry began to take shape between Boca and River. The two Buenos Aires giants still dominate Argentine soccer with occasional breakthroughs by Rácing, Independiente, Estudiantes, San Lorenzo and Newell's Old Boys.

Though both clubs fielded many great teams during these years, perhaps the most invincible of them all was River's 1941-47 side, which included one of the great forward lines in the history of the game: Munoz, Moreno, Pedernera, Labruna, and Loustau or Deambrosi.

Argentina burst onto the world scene in 1928 at the Olympic Games, the world's premier international competition at that time, on the heels of Boca's triumphant European tour of 1925 and the national side's excellent record against the 1924 gold medalists, Uruguay.

Its European debut in Amsterdam was an 11-2 drubbing of the U.S.A., and after easy wins over Belgium and Egypt, the stage was set for the first all-South American Olympic final against Uruguay. The Dutch spectators were treated to tantalizing displays of skill by both teams, and after a 1-1 draw a replay was forced, won finally by Uruguay.

After Argentina's first exposure in Europe, however, a pattern emerged that was to haunt the future of its game: the poaching of Argentine players by wealthy European clubs, especially those of Italy and Spain.

The first to go was Independiente's star outside left Raimondo Orsi, lured to Juventus after the Amsterdam Olympics after much protest from Argentine officials. By 1934, Orsi, Luisito Monti, and others were playing for Italy in the World Cup on the basis of their Italian parentage, and Argentina's international hopes suffered until after World War II.

In the first World Cup at Montevideo in 1930, Argentina entered as co-favorites with mighty Uruguay, and Argentine center forward Guillermo Stabile was the high scorer in the tournament. Argentina eliminated France, Mexico, and Chile in three poorly played and badly officiated first round matches, and had only to breeze past the U.S.A. to gain the final against Uruguay.

The Uruguayans' superiority was more clearly pronounced than in 1928, and, in front of thousands of Argentine fans who had crossed the Rio de la Plata, they came back from a halftime deficit to win by 4-2.

Argentina's frustration after two second-place finishes in world competition—and to archrival Uruguay at that—was unleashed in public displays of anger, and in Buenos Aires the Uruguayan consulate was sacked by rioters.

In the 1934 World Cup, Argentina was eliminated after only one game (to Sweden) and a long transatlantic ocean voyage. Piqued by FIFA's rejection of its bid to host the next World Cup, the AFA declined to enter the 1938 edition altogether.

When FIFA passed over them again in 1950 in favor of Brazil, the AFA again declined to participate, and it was not until the 1958 edition in Sweden that Argentina consented to enter, only to be eliminated in the first round by Germany FR, Czechoslovakia, and Northern Ireland.

In the intervening years, it gained some sustenance by dominating the South American Championship between 1937 and 1957. Five titles during this period were won without losing a game, and in three of those won by others, Argentina did not even participate.

Drawing heavily on Boca and Ríver players, Argentina remained the lord and master of South American soccer during a time when Uruguay won its second World Championship and Brazil was rising rapidly to world prominence.

The litany of disappointing World Cup results continued to mount. In the familiar setting of Chile, Argentina once again failed to advance beyond the first round in 1962 (England and Hungary qualified from its group), and from the 1966 World Cup in England it departed under a hail of criticism after a series of ugly scenes.

Having reached the quarterfinals, Argentina met England at Wembley, and when captain Antonio Rattin was ordered off, he refused to go. It took ten minutes to clear him off the field, and at the end of the game (which England finally won 1-0) the Argentine reserves besieged the referee and drew the protective intervention of the police.

Argentina's antics in England intensified the traditional rivalry between Europe and South America; in fact, it signaled the beginning of a particularly belligerent era in the transoceanic rivalry.

In the coming years, Argentina would be feared and ostracized in Europe, and a vicious war of words would detract attention from its otherwise high standard of play.

Meanwhile, the national team failed to qualify for the 1970 World Cup in Mexico, and in 1974 in West Germany, it placed last in its first-round group. There was tremendous glory just ahead, however.

Playing at home before adoring crowds, Argentina won its first World Cup in 1978, capturing a thrilling final game against Holland, 3-1 after extra time was needed to resolve the issue.

Led by Mario Kempes, Daniel Passarella, and a host of players willing to work hard in the important supporting roles, Argentina played well throughout the tournament but still needed a remarkable 6-0 victory over Peru in its last second round match to advance to the final.

That score enraged the Brazilians, who had beaten Poland 3-1 earlier in the day and expected to reach the championship game.

Previously Argentina had come through a difficult first-round group, defeating Hungary and France but losing to a strong Italian team. In the second round, played in the controversial group format that was not abandoned until 1986, the hosts defeated Poland, 2-0 and drew with Brazil, 0-0, before routing the Peruvians to reach the final on goal difference.

The final itself was a game of high drama watched by 78,000 fans in the Ríver Plate Stadium. Kempes, who emerged as the scoring hero of the tournament, scored twice and Daniel Bertoni once for the winners who were nearly beaten in regulation time by a stirring Dutch comeback. Dirk Nanninga equalized, then Rob Rensenbrink, another of the tournament's stars, came close to grabbing a winner before the teams played the extra 30 minutes.

Four years later the Argentines crashed out of their World Cup title defense in Spain, perhaps the victims of unreasonable pressure. Diego Maradona, who had been overlooked as a teenager for the 1978 tournament, came into the 1982 competition expected to work miracles, facing additional scrutiny because he had just signed a contract to play with FC Barcelona, the city that would host Argentina's games.

The tournament began badly with a 1-0 loss to Belgium on opening day and Argentina never regained momentum. They were eliminated by defeats from Brazil and Italy in the second round.

The roller-coaster was heading upwards again four years later when Argentina again ruled the soccer world. This time their triumph was somewhat unexpected, the French European Champions and a very creative Brazilian team were generally thought to be the class of the 24-team field.

Maradona was at the top of his powers, however, scoring a brilliant individual goal in the quarterfinal victory over England and two more remarkable strikes against Belgium in the semifinal. The final was a 3-2 victory over West Germany, which had to suffer through a second straight championship game defeat.

For some, Argentina's second World Cup win was marred by Maradona's hand goal scored against England in the quarterfinal, but others saw the little midfielder as the undisputed player of the tournament and thought Argentina deserved its title on the basis of a strong, cohesive style of play.

But in 1990 the mistakes of 1982 were repeated. Once again a team that relied too much on its past stars attempted to defend the title, but Maradona was not able to recreate his form of Mexico and had it not been for a completely unexpected hero, goalkeeper Sergio Goycochea, Argentina never would have reached the final.

Taking over in the tournament's second game when regular keeper Nery Pumpido suffered a broken leg, Goycochea went on to dazzle the crowds with his saves in penalty kick tie-breakers, the route Argentina used to get past Yugoslavia in the quarterfinals and Italy in the semifinal.

Ironically, Goycochea could not save the penalty kick taken by Andreas Brehme which decided a generally unsatisfactory final, but with two men ejected from the game by a vigilant Mexican referee, Argentina had little to argue about in terms of the result.

The Argentine first division is a national league. Its annual championship is patterned on the European league format with 20 teams playing each other home and away.

ARMENIA

Address: Football Federation of Armenia, 9. Abovian Street, 375001 Erevan. *Founded:* 1991.

One of the new countries formed with the dissolution of the Soviet Union, Armenia has applied for FIFA and UEFA membership but has yet to be granted entry into international or European competition.

In the old Soviet League, Ararat Erevan was a member of the First Division, but the political unrest in the region has made it impossible to monitor the current state of soccer.

AUSTRALIA

Address: Australian Soccer Federation, 1st Floor, 23-25 Frederick St., Rockdale, N.S.W. 2216. *Founded:* 1961. *FIFA:* 1963. *National stadium:* Olympic Park, Melbourne (48,500); *largest stadium:* Olympic Park. *Colors:* Yellow jerseys with green trim, white shorts. *Season:* March to October.

Soccer in Australia has suffered mightily from intense competition with three other types of football—Rugby Union, Rugby League, and Australian Rules—all of which have a stronger tradition than soccer in many parts of the country. To make matters more difficult, all four sports run simultaneously during the winter months.

A second major obstacle has been Australia's geographical location. With 10,500 miles between Melbourne and London, and 8,200 miles between Melbourne and Rio de Janeiro, much of the world's best soccer has been out of reach.

Geographical competitiveness has been a problem even within Australia itself, as the Australian Soccer Federation has sought to establish ties with Asia at the expense of its own Oceania Football Confederation.

Soccer was brought to Australia by British coal miners as early as 1870. By 1881, there were at least five clubs in New South Wales, and the first association, the New South Wales Football Association, was founded in 1882. The first organized competition was the Rainsford Trophy, a knockout tournament introduced in 1885 and first won by Granville FC of Sydney.

An Australian Soccer Association (ASA), operating almost exclusively in New South Wales, was established in 1921 and became affiliated with the Football Association in London. A year later, the first officially sanctioned national team was put on the field, though the ASA's non-independent status precluded its team's recognition as a full international side.

The ASA formed a limited company in 1945, but in 1957 the New South Wales Federation of Soccer Clubs was founded, and within a few years had ousted the old association from its official position. This led to the formation of the Australian Soccer Federation (ASF) in 1961, which in turn was recognized by FIFA two years later.

The time had come for Australia to enter the international arena outside the British Commonwealth. An attractive inducement to expand its interests now existed in the 1966 World Cup, scheduled to be held in England. FIFA allotted one berth to Asia-Oceania, which was sought by only two countries, North Korea and Australia. The Koreans won both qualifying matches in Phnom Penh (6-1 and 3-1).

In 1966, FIFA authorized the formation of the Oceania Football Confederation (OFC). Australia was its chief instigator and ultimately its most important component, though there were only four charter and two provisional members. Increasingly, however, the ASF sought to establish ties with East and Southeast Asian countries in an effort to improve their level of opposition in international competition.

On the playing field, the "Socceroos" have continued to improve. In 1970, Australia missed qualification for the World Cup in Mexico by an own goal against Israel in Tel Aviv. Four years later, it advanced to the World Cup finals for the first time after eliminating New Zealand, Iraq, Indonesia, Iran, and South Korea in the Asia-Oceania group.

In West Germany, its presence marked a new high point in the history of Australian soccer. Instructed in no uncertain terms to play defensively against its stiff opposition, the Australian's managed to lose to West Germany and East Germany by only 3-0 and 2-0 respectively, and in its best showing, gained a scoreless draw with Chile.

Although 1974 remains the only World Cup finals appearance, Australia has enjoyed success at youth levels, twice hosting the FIFA Under-20 World Cup.

In 1977, the five regional leagues at home, New South Wales, Victoria, South Australia, Queensland, and Western Australia, gave way to the creation of Australia's first national league. The NSL continues in the 1990s, still not as popular as VFL or rugby football, but making steady growth.

With its international affiliation in limbo, and while awaiting the success or failure of the experimental national league, soccer in Australia is now passing through a period of transition.

AUSTRIA

Address: Österreichischer Fussball-Bund, Praterstadion, Sektor A/F Meierstrasse. A-1020, Vienna. *Founded:* 1904. *FIFA:* 1905. *UEFA:* 1954. *National stadium:* Prater, Vienna (73,243); *largest stadium:* Prater. *Colors:* White jerseys, black shorts. *Season:* August to December, February to June. *Honors:* World Cup third place (1954); Olympic Games runner-up (1936).

Austria was one of the great powers in world soccer until its downfall in international competition during the 1960s, but the legacy of two golden eras lives on. Vienna, the old capital of Austria-Hungary, became one of Europe's early soccer hotbeds, and in 1902 Austria was the winner of the first officially recognized international played by two non-British countries.

Its opponent on that day was its historic archrival Hungary. Together, Austria and Hungary rose to prominence over the decades and have thrived on a friendly competitive spirit.

In the early 1930s, Austria's national team was probably the best in Europe and achieved lasting fame for its "Danubian style" that was based on short passing in the classic Scottish mode. A second great era occurred when a new generation of superbly skilled players won third place in the 1954 World Cup.

Soccer was first played in Vienna and Graz in the 1880s. In Austria-Hungary as a whole, teams were organized earlier in Bohemia than in Austria proper, but the first two Austrian clubs were founded as early as 1894 by British workers and businessmen.

They were First Vienna Football Club, still known today as First Vienna, and Vienna Cricket and Football Club, which was commonly known as Cricketer and ultimately became FK Austria in 1925. The first meeting of these two famous clubs in 1894 was the first official match ever played on Austrian soil.

Graz soon receded into a secondary role as a soccer center, and Vienna's natural leadership came to the fore. A handful of Viennese clubs, as well as some in Graz and Innsbruck, appeared after 1894, and in 1897 the first competition, a knockout tournament called Der Challenge-Cup, was introduced.

In 1905, the WSV's soccer section, known as the Österreichischer Fussball-Verband (oFV) became one of the first associations to join FIFA after the seven charter-members had founded the federation one year earlier.

The two greatest personalities in Austrian soccer emerged during this period. Hugo Meisl, the "father of Austrian soccer," was one of the founders of Wiener Amateur Sport Club in 1911, which was an outgrowth of Cricketer and would later become FK Austria.

Already a force in the ÖFV, Meisl became an international referee in 1907, and in 1912 he brought the English coach Jimmy Hogan, the second legendary figure in the Austrian game, to work with the Amateur.

Hogan coached the Austrian national team briefly before the 1912 Olympics in Stockholm, and with Meisl's blessing introduced the fluid and effective Scottish short passing game to Austrian players. In so doing, Hogan created a tactical revolution that was to bring fame and glory to Austrian soccer for 45 years. The fruits of his teachings, however, were not immediately seen, and Austria bowed out of the 1912

P.A. Reuter Features Ltd., London

Jimmy Hogan

Olympics in the second round after a surprising loss to Holland.

The Austrian national league was introduced in 1911-12, but it was limited to Viennese clubs and took the name Wiener Liga (Vienna League). Provincial clubs were finally accepted in 1949-50. It was in this league that Rapid Vienna started to make its mark on Austrian soccer by winning eight of the first 12 championships, including the first two in 1912 and 1913.

Meisl and Hogan's impact became fully evident in the years following World War I. While Hogan took coaching jobs in Hungary, Germany, North Africa, and Switzerland, Meisl guided Austrian soccer as the secretary of the ÖFV and manager of the national team, in addition to having close ties with SK Admira.

Under his tutelage, both Austria and Admira played the slow and attractive short passing game, and, while Admira became the greatest club of its day, Austria began to achieve excellent international results on a relatively consistent basis in 1924.

Hungary and Czechoslovakia continued to be Austria's most difficult opponents throughout this period, and accounted for nine of its 13 losses between 1924-30. Against these 13 losses, however, were 30 victories and nine draws.

In 1931, Meisl's famous Wunderteam was born when Scotland went down to a 5-0 defeat in Vienna. It was an historic performance, and in this and the 26 matches that followed (1931-34) Austria lost only twice (to England and Czechoslovakia), accumulating a goal difference of 97-39.

There were 6-0 and 5-0 wins over Germany, an 8-2 defeat of Hungary, an 8-1 victory over Switzerland, 6-1 wins over Belgium and Bulgaria, and Austria won its first honor at full international level by capturing the International Cup of 1931-32.

In 1932, Jimmy Hogan returned to Vienna and took over the national team from Meisl, infusing yet more of the philosophy that had carried Austrian soccer so far. Meisl remained the father figure of the team and its guiding light, but Hogan gave it polish and was an important factor behind Austria's extraordinary success after 1931.

Center forward Matthias Sindelar of FK Austria, nicknamed "the man made of paper," because of his thin build and his ability to weave on the pitch like a piece of paper flowing in the wind, was perhaps the greatest Austrian player of all time.

Josef Bican of Rapid and Admira, who played inside right or center forward after 1933, was Sindelar's equal in skill and undoubtedly his country's most gifted goal scorer in history.

The Wunderteam's downfall came sadly with a 1-0 semifinal loss to Italy in the 1934 World Cup in Milan. Meisl had warned of his team's age and tiredness and of the decided advantage afforded to Italy by passionate home crowds cheering from the stands, and he was right. The end of an era was sealed when Germany won the third place game over a disconsolate Austria.

Tragedy lay ahead as 1937 approached. In this bleak year, Hugo Meisl died, the national team seemed headed for a poor finish in the 1936-38 International Cup, and Austria barely qualified for the 1938 World Cup with a 2-1 win over lowly Latvia in Vienna.

Hitler's occupation of Austria in March 1938 ended the International Cup before it could be completed, and, sadly, it also prevented Austria from entering the 1938 World Cup.

Austrian clubs were actually absorbed into German competitions for a time; four Austrian clubs participated in the German league, Rapid Vienna actually winning the German cup in 1938 and the German championship in 1941.

When international competition was resumed after the war, semiprofessionalism (recognized in the early 1920s) was not reintroduced, and this enabled the full national team to enter the 1948 Olympics in London.

Its hopes were dashed in the first round by a defeat to Sweden, the eventual winner, but the seeds of another great era in Austrian soccer were sown.

A winning Austrian team was again assembled by 1950, and in May of that year Austria conquered mighty Hungary in what was to be the Magyars' last defeat in four years. This 5-3 victory launched Austria upward again, and was followed by lopsided wins over Yugoslavia, Denmark, Scotland, Belgium, the Republic of Ireland, and a rare 2-2 draw in England.

Finally, Austria qualified for the 1954 World Cup final rounds with a 9-1 thrashing of Portugal. The backbone of this extraordinary new Austrian team was attacking center half Ernst Ocwirk of FK Austria, who orchestrated another version of the old "Danubian style."

Despite their longstanding success, the tactics taught long ago to Austrian players by Jimmy Hogan were finally abandoned before the 1954 World Cup.

Ocwirk became an orthodox wing half and with outstanding Rapid Vienna players such as Gerd Hanappi at right back and Ernst Happel in the role of stopper center half, the Austrians took third place in the 1954 World Cup, their highest honor ever.

This was Austria's last hurrah to date. Though it qualified for the 1958 World Cup, Austria's fortunes came to an end with the decline of the Ocwirk ensemble.

Austria's qualification for the 1978 World Cup was impressive (six games without a defeat), but its long range effect on the Austrian game remained questionable. It was another 12 years before Austria qualified again, when their only World Cup victory came against the weak United States. Despite introducing several promising individual stars, the Austrians found the old magic elusive.

BAHAMAS

Address: Bahamas Football Association, P.O. Box 8434, Nassau, N.P. *Founded:* 1967. *FIFA:* 1968. *Largest stadiums:* Clifford Park (5,000), Queen Elizabeth Sports Centre (5,000). *Colors:* Yellow jerseys, black shorts, yellow socks. *Season:* October to May.

The Bahamas is one of the least active FIFA members in international competition, probably since the 200,000 people over its 700 islands are more preoccupied with cricket than soccer. They did not even enter the 1994 World Cup.

BAHRAIN

Address: Bahrain Football Association, P.O. Box 5464, Bahrain. *Founded:* 1951. *FIFA:* 1966. *AFC:* 1970. *National stadium:* Isa Town Stadium, Isa Town (16,000); *largest stadium:* Isa Town Stadium. *Colors:* White jerseys, red shorts. *Season:* October to June.

Bahrain is one of the Persian Gulf states whose rapid economic rise has prompted a concerted effort to advance the level of native soccer. Like neighboring rivals Qatar and United Arab Emirates, it is trying to achieve regional success by importing coaches. Although some progress can be seen, Bahrain has yet to equal Kuwait, Qatar or the U.A.E. in its region.

Soccer arrived on Bahrain Island after World War II with the influx of workers who were brought in to develop the fledgling petroleum industry. The Bahrain Football Association, founded in 1951 as the Football Association of Bahrain, was the first national association established in the region, and the first in the immediate area to join FIFA and the Union of Arab Football Associations.

BANGLADESH

Address: Bangladesh Football Federation, Stadium, Dacca 1000. *Founded:* 1974. *FIFA:* 1974. *National stadium:* Dacca Stadium, Dacca (23,000); *largest stadium:* Dacca Stadium. *Colors:* Orange jerseys, white shorts, green socks.

The Bangladesh Football Federation joined FIFA in 1974. The game, however, had been well established in Bangladesh for many decades, when the area was known as East Pakistan.

With the formation of the Pakistan Football Federation in 1948, a Bangladesh regional association for East Pakistan was formed to administer one of Pakistan's four provincial championships, the Dacca League, traditionally held between March and November.

The South Asian custom of barefooted play was officially banned in the early 1950s, and at the same time the official duration of league matches was increased from 70 minutes to the standard 90. Prior to independence in 1972, the Dacca regional selection was an important participant in the national championship of Pakistan.

Today, despite strong interest in field hockey throughout South Asia, soccer is unquestionably the national sport of Bangladesh, and since 1974 efforts have been made to enter the Asian mainstream. The 1994 World Cup qualifying bid included a victory over Sri Lanka, but the sport is still in infancy in the region.

BARBADOS

Address: Barbados Football Association, P.O. Box 833 E, Bridgetown. *Founded:* 1910. *FIFA:* 1968. *CONCACAF:* 1968. *Stadium:* Barbados National Stadium, St. Michael (12,000); *stadium of equal size:* Kensington Oval Bridgetown (12,000). *Colors:* Royal blue-and-gold jerseys, gold shorts. *Season:* February to May.

Barbados has only recently entered international competition on a regular basis, but soccer has been established there for many decades. At first, the game in Barbados was closely linked with cricket, as was the custom in all British colonies. The formation of the Barbados Amateur Football Society in 1910 occurred about the same time Jamaica and Trinidad started their associations. Indeed, these three got a head start on all the Caribbean colonies.

With such a small number of players at its disposal, Barbados rarely has the opportunity to engage in international friendlies; they did not enter the 1994 World Cup qualifying rounds.

BELARUS
(Formerly part of the U.S.S.R.)

Address: Football Federation of Bielorussia, 8-2 Kyrov Street, 220600 Minsk. *Founded:* 1991.

Dynamo Minsk was a strong Soviet team in its heyday of competing for the U.S.S.R. champi

onship, so there is reason to believe that Belarus may be able to compete internationally and in European club tournaments with some impact when its entry to both FIFA and UEFA is completed.

The national team has already taken a short tour of South America in early 1993, while the creation of a 1993 Belarus League competition is already in the process of determining a champion to enter the European Cup.

BELGIUM

Address: Union Royale Belge des Societes de Football-Association/Koninklijke Belgische Voetbalbond, Rue de la Loi 43, Boite 1, B-1040 Bruxelles. *Founded:* 1895. *FIFA:* 1904. *UEFA:* 1954. *Colors:* White with red-, black-, and yellow-trimmed jerseys, white shorts. *Season:* August to May. *Honors:* Olympic Games winner (1920).

Cycling is the traditional national sport of Belgium, but soccer is the most popular. Proximity to England meant that Belgium was destined to become one of Europe's first soccer playing countries and one of the first to establish a governing body and a league.

Belgium was one of the founding members of FIFA and has remained active in international administration through the years. Its profile has recently become more visible with the success of its greatest club, RSC Anderlecht, in European championships and the boost given to its domestic game by World Cup successes in 1982, 1986, and 1990. The 1994 national team is well-placed to qualify once again.

Various hybrid forms of football—some resembling soccer and others rugby—appeared in Belgium around 1860. Football was included in the athletic programs of English schools in Brussels, Jenkins College, Harlock College, Xavierian College in Brussels, and St. Andries in Bruges.

British workers and residents in the port city of Antwerp and in the industrial city of Liege preferred the round ball game as early as 1860-65, and at Melle, near Ghent, students at the local Josephite college took to the game enthusiastically in 1865. Belgian students finally began to play in significant numbers by learning from British teachers in the schools.

Soccer surpassed rugby in the race for supremacy during the formative years between 1865-90. The first club, Cercle des Regates de Bruxelles, was founded in Brussels in 1878, and two years later Sporting de Bruxelles and Antwerp Harriers appeared. All three of these early clubs were founded by Belgians who had learned the game either in Britain or from British residents in Belgium.

In 1881, organized soccer spread to Ghent with the founding of the Ghent Athletic Association's soccer section. Under the name AA Gent, or FC Ghent, this remains the oldest Belgian club still in existence.

A similar team sponsored by Brussels' Athletic and Running Club was formed in 1883. Antwerp FC was founded in 1890, and Rácing de Bruxelles, Antwerp Lyon's Club, FC Brugge, and Leopold Club were founded in 1891. Antwerp, FC Brugge, and Leopold Club were founded in 1891. Antwerp, FC Brugge, and Rácing de Bruxelles (as part of RWD Molenbeek) all exist today.

The Belgian championship was introduced during the calendar year 1896, lasting several weeks, and the first winner was FC Liege from the big industrial city of the same name on the Meuse River. The league trophy was donated by King Leopold II. Rácing Club Brussels won its first championship in 1897 and with Liege domi-

nated the first eight league seasons. Rácing won four in succession from 1900 to 1903.

Rácing Club Brussels became the first Belgian team to go abroad in 1900 with a visit to Hastings, England. On May 1, 1904, Belgium and France met in their first full international at Uccle, just south of Brussels—the game ended in a 3-3 draw—and officials of the two governing bodies decided that an international federation should be formed to oversee such contests in the future.

The Belgian and French associations contacted those of Denmark, Holland, Spain, Sweden, and Switzerland, and at their behest convened the charter meeting of FIFA in Paris three weeks later. Belgium's L. Miihlinghaus became the first secretary.

In 1912, the present governing body for soccer was formed under the name Union Belge des Societes de Football-Association by separating the soccer section from the UBSSA.

King Albert I bestowed the title of "Royal" on the union in 1920. Its current name—Dutch as well as French—dates from that time, and in deference to the sensitive issue of ethnic equality, it became known by the abbreviation URBSFA/KBV.

The Coupe de Belgique (Belgian Cup) was introduced in 1911-12, and Rácing Club Brussels won the first edition by defeating Rácing Ghent in the final.

In 1920 Belgium's great port city in the north, Antwerp, was the site of the sixth Olympic Games, and it was here on its own turf that Belgium entered its first official competition and gained its first and only international honor.

As host Belgium had a bye to the second round, where it easily defeated fledgling Spain (itself the conqueror of experienced Denmark), and in the semifinal achieved its biggest win over Holland since 1906 with a 3-0 shutout.

The 1920 final, refereed by the Englishman J. Lewis, was a hard-hitting affair between Belgium and Czechoslovakia. When Lewis finally sent off a Czech player with Belgium leading by 2-0, the entire Czech team walked off the field in protest. The score was allowed to stand, and Belgium won the gold medal.

The momentum that might have materialized from Belgium's Olympic victory never occurred. Sweden overwhelmed the Belgian XI in the first round of the 1924 Olympics, 8-1, and Argentina did the same in the second round of the 1928 edition by a score of 6-3.

Belgium played in its first full internationals against England during the 1920s—eight in all—and lost all but one, a draw in 1923. The growth of soccer in Scandinavia, Central Europe, and South America left Belgium far behind, and the national team emerged from the 1920s having lost twice as many games as it won.

The first post-war bright spot in Belgian soccer history was the period between 1948 and 1954. This was the era of Anderlecht's goal scoring center forward Josef ("Jef") Mermans, Beerschot's center-forward Henri ("Rik") Coppens, FC Liege's inside left Leopold ("Pol") Anoul, and the FC Liege stopper Louis Carry.

This gifted group was brought together by national team manager Bill Gormlie, an Englishman hired by the URBSFA/KBV in 1946 to direct all nationwide soccer activities.

Gormlie's team played nine consecutive games in 1948-49 without a defeat, including important wins over Sweden and Yugoslavia (away) and Italy and Wales at home. The brief success continued with Belgium qualifying for the 1954 World Cup in Switzerland at the expense of Sweden and Finland.

A final gallant effort by this fine team was seen in the famous 4-4 draw with England in Basle after the English had been ahead by 3-1. Belgium equalized before the end of regulation time, and in extra time it was lucky to equalize again on an own goal.

This was Belgium's last hurrah in international competition for several years, as it lost to Italy 4-1 in the next match, and for the fourth time in as many attempts bowed out of the World Cup in an early round.

Semi-professionalism had appeared in the 1950s in big clubs such as Royal Sporting Club Anderlecht and Royal Standard Club, Liege, but official sanctioning of full-time professionalism was not immediately forthcoming.

After World War II, Anderlecht and Standard began their strong hold on league and cup honors. Between them they consistently managed to attract many of Belgium's finest players, and Anderlecht especially enjoyed several successive runs of league titles.

Anderlecht's rise to the top was achieved under the tutelage of Bill Gormlie, who took over the club in 1949 after leaving his national post; he stayed with Anderlecht for ten years. Standard's rise started in the late 1950s under the leadership of Paul Henrard, the former chairman of the huge steel factory that sits next to the stadium.

Standard Liege, in the meantime, advanced to the semifinals of the European Cup in 1961-62, and the national team qualified for the World Cup a fifth time in 1970, boldly eliminating Yugoslavia and Spain in the process.

This appeared to be the finest Belgian team since 1949, but after an easy win over war-torn El Salvador, Belgium was thwarted by the technically polished Soviets and Mexico, the home team, both of whom won handily.

It was later understood that this fine Belgian team was drained by internal disputes over shoe sponsorships, and its morale was broken as a result. Whatever the cause, the team's potential vanished in a series of poor performances.

As the nagging question of professionalism continued to smolder and Paul van Himst went on to become the most famous Belgian player of all time, Anderlecht and Standard Liege furthered their reputations in the 1970s. Anderlecht began to import top players from Holland and Sweden, and in 1976 its ceaseless knocking at the gates of international success finally reaped a big reward.

This was Anderlecht's first winning of the European Cup Winners' Cup behind the extraordinary artistry of Dutch left winger Robby Rensenbrink and the subsequent upset of Bayern Munchen in the unofficial Super Cup some months later.

After reaching the final of the Cup Winners' Cup again in 1977 and losing to Hamburg, the Rensenbrink-led club repeated its win in 1978 over FK Austria.

In recent years, FC Brugge has become the third important club in Belgium, threatening to win international honors, and the floodgates of professionalism have broken open for the big clubs that can afford it.

The big three clubs and a few others are making Belgium a lucrative magnet for Dutch as well as Belgian players, and the recent successes of Belgian clubs in international competition are the first products of that transformation.

Anderlecht still commands with 22 titles, including 1992-93, but Brugge has won nine. Anderlecht has seven Belgian cups to the five for Brugge.

Real International success had to wait until the 1970's. Then Belgium finished third in the 1972 European Championship it hosted. In 1980 the national team was European Championship runner-up, setting the stage for the World Cup qualification two years later.

BENIN

Address: Federation Dahomeenne de Football, B.B. no. 965, Cotonou. *Founded:* 1968. *FIFA:* 1969. *CAF:* 1969. *Largest stadium:* Charles de Gaulle, Porto-Novo (15,000). *Colors:* Green jerseys, yellow shorts. *Season:* November to June.

The Republic of Benin, formerly Dahomey, has been one of the least successful participants among active African nations, especially when measured by the level of play in other countries of French West Africa. The Federation Dahomeenne de Football was not founded until eight years after independence, though a league had been established for some years.

In addition to a Dahoman national championship, the FDF has recently launched a national cup competition, which, despite Benin's weak showing in international competition, demonstrates an active domestic organization. Benin is also a member of FIFA and the African Football Confederation, as well as the regional West African Football Union.

BERMUDA

Address: Bermuda Football Association, P.O. Box H M 745, Hamilton 5 HMCX. *Founded:* 1928. *FIFA:* 1962. *CONCACAF:* 1966. *National stadium:* The National Stadium, Prospect-Devonshire, (10,000); *largest stadium:* The

National Stadium. *Colors:* Royal blue jerseys, white shorts. *Season:* October to April.

Bermuda, a cricket-loving British dependency in the Western Atlantic, has maintained separate affiliation with FIFA since a large measure of self-government was achieved in the early 1960s. Before 1962 the Bermuda Football Association was affiliated with The Football Association in London.

Despite its closeness to the North American mainland, Bermuda's historical and cultural connections with other British colonies of the Caribbean have resulted in administrative links with that section of CONCACAF rather than the U.S.A., Canada, and Mexico.

With a shortage of funds and many of its better players in the U.S.A., Bermuda has not been consistently active in either Olympic or World Cup qualification rounds.

In 1994, however, the team advanced to the CONCACAF second round and scored a 1-0 victory over El Salvador, gaining honorable draws with both Canada and Jamaica before being eliminated. There also was a 1-0 victory over the USA in 1991 which may have sparked the later 1994 qualifying bid.

BOLIVIA

Address: Federacion Boliviana de Fútbol, Av. 16 de Julio No. 0782, P.O. Box 474, Cochabamba. *Founded:* 1925. *FIFA:* 1926. *CONMEBOL:* 1926. *National stadium:* Hernando Siles, La Paz (60,000); *largest stadium:* Hernando Siles. *Colors:* Green jerseys with white trim, white shorts. *Season:* April to December. *Honors:* South American Championship winner (1963).

Bolivia is one of the weakest soccer nations in South America, ranking just above Ecuador and Venezuela on its record, though the game has been pursued throughout the country with vigor and keen interest since the turn of the century.

There are signs of recent gains despite the fact that for decades foreign players have winced at the thought of having to play in Bolivia, where the altitude of La Paz, the capital city and location of most leading clubs, is 12,000 feet.

The national team has won the South American Championship only once—in 1963 when the competition was held in La Paz—and has never been a runner-up, but improved youth team performances, especially by the famous Tahuici club, have bought attention to the country's soccer.

Leoncio Zuaznabar is credited for having introduced the game in the 1890s, uniforms and all, to Oruro, an important railway and mining center. In 1896, Zuaznabar founded the first Bolivian club, Oruro Royal Club, and became its first captain and treasurer.

The game spread to La Paz, Sucre, Cochabamba, and other important mining districts, and in 1908, The Strongest, which remains today the senior club of La Paz, was founded in the two-mile high capital. The Stormers, the first important club in Sucre, was formed in 1914; Highlands Players in Potosi and Rácing in Cochabamba were founded in 1922.

The mid-1920s was a watershed in Bolivian soccer. The Federacion Boliviana de Fútbol was founded at Cochabamba in 1925, and remains the national governing body. One year later, the Torneo Nacional was introduced as a knockout tournament for regional selections and remained the only truly nationwide competition until 1978.

The year 1926 also marked Bolivia's official entrance into international competition. The newly formed national team competed in the South American Championship in Santiago and lost all four matches to Argentina, Uruguay, Paraguay, and Chile.

In 1930, the national stadium was built in the center of La Paz and named for the President of Bolivia, Hernando Siles. In the same year, Bolivia entered the first World Cup in Uruguay. Grouped with Yugoslavia, Bolivia's first European opponent, and Brazil, the Bolivians suffered 4-0 losses to both.

Bolivia's only subsequent appearance in World Cup final rounds occurred in 1950, when Uruguay, its only first round group opponent, delivered an 8-0 thrashing.

Bolivia's first relative success in the South American Championship was achieved in 1949 with a fourth place finish in a field of eight. The nation has not appeared in a World Cup finals in the modern era.

The domestic organization, meanwhile, was bewildered by extraordinary logistical problems caused by alpine terrain and primitive transportation. The La Paz League, formed in 1914, emerged as a kind of national championship, and was officially designated as Bolivia's first division. It was dominated until the mid-1930s by The Strongest.

Bolivar Independiente Unificada was founded in 1927, and La Paz's greatest rivalry (Bolivar against The Strongest) was born. Professionalism was introduced in the La Paz League in 1950 and the name of the league was changed to the Campeonato Professional de Fútbol.

With the advance of professionalism, new clubs, such as Jorge Wilsterman and Deportivo Municipal, arose to challenge the supremacy of The Strongest and Bolivar.

BOTSWANA

Address: P.O. Box 1396, Gaborone. *FIFA:* 1976.

The game was being organized during the late 1960s and early 1970s, but some members of the African Football Confederation ostracized Botswana because it did not openly oppose South Africa's racial policies in sport during the early 1960s.

Growth has been slow since then, but Botswana did enter the 1994 World Cup, being eliminated in the opening round by the Ivory Coast and Niger. A 0-0 home draw with group and African Champion Ivory Coast was a notable achievement.

BRAZIL

Address: Confederacao Brasileira de Desportos, Rua de Alfandega 70, P.O. 1078, Rio de Janeiro. *Founded:* 1914. *FIFA:* 1917. *CONMEBOL:* 1916. *National stadium:* Estadio Mario Filho, o Maracana Rio de Janeiro (170,000); *largest stadium:* Estadio Mario Filho. *Colors:* Yellow jerseys with green trim, blue shorts. *Season:* January to June, August to December.

Honors: World Cup winner (1958, 1962, 1970), runner-up (1950), third place (1938, 1978); South American Championship winner (1919, 1922, 1949, 1989), runner-up (1921, 1925, 1937, 1945, 1946, 1953, 1956, 1957, 1959, 1983, 1991); World Cup Under-20 Champion (1983, 1985, 1993).

It is perhaps extraordinary that in a world where more than 125 sovereign nations claim soccer as their national sport, there is one that stands out as the standard bearer of the game. For 40 years, this has been Brazil's distinction.

A vast and sprawling, multiracial country comprising half of South America's land mass and population, it is at once the world's greatest and most complex soccer power.

Brazil's standing in the world soccer community is the result of a unique combination of factors: first, a seemingly endless reservoir of talented and creative players; second, the unequaled stature of the game in the country's national life, even by Latin America standards; and third, the support and administration of Brazilian soccer by a bewildering, controversial organizational structure, whose arms have penetrated to the farthest reaches of the country.

Surprisingly, no national league exists in Brazil, the state leagues and wealthy clubs of Rio de Janeiro and Sao Paulo remaining the dominant competitions.

In international competition, Brazil is the only country in the world to qualify for all 14 World Championships, and the only country to win permanent possession of a World Cup, the Jules Rimet trophy in 1970. Germany and Italy have also won three times, but a new trophy was introduced in 1974, so neither country has three legs on that reward.

Ironically, Brazil's international standing in the South American Championship and the Copa Libertadores is a distant third to that of Argentina and Uruguay, caused by some important historical differences: the game itself was introduced in Brazil three decades later than in either Argentina or Uruguay, and the working classes of Brazil, especially blacks and mestizos, were excluded from top flight competition until the 1920s, when racial barriers finally broke down.

The ultimate turning point in Brazil's development came with the 1938 World Cup in France, when the acrobatic center forward Leônidas, instructor to the world on performing the bicycle kick, dazzled European audiences and led Brazil to a third-place finish.

Soccer was introduced in Brazil by Charles Miller, the Brazilian-born son of English parents who is said to have returned home from school in Southampton in 1894 with two soccer balls in his luggage.

Miller immediately began to organize teams among fellow British residents at the English Gas Company, the London Bank, and the Sao Paulo Railway Company, where he was employed. He eventually persuaded the Sao Paulo Athletic Club, of which he was a member, to play soccer as well as cricket.

These teams, as well as others in Sao Paulo and Rio de Janeiro before the turn of the century, were almost entirely comprised of British residents. The first team of native Brazilians was that of Mackenzie College, Sao Paulo (founded 1898), which continued to be a force in the Sao Paulo league until World War I.

British residents in Rio de Janeiro, then Brazil's largest and most important city, were not far behind Miller in their determination to introduce soccer to the capital city. In 1895, the Clube de Regatas do Flamengo (Flamengo Sailing Club) formed a team, and encouraged other sporting and athletic clubs in the city to do the same. Today, CR Flamengo is the oldest club in Brazil.

In 1902, British residents in Rio founded the Fluminense Foot-Ball Club, the second-oldest Brazilian club in existence today. The first match between teams from Rio and Sao Paulo took place in 1901, when the Sao Paulo Scratch Team and the Rio Team fought to a 1-1 draw.

In 1901, the first regional league was founded, the Campeonato Paulista de Futebol (Sao Paulo), by five clubs: Sao Paulo A.C., CA Paulistano,

EC Germania, A.A. Mackenzie, and EC Internacional, all of which are now extinct as independent clubs or have been absorbed into other clubs.

The eventual giants of Paulista competition, Corinthians and SE Palmeiras (originally Palestra Italia), were not founded until 1910 and 1914, respectively. Their domination of the Sao Paulo leagues along with Sao Paulo FC and Santos continues today.

In Rio, Brazil's second league was founded in 1905, the Liga Metropolitana de Foot-Ball do Rio de Janeiro, by six clubs: Fluminense F.C., America F.C., Bangu AC, Botafogo F.C., Sporte Clube Petropolis, and Foot-Ball and Athletic.

America and Petropolis dropped out before the start of the first season (1906), while Paissandu AC and Rio Cricket and Athletic Club took their place. The first champion was Fluminense, which dominated Rio (carioca) soccer during the first five seasons along with Botafogo.

In 1907, the Liga Metropolitana de Foot-Ball was dissolved and replaced by the Liga Metropolitana de Esportes Athleticos (LMEA). Flamengo did not join the carioca league until 1912, but rose to the top rapidly once it did. South America's greatest archrivalry, Flamengo versus Fluminense (or Fla-Flu), was launched that same year and Flamengo won its first championship in 1914. The early carioca league was dominated decisively by Flamengo and Fluminense, but today Vasco da Gama and Botafogo regularly make the title chase a four way affair.

Brazil's first unofficial international was played in 1906 at Sao Paulo between a Paulista selection of British-born players and a team representing the Cape Colony and Natal of British South Africa. For the first 20 years, the administration of Brazil's game was carried on separately by the Rio and Sao Paulo leagues, but an umbrella governing body for all sports in Brazil, the Federacao Brasileira de Sports (FBS), was created in 1914.

The Federacao immediately gained international recognition from several world bodies, though FIFA was not among them. A rival administrative organization, the Comite Olimpico Nacional, was also formed in 1914. When the Comite managed to win its own measure of international recognition, an intense struggle between the two groups ensued, and in 1916, the two merged under the banner of the FBS.

The new governing body was provisionally admitted to FIFA one year later, gaining full membership in 1923. Its name was eventually changed to the Confederaqao Brasileira de Desportos (CBD). The CBD is today the administrative body for all sports in Brazil, with soccer its primary concern and main source of revenues.

Two months after the founding of the FBS in 1914, the first representative team of Brazil was assembled at Fluminense's ground in Rio to meet the visiting Exeter City F.C. of England's Southern League.

The victorious Brazilian team (2-0) was composed of three players who were destined to become the first immortals of Brazilian soccer; goalkeeper Marcos de Mendonca, center half Rubens Salles, and center forward Artur Friedenreich, who lost two teeth in a collision with an Exeter fullback. Two month later, Brazil's first unofficial international involving national teams occurred in Buenos Aires. Brazil won 1-0 on a goal by Salles.

By World War I, the game in Brazil had moved away from the influence of the class-conscious British and with the influx of workers from Italy, Spain, and Portugal found a new and vital acceptance among all strata of society—with one major exception.

Clubs throughout the country refused to sign black players or those of mixed black-and-white or black-and-Indian parentage. The first widely known mestizo to break the race barrier was Artur Friedenreich, who started with Germania FC of Sao Paulo in 1909.

Friedenreich's incomparable artistry on the field and his tawny appearance made him the first idol of impoverished Brazilians and led directly to the eventual entry of blacks into senior-level competition. The first black player to gain a regular place on a major team was Manteiga of America F.C. (RJ), but his signing caused many America players to leave the club.

The most important breakthrough occurred in 1923, when the second division Rio club Vasco da Gama, which had adopted a nondiscriminatory policy in the late 1910's, gained promotion to the Carioca first division and won the championship that same year.

More than half of Vasco's first-string team was nonwhite, an unprecedented occurrence in the upper reaches of Brazilian soccer and one that prompted the established clubs of Rio to break away temporarily and form their own league in 1924 (the AMEA).

By 1930 the racial barriers had further broken down, and black and mestizo heroes such as Fausto, the Maravitha Negra ("Black Wonder") became almost commonplace. Brazilian historians do not hesitate to point out that Brazil's earliest challenge to Argentina's and Uruguay's domination of South American soccer coincided with the opening of Brazilian soccer to all segments of the population.

In the six South American Championships held between 1924 and 1935, Brazil participated only once, and while Uruguay and Argentina were blazing their way to international glory in the Olympic Games, the CBD showed little interest in what was then the only worldwide competition available.

The first World Championship in 1930, however, was an opportunity not to be missed, especially since it was being held in neighboring Uruguay. A disorganized if gifted Brazilian team, lacking European tactical expertise and the international experience of Argentina and Uruguay, was grouped in the first round with Bolivia and Yugoslavia.

The surprising Yugoslavs, Brazil's first full international European opponents, proceeded to win 2-1, but Bolivia was clearly (4-0) outclassed by a goal-scoring efficiency that was already becoming characteristic of Brazilian teams.

Three of Brazil's five goals in the competition were scored by the captain, Neto. Eliminated and disappointed, the team came home and played a friendly with the U.S.A. in Rio, winning by 4-3.

In spite of the destructive power struggle at home between rival national governing bodies from 1930 to 1936 (the CBD favored amateurism and the new Federacao Brasileira de Futebol, founded in 1930, supported professionalism), Brazil was one of two South American nations to make the long voyage to the 1934 World Cup in Italy.

Under the knockout format of the early World Championships, Brazil was eliminated after only one match (a loss to Spain) before stepping onto an Italian liner once again to sail for Rio. The loss to Spain was a nervous contest, in which Brazil's star inside forward Waldemar de Brito (discoverer of Pelé) missed a penalty. Genoese spectators were generally deprived of seeing a Brazilian XI on form.

European audiences were by now aware of Brazil's ability to produce players of dazzling skill, as proven by the first and second World Cups. But this reputation had existed as early as 1925, when the Sao Paulo club A.C. Paulistano made a spellbinding tour of Europe with Friedenreich at center forward.

The legacy of this famous club found its national counterpart in Brazil's World Cup squad of 1938. Indeed, it was at this juncture that Brazil made its debut as a potential world power, and in coming to France, became the only South American country to participate in all three prewar World Cup competitions.

With the breathtaking Leônidas at the center of the attack, the Brazilians slipped by Poland in the first round by 6-5 in extra time on a rain soaked pitch. Leônidas and Poland's Willimowski scored four goals apiece. In the second round, the Brazilians' redoubtable spirit was unleashed against Czechoslovakia in the

first of Brazil's many violent matches in World Cup competition.

The first game against Czechoslovakia, which ended in a draw after extra time (and subsequently known as the "Battle of Bordeaux") featured three ejections as well as broken limbs for two of Czechoslovakia's greatest stars, Planicka and Nejedly.

The replay, in which there were 15 new players on the field, was won uneventfully by Brazil. Overconfident and lacking two of its most important players, Leônidas and Tim, Brazil fell to the eventual winner of the tournament, Italy, in the semi-finals.

In the third-place match, Leônidas increased his scoring total to eight (best in the competition), and Brazil defeated the gentlemanly Swedes. It was now abundantly clear, as Brazil entered the

Maracana Stadium

war years with its first World Cup honor, that reaching the world summit would depend primarily on its ability to coordinate a plethora of dazzling ball artists into a cohesive tactical unit. This was not to be accomplished until 1958.

Brazil played host to the 1950 World Cup. Under the sponsorship of the Rio de Janeiro government, the gigantic Maracana Stadium, easily the world's largest with a capacity for 200,000 spectators (later increased to 220,000), was built as the showpiece of the fourth World Championship and as a testament to the future of Brazilian soccer.

The interior of the stadium was barely finished in time for the opening game, and the area around it resembled a battlefield of mud and construction material for the duration of the competition. But the stadium's staggering dimensions and futuristic appearance contributed much to Brazil's stature in the world sporting community.

The Brazilian team, more aware than ever of its need to coalesce raw talent into winning form, entered the competition firmly set on winning the trophy. Nothing less would do, and the pundits in Europe as well as in South America declared the Brazilians a strong favorite. In the first round they were grouped with Mexico, Switzerland, and Yugoslavia.

However, Brazil's ultimate goal looked attainable in the second round (played under a controversial league system), as manager Flavio Costa set free his extraordinary new front three, Zizinho, Ademir, and Jair.

The Brazilians vanquished Sweden and Spain by an aggregate of 13-2 and awaited the final match against talented Uruguay sitting on top of the table with a one point lead.

Uruguay, however, which had drawn with Spain and edged by Sweden uncomfortably, rose to the occasion as it always had against its northern archrival. Brazilian overconfidence may have contributed to a losing result, and little Uruguay won its second World Championship in one of the most exciting international contests ever played.

A world record 199,850 spectators watched Brazil attack unmercifully in the first half, but the Brazilian defense was caught off guard by an unexpected Uruguayan onslaught after the interval. The final score was 2-1 in favor of Uruguay. The host country, which had virtually ground to a halt during the tournament, was stunned.

In the three World Championships before the war, Rio clubs had supplied 74 players to the national side while only five had come from the great clubs of Sao Paulo. In 1950, this trend reversed itself to some extent and began to edge toward a balance, though as late as 1974 the numbers still reflected an imbalance in favor of Rio. In the 1954 World Cup, Paulista players were dominant for the first time, and the seeds of Brazil's later glory were sown.

Brazil's two backs in 1954 were Djalma Santos and Nilton Santos, probably the greatest backfield in the history of the game and holders of their position on the national team for three successive World Cups. At inside right, Fluminense's Didi (later of Botafogo) drew worldwide attention with his rare combination of leadership abilities and skillful play making.

The 1954 World Cup, however, provided a dark sequel to the 1938 "Battle of Bordeaux." In Switzerland, it was the notorious "Battle of Berne," and the opponent was another Central European team, the incomparable Hungary. It is clear from hindsight that this quarter final match might have erupted into a pitched battle.

Hungary was undefeated in four years and determined to crown its record breaking achievement with a World Championship. Brazil felt it had been denied the World Cup its last two times out: the defeats of 1938 and 1950 still stung, and Brazil was determined to vindicate its claim.

Billed appropriately as a contest between the two best teams in the competition, the 4-2 result in favor of Hungary was not a fair test of relative worth, and brawls in the locker room after the game were among the ugliest ever associated with a major international competition. In the end, the Brazilians were eliminated and bitter.

Fortunately, the fanciful memories of international fans continued to be focused on images of the giant Maracana and the skills of players like Friedenreich, Fausto, Leônidas, Zizinho, Ademir, Jair, Djalma Santos, Nilton Santos, and Didi rather than on rough play on the field, but knowledgeable observers continued to hold that without a cohesive tactical approach Brazil would not achieve its ultimate goal.

In 1955 a new phenomenon appeared at the Paulista club Santos FC from the coastal city of the same name, and Brazilian soccer would never be quite the same again. The spark that ignited Santos' fire was a 15-year-old boy wonder named Pelé. The "Black Pearl" transformed an already excellent side into an astonishing goal-scoring machine.

With one previous Sao Paulo championship to its credit (1935), Santos won the title in 1955, 1956, and nine additional years in the period after that and, with Pelé at inside left, became the most famous club in the world, eclipsing even Arsenal and Real Madrid in the minds and hearts of fans around the world.

At the same time Santos was on the rise, a tactical breakthrough transformed the national team. Manager Vincente Feola decided to drop the traditional third-back game in favor of the little-known 4-2-4 system, introduced in 1953 by Paraguay manager Fleitas Solich in the South American Championship.

At the 1958 World Cup in Sweden, Brazil brought the new system into full bloom. The forward line, which under the 4-2-4 was freed from a defensive role altogether, featured an array of sublimely skilled players: Garrincha, Vava, Pelé, and Zagalo. This awesome group, in addition to midfielder Didi, won the 1958 World Cup for Brazil.

Everything finally seemed to come together for Brazil at the sixth World Championship. Pelé and Garrincha, both in the flower of their youth, were the two most gifted ball artists of the postwar era; the unique Didi was at the height of his form; Vava ranked close to Pelé as an intuitive goal scorer, though their styles were completely different; Zagalo's ceaseless stamina absorbed the whole left side of the field like a sponge; Zito was appropriately versatile at right half; Djalma Santos and Nilton Santos continued to justify their deserved international reputations; and Gilmar was and remains the finest goalkeeper Brazil has ever produced.

To these attributes were added the facts that the 4-2-4 suited Brazil's talent admirably, and that Sweden proved to be an agreeable locale. The entire team and coaching staff entered the competition with what can only be described as a joyous spirit and an eager desire to win.

After eliminating England, Austria, and the U.S.S.R. in the first round, Brazil defeated the strong Welsh team in the quarterfinals and France, perhaps the second most exciting team in the tournament, in the semifinals. In game after game, Brazil staged dazzling displays of wide open yet modern soccer, especially against the U.S.S.R. and France, and Pelé and Vava scored one memorable goal after another.

In the final against Sweden, the front four and Didi beat their defenders and dominated the game. Pelé and Vava scored a pair each, Zagalo scored once, and the final result was 5-2. Brazil was finally the World Champion, and the wealthy clubs of Europe came rushing to its doorstep, contracts in hand.

In Chile, Brazil won its second World Championship, but the exuberant atmosphere of Sweden was absent. In the more familiar surroundings of South America, the Brazilian approach was less intense though every bit as skillful. A 4-3-3 replaced the 4-2-4, and Feola was forced to step down prior to the competition due to illness.

In the opening round against Czechoslovakia, Pelé was injured and sadly rendered unable to play for the remainder of the series. Vava, Didi, Zagalo, Zito, Nilton Santos, Djalma Santos, and Gilmar were all present again, the two Santoses for the third World Cup in succession, but Brazil's heroes were Garrincha, scorer of two goals each against England and Chile, and Pelé's replacement Amarildo, who almost single-handedly beat Spain in the opening round and equalized in the final against Czechoslovakia. The final was won 3-1 with an on-and-off performance, and the Jules Rimet Cup was again enveloped by the musical sounds of samba.

Pelé, injured Garrincha, and the aging Djalma Santos and Zito returned for the 1964 title defense, as did Bellini and Orlando from 1958. Feola was back at the helm, and there were gifted newcomers in Gerson and Tostao, but in

Brazilizn fans carry Pelé off the field following Brazil's 1970 World Cup victory in Mexico City.

the first round it became apparent that less talented players—and that meant nearly everyone else in the competition—were intent on fouling the redoubtable Brazilian strikers to the turf.

Pelé especially was victimized so consistently by fearful defenders that his saga became little more than a tragedy. Brazil's hopes suffered with each foul, and after first round losses to Hungary and Portugal, it was eliminated.

Despite that loss, the 1960s also saw the beginning of a boom in the construction of giant stadiums up and down the country that was still in full swing in the late 1970s.

Stadiums with capacities for over 100,000 spectators were built in Sao Paulo, Belo Horizonte, Curriba, Porto Alegre, Belem, Fortaleza, Salvador, and Maceio. Individually or collectively, these huge futuristic edifices remain unrivaled anywhere in the world.

The national team, revitalized by Pelé's newly found enthusiasm and a fresh crop of supremely talented players, returned to winning form by 1968. Between the summer of 1968 and the 1970 World Cup, Brazil won 21 matches and lost only three.

In the midst of this was the national jubilation over Pelé's one-thousandth goal, scored for Santos in a 1969 league match, and the promise that he would be available for Mexico after all.

The festive atmosphere of Mexico's soccer-crazed cities was well suited to a Brazilian comeback, but England, Italy, and West Germany were serious threats to Brazil's chances. Three months before the World Cup began, former international hero Mario Zagalo replaced controversial Joao Saldanha as a national team member. Well liked and respected by all concerned, Zagalo turned out to be the necessary stabilizer.

The World Cup of 1970 was a brilliant high point in soccer history. This was due to the manner in which Brazil won its third World Championship. For 15 years, the game was dominated by the negative tactics of *catenaccio,* with brief respites provided by Brazil and Portugal. Zagalo's open and exciting team showed the world once again how the game might be played.

With Pelé and the splendid Tostao in the middle of the attack, the right and left flanks were occupied by Jairzinho and Rivelino, respectively, both players of world class stature. Out of the midfield came the orchestrator Gerson, and from even further back came the elegant, attacking right fullback Carlos Alberto, the new captain. The striking potential of these six alone was among the greatest the game has ever seen.

Czechoslovakia, England, Rumania, Peru, and Uruguay all succumbed in due course, and in the final against Italy, Brazil painted a canvas of delights. Though Italy played superbly in the adversary role and even managed to score a goal, Pelé, Gerson, Jairzinho, and Carlos Alberto each hit the back of the net, leaving no doubt that Brazil was back on top.

Brazil's domination of world soccer was thus extended from the 1950s to the early 1970s, but Brazil was not to repeat its accomplishment in 1974. In 1975, Brazil was eliminated from the revitalized South American Championship by Peru, and the Brazilian game sank to an all-time low. The rebuilding process did nor begin in earnest until 1977, when the national team manager, Claudio Coutinho, set out to introduce elements of European teamwork.

In Brazil's eleventh attempt to gain World Cup honors in 1978, Coutinho's idea backfired. Individual skills were apparent, as always, but apart from a splendid 3-0 defeat of Peru, the Brazilian team was disorganized and ineffective. It finally settled for an uneasy third place, despite the fact that it finished as the only unbeaten team in the competition.

A Brazilian Championship has finally been started but remains controversial. Provincial clubs have won the competition three times (Atletico Mineiro in 1971 and Internacional Porto Alegre in 1975 and 1976), and in 1975 the two finalists were both from provincial leagues (Internacional and Cruzeiro). Sao Paolo's Palmeiras, meanwhile, has excelled in winning four National Championships (1967, 1969, 1972, 1973).

In the Liga Paulista, the big five clubs down through the decades have been (in descending order of points accumulated): Palmeiras, Santos, Sao Paolo, Corinthians, and Portuguesa. In the Liga Carioca, the big five are (in order): Fluminense, Flamengo, Vasco da Gama, Botafogo, and America.

Cruzeiro's winning of the 1976 Copa Libertadores, however, was the clearest signal yet that the hegemony of these giant sporting establishments is open to challenge. Cruzeiro, Atletico Mineiro, and Internacional have reached the front ranks of Brazilian soccer, and in future years other provincial clubs are likely to have a heavy impact on the National Championship.

Soccer is the outstanding passion of the Brazilian people. The depth of their *religiao Brasileira* (a term used frequently by Brazilians themselves) may be felt not only on the terraces of giant stadiums, but up and down the beaches and in the wet jungles.

BRUNEI

Address: Brunei Amateur Football Association, P.O. Box 2010, 1920 Bandar Seri Begawan. *Founded:* 1959. *FIFA:* 1969. *AFC:* 1970. *Col-* *ors:* Gold jerseys, black shorts. *Season:* September to March.

The Brunei State Amateur Football Association was founded in 1959, the year of the first national constitution, and affiliation with FIFA was sought in anticipation of full self-government in 1971. Soccer is now played by Malay as well as Chinese natives, most of whom are not officially registered with the national association. They did not enter the 1994 World Cup.

BULGARIA

Address: Bulgarska Football Union, Gotcho Gopin 19, 1000 Sofia. *Founded:* 1923. *FIFA:* 1924. *UEFA:* 1954. *National stadium:* Vassil Levski Stadium, Sofia (60,000); *largest stadium:* Vassil Levski Stadium. *Colors:* White jerseys, green shorts. *Season:* August to December, March to June. *Honors:* Olympic Games runner-up (1968), third place (1956).

Since its entry into the international mainstream at the 1956 Olympics, Bulgaria's record among European countries has been reasonable. Bulgaria qualified for four successive World Cups between 1962 and 1974 and again in 1986 but failed to move beyond the first round in any of them. In the European Football Championship, it has participated in every edition but has not won honors.

In the Olympic Games, Bulgaria has achieved a degree of success, but its overall Olympic record is inferior to the other formally Communist Eastern European states. At the club level, its achievements have also been limited.

Soccer was introduced to Bulgaria in 1894, when Georges de Regibus, one of a dozen Swiss athletic instructors hired by the newly independent Kingdom of Bulgaria to establish a sports program, taught the game as a warm-up exercise to youth organizations in Varna.

The "English game" did not take root, however, and Bulgarian soccer actually received its first impetus from Bulgarian students at universities in Constantinople, Turkey, who in 1909 formed Football Club 13, named for its 13 members. In 1910, Football Club 13 was joined by Slavia Sofia and Levski Sofia, which remain the oldest clubs in Bulgaria.

An unofficial championship was held in Sofia in 1913, won by Slavia over F.C. 13, but before World War I Bulgarian soccer continued to be held back by the political turbulence of the period and the state's inability to organize and administer sports programs.

The first era of concentrated growth occurred immediately after World War I. The Bolgarska Nationalna Sportna Federatia (BNSF) was founded in 1923, admitted to FIFA six months later, and in 1924 the first national championship was established.

In 1937, a true national league was established. Today it consists of 16 clubs. The league has been dominated by CSKA, the Communist Army Club, with 27 titles and Levski with 16.

Bulgaria made its international debut in Vienna against Austria in 1923, losing by a predictable 6-0 score. Within a year, Bulgaria entered the Olympic Games in Paris, but again it lost, this time to the Irish Free State by 1-0. It lost its first seven games, and did not win until its 15th game, which took place in 1930 against Rumania in the first Balkan Cup.

With the birth of the Communist state in 1944, Bulgaria entered a splendid period of growth in all sports, and soccer was one of the primary beneficiaries. The reconstituted Supreme Committee for Physical Culture and Sports threw all its weight behind the new showcase club, CDNA (later, CSKA).

Funds and personnel were channeled to the army club, and in its first 15 years it won the league title 12 times, including 1948, its first year in existence, and nine in a row between 1954 and 1962.

Levski continued as the most popular club, winning a well deserved share of honors (six league and eight cup titles between 1953 and 1977), and in 1969 it was ordered to merge with Spartak Sofia as Levski-Spartak.

Bulgaria's winning the 1956 Olympic bronze did not represent the birth of a major international power—the presence in Australia of only one genuine world class team (Yugoslavia) relegated the competition to obscurity—but in 1962, after failing in two previous tries, Bulgaria qualified for the World Cup in Chile by eliminating France and Finland.

The 1956 Olympic Games and the 1962 World Cup were spanned by the career of Bulgaria's first international star, the inside left Ivan Kolev, on whose shoulders fell the distinction of attracting some international attention to the Bulgarian game.

The early 1960s saw the emergence of several important Bulgarian players. The most gifted, and probably the greatest Bulgarian player of this era, was Georgi Asparoukhov, Levski's goalscoring center forward, whose injuries sadly kept him at half pace in the 1966 and 1970 World Cup finals.

Had Asparoukhov been in form, it is difficult to imagine Bulgaria suffering two winless World Cup final rounds in a row. Tragically, in 1971, Bulgarian soccer was dealt a severe blow when Asparoukhov was killed in an automobile accident.

A new generation of stars emerged late in the 1980s, giving rise to Bulgarian hopes that they would make a major impact on the game in the 1990s.

The leading personality was the Barcelona forward Hristo Stoichkov, who helped lead the Spanish team to the 1992 European Cup, but there were several talented Bulgarians elsewhere in both Portuguese and Spanish soccer.

BURKINA FASO
(Formerly Upper Volta)

Address: Federation Burkina-Faso de Foot-ball, B.P. 57, Ouagadougou. *Founded:* 1960. *FIFA:* 1964. *CAF:* 1964. *National stadium:* Stade Municipal de Ouagadougou, Ouagadougou (4,000); *largest stadium:* Stade Municipal de Ouagadougou. *Colors:* Black jerseys, white shorts.

One of the poorest countries of West Africa, Burkina Faso is an underdeveloped soccer nation as well. It ranks in the bottom quarter of African members of FIFA when considered on the basis of international success at both national and club levels.

Burkina Faso's inferior standing, though, is a result of financial and organizational woes rather than the inferiority of its players. The country did not organize a team to compete in the 1994 World Cup.

Soccer had been brought to the capital, Ouagadougou, by French colonists around 1896, but as was the case in all countries of the Sahel, it got off to a slow start even after the French partition of 1932.

During the colonial period, soccer in Burkina Faso was under the aegis of the Ligue de l'Afrique Occidentale Francaise in Dakar, which administered the game in all of French West Africa, but little evidence of its activities existed.

Enthusiasm increased considerably after World War II, however, and the Federation Voltaique de Foot-ball (FVF) was founded immediately after independence in 1960, followed closely by affiliation with FIFA and the African Football Confederation.

BURMA
(Now Myanmar)

Address: Burma Football Federation, Aungsan Memorial Stadium, Kandawgalay Post Office, Yangon. *Founded:* 1947. *FIFA:* 1947. *AFC:* 1958. *National stadium:* Aungsan Memorial Stadium, Yangon (45,000); *largest stadium:* Aungsan Memorial Stadium. *Colors:* Red jerseys, white shorts. *Season:* May to February.

Myanmar, the former Burma, is largely isolated from international play and has made few inroads outside its own area. The popularity of soccer in Burma is attributable to the country's strong colonial links with Great Britain.

Soldiers and residents in British outposts and major population centers played the game throughout the period when Burma was a province of India (1885-1942).

The major turning point was World War II, which brought a huge influx of British military personnel and cultural staples, such as soccer and cricket. By the time the Burma Football

Federation was founded in 1947, shortly before independence, there was a thriving league of first and second divisions and two annual cup competitions.

Burma was one of six participants in the first soccer tournaments of the Asian Games (1951), losing its only match to Iran in the first round. It has won the Merdeka Football Tournament of Malaysia three times, the Djakarta Anniversary Tournament, and the South Korean President's Cup three times, but has suffered recent political turmoil. The country, which has not competed on an international level since it has become Myanmar, entered, but then withdrew from, the 1994 World Cup before qualifying began.

BURUNDI

Address: Confederation des Sports (CSB), B.P. 3426, Bujumbura. *Founded:* 1948. *FIFA:* 1972. *CAF:* 1972. *National stadium:* Federation de Football du Burundi Stadium (6,000); *largest stadium:* FFB Stadium. *Colors:* Red jerseys, white shorts.

Burundi has enthusiastically adopted soccer as the national sport. It is uncertain whether the game was introduced to the territory of Ruanda-Urundi by Germans, who took control of the area in the late nineteenth century, or by Belgians, who leased the colony during World War I. In any case, the country's concerted effort to organize the domestic game and actively seek international arenas is a testament to the people's enthusiasm for soccer.

The years of continuous civil unrest following independence from Belgium in 1962 impeded the growth of the game, but in 1972 sports officials closed ranks and sought membership in FIFA and the African Football Confederation.

Actual control of soccer in Burundi is in the hands of the Federation de Football du Burundi (FFB), an adjunct of the Confederation des Sports, which was founded with Belgian initiative immediately after World War II.

Burundi's potential as a regional power may be minimal. Yet, it has proven convincingly that it cannot be overlooked.

In the 1994 World Cup qualifying competition, Burundi upset highly-favored Ghana, 1-0, a result that effectively eliminated one of Africa's strongest teams from the 1994 tournament.

CAMBODIA
See: Kampuchea

CAMEROON

Address: Federation Camerounaise de Football, B.P. 1116, Yaounde. *Founded:* 1960. *FIFA:* 1962. *CAF:* 1963. *Largest stadium:* Stade Ahmadou Ahidjo. *Colors:* Green jerseys, red shorts. *Season:* October to August. *Honors:* World Cup quarterfinalists 1990; World Cup finals participant 1982; African Championship Winners 1984, 1988, runner-up, 1986.

Cameroon (or Cameroun) is the home of two great African clubs, Canon de Yaounde and Tonnerre Kalara Club Yaounde, and the location of two of the most modern stadium facilities in sub-Saharan Africa: the national stadium in Yaounde, the capital, and the Stade Reunification in Douala.

Cameroon is the most famous nation in African soccer, following its stunning performance in the 1990 World Cup. As a direct result of the

Indomitable Lions' quarterfinal performance, FIFA extended the number of African teams in the World Cup finals from two to three.

The game was introduced to Cameroon by German colonists in Buea before World War I, but the French did more to popularize it during their League of Nations mandate between the wars. The biggest surge of interest was seen after World War II, when an organizational structure of sorts rose from the chaos of French Equatorial African soccer.

This was the only area in French Africa that was not governed by one of the primary colonial soccer administrations linked to the French Football Federation, thus relegating it to relative obscurity until independence in 1960.

Great encouragement was given to Camerounais soccer when Oryx de Duuala romped through the inaugural African Champions' Cup in 1964, and brought home the first African club trophy.

Cameroon clubs were to figure prominently in African club championships for years to come, although the 1980 victory by Canon de Yaounde, the country's fifth African Club Championship, is their last success in this tournament. Canon also has one Africa Cup Winners Cup (1980) to its name, while both Tonnerre Yaounde (1975) and Union Douala (1982) have also won that competition.

CANADA

Address: Canadian Soccer Association, 1600 James Naismith Drive, Gloucester, Ontario K1B 5 NY. *Founded:* 1912. *FIFA:* 1912-26. *Largest stadium:* Stade Olympique, Montreal (72,000). *Colors:* Red jerseys, red shorts. *Season:* April to August.

Soccer in Canada was rejected in the early stages of its development for the more idiosyncratic Canadian football (akin to American football) and other than a period of moderate growth in the 1920s, soccer did not show signs of taking root again until the formation of the North American Soccer League in 1968.

The losing battle with rugby began in 1874, when McGill University in Montreal formed a rugby team. It was McGill that introduced the rugby game to Harvard in the same year, leading to the birth and ultimate domination of gridiron football in the United States.

Association rules were played at Queen's University, Kingston, Ontario, in the early 1870s. Queen's played two games in Toronto in 1874 against local teams and lost both.

Upper Canada College played under association rules until 1876, but subsequently switched to rugby. Both types of football were reserved exclusively for students and graduates of boarding schools during the 1870s and 1880s.

Canada's first and only international honor was won at the 1904 Olympic Games in St. Louis, but, unfortunately, the tournament was only an exhibition series and never entered the record books. Ontario's Galt F.C., representing Canada, defeated a team called USA I (actually Christian Brothers College, St. Louis) by 7-0 and USA II (St. Rose, St. Louis) by 4-0. No other teams were entered, and Canada was declared the winner.

The Dominion of Canada Football Association (DFA as it was known) was founded in 1912 in Toronto, and held its first meeting in Winnipeg the same year. The DFA was the first truly national governing body, and became the precursor of the Football Association of Canada and eventually the present Canadian Soccer Association. Representatives from Quebec,

Ontario, Manitoba, Saskatchewan, and Alberta were charter members.

From the beginning, the DFA was beset by problems concerning professionalism and provincial antagonism. In British Columbia, where soccer had become particularly strong, many clubs had broken away from the provincial British Columbia Football Association to form a professional league.

During the first year of the DFA's existence, rival associations were set up in Vancouver: the British Columbia Provincial F.A., which affiliated with the ISFA, and the British Columbia F.A., which joined the Amateur Athletic Union of Canada.

In the 1920s, there was a soccer revival caused by vast numbers of European immigrants who had arrived after World War I. Numerous British teams visited Canada, and Canadian teams toured Australia and New Zealand. While Canadian teams at home won a portion of these international friendlies, the relative lack of interest shown by Canadian fans was not enough to make the tours financially viable.

Canadian tours abroad, on the other hand, were more successful. On the 1929 tour of New Zealand, the Canadian national team won 20 matches while losing and drawing only one each.

In domestic competition between the wars, important rivalries between new immigrant communities took their place beside English, Scottish, Welsh, and Irish rivalries.

After World War II, the game at club level was played almost exclusively by immigrants, and was seen less and less outside the major urban areas of Ontario, Quebec, and British Columbia.

The participation in the NASL by teams from Montreal, Toronto and Vancouver had limited success, while a Canadian soccer league existed briefly in the 1980's, but interest never rivaled that of Canadian football for spectator support.

After its anomalous victory in 1904 at St. Louis, Canada did not attempt to qualify for the Olympic tournament until 1968. Its first participation in the final rounds was as the host country in 1976, when it lost to the U.S.S.R.'s full international team by only 2-1 and North Korea by a more decisive 3-1 in the first round.

In international competition, Canada has suffered from a lack of funds and the difficulty of molding a cohesive national unit of players who must travel thousands of miles to prepare for a match. Canada's most frequent opponent has been the USA, and they eliminated the USA from both the 1974 and 1978 World Cup qualification rounds in Canada's first World Cup attempts.

CAPE VERDE

Address: Federacao Cabo-Verdiana de Futebol, P.O. Box 234, Praia, Cape Verde. *Founded:* 1982. *Colors:* Green.

Cape Verde is not currently participating in African Championship or World Cup play.

CAYMAN ISLANDS

Address: Cayman Islands Football Association, P.O. Box 178, George Town, Grand Cayman, Cayman Islands, West Indies. *Founded:* 1991.

The tiny Cayman Islands have entered some Caribbean regional competition, like the Shell Cup, which qualifies teams for the CONCACAF Gold Cup, but they have not attempted a World Cup qualification.

CENTRAL AFRICA

Address: Federation Centraficaine de Football, B.P. 344, Bangui. *Founded:* 1937. *FIFA:* 1963. *CAF:* 1965. *National stadium:* Barthelemy Boganda, Bangui (35,000); *largest stadium:* Barthelemy Boganda. *Colors:* Grey-blue jerseys, white shorts. *Season:* October to July.

While the domestic game in Central Africa is widespread and active, soccer in the Central African Empire is virtually an unknown quantity.

The game was introduced in the Ubangi Chari Territory of French Equatorial Africa after World War I by French colonists and missionaries along the settlements of the Ubangi River. Bangui, Fort de Possel, and Fort Crampel (up-country) were probably the first locations to have organized competitions.

The original sports federation of 1937 was established primarily for Europeans. International participation has been sporadic. CAR did not enter the 1994 World Cup.

CEYLON
See: Sri Lanka

CHAD

The former French Equatorial African colony of Chad was a member of FIFA from 1962-71 but was expelled for repeated non-payment of dues.

CHILE

Address: Federacion de Football de Chile, Calle Erasmo Escala No. 1872, Casilla No. 3733 Santiago de Chile. *Founded:* 1895. *FIFA:* 1912. *CONMEBOL:* 1916. *National stadium:* Estadio Nacional de Chile, Santiago (77,127); *largest stadium:* Estadio Nacional de Chile. *Colors:* Red jerseys, blue shorts. *Season:* April to December. *Honors:* World Cup third place (1962); South American Championship runner-up (1955, 1956, 1979, 1987).

Soccer has a long and distinguished history in Chile, but the game entered the 1990s under a cloud. Like its more famous soccer-playing neighbors to the east, Argentina and Uruguay, Chile was introduced to the game as early as the mid-nineteenth century, and its pioneers were able to organize clubs and competitions earlier than in many European countries.

Chile has been a leader in promoting soccer throughout South America, and its continental rank as a power to be reckoned with hovers just behind the mighty Argentina, Brazil, and Uruguay. Many Chilean players down through the years have been actively pursued by wealthy foreign clubs.

In 1889, the first club in Chile, Valparaiso Football Club, was founded by David Scott, but expansion was halted temporarily during the political upheavals of 1891. In 1892, other British-based clubs were formed to take up the challenge posed by the already famous Valparaiso F.C.: Mackay and Sutherland, English Stocking, Hall School, and Rogers F.C. founded by a firm importing tea by that name.

Few of these clubs included any Chileans until 1893, when Mackay and Sutherland met the all-British Valparaiso F.C. in a showdown at the Parque Cousino (now the Parque O'Higgins) with a mixed Chilean-British lineup.

Late in 1893, the first international involving Chile was played at the Sporting Club between Valparaiso and an Argentine selection with a 1-1 result. Both teams were made up entirely of British players. In 1895, a group of nine clubs from Valparaiso, Santiago, Viria del Mar, and Concepcion met to form the Football Associacion of Chile, forerunner of the present governing body, and to organize a formal competition.

After 1895, soccer gained a stronger foothold in Santiago under the stewardship of Juan Ramsay, the "father of Santiago soccer," and the first truly Chilean club in the capital, Santiago Rangers, was founded in 1896.

By 1897, the game had spread north to Coquimbo and Antofagasta, and the following year Iquique Wanderers F.C. was founded in the city of that name, Chile's northernmost population center. In 1912, the old Football Association of Chile was reorganized as the Asociación de Fútbol de Chile (AFC). For five years the AFC struggled with the Federacion Sportiva Nacional over the question of jurisdiction, but in, 1917 the latter gave up all claims of control.

In 1910, Chile made its international debut in Buenos Aires in a tournament with Argentina and Uruguay to commemorate Argentina's centennial. The Chilean team played three games, losing to Argentina 3-1 and 5-1 and losing to Uruguay 3-0.

Chile's next international appearance was in the first South American Championship in 1916 at Buenos Aires, where it met Argentina and Uruguay again and, for the first time, Brazil. The Chileans gained a 1-1 draw with Brazil but lost again to Argentina, 6-1, and Uruguay, 4-0, to settle for last place in the standings.

The clubs that were to figure prominently in Chilean soccer were all founded between 1900 and 1925. Magallanes (Magellan) appeared in 1904; Union Deportiva Espaniola was founded in 1921; Audax Italiano was originally an Italian-based cyclists' club; Green Cross F.C. in 1916; and the most important of all Chilean clubs, Club de Deportes Colo Colo, was organized in 1925 by dissident members of Magallanes. All of these famous clubs are located in Santiago. Cobreloa, the current champion, is a much more recently founded club.

For several decades, domestic competition in Chile centered on the regional leagues, each of which was affiliated with a regional association, which in turn was affiliated with the FFC. The Santiago league, called the Liga Metropolitana, became the most important of these regional leagues after World War I. The birth of Santiago's Colo Colo in 1925 marked a watershed in Chilean soccer history.

The new club, under captain and founder David Arellano, became a huge hit with the public because its style was flashy and outgoing, and Arellano developed a sense of urgency and comradeship that Santiago fans appreciated.

The rise of Colo Colo and the new enthusiasm for the game that it generated led directly to the growth of professionalism and the founding of the first national—and professional—league in 1933. Colo Colo went on to gain a record number of championships, accumulating 16 by 1990. Today their main rivals are Cobreloa, Universidad Catolica, and Universidad de Chile.

In 1930 Chile had participated in the first World Cup in 1930, held in Montevideo, Uruguay and had acquitted itself well with a strong win over Mexico and a 1-0 shutout of France. Argentina, on the other hand, whom Chile has not managed to defeat in nine attempts, won an easy victory, 3-1, on the goal-scoring might of Guillermo Stabile.

In 1934 and 1938, Chile decided not to make the long trip to Italy and France, and until the 1950 World Cup Chile's international schedule was restricted to the South American Championship.

Chile was not one of the glamorous South American teams in the 1950 World Cup, but its showing drew some praise. Chile hosted the 1962 World Cup, which ultimately served to draw world attention to the terrible devastation caused by the 1961 earthquake. To Chileans the games brought much pride and great excitement.

As host, Chile automatically qualified for the final rounds, and Chilean soccer finally arrived in the international spotlight. Splendid new stadiums were built in Santiago, the Estadio Nacional, and Vina del Mar, the resort town near Valparaiso, and matches were also played in a copper mining company's stadium in Rancagua, and at Arica.

Chile's 1962 team was managed by Fernando Riera, a former player in France, and it played under a 4-2-4 system that was sparked by Universidad de Chile's left winger Leonel Sanchez. Before the competition, Chile had lost to the U.S.S.R. and played Hungary twice, winning by a huge score and then drawing.
In the first round, Chile showed its worth by coming from behind to defeat Switzerland 3-1, but the second game against Italy was a brawl.

The situation had been exacerbated by the Chilean and Italian presses, which made certain charges about drugs in Italian soccer and living conditions in Chile, respectively, and before the game was over there were two ejections and an injured referee. Sanchez broke Humbert Maschio's nose with an internationally televised punch, and goals by Ramirez and Toro gave the home team a 2-0 upset victory.

Chile's third game of the round was against West Germany, and here Chile was no match for European tactical sophistication; the Germans won 2-0. West Germany and, to everyone's surprise, Chile went on the quarter-finals.

In Arica, Chile upset the U.S.S.R. by 2-1 on goals by Sanchez and Rojaz, causing excited Chilean fans to erupt in festive celebration. Astonishingly, this put Chile into the semifinals with Brazil, Yugoslavia, and Czechoslovakia.

Chile's unlucky draw for the round was Brazil. This game was the biggest event in Chilean sports history, as evidenced by public demonstrations of euphoria, but the defending champion Brazilians were in an entirely different class on the field, and the home team never had a chance.

Garrincha and Vavd both scored a pair of goals for Brazil, and one of Chile's two goals was scored from a penalty, leaving the final result, 4-2. The Chileans, however, still had a chance to win a medal with the third place game, and their determination showed in a 1-0 defeat of Yugoslavia on a goal scored in the last minute by Rojas.

Chile's third-place finish in the 1962 World Cup was by far its highest accomplishment in international competition. The political upheavals of the post-Allende era worked ironically in Chile's favor in the 1974 World Cup. It was scheduled to meet the U.S.S.R. to decide a berth in the final rounds, but the Soviets refused to play Chile in Santiago's national stadium because the stadium had been used to hold political prisoners after the Pinochet coup d'etat. On that basis, Chile received free passage to the finals.

In West Germany, Chile's defensive tactics produced two draws with East Germany and Aus tralia, and a 1-0 loss to eventual world champion West Germany. In qualification rounds for the 1978 finals, Chile was eliminated by Peru.

The 1982 Chilean performance in Spain was reasonable if not successful as they were eliminated after the first round. However they did play a part in the controversy which surrounded their section when holding Algeria to a 3-2 victory in their final group game. That ultimately put Algeria out of the tournament when Austria and West Germany played a draw which many observers thought was a contrived result.

If the Chileans can justly claim to have been innocent bystanders in 1982 they were smack in the middle of one of the major World Cup incidents in the qualifying rounds for the 1990 tournament.

Facing defeat in Brazil and elimination from the competition, the Chileans walked off the field at Maracana Stadium after a flare shot from the crowd landed near goalkeeper Roberto Rojas. He later admitted that he was not injured by the device but was carried off the field bleeding from a cut which apparently occurred sometime after the Chilean training staff came onto the field.

Rojas was later suspended for life from world soccer and the country was banned from competing in the 1994 tournament.

CHINA, PEOPLE'S REPUBLIC OF

Address: 9 Tiyuguan Road, Beijing. *Founded:* 1924. *FIFA:* 1976.

China has two separate histories of football. One is the story of *tsu chu,* the ancient Chinese ritual that is widely thought to be the world's first football game. The second is that of modern

soccer, entering China just as it did other countries of the Far East—via European colonists.

The exact date and location of the modern game's importation to China are uncertain, but it is likely that the British introduced it in their treaty ports (Shanghai, Ningpo, Amoy, Hong Kong, and Canton) during the 1860s. By the turn of the century, substantial numbers of Chinese were playing, and some Chinese teams had been formed.

The revolution of 1912 prompted the creation of a national team and the semblance of administrative organization, despite the political chaos of the period.

In February 1913 a Chinese team of students traveled to Manila to play the Philippines in the first Football Tournament of the Far East Games, and lost 2-1. This was the earliest officially recognized international on the continent of Asia, and it launched the oldest soccer rivalry East of Suez, Australasia included.

China's second and only other consistent opponent at this time was Japan, again in the Far East Games, the first in 1917, resulting in an 8-0 win for China. China met Japan seven times in the Far East Games from 1918-34, winning six and drawing one with a 31-9 goal difference.

In 1924, the China National Amateur Athletic Federation (CNAAF) was founded in Nanking as an attempt to create an umbrella body for all organized sports. It became affiliated with FIFA in 1931, and five years later a more autonomous soccer association was established (claimed by Chinese Tapei, an Olympic unit but no longer a FIFA-recognized entity) to supervise the direct administration of the game from the CNAAF's soccer section.

By the immediate postwar period, there were over 20 stadiums in China capable of holding large soccer crowds (almost 300,000 seats in all). The main centers of activity until general reorganization in the 1950s were: Peking, Shanghai, Tientsin, Canton, Mukden, Hankow, Wuchang, Chungking, and Sian. Domestic competitions were plentiful, and more than 1,000 clubs and 20,000 players were affiliated with the federation.

A few weeks after the founding of the People's Republic of China in October 1949, a new umbrella governing body was formed in Peking, the All-China Athletic Federation (ACAF). The administration of soccer in the People's Republic was immediately put under the collective aegis of the ACAF, where it remains to this day.

After the revolution, FIFA continued to recognize the mainland governing body as a matter of course, since the geographical area it represented was the same as pre-1949 China. China's isolation, however, precluded any significant international contact on the playing field except with North Korea and the Soviet Union.

It remained a member de jure of FIFA until 1958, when the ACAF withdrew of its own volition in protest over FIFA admitting Chinese Taipei four years earlier. In the aftermath of "ping-pong diplomacy" during the early 1970s, Chinese participation in international competition increased dramatically. The number of countries or territories visited or hosted by Chinese soccer teams during 1971-77 eventually rose to over 50.

Other than Albania, the first European team to tour China was the Yugoslav national amateur team in 1975. The Yugoslavs won all three matches against selections from Shanghai (1-0), Canton (1-0), and Northwest China (2-0). The first Chinese foray into the Western Hemisphere occurred in 1977 in the United States. A Chinese national selection drew once with the U.S.A.

Against club opponents on the same tour, China fared slightly better (1-1 against Cosmos and a 2-1 win against Tampa Bay). By 1980, Chinese teams had played their first matches in Western Europe, probably against West German and British Amateur teams.

In 1976, the Asian Football Confederation expelled China National and admitted the People's Republic, setting off a chain of reactions and counteractions that threatened to split the world soccer community. China National, seeking nations willing to compete on the field, looked to Oceania for opponents and increased its international fixture list with numerous island republics and territories.

This new association with Oceania resulted in Taiwan's grouping with Australia and New Zealand in the qualification rounds for the 1978 World Cup, which resulted in four consecutive losses and a dismal goal difference of 1-17.

COLOMBIA

Address: Federacion Colombiana de Fútbol, Avenida 32, No. 16-22, Apartado Aereo No. 17.602, Bogota, D.E. *Founded:* 1924. *FIFA:* 1931. *CONMEBOL:* 1940. *National stadium:* Estadio distrital nemesio camacho "El Campin," Bogota (57,000); *largest stadium:* Pascual Guerrero, Cali (61,000). *Colors:* Yellow jerseys with orange, blue, and red stripes, cream shorts. *Season:* February to December. *Honors:* South American Championship runner-up (1975).

Colombian soccer authorities have suffered in trying to organize its domestic game. Colombia has been in conflict with FIFA repeatedly over the past 30 years, but its good standing was restored and its image improved in the last two decades.

Soccer in Colombia was first established in the Caribbean port city of Barranquilla, where the influence of British and other European commerce was strongly felt after the turn of the century. The influx of European military and commercial visitors during World War I accelerated growth, and in the early 1920s Colombian soccer enjoyed its first great expansion.

In 1924, the Liga de Football del Atlantico (LFA), forerunner of the present governing body, was founded in Barranquilla, and was admitted to FIFA in 1931. The LFA, which was really a regional association restricted to the Atlantico Department (Barranquilla and environs) was reorganized in 1936 under the name Asociación Colombiana de Fútbol (ACF).

Regional leagues were introduced in major population centers, and clubs became affiliated directly to the local associations that administered their leagues. Clubs did not affiliate directly with the national association until after World War II. The only national championship before World War II was an annual tournament for representative teams of each regional association.

The ACF looked to the Caribbean and Central America rather than South America when it sought regional international affiliation in the 1930s. In 1938, it became a charter member of the Confederacion Centroamericano y del Caribe de Fútbol (CCCF), and participated in the soccer tournament of the third Central American and Caribbean Games that took place in Panama. This was Colombia's debut in international competition, and it produced mixed results in a relatively weak field.

In 1940, the ACE also joined CONMEBOL, the South American Football Confederation, but continued its affiliation with the CCCF at the same time. Colombia is the only country in the world that has been a member of two regional confederations simultaneously. Its first partici-

pation in the South American Championship came with the eighteenth edition in 1945, and it finished a distant fifth in a field of eight. Its only victory in six games was over Ecuador (3-1).

In 1948, professionalism was recognized (15 years later than in most South American countries), and a national league was finally introduced. The focus of Colombian soccer switched from Barranquilla to Bogota, and the big Bogota clubs, Millonarios and Independiente Santa Fe, came to the fore.

The latter won the first league title in 1948, but in 1949 Millonarios secured the services of Alfredo Di Stefano from Ríver Plate in Buenos Aires and became the strongest team ever seen in Colombia.

The two-year-old Millonarios, which seemed to have a millionaire's bank account, won its first championship in 1949, and in 1950 it and several other clubs broke away from the ACF to form a renegade league, resulting in Colombia's suspension from FIFA.

Millonarios signed River Plate's great center forward Adolfo Pedernera, as well as Nestor Rossi, and with Di Stefano and Pedernera spearheading the attack, the team easily won three more league titles in succession.

Dozens of leading foreign players were lured to the renegade league, many of them from Argentina and several from Great Britain. Since the renegade clubs were now outside the jurisdiction of FIFA, they were not obligated to pay transfer fees, and Colombian soccer received the wrath of soccer officials all over Europe and South America.

In 1953, most of the foreign players left in frustration; Pedernera stayed on as player-coach of Millonarios and, later, the Colombian national team, and order was finally restored with the reinstatement of the ACE in FIFA in 1956.

Colombian clubs have participated in the Copa Libertadores since the first edition in 1960. Atletico Nacional of Medellin won the trophy in 1989, the first major regional victory for a Colombian club. Colombia eventually became a regular entrant in World Cup qualifying rounds, but it has advanced to the final rounds only in 1962 and 1990.

The first appearance coincided with another strong period for Millonarios, and its players figured prominently in the 1962 World Cup squad. The Colombians lost narrowly to Uruguay, 2-1, in the first round, and nearly caused one of the greatest upsets in recent years by holding the U.S.S.R. to a 4-4 draw—this after losing early in the game 3-0 and 4-1. But the highly skilled team of Yugoslavia proved far too advanced in technique and stamina, and it crushed Colombia in its third and final game, 5-0.

The 1990 Colombian World Cup team, however, proved a revelation to both its passionate fans and the world. Led by an eccentric goalkeeper Rene Higuita, whose forays well beyond the goal made him famous and infamous, one such wandering led to the strangest goal of the 1990 finals, when Cameroon's Roger Milla stole the ball from Higuita and scored unmolested.

The national team won a difficult entry into the finals by defeating Israel in a TransContinental two game playoff for the final available spot. Once in Italy the Colombians acquitted themselves well, gaining a 1-1 draw against eventual champion West Germany before bowing out with honor.

The first division of the national league now has 16 clubs, and the season is divided into three phases. In the apertura, or first phase, all 14 clubs compete on a home and away basis. The top eight go on to Group A of the finalizacion, or second phase, and the bottom eight play in Group B of the finalizacion, each club playing on a home and away basis within its group and accumulating points from the first and second phases.

The top clubs of the finalizacion (based on points) enter a third round to determine the national champion and runner-up, and these two clubs represent Colombia in the Copa Libertadores. The most prominent teams today are America-Cali and Atletico National-Medellin.

The 1989 Colombian season was disrupted and ultimately suspended because of threats made against referees. In the politically uncertain situation, with the government attempting to crack down on drug trafficking in the country, it was considered wise to suspend play.

As a result, the Colombian national team and its Copa Libertadores representatives played many of their matches in Miami and at other United States sites where a large Colombian-American population was present for support.

Congo

Address: Federation Congolaise de Football, B.P. 4041, Brazzaville. *Founded:* 1962. *FIFA:* 1963. *CAF:* 1966. *National stadium:* Stade de la Revolution, Brazzaville (50,000); *largest stadium:* Stade de la Revolution. *Colors:* Red jerseys, red shorts. *Season:* February to October. *Honors:* African Nations' Cup winner (1972), C.A.R.A., African Cup of Champions (1974).

One of Africa's leading soccer nations, the Congo (formerly Congo-Brazzaville) has achieved success on both the national and club levels out of proportion to its population.
Soccer in French Congo gained its first foothold in Brazzaville and, as elsewhere in colonial Africa, was first played by resident colonists. As a result of Brazzaville's location directly across

the Stanley Pool from Leopoldville, the capital of the Belgian Congo (now Zaire), Belgians as well as French influenced the local game.

When the Federation de Football Association du Pool was founded in 1924 at Leopoldville, clubs from Brazzaville were invited to join the new league. The affiliation was retained until independence. As a result, the leading Brazzaville club, Cercle Athletique Brazzavillois, won the Pool championship in 1931, 1937, 1941, 1945, and 1949, as well as the Cup de Leopoldville in 1937.

The Federation Congolaise de Football was founded two years after independence and joined FIFA the following year and the African Football Confederation in 1966. The Congo's strong, historical interest in soccer was revitalized after the coup of 1963. Then, prophetically, a national selection won the soccer tournament of the 1965 African Games.

Since the 1960s, the Congolese game developed rapidly. After losing all three matches in the final rounds of the 1968 African Nations' Cup to Congo-Kinshasa, Senegal, and Ghana, and failing to qualify for the 1970 edition, a strong Congolese national side prevailed against Africa's best teams and won the eighth Nations' Cup in 1972.

In 1974, the Congo placed fourth after winning a first round group that included eventual winner Zaire. They have not figured in the top four since, however, and have not made an impact in World Cup qualifying play.

On the club level, C.A.R.A., or Club Athletique Renaissance Aiglons, won the African Cup of Club Champions after defeating the Egyptian champions Mehalla in both home and away legs of the final in 1974, for the only such Congolese success in that tournament.

COSTA RICA

Address: Federacion Costarricense de Fútbol, Calle 40-Ave, San Jose. *Founded:* 1921. *FIFA:* 1921. *CTLI CONCACAF:* 1962. *National stadium:* Estadio Nacional de Costa Rica, San Jose (30,000); *largest stadium:* Estadio Saprissa (40,000). *Colors:* Red jerseys, blue shorts. *Season:* March to October.

For 30 years, Costa Rica was the runaway powerhouse of Central America, but curiously it was never able to capitalize on its apparent strength and carry that momentum into major international competitions until the 1990 World Cup. Then it stunned Scotland and Sweden in reaching the second round in Italy.

As the nine-time champion of either the Central American and Caribbean region or CONCACAF (Central America, the Caribbean, and North America), Costa Rica had early dominance of its closest challenger, Mexico, but the Mexicans turned that around in the last two decades.

When Costa Rica beat Mexico in a 1992 World Cup qualifying match, it marked the team's first win over their rivals in two decades.

The Costa Rican governing body has gone through several name changes and reorganizations. It was founded in 1921 as the Liga Nacional de Football, the British influence evident at this early date, and in 1927 it was incorporated into an umbrella sports union called the Federacion Deportiva de Costa Rica.

It reemerged in 1940, shortly after the Central American and Caribbean Football Confederation was founded, as the Federacion Nacional de Fútbol. The present name was adopted around 1961.

A remarkable winning streak began with the first championship of the Central American and Caribbean Confederation in 1941, and went on to include the third, fourth, sixth, seventh, ninth, and tenth editions, none of which included Mexico in the field of competitors, and the first and fourth editions of the CONCACAF Championship, which succeeded the earlier series.

Much of Costa Rica's opposition in these tournaments came from the five other republics of Central America, and occasionally from Curacao, Colombia, Venezuela, and Puerto Rico.

The Costa Rican league was well structured by the late 1940s. The present first division consists of 12 clubs, several of them from San Jose.

Costa Rica's most successful club has been Deportivo Saprissa, with Alajuelense offering a strong challenge in recent years.

CROATIA

Address: Illica 21/11, CRO-41000, Zagreb. *Founded:* 1991.

Croatian nationalists first organized a quasi-official national team for a brief two-year period under the German occupation around 1942. The significance of its international results are negligible, since it was impossible to put together a truly representative "national team."

Its rebirth in 1991 came as a result of the dissolution of Yugoslavia into Civil War. The Croatian league played a 22-game 1991-92 season with 12 clubs and sent champion Hajduh Split, a former top Yugoslav League team, into the 1992-93 European Cup.

CUBA

Address: Asociación de Fútbol de Cuba, c/o Comite Olimpico Cubano, La Habana ZP 4. *Founded:* 1924. *FIFA:* 1932. *CONCACAF:* 1961. *National stadium:* Juan Abrantes de la Universidad de Occidente, Havana (18,000); *largest stadium:* Estadio Latino-Americano, Havana (55,000). *Colors:* White jerseys with red trim, dark blue shorts. *Season:* July to November. *Honors:* Central-American and Caribbean Championship (1930); North American Championship (1947).

The first Cuban association, the Asociación de Football de la Republica de Cuba, was founded in 1924 and became affiliated with FIFA in 1932. A national championship was launched in 1929, and was first won by Real Iberia Football Club. The league has had a continuous existence ever since.

Cuba made its international debut in 1930 when it was host to the first Central American and Caribbean Games in Havana. The Cuban team finished the tournament undefeated with wins over Jamaica (in Cuba's first international), 3-1, Honduras (twice), Costa Rica, and El Salvador.

In 1934, Cuba tried to qualify for the World Cup but was eliminated by Mexico in three consecutive losses after earlier defeating Haiti twice.

In 1938, it qualified for the final rounds of the World Cup in France when Colombia, Costa Rica, Mexico, Surinam, and El Salvador all withdrew from the qualifying round. In France, Cuba had its first encounter with a European team, and drew with Rumania, 3-3, forcing a replay which it won 2-1.

Facing Sweden in the second round, Cuba succumbed to a goal scoring bonanza by the Swedish forward Gustav Wetterstrom and lost 8-0, ending its first and only World Cup experience.

Cuba's international opponents in recent years have sometimes reflected the country's directions in international relations. In 1977, for example, Cuba defeated Mozambique "A" in Maputo by the score of 2-0. But unlike the East European Communist nations, Cuban Olympic team preparation did not include a major commitment to soccer.

Cuba's traditional love of baseball continues to keep soccer a secondary game. The country entered, but withdrew before competing in, the 1994 World Cup qualifying.

CURACAO

See Netherlands Antilles

CYPRUS

Address: Cyprus Football Association, Stasinos Street 1, Engomi 152, P.O. Box 5071, Nicosia. *Founded:* 1934. *FIFA:* 1948. *UEFA:* 1962. *National stadium:* G.S.P. Nicosia (12,000); *largest stadium:* G.S.P. *Colors:* Blue jerseys, white shorts. *Season:* October to June.

One element of Cypriot soccer that is a constant source of encouragement is the Cypriots' devotion to the game, as soccer is the major cultural pastime on the island. Clubs are strongly sup

ported, and international matches at both club and national levels are eagerly anticipated.

In international competition, Cyprus is near the bottom of the list of European countries, but has improved dramatically in the last decade. Ethnically divided into two camps, Greek and Turkish Cyprus has not experienced solid political stability for decades. The Cypriot game is controlled and dominated by Greeks and Greek-based clubs.

Soccer was played in Cyprus as early as the 1870s by British soldiers and sailors, but it got its real impetus from the infusion of British troops during World War I. British residents helped to set up the Cyprus Football Association in 1934, and an official Cypriot league and cup competition were introduced in 1934-35.

After World War II, buoyed by the swarm of foreign troops on the island, Cypriot soccer made important organizational gains. In 1948, the Cyprus F.A. became affiliated with the Football Association in London, and only three months later secured permission from the English to seek separate membership in FIEA.

This was granted without hesitation, and Cyprus entered the mainstream of international soccer, though political independence was still 12 years away. Cyprus's first international in 1949 was a loss to Israel's "B" team.

In 1962, two years after political independence, Cyprus joined UEFA and began to participate in the European Football Championship and to attempt World Cup qualification. Cypriot clubs have also participated in all three European club championships but are usually overmatched by stronger, wealthier opponents.

The Cypriot first division has 14 clubs topped by the Nicosia pair, Omonia (16 titles) and Apoel (15 championships).

CZECHOSLOVAKIA

Address: Ceskoslovensky Fotbalovy Svaz, Na Porici 12, 11530 Praha 1. *Founded:* 1901. *FIFA:* 1906. *UEFA:* 1954. *Largest stadium:* Zbrojovka, Brno (70,000). *Colors:* Red jerseys, white shorts. *Season:* August to November, March to June. *Honors:* World Cup runner-up (1934, 1962); Olympic Champion 1980, runner-up (1920, 1964); European Football Champion (1976).

Czechoslovakia has been a mainstay of European soccer since the turn of the century, but its future is uncertain in 1993. It represented one-third of the great triumvirate of Central European powers that also includes Austria and Hungary, but today is no longer a single country. The Czechs have been remarkable in achieving success consistently over the decades and have many important honors to prove it.

Like the Austrians and Hungarians, they were exposed early to the Scottish short passing game, and became masterful practitioners of its derivative, the so-called "Danubian style." Soccer in Bohemia and Moravia have historically been more advanced than the game in Slovakia, but this has changed since the 1960s, when clubs from Bratislava and Trnava dominated the league and cup. Prague, however, is still the traditional center of Czech soccer.

Of the three great capital cities of the Austro-Hungarian empire, Prague was the first to produce really competitive teams. Soccer was first played in the Bohemian capital during the 1880s, and the first important club was founded in 1892. The Bohemian Football Association (BFA), whose jurisdiction included Bohemia

and Moravia (Slovakia was not then part of Austria-Hungary), was founded in 1901.

The BFA became a pioneer in organizing Central European soccer. It joined FIFA in 1906 and in that same year was one of six continental associations that formulated the revised laws of the game with the International Football Association Board, a revision that has remained very influential in twentieth-century soccer.

Between 1903-08, Bohemia played in seven full internationals and it also entered the 1908 Olympic Games, the world's first officially recognized international soccer competition. However, it withdrew before its opening round match with France "A." The social and political turmoil that was starting to brew in the empire took its toll, and Bohemia never again competed in international competition.

The first official Czech league, which was restricted to Bohemian clubs, was introduced in 1912. Sparta and Slavia, Prague clubs, won the first two championships, before the league was promptly suspended for five years with the outbreak of war in 1914. The birth of the Czechoslovak republic in 1918 signaled a major reorganization, and Slovakian soccer was included for the first time, as the league was reintroduced in 1918-19.

Though the official Czech governing body had not yet been formed, Czechoslovakia entered the 1920 Olympic Games in Antwerp, but unfortunately its international debut was seriously marred. Czechoslovakia's strength on the playing field was unquestioned as it rolled to sweeping victories over Yugoslavia (7-0), Norway (4-0), and France (4-1) to reach the final against Belgium.

As the heavy favorite, Czechoslovakia found itself down by 2-0 in a violent final. After strong objections to Belgium's second goal and the expulsion of one of its own players, the Czech team walked off the field, handing the gold medal over to Belgium by forfeit. Olympic authorities ruled that Czechoslovakia was ineligible for a medal of any kind, and a special game was scheduled between Spain and Holland for the silver and bronze.

In 1922, the Ceskoslovenska Asociace Footballova (CAF), Czecholovakia's first governing body, was founded and the CAF was officially admitted to FIFA in place of the BFA in 1923. The CAF sanctioned professionalism almost immediately, and the quality of soccer in Czechoslovakia continued to grow, but another major disappointment in Olympic competition occurred in 1924 when unheralded Switzerland eliminated the Czechs in the first round.

In the 1934 World Cup, Czechoslovakia emerged as one of Europe's three strongest teams. Its gifted duo of Slavia's Antonin Puc on the wing and Sparta's Oldrich Nejedly at inside was probably the finest left side pair in Europe, and Slavia's Frantisek Planicka, the captain, ranked with Spain's Ricardo Zamora as the safest goalkeeper anywhere. Planicka, indeed, had already become the greatest sports idol in his country's history. Playing its "Danubian" game in the World Cup, the Czechs slipped by Rumania and Switzerland, and outwitted cumbersome Germany in the semifinals with relative ease.

Nejedly had scored four of Czechoslovakia's eight goals in these three games, but his finishing power was not enough to raise his team above the role of underdog in the final against Italy. In Rome, the Italians had the home advantage and manager Vittorio Pozzo instilled high motivation in his team, yet Italy still managed to achieve only a 1-1 draw at the end of regulation time. Italy's goal was a fluke scored by Raimondo Orsi from an impossible angle, which Planicka has always maintained was his fault. In extra time, Italy's goal by Schiavio proved to be the

difference, and Czechoslovakia lost the World Cup final by 2-1.

This may have been the best team Czechoslovakia has ever produced, but four years later in the World Cup, events were to take a different course. In the first round of the 1938 World Cup, Czechoslovakia and Holland played to a scoreless draw at regulation time, but the Czechs scored three goals after the restart.

In the second round, Planicka's team engaged Brazil at Bordeaux in what became known as "the Battle of Bordeaux," one of the most vicious early international matches on record. Nejedly, the sublime scoring artist, had his leg broken, Planicka's right arm was also broken, and the stomach of right half Kostalek was badly injured.

There were several minor injuries to Brazilian players as well, and at the end of extra time the score remained 1-1. Czechoslovakia's goal came on a penalty by Nejedly, whose leg miraculously held together. The replay, in which the Czechs fielded six new players and Brazil nine, was won by Brazil 2-1 in a plodding anticlimax.

The burden of responsibility for "the Battle of Bordeaux" was placed on Brazil, but it was Czechoslovakia who suffered for it with elimination from the tournament and physical decimation. Czechoslovakia played only three more internationals before the German takeover of Sudetenland in 1938 initiated a seven-year-long hiatus.

It took many years for the game in Czechoslovakia to get itself back on its feet after World War II, and the 15-year period from 1945-60 was—relatively speaking—its worst ever.

The reorganization of Czech soccer after the Communist takeover in 1948 spelled the end of Sparta's and Slavia's domination of the league.

Even their venerable names were changed for a while to drive the point home further.

As in other countries of the Warsaw Pact, an elite army club was founded in Prague called ATK, later to be renamed UDA and still later Dukla, and considerable resources and money were channeled into the club. The army club was given first choice of the best players, and by 1953 it had already won its first championship after only five years in existence.

Before the era of Dukla began, however, the province of Slovakia, now a fully recognized part of the Czech soccer scene, produced its first champion, NV Bratislava winner of three league titles from 1949-51.

Slovan Bratislava eventually emerged as the top Slovakian club, winning 7 titles by 1992, but Sparta (20) still commands the league honors list. Dukla has won 11 titles, one fewer than Slavia.

A comeback for the national team began with the winning of the 1955-60 Dr. Gero Cup and an appearance in the 1958 World Cup. The Czechs were barely eliminated in the first round after a special play-off with Northern Ireland. Another good Czech team was in the making.

Its backbone was in the midfield and defense and featured Dukla's right back Ladislav Novak, captain of club and country, and Dukla's attacking left half Josef Masopust, Czechoslovakia's only European Footballer of the Year (1962).

Novak's team qualified for the 1962 World Cup in Chile by eliminating Scotland (after a play-off in Brussels) and the Republic of Ireland in qualification rounds, and entered the final rounds with one of the world's most solid defenses. Its style was by now completely transformed from the delicate "Danubian style" to a robust and physical approach, but individual Czech players retained their reputation for good technique.

In the 1962 quarter-finals, the Czechs met Hungary for the first time since 1955 and won in spite of Hungary's domination of the game. A tight defense and mistakes by Yugoslavia in the semi-finals put Czechoslovakia through to the final and a rematch of the 1938 "Battle of Bordeaux" against Brazil.

Czechoslovakia scored first through Masopust, but Amarildo and Zito took advantage of defensive mistakes, scoring brilliantly for Brazil. Brazil's third goal was kicked in by Vava after goalkeeper Schroiff dropped the ball at his feet. For the second time, Czechoslovakia had gained and lost the World Cup final, but this time it was to an obviously superior team. Czechoslovakia has not gotten as close again, although it qualified for the World Cup final phase in 1970, 1982, and 1990.

In the European Championship, Czechoslovakia dutifully participated In the first edition (1960) with its eastern bloc neighbors, and finally bowed out in the semi-finals against the U.S.S.R. In the next three editions, however, Czechoslovakia failed to reach the second round.

Finally, in 1974-76, the Czechs struck gold and won their greatest victory in history by nosing out World Cup champion West Germany on penalty kicks in the European Football Championship final. They finished third again in 1980, but missed out on the last three final rounds.

In the 1994 World Cup, a combined Czech-Slovak side labeled the RCS competed, and the 1992-93 league season continued after the country officially divided on January 1, 1993. It is not certain what the future will hold.

DENMARK

Address: Dansk Boldspil-Union, Ved Amagenbanen 15, DK-2300, Copenhagen 5. *Founded:* 1889. *FIFA:* 1904. *UEFA:* 1954. *National stadium:* Copenhagen Park Stadium (55,000). *Colors:* Red jerseys, white shorts. *Season:* April to November. *Honors:* Olympic Games runner-up (1908, 1912, 1960), third place (1948); European Champions 1992.

Little Denmark was a giant in European soccer for many years before the outbreak of World War I, and since that time has continued faring disproportionately well in international competition. In 1992, they stunned the experts by winning the European Championship.

Denmark was one of the first countries to learn the game from British travelers, and historically and by temperament has maintained a strong link with the British style of play.

But as one of the last Western European nations to relinquish its amateur status, having done so in 1978, and this has been both its legacy and an impediment.

Although the first official international match on the European continent was Austria against Hungary in 1902, a Danish selection is known to have traveled to Athens in 1896 to play a team representing Greece in an exhibition game at the first modern Olympics.

The Danes won by an unknown score, and with this match helped to initiate international competition outside the British Isles.

Danish association with the Olympic Games was to be long and extraordinarily successful. In 1906, a Danish selection won the soccer competition of the unofficial Intermediate Olympic Games in Athens. Denmark's first FIFA-recognized internationals were played at the 1908 Olympics in London, where a full international team defeated the so-called France "A" and France "B" teams 17-1 and 9-0, respectively. This 17-1 score is still a record for any international match.

In the 1908 final, Denmark lost to Britain, 2-0, but in so doing, established itself as a frontrunner among soccer nations. Its second place finish was repeated in 1912 at Stockholm when again it lost to Great Britain in the final, this time by 4-2.

Despite the fact that Britain did not field its best team in either of these Olympic tournaments, Denmark's 7-0 defeat of Norway and 4-1 defeat of Holland at Stockholm indicated the relatively high level of play in Denmark during this period.

Although Denmark had been one of the founding members of FIFA in 1904, its continental opponents between the wars were restricted to Germany, Poland, and the Benelux. Denmark did not qualify for the final rounds of the Olympics between 1920 and 1948.

At the 1948 games, however, it defied the pundits again by defeating Egypt and the Olympic teams of Italy and Great Britain to gain third place.

At the Rome games in 1960, Denmark achieved its most impressive success ever by reaching the final against Yugoslavia after defeating the full international teams of Poland (2-1) and Hungary (2-0). Its appearance in the final and eventual 3-1 loss to the talented Yugoslavs was a moral victory and one of the great moments in Danish sports history.

Having qualified for the final rounds of the Olympic Games at Munich in 1972 the Danish team advanced to the semifinal group of eight, which was dominated by four Eastern European powers, and in the major upset of the tournament managed a 1-1 draw with Poland, the eventual gold medal winner. Denmark's international reputation as spirited amateurs with an old-fashioned will to succeed was assured with those three postwar Olympic showings.

Real World Cup success, on the other hand, has eluded Denmark. Danish teams failed to qualify until the 1986 finals when a strong team crushed Uruguay 6-1 only to lose by a surprisingly high 5-1 scoreline to Spain.

In 1976, the DBU reversed its previous policy and for the first time allowed Danish professionals under contract to foreign clubs to be selected for the national team. This helped to solve a major problem that has existed for Danish national managers since Juventus attracted Denmark's Olympic forward line of 1948 to Turin (Karl Aage, John Hansen, and Carl Praest), and Danish clubs were long depleted of all their best talent. The DBU's acceptance of professionalism in 1978 was an inevitable outgrowth of this decision. The 1992 European win, accomplished with home-based and "outside" pros confirmed the wisdom.

Danish clubs have not done as well in any of the European competitions, but have proven increasingly difficult to beat. In the 1991-92 UEFA Cup, 1903 stunned perennial German power Bayern Munich 6-2, a precursor of the European Championship success that lay just ahead.

DOMINICAN REPUBLIC

Address: Federacion Dominicana de Fútbol, Apartado de Correos No. 1953, Santo Domingo. *Founded:* 1953. *FIFA:* 1958. *CONCACAF:* 1964. *National stadium:* Estadio Olimpico-Juan Pablo Duarte, Santo Domingo (22,000); *largest stadium:* Estadio Olimpico. *Colors:* Navy blue jerseys, white shorts. *Season:* March to September.

The Dominican Republic, an independent, baseball-mad nation under various foreign influences, including American, since the early nineteenth century, has been, with Puerto Rico, the least active Spanish-speaking state in the Central America-Caribbean region. With most top athletes preferring a shot at baseball's major leagues, the Dominican has not developed a soccer pedigree.

EAST GERMANY
See: German Democratic Republic

ECUADOR

Address: Asociación Ecuatoriana de Fútbol, Calle Jose Moascote 1.103 (Piso 2), Luque, Casilla 7447, Guayaquil. *Founded:* 1925. *FIFA:* 1926. *CONMEBOL:* 1930. *National stadium:* Estadio Modelo Guayaquil (48,772); *largest stadium:* Estadio Modelo Guayaquil. *Colors:* Yellow jerseys with blue fringe, blue shorts. *Season:* May to December.

This small Andean republic-with South America's highest population density-has struggled long and hard to make a dent in international competition, but, with the exception of fledgling Venezuela, it remains the least successful country in the South American group.

The chief interest of Ecuadorean soccer is the intense rivalry between the two great cities of the country, Guayaquil, the commercial and industrial center, and Quito, the capital.

Soccer was introduced in Ecuador via the port city of Guayaquil after the turn of the century, and some form of organized competition emerged before World War I. The country's exposure to foreign players during that war increased local interest considerably, and in 1922 a league was organized in Guayaquil.

An umbrella sports association, the Federacion Deportiva Guayaquil, was founded in 1925 to control soccer as well as all other sports, and it was admitted to FIFA in 1926. A national team was organized in 1938 to join other Ecuadorean athletes taking part in the first Bolivarian Games at Barranquilla, Colombia. It was here that Ecuador made its international debut against Peru, losing 9-1, and in five games won only once-over Colombia 2-1-capturing third place in a field of five.

A separate governing body for soccer, the present Asociación Ecuatoriana de Fútbol, was created in 1957, and a national championship was introduced with no restrictions on professionalism. The national league eventually unified the May-to-December schedule to conform to the summer season prevalent throughout South American leagues.

Ecuador has never qualified for the final rounds of the World Cup or Olympic Games, but Barcelona of Guayaquil reached the 1990 final of the Copa Libertadores, signalling the country's recent success. As host of the 1994 South American Championship, Ecuador is hoping for further development of the game.

The Campeonato Ecuatoriano, as the first division is called, includes 12 clubs. Aside from Guayaquil and Quito, the leading clubs hail from Portoviejo, Manta, Ambato, and Cuenca. The biggest rivalry in Quito is between El Nacional and Liga Deportiva Universitaria; in Guayaquil it is between Emelec and Barcelona.

EGYPT, ARAB REPUBLIC OF

Address: Al Ettihad el Masri Ii Korat el Kadam (Egyptian Football Association), 5 Shareh Gabalaya, Guezira, Al Borg Post Office, Cairo. *Founded:* 1921. *FIFA:* 1923. *CAF:* 1956. *National stadium:* Nasser Stadium, Cairo (100,000); *largest stadium:* Nasser Stadium. *Colors:* Red jerseys, white shorts. *Season:* September to June. *Honors:* African Nations' Cup winner (1957, 1959, 1986), runner-up (1962).

Egypt was the undisputed leader of soccer in the Arab world and Africa for more than 40 years, but today it is being strongly challenged by Algeria, Morocco and Tunisia on the one hand, and several black African states on the other. On the African continent, Egypt has had more experience in organized competition and administration than any other country.

Although soccer first reached Africa via the South African colonies, and Ghana was the pioneer among black African states, soccer flourished in Egypt as nowhere else on the continent.

Egypt was the only African country to be represented in major international tournaments before World War II, and as early as the 1920s three European countries—Hungary, Holland, and Portugal—fell to Egyptian teams on European soil. Cairo's Nasser Stadium, where crowds of 100,000 fans are routine for big games, was the first facility in Africa to hold 100,000 people.

Soccer was played in Egypt for the first time by the British around 1895, some 30 years after its introduction to South Africa and about fifteen years after it was played by colonists on the Gold Coast. The earliest clubs were formed in Cairo in 1903 by British players, and a handful of Egyptian clubs, such as the famous Al-Ahly, emerged before World War I.

The first major competition, the Sultan's Cup, named for Sultan (later to be King) Fouad, was introduced in 1916 for clubs of the Cairo and Alexandria districts.

The Egyptian Football Association (EFA) was founded in Cairo in 1921 under the patronage of the king and was admitted to FIFA in 1923, thus becoming the first member of the world body from the African-Asian bloc.

In 1924 Egypt entered the Olympic Games again, and in the first round it beat Hungary 3-0 in one of the great upsets in Olympic history. Egyptian glory was short-lived, however, and in the second round the stronger and more cohesive Swedish team knocked Egypt out of the tournament with a 5-0 thrashing.

Egypt returned in 1928 with more surprises for the confident Europeans, defeating Turkey in the first round 7-1 and Portugal in the second round 2-1, bringing Egypt's record against European opposition from 1920-28 to four wins and one defeat.

In the 1928 semifinals, mighty Argentina buried Egypt 6-0, and in the third-place game a vastly improved Italy dealt demoralized Egypt its worst defeat ever in international competition, 11-3.

Egypt went on to enter Olympic qualification rounds, but it has failed to win any medals, the best finish a fourth place in 1964 that equalled the 1928 team's achievement.

Egypt made its first appearance in the final rounds of the World Cup in 1934, but Hungary avenged its 1924 Olympic loss by defeating Egypt 4-2 in the first round. It was not until 1990 that Egypt qualified again, losing honorably in the first phase 1-0 to England after draws with favored Holland and the Irish Republic.

Sadly, the 1994 qualifying bid ended in contentious circumstances. Egypt had apparently won its first round group, but FIFA ordered the final match against Zimbabwe to be replayed following crowd trouble in Cairo. In the replay, staged in neutral Lyons, France, Zimbabwe held the Egyptians to a 0-0 draw and advanced to the second round as a result.

In 1956, Egypt was one of the three founding members of the African Football Confederation (CAF) in Khartoum, and, after 35 years as the most successful representative of the non-Western world in international competition, Egyptian soccer changed its focus radically. In 1957, the CAF introduced the African Nations' Cup.

Egypt won the first two editions, in 1957 and 1959, placed second in the third edition in 1962, third in the fourth edition in 1963, and would surely have done well throughout the 1960s had not the national team been almost dormant from 1965-69 due to Arab-Israeli conflicts. Despite the disorganization of this troublesome period, the national teams managed to qualify for the 1970 African Nations' Cup, and gained another third place finish in a powerful field.

In 1974, when the final rounds were held in Egypt for the second time, Egypt again placed third, and two years later it placed fourth, but victory eluded them until 1986 when Egypt again hosted the finals.

Al-Ismailia National of Cairo and Arab Contractors have all won either the African Champions' Cup or the Cup Winners Cup. Al-Ahli (1982, 1987) and Zamalek (1984, 1986) have two Africa Cup wins, while National-Cairo won the Cup winners Cup three consecutive times from 1984-1986, completing a five- year Egyptian hold on the trophy begun by Arab Contractors in 1982-83.

EIRE

See Ireland, Republic of

EL SALVADOR

Address: Federacion Salvadorena de Fútbol, Av. Jm. Delgado, Col. Escalos, Centro Espanol, San Salvador. *Founded:* 1936. *FIFA:* 1938. *CONCACAF:* 1962. *National stadium:* Estadio Nacional de Flor Blanca, San Salvador (30,000); *largest stadium:* Estadio Nacional de Flor Blanca. *Colors:* White jerseys with blue trim, white shorts. *Season:* January to November.

Tiny, populous El Salvador has broken through to the front ranks of Central American soccer on three occasions but over the long run has been forced to take a secondary position to Costa Rica, the major Central American power, and to Mexico.

Its notoriety, however, is dominated by the tragic "Fútbol War" it waged with neighboring Honduras in 1969, and it is unlikely that such an indelible legacy will be worn down for many years to come.

The game began to establish itself in San Salvador sometime after World War I. The Federacion Salvadorena de Fútbol was founded in 1935, and became affiliated with FIFA three years later.

Following World War II, the association's name was changed to Federacion Nacional de Football de El Salvador, and eventually it was reconstituted as the present FSF. El Salvador was the first CONCACAF member outside North America to support full professionalism.

Like many Central American and Caribbean states, El Salvador's international debut was made at the first championship of the Central American and Caribbean Confederation at Havana in 1930, where its first opponent was Guatemala. The Salvadoran team won by 8-2, but lost its four remaining games in the tournament and finished fourth in a field of six.

To their credit, Salvadorans have competed regularly ever since but the relative level of the Central American game has often been exposed by vastly superior Mexico, except in the bizarre case of the 1970 World Cup at Mexico City.

By eliminating Honduras, whose government was then in a state of war with El Salvador, the Salvadoran national team went through to the final rounds, occupying the lone Central American berth in the competition. Mexico qualified automatically as host country.

Belgium and the U.S.S.R. quickly disposed of El Salvador, 3-0 and 2-0 respectively, but the third opponent in its first round group was Mexico. In this match, El Salvador became the victim of one of the most flagrant errors ever committed by a referee in World Cup competition. Late in the first half, the Egyptian referee, Hussain Kandil, awarded El Salvador a free kick.

The kick, however, was taken by the Mexican Perez and went to his left wing Padilla, who crossed the ball to Mexican right wing Valdivia. In an instant, Valdivia had scored. Kandil allowed the goal to stand. Emotional appeals and cries of despair from Salvadoran players were to no avail, and a thoroughly demoralized El Salvador went down to a 4-0 defeat. Coming as it did after its bitter qualifying round victory over Honduras, Kandil's injustice was little short of tragic.

El Salvador rebounded despite ongoing political unrest and qualified again for the 1982 finals in Spain. There they suffered a humiliating 10-1 defeat in the opening game against Hungary but preserved honor by losing just 1-0 to Belgium and 2-0 against world champion Argentina. The 1994 national team reached the finals of the CONCACAF qualifying tournament as the came continued to grow in the country.

ENGLAND

Address: The Football Association, 16 Lancaster Gate, London, W2 3LW. *Founded:* 1863. *FIFA:* 1905-20; 1924-28; 1946. *UEFA:* 1954. *National stadium:* Empire Stadium, Wembley (100,000); *largest stadium:* Empire Stadium. *Colors:* White jerseys with red-and-blue trim, royal blue shorts with red-and-white trim. *Season:* August to June. *Honors:* World Cup winner, 1966.

England is the birthplace of soccer and the source of all modern football games. Soccer, rugby, American football, Canadian football, Gaelic football, and Australian Rules were all derived from the rough and tumble English games of centuries past. The expansion of the British Empire and dissemination of British learning and technology eventually served as a vehicle for exporting the game to all parts of the globe.

England also exported soccer to the other countries of the United Kingdom—Scotland, Wales, and Ireland—which in turn did much to spread the game to all parts of the world. The unique political structure of the United Kingdom, with its separate national identities, gave rise to autonomous governing bodies for control of the game in their respective countries.

The world governing body—FIFA—has continued to respect this tradition, in deference to the unique position of Great Britain as the birthplace of the modern game.

On the playing field, England has watched with mixed emotion as the major soccer countries of the world have emulated and surpassed its own level of expertise, beginning, in fact, with Scotland in the 1870s.

From the middle of the nineteenth century until the 1920s, there was little doubt that the finest soccer in the world was being played in the British Isles, but the rise of Uruguay, Argentina, Austria, Italy, Hungary, Brazil, and West Germany, in succession, put an end to England's presumption of superiority.

England's league play was deep and balanced and English teams had certainly won their share of international honors until a ban on their participation in European tournaments followed the Heysel Stadium disaster.

The five-year absence from Continental play has left its mark although Manchester United did beat the odds by winning the European Cup Winners Cup in 1991 immediately after the ban was lifted.

Modern football took shape in the English public schools (private schools to Americans), and eventually made its way to the universities, particularly Cambridge. Between 1820 and 1863, dozens of schools played according to idiosyncratic rules that were largely dependent on shapes and sizes of existing playing areas.

The first football clubs, Sheffield and Hallam, were founded in Sheffield, Yorkshire, in 1857, but each developed its own set of rules and wavered in its allegiance to the dribbling code.

The first club to devote itself exclusively to the dribbling game was the Forest Football Club, founded in 1859 at Snaresbrook in Epping Forest, about two miles from the present location of Orient F.C. in East London.

The other pioneer dribbling clubs were Crystal Palace, South London (1861), which bears no relation to the modern club of the same name; Notts County, Nottingham (1862), which played by rules closely resembling those of Sheffield; Barnes, Southwest London (1863), which had a strong interest in rowing; Civil Service London, (1863); and Stoke City, Stafford (1863), which was started by Old Carthusians (Charterhouse). Notts County and Stoke City are still members of the English Football League and are thus the oldest extant soccer clubs in the world.

On October 26, 1863, the representatives of 14 London clubs and schools met at the Freemasons' Tavern near Lincoln Inn Fields, London, to establish the Football Association (F.A.) and propose a uniform set of rules.

The resulting code became the basis for the modern game and the creation of both league and international play. The Football Association, the world's first governing body for soccer, did not develop into a truly national association until the 1870s, because ten years were spent unifying England according to mutually acceptable rules.

In 1871, the Football Association Challenge Cup (F.A. Cup) was introduced as the world's first organized competition with 15 entrants. The first trophy was won in 1872 by Wanderers F.C. (formerly Forest F.C.), a club of public school graduates that went on to become the first dominant team in English soccer, winning five F.A. Cups between 1872-78.

The 1870s was the era of the "gentlemen's" game, in which most of the leading teams were either named for or consisted of public school and university graduates, but by 1879 most of the participants in the F.A. Cup were located in the industrial regions, and officials soon introduced a series of regional elimination tournaments to accommodate them.

With the F.A. Cup of 1882-83, a non-London-based club won the cup for the first time, and the trophy was not to return to the capital city for another 20 years. Blackburn Rovers became the first important club from the industrial north, winning five cups during the 1880s. The southern clubs of upper- and upper-middle-class composition fell by the wayside and eventually receded into amateur competition as the rising tide of professionalism swept the country.

International competition, meanwhile, was introduced in 1870 when representative teams from England and Scotland met in London and played to a 1-1 draw. In 1872, the first official international between England and Scotland took place in Glasgow, ending in a scoreless draw. This rivalry, the world's oldest, continued on an annual basis until 1990 when a combination of crowd troubles and the ever-increasing demands of the international fixture schedule led to its abandonment.

After the formation of the Scottish F.A. (1873), the Welsh F.A. (1876), and the Irish F.A. (1880), England initiated the formation of an International Football Association Board in 1882 to regulate differences among the four governing bodies and organize an international championship. The introduction of the Home (British) International Championship followed in 1883 between England, Scotland, Wales, and Ireland.

Photo by H. Tonge and S.L. Martin; copyright by Thomson Organization, Ltd.

Queen Elizabeth presents the 1965 F.A. Cup

The meteoric rise of worker-based clubs in the north and midlands during the 1880s resulted in the formation of The English Football League in 1888. All 12 original members came from Lancashire County or the Midlands, and all emerged from the great debate over professionalism during the 1880s as fully professional clubs. The number of clubs clamoring to gain membership in the league grew steadily, and in 1892 a second division was added.

The third and fourth divisions were added in 1920 and 1958, respectively. The first southern member of the league was Royal Arsenal F.C. (later to become the famous Arsenal F.C.), elected in 1893. This divisional structure remained largely unchanged until 1992-93 when the English Football Association formed its own FA Premier League, taking the country's top clubs. The Football League continues to operate, but now as a separate entity from the FA's League.

Preston North End, which won the first league championship without conceding a defeat, also won the F.A. Cup of 1888-89 and the first double. After Preston, the first dominant clubs of the league were Aston Villa and Sunderland.

In 1895, the F.A. Cup Final, that most venerable of English soccer institutions, found its first permanent home at Crystal Palace, South London and, at the 1901 final an attendance figure above 100,000 was reached for the first time when the London club Tottenham Hotspur drew with Sheffield United. Soccer as a spectator sport for everybody had arrived.

After the turn of the century, Newcastle United achieved fame and fortune with the winning of three championships and appearances in five F.A. Cup finals. Northern and Midlands clubs continued to dominate both league and cup, and the first London-based league champion did not emerge until 1930 when Arsenal prevailed.

When FIFA was founded in 1904 (at the urging of France and Belgium), the F.A. rebuffed an invitation to join, dismissing the notion of an international governing body as an unattainable dream. Actually, the F.A. was fearful that the new organization would tamper with the authority of its own International Football Association Board, but when it became apparent that the seven charter members of FIFA were serious in their intent, and at the same time respectful of British authority on matters relating to rules and regulations, there was a change of heart.

In 1905, the F.A. became affiliated with FIFA, and in 1906, D.B. Woodfall of the F.A. Council was elected President of the world body. The International Football Association Board was acknowledged as the sole authority over the Laws of the Game.

The relationship with FIFA was not always smooth. In 1920, England, as well as the other

British associations, withdrew from FIFA, declaring that they would not intermingle with their former enemies of the Great War.

The English rejoined in 1924, but four years later withdrew again over FIFA's sanctioning of part-time wages for amateur players at the 1928 Olympic Games. All the British associations finally reaffiliated in 1946. As a result of the disputes, England did not enter its first World Cup until 1950.

England's first official international against a non-British team was with Austria in 1908, won in Vienna 6-1 and followed within a week by a second win over Austria (11-1) and defeats of Hungary (7-0), and Bohemia (4-0).

Prior to World War I, there were only three additional full internationals with non-British teams (against Austria and Hungary), all victorious. Belgium became the first European country to play on English soil at full international level in 1923.

Between 1919-29, only 18 of England's 50 full-level internationals were played against continental opponents. Its first loss to a foreign team was against Spain in 1929 at Madrid (4-3), but Belgium, France, Sweden, and Luxembourg all fell to England's superiority during the 1920s.

During the next decade, England lost seven of its 27 matches with European teams (all away), and its claim to supremacy on the playing field was suspect for the first time. Without membership in FIFA, however, England did not participate in the three World Cups of this period, depriving everyone of a chance to know its true strength.

On the domestic front, the dominant clubs between the wars were Huddersfield, which had risen from relative obscurity in the 1920s to league champions three times in succession, and

Nordbild

Matt Busby

Arsenal. Under Herbert Chapman, who had previously taken Huddersfield to its glory, Arsenal won five championships and two F A. Cups between 1930-38.

Chapman, meanwhile, wrote a chapter in English soccer annals by creating two teams that won a hat trick of league championships. His reputation as the greatest manager in England's history has been challenged only rarely: Sir Matt Busby of Manchester United, Liverpool's Bill Shankly, and Brain Clough of Nottingham Forest are managers who have achieved similar acclaim in the post World War II era.

Realities of the new balance of power on the playing field began to appear when England entered the World Cup for the first time. After defeating Chile, its first South American opponent in international competition, England re ceived the greatest shock in its 80-year soccer history, a 1-0 defeat by the United States. It failed to recover from the trauma, and was eliminated after losing to Spain.

Later that year, Yugoslavia became the first non-British country to gain a draw at Wembley, and in 1951, France and Austria managed to attain the same result. In 1953, undefeated Hungary, already touted as the greatest team ever seen, buried the English by 6-3 and became the first foreign country to defeat England at home. The decisiveness of Hungary's victory was sobering. In Budapest seven months later, Hungary crushed England by 7-1 and sealed the end of an era.

Having been toppled from its international throne—apocryphal as that seat might have been—England struggled through the remainder of the 1950s. Its World Cup results in 1954 and 1958 were a disappointment. In 1954, Uruguay defeated England in the quarter-finals for the second time in two years, displaying superior ball control skills, and in 1958, three draws against Brazil, the U.S.S.R., and Austria, were followed by a loss to the Soviets. In 1959, England made a disastrous tour of South America, in which it lost to Brazil, Peru, and Mexico by an aggregate score of 2-8, and on its return home lost at Wembley to Sweden.

The state of England's domestic game, however, was healthy and vibrant. This was an era of exciting, attacking teams in league and cup competition. It was the era of "Busby's Babes," the Manchester United team said to be the finest in England and one destined to challenge Real Madrid's supremacy in Europe. The tragic airplane disaster at Munich that killed most of the team brought the nation to a grinding halt in 1958.

This was also the era of Wolverhampton Wanderers, winner of three championships during the 1950s, led by English captain Billy Wright;

Upa, Deutsche Presse-Agentur GmbH

Wembley Stadium

and of Newcastle United, whose spearhead was the redoubtable Jackie Milburn. Stanley Matthews, the world's most famous player, continued to dazzle fans with his genius after more than 25 years in senior-level competition, and the other heroes of this golden era, Finney, Mortensen, Lofthouse, Dickinson, and Mannion, left an unforgettable legacy in the hearts and minds of English fans.

On the national team, spirits were revived under the tutelage of manager Alf Ramsey and captain Bobby Moore in the mid-1960s, aided no doubt by the prospect of staging the 1966 World Cup in England itself.

With the exception of Moore, Gordon Banks, and Bobby Charlton, there were few in the lineup who could claim world-class status, but with the best coordinated backfield in international competition and a confidence of purpose, England won the eighth World Cup, a dramatic final with a most controversial of goals off the right foot of Geoff Hurst. It came in overtime against the West Germans and led to an eventual 4-2 victory. Hurst scored three times in that final, still a championship game record.

The winning of the World Cup sparked a revival of interest in the game. Manchester United, now rebuilt by Busby into a glorious array of world class talent, became the first English club to win the European Cup in 1968. Though London teams Tottenham Hotspur and West Ham United had earlier won the European Cup Winners' Cup in 1963 and 1965, respectively, the major trophy in European club competition had previously been unattainable.

In addition, United's championship team included no less than three recipients of the European Footballer of the Year award—more than any other European club since the prize has been awarded. Coupled with a considerable holdover of sentiment from the Munich air disaster, these factors resulted in an unprecedented following for the new Manchester United.

Liverpool and Leeds United emerged as two new powers in the 1960s, later dominating the 1970s as well, while Tottenham and Arsenal enjoyed League and F.A. Cup doubles in 1961 and 1971, respectively. Liverpool (4 times), Nottingham Forest (twice) and Aston Villa all won the European Cup between 1977-84 while English League teams were also regularly successful in the other two European club competitions.

Unfortunately, crowd violence that culminated in the Heysel Stadium on the night of the 1985 European Cup final not only marred English clubs' achievements but also prevented them from competing in the major competitions for five years. At Heysel, where Liverpool and Juventus were to meet in the final, 39 Italian fans were killed when rioting broke out at one end of the stadium.

The English fans, who had become notorious in the late 1970s and early 1980s for provoking trouble on the continent, were blamed for the disaster, and English clubs were banned from all European club tournaments until 1990-91. Ironically, Liverpool's other great club, Everton, had won the European Cup Winners Cup just two weeks before the grim incidents in Belgium. It was to be the last prize until Manchester United's return to the winner's circle in 1991.

Since 1966, English soccer has suffered somewhat in comparison to more advanced styles of play on the continent. Its club successes in were often due to an occasional coalescence of traditional English characteristics on the playing field: superb conditioning and speed, decisive tackling, strength, excellence in the air, and consistent goalkeeping as well as the presence of gifted players from Ireland, Scotland and Wales who often held the specialist goal-scoring roles on the most successful English League teams.

The attractive ball control skills that were prevalent in England during the 1930s and 1950s appear to have been lost in favor of a speed and power. Failure to advance to the final stages of the 1974 and 1978 World Cups or to the 1974-76 European Championship) marked a low point England.

English international prestige rebounded somewhat in the 1980s but the national team performance still followed achievement with failure. The 1980 European Championship team qualified for the finals in Italy but made no impression in a tournament won by Germany.

In the 1982 World Cup there was a flash of the old English form in an opening game victory over France, but the remainder of the tournament was generally unsatisfactory as a plodding, unimaginative team made it to the second round without impressing.

The 1984 European Championship side didn't even reach France for the final eight, so it was somewhat unexpected when the 1986 World Cup entry reached the quarterfinals in Mexico. Even that achievement seemed unlikely after a dismal start, a loss to Portugal and a draw against the unknowns from Morocco.

Gary Lineker took over thereafter, personally inspiring the victories over Poland and Paraguay that lifted England to the match with Argentina that was turn out to be one of the most notorious of the 1986 World Cup.

Lineker's six goals ultimately made him the top scorer in Mexico, but it was the other Mexico star, Argentina's Diego Maradona, who figured in the memorable Azteca Stadium events. England may have only itself to blame for the fact that it fell behind 2-0, an overly cautious style allowing Argentina to dominate much of the first hour of the match.

Still, when Maradona fisted in the opening goal—an event caught by BBC television cameras and shown at home—there was an outraged response from most English supporters. The fact that the little Argentine followed that score with the goal of the tournament did not take away from the fact that many England fans felt they were unfairly beaten.

In the closing 15 minutes, when England did come out of its shell into all-out attack, a goal materialized, but it was too late. The combination of Maradona's self-proclaimed "hand of God" and England's lack of a confident approach to the match had ended their tournament.

That same lack of confident control was seen in the 1988 European finals when an England team that entered with high hopes was crushed by three consecutive defeats. The opener, against the Republic of Ireland, set the tone for a tournament when both the press and public were scath-

ing in their criticism of the team and manager Bobby Robson.

It was against that background that Robson, often the subject of harsh media attacks, prepared the team for the 1990 World Cup finals. This time little was expected from the English, tucked away on the island of Sardinia because of their potentially dangerous fans. The opening round, a pair of draws with the Irish Republic and Holland and a 1-0 victory over Egypt, did not presage the drama to follow.

Paul Gascoigne, the erratic but creative midfielder, had struggled to find a permanent place in Robson's team until a magnificent pre-finals performance against Czechoslovakia in London. But he suddenly emerged as the star of the English team, and the missing element of the unexpected was injected into an otherwise dour attack.

Gascoigne's free kick set up David Platt for a last-minute overtime goal that defeated Belgium, and Lineker scored two penalty kicks as England got past the impressive, powerful Cameroon in the quarterfinals.

That sent the team to Turin for a totally unexpected semifinal against West Germany, a match that turned out to be one of the best in the championship. It finished 1-1 after 120 minutes, England ultimately losing on penalty kicks. A fourth place finish was more than anyone had expected six weeks before the competition began.

But the uncertain future of the English game continues today. Their 1992 European Cup final appearance in Sweden was as bereft of genius as the 1990 World Cup had been crowned by it.

They failed to get past the first round, new manager Graham Taylor now the target of the media and the English style of play again criticizcd as outmoded and lacking in the necessary skills to compete in the modern era.

The vast majority of England's international meetings over the decades have been in the British Championship which lasted through 1983-84. England's consistent superiority over Wales and Ireland (including Northern Ireland) in this series helps to account for its very high success rate in cumulative won-lost tabulations. Ireland did not defeat England at all until 1920. England and Scotland, on the other hand, finished nearly level after 107 matches. Through 1989 England had 43 wins, Scotland 40 and 24 matches were draws.

ESTONIA

Address: Refati PST 1-376, 200103 Talinn. *Founded:* 1921. *Readmitted to FIFA:* 1992. *Largest Stadium:* Tallinn. *Colors:* White shirts, black shorts, white socks.

One of the expressions of self-assertion made by the Baltic states during their 20-year period of independence between the world wars was to engage other countries in soccer. When independence came again with the collapse of the Soviet Union, Estonia immediately applied for FIFA readmission to the game in time to enter the 1994 World Cup.

Estonia had already played 44 matches against European teams other than those from Latvia and Lithuania in its earlier independent existence so its request was quickly granted.

Estonia had beaten Rumania, 2-1 in 1937 at Tallinn and managed to draw once with Poland, but its biggest win occurred at home in 1930 over Finland (4-0). It was also Finland that dealt Estonia its severest blow, a 10-2 loss at Helsinki in 1922.

Estonia's World Cup debut match came in August of 1992 when Switzerland won 6-0 in Tallinn, but the historic dimensions of the game overshadowed the result. In October of 1992 the Estonians gained their first World Cup point in a 0-0 draw with Malta while the league champion Norma Tallinn played in the European Cup to mark the country's debut in club tournament soccer.

ETHIOPIA

Address: Yeitiopia Football Federechin, Addis Ababa Stadium, Box 1080, Addis Ababa. *Founded:* 1943. *FIFA:* 1953. *CAF:* 1957. *National stadium:* Addis Ababa Stadium (30,000); *largest stadium:* Addis Ababa Stadium. *Colors:* Green jerseys with yellow trim, yellow shorts. *Season:* September to June. *Honors:* African Nations' Cup winner (1962).

Ethiopia was one of the early pillars of organized soccer in Africa. Before the rise of sub-Saharan soccer-playing countries in the mid-1960s, no country on the African continent was more respected for its contribution to the game's growth, and there were few who were able to match wits with the skill and determination of Ethiopian players.

The level of play in Ethiopia, however, did not stay ahead of its new rivals in the south, and, while Ethiopian national teams once had a high overall ranking, they are no longer a major force. The political turmoil and famine of the past three decades have wreaked havoc on the game, casting serious on its immediate future.

Soccer was introduced to Ethiopia in Addis Ababa around 1924 by Italians and other immigrants, including, Greeks, Armenians, and Indians. Despite soccer's growth, the first important Ethiopian players were better known as stars of track and field, Ethiopia's traditional national sport.

Most of the early clubs, however, were restricted to Italian, Greek, or Armenian players, and Ethiopians themselves were left out of the mainstream of their country's soccer growth until the liberation of 1941. The first important Ethiopian-based club was Saint George Sports Association, founded in 1935.

Finally, in 1943, the Yeitiopia Football Federechin was founded in Addis Ababa by a group of nine prominent clubs, none of which was Italian. A league based in Addis Ababa (the Ethiopian Cup) was introduced simultaneously.

Ethiopia's first unofficial international was played in 1948 in Addis Ababa against a representative team from Djibouti, capital of neighboring French Somaliland, resulting on a 5-0 win. Ethiopia met Djibouti selections on six occasions between 1948-56, winning each time but failing to gain real international experience.

Ethiopia's first full international was a 4-1 loss to Egypt in 1956 at Addis Ababa. This was also the year in which Ethiopia joined forces with Egypt and Sudan (and abortively with South Africa) to establish the African Football Confederation. In 1957, the three founding members met in Khartoum to play out the first African Nations' Cup.

Egypt defeated both Ethiopia (4-0) and Sudan to win the first trophy. In 1959, Ethiopia paid its first visit to Europe, and lost to the U.S.S.R in Moscow, 12-3. In the second African Nations' Cup (1959), Ethiopia, Egypt, and Sudan were again the only participants, and Ethiopia lost to Egypt 4-0 and to Sudan 1-0 for another third place finish.

In the third edition in 1962, the slightly expanded competition was held in Ethiopia the Haile Selassie Stadium in Addis Ababa was then one of the finest grounds in Africa—and the home team defeated Tunisia and, in the final, Egypt, to win its first and only international trophy.

The final was witnessed by Emperor Haile Selassie himself and went into an exciting overtime, during which the Ethiopian team bombarded Egypt's goal with countless shots and finally won, 4-2.

Ironically, the captain and guiding spirit of this team was Luciano Vassalo, the son of Italian immigrants. In the 1963 African Nations' Cup, Ethiopia lost the third place game to its old rival Egypt, and again lost in a third place game in the 1968 competition, this time to Ivory Coast. Those performances still mark the best Ethiopian performances in African Championship history.

FAROE ISLANDS

Address: Faroes FA, Gundalur PO Box 1028, FFR, Torshavn. *Founded:* 1979. *Colors:* Blue jerseys, white shorts.

The semi-autonomous Faroe Islands, a Danish possession located midway between Iceland and Norway, were exposed to soccer in the early years of this century as Danish settlements took root. The Faroes began engaging in friendly internationals in 1959 with various national teams of Iceland and made their official UEFA debut in the 1992 European Championship qualifying competition.

That debut resulted in one of the great shocks in European soccer history when Austria, which had just participated in the 1990 World Cup finals, was beaten by Faroe 1-0 in a match played in Sweden—no grass were fields available on the islands to stage the game. The creation of a new grass playing surface was completed in time for 1994 World Cup qualifying.

Fiji

Address: Fiji Football Association, Government Buildings, PO Box 2514, Suva. *Founded:* 1936. *FIFA:* 1963. *OFC:* 1963. *Largest stadium:* Burkhurst Park, Suva (20,000). *Colors:* White jerseys, black shorts. *Season:* March to September.

Among the dozens of small island nations and protectorates in Oceania, Fiji was the first full-fledged member of FIFA and the Oceania Football Confederation (OFC).

The game was brought to the Fiji Islands by British colonists, and by the early 1950s Fiji selections had become active in international competition.

Though the Fiji Football Association was founded in 1936, it was not affiliated with The Football Association in London. Competitive links were established early with New Zealand and other British colonies in the area, and from the early 1960s Fiji became active in all regional competitions in Oceania.

Fiji has been an active participant in all the area's regional tournaments but it has not been able to complete effectively against much stronger Australian and New Zealand teams.

Fijian soccer must compete against rugby, the more popular game in the islands, for the best athletes. A national championship and an annual cup competition are held, and regional leagues do exist on the outlying islands, but Fijian club soccer has not yet achieved international notice.

Finland

Address: Suomen Palloliitto-Finlands Bollforbund, Kuparitie 1, PO Box 29, SF-00441 Helsinki. *Founded:* 1907. *FIFA:* 1908. *UEFA:* 1954. *National stadium:* Olympiastadion, Helsinki (50,000); *largest stadium:* Olympiastadion. *Colors:* White jerseys, blue shorts. *Season:* April to October.

The weakest of the Scandinavian countries except Iceland, Finland nevertheless remains well above the poorest level in Europe. Finnish soccer is dominated by the question of amateurism, but like many of the so-called amateur countries, players in the higher echelons of the Finnish league receive bonuses and ad hoc payments.

Full-fledged professionalism is unlikely to surface, however, in a country where a small population is strewn over such a sparse landscape. On the playing field, Finnish teams have won few honors, but their selection competes well and is never easy to defeat.

English businessmen and workers brought soccer to Helsinki around 1890, but the game was slow to emerge. Its stature as a national pastime is still below that of track and field and any number of winter sports, though it has probably become the leading team sport. The SPB-FBF was founded in 1907, and one year later a league was introduced that centered in Helsinki and Turku.

The formation of a national team was accomplished in 1911 when Finland played host to a visiting Swedish selection and lost 5-2. Its first and perhaps most laudable victory occurred the following year at the 1912 Olympic Games in Stockholm with a 3-2 win over Italy, not yet the international power of later years, and a solemn 2-1 defeat of Czarist Russia the next day.

In the next two rounds of the 1912 games, however, the future of Finnish soccer was presaged in a 4-0 defeat at the hands of an amateur British side and a 9-0 trouncing by Holland, yet another minor continental team at the time.

On the club level the cities of Helsinki and Turku dominated league play but after World War II the top clubs from Vaasa, Kotka, Kuopio, and Lahti began to receive their share of the honors. HJK Helsinki has won eight titles since league play was organized in 1949 while Turun and Kuopion have both won five.

The First Division is comprised of 12 clubs while a national cup competition was introduced in 1955. Top Finnish players seeking professional contracts usually go outside the country. Some have made star names for themselves in Scotland and Germany in recent years.

FRANCE

Address: Federation Francaise de Football, 60 bis, Avenue d'Iena, F-75783 Paris, Cedex 16. *Founded:* 1918. *FIFA:* 1904. *UEFA:* 1954. *National stadium:* Parc des Princes, Paris (50,000); *largest stadium:* Stade Yves du Manoir, Colombes-Paris (65,000). *Colors:* Blue jerseys with red trim, white shorts. *Season:* August to June. *Honors:* World Cup third place (1958, 1986); European Championship (1984).

The French long having made enormous contributions to the world game as administrators and organizers of soccer, have seldom begun to achieve the success one would expect on the playing field. Frenchmen were the principal organizers of FIFA, the World Cup, various European championships, and several other international competitions and awards, and *France*

Football, the Paris weekly, has been the world's most respected soccer publication for decades, helping to launch the European Cup.

Ironically, the game in France was in organizational chaos for over forty years, and it was not until after World War II that soccer finally mounted a strong challenge to the popularity of rugby.

In soccer, France had one bright period during the 1950s, when the immortal Raymond Kopa and Just Fontaine led the national team and their club, Stade de Reims, to high honors in the World and European Cups.

Twenty years later, French teams began to make their mark on international competition, employing a highly attractive style that featured several great players in the 1980s. This era included two World Cup semifinal appearances and a European Championship victory (1984).

Modern soccer was imported to France by British sailors and in 1891, the first two clubs in France devoted exclusively to soccer were founded in Paris by British residents: White Rovers F.C., comprised entirely of Scots, and Gordon F.C., later renamed Standard A.C. A pivotal year for French soccer was 1892, when White Rovers defeated Standard, 10-1, at Becon-les-Bruyeres in the first soccer game between French clubs.

Club Francais, the first soccer club founded by Frenchmen, also appeared in 1892. In 1894, the USFSA introduced the first competition, the Championnat de France, for the six Parisian clubs. The six competed over a four week period in a knockout series, and Standard won the first edition with an all British roster.

After the first year, the Championnat de France was decided on points. The major issue during this period was selecting the minimum number of French nationals for each team.

In 1895, the first unofficial international involving a French team took place in Paris, when Folkestone A.C., a minor English club, defeated a Parisian selection, 3-0. The English club won 8-0 six weeks later in Folkestone.

The soccer section of Rácing Club de France, later to become the most famous club in the country, was started in 1896, but by 1897 there were still only 30 soccer clubs in all of France, and rugby continued to be the most popular form of football in the country.

French officials had already become pioneers in organizing international competition before the turn of the century, and after 1900, despite the game's second-class status at home, the French continued to take the lead in bringing together the soccer-playing nations of Europe.

Robert Guerin, a founder of the USFSA, was a primary instigator of FIFA, the world governing body, and with the Dutch banker C.A.W. Hirschman, Guerin did more than anyone to get the new federation off the ground. Not only was the first FIFA Congress held in Paris, but Guerin became the first president of FIFA in 1904 and helped to establish an Anglo-French hold in the FIFA leadership that lasted until 1974.

The first president of the FFF, created in 1918 after years of organizational rivalries, was Jules Rimet, who in 1921 also became the president of FIFA, a post he held for 33 years. Rimet became the prime mover in launching the World Cup during the 1920s, and for many years the World Cup trophy bore his name.

Henri Delaunay became the first general secretary of UEFA, the European governing body, in 1954. The trophy of the European Football Championship is named for Delaunay.

France's first full international took place at Brussels in 1904, a 3-3 draw with Belgium. The next two games against Belgium resulted in 7-0 and 5-0 losses, and these crushing defeats set the tone for the French national team in the years ahead.

The chaos that was raging in domestic administration during the pre-World War I era, in addition to the country's relatively late start in adopting the game, took a serious toll on international results for decades.

The French entered all three Olympic tournaments during the 1920s, reaching the semifinals in 1920 but failing to advance beyond the second round in 1924 and 1928. When the first World Cup was assigned to distant Uruguay in 1930, Rimet was obliged to keep France in the competition despite the widespread boycott by European countries, because he and France had been so instrumental in organizing the series.

In Montevideo, the French, respected for their role in FIFA though not on the playing field, defeated Mexico and suffered surprisingly low 1-0 shutouts to Argentina and Chile.

In 1934, they were unfairly eliminated in the first round by the great Austrian team when the winning goal was scored in overtime by inside left Schall, who was clearly offside. France itself was chosen to stage the 1938 World Cup in recognition of Rimet an his tireless work on behalf of soccer.

The atmosphere was in marked contrast to Mussolini's dour show in Italy four years earlier, and the biggest event was France's second-round rendezvous with the world champion Italians, who were scorned by French fans.

This match was played in Paris at the Colombes Stadium, the largest in the country, and it was decided in the second half by Italian center forward Piola, scorer of two goals in a 3-1 Italian win.

After an unofficial wartime league that lasted for six seasons—the Coupe de France was played officially throughout the war without a break—the regular league reappeared in 1945-46 with another win by Lille OSC. Lille proceeded to win three cups in a row and then achieved the extraordinary feat of placing second in the first division for four consecutive seasons (1948-51) while OGC Nice and Stade de Reims won titles and built up winning reputations. Reims' win of 1949, in fact, inaugurated an unprecedented era of success in French and European competition.

After winning another championship in 1953, the famous Champagne club won the Latin Cup that same year with a magnificent 3-0 defeat of AC Milan, a club widely touted as the best on the continent. Reims' victory in this elite competition was the first and still the only major international honor won by a French club, initiating Reims' lasting fame as the finest team ever produced in France.

Reims shone with Robert Jonquet and Roger March in the backfield and the immortal Raymond Kopa—the most talented French player of all time—on the forward line (replaced in 1956 by France's greatest goalscorer, Just Fontaine).

The club gained the European Cup final twice (1956 and 1959) only to face the unbeatable Real Madrid on both occasions. Led by manager Albert Batteux, Reims brought glory to French soccer, and had it not been for the presence of Real Madrid, Reims might have been the first club in Europe to dominate the European Cup.

After early elimination by Yugoslavia in the 1954 World Cup, the Reims-based French national team entered its golden era under manager Paul Nicholas. At the 1958 World Cup in Sweden, France won its first-round group despite a loss to Yugoslavia, and delighted observers with its entertaining and attacking style. A crushing win over Northern Ireland in the quarter-finals confirmed its status as a major international power, and in the semifinals its reputation suffered little in a 5-2 loss to the scintillating Brazilian team featuring Pelé and Garrincha.

The stalwart center-half Jonquet and a forward line made up of both Kopa and Fontaine were highlights of the competition. In the third place game, it was hardly surprising when the French demoralized West Germany with a 6-3 win. Fontaine scored four goals, each assisted by Kopa—who also scored from the penalty spot—and France won third place in the World Championship, its highest achievement to date at the national level.

France's place in the sun, however, was short-lived. Kopa and Fontaine began to suffer from injuries, the latter bowed out of organized competition altogether in 1961, and Nicholas was killed in an accident in 1959.

France again took a leading role in international organization and was instrumental in setting up UEFA, the European governing body, in 1954. When UEFA introduced the European Nations' Cup in the late 1950s, the final rounds of the first edition in 1958-60 were staged in France.

In a repeat of the circumstances surrounding the first World Cup in 1930, the French were nearly alone in representing Western Europe (Eastern Europe was fully represented), and this enabled France to gain the semifinals with relative ease, where once again its old nemesis Yugoslavia kept the tricolors out of the final. France's 5-4 loss to the Yugoslavs was its last hurrah in international competition until the rise of a new generation of talented players during the mid-1970s.

French soccer in the 1980s suddenly became the envy of Europe and was even likened to that of Brazil for its breadth of ideas and its wonderful attacking philosophy. The 1982 World Cup team was denied a place in the final only by one of the dramatic comebacks in World Cup history, the 1984 side won the European Championship, and the 1986 World Cup team was again deprived of a place in the final by West Germany, the *bete noire* of a French side that many feel deserved more than the record will report.

At the heart of the team was Michel Platini, perhaps the greatest player France ever nurtured, certainly earning the comparisons with Raymond Kopa, who had previously been unchallenged as the paragon of Gallic play. A midfielder with a gift for picking the right moment to attack, Platini was also one of the most dangerous free kick takers of the sport.

His running mates in the French side were also brilliant individualists as well as willing workers in the supporting cast. They included the silky Jean Tigana; tiny, tenacious Alain Giresse; the quicksilver Dominque Rocheteau; and the unpredictable Didier Six. What France lacked was a completely reliable set of defenders, perhaps because the team's style of play, encouraged by manager Michel Hidalgo, never accented safety first.

France's 1982 World Cup campaign began badly, a defeat to England in the opening match, but the Tricolors gathered steam thereafter and went into the Seville semifinal favored to win against a West German team that was characterized as more plodding than gifted. After a 90-minute battle finished 1-1 the teams moved into a punishing 30 extra minutes, but France was deprived of one of its central defensive stalwarts, Patrick Battiston.

Battiston had been hacked down by German goalkeeper Tony Schumacher in an incident that was replayed often after the competition ended. Schumacher was not even cautioned for the foul, and Battiston was carried off the field. Nevertheless, France scored twice in the first extra period to take a 3-1 lead as their fans began to celebrate.

The Germans, however, drew on their resources, a limping Karl-Heinz Rummenigge came off the substitutes' bench to score, and an equalizing goal in the second half of extra time meant the first World Cup match ever to be decided on penalties. West Germany prevailed, but many felt France to have been the true moral winners on the night.

The 1984 European Championship showcased the French at their rampant best, although victory over Portugal in the semifinal was hard won and the style of the 2-0 championship win over Spain was not as lavish as might have been expected. Platini, however, could hold a well-deserved trophy high, and French achievement finally matched the expected goals.

The 1986 Mexican World Cup brought further frustration, though. Instead of a more mature, experienced French side, the World Cup eleven looked like a team which had just begun to slip downhill. Despite progressing to the semifinals, when their quarterfinal game against Brazil was the highlight of the tournament, this wasn't the France of '82 Spain.

A 2-0 semifinal loss to the Germans was not all that unexpected, harsh as it may have seemed at the time. The romantic, all-attack French simply were not powerful enough against a West German team that may have been less creative but was better organized.

Indeed, the French team needed a complete overhaul at the end of the 1986 event, so much so that it failed to reach the 1990 World Cup finals altogether. It's 1992 European Championship team, now guided by Platini, advanced to the finals without a loss or tie, but its lack of balanced attack proved fatal in Sweden, where a first round loss to Denmark sent France home before the semifinals. Platini resigned as national boss after that defeat, leaving Gerard Houlier to put together a 1994 team capable of reaching the United States.

In domestic competition, the legacy of Stade de Reims was assumed in the 1960s by Saint Etienne from the industrial city of the Massif Central region. Under former Reims manager Batteux, Saint-Etienne raced to the top of the first division in 1964 and won four titles in succession from 1967-70.

In 1974, it won three more in a row, and in 1976, it reached the European Cup final. Saint-Etienne's loss to Bayern Munchen in that final resulted from its lack of experience in big international matches rather than from inferior talent.

When Marseille took over in the 1980s, winning five straight titles, they became the second French side to play in a European Cup final, losing a penalty kick decision to Red Star-Belgrade in 1991, a match in which the Yugoslavs played so defensively that many observers felt Marseille was the moral victor.

GABON

Address: Federation Gabonaise de Football, B.P. 181, Libreville. *Founded:* 1962. *CAF:* 1967. *FIFA:* 1963. *National stadium:* Stade Reverend Pere Lefebre, Libreville (7,000); *largest stadium:* Stade Reverend Pere Lefebre. *Colors:* Blue, yellow, and green jerseys, white shorts. *Season:* October to July.

In the Gabon Republic, a tropical African rain forest, practically all competitive soccer activity is confined to the capital, Libreville, where the country's one modern stadium is located.

A national league and a national cup competition, which are contested by clubs from Libreville and Port Gentil, the oil production center on the Atlantic coast are played annually.

Gabon has never qualified for the final stages of the African Nations' Cup, and has seen little playing time in Olympic or World Cup qualification rounds, but the national team nearly created a sensation in 1993 when they took Senegal to the final qualifying game before losing out in the 1994 World Cup qualifying tournament.

GAMBIA

Address: Gambia Football Association, P.O. Box 523, Banjul. *Founded:* 1952. *FIFA:* 1966. *CAF:* 1962. *National stadium:* Box-Bar Stadium, Bathurst (6,000); *largest stadium:* Box-Bar Stadium. *Colors:* White jerseys with red, blue, and green stripes; white shorts. *Season:* October to July.

Soccer has been slow to gain a foothold in Gambia, despite the former British presence. The relatively early founding date of the Gambia Football Association reflects the interest of British residents rather than Gambians themselves.

Its early affiliation with the African Football Confederation and then with FIFA immediately after independence has been unfulfilled. Gambia entered the 1994 World Cup, but withdrew without having played a single match in the qualifying round.

GEORGIA

Address: Football Federation of Georgia, 5, Shota Iamanidze Street, 380 012 Tbilisi.

Dynamo Tbilisi earned a deserved reputation in the former Soviet First Division and in European soccer, but the demise of the old Soviet Union has not meant an easy transition into international and UEFA play for the republic it represented. Instead, a lengthy civil war and an acrimonious withdrawal from old the Soviet League has combined to keep Georgia from becoming a recognized UEFA and FIFA participant.

Dynamo Tblisi won the European Cup Winners Cup in 1980-81, defeating Carl Zeiss Jena of the old German Democratic Republic in the only major club final to match East European teams. It was a consistent challenger in the old Soviet league, developing players of world class and contributing to the Soviet national team.

Ironically, when Georgia summarily pulled out of the Soviet league in 1990, before the complete collapse of the old government, it left Dynamo and its players without a top-level competitive counterpart.

The future of Georgian soccer remains clouded by the ongoing fighting in the region that has kept both major federations from sanctioning its entry into international competition. It was expected that Georgia would receive full FIFA membership in the summer of 1993, but UEFA's stance on the nation was not clear.

GERMANY, FEDERAL REPUBLIC OF

Address: Deutscher Fussball Bund, Otto-Fleck-Schneise 6, Postschliessfach 710265, D-6000 Frankfurt (Main)-71. *Founded:* 1900. *FIFA:* 1904-46, readmitted 1950. *UEFA:* 1954. *Largest stadium:* Olympia-Stadion, Berlin (85,000). *Colors:* White jerseys with red-and-yellow piping, black shorts. *Season:* August to June. *Honors:* World Cup winner (1954, 1974, 1990), runner-up (1966, 1982, 1986), third-place (1934, 1970); European Football Championship winner (1972, 1980), runner-up (1976); World Youth Champion (1981).

If England was once the titular leader of European soccer, Germany is its practicing master, having amassed an extraordinary record of consistent success at all levels of competition. The Bundesliga, the national league formed in 1963, ranks with the Italian First Division as the showplace of modern soccer in Europe.

From a global perspective, Germany now threatens to surpass even Brazil's record at the highest reaches of organized competition. In so doing, the newly reunited nation has sparked a renaissance of tactical innovation on the playing field.

Germany's growth from a moderately successful European power during the Hitler era to that of standard-bearer in the postwar years has resulted from the unification of long-range planning, exceptional coaching techniques and practices, and a fair share of highly skilled players.

The Deutscher Fussball-Bund (DFB) has established a national coaching school, which is widely regarded as a model of its kind, providing a level of continuity and uniformity of standards that seeps down through the domestic game. These factors have resulted in the large number of excellent players who have turned German methods and practices into victories on the field.

The prosperity of western Germany's soccer from 1960 to 1990 amid the political realities of a divided country was dictated by historical precedent. Geographically, most of the first and strongest clubs in Germany hailed from the west. Soccer had been introduced to Germany by British residents through the North Sea ports and Berlin in 1870.

The growing popularity of the game sparked the formation of football clubs as early as the 1880s. Most of the earliest clubs were established along the Elbe or Weser Rivers in the North and in Berlin, but by 1900 nearly all regions of the

German Empire supported some clubs devoted to association rules.

In 1890, the Bund-deutscher Fussballspieler, the first regional association, was founded in Berlin to unify soccer activities in the capital, but it was supplanted one year later by the Deutsche Fussball und Cricket Bund, also a Berlin-based organization.

The regional leagues that would figure prominently in German soccer for the next 70 years began to take shape during the 1890s, and in 1896 the first inter-city match was held between representative teams from Berlin and Hamburg. The Berliners won 13-0.

A truly national association was not formed until 1900, when regional delegates met in Leipzig and established the Deutscher Fussball-Bund. The DFB introduced the first national championship in 1902-03, but decided to retain the various regional leagues and bring the regional champions together at the end of the season for a playoff to determine the overall German champion. This format was followed without change until 1962.

In 1904, the DFB became one of the first governing bodies to join FIFA. A properly authorized national team was not organized until 1908, however, and it was only then that the first official full international was played against Switzerland in Basle, resulting in a 5-3 win by the Swiss. Later in the year, Germany lost to Austria in Vienna by 3-2.

Before World War I, the eleven national championships were widely divided between clubs from Berlin, Leipzig, and Karlsruhe, as well as Freiburg, Kiel, and Furth. Between the wars, however, two clubs, FC Nürnberg and Schalke 04, came to dominate and establish once and for all their fame and popularity.

During the Weimar Republic, FC Nürnberg won an astounding five national titles, and during the Third Reich won another title and placed second twice.

Nürnberg also won two German cups in the 1930s and lost an additional cup final in 1940. The north Bavarian club became so popular with its attractive, fluid style, particularly during the 1920s, that it became known simply as *der Club,* and it influenced German soccer for a generation.

The second team to emerge during the period between the wars was Schalke 04 from the Ruhr city of Gelsenkirchen, a region that was to take over as the soccer hotbed of the industrialized Third Reich and postwar Germany. Schalke was the major power during the Hitler era, winning six championships, placing second three times, and advancing to five cup finals, all between 1934 and 1942.

During the Ostmark and German occupation of other neighboring countries between 1938 and 1944, 18 leading clubs from the occupied regions participated in the German regional leagues. Rapid Vienna, Austria's greatest club, went so far as to win the German Cup in 1938 and a national championship in 1941. Six of these clubs were from Sudetenland, five from Poland, four from Austria, two from Alsace, and one from Luxembourg. The German national team was also open to certain players from occupied lands.

The leagues were not suspended until after the 1943-44 season, but then remained closed for three years. The finals of the national cup, which since 1937 had been held at the new Olympic Stadium in Berlin, drew capacity crowds of 95,000 to 100,000 spectators until 1943, but were themselves halted after 1944, when the attendance figure dropped to 70,000.

Most of Germany's international opposition before 1933 came from Central Europe, Scandinavia, and the Benelux. Germany entered the Olympic soccer tournaments of 1912 (in which it achieved its best result ever, a 16-0 drubbing of Czarist Russia) and 1928 (to face elimination by the sensational Uruguayans).

With numerous wins over Switzerland, Denmark, Norway, and Finland, in addition to mixed results against the stronger teams from Central Europe, Germany became a middle-level power in continental soccer.

Under Hitler, the motivation to achieve better results was heightened considerably. Using Schalke as a base for the national team, a strong challenge was made to the major powers of Europe during the 1930s, beginning with the 1934 World Cup in Italy, and Germany achieved third place after losing in the semifinals to Czechoslovakia in Rome.

Political hopes on the playing field, however, were not enough to compensate for a lack of cohesion created by sectionalized league competition at home, and Germany suffered humiliating defeats in the 1936 Olympic Games in Berlin (elimination by unlikely Norway) and in the 1938 World Cup in France (elimination by Switzerland).

At the 1946 Congress in Luxembourg, FIFA delegates voted to expel the DFB from the world body, and German soccer entered a five-year period of international ostracization and domestic reorganization. An East German national association, the Sektion Fussball in der DDR, was formed in 1948, and soccer in the German Democratic Republic was launched on its own path, gaining separate membership with FIFA four years later.

Meanwhile, the old DFB became dormant during the Allied occupation, and in January of 1950, it was reconstituted under its original name to continue its administration of the game in West Germany. In June of 1950, at the FIFA Congress in Rio de Janeiro, the DFB was readmitted to the world body. The regional leagues were revitalized, and in the 1953-54 season, the reorganization process was concluded with a domestic structure consisting of five separate leagues.

Repeating its debut in 1908, West Germany reentered international competition in November of 1950, with a friendly against Switzerland a 1-0 win in Stuttgart. Friendlies were arranged with Turkey, Austria, Ireland, Luxembourg, and others, and under the leadership of Sepp Herberger it soon became apparent that the Germans had resurfaced with a strong national team.

Despite some excellent results against Austria and Yugoslavia between 1951 and 1953, West Germany entered the 1954 World Cup with a slim chance of overcoming the likes of Uruguay, Brazil, England, Scotland, and mighty Hungary, not to mention Austria and Yugoslavia, but in the end the cunning of Herberger, master strategist, and extraordinary performances by captain Fritz Walter and his teammates caused one of the great upsets in World Cup history.

In the final against unbeatable Hungary, two goals from Helmut Rahn were enough to defeat the overconfident Magyars and proclaim in no uncertain terms the reentry of German soccer on the world scene. The score on that rain-soaked day in Berne was 3-2, and it was all the more remarkable because at one point in the first half the Germans were down by 2-0.

In the 1958 World Cup, Germany took fourth place after conceding six goals to France in the third place game, and its performance throughout the competition was otherwise impressive. It won its first round group over Argentina, Czechoslovakia, and Ireland, and in the quarter-finals eliminated Yugoslavia. Fritz Walter, the first of West Germany's influential postwar stars, was joined by a new idol, Uwe Seeler of Hamburger SV, whose international career would eventually overlap elements of both the 1954 and 1974 World Championship teams.

In the early 1960s, the DFB set out to reorganize the domestic structure of the game again. Two important changes were advanced that were calculated by design to thrust West Germany into the front ranks of international competition.

One was to sanction full-time professionalism for the first time, though semi-professionalism had surfaced by the early 1950s. The second was to realign the domestic format by creating a national league and reassigning the regional competitions to lower divisions.

The Bundesliga (Federal League) was introduced in the 1963-64 season, and drew its 16 charter members from the regional leagues. Each of the 16 clubs were top finishers in their respective leagues the year before. This new league became the linchpin for Germany's later strength in both European tournament play and international competition.

The national team meanwhile, spurred by Uwe Seeler and the revelation of young Franz Beckenbauer, advanced to the final of the 1966 World Cup. Its performance in this event was significant, because it marked the beginning of a more delicate, fluid style of play than had previously been associated with German soccer, and it signaled the debut of tactical innovations that were to carry West Germany to the summit of world competition in the years ahead.

Sven Simon

1973 German National Team

The 1966 World Cup final against England at Wembley was perhaps the most controversial international match ever played. In overtime, with the score 2-2, England's Geoff Hurst tallied home a shot that hit the German crossbar and bounced downward to the edge of the goal line. English players insisted it was a goal; German players insisted it was not; neutral observers were unable to agree.

The linesman, on appeal from the referee, awarded the goal. Hurst eventually put away a fourth England goal to make the final score 4-2. The West German team, which was now led by Herberger's former assistant Helmut Schon, left the field at the end of the game certain that a second World Championship had been stolen from them, and to this day there are many who agree.

Vindication, however, was forthcoming. In succeeding years, Schon's attractive and intelligent methods were masterfully combined with the flowering of great players, including Franz Beckenbauer, who innovated a fluid, all-purpose role for the sweeper position; goalkeeper Sepp Maier; and goalscoring genius Gerd Müller. These players, all of Bayern Munchen, provided the backbone of what was to become one of the finest national teams of the 1970s.

At the 1970 World Cup in Mexico, West Germany gained third place, and the team might just as easily have advanced to the final but for a superbly played 4-3 loss to Italy in the semifinals. In 1972, West Germany's exciting, attacking style reached its peak in the European Football Championship, which was won with an incomparable 3-0 victory over the U.S.S.R.

The Bayern threesome were joined at that time by Gunter Netzer, perhaps the most elegant German midfielder of all time and orchestrator of Borussia Monchengladbach, a club that had come to share domination of the Bundesliga with Bayern in the late 1960s. West Germany

again reached the final of the European Championship in 1976, which was won by Czechoslovakia on penalty kicks.

The crowning achievement came in 1974 with the winning of the tenth World Championship. Though the 1972 European Championship team was retained nearly intact (Netzer had fallen out of favor), Holland was touted by some to win the cup as David to West Germany's Goliath. Indeed, it was Holland and West Germany that met in the final with similar styles of play and immense reserves of talent.

At 1-1 in the first half, the intuitive Gerd Müller drove home the winning goal, and West Germany's containment of Dutch star Johan Cruyff for the remainder of the game sealed Holland's fate.

Though its World Championship team was thought to be marginally inferior to that of 1972, there was no question that West Germany had now arrived as the preeminent power in world soccer. The strength of West Germany's game was borne out by the emergence of a new generation of brilliant players.

No team in the world can match Germany's performance of the last two decades, built first around that 1974 World Cup triumph and the very powerful Bundesliga but reinforced by a consistency which has never been equalled in the world game. Perhaps only Argentina can claim the same mastery of regional and world competition, but even that is questionable in light of the German record since 1980.

In succession, Germany has won the European Championship (1980), finished second in the World Cup (1982), qualified for the final rounds of the European Championship (1984), ended as runner up in the World Cup (1986), fallen in the semifinals of the 1988 European Championship, won the 1990 World Cup, and finished second in the 1992 European Championship.

That success rate was built around two rather different teams. The 1982 and 1986 World Cup runners-up were not stylish as the 1974 team had been but were physically powerful, thoroughly professional in their approach and were almost impossible to outwork.

In 1982 they came from a two–goal deficit in overtime to eventually prevail in the remarkable semifinal game against France in Seville, and in the 1986 World Cup final marked by long-time Argentine domination, a frantic West German team comeback from 0-2 in the closing quarter hour before falling 3-2 to a deserved, championship Argentine squad. Those games showed German character at its highest level.

What the 1982 and 1986 teams lacked, however, was the driving force of leadership that Lotthar Matthaus contributed to the 1990 World Cup winners. A powerful midfielder every bit as capable of the high work rate that had come to characterize the West German teams, Matthaus added that little touch of class that was reminiscent at times of the wily Beckenbauer. Although a traditional midfielder, Matthaus had some of Beckenbauer's ability to pop up in unexpected places to turn a match.

It was perhaps not unimportant that Beckenbauer served as coach of the team that brought West Germany its third world title. His stoic, handsome face was seen by the world's television audience as he stood next to the team bench throughout the tournament, seemingly able to communicate with his players by means of a nod of the head or a look.

The Matthaus-led team opened impressively with victory over Yugoslavia and had no trouble with the inexperienced United Arab Emirates, and so was safely into the second round when it suffered its only embarrassment of the tournament, a 1-1 draw against Colombia when the defense uncharacteristically let a 1-0 lead slip away in stoppage time.

The second round began with an emotional, volatile game against Holland, won by the Germans 2-1 in Milan only after two players had been ejected during the first half. Matthaus scored the goal that beat Czechoslovakia in the quarterfinal, and England was overcome, although not without great difficulty, in the semifinal at Turin. That match was actually a 1-1 draw, the West Germans prevailing on the penalty kick tie-breaker.

The final in the Rome Olympic Stadium proved a disappointment. Argentina, with its best striker Claudio Caniggia suspended and its midfield genius Diego Maradona unable to realize anything like top form in the tournament, played a grinding, defensive game, apparently content to go 120 scoreless minutes and take its chances with goalkeeper hero Sergio Goycochea in the penalty kick session.

It never got that far, as Argentine fouls mounted, two players were sent off by the Mexican referee, and Andreas Brehme ultimately settled matters with a penalty kick that even Goycochea couldn't stop.

At the club level Bayern Munich won three European Cup titles in succession (1974-76), SV Hamburg another in 1983. Werder Bremen captured the European Cup Winners Cup in 1993 while Borussia Moenchengladbach (1975 and 1979), Eintracht Frankfurt (1980) and Bayer Leverkusen (1988) all have won the UEFA Cup.

Borussia Dortmund was the 1993 UEFA Cup finalist to continue the proud German record of making an almost yearly impact in the top club tournaments.

Soccer in the former Soviet zone of Germany proved to be an interlude in German history that included one World Cup appearance by two German teams, but no European Championship qualifications by the old East Germany.

Other than VfB Leipzig, which won the first German championship in 1903 (and two others), and Dresdner SC, which dominated German competitions during World War II, eastern Germany had been far less important in its impact on the German game before 1945 than the western regions of the Ruhr and Bavaria. Thus, a long road lay ahead when in 1948 the Sektion Fussball in der DDR was founded.

The Sektion immediately organized a national championship, won in 1948 by SG Planitz, and a national cup was introduced one year later. The new league was comprised of a first division of 14 clubs and a second division of two sections with 14 clubs each. In 1952, the DDR was admitted to FIFA, and two months later an East German national team began to haul itself out of obscurity.

The first match, against Poland in Warsaw, was won by the home team, 3-0. Poland, Rumania, and Bulgaria remained its only opponents through 1956, a western embargo was in full force. It was noteworthy when Wales, drawn in the same World Cup qualifying group with East Germany and Czechoslovakia, ventured to Leipzig in 1958 and became East Germany's first non-Warsaw Pact adversary.

In 1961, the national association, now renamed Deutscher Fussball-Verband der DDR (DFV), hired Hungarian coach Karoly Soos to manage the national team. Soos's seven-year stint proved to be the turning point in East German soccer. His knowledge and experience was decisive in reversing the losing East German record. During Soos's stewardship, a winning trend was established that was maintained into the 1970s.

Much of East Germany's opposition continued to be the other Warsaw Pact states with a sprinkling of some "politically suitable" African countries. The exceptions have been in World Cup, European Football Championship, and especially Olympic competition.

The World Cup finals were not reached until 1974, and advancement in the European Football Championship eluded East Germany on each occasion, except in the 1962-64 edition when it reached the second round by surprising Czechoslovakia (2-1 and 1-1) before elimination by Hungary.

In the Olympic Games, however, the East Germans distinguished themselves, following the tradition of Eastern European dominance in this competition from 1956 through 1980. In 1964, they were bronze medalists, defeating Iran, Mexico and the full Yugoslav national team before succumbing to powerful Czechoslovakia in the semifinals.

Disappointed at being knocked out of the 1968 Olympic qualification tournament, East Germany began its most successful era with its entry into the 1972 games at Munich. Disposing easily of Ghana and Colombia by an aggregate score of ten to one, it found Poland, the new European powerhouse and eventual winner, an impossible obstacle in first round competition. In the semifinal round, however, it was grouped with host team West Germany as well as Hungary and Mexico.

While its match with the amateur West Germans was not taken seriously in the west, the fans at home had come to realize a near-impossible dream. In the end, East Germany's 3-2 win was put in its proper perspective since the West German amateur eleven was not at all the same team that a few weeks before had won the European Football Championship. In the third place game, the East Germans battled the U.S.S.R. to a draw, and the bronze medal had to be shared.

East Germany's highest achievements came under former Carl Zeiss Jena manager Georg Buschner, who led the national team into its only World Cup in 1974. It was here the ultimate consolation prize was attained. There was an easy win over Australia, followed by a disappointing draw with defensive minded Chile, and finally a meeting of the two Germanys, picked by luck (or design) to play in the same group.

Both teams, sensitive to the occasion, played a close, controlled passing game, but a goal by East Germany's attacking midfielder Jurgen Sparwasser was the only score of the day, and a polite West German team, some would say deferential, took its lone upset of the competition with poise. Across the border, a nation of unparalleled sports enthusiasts celebrated its finest hour.

In the less challenging Olympic Games of 1976, East German soccer fortunes were commensurate with its domination of the entire games. A scoreless draw with Brazil's amateurs was the only blemish in its successful run for the gold medal. Once again, the primary opposition came from Eastern European teams; the U.S.S.R. fell in the semifinals, and in the final Poland's great World Cup team from 1974 succumbed 3-1. East Germany won its only major victory in international competition, and observers could not overlook the impressive growth of its game.

East German clubs never reached the European Cup final, but I. FC Magdeburg won the Cup Winners Cup in 1974 and Carl Zeiss Jena and Lokomotiv Leipzig were both losing finalists in the same competition. When reunification came, Dynamo Dresden established itself in the Bundesliga and three former East German internationals, Matthias Sammer, Thomas Doll, and Ulf Kirsten found places in the unified German selections.

GHANA

Address: Ghana Football Association, P.O. Box 1272, Accra. *Founded:* 1957. *FIFA:* 1958. *CAF:* 1958. *National stadium:* Accra Sports Stadium,

Accra (30,000); *largest stadium:* Accra Sports Stadium. *Colors:* Yellow jerseys, yellow shorts. *Season:* January to October. *Honors:* African Nations' Cup winner (1963, 1965, 1978, 1982), runner-up (1968, 1970, 1992); World Under-16 Champions (1991); Olympic Games bronze medal (1992).

Ghana is the preeminent soccer power in black Africa, though not by a wide margin, and it is also the birthplace of African soccer north of the Zambezi. It was the first black African country to form a governing body, the first to join FIFA, the first to win a place in the final rounds of the Olympic Games, and the first to win the African Nations' Cup and the second to win a World 16-Under title.

But there has been disappointment at the highest level. Elimination in the first round of the 1994 World Cup qualifying stage meant that this talent-laden nation would again miss the ultimate showcase. Ghana has yet to appear in a World Cup finals.

A Jamaican introduced soccer on the Gold Coast around 1880. This represents the earliest known date associated with soccer on the African continent with the sole exception of South Africa (ca. 1865). That a Jamaican, rather than a Brit, should take credit for this astonishing historical oddity makes the event all the more intriguing, but, unfortunately, little is known of the game's development until the British established the Gold Coast Football Association in 1922. (This founding date is officially superseded by the formation of the Ghanaian association in 1957.)

By this time, much of the Gold Coast's soccer activity was being carried out by British residents, though many African-based clubs were founded during the 1920s and 1930s.

Ghana's dominant club, Asante Kotoko Sporting Club, was founded in Kumasi in 1926 as Ashanti United. The City Championship Cup was introduced in 1922 for clubs in Accra, remaining the most important competition until the 1950s, and the Asantehene Cup was established soon thereafter for clubs in Kumasi. In 1938, the first national cup competition, the Gold Coast Football Championship, was introduced under the sponsorship of the governor. Several local championships emerged before World War II in secondary cities such as Obuasi, Sekondi, and Tarkwa.

The Gold Coast Football Association became affiliated with FIFA in 1948, and two years later a Gold Coast national team made its unofficial international debut against Nigeria in Accra, winning 1-0. The governing body was renamed the United Gold Coast Amateur Football Association in 1952. In 1957, the year of Ghanaian independence, the Ghana Football Association was established, and a national championship was introduced under a league format.

In 1963, Ghana played host to the fourth African Nations' Cup—the first to be held in black Africa—and defeated Sudan in the final to win its first big trophy. The star of this series was Wilberforce Mfum, who in 1971 became one of the first players signed by the fledgling New York Cosmos.

In 1965, Ghana reached its peak with a stunning sweep of Congo-Leopoldville, Ivory Coast, and Tunisia, to take its second consecutive Nations' Cup. Left winger Frank Odoi scored the winning goal in the 3-2 final after extra time.

In the 1968 edition, Ghana reached the final for a third straight time after going undefeated in its first round group and defeating Ivory Coast in the semifinals.

The final was lost to Congo-Kinshasa 1-0, but Ghana played to attack while the Congolese merely shut off the goalmouth. Ghana's capacity to rejuvenate itself and produce fine players seemed endless, and in 1970 it reached the

Nations' Cup final yet again after placing second in its first round group.

In the final against Sudan, Sudanese fans clashed with Ghanaian players on the field and the home team held on to a 1-0 lead, leaving Ghana frustrated and physically battered.

In 1972, 1974, and 1976 Ghana failed to qualify for the final rounds with a new generation of players. The 1978 edition of the Nation's cup was held in Ghana, giving the "Black Stars," as the national team is called, automatic entry, and this led to an unprecedented third African Nations' Cup triumph.

A fourth followed in 1982 when Ghana beat host Libya on penalty kicks in the final and there was a somewhat disappointing second place finish in 1990 when Ghana's top player, Abedi Pelé was suspended from the final against Ivory Coast. Lacking his striking power, Ghana lost on penalties after a final that was dour and goalless.

Ghana has also had Olympic Games success including a 1992 bronze medal while at club level there have been limited rewards. Ashanti Kotoko (1970, 1983) has won the African Champions Cup twice but no Ghanaian side has lifted the Cup Winners Cup trophy.

That can be explained in part by the fact that its top players—notably Abedi Pelé and Anthony Yeboah—have been snapped up by European clubs rather than remaining at home.

GREECE

Address: Elliniki Podosfairiki Omospondia (Greek Football Federation), Singrou Avenue 137, Athens. *Founded:* 1926. *FIFA:* 1927. *UEFA:* 1954. *National stadium:* Olympic Stadium, Athens (75,000); *others:* Kaftantzoglion,

Salonica (47,000). *Colors:* White jerseys, blue shorts. *Season:* September to June.

Greek soccer has long been the victim of political and cultural hostilities, though the game has been a passion among Greeks since the turn of the century. Before World War I, Greek soccer suffered from political strife involving Turkey and Bulgaria and from upheaval caused by the Balkan Wars. The instability of domestic politics between the world wars put a newly organized Greek game on rocky footing.

After World War II, when soccer in Greece had its first real chance to settle down and modernize, the ceaseless clash between Athenians and Salonicans, the two principal parties in Greek soccer, continuously got in the way of unifying national soccer interests.

As a result of these many troubles, Greece has little to show for itself in international competition. That is about to change as a place in the 1994 World Cup finals seems all but certain with qualification beyond the halfway stage.

In Greece, as elsewhere, the introduction of soccer was left to British sailors and engineers in the 1880s. Greek residents in Piraeus, Athens, Salonica, and Smyrna (now Izmir and part of Turkey) saw the British play soccer near the docks and in city squares, and from the beginning they too took an interest in the game.

An unofficial exhibition match was held in conjunction with the first modern Olympic Games in Athens in 1896 between a Danish selection and a "Greek" team that was probably made up of British players. The result of this game is unknown, but it surely accelerated Athenian curiosity.

The first important Greek club was Panhellenic, whose English name was later changed to the Greek "Panathinaikos" (Pan-Athenian) in 1908. Olympiakos (Olympian) was founded in Athens's port city of Piraeus in 1914. Together these two clubs have dominated Greek soccer decisively over the decades, Olympiakos owning 20 titles by 1992 to the 13 for Panathinaikos. Panathinaikos, however, can claim the distinction of being the only Greek club to appear in a major European final, the 1971 European Cup final.

Greece's first genuine foray into international competition came with the 1920 Olympic Games at Antwerp. With the formation of a Greek soccer association still several years away, a Greek national team banded together and was pitted against experienced Sweden in the first round. This resulted in an overwhelming 9-0 loss, and Greece was not seen in international competition again for nine years.

The Greek republic was proclaimed in 1925, and the following year a governing body for soccer, the Elliniki Podosfairiki Omospondia (EPO), was founded in Athens. A national championship was finally introduced in 1927-28, but it was restricted to clubs from the two major cities, Athens (including Piraeus) and Salonica, until 1959, when the first real national league was launched.

To the dismay of Athenians, the first champion was Aris Salonica, but Olympiakos, Panathinaikos, and AEK rapidly took over. AEK has won nine titles to claim third place overall.

Under a succession of British and Western European coaches, Greek clubs have been regular participants in the European club championships. The finest hour in Greek soccer occurred in 1971 when Panathinaikos, under the managership of Hungarian immortal Ferenc Puskas, advanced to the final of the European Cup. "Panas" eliminated Jeunesse Esch and Slovan Bratislava in early rounds, and in the quarterfinals slipped by Everton on the away-goals rule, startling the English champions.

In the semifinals, Panathinaikos again won on the away-goals rule, this time over Red Star Belgrade, and gained the final. Its opponent in the final at Wembley was Ajax Amsterdam, which played cautiously and won by a comfortable 2-0 margin. Three-hundred thousand people greeted the Athens team on its return home, and Greek soccer basked in world glory for the first time. When Ajax refused to meet Nacional Montevideo in the Intercontinental Cup, "Panas" happily substituted.

The Greek heroes performed admirably in holding Nacional to a 1-1 draw in the Athens leg, and in Uruguay succumbed by 2-1, losing the "world club championship" by an aggregate of only 3-2. That marked Greek soccer's high point until 1992-93 when Alkis Panagoulias' national team defeated Hungary 1-0 in Budapest to edge close to the first-ever place in the World Cup finals.

GUADELOUPE

This French Overseas Department has long been a production center for fine players, many of whom migrate to France to play with major clubs. The most famous of these in recent years has been the captain of Olympique Marseille and the French national team, Marius Tresor, an elegant attacking sweeper. Guadeloupe's political status entitles it to send representative teams each year to play in the Coupe de France.

They do not compete as a separate nation in World Cup competition.

GUATEMALA

Address: Federacion Nacional de Fútbol de Guatemala C.A., Palacio de los Deportes, 20 piso, Zona 4, Guatemala C.A. *FIFA:* 1933. *CONCACAF:* 1961. *National stadium:* Mateo Flores, Guatemala (50,000); *largest stadium:* Mateo Flores. *Colors:* White jerseys, white shorts. *Season:* May to October.

Internal disorder has kept Guatemala from dominating soccer in Central America, despite its large population and historical importance in the region. The Federacion Nacional de Fútbol was founded in the 1920s (exact date uncertain), and joined FIFA in 1933, the second Central American federation to do so.

Before World War II, a multidivisional league was established with the Liga Mayor (national league), consisting of a Division Mayor and a Division Primera, and the Liga Menor (regional leagues). Guatemala made its international debut in the first Central American and Caribbean Games in 1930, and played two matches in that competition, losing both, to Costa Rica 8-1 and to El Salvador 8-2.

That same year, Guatemala qualified for the final rounds of the 1968 Olympic Games in Mexico City, and found itself grouped in the first round with two teams from Eastern Europe, Czechoslovakia and Bulgaria. Guatemala held Bulgaria to a respectable 2-1 win and, after defeating Thailand convincingly 4-1, stunned Czechoslovakia with a 1-1 draw, preventing the Czechs from moving on to their expected berth in the quarter-finals. Instead, it was Guatemala that advanced, poised to meet the excellent Hungarian team that was about to win its second consecutive gold medal. Hungary squeaked by Guatemala 1-0.

Guatemala qualified for the Olympic final rounds again in 1976, and on this occasion its best result in the first round was a 1-1 draw with Mexico, though it also drew with Israel before losing to the French amateurs. The expectations that both these Olympic runs created, however, did not materialize, and Guatemala failed to mount a real challenge to Haiti and Mexico in the 1974 and 1978 World Cup qualifying rounds. They did appear again in 1988, however, when Mexico was banned for using overage players in a FIFA qualifying tournament for the World Youth Cup.

The center of Guatemalan soccer is located in the big earthquake-bound cities of the south—Guatemala City, Quezaltenango, Mazatenango, and Escuintla. The national stadium in Guatemala City, Mateo Flores, is the largest in Central America, but all of Guatemalan soccer suffered tragically in the massive earthquake of 1976.

Guatemala has never reached the World Cup finals. It's most recent qualifying bid ended with a defeat by Honduras in the 1994 qualification stage.

GUINEA

Address: Federation Guineenne de Football, P.O. Box 262, Conakry. *Founded:* 1959. *FIFA:* 1961. *CAF:* 1962. *National stadium:* Stade du 28 Septembre, Conakry (40,000); *largest stadium:* Stade du 28 Septembre. *Colors:* Red-and-white jerseys, yellow-and-white shorts. *Season:* October to June. *Honors:* African Nations' Cup runner-up (1976).

Guinea's fierce archrivalry with neighboring Ivory Coast is one of the most intense in all of French-speaking West Africa and has generated a high standard of play in domestic competition. The country's relatively early date of independence helped to coalesce soccer interests, especially in the capital of Conakry, and by 1970 Guinea had emerged as a leading continental power. In the mid-1970s, the national team's forward line was thought to be the most sophisticated and effective in Africa.

Guineans learned the game from French colonists after World War I and by the late 1940s were active in local tournaments. The Federa-tion Guineenne de Football introduced a league and cup competition based in Conakry shortly after its founding in 1959. Guinean clubs became active in the African Champions' Cup in the late 1960s, when Hafia Football Club of Conakry emerged as the major force in the league. Hafia remains the runaway record holder in league championships with eight (1967-69 and 1971-75).

In 1972, Hafia eliminated two powerful African champions, Cameroon's Canon de Yaounde and Zaire's T.P. Mazembe, to reach the final of the Champions' Cup, and there defeated Uganda's Simba Club in two hard fought games to gain its first African title. In 1975, Hafia won a second time, having eliminated two more continental powers, Zaire's Vita Club and Congo's C.A.R.A. In the final, it won both legs over Nigeria's leading club, Rangers.

The following year, Hafia again had to overcome a major African club, Ivory Coast's ASEC Abidjan, to gain the final against Algeria's surprising Mouloudia Chalia. After splitting the two legs of the final with Mouloudia, 0-3 and 3-0, Hafia was unlucky to lose a second trophy in as many years on penalty kicks. In 1977, however, Hafia returned and became the first club to win the champions' cup three times. They have not enjoyed such success again, though. Horoya Conakry's 1978 Cup Winners Cup triumph marks the country's last club win in Africa.

Guinea's first big international success at the national level was in qualifying for the 1968 Olympics in Mexico City, but in the first round the Mexican and French amateurs defeated Guinea convincingly, and Guinea's 3-2 win over Colombia was not sufficient to prevent a last place finish in its first round group.

In 1973, Guinea placed second in the soccer tournament of the African Games in Nigeria. Guinea first qualified for the final rounds of the more coveted African Nations' Cup in 1970. A loss to Egypt and draws with Congo-Kinshasa and Ghana, however, proved fatal, and it bowed out after the first round. There were similar results in 1974, but in 1976, behind the gifted inside forwards Nabylaye Papa Camara and Ibrahim "Petit" Sory Keita, Guinea went undefeated in six games and took second place to the talented Moroccans.

That is still the best African Championship finish, but the 1994 World Cup qualifying tournament saw Guinea advance to the African final round. There they were matched with the powerful Cameroon and surprising Zimbabwe for a place in the 1994 tournament.

GUINEA-BISSAU

Address: Apartado 375, 1035 Bissau-Codex, Rua 4 no. 10 C. *Founded:* 1974. *FIFA:* 1986.

Relatively new members of FIFA, Guinea-Bissau has yet to make an impact at international or club level.

GUYANA

Address: Guyana Football Association, PO Box 10727, Georgetown. *Founded:* 1902. *FIFA:* 1968. *CONCACAF:* 1969. *National stadium:* Guyana Sports Club, Georgetown (5,800); *largest stadium:* Georgetown Cricket Club (15,000), *Colors:* Green-and-yellow jerseys, black shorts. *Season:* March to December.

The British Guiana Football Association, founded at Georgetown in 1902, was the first regulatory body of soccer in any of the three Guianas. The Guyana Football Association was reconstituted two years after independence was achieved in 1966, and in 1969 Guyana joined CONCACAF. Guyana's has yet to make any World Cup impact, cricket remaining the major sporting interest.

HAITI

Address: Fédération Haïtienne de Football, Stade Sylvio Cator, Port-au-Prince. *Founded:* 1912. *FIFA:* 1937. *CONCACAF:* 1957. *National stadium:* Stade Sylvio Cator, Port-au-Prince (15,000); *largest stadium:* Stade Sylvio Cator. *Colors:* Black-and-red jersey, black shorts. *Season:* October to June.

The success of Haiti, for many years one of the leading soccer-playing countries of the Caribbean, has become unsure in an ear of political unrest and national instability.

The Fédération Haïtienne de Football Amateur has been an autonomous body from its founding in 1912, though French influence left over from the colonial experience was considerable. Still, Haitian soccer has developed quite independently from outside domination. Haiti's first official international matches date from a seven-day World Cup qualifying tournament in Port-au-Prince in 1934 with a Cuban selection that was superior in technique and skills.

Haiti's first and only foray into genuine world class competition was at the 1974 World Cup in West Germany. It gained the berth by crushing Puerto Rico and going on to defeat Netherlands Antilles, Trinidad, Honduras, and Guatemala, though it lost to Mexico, 1-0. Its record in the final rounds was only marginally better than that of Zaire, but it did manage to impress by holding mighty Italy to a 3-1 win. The great Polish side crushed them 7-0, and Argentina probably should have done better by its 4-1 victory over the Haitian amateurs. Since then, Haiti has not been able to support a major soccer investment. In 1994 qualifying a measure of its weakness was seen in first round elimination.

HONDURAS

Address: Federación Nacional Deportiva Extraescolar de Honduras, Apartado 827, Costa Oeste Del Est. Nacional, Tegucigalpa, De.C. *Founded:* 1935. *FIFA:* 1946. *CONCACAF:* 1961. *National stadium:* Estadio Nacional, Norte e Sur (22,000); *others:* Francisco Morazan, San Pedro Sula (22,000). *Colors:* Blue jerseys, white shorts. *Season:* February to October.

For Honduras, the 1980s were the first era of encouraging international results at the national level. Qualification for the 1982 World Cup in Spain sparked interest, which has carried into the 1990s. The country has developed two distinct centers of soccer activity in recent years—Tegucigalpa, the capital, and San Pedro Sula, the industrial center on the other side of the country. Like Ecuador, Honduras promises to profit from this sort of inter-city rivalry.

The post-World War I soccer boom in Central America took place in Honduras as it did in Costa Rica, Guatemala, and El Salvador. The national association was founded as part of the Federación Nacional de Cultura Fisica y Deportes de Honduras in 1935, and joined FIFA in 1946 with over 40 clubs registered and a thousand players on the rosters.

A national team played in the first Central American and Caribbean Games in 1930, winning in its international debut over Jamaica (5-4) and crashing to Cuba only two days later by a score of 7-0.

The appearance in Spain in 1982 proved that Honduran soccer could compete. Unlike El Salvador, crushed 10-1 by Hungary in its first game, Honduras opened by drawing 1-1 with the host. Another draw, 1-1 with Northern Ireland, kept them alive for second-round qualification, but the dream ended in an honorable 1-0 defeat against Yugoslavia.

Since then, Honduras has not reached the finals again, but the exposure given the country's players has greatly increased. Veteran captain Gilberto Yearwood has earned recognition as one of the region's great players.

HONG KONG

Address: Hong Kong Football Association, 55 Fat Kwong Street, Homantin, Kowloon, Hong Kong. *Founded:* 1915. *FIFA:* 1954. *AFC:* 1954. *National stadium:* Hong Kong Government Stadium, Hong Kong (28,000); *largest stadium:* Hong Kong Government Stadium. *Colors:* Red jerseys, blue shorts. *Season:* September to June.

Hong Kong, the first Asian country to adopt full professionalism in senior-level competition, has often seemed about to become a major soccer power in East Asia but has not been able to beat larger nations to reach a World Cup finals. Hong Kong has produced highly skilled players for many years, but in general has been unable to overcome the Koreans or the increasingly stronger Arabic Gulf States.

Soccer was introduced in the Hong Kong colony by British missionaries, military personnel, and technicians in the 1880s or before. The game was primarily played by the British for several decades, though some Chinese schoolboys learned it in British schools, and the British founded the Hong Kong Football Association (HKFA) in 1915.

The HKFA was affiliated with the Football Association in London until 1954, when it secured permission from the English to join FIFA. Many clubs were established before and after the First World War by the British, but the Chinese did not become important participants until the 1920s.

The first recorded Hong Kong internationals were a series of three unofficial matches against the Philippines in the late 1940s. Hong Kong won all three, by 4-1 in 1948 (in Hong Kong), 5-1 in 1949 (Manila), and 5-1 in 1950 (Hong Kong).

There are 14 First Division clubs and an annual cup competition that attracts a wide following. In recent years the teams have imported players from overseas to strengthen the level of play, but genuine home-grown stars are also a feature of the league and cup competition.

HUNGARY

Address: Magyar Labdarugok Szövetsége (Hungarian Football Association), Népköztársaság utja 47, H-1061 Budapest VI. *Founded:* 1901. *FIFA:* 1907. *UEFA:* 1954. *National stadium:* Népstadion, Budapest (80,000); *others:* Ferencvárosi T.C. Stadion, Budapest (80,000). *Colors:* Red jerseys, white shorts. *Season:* August to November, March to June. *Honors:* World Cup runner-up (1938, 1954); Olympic Games winner (1952, 1964, 1968), runner-up (1972).

If England was once the most respected country in world soccer and Brazil the most attractive, then Hungary was once a sentimental favorite. This exalted reputation stems from the extraordinary Hungarian national team that nearly dominated international competition in the early 1950s. The "Magic Magyars" were the greatest team ever assembled up to that time, but the fine Hungarian teams that preceded or followed it have been overshadowed and recent success has been elusive.

In company with Austria and Bohemia, Hungarian teams learned the sophisticated Scottish short passing game from British coaches and combined it with their growing high standards of skill. Unlike Austria and Czechoslovakia, however, the focus of Hungarian soccer has remained on the capital city—Budapest—throughout the post-World War II era.

AP/Wide World Photos

Perhaps the greatest team ever assembled: the incomparable "Magic Magyars" of Hungary, shown here in 1953. (back row, left to right) Landor, Palotas, Hidegkuti, Varhidi, Kovacs, Czibor, Budai II, Zakarias; (front row) Geller II, Csordas, J. Toth, Puskás, Grosics, Buzanszky. Missing: Bozsik.

Ujpest Sport Club (later Ujpest Dozsa) was formed in the Budapest suburb of Ujpest in 1885. The Budapest Gymnastic and Athletic Club introduced a soccer team in 1888 under the name Magyar Testgyakorlok Kore (MTK), or "Hungarian Gymnastics Club," and other British-based clubs followed. Despite the later fame of Ujpest and MTK, the first important name in Hungarian soccer was Budapesti Torna Club (BTC), or "Budapest Gymnastics Club," which arranged the first public soccer match in the country.

In 1901, the Magyar Labdarugok Szovetsege (MLS), the first and only national governing body in Hungary, was founded in Budapest by 13 clubs, and an annual championship was introduced. Lacking the experience of Austrian players who had competed annually since 1896 with Bohemian teams, Hungary was a participant in the very first full international played outside the British Isles in 1902. This was Austria's historic 5-0 defeat of the Magyars in Vienna, and it was the beginning of the world's longest-running non-British rivalry.

The MLS joined FIFA in 1907 and entered the soccer competition of the 1908 Olympic Games, the first officially recognized international tournament, but withdrew before its opening round match with Holland because of political tensions at home.

During this period Hungary produced its first great star, Imre Schlosser, a goalscoring inside left who became famous throughout Europe after his international debut in 1906 and who led FTC to seven championships between 1905-13. FTC's hold on the league was broken in 1914 by MTK, FTC's keen crosstown rival.

In 1916, English coach Jimmy Hogan arrived at MTK from an internment camp in Vienna and changed the course of Hungarian soccer. Hogan brought with him the philosophy and tactics of the Scottish short passing game that he had earlier taught in Austria, and he transformed MTK into an all-conquering team. One of his first important acts was the discovery of Gyorgy Orth in a Budapest park in 1916, and it was Orth who led MTK to 10 successive Budapest championships through 1925.

Hogan's teachings spread throughout Budapest, and by the time his all too brief stay was over, a Hungarian version of the "Danubian style" emerged. It was based on skilled passing and a sophisticated sense of positioning, and contributed significantly to Hungary's development as an international power.

The rivalry with Austria continued after World War I until the Olympic break of 1924 with mixed results. This combination of success and failure was typical of Hungary's overall status in international competition at that time. At the 1924 Olympics, Hungary suffered one of its worst upsets of all time: after a 5-0 defeat of Poland the Magyars were eliminated by Egypt (3-0) in the first round.

In 1926 professionalism was sanctioned by the MLS, signaling an important change. Ferencvaros, as FTC was now called, won the important Mitropa Cup in 1928 and Ujpest did the same in 1929. These two clubs, along with MTK, have dominated Hungarian League play ever since. Ferencvaros had 24 titles by 1992, along with 15 Cup triumphs. MTIC and Ujpest each have won 19 championships.

In the 1934 World Cup, gained after eliminating Bulgaria with considerable ease, Hungary partially avenged its 1924 Olympic loss to Egypt by defeating the Egyptians 4-2. In the second round, Hungary faced its old rival Austria and was defeated 2-1.

Hungary's national team was by now one of the best in Europe despite its failure to beat mighty Austria. Hungary's 11-1 trouncing of Greece in the World Cup qualification rounds set the stage for its entry into the 1938 World Championship in France.

In the first round at Reims, Sarosi and his exceptional inside left Gyula Zsengeller scored two goals apiece in a 6-0 rout of the Dutch East Indies, and in the second round Zsengeller scored both goals in a 2-0 win over Switzerland. Hungary's opponent in the semifinal was Sweden, which like Brazil, was coached by a Hungarian, but the so-called "team of steel" proved to be Hungary's easiest opponent. Zsengeller converted a hat trick, and Hungary was merciful in holding the score down to 5-1.

With its advance to the final of the 1938 World Cup, Hungary had deservedly reached the pinnacle of international competition. Italy, however, was a most formidable opponent, and the Italian forward trio of Meazza, Piola, and Ferrari was too highly motivated to be contained by the Hungarian defense.

Despite the presence of Hungary's excellent goalkeeper, Antal Szabo, and speedy left back Sandor Biro, both of MTK, Meazza was able to set up three goals and keep Italy in Hungary's half of the field for most of the game. The final score was 4-2 but, as in 1934 against Austria, Hungary had lost to the best team in Europe.

After World War II, all official competitions except the national league came to a halt while political matters were resolved. The cup did not resume until 1952, and then only sporadically. Meanwhile the domestic structure of the Hungarian game changed considerably after the birth of the Communist government in 1947.

The most important event was the founding of the army club, Honved Sport Egyesulet, in 1948, which absorbed the suburban club Kispest in the process. Honved was given priority treatment from the beginning and got first choice of the best players. In 1948-49, its first season in the

first division, Honved won the first of its 12 championships. Other clubs were reorganized by the new Ministry of Sport. Ujpest became Ujpest Dozsa, and MTK went through several more name changes including Bastya and Voros Lobogo.

In all this reorganization a stunning array of talent was developing. Honved alone came alive with inside left Ferenc Puskas and right half Jozsef Bozsik on the roster, and in 1950 the club acquired inside right Sandor Kocsis and goalkeeper Gyula Groscis; MTK had inside right Nandor Hidegkuti and Ferencvaros had outside left Zoltan Czibor.

These gifted players were eventually rated as the world's greatest at their respective positions. Gustav Sebes emerged in the later 1940s as overseer of the national team, and while the Ministry of Sport kept Hungary virtually out of postwar international competition, Sebes was able to bring together the unique talents of his players to build a remarkable team.

Between May of 1950, when it lost to Austria in Vienna, and February of 1956, a loss to Turkey in Istanbul, Hungary played 48 games with only one defeat. Hungary managed to score at least once in every match, and averaged almost four goals per game.

A stretch of 29 consecutive matches passed without a defeat from 1950-54. In fact, excluding the war years, Hungary was undefeated at home for 17 consecutive years from 1939-56. Included was the 1952 Olympic gold medal.

No single game in soccer history has achieved more fame and attention than the November of 1953, 6-3 win in England. It not only shocked English soccer, but solidified Hungary's reputation as the greatest team of the era. Hungary again flogged the English 7-1 in Budapest five months later.

The "Magic Magyars" entered the 1954 World Cup in Switzerland as the odds-on favorite. Sebes had been elevated to deputy minister of sport, though he was still in charge of the national team, and Gyula Mandi took care of discipline and day-to-day training as field coach.

In the first round, Hungary scored 17 goals to its opponents' three in huge wins over South Korea and cunning West Germany. In its 8-3 defeat of the Germans, however, Hungary lost Puskas, its captain and supreme player, on a tackle by Werner Liebrich. Kocsis scored seven goals between these two matches, Puskas another three, and five other players also scored.

Even without Puskas, Hungary went on to defeat Brazil in the quarter-finals and Uruguay, world champion, in the semifinals. The game with Brazil was particularly violent—known as the "Battle of Berne"—and is still a subject of great discussion. The final result, 4-2, was overshadowed by rough play, fights, and hurled missiles from the sidelines and afterward a wholesale invasion of the Hungarian locker room was undertaken by Brazilian players.

Bozsik, who by now had become a member of the Hungarian House of Deputies, was sent off, and players on both teams were stained with blood and caked with mud. This game was billed as the unofficial "final" between the world's two best teams, but neither would comment later on their belligerent behavior.

The semifinal against Uruguay, on the other hand, was won by a similar score. But the quality of play was close to perfection, and the game still ranks as one of the most memorable internationals on record. Hungary led by two goals until late in the second half, but Uruguay equalized on two goals by Juan Hohberg to force an overtime period. Kocsis scored twice in extra time to bring his total in the competition to 10, and Uruguay lost its first match ever in the World Cup.

Against the wishes of Sebes and Mandi, Puskás insisted on playing in the final against West Germany despite his nagging injury. This proved to be one of the key elements in Hungary's loss of the World Cup final—its only defeat during that 48-game run between 1950 to 1956.

The other key element was German manager Sepp Herberger's shrewd unleashing of his team's emotional energy after holding the Germans back in that deceptive first round loss. Through Puskas and Czibor, Hungary was leading 2-0 after eight minutes, but the limping Puskas and soaking rain neutralized Hungary's momentum. By sheer determination, the Germans came back with three goals before the final whistle, and Hungary went down to defeat.

To prove that the World Cup result was indeed a fluke, the MLS drew up a heavy schedule for its national team in the remaining months of 1954 and throughout 1955. The upshot was another stunning series of 15 wins and three draws in only 16 months, including decisive victories over Austria, Czechoslovakia, Scotland, Italy, and Sweden.

In 1956, Hungary's watershed loss to Turkey was followed by two more to Czechoslovakia and Belgium, and the entire glorious era was finally shattered in November by the Soviet invasion of Budapest. Puskás, Kocsis, and Czibor fled to the West, and international opinion turned against the remaining members of the world famous team.

The 1956 political uprising would surely have ended Hungary's rank as an international power, but the depth of talent in the country, the players' sureness of style, and productive training techniques ensured another generation of potential excellence. Hungary qualified for the 1958 World Cup by eliminating Norway and Bulgaria, but in the final rounds a nervous and intimidated team—taunted by heckling fans and police—lost to

Sweden and drew with Wales to force a replay with the latter.

Wales won after center back Ferenc Sipos was sent off, and Hungary was eliminated from its first post-1956 World Cup. Better results were seen in the 1962 World Cup, which the Hungarians reached by eliminating the Netherlands and East Germany, but the much improved Czechs stopped the Albert-Tichy scoring machine with a 1-0 quarterfinal shutout, and Hungary bowed out again.

As its World Cup role declined, Hungary moved aggressively into Olympic tournaments. In Olympic competition, Hungary won gold medals in 1964 and 1968, and in 1972 won the silver medal.

The 1966 World Cup, however, offered Hungary a comeback. This team, led by Albert and Bene, had the misfortune of being in a first round group with Brazil and Portugal, the latter a sentimental favorite to challenge Brazil's hegemony.

Portugal won its match after Hungarian goalkeeper Szentmihalyi was injured, but in the next game Albert gave one of the finest performances of the competition and led his team to a 3-1 defeat of Brazil, the latter's first World Cup loss since 1954.

The game was a delight, and it endeared Hungary to the hearts of international fans once again. In the quarter-finals, however, Hungary's growing nemesis, the U.S.S.R., played with power and intelligence—mainly power—and neutralized Albert to win.

Despite its 1968 Olympic gold medal, Hungary decline had begun after the 1966 World Cup. Hungary did not qualify for the final stages again until 1982, but failed to advance past the first round despite opening with a 10-1 route of El Salvador. The next game was a 4-1 loss to

Argentina that put Hungarian strength in true perspective.

They appeared again in Mexico in 1986 but were hammered 6-0 by the U.S.S.R. and went home again with only a victory over Canada to show for their efforts. Hungary missed the 1990 finals and seemed destined to fail again in 1994 when defeated at home by Greece and Iceland, teams which never have played in the finals, in the initial qualifying phase.

ICELAND

Address: Knattspyrnusamband Islands (Football Association of Iceland), P.O. Box 8511, 128 Reykjavik. *Founded:* 1947. *FIFA:* 1929. *UEFA:* 1954. *National stadium:* Laugardalsvollur, Reykjavik (15,000); *largest stadium:* Laugardalsvollur. *Colors:* Blue jerseys, white shorts. *Season:* May to October.

Tucked away on the Arctic Circle, Iceland has made the most of difficult circumstances and may no longer be ranked at the bottom of the European charts. In the mid-1970s, within the space of two years, the Icelandic national team defeated East Germany, Norway, and Luxembourg.

Since then, they have beaten the likes of Hungary and Spain, taking advantage of native players with professional experience in Europe and their own increased confidence borne from victories. For decades, soccer has been enthusiastically supported by Icelanders and has served as a primary link between Iceland and its European cousins, though it is one of the smallest of all UEFA member-nations.

Inhabitants of Iceland, the oldest republic in the world, began playing the game in 1895, when a Scottish printer and bookseller named James Ferguson introduced it in Reykjavik. Little time was wasted in organizing clubs, and by 1912 an Icelandic championship was under way. International competition was still many years away, but in 1929 the Ithrottasamband Islands (Athletic Union of Iceland, founded in 1912) was admitted to FIFA, and Iceland has remained a respected member of the world body ever since.

The Knattspyrnusamband Islands (KSI) was formed in 1947 as an independent governing body for soccer and immediately received FIFA's blessing. In 1954 Iceland became a charter member of UEFA, and today it remains almost entirely amateur.

Iceland made its international debut against Denmark in Reykjavik, losing 3-0 in 1946, and two years later won for the first time in a home friendly against Finland (2-0). In 1958 an inexperienced national team entered the World Cup qualifying rounds and dropped two games apiece to France and Belgium by an aggregate of 6-26.

Financial difficulties kept Iceland out of further World Cup qualifying rounds until 1974, but it has regularly competed since. Although never a finalist, Iceland is no longer an easy opponent for any rival at home or away.

In domestic competition, the big Reykjavik clubs Fram, KR and Valur have been dominant. KR owns 20 titles, Valur 19 and Fram 18 since league play began in 1912. IA Akranes, a provincial club, won its 13th crown in the 1992 season to close in on the leading trio.

INDIA

Address: All India Football Federation, Netaji Indoor Stadium, Eden Gardens, Calcutta 700 21. *Founded:* 1937. *FIFA:* 1948. *AFC:* 1954. *National stadium:* National Stadium, New Delhi (40,000); *largest stadiums:* Eden Garden Stadium, Calcutta (100,000), Corporation Stadium,

Calicut (100,000). *Colors:* Light blue jerseys, white shorts.

In India, soccer play is centered primarily in Calcutta. In much of the rest of the country, soccer takes a back seat to the traditional national games of field hockey and cricket. The All India Football Federation (AIFF), a truly national association, was founded in 1937 and claimed an affiliated membership of 14 regional associations.

India made its official international debut at the Olympic Games of 1948 in London, losing in the first round to France (Amateur) 2-1. This was followed by two friendlies with Wales (Amateur), lost 4-1 and drawn 0-0 in Wrexham and Swansea, respectively. In 1950 India qualified for the World Cup in Brazil after the withdrawal of Burma (the only other country in its qualifying group), but India also withdrew before the start of the competition, citing financial and organizational pressures.

India qualified for the Olympics again in 1956, and competing against a sparse field of 11 countries—only one of them a top flight team. India just missed collecting a bronze medal by losing to powerful Yugoslavia in the semifinals. In its final appearance in the Olympic Games in 1960, India placed last in its first round group and effectively bowed out of world competition until again entering the 1986 qualifying rounds where two wins over Bangladesh marked an unsuccessful try at the finals.

INDONESIA

Address: Persatuan Sepakbola Seluruh Indonesia (All Indonesia Football Federation), Main Stadium Senagan, Gate VII, P.O. Box 2305, Djakarta. *Founded:* 1930. *FIFA:* 1952. *AFC:* 1954. *National stadium:* Senagan Stadium,

Djakarta (110,000); *largest stadium:* Senagan Stadium. *Colors:* Red jerseys, white shorts.

In the world's largest archipelago, soccer officials have coped surprisingly well with major organizational difficulties. While only a small number of Indonesia's 130 million citizens (spread across 13,000 islands) compete in soccer leagues, the game is very popular and the government has gone to great lengths to accommodate this following.

Indonesia has surfaced in the final rounds of two worldwide competitions. As Dutch East Indies, a representative team of the colonial *voetbalbond* qualified for the 1938 World Cup in France, where it was defeated in the first round. In 1956 Indonesia, a fledgling competitor on the international circuit, went through to the final rounds of the Olympic Games in Melbourne, and held the mighty Soviet Union to a scoreless draw before losing the replay 4-0. These were great moments in Indonesian soccer.

The Dutch were very handy in organizing soccer in their colonies, and in Batavia (Djakarta) they established a governing body as early as 1930. In 1949 the new government of Indonesia gave soccer's governing body its present name, known under the abbreviation PSSI, and introduced a national championship in 1951. Indonesia made its official international debut in the first Asian Games in 1951 at New Delhi. To date Indonesia has been unsuccessful in World Cup qualifying.

IRAN

Address: Iranian Football Federation, Ave Varzandeh No. 10, P.O. Box 11-1642, Tehran. *Founded:* 1922. *FIFA:* 1948. *AFC:* 1958. *National stadium:* Aria Mehre, Karadj Auto Band (100,000); *largest stadium:* Aria Mehre. *Colors:* Green jerseys, white shorts. *Season:* April to February. *Honors:* Asian Cup winner (1968, 1972, 1976).

Iran's solid position as the leader in Asian soccer was virtually assured until the Islamic revolution and the following lengthy war with Iraq. The solidity of Iranian soccer before the revolution was demonstrated by a high degree of organization at both domestic and international levels.

Several cities in Iran were genuine soccer hotbeds, and beginning in the 1960s, this unusual combination of official support and grass roots enthusiasm reaped one reward after another on the playing field. Soccer in the Islamic republic does not occupy a similarly central place in policy, but Iran seems ready to make an impact internationally again in the 1990s.

Other than the presence of European soccer-playing residents, the game gradually infiltrated the country by means of Iranian students returning home from school in Europe. The Persian Amateur Football Federation was founded as early as 1922 ("Iranian" became part of the name in the late 1940s), and until World War II this body functioned primarily to promote the development of soccer as part of the overall sports program.

In 1948 the Iranian federation was admitted to FIFA, and Iran entered international competition in earnest. Its officially recognized debut was a friendly against Turkey at Ankara in 1950, which the Iranians lost 6-1.

Later in that year, Iran played Pakistan in Tehran and lost again, 5-1. In 1951 Iran was one of six countries to compete in the soccer tournament of the first Asian Games in New Delhi, and here it achieved its first victories, a 2-0 win over Burma and a 3-2 defeat of Japan (in a replay after a scoreless draw).

Iran did not enter the Asian Cup until the fourth edition in Tehran in 1968, winning this and the next two editions. In 1968 it went undefeated in four games with victories over Hong Kong, Republic of China, Burma, and Israel. In 1972 at Bangkok, Iran was again undefeated in four games, winning this time over Thailand and Iraq in the first round, Khmer in the semifinals, and Republic of Korea in the final.

At Tehran in 1976, the Iranians continued their winning streak with victories over Iraq and Yemen PDR in the first round, the People's Republic of China in the semifinals (after extra time), and Kuwait in the final. In its three consecutive Asian Cup triumphs, Iran won 12 straight games and amassed a goal difference of 34-6, elevating itself to the top of the overall Asian Cup standings.

Much of Iran's growth as an international power during the 1960s and 1970s was due to the steady influx of good European coaches. Irishman Frank O'Farrell guided Iran through the successful qualifying rounds the 1978 World Cup before handing the reins over to his assistant, Heshmat Mohadjerani, the first Iranian to manage the national team.

To qualify for the 1978 World Cup, Iran played 12 games without a defeat. It drew with Republic of Korea both home and away and defeated Saudi Arabia, Syria, Kuwait, Australia, and Hong Kong twice each.

In the 1974 World Cup qualifying rounds, Iran had been narrowly edged out of the running by Australia after eliminating Syria, Korea PDR, and Kuwait, so qualification for the Argentina finals was celebrated.

In Argentina, Iran gained an unexpected 1-1 draw with Scotland but lost 3-0 to eventual finalist Holland and lost 4-1 to Peru. Iran did not attempt qualification again until 1990 when it was eliminated in the opening round by China.

Iran is back in the tournament qualifying phase in 1994.

IRAQ

Address: Iraq Football Association, Youth City, P.O. Box 484, Baghdad. *Founded:* 1948. *FIFA:* 1951. *AFC:* 1971. *National stadium:* Sha'ab Stadium, Baghdad (50,000); *largest stadium:* Sha'ab Stadium. *Colors:* White jerseys, white shorts. *Season:* October to May.

Iraqi soccer has taken a sharp swing upward in the 1970s and 1980s. The national team first attempted to qualify for the World Cup in 1974. Grouped with Australia (the eventual qualifier), Indonesia, and New Zealand, it lost only one match in six (away to Australia), and won three, including two against New Zealand; the rest were drawn.

Despite political unrest and the long war with Iran, the Iraquis qualified for the finals in 1986 as soccer continued to grow despite the troubles at home. In Mexico, though, the team was beaten 1-0 by both Paraguay and Mexico and 2-1 by Belgium.

In 1990 qualifying, when the Iraquis were among the favorites, Qatar upset them in the opening phase. The subsequent Gulf War and United Nations' sanctions have cast doubts on the status of the national team, but it will attempt qualification for the 1994 event in the United States.

IRELAND, NORTHERN

Address: Irish Football Association Ltd., 20 Windsor Avenue, Belfast BT9 6EG. *Founded:* 1880. *FIFA:* 1911-20, 1924-28, 1946. *UEFA:* 1954. *National stadium:* Windsor Park, Belfast (58,000); *largest stadium:* Windsor Park. *Col-*

ors: Green jerseys with white trim, white shorts. *Season:* August to May.

For almost 60 years, Irish soccer has been split into two camps: Northern Ireland (Ulster) and the Republic of Ireland. But during the four decades between the first appearance of organized soccer on Irish shores in 1878 and the birth of the Republic in 1921, there was only one Ireland and one Irish Football Association.

In 1921 the Republic of Ireland formed its own governing body—the Football Association of Ireland—and set out on its own.

Because the focus of Irish soccer and the original Irish Football Association had always been in Ulster, soccer in Northern Ireland suffered little when the south broke away, and, to a great extent, Northern Ireland remained the more significant of the two Irelands in international competition until the 1988 European Championship and the 1990 World Cup.

Northern Ireland has produced several players of world–class caliber, including the incomparable George Best and goalkeeper Pat Jennings, but it has always struggled when facing larger rivals.

The Irish Football Association, as one of the four British governing bodies, sits permanently on the International Football Association Board. In international competition, the Irish F.A. was the last British association to play a non-British international, facing France in 1951. Seven years later, however, it qualified for and reached the quarterfinals of the World Cup.

The first Irish club devoted entirely to soccer was Cliftonville F.C., founded in 1879 by J. M. McAlery in Ballyclare, County Antrim. Most Irish clubs that sprang up immediately after Cliftonville contained Scottish players, and Scot

tish-based clubs dominated Belfast competition for almost a decade.

In 1880 McAlery led the formation of the Irish Football Association (IFA) in Belfast with jurisdiction over all of Ireland. Its ties to the English, Scottish, and Welsh associations were made official, and an IFA Cup, Britain's fourth cup competition, was introduced that same year.

In 1890-91, the Irish League was formed by Clarence, Cliftonville, Distillery, Glentoran, Linfield, Milford, Old Park, and Ulster. Linfield has been the power ever since, accumulating 40 titles by 1992. Glentoran, another original member, had 16 but neither Distillery (6) nor Cliftonville (2) have been that successful despite their historical importance to the game.

In 1882 Ireland entered international competition with a 13-0 loss to England in Belfast. The following week it met Wales in Wrexham, Ireland, losing 7-1. Further crushing defeats to England and Wales followed.

In 1884, in what became the first edition of the Home International Championship, Ireland made its debut against Scotland, losing 5-0 in Belfast. More often than not, Ireland finished last in those early editions of the Home Internationals, but for the next 70 years this series provided the entire Irish international schedule.

With the formation of the Dublin-based Football Association of Ireland in 1921, some Ulster clubs defected to the south. The famous 1923 meeting of the four British associations determined the autonomy of the Dublin association and required the defectors to return to the fold.

From that point on, all clubs located in the five counties of the north remained affiliated with the Belfast association—until Derry City joined the Republic of Ireland's league in the mid-1980s.

The 1950s began a successful era in international competition, culminating in the 1958 World Cup appearance. With home defeats over Italy and Portugal, this marvelously talented team advanced to the final rounds in Sweden under the management of Peter Doherty, holding Italy to a 1-0 win in Rome and winning the return match in Belfast.

Meanwhile, Portugal was disposed of by a 4-1 aggregate. In Sweden, the Irish outplayed Czechoslovakia in the first round, winning 1-0 on a goal by the Leeds United left half Wilbur Cush.

A 3-1 loss to Argentina, Northern Ireland's first South American opponent, temporarily derailed the Irish, but they reemerged with great flair against the physically strong West Germans. Only a mighty 35-yard goal by German star Uwe Seeler prevented the Irish from upsetting the World Cup holders, and the final result was a surprising 2-2 draw.

This exciting match represented a high point in Irish soccer, enabling Northern Ireland to meet Czechoslovakia in the play-off. The Irish team defeated the Czechs 2-1, after extra time, on two goals by the Aston Villa left wing Peter McParland, who had also scored three of his team's four goals in earlier games.

Northern Ireland advanced to the quarter-finals with this win and found itself pitted against the French team of Kopa, Fontaine, and Jonquet, whose goal-scoring might was overwhelming.

The Irish lost 4-0 and bowed out of its first World Cup. The backbone of the World Cup team was Tottenham Hotspur's right half Danny Blanchflower, a virtual midfield coach on the field whose knowledge of the game made him one of the most respected British players of the postwar era.

Unfortunately, the George Best era of the 1960s and early 1970s did not produce the desired international results, and Northern Ireland teams during the strife-torn years of the 1970s were decidedly weak.

There were two more World Cup final appearances for Northern Ireland in the 1980s, the first a surprisingly strong performance in Spain, when a team led by goalkeeper Pat Jennings was in its prime, and a second in 1986 in Mexico that saw the team on the other side of its best.

In 1982, when Norman Whiteside became the youngest player ever to take part in a finals match, the Northern Irish surprised many by qualifying for the second round. Among their victories was a 1-0 decision over the host country after drawing two matches against Yugoslavia and Honduras.

The second round showed the fighting spirit of the Irish side as it gained a 2-2 draw with a good Austrian team before bowing to the by-then rampant French 4-1. By all standards it had been a most successful World Cup campaign.

Jennings was the star of the 1986 appearance, ending his long and wonderful career in Guadalajara against Brazil, but the Irish side was not up to the form of the 1982 eleven. After opening with a 1-1 draw against Algeria, Northern Ireland lost to both Spain and Brazil and failed to advance past the opening stage.

Northern Ireland and the Republic of Ireland had never met on the playing field before they were finally drawn together in the same qualifying group for the 1978-80 European Football Championship. Their first meeting, held in Dublin in 1978, resulted in a scoreless draw. Subsequently they have met five more times, including twice in 1994 World Cup qualifying rounds.

IRELAND, REPUBLIC OF

Address: Cumann Peile Na h-Eireann (Football Association of Ireland), 80, Merrion Square, South Dublin 2. *Founded:* 1921. *FIFA:* 1923. *UEFA:* 1954. *Largest stadium:* Landsdowne Road, Dublin (48,000). *Colors:* Green jerseys with white trim, white shorts. *Season:* August to May.

The liabilities of international politics long remained at the center of Ireland's game since the founding of the independent state in 1921, confusion over international recognition and the question of birthrights of Ireland and Ulster players preventing the country from developing to its fullest potential until Jack Charlton took charge of the national side in 1987.

Capitalizing on the support and enthusiasm of Irish Republic fans Charlton convinced Ireland's best players that there was a future with the Republic's national team. The result was qualification for the 1988 European Championships, a berth in the 1990 World Cup quarterfinal and the great era in Ireland's soccer history. Ironically, Charlton is English, a member of the 1966 World Cup winners, but Irish fans have adopted him as "King Jack."

When the first Irish Football Association (then responsible for all Ireland) was founded in 1880, it was unhesitatingly located in Belfast rather than in Dublin. It followed that with the exception of Shelbourne F.C., all the leading clubs of pre-independence Ireland came from the North, with its concentration of population, industry, and experienced players from England and Scotland.

The first soccer club founded in present-day Ireland was the Dublin Association in 1883, though some historians have placed the formation of Bohemians F.C., also of Dublin, in 1882.

Dublin Association played against a team from Dublin University in the year of its birth, and competitive soccer in the South got under way.

Shelbourne's Irish Cup victories in 1906, 1911, and 1920, and Bohemians' cup win in 1908, were the only honors won by southern teams under a unified Irish association. The league championship trophy never left Ulster.

The proper history of Republic of Ireland soccer begins with independence from Great Britain in 1921. Immediately after World War I, many southern clubs defected from the Irish Football Association, which was still centered in Belfast.

The Irish F.A. did not sanction these defections, but there was little it could do about it. In 1921, the year of Great Britain's offer of dominion status to Ireland, the Football Association of Ireland was founded in Dublin.

The Irish Republic's international debut was made at the Olympic Games of 1924 in Paris, where it defeated Bulgaria 1-0 and lost to the Netherlands 2-1 after extra time. Having declined to enter the World Cup of 1930 in Montevideo, the Irish Free State enthusiastically tried to qualify for the 1934 and 1938 world championships. It was eliminated from the final rounds in 1934 by the Netherlands and in 1937 by Norway after an aggregate score of 5-6, a narrow defeat.

Though the Republic of Ireland and Northern Ireland did not play each other until 1978, the ice was broken with other British associations in 1946, when England won a friendly in Dublin by 1-0 despite superior play by the Irish team. The

return friendly in Liverpool three years later resulted in England's first defeat by a foreign country on home soil. The score was 2-0, and the Irish team was made up entirely of players from English clubs.

England figured prominently in Irish fortunes again in 1957 when Ireland was grouped with England and Denmark in World Cup qualifying rounds. After Denmark was easily vanquished, Ireland lost decisively in England. In the return match at Dublin the result was a 1-1 draw, but England did not equalize until the final seconds of the match and only after consistent domination of the game by the Irish.

Ireland has attempted to qualify for each World Cup since 1934 and each European Championship since 1958, succeeding finally in the 1988 European tournament. There the Irish upset England 1-0, but did not reach the semifinals.

The 1990 World Cup team was based on this fine set of players and went all the way to the final eight before bowing 1-0 to host Italy. That game ended with Jack Charlton called back by the adoring Irish fans in the Rome Olympic Stadium to accept a late night salute.

Among the nagging problems that lingered for many decades after independence was the question of both Irish associations claiming the rights to field certain Irish players. The FIFA ruling on this matter for many years was that Northern Ireland could select players born in Ireland for its matches with other British associations, but was restricted to Ulster-born players for matches with anyone else. The F.A. of Ireland vehemently, but unsuccessfully, opposed this ruling.

In 1954 the FIFA ruled on the names of the two Irelands, the Republic of Ireland and Northern Ireland. The FAI's recognition of eligibility through grandparental heritage has helped the Republic to widen its pool of available talent.

The League of Ireland in 1921 consisted entirely of Dublin clubs. The first outsider was Athlone Town, elected in 1922. By far the most successful club has been the famous Shamrock Rovers, which has won a record 14 championships and 23 cups.

ISRAEL

Address: Hitachdut Iekaduregel Beisrael (Israel Football Association), 12 Carlibach Street, P.O.B. 20188, Tel Aviv. *Founded:* 1928. *FIFA:* 1929. *National stadium:* Ramat-Gan (55,000); *largest stadium:* Ramat-Gan. *Colors:* Blue jerseys, white shorts. *Season:* September to June. *Honors:* Asian Cup winner (1964), runner-up (1956, 1960).

Israel has had a difficult soccer history for political reasons. Israeli teams at both national and club levels won international competitions and have placed high in the standings of almost every Asian tournament they entered. From the beginning, however, Israel has been forced to seek international opposition on the playing field outside of its immediate region because of Arab opposition to their state's existence.

One exception to this, ironically, was a 1934 match against Egypt, when a Jewish-based national team played under the name Palestine. In World Cup and Olympic qualification rounds and other official Asian tournaments, international administrators long have had to schedule Israeli teams around potential confrontation with Arab opposition.

Eventually, Israel was relocated as a European member nation for the 1994 World Cup and Israeli clubs began participation in the UEFA club tournaments.

That solution was long in coming. In the mid-1970s the power base in the Asian Football Confederation changed drastically. In 1976, in one of the most overtly political moves by an official governing body in the history of soccer, Israel was expelled from the AFC. The Arab bloc and friends of the People's Republic of China struck a deal to get the necessary votes to admit China and remove Israel.

FIFA deplored this action and set about to have Israel reinstated or find it a new home. In 1978 the European confederation turned down Israel's request for membership, citing logistical and financial difficulties, leaving the Israel Football Association to seek membership with Oceania. This created a fine Israeli rivalry with Australia but did little to support the idea that sport and politics could be kept separate.

Soccer had been brought to Palestine along with the infusion of British military personnel during World War I. Interest in the game was compounded immediately after the war by the immigration of European Jews who had been exposed to soccer in their native countries. Clubs and local tournaments sprang up quickly during the 1920s, and the Palestine Football Association was founded in 1928 in Tel Aviv.

The new association introduced the annual Palestine Challenge Cup—a knockout competition—that same year and a national league in 1932. The early winners of the league and cup were the same clubs that still dominate the Israeli game—Hapoel Tel Aviv and Maccabi Tel Aviv.

In 1934 Palestine entered World Cup qualification rounds and made its international debut against Egypt in a home and away series to determine the Asia-Africa berth. In 1948 the authority of the Palestine Football Association was passed on to the new Hitachdut Lekaduregel Beisrael (Israel Football Association).

In its first international game under the name of Israel, the national team was initially grouped with European opposition in qualifying rounds for the 1950 World Cup, this time with Yugoslavia, which won both legs and qualified. Israel then played home and away friendlies with Turkey; in Tel Aviv it won its first international as an independent country, 5-1.

Full international opposition was exceedingly difficult to find during the 1950s, though many European clubs and representative teams visited Israel. Seeking a berth in the World Cup continued to provide Israel with its most strenuous challenge.

Greece and Yugoslavia both won home and away legs in 1954 to eliminate the Israelis, and in 1958 Israel was grouped with Turkey and Indonesia after FIFA's original choices for that group (all African) refused to play them.

Turkey and Indonesia also refused to meet Israel, and it appeared that Israel would enter the final rounds of the World Cup in Sweden without having played a single game. This being unacceptable, FIFA selected Wales to play a home and away qualifying series with Israel, and Wales won both legs 2-0 to gain the berth.

Having joined the Asian Football Confederation in 1956, Israel entered the first Asian Cup that same year. All matches were played in Hong Kong and there were only four participants. Israel placed second, defeating Hong Kong and South Vietnam and losing to South Korea, the winner. Israel also entered the second Asian Cup in 1960, held in Seoul, and placed second by defeating South Vietnam and Taiwan and again losing to South Korea.

In 1964 Israel itself was the host, and the field was again limited to four. This time Israel emerged with its first international triumph by defeating Hong Kong, India, and South Korea.

The Israelis' last chance to compete in the Asian Cup came in 1968 in Tehran, where they finished a distant third in a field of five, winning over Taiwan and Hong Kong and losing to Burma and Asia's emerging power, Iran.

In 1968 the Israelis qualified for the Olympic Games in Mexico and achieved their first great international success by advancing to the quarterfinals at the expense of Ghana and El Salvador.

Israel battled Bulgaria to a 1-1 draw and then had the misfortune of losing the coin toss for the semifinal.

Having gained valuable experience playing in Mexico's high altitudes in 1968, Israel achieved its greatest feat in 1970 when it qualified for the World Cup final rounds—held in Mexico.

The Israelis had to eliminate South Korea and Australia to get there, but in their first round group there was a whole new set of challenges with the presence of Italy, Uruguay, and Sweden—each great international competitors. Israel began by losing to Uruguay 2-0, a respectable outcome, but in its next match held Sweden to a 1-1 draw on a goal by inside left Mordecai Spiegler.

In the third match of the first round group, the Italians tried desperately to punch their way through Israel's defense in an unattractive game, but Israel held on for a scoreless draw. It was Israel's first success against a proven world power, though in the standings it finished at the bottom of its group.

Since then Israel has not reached another final round despite several near misses. In 1990 it lost a playoff against Colombia by a single goal after winning the Oceania zone.

But Israel's return to Europe in 1994 World Cup qualifying revealed the gap between the Israeli team and the more powerful continental sides as it was beaten at home by Bulgaria, France, and Sweden in the first half of the qualifying competition.

ITALY

Address: Federazione Italiana Giuoco Calcio, Via Gregorio Allegri, 14, C.P. 2450, 1-00198-Roma. *Founded:* 1898. *FIFA:* 1905. *UEFA:* 1954. *National stadium:* Stadio Olimpico, Rome (78,000); *largest stadium:* Stadio Olimpico. *Colors:* Blue jerseys, white shorts. *Season:* September to June. *Honors:* World Cup winner (1934, 1938, 1982), runner-up (1970); Olympic Games winner (1936), third place (1928, 1960); European Football Championship winner (1968).

Italy's place among the elite of world soccer is assured on several counts. The Italians dominated international competition during the 1930s with two World Championships and an Olympic gold medal, adding a third World Cup in 1986.

Italian clubs have constantly been at the forefront of the European game since international club competitions became popular in the 1950s, and Italian soccer has been one of Europe's greatest spawning grounds for talented players.

The successful marketing of postwar Italian clubs has led to a high concentration of international stars, helping to make the Italian League a showcase for the world's best talent. From the 1960s to the 1980s, Italy was also the bastion of defensive soccer, but that image seemed to be changing with the arrival of a new collection of attacking stars.

The Roman football tradition in Italy, however, was carried at least into the Renaissance itself, because in Florence, between the 15th and 17th centuries, was the most glorious example of soccer ancestry before the modern era.

This was the ritualized football game known as *giuoco del calcio fiorentino* ("Florentine kickball"). *Calcio* was a regulated game, more closely resembling rugby than soccer, that was played by the aristocracy during the Medici epoch, and it featured much running, jumping, and tackling (in the American football sense). Goals were scored by throwing the ball over a designated spot on the perimeter of the field.

The "field" was actually the Piazza di Santa Croce, and games were held every night between Epiphany and Lent. Its avowed purpose was to express the aristocratic graces and celebrate the common rank of all participants, but, as in the art and literature of the period, it was also typical of the Renaissance revival of classical mores.

Calcio was an aristocrat's game—meant for a certain time and place—and it did not survive into the modern era, except as an annual pageant for tourists. Its only legacy is the use of the word itself in place of an Italian adaptation of the English word "football," e.g., Federazione Italiana Giuoco Calcio (Italian Kickball Game Federation).

The British imported modern soccer to Italian shores, though an Italian businessman, Edoardo Bisio, is generally credited with introducing it in Turin in 1887. The game first took root in that city, spreading rapidly to Genoa and Milan, and from there to other cities in the northern provinces. The first club was Football Club Internazionale (not to be confused with modern Internazionale Milan), founded in Turin in 1890.

F.C. Torinese was formed in Turin in 1894, and the Sezione Calcio della Societe Ginnastica di Torino followed soon after that. A fourth major Turin club, Sport Club Juventus, was formed in 1897. In 1893 the Genoa Cricket and Football Club—il vecchio Genoa—was established, destined to become the first great club in Italian soccer. A second Genoa club, Sezione Calcio

dell'Andrea Doria, was started in 1895. In Milan, the first club was the Milan Cricket and Football Club, founded in 1899.

All but one of these pioneering clubs were to figure prominently in the development of the Italian game. In 1906 F.C. Internazionale merged with F.C. Torinese to form the venerable F.C. Torino (later Torino).

In 1899 S.C. Juventus became F.C. Juventus, Italy's most popular club after the 1920s. Milan C.F.C. was eventually renamed AC Milan, and in 1908 spawned F.C Internazionale when a group of dissident Milan players broke away to form their own club.

Genoa Cricket and Football Club proudly holds on to its original name to this day, as do dozens of other Italian clubs with English-sounding names. In 1946 Andrea Doria merged with another Genoese club, Sampierdarenese, to form UC Sampdoria, Genoa's archrival. Of the seven pioneering clubs, only Ginnastica Torino did not survive the first years of Italian soccer.

Meanwhile, the game spread across the northern provinces from the early centers in Piemonte, Liguria, and Lombardy. It was being played by students in Vicenza by 1898 and in Padua by 1899. In Bergamo, Busto Arizio, Vercelli, Udine, Ascoli, and Palermo, sports clubs or gymnastic societies that in later years would become the parent bodies of important soccer clubs were founded before the turn of the century. Juventus still has the most Italian titles (22) with Inter (13), AC Milan (12) and Genoa (9) well behind.

In 1898 the Federazione Italiana del Football was founded in Turin, and in 1905 it became one of the first associations after the charter group of seven to join FIFA. Its present name, Federazione Italiana Giuoco Calcio (FIGC), was adopted in 1909.

An Italian championship was also introduced in 1898, but did not become a national league until 1929-30. The FIGC was 12 years old before Italy finally entered international competition.

In 1910 Italy hosted France in Milan and won 6-2. Ten days later, the Italians traveled to Budapest and lost 6-1 to Hungary. Before the outbreak of World War I, Italy played in 19 full internationals, winning six and losing nine.

The sophisticated Central European teams, Austria and Hungary, were responsible for five of these losses. Italy's biggest disappointment was a loss to lowly Finland in extra time at the 1912 Olympic Games in Stockholm and subsequent eliminating from the competition.

The manager of the 1912 Olympic team was a Piemontese named Vittorio Pozzo, destined to become an outstanding figure in Italian soccer history. Among other things, he was to be the guiding force behind Italy's great successes of the interwar years and a prime mover in the creation of a national league.

He returned briefly as manager of Italy at the 1924 Olympics, and in 1929 he became the permanent Commissario Tecnico of the national team, a post he held for 20 years. His influence was seen in Italy's winning of the first International Cup in 1927-29 and the bronze medal at the Amsterdam Olympics in 1928, but the ultimate effect of his leadership was Italy's outright domination of world soccer during the 1930s.

Pozzo developed a system, known as *metodo,* from similar tactics used by Manchester United, the club he had watched closely during the first decade of the century as a resident in England. The key was an attacking center half who distributed freely to either wing, and Pozzo's ideal center half was eventually found in Luisito Monti, the Argentine *oriundo* ("foreigner of Italian extraction"), who joined the national side in 1932.

Italy's winning form commenced immediately after Pozzo took over in 1929. Between 1930 and the outbreak of war in 1940, Italy lost only seven games out of a total 67 full internationals, a mere two of these at home. Austria and Czechoslovakia accounted for two apiece, and international powers England and Spain accounted for two more between them.

Austria, the second great international power during the 1930s, was Italy's strongest opposition until the German occupation in 1938. Italy's tough blend of hard tackling and scintillating skills were in marked contrast to the slower, short passing "Danubian" game of Austria. This endlessly fascinating contrast, as well as the presence of Europe's two most celebrated national managers, Pozzo and his Austrian counterpart Hugo Meisl, resulted in one of the greatest rivalries in soccer history.

In 1934, with Italy itself playing host, the *Azzurri* ("blues"—so-called for the uniform color) won the World Championship before zealous home crowds. Mussolini, a devoted *Azzurri* supporter, witnessed the victorious final in the Stadio PNF (Rome) against Czechoslovakia, but the big match of the tournament was played in the semifinals at Milan's San Siro, where an off-form Austria allowed Italy to advance to the final with a 1-0 win. Italy's goal was fittingly scored by its Argentine right wing Guaita. Its earlier wins in the first round had been against the United States (7-1) and Spain, the latter a replay after a 1-1 draw the day before.

In the final, Italy won 2-1 on goals by the sublime Orsi, another *oriundo,* and Schiavio. Away from the playing field, the entire competition was dominated by Fascist salutes and martial music, celebrations, and tributes to Il Duce. On the field, the *Azzurri* had won their first World Championship with a fair bit of muscle and Vittorio Pozzo's wholly genuine enthusiasm.

In 1938, under more tenuous conditions in France, Italy returned to the World Cup without Monti, Orsi, or the veteran goalkeeper Combi. But Giuseppe Meazza, the gifted inside right, was joined on the forward line by Silvio Piola, who was to be the hero of this World Championship and an Italian idol for years to come. In the first round, however, Italy stumbled over its 1936 Olympic nemesis, Norway, and was barely able to achieve a 2-1 win in extra time on a goal by Piola.

None of its later opponents—France, Brazil, and Hungary—were as troublesome as Norway, though Brazil and Hungary were astonishingly gifted teams. In the final against Hungary, Italy was superior in all respects. Piola and the left wing Colaussi scored a pair of goals each, Hungary managed only two, and Italy won its second World Championship.

In contrast to 1934, Italy's success in France was untainted by political factors, and not only was Italy's the best team in the competition, but its style had become less physical and more attractive in appearance. This was the finest team Italy had ever produced, and its victory represented the high point in Italian soccer.

After World War II Torino had risen to the forefront, destined to become the finest club team Italy had yet seen. Torino won the 1942-43 series, and when the league resumed in 1945-46 (a 1943-44 season was cut short by the Allied invasions), Torino emerged on top again. It won in 1947 (by 10 points) and 1948 (by an astounding 16 points and scoring 125 goals in 40 games). Among its stars was the legendary inside left Valentino Mazzola, the father of Sandro Mazzola of later Inter Milan fame, and eight members of the national team.

Four weeks before the end of the 1948-49 season, Torino was four points clear at the top of the standings and sure of the league title for a fifth consecutive year. But the airplane that was carrying the team home from a friendly in Lisbon crashed in the Turin suburb of Superga, killing all aboard, including the entire first and second team, manager, coach, and trainer. A state funeral was held, and the nation went into deep mourning.

The remaining four games in its league schedule were played out by Torino's youth team against the youth teams of the opposition, and all four were won. Torino was awarded the championship on the basis of these results.

The Torino disaster shook Italian soccer to its foundation, for the national team was undone. To add to the confusion, the game in Italy was in the throes of a revolutionary tactical transformation. Pozzo had finally given way during the 1940s to his *Sistema* ("system")—the nomenclature here is significant—in which he replaced the attacking center half with a full-blown stopper.

This change, made with great reluctance by Pozzo, was noteworthy because it anticipated Italy's preoccupation—begun in the late 1940s—with defensive tactics. *Catenaccio,* the defensively oriented system in which there were four positioned defenders as well as one mobile defender (the *libero,* or sweeper) behind them, began at Triestina in 1948 with considerable success under manager Nereo Rocco.

By the early 1950s, *catenaccio* ("great chain" or "bolt") had spread to some clubs of the upper divisions, especially the smaller ones which found the going very difficult against the Milan and Turin giants that were importing one lethal goalscorer after another.

Unfortunately, the influx of foreign stars, particularly in forward positions, and the negative attitude engendered by *catenaccio* resulted in a disappointing period for the *Azzurri* in international competition. Though Italy qualified for the World Championships of 1950, 1954, 1962, and 1966, it failed to advance to the second round each time.

In 1958 Italy failed to qualify altogether when the Northern Ireland team with Danny Blanchflower and Jimmy McIlroy won both Rome and Belfast legs in the qualifying round.

These results were shocking to a country used to hovering near the top echelons of world soccer, and the FIGC finally accepted the fact that Italian players were not getting enough top-flight playing time. In 1964 the floodgates were closed to foreign players completely, not to reopen again until the final two decades of the 20th Century.

But the ultimate shock came at the 1966 World Cup in England, when the resourceful North Koreans defeated a star-filled Italian team 1-0 in the opening round. Embarrassed and fearful of widespread reaction at home, the team flew back to Genoa in the early hours of the morning and was greeted by a barrage of vegetables.

Many jobs were lost, and *Azzurri* team members were dogged for months by derisive fans at league matches. A semblance of order was finally restored in time for the 1966-68 European Nations' Cup, but it was an uninspiring team that ultimately won that competitio—in Rome—after a replay against Yugoslavia.

At the World Cup of 1970 in Mexico, a team replete with world class talent was expected to atone for the sins of 1966, and left side striker Gigi Riva was expected to do more than the others. Its droll *catenaccio* was still at the heart of the plan, but with Mazzola, Rivera, and Riva, there was thought to be enough striking power to have an effective counterattack.

Concern mounted when Italy won its first round group after scoring only one goal. The team next faced Mexico, the weakest of the eight

quarterfinalists, and advanced with ease to the next round. Its best match was the semifinal against Germany FR, that it won 4-3 in a thrilling—though not necessarily good—end-to-end contest between strikers and defenders.

In the final, Italy was given the thankless task of holding back one of the greatest goal-scoring machines ever assembled, as Brazil offered Italy and the world a textbook lesson on ball control skills and intuitive playmaking. The result was a respectable 4-1 loss to Pelé and company, and the Italians went home with a second place medal. In 1974 Italy was once again shut out of second round World Cup competition by Argentina, its old South American adversary, and Poland, the revelation of the tournament.

The Italian story from Argentina to the present is something of a roller-coaster. The 1978 squad performed well in South America, ultimately finishing fourth in a World Cup dominated by the two South American powers, host Argentina and Brazil, and the reigning European power, Holland. While Italy's opening round included a 1-0 victory over Argentina—the only loss suffered by the winners on their way to the title—there was a hint of fragility about the team that was exposed in the second round.

An opening 0-0 draw with defending champion West Germany was followed by a slender 1-0 victory over Austria. A place in the final vanished when Holland put the *Azzurri* out, 2-1 in what effectively was a semifinal game even though the second round was played in the group system.

Goalkeeper Dino Zoff took some criticism for allowing a long-range Aarie Haan goal in Argentina but he had more than redemption four years later when Italy, in Spain, won its third world championship. It was almost completely unexpected, especially after the 1980 European Championship had been staged in Italy without home team success. There Italy had finished fourth in the finals and fostered little expectation that they would emerge from Spain as champions in a tournament that featured a powerful Argentine team, a Brazil that reminded some observers of the great 1970 side, and the usual strong German presence.

To make matters even more improbable, the man who emerged as Italy's hero alongside Zoff was striker Paolo Rossi, who had just come off a year's suspension from top-level play. It took him the first round to regain his touch, but from there to the finish he was the star of the championship. Italy, in fact, barely made it to the second round on goal difference after an unimpressive first phase that consisted of draws against Poland, Peru, and Cameroon.

The second round presented a totally different story. Argentina was upset 2-1, and then Rossi beat Brazil with a hat trick that put Italy into the semifinals and sent arguably the best team in the tournament home without a trophy. Helped by the absence of suspended Zbigniew Boniek, Italy brushed aside Poland in the semifinals, with Rossi again scoring both goals.

In the final against West Germany, Rossi opened the scoring, then Marco Tardelli and Alessandro Altobelli finished off a remarkable 3-1 victory in the Bernabeu Stadium.

The rocky ride resumed almost immediately, though, when Italy failed to qualify for the 1984 European Championship and made a generally unimpressive appearance in the 1986 World Cup as the defending champions. France eliminated the *Azzurri* from that World Cup in the second round.

Italian soccer did another turnaround with a rebuilt side, performing well enough in the 1988 European Championship to reach the semifinal and lay the groundwork for the squad that would serve as 1990 World Cup host.

That Italy did not prevail in 1990 is well known, but it is harder to summarize what went wrong. Indeed, fate seemed to be smiling on the *Azzurri* when Salvatore Schillaci came off the substitute's bench in Italy's opening game to power home a header that defeated Austria.

After a lackluster 1-0 win over the weak United States, Italy gained momentum, defeating Czechoslovakia, Uruguay, and Ireland as Schillaci—the tournament scoring leader—became the hero of the nation.

It all went dreadfully wrong in the theatrical semifinal played in Napoli, where Diego Maradona's Argentina prevailed on a penalty kick tiebreaker after a night of incredible tension and drama.

Maradona, of course, had added to the script by appealing to the fans of his Italian League club to support him; there was even a hint of his using the traditional rivalry between Naples and the rest of Italy to stir up the pot. Whatever the motive, the Sao Paulo Stadium crowd was not as boisterously supportive as the Rome Olympic Stadium faithful had been, even when Schillaci, again, put Italy ahead.

Argentina drew level through Claudio Caniggia and the extra time, the first period of which lasted almost 23 minutes (for reasons known only to the French referee), was almost unbearable. The Italian crowd seemed to sense a operatic ending, and it came when Sergio Goychochea, Argentine's penalty-kick saving hero of the World Cup, prevailed in the tiebreaker.

The World Cup seemed to end that night in Naples even though three games—including Italy's eventual third place victory over England at Bari—remained to be played. A country that had turned the World Cup into a festival returned to normal and let the rest of the soccer world get on with its business.

Despite the pervasive influence of *catenaccio,* Italy's biggest contribution to postwar soccer has been its great success in European club competition. Juventus, Inter Milan, and AC Milan have all won the European Cup. Fiorentina, AC Milan, Juventus, and Sampdoria have captured the Cup Winners Cup and Roma, Juventus, Napoli and Inter have all won the UEFA Cup. Juventus is one of only three European clubs (Ajax and Barcelona, the others) to have won each of Europe's prestigious club prizes.

In the 1990s, Italian clubs continue to line up the finest talent, so much so that the dominant AC Milan side signed six of the world's best players even though league rules allowed only three to play in any match.

With the changing nature of the European Economic Community and UEFA's concern about the stockpiling of talent it seemed likely that the issue of powerful Italian clubs controlling a large share of the game's big names would continue to percolate well into the 1990s.

IVORY COAST

Address: Federation Ivoirienne de Football, Stade Felix Houphouet Boigny, B.P. 1202, Abidjan. *Founded:* 1960. *FIFA:* 1960. *CAF:* 1960. *National stadium:* Stade Houphouet-Boigny, Abidjan (27,456); *largest stadium:* Stade Houphouet-Boigny. *Colors:* Orange jerseys, white shorts. *Season:* November to August. *Honors:* African Championship (1992).

Ivory Coast ranks with Guinea and Senegal as the leading exponent of soccer in French-speaking West Africa. Ties with the French have always been strong in the Ivory Coast, and this fact quickened public interest in the game.

After World War II, there were links with the colonial soccer federation of French West Africa in Dakar, and by the 1950s Abidjan, the capital, had become one of the most active soccer-playing cities in the region. A national championship and cup competition (Coupe Nationale) were established in the early 1960s.

The national team, known as *les elephants,* became one of the first representatives of the former French colonies to qualify for the final rounds of the African Nations' Cup in 1965 and won the trophy in 1992. They had won third place in 1965, 1968, and 1986 before breaking through. Ivory Coast has not been able to translate that success in Africa into a World Cup finals place as yet. Their best opportunity may come in 1994, as their 1992 African title side is the basis for the Cup entry.

At club level, Stade Abidjan made an early impression by winning the 1966 African Champions Cup but it was again not until 1992 that another team, Africa Sports, won a major title. They captured the African Cup Winners Cup.

JAMAICA

Address: Jamaica Football Association, Room 9, National Stadium, Kingston 8. *Founded:* 1910. *FIFA:* 1962. *CONCACAF:* 1963. *National stadium:* National Stadium, Kingston (40,000); *largest stadium:* National Stadium. *Colors:* Green jerseys, black shorts. *Season:* August to April.

British residents introduced the game of soccer to Jamaica during the last years of the nineteenth century, and the Jamaican Football Federation (JFF), founded in 1910, was affiliated with the Football Association in London until indepen dence in 1962. The Federation in its name was changed to Association in the early 1970s.

The first recorded international by a Jamaican team was during the first Championship of the Central American and Caribbean Confederation in 1930 in Havana. Financial limitations were long an obstacle for the JFA but recent years have seen growth in soccer.

When Jamaica won entry into the 1991 CONCACAF Gold Cup as Caribbean champion, the resulting interest in the team gave the game a needed boost. There were large crowds to see the 1994 World Cup qualifying competition, but the Jamaicans failed to reach the final stage of that event.

JAPAN

Address: Nippon Shukyu Kyokai (Football Association of Japan), 1-1-1 Jinnan, Shibuya-Ku, Tokyo. *Founded:* 1921. *FIFA:* 1929-45, 1950. *AFC:* 1954. *National stadium:* National Stadium of Tokyo (72,000); *largest stadium:* National Stadium. *Colors:* Blue jerseys, white shorts. *Season:* March to January. *Honors:* Asian Cup winner (1992).

Japan is taking steps to become a force in soccer in the next century. While Japanese national teams have a long history of participating in Asian competitions, the game made limited headway. With strong sponsorship from industrial and commercial enterprises, Japan will launch a professional league in 1993 and is bidding to host the 2002 World Cup. Japan's customary devotion to excellence has already made its mark on the domestic game, and Japanese players and officials have impressed foreign observers.

It is believed that modern soccer was introduced in Japan by an English teacher named Johns in 1874 at the Kogakuryo School just north of Tokyo. In a pattern not unlike that of China, the game was primarily restricted to a small number of schools until well after the turn of the century; few Japanese were exposed to soccer unless they had connections with British-oriented learning institutions. The growth of the Olympic movement in Japan resulted in the first steps toward organized teams.

In 1921 the Nippon Shukyu Kyokai (Football Association of Japan) was founded in Tokyo, and a national cup competition was instituted that same year. The association was admitted to FIFA in 1929. In the national championship that began in 1921, champions came from every part of Japan. The first winner was Tokyo Club, but many titles were won by university teams and clubs from other cities.

Japan's greatest achievement before the war occurred at the 1936 Olympic Games in Berlin. In the first round, a national team made up almost entirely of Koreans defeated Sweden 3-2 before a stunned European crowd. In the second round, however, the Italian amateurs out-muscled the upstarts and handed them an 8-0 drubbing. After the war, at the FIFA Congress of Luxembourg in 1946, Japan was expelled from the world body for its part in the war, but it was reinstated in 1950 at the Congress of Rio de Janeiro.

A first turning point in Japanese soccer occurred in 1960 with the hiring of West German coach Dettmar Cramer to prepare the national team for the Tokyo Olympics in 1964. Cramer introduced sophisticated European techniques to an already enthusiastic soccer community and took the national team to the quarterfinals of the

Olympics with a first round win over Argentina's amateurs.

In its other first round match, Japan lost to the group winner, Ghana. The state-sponsored "amateurs" of Czechoslovakia knocked Japan out of the quarterfinals, but Japan's fine showing in the tournament and exposure to top flight foreign teams made a great impression on the Japanese public. In the post-Olympic fervor, Japanese soccer was reborn.

A Japanese Football League was introduced in 1965 with eight participating clubs. The Japan FA rehired Cramer for the 1968 Olympic Games in Mexico, and he led Japan to its highest achievement in international competition.

In a first round group consisting of Spanish and Brazilian amateur national teams, as well as the full Nigerian national team, Japan placed second after defeating Nigeria and drawing with Spain and Brazil.

In the quarterfinals, France was eliminated 3-1, setting up a semifinal confrontation with the full international team of Hungary. Japan lost to the Hungarian gold medal winners, but in the third place game defeated Mexico's amateurs to take the bronze medal. The star of this fine Japanese team, and the leading scorer in the tournament, was striker Kunishige Kamamoto, Japanese Footballer of the Year in 1966, 1968, 1971, and 1974, and the first Asian Footballer of the Year in 1976.

Another internationally acclaimed player was left winger Yasuhiko Okudera, who became the first Japanese to enter top level European competition when he joined West Germany's FC Köln in 1977, helping his adopted team to a national championship in his first year.
Although unsuccessful to date in World Cup qualifying attempts, Japan made continued strides through the 1980s, culminating in the 1992 Asian Cup victory at Hiroshima where they defeated Saudi Arabia in the final.

The creation of the new J-League, following years of hosting the prestigious international Toyota Cup club finals, may provide the impetus for further achievement. England's Gary Lineker and Brazil's Zico are among the players who have signed for the new Japanese circuit.

JORDAN

Address: Jordan Football Association, P.O. Box 1954, Amman. *Founded:* 1949. *FIFA:* 1958. *AFC:* 1970. *National stadium:* Amman International Stadium, Amman (30,000); *largest stadium:* Amman International Stadium. *Colors:* White jerseys, white shorts. *Season:* June to December.

Even among the membership of the Union of Arab Football Associations, Jordanian soccer is considered weak and undeveloped. Each of the surrounding Arab states have considerably more experience in international competition and a more ambitious domestic program.

The Jordan Football Association was founded in 1949, but affiliation with FIFA was not sought for nearly ten years, and membership in the Asian Football Confederation did not occur for another 21 years. These delays indicate the preoccupation of the JFA with domestic organization and Jordan's lack of international exposure. Indeed, Jordan's first World Cup qualifying attempt did not come until 1986.

KAMPUCHEA

Address: Fédération Khmère de Football Association, C.P. 101, Complexe Sportif National, Phnom-Penh. *Founded:* 1933. *FIFA:* 1953.

AFC: 1957. *National stadium:* Complexe Sportif National-C.S.N., Phnom-Penh (stadium capacity unknown); *largest stadium:* Complexe Sportif National. *Colors:* Blue, red, and white jerseys; white shorts. *Season:* November to October.

The state of soccer in Kampuchea is uncertain. Prior to 1975, the Cambodian league had 14 clubs in senior competition, six of which were in the first division. Four hundred players participated in a national championship, an annual cup competition, and regional championships, and there were eight stadiums in the country with capacities of 15,000 or more. Nearly 40 years of war, however, have wracked the country in the second half of the 20th century. As late as 1993, political disputes continued to make sport a secondary facet of Kampuchea's existence.

The Fédération Cambodgienne de Football Association was founded in 1933, ten years after the Cochinchina Federation was formed in Saigon. The Cambodian game did not advance as rapidly as did the Vietnamese, but it had already been well established for many years by the time Laos formed a governing body in the early 1950s.

Kampuchea's highest achievement to date in international competition was a fine run for the Asian Cup in 1972. The national team of the then-Khmer Republic advanced to the final rounds in Bangkok, and in its first round group defeated Kuwait 4-0 after losing to South Korea, a major continental power, to finish second in a field of three. This entitled Khmer to a spot in the semifinals, where mighty Iran won 2-1. In the third place game, Thailand won on penalty kicks, and Khmer finished fourth.

KENYA

Address: Football Association of Kenya, Nyayo National Stadium, P.O. Box 40234, Nairobi. *Founded:* 1960. *FIFA:* 1960. *National stadium:* City Stadium, Nairobi (18,000); *largest stadium:* City Stadium. *Colors:* Red, green, and white jerseys; red, green, and black shorts. *Season:* June to March.

Kenya is not among Africa's more successful soccer squads. This is perhaps the one country on the continent where soccer still plays a subordinate role to track and field, the traditional sport of East Africa.

The strong British presence in Kenya assured an early founding date for the national association (sometime during the 1920s or early 1930s), but this was mainly for the benefit of the British themselves. The Football Association of Kenya was directly affiliated with the Football Association in London from its formation until well into the 1950s.

Kenya secured permission from London to join FIFA separately three years before independence, yet internal organization remained uncertain for 15 years.

In the early 1970s, the fledgling Kenya Football League and the Football Association of Kenya feuded over the formation of a new league, and the present national championship was not established until 1974.

Club side Gor Mahia won the 1987 African Cup Winners Cup to achieve the country's only major title.

KOREA, DEMOCRATIC PEOPLE'S REPUBLIC OF
(North Korea)

Address: Munsin-Dong 2, Dongdaewan District, Pyongyang. *Founded:* 1945. *FIFA:* 1958. *National stadium:* Moranbong Stadium, Pyongyang (60,000); *largest stadium:*

Moranbong Stadium. *Colors:* Red jerseys, white shorts. *Season:* March to November.

A North Korean football association was formed immediately after Soviet troops entered the region in 1945 and defection from the old Korean Football Association in Seoul was declared. In the 1950s the North Korean F.A. set its sights on the World Cup, and in 1958 it was admitted to FIFA as Korea DPR.

At the time few would have guessed that by 1966 the unknown North Koreans would come close to reaching the summit of world soccer, advancing to the final rounds of the World Cup in England because Asian and African entries withdrew from qualifying rounds *en masse* to protest FIFA's awarding a solitary berth in the finals to the Asian-African bloc. North Korea's only hurdle was Australia (representing Oceania), whom it defeated soundly in neutral Phnom-Penh, 6-1 and 3-1.

Word of this surprisingly good team reached Europe, but when the Koreans stopped off on their way to England to receive a 7-0 thrashing by Hungary, the rumors lessened. All that anyone knew about the Koreans was that the team was comprised entirely of players picked from the highly disciplined army, and they apparently dedicated themselves exclusively to playing soccer.

In the first round at Middlesborough, North Korea was grouped with Chile, the powerful Russians, and Italy, one of the favorites to win the cup and a team resplendent with world class players. Playing nervously and unable to compensate for its small size, North Korea lost to the Soviets 3-0.

In its next match, against Chile, however, it found its stride in the second half, and Pak Seung Zin equalized two minutes before the final whistle to give North Korea its first point in world competition. A true Cinderella story was emerging, and it became the talk of the tournament, bolstered by an exotic image perpetuated in the press.

Mighty Italy was waiting in the wings. In the greatest World Cup upset since 1950, the soldiers from Pyongyang dazzled the English crowd and forced the cumbersome Italian defense into submission. At 42 minutes, shortly after Italy lost midfielder Giacomo Bulgarelli to injury, inside-left Pak Doo Ik scored against Enrico Albertosi after stealing the ball from Rivera.

The 1-0 score stood at game's end, and the stunned Italians warily returned home to a hostile reception, knowing they had been outplayed. Moreover, the Koreans were through to the quarterfinal round. Their famous team on the field against Italy was Li Chan Myung, Sim Zoong Sun, Shin Yung Kyoo, Ha Jung Won, Oh Yoon Kyung, Im Seung Hwi, Pak Seung Zin, Han Bong Zin, Pak Doo Ik, Kim Bong Hwan, and Yang Sung Kook.

The quarterfinal opponent was Portugal, with the incomparable Eusebio at his peak, but the North Koreans did not disappoint. At Goodison Park, Liverpool, 52,000 spectators were treated to the best game of the tournament. North Korea scored a goal at 60 seconds and two in rapid-fire succession to give them a 3-0 lead at the outset.

With the crowd clearly on their side, the Koreans again played brilliantly, but on four goals by Eusebio—two from the penalty spot—Portugal came from behind to gain a 5-3 win. North Korea was out of the World Cup. There has been such magic since.

North Korea withdrew from World Cup qualification rounds in 1974 (over the South Korea issue) and in 1978 (to protest having to compete against Israel) and then was overshadowed by South Korean qualification in both 1986 and 1990.

An indication that a unified Korea may someday appear in international play came in the 1991 World Youth Cup when a single team appeared in Portugal, but separate teams were again entered in the 1994 World Cup qualifying competition leaving the issue of a unified Korean FA unresolved.

KOREA, REPUBLIC OF
(South Korea)

Address: Korea Football Association, 110-39 Kyoenji-Dong, Chongro-Ku, Seoul. *Founded:* 1928. *FIFA:* 1948. *AFC:* 1954. *National stadium:* Seoul Olympic Stadium (80,000); *largest stadium:* Seoul Olympic Stadium. *Colors:* Red jerseys, white shorts. *Season:* March to November. *Honors:* Asian Cup winner (1956, 1960), runner-up (1972, 1980).

South Korea has been one of Asia's leading soccer-playing countries since World War II, having won more tournaments—large and small—than practically anyone on the continent. Once outside its own sphere of influence, however, South Korea has been frustratingly close to greater achievement. Though it has reached the final rounds of the World Cup three times, it has yet to collect a point despite close losses to the likes of Italy, Argentina and Uruguay.

Soccer found its way to the Korean peninsula long before baseball and other American sports entered the scene. European technicians and missionaries introduced the game before the Japanese annexation in 1910. The Korean Football Association was founded in 1938 in Seoul, but stayed under the wing of the Japanese association. It finally joined FIFA in 1940 in order to play in Olympic qualifying rounds, but those never materialized because of World War II.

In 1953 a national team representing South Korea made its international debut with an ex

tended tour of Hong Kong and Singapore, playing several teams in those colonies over a period of one month. In Hong Kong, the team played four matches, winning two and losing two, and in Singapore it played nine, winning four and losing three.

After eliminating Japan in the qualifying round, South Korea found itself in the company of the world's best teams at the 1954 World Cup in Switzerland. Its first opponent in the opening round was none other than Hungary—in what should have been the greatest mismatch in World Cup history. Kocsis and Puskás were held to five goals, however, and South Korean lost only 9-0. Far worse was a 7-0 loss to less imposing Turkey several days later, and South Korean luckily did not have to play West Germany, the other country in its group.

South Korea's strength in Asia, however, was demonstrated in no uncertain terms when it won the first two editions of the Asian Cup in 1956 and 1960. Since 1964 South Korea has not won a major tournament, but the 1986 and 1990 World Cup qualifications were excellent achievements. In addition, the country has been a regional power in events like Malaysia's Merdeka tournament and the King's Cup Tournament of Thailand, as well as its own President's Cup.

KUWAIT

Address: Udailiyya BL, 4 Al-Ittihad St., P.O. Box 2029 (Safat), Safat. *Founded:* 1952. *FIFA:* 1962. *AFC:* 1964. *National stadium:* Shuweikh Secondary School Stadium, Kuwait (25,000); *largest stadium:* Shuweikh Stadium. *Colors:* Blue-and-white jerseys, white shorts. *Season:* October to May. *Honors:* Asian Cup winner (1980), runner-up (1976).

In the aftermath of the Middle East soccer boom of the 1970s, Kuwait emerged as a genuine power among countries of the Gulf region. Little was heard of Kuwaiti soccer until 1970, but the vast financial reservoir of the Kuwait Football Association (KFA) has since attracted some of the world's best coaches to establish a stable domestic program and carry the national team to international honors. By any standards, this effort has succeeded.

Soccer was first played in Kuwait by British sailors and civil servants shortly after colonization in 1889. The KFA was founded in 1952, but it did not join FIFA until after Kuwait had gained its full independence from Great Britain in 1961. In the 1960s, most of the KFA's resources were put into building a sound league structure.

Kuwait has participated in regional tournaments since their inception in 1970, nearly reaching the 1978 World Cup finals. Kuwait handily won all of its games against Bahrain and Qatar in the opening group, and in the deciding round defeated Hong Kong and Australia (twice).

Its elimination from the finals came at the hands of mighty Iran and South Korea, but among the 17 Asian nations attempting to qualify for the 1978 World Cup, Kuwait finished third.

It made it all the way in 1982, finishing first in a four-team final play-off that included China, Saudi Arabia, and New Zealand. Its performance in Spain was marred, however, when team officials protested a decision in a 4-1 loss to France, nearly taking the team off the field. The other matches produced surprising results— a 1-1 draw against favored Czechoslovakia and a narrow 1-0 loss against England—so the overall effort was strong.

Kuwait was upset by Syria in 1986 qualifying and by the United Arab Emirates in the 1990 tournament. Despite occupation by—and the war with—Iraq, Kuwait resumed international play by reaching the 1992 Olympic final stages and was ready to take part in 1994 World Cup qualifying.

Laos

Address: Fédération Lao de Foot-ball, c/o Dir. of Sports and Physical Education, Vientiane. *Founded:* 1951. *FIFA:* 1952. *AFC:* 1968. *National stadium:* Stade National Vientiane, Vientiane (5,000); *largest stadium:* Stade National Vientiane. *Colors:* Red jerseys, white shorts. *Season:* October to May.

Ravaged by the long Indochina war, Laotian soccer has made little impact on the Asian game as a whole, or in its own Southeast Asian region. Its inland geographical position and small, sparse population had thwarted the pervasive foreign influence of other French colonies in Indo-China and the larger British colonies to the west. Once soccer in Laos began to be organized after World War II, the war put a damper on what progress had been made. French colonists introduced soccer after the turn of the century in Luang Prabang and Kiang Kwang (now Xieng Khouang), but there is no record of a Laotian football association before World War II.

Some teams had formed by 1949, the year of independence, and the new government eventually helped to form a national association. The Fédération Lao de Foot-ball was founded in 1951 and gained membership in FIFA less than one year later, but Laos has never been a factor in international soccer.

Latvia

Address: 4 Terbatas Str., 226723 Riga. *Founded:* 1922. *FIFA:* 1992.

As with Estonia and Lithuania, Latvia formed a national association and initiated an international schedule in Europe during the Baltic states' 20-year-long independence between the world wars. Latvian teams completed 35 full internationals (other than their matches with Estonia and Lithuania) between 1923-38, including 11 matches each against Finland and Sweden. Latvia met Poland on seven occasions between 1931-38.

Aside from one win in Riga, its record against the Poles was more successful away than at home. In three matches away, Latvia drew once with Poland and lost twice 2-1. Perhaps its most astonishing performance was a 2-1 loss to Austria in 1937 at Vienna in a World Cup qualifying round. In 1935 and 1937, Latvia lost to Germany 3-0 and 3-1. Among its further international accomplishments were three draws with Sweden, one of them at Stockholm in 1938.

After the dissolution of the Soviet Union, Latvia regained its independence and returned as an international team in time for the 1994 World Cup. Its first qualifying game was a 2-1 loss to old rival Lithuania on August 12, 1992, but gained its first World Cup point two weeks later by holding the European Champions, Denmark, to a 0-0 draw.

LEBANON

Address: Fédération Libanaise de Football Association, Rue Omar Ibn Khattab, B.P. 4732, Beirut. *Founded:* 1933. *FIFA:* 1933. *AFC:* 1964. *National stadium:* Cité Sportive-Camille Chamoun, Beirut (60,000); *largest stadium:* Cité Sportive-Camille Chamoun. *Colors:* Red-and-white jerseys, white shorts. *Season:* October to June.

Lebanon was one of the first countries in the Middle East to establish an administrative body for soccer (the F.A.'s of Egypt, Israel, and Iran are older), and it was an early participant in international competition (only Egypt and Israel started earlier).

Lebanon's poor standing even among Middle East countries was initially caused by the absence of a large working class population to support the game, then by a nearly 20-year civil war. Therefore, the staging of World Cup qualifying games in Beirut in May of 1993 was of more than just symbolic significance in a country which had fought long to preserve its identity.

The heyday of Lebanese soccer was perhaps the 1930s, when the French mandate was still in full swing, and French soldiers and workers in residence provided a strong impetus. The oldest clubs had been founded in the 1920s, and in 1933, one year after the formation of the Fédération Libanaise de Football Association, the Lebanese league was introduced.

Lebanon made its international debut in 1940 at Tel-Aviv against Palestine, losing 5-1, but there followed precious few forays into international competition. The 1994 World Cup campaign marked the nation's reentry into international soccer.

LESOTHO

Address: Lesotho Sports Council, Maseru 100. *Founded:* 1932. *FIFA:* 1964. *CAF:* 1964. *National stadium:* Lesotho National Stadium, Maseru (10,700); *largest stadium:* Lesotho National Stadium. *Colors:* Blue, white, green, and red jerseys; white shorts. *Season:* November to October.

Soccer in Lesotho has been characterized by activity at the club level and a certain degree of exclusion by some other black African states over the question of the kingdom's close relations with South Africa. Most of Lesotho's international exposure has been at the club level. At the national level, Lesotho has failed to qualify for the final rounds of the African Nations' Cup.

The game arrived early in Lesotho because of geographical proximity to South Africa, the first stronghold of soccer on the continent. The Lesotho Sports Association (later Council) took over administration of the game from the old Basutoland Association when Lesotho became independent in 1966.

LIBERIA

Address: Liberia Football Association, P.O. 1066, Monrovia. *Founded:* 1962. *FIFA:* 1962. *Largest stadium:* Antoinette Tubman Stadium, Monrovia. *Colors:* Red-and-white jerseys, white shorts.

Liberia remains a little known quantity in African competition, as civil war in recent years stalled an apparently slow development begun in the 1980s. The primary reasons for Liberia's low position in African soccer is the country's unique absence of a colonial past.

Much of Liberia's international relations over the decades has been with the United States, the only western power that did not export soccer to the developing countries. Liberia's relative political isolation in Africa has contributed further to its slow progress on the playing field.

LIBYA, ARAB REPUBLIC OF

Address: Libyan Arab General Football Federation, P.O. Box 5137, Tripoli. *Founded:* 1963. *FIFA:* 1963. *CAF:* 1965. *National stadium:* Tripoli Sports City Stadium, Gurgi (70,000); *largest stadium:* Tripoli Sports City Stadium. *Colors:* Orange-and-white jerseys, white shorts.

Season: September to April. *Honors:* African Championship runner-up (1982).

Soccer was introduced to the coastal cities of Libya by Italian soldiers and workers shortly after the occupation in 1912, but the game did not really take root among Libyans themselves until well into the post-World War II era. The Libyan General Football Federation, as it was then called, did not surface until 1963, but it wasted no time in joining FIFA and the African Football Confederation.

Libya's first participation in international competition was in the fifth Mediterranean Games in 1967. Libya has only sporadically played in the African Nations's Cup, and it first entered World Cup qualifying rounds in 1976, only to be eliminated in the preliminary round by neighboring Algeria.

The country did stage the 1982 African Championship and finished second, losing the final to Ghana on penalty kicks. In recent years, however, Libya has usually found a political reason for either not entering or making a late withdrawal from international play. That trend continued in the 1994 World Cup qualifying phase when they did not participate.

LIECHTENSTEIN

Address: Liechtensteiner Fussballverband, Postfach 165, 9490-Vaduz. *Founded:* 1933. *FIFA:* 1974. *UEFA:* 1974. *National stadium:* Landessportplatz, Vaduz (10,000); *largest stadium:* Landessportplatz. *Colors:* Blue jerseys, red shorts. *Season:* July to June.

The Principality of Liechtenstein is a tiny FIFA member holds a number of unique aspects to its administrative structure and official relationship with the rest of European soccer. Six of the seven major Liechtensteiner clubs play in a Swiss League and there is no national league, as the principality is too small to support any regional competitions. The only national team in international competition is at the under-21 level. This precludes Liechtenstein's participation in any of the major FIFA or UEFA-sponsored tournaments.

Liechtenstein did play an unofficial full international against the United States in 1990, losing 4-1 to the American side that was in the closing stages of its preparation for the 1990 World Cup finals in Italy. The national team has not played a full international since.

LITHUANIA

Address: 6 Zemaites Street, 232675 Vilnius.

The most insular of the Baltic states, Lithuania was also the least successful in its encounters on the playing field between the wars. It formed a national association during the early 1920s after independence from Russia, but the Lithuanian game was not as active as that of Estonia or Latvia, and the level of play was somewhat lower.

Of its ten full internationals against European opponents (Finland, Rumania, Sweden, Switzerland, and Turkey), it was victorious only once, against Finland at Kaunas in 1934 (1-0). Paradoxically, Lithuania emerged from the long years of Soviet occupation stronger than its Baltic neighbors because the club side, Zalgiris Vilnius had achieved some success in the Soviet League, even qualifying for European club tournament competition.

Thus, when Lithuania regained independence and returned to World Cup soccer in 1992, it was no surprise that it took points from both North

ern Ireland and Denmark at the start of its 1994 World Cup qualifying scheduled. It remains well-placed to make an impact in European soccer sooner than its Baltic neighbors.

LUXEMBOURG

Address: Fédération Luxembourgeoise de Football, 50, rue de Strasbourg, L2560 Luxembourg. *Founded:* 1908. *FIFA:* 1910. *UEFA:* 1954. *National stadium:* Stade Municipal de la Ville de Luxembourg, Luxembourg (15,000); *largest stadium:* Stade Municipal de la Ville de Luxembourg. *Colors:* Red jerseys, white shorts. *Season:* August to June.

Little Luxembourg continues to compete relentlessly among the titans of European soccer. They have played in international competition since 1911 and have never softened in their devotion to the game, yet their full international team struggles to get results. With an area the size of Rhode Island and a population one-third of Rhode Island's, there is little else to do but play hard for an occasional victory or draw.

Like other industrialized countries of Western Europe, soccer in the Grand Duchy is centered on factory life—in Luxembourg's case, steel mills—and reaches high levels of emotional intensity. In addition to the capital city of Luxembourg, the game has been strongest in the industrial cities of the South—Esch-sur Alzette, Dudelange, Differdange, and Rumelange. More than 80 percent of Luxembourg's championships have been won by clubs from these four cities.

The first clubs in Luxembourg were founded in the capital around the turn of the century, and in 1908 an umbrella governing body called the Fédération des Sociétés Luxembourgeoises de Sports Athlétiques was founded to administer soccer and other sports. This body gained admission to FIFA in 1910, and, the following year, Luxembourg played host to France in its first international (won by the visitors 4-1). The Luxembourg league was introduced in 1909-10, and the first and second champions, respectively, were Rácing Club Luxembourg and Sporting Club Luxembourg, both from the capital.

The ever-increasing gulf between Luxembourg and bigger countries grew wider after World War II, except on a few noteworthy occasions. Only weeks after the liberation from Germany, Luxembourg defeated Belgium 4-1 in its first full international victory since 1914. Luxembourg has continually entered every international competition at its disposal.

Perhaps its finest achievement to date was a stunning upset over Portugal in 1961 during qualifying rounds for the 1962 World Cup. This famous game—made legendary because it was Eusebio's first international for Portugal—took place in Luxembourg, and was all the more decisive because the home team led throughout the entire game. The final score was 4-2, and a hat trick was scored by center forward Andy Schmidt, a 21-year-old locksmith.

Since then Luxembourg has managed to defeat Holland twice (once in the European Nations' Cup of 1962-64), Norway a second time, Mexico, and Turkey, but it cannot really hope for European Championship or World Cup places. Its best club has been Jeunesse Esch with 21 league titles, but Red Boys, Differdange take honors in the Luxembourg Cup with 16 triumphs.

MACAO

Address: P.O. Box 920, Macao. *Founded:* 1939. The Portuguese introduced soccer to Asia's oldest European colony in the early decades of this century, but the cultural separation between the native Chinese and Portuguese colonists hampered growth of the sport. The Associaçao de Futebol de Macáo was founded in 1939 and became affiliated with the Portuguese governing body in 1950 with eight clubs registered.

Macao's infrequent internationals are generally played against teams from Hong Kong, but in 1975 the top Macao selection managed to draw 1-1 with visiting New Zealand. The country did not enter the 1994 World Cup.

MADAGASCAR

Address: c/o National Football Committee, BP 4409, Antananarivo 101. *Founded:* 1961. *FIFA:* 1964. *CAF:* 1963. *National stadium:* Stade Municipal de Mahamasina, Antananarivo (13,600); *largest stadium:* Stade Municipal de Mahamasina. *Colors:* Red jerseys, white shorts. *Season:* November to October.

The island republic of Madagascar has not yet emerged in African soccer, but it inherited a solid soccer tradition from its French colonial days. Financial and geographical considerations have impeded international competition, yet there is no lack of enthusiasm for the game at home, and soccer ranks as the leading sport.

In the 1994 World Cup, the country came close to reaching the second round in Africa before bowing to heavily favored Zambia in the final group match and being eliminated on goal difference.

The colonial governing body was founded as an outgrowth of World War II and became affiliated with the Fédération Française de Football in 1947. In 1958, the year of self-proclaimed political autonomy, France "Amateur" traveled to then-Tananarive and defeated a Tananarive selection 5-1 before an identical win over a West Coast of Madagascar selection at Majunga. These were the first officially recorded internationals played by Madagascar teams.

The national team has not yet been able to gain the final rounds of the African Nations' Cup, but Madagascar clubs have participated actively in African club championships.

MALAWI

Address: National Football Association of Malawi, P.O. Box 865, Blantyre. *Founded:* 1966. *FIFA:* 1967. *National stadium:* Kamuzu Stadium, Blantyre (52,970); *largest stadium:* Kamuzu Stadium. *Colors:* Red, green, and black jerseys; red shorts.

This small, picturesque country—formerly Nyasaland—was introduced to soccer by British colonists, but the game was slow to spread among the African population. Ostracism from by other black African states—because of the government's political ties to white Rhodesia from 1953-63—also hindered development.

The Football Association of Nyasaland was established in Limbe during the colonial era and was affiliated with The Football Association in London until self-government came about in 1964.

The reconstituted Football Association of Malawi was founded under the office of the Director of Sports and Culture in Blantyre immediately after independence two years later, and it adopted its present name in the early 1970s.

Malawi did not become active in international competition until the mid-1970s. Its first attempt to qualify for the World Cup was for the 1978 edition, when it was eliminated by Zambia, and no real progress has been made in the African Nations' Cup. A sign of the lack of progress was seen in 1992, when Malawi en-

tered but then withdrew from the 1994 World Cup.

MALAYSIA

Address: Football Association of Malaysia, Wisma Fam., Tilgat 4, Jalan SS 5A/9, 47301 Petaling, Jaya Selangor. *Founded:* 1933. *FIFA:* 1956. *AFC:* 1954. *National stadium:* Merdeka Stadium, Kuala Lumpur (29,000); *largest stadium:* Sultan Mohamed IV, Kelantan (30,000). *Colors:* White jerseys with black-and-gold sleeves, black shorts.

Malaysia is one of the most active soccer nations in Southeast Asia. During the postwar era, Malayans have played an important role in organizing Asian soccer, even after the separation of Malaya and Singapore in 1965.

After its introduction in Singapore by British colonists, soccer was first played on the Malay peninsula in Perak and Selangor states. The old Football Association of Malaya was founded in 1933 and became affiliated with the English governing body in London shortly thereafter. Its headquarters for many years was divided between Kuala Lumpur and Singapore.

In 1956 the F.A. of Malaya was granted separate membership in FIFA, and one year later it introduced the ambitious Merdeka Anniversary Football Tournament to celebrate Malayan independence and the opening of a grand national stadium. The annual Merdeka Tournament is open to invited national teams of Asia and is the largest and most respected competition of its kind on the continent.

Malaysia has continued to be one of the busiest Asian countries in international competition. Its champion teams competed in all editions of the Asian Champions' Cup, and the Malaysia national team has been active in World Cup and

Olympic qualification tournaments. Though a regular entrant in the Asian Cup, it has advanced to the final rounds only once (1976), when it lost to Kuwait and drew with China PR. Victory in that regional event has eluded the country, but it has not hindered the growing popularity of the sport.

The political separation of Singapore from the rest of Malaysia was unquestionably a blow to Malaysian soccer, because Singapore's Chinese population had been instrumental in organizing the game in Malaya and Asia as a whole, but it did not dampen the Malays' enthusiasm.

MALI

Address: Fédération Maliènne de Football, Stade Mamdou Konate, B.P. 1020, Bamako. *Founded:* 1960. *FIFA:* 1962. *CAF:* 1963. *National stadium:* Stade Omnisport, Bamako (30,000); *largest stadium:* Stade Omnisport. *Colors:* Green jerseys, yellow shorts. *Season:* October to June. *Honors:* African Nations' Cup runner-up (1972).

Among the numerous strong soccer nations of West Africa, Mali once ranked just below the established continental powers Ghana, Nigeria, Ivory Coast, and Guinea. The exceptional quality of Mali's best players has become widely known both in Africa and Western Europe.

The game arrived in French Sudan through Bamako from Dakar when French traders settled in the commercial centers along the Niger River. As an Islamic religious capital, however, Timbuktu was less exposed to the recreational activities of the commercial world. As a result, the ancient city's impact on the Mali game is minimal compared with Bamako, Segou, Kayes, Gao, and Sikasso.

In 1972 Mali reached the final rounds of the African Nations' Cup for the first and only time.

On five goals by the tournament's leading scorer, Fantamady Keita, it qualified for the semifinals by drawing with each of its first round group opponents—Togo, Kenya, and Cameroon—and upset Zaire, 4-3, in the penultimate round.

The Congo, led by the skillful M'Pelé and M'Bono, scored three goals in the second half of the final and defeated Mali's greatest national team 3-2. Salif Keita, Mali's famous striker with St. Etienne and later Olympique Marseille in France, was the driving force behind its great success.

That high level of performance has not been maintained, however, and the 1994 World Cup qualification attempt ended in withdrawal before it began.

MALTA

Address: Malta Football Association, 280 St. Paul Street, Valetta. *Founded:* 1900. *FIFA:* 1959. *UEFA:* 1960. *National stadium:* The Stadium, Gzira (15,000); *largest stadium:* The Stadium, Gzira. *Colors:* Red jerseys, white shorts. *Season:* September to May.

There was never any doubt that tiny Malta would become a soccer hotbed. A British possession since the early nineteenth century, Malta and the Maltese were exposed to the game from the beginning, mainly through British naval personnel stationed at the Royal Navy's Mediterranean base.

The Royal Navy officially sponsored many of the first competitions, and eventually games between military teams and local citizens were encouraged. The problem was that the first soccer field was not constructed until the 1890s, and all previous contests were played in the streets and makeshift grounds. Nevertheless, dense population conditions and the Mediterranean climate contributed significantly to the growth of the Maltese game.

The Malta Football Association was established in 1900 and remained affiliated with The Football Association in London until 1959, two years before Malta's independence. Membership in FIFA and UEFA followed almost immediately.

Malta, the colony, first engaged in international competition in 1953 by hosting an Austrian selection which won 3-2. Since then Malta has remained in the European soccer community and resisted the temptation to align itself with African countries, against whom Maltese teams would doubtlessly fare better on the field.

Since the early 1960s, Malta has been a regular participant in the European Football Championship and World Cup qualifying rounds. One of its finest achievements occurred in 1971 when The Stadium filled to capacity for the only time in its history as England, playing its first full international in Malta, defeated the national team 1-0.

Maltese fans were jubilant when world champion West Germany was held to the same result in 1974 and East Germany in 1977, but there have been few successes despite the fact that Maltese teams often are difficult to beat at home.

The first Maltese club and the pioneer of Maltese soccer was St. George's F.C., founded at Valetta in 1890. Floriana F.C., located in Valetta, was founded in 1900, and through the decades has won the lion's share of honors in league and cup competition along with its archrival Sliema Wanderers, which hails from the Valetta suburb of Sliema.

In the 1930s, Valetta F.C. emerged as a third leading club and has closed in on Floriana's 24 league championships and 14 cup wins, and Sliema's 22 championships and 17 cup wins.

Valetta had collected 14 titles and 6 cups by 1992.

MAURITANIA

Address: Fédération de Foot-Ball de Ia République Islamique de Mauritanie, B.P. 566, Nouakchott. *Founded:* 1961. *FIFA:* 1966. *CAF:* 1968. *National stadium:* Stade National, Nouakchott (6,000); *largest stadium:* Stade National. *Colors:* Green jerseys, yellow shorts. *Season:* November to July.

Sand-swept Mauritania, three-fourths of which is uninhabitable, is a country held together by one major highway and a handful of cultural activities, such as soccer. There is no lack of interest in the game by the Moorish residents who make up 80 percent of the population.

Though all indications point to a vigorous domestic game, Mauritania rarely entered international competition until the mid-1970s and did not compete in the 1994 World Cup.

As an Overseas Territory of French West Africa, Mauritania first saw the game being played by French colonists and soldiers of the French Foreign Legion.

The Mauritanian federation was founded in 1961, one year after independence, and affiliation with FIFA followed five years later. The federation made provisional ties with the CAF in 1968.

MAURITIUS

Address: Mauritius Football Association, Chancery House, 14, Liset Geoffroy St. (2nd Floor, Nos. 303-305), Port Louis. *Founded:* 1952. *FIFA:* 1962. *CAF:* 1963. *National stadium:* King George V Stadium, Curepipe (39,000);

largest stadium: King George V Stadium. *Colors:* Red jerseys, white shorts.

Soccer did not become fully organized in Mauritius until after World War II, when an umbrella governing body for all sports on the island was founded in 1952. Soccer has remained under its aegis ever since.

In 1962, six years before independence, Mauritius was given permission to join FIFA, and membership in the African Football Confederation came along one year later. The Mauritius national team—known as the "Islanders"—has never attained international success.

MEXICO

Address: Federación Mexicana de Fútbol Asociación, Abraham Gonzalez, 74, Col Juárez, Mexico, 6, D.F. *Founded:* 1927. *FIFA:* 1929. *CONCACAF:* 1961. *Largest stadium:* Estadio Azteca, Mexico City (108,499). *Colors:* Green jerseys, white shorts. *Season:* July to October.

Mexico is easily the dominant soccer power in the North-Central American and Caribbean region. Its predominance is based on a strong professional league, and its prestige has been enhanced by its successful staging of the 1970 and 1986 editions of the World Cup.

It is also the home of Estadio Azteca, the stadium in Mexico City which is thought by many to be the finest soccer facility in the Americas.

Yet Mexico's isolation from the mainstream of top flight soccer in Europe and South America has limited it from having a real impact on the world game. There have been occasional efforts to seek affiliation with South America's governing body because of the lack of CONCACAF competition, but the growth of the game in both the United States and Central America has re-

cently closed the gap between the Mexicans and the rest of the world.

Soccer was introduced in Mexico during the last decades of the nineteenth century by British, Spanish, and French technicians who were brought in to modernize technology and commerce in the cities.

The national league, founded in 1903, is one of the oldest in the Western Hemisphere and explains Mexico's regional preeminence. A great rivalry has developed between the America Club of Mexico City and Guadalajara. Their matches regularly fill both the giant Azteca Stadium and 70,000 seat Jalisco.

In international competition, Mexico long was dominant in the CONCACAF region, but, significantly, its first full international was played in 1928 against a European opponent—Spain— at the Amsterdam Olympics; Spain won 7-1. A few days later, the Mexicans played against Chile, also eliminated from the Olympics, in a friendly at Arnhem and lost 3-1. These teams were sponsored by the new Federación Mexicana de Fútbol Asociación (FMFA), which had been founded the year before as an independent governing body.

In 1930 Mexico entered the first World Cup in Montevideo and lost all three of its matches to France, Chile, and Argentina. Unfortunately, this was to set the tone for its poor record (just six wins overall) in subsequent editions. At home, however, Mexico reached the 1986 quarter finals before losing a penalty kick tie-breaker to West Germany.

These lopsided statistics, however, obscure Mexico's achievements in dominating the CONCACAF region. Mexico had been eliminated from the World Cup in qualification rounds only three times (1934, 1974, 1982). In 1938 it did not enter, and it was suspended from the 1990 event. However, by the 1980s, it was clear

Schirner

Estadio Azteca

that Mexican national teams no longer were sure winners in the region. A 1991 CONCACAF gold cup semifinal loss to the United States confirmed that fact.

The Mexican game at the club level is as well established as the more famous leagues of South America. After World War II there was a strong Argentine influence, as many players from the big Buenos Aires clubs came north. This gave way to large numbers of Brazilian players in the 1960s, and today some Mexican clubs compete financially with Spanish and Brazilian clubs for South American players.

The multidivisional national league includes a first division of 20 clubs and more than 1500 professionals, and Mexico City boasts the two largest soccer stadiums north of the Amazon.

Great impetus was given to Mexican soccer by the FMFA's successful staging of the 1970 and 1986 World Cups. Players and spectators everywhere remember the 1970 World Championship as the happiest and most festive in the history of the competition, while the 1986 event, staged by Mexico when Columbia could not handle the task, was another success.

MOROCCO

Address: Fédération Royale Marocaine de Football, Av Ibn Sing, CNS Bellevue, B.P.51, Rabat. *Founded:* 1955. *FIFA:* 1956. *CAF:* 1966. *National stadium:* Stade d'Honneur, Casablanca (40,000); *largest stadium:* Stade d'Honneur. *Colors:* Red jerseys with green sleeves and trim, white shorts. *Season:* September to June. *Honors:* African Nations' Cup winner (1976).

Morocco emerged in the late 1960s as the early front-runner of the post-independence era in North African soccer and became the first new African country to participate in final rounds of the World Cup.

Historically, French North Africa has been the strongest bloc of soccer-playing nations in the Arab world. Algeria and Tunisia were more advanced than their neighbor to the west, but this changed in the 1960s, as the stability of Morocco's government served to bolster the Moroccan game.

The rise of Tunisia since 1974 has evened the balance of power in the area, but Morocco is still a major force in African soccer, most recently eliminating their Tunisian rivals from the 1994 World Cup.

While it is possible that Spanish colonists played soccer at Cueta and Ifni before the turn of the century, soccer was surely played by the French in Tangier, Casablanca, and Fez immediately after 1900, and the French influence ultimately had the greater impact. Soldiers of the French Army and Foreign Legion did much to spread the game, especially after the 1910 uprising and during World War I.

At about this time, leagues were introduced all across French North Africa, and the Moroccan championship, which encompassed Tangier as well as Morocco, was the first to be established (1916). A governing body, the Ligue du Maroc, was founded in 1923 and became affiliated with the French federation in Paris.

Morocco's first internationals were inter-association matches with other representative teams of French North Africa. A and B selections were put on the field as early as 1927, when a draw was achieved with Oran, and Algiers fell to defeat.

In 1930 and 1931, Moroccan selections played host to France B and lost 3-1 and 4-0. There were further losses to France B in 1934, 1937, 1942, and 1948, though none of these are officially recognized by France.

In 1955 the colonial association was reconstituted as the Fédération Royale Marocaine de Football (FRMF), and separate membership with FIFA was obtained one year later. The international schedule was increased substantially, and in 1962 the FRMF invited Switzerland, Poland, and Hungary B to Casablanca for a mini-series.

Though achieved by a toss of the coin, Morocco's finest hour was in qualifying for the 1970 World Cup in Mexico. Not only was Morocco the first modern African nation to be represented in the competition, but its performance was widely praised.

Led by the great Mohammedia striker Ahmed Faras, the Moroccan amateurs nearly upset West Germany, eventually losing 2-1, and drew 1-1 with Bulgaria.

Faras led the national team to its first qualification for the final rounds of the African Nations' Cup and the Olympic tournament in 1972, and in 1976 he was the driving force behind Morocco's winning of the Nations' Cup in Ethiopia.

Undefeated in six matches, it drew the stiffest opposition in the competition, finishing ahead of Nigeria, Sudan, and Zaire in the first round, and Guinea, Nigeria, and Egypt in the final pool. The best finish since then came in 1980 when Morocco finished third in Nigeria.

Morocco's most famous player is still the legendary Larbi Ben Barek, a dazzling inside left whose juggling and dribbling impressed French crowds during the late 1930s and 1940s. Ben Barek played for several Moroccan clubs before signing with Marseille and Stade Françis in France, and in 1938 he made his first of 17 appearances for the French national team.

But the country also can be proud of club success in Africa. FAR Rabat (1985), Raja Casablanca (1989) and WAC Casablanca (1992) all have won the African Champions Cup.

MOZAMBIQUE, NEW PEOPLE'S REPUBLIC OF

Address: Mozambique Football Federation, Av. Samora Machel 11-2, Caixa Postal 1467, Maputo. *Founded:* 1978. *FIFA:* 1978.

Soccer in Mozambique has been organized for more than 70 years, Portuguese colonists having introduced the game after World War I. The Associaço de Futebol de Lourenço Marques was founded in the capital in 1923. After attaining independence in 1975, Mozambiquan soccer organized a national association in 1978.

Mozambique's best players, like those of other Portuguese colonies, had often been poached by clubs in Portugal; the greatest of them all, the Benfica star Eusebio, who put his country—and to some extent Portugal—on the soccer map. Mozambique quickly moved into World Cup play, entering the 1982 qualifying process and has continued to seek its own place in the game.

NAMIBIA

Address: Namibia Football Federation, 18, Curt von Francois Strasse, P.O. Box 1345, Windhock 2000. *Founded:* 1991.

Namibia, the former Southwest Africa, secured its independence after a long struggle in Southern Africa and immediately took advantage of its new status by joining FIFA and entering the 1994 World Cup.

Although beaten in all four of its matches by Madagascar and group winner Zambia, Namibia's entry was probably of more symbolic importance than the results on the field. It is expected that Namibian clubs will take part in African club tournaments soon.

NEPAL

Address: All-Nepal Football Association, Dasharath Rangashala, Tripureshwor, Katmandu. *Founded:* 1951. *FIFA:* 1970. *AFC:* 1971. *National stadium:* Dasarath Rangashala, Katmandu (25,000); *largest stadium:* Dasarath Rangashala. *Colors:* Red jerseys, white shorts.

There was little soccer in Nepal until the immediate postwar years. By 1951, when the Shah King abolished the old autocracy and adopted some forms of modern government.

A gradual influx of English-speaking teachers and businessmen—especially from India—occurred, and the All-Nepal Football Association was founded. Nepalese teams have not yet made a mark, but they did enter both the 1986 and 1990 World Cups.

NETHERLANDS

Address: Koninklijke Nederlandsche Voetbalbond, Woudenbergseweg 56, Postbus 515, NL-3700 AM, Zeist. *Founded:* 1889. *FIFA:* 1904. *UEFA:* 1954. *National stadium:* Olympic Stadium, Amsterdam (67,000); *largest stadium:*

Olympic Stadium. *Colors:* Orange jerseys, white shorts. *Season:* August to June. *Honors:* World Cup runner-up (1974, 1978); European Champion (1988); Olympic Games third place (1908, 1912, 1920).

The rise of Dutch soccer since the 1960s continues to be Europe's greatest success story of the postwar era. The Netherlands, whose early jump (along with Denmark) on the rest of Europe led to prominence after the turn of the century, floundered in amateurism for decades as larger—and professional—competitors moved steadily up the European ladder.

But the advent of professionalism in the 1950s changed the course of the Dutch game, and with the miraculous appearance of gifted players in the 1960s and an infusion of enlightened tactical innovations, Holland rose to the pinnacle of world soccer. It continues to produce great individuals and powerful national teams.

The association game was imported to Holland about 1865 by English textile workers, and in 1870 it was played by schoolboys at "Pim" Mulier's school in Noordwijk. The first club was the Haarlem Football Club, founded in 1879.

In 1889 the Nederlandsche Voetbalbond, the second oldest national association outside the British Isles, was founded at The Hague. The title "Royal" was added to the name in 1929, resulting in the present Koninklijke Nederlandsche Voetbalbond (KNVB).

Holland became one of Europe's first soccer powers, displaying strength and speed in the northern European tradition, but unlike Denmark, France, and Belgium, it did not participate in the first unofficial Olympic soccer competitions of 1900 and 1904.

Its first official international was against Belgium in 1905 at Antwerp—a 4-1 loss—and in Rotterdam one month later, Belgium won again in Holland's home debut. The week after Belgium's crushing victory in Rotterdam (4-0), the NVB became one of the seven founder-members of FIFA, and thus helped to chart the course for the game's world governing body.

Every major town in the country had by now spawned one or more clubs. In 1897-98 a national championship was introduced, and the following season a national cup competition got under way, producing the continent's first complete schedule of league and cup fixtures.

The momentum of Holland's early start resulted in three consecutive Olympic bronze medals in 1908, 1912, and 1920 (the last achieved after Czechoslovakia defaulted), and a fourth place finish in 1924. This record put the Dutch high among the early European elite behind the British and Denmark.

Sweden, Austria, Germany, and France were all regular victims of Dutch national teams during this period, but an indication of Europe's relative weakness compared to Great Britain is seen in Holland's results against English amateur teams between 1907-13. In nine games Holland failed to gain a single win and scored only seven goals to England's 45.

Between the world wars, Holland continued to participate actively in international competition, but the growth of soccer in more populous—and more professionally oriented—countries left Dutch soccer in its wake. Holland qualified for the World Cups of 1934 and 1938, but it was eliminated in the first round by Switzerland and Czechoslovakia, respectively.

In the years before and immediately after World War II, league and cup titles were spread widely among the major clubs of The Hague, Rotterdam, Amsterdam, Deventer, Eindhoven, Groningen, and other cities, but in the early 1950s, a movement—led, among others, by Fortuna Geleen—was brewing to end the stagnation of amateur competition.

Semi-professionalism was adopted in 1954, and full professionalism was finally sanctioned by the KNVD in 1956. This led directly to the rise of Ajax and Feyenoord as the preeminent clubs of the Dutch game. By the mid-1960s, their hold on the league and cup was almost complete, and it was not to be broken until the emergence ten years later of PSV Eindhoven (the club of the giant Philips consortium). By 1992 Ajax had 23 titles, while Feyenoord and PSV held 13 apiece.

The effect of professionalism on the development of Dutch soccer was slow and steady, but eventually it reaped the highest rewards. An all-time low in Holland's international fortunes was reached with its elimination from the European Nations' Cup by tiny Luxembourg in 1963, but in that same year a Dutch club—Feyenoord—achieved its first success in the European Cup, advancing to the semifinals.

In 1965 Ajax signed a new manager, Rinus Michels, and a forward of unparalleled ability, Johan Cruyff, and the club was instantly transformed. It won three Dutch championships in a row, and in 1968-69 it advanced to the European Cup final after eliminating mighty Benfica in the semifinals. In 1970 Ajax gained the semifinals of the Fairs Cup, and the depth of a revitalized Dutch soccer was demonstrated unquestionably when Feyenoord won the European Cup that same year with a convincing victory over Celtic.

The benefits of a highly competitive domestic rivalry between two strong clubs helped to speed up the growing Dutch onslaught in Europe, and in 1971, after winning the domestic league and cup double, Ajax brought the European Cup to Holland for the second consecutive year.

Ajax's win over Panathinaïkos was even more convincing than Feyenoord's over Celtic, but Ajax's best days were still to come. Michels moved to Barcelona, and Steaua Bucharest manager Sefan Kovacs was brought in to take his place. Kovacs instituted a more fluid *catenaccio*-based system in which players improvised with freedom and an attacking sweeper provided a constant threat.

With an astonishingly high caliber of talent at its disposal—Wim Suurbier, Ruud Krol, Arie Haan, Johan Neeskens, Arnold Muhren, Johan Cruyff, and Piet Keizer—Ajax's mature and elegant style flourished. Second and third European Cups were won in 1972 and 1973, and the era of Ajax and "total football" took Europe by storm.

Cruyff's departure for Barcelona in 1973 signaled a temporary decline of Ajax. Feyenoord grabbed one more European title—the UEFA Cup—in 1974, but the era of Dutch preeminence in European club competitions was virtually over until PSV Eindhoven's European Cup win of 1988. Ajax went on to win Europe's two other club trophies by 1992, joining Barcelona and Juventus in that unique category of success.

This success in the 1970s failed to be translated into international prizes at the national level. Yugoslavia and East Germany had proved to be too difficult in the 1970-72 European Football Championship, and in qualifying for the 1974 World Cup, Belgium held the Dutch to two scoreless draws. In the 1974 finals themselves, however, the magical Cruyff and his supporting cast of improvisors captured the imagination of everyone.

Uruguay, Bulgaria, Argentina, East Germany, and Brazil fell to defeat decisively, and Holland became the sentimental favorite to win the World

Championship. In the final, however, Dutch failure to build on a quick 1-0 lead in the first half, coupled with a stalwart West German defense in the second half, undid the Dutch masters, and the ultimate prize was lost, 2-1.

Though many stars were lured to more lucrative pastures in other countries, Holland had by now produced so many world-class players that the future of the national team looked bright. After a worrisome slump in 1975, Holland rapidly regained its form and qualified for the 1978 World Cup as a co-favorite to win, despite Cruyff's retirement from the team.

The dispersion of its great players and the XNVG's curious lack of confidence in Dutch coaches was seen as a likely cause for decline, but the Dutch once again advanced to the final of the World Cup in 1978, and they mounted a bold challenge to Argentina.

After a disappointing first round, Holland defeated Austria and Italy decisively, and in the final tenaciously held on before Argentina won in extra time, 3-1, in front of a delirious Buenos Aires crowd. Holland became only the third country in history to gain back-to-back finals in the World Cup, and, unfortunately, the first to lose twice in a row.

A new generation of great players, led by Ruud Gullit and Marco van Basten finally brought the Netherlands that elusive title. They won the 1988 European Championship in spectacular fashion, defeating host West Germany in a tremendous semifinal, then downing the U.S.S.R. thanks to a Gullit header and a wondrous van Basten volley.

The 1990 World Cup finals, however, were disappointing—eventual elimination coming in the second round against West Germany. And the 1992 European Championship also brought frustration. Although many felt that the Dutch had the best team, upstart Denmark played them to a draw in their semifinal and then won the penalty kick tiebreaker when the usually unstoppable van Basten failed on his spot kick.

NETHERLANDS ANTILLES

Address: Nederlands Antilliaanse Voetbal Unie, P.O. Box 341, Curaçao, N.A. *Founded:* 1921. *FIFA:* 1932. *CONCACAF:* 1961. *National stadium:* Rif Stadium, Willemstad (6,000); *largest stadium:* Rif Stadium. *Colors:* White jerseys with red and blue stripes; white shorts. *Season:* August to February.

The Netherlands Antilles—comprised of three tiny islands in the upper Leeward group and three larger islands off the coast of Venezuela—has a long and venerable tradition in Caribbean soccer, as does the region's other former Dutch colony, Surinam. It was characteristic of Dutch colonies that they developed their game earlier than many of their British counterparts.

The Netherlands Antilles, under the name Dutch West Indies, was a participant in the 1952 Olympic Games, and both Curaco, the most important of the Netherlands Antilles, and Surinam maintained the busiest international schedule of any colonies in the Caribbean region between 1934 and 1961.

With the growth of soccer in the CONCACAF region, however, the Netherlands Antilles have found it increasingly difficult to compete. It was eliminated from the 1994 World Cup qualifying tournament in the preliminary round by Antigua, an example of the emerging soccer nations in the region that have contributed to a much more balanced level of competition among the small federations.

NEW HEBRIDES
(Now Vanuatu)

Address: P.O. Box 266, Port Vila. *Founded:* 1934 as New Hebrides. *FIFA:* 1991. *Colors:* Gold and black.

The New Hebrides, a joint French-British condominium in the Southwestern Pacific, has been active in regional Oceania competitions since the early 1960s. The first internationals were played shortly after World War II.

In 1951 New Zealand crushed their small rival 9-0 at a tournament in Nouméa, New Caledonia, and in 1963 New Hebrides entered the first South Pacific Games Soccer Tournament.

It was also one of the five participants in the first Oceania Cup at Auckland in 1973, placing fourth in the table ahead of Fiji. New Hebrides lost all of its matches with New Zealand, Tahiti, and New Caledonia, but emerged victorious over Fiji. Its most frequent opponents in the past 30 years have been New Zealand and New Caledonia.

In 1992, competing under its new name of Vanuatu, World Cup qualifying ended with four defeats and just one goal scored against Fiji and New Zealand.

NEW ZEALAND

Address: New Zealand Football Association, Inc., Central Park, Green Lane, P.O. Box 62-532, Auckland 6. *Founded:* 1891. *FIFA:* 1948. *OFC:* 1966. *Largest stadium:* Newmarket Park, Auckland (18,000). *Colors:* White jerseys with black trim, black shorts. *Season:* March to October.

Soccer was introduced to New Zealand during the 1880s, but it immediately took a distant second seat to rugby, a position it has never escaped despite reaching the 1982 World Cup finals. The association game was played in Dunedin as early as 1880 and in Auckland, Wellington, and Christchurch shortly thereafter.

The oldest extant club is North Shore, founded in 1886 at Auckland, and the first governing body, the Auckland Football Association, was formed the same year. The Otago (Dunedin) and Canterbury (Christchurch) associations were formed in 1889, and the Wellington association was formed in 1891. It was also in 1891 that an umbrella body, the New Zealand Football Association, was established and sought affiliation with the Football Association in London.

The first unofficial internationals were played in 1904 at home by regional and national representative teams against New South Wales. In a series of nine games, the Australian team defeated New Zealand 1-0 and, seven days later, held them to a 3-3 draw. Regional New Zealand selections won twice, drew once, and lost four times.

One year later a national representative team played various Australian clubs and a New South Wales selection, and New Zealand won six, drew two, and lost three, including one each against New South Wales. The other opponents on the Australian tour were clubs from New South Wales.

New Zealand did not participate in international competition again until similar tours were set up in 1922 (in New Zealand), and 1923 (in Australia). The results were again mixed, but curiously enough, New Zealand fared better away than at home.

In 1924 there was an extensive 22-game tour of New Zealand by a Chinese university selection, dominated by regional New Zealand teams.

A Canadian representative team descended on New Zealand in 1927 and won 20 out of 23 games, and, after two further series with various Australian teams in 1933 and 1936, England "Amateur" paid a visit in 1937 and won all nine contests against a representative New Zealand team and assorted regional selections. New Zealand's goal difference against England "Amateur" was 6 for and 84 against, a startling indicator of the relative level of play in New Zealand soccer.

World War II provided increased exposure to the game as New Zealand troops fought their way across North Africa and Europe. As a result, a surge of interest occurred after the war, and in 1948 the New Zealand Football Association, Inc. joined FIFA.

In subsequent weeks, New Zealand played its first official internationals against Australia—a series of four games at home—all of which were lost with an aggregate score of 1-25.

In 1951 a national team made its first tour of Oceania, defeating New Caledonia three times and Suva, New Hebrides, and Fiji once each; New Caledonia also won once. This was the beginning of a long and steady association with the islands of the South Pacific, many of which have been among New Zealand's friendliest opponents.

The rivalry with Australia, however, has dominated New Zealand soccer over the past 30 years. Only in 1982, when Winton Rufer led the All Whites to the World Cup finals, has the national team been able to get past its neighbor in qualifying play.

The presence of Israel in the same Oceania qualifying section also proved an obstacle to success. In 1993 it again must get by Australia in a head-to-head showdown to have any chance to reach the 1994 finals.

NICARAGUA

Address: Federacion Nicarauguense de Fútbol, Inst. de Deportes, Apartado Postal 976 0383, Managua, D.N. *Founded:* 1931. *FIFA:* 1950. *CONCACAF:* 1968. *National stadium:* Estadio Nacional, Managua (30,000); *largest stadium:* Estadio Nacional. *Colors:* Blue-and-white striped jerseys, blue shorts. *Season:* June to September.

Nicaragua is the only Central American country other than the infant Belize that has failed to win a single international tournament. As a national sport, soccer is still seriously challenged by much-loved baseball.

Nicaragua entered international competition with its participation in the 1941 Championship of the Confederación Centroamericano y del Caribe de Fútbol (forerunner of the Championship of CONCACAF).

Nicaragua did not attempt to qualify for the World Cup until 1992 when it was easily eliminated by El Salvador 10-1 over two matches in the opening phase of qualifying competition.

NIGER

Address: Fédération Nigérienne de Foot-Ball, Stade National Niamey, B.P. 10299, Niamey-Balafon. *Founded:* 1967. *FIFA:* 1967. *CAF:*

1967. *National stadium:* Stade National, Niamey (7,082); *largest stadium:* Stade National. *Colors:* White jerseys, white shorts. *Season:* January to June, September to December.

Niger, home of the world's largest sand dunes and unspoiled natural game reserves, is just starting to make an impact in Africa. Though French soldiers sometimes played the game in their garrisons at Niamey or Agades during the first decades of this century, the growth of soccer in this part of the Sahara has come about only since independence in 1960.

Little connection was made between soccer interests in Niamey and the French West African governing body at Dakar during the colonial era, and a Nigerien (not to be confused with Nigerian) association was not founded until 1967. A national league was introduced in the 1960s, and Nigerien champion clubs entered the African Champions' Cup as early as 1970.

A national cup competition is also held, and its winners have been participants in the new African Cup Winners' Cup. In 1994 qualifying for the World Cup, Niger held African champion Ivory Coast 0-0 at home and then lost 1-0 at Abidjan to just miss advancing to the second round. These games may mark the start of stronger national team showings in the future.

NIGERIA

Address: Nigeria Football Association, Nigeria National Stadium, P.O. Box 466, Lagos. *Founded:* 1945. *FIFA:* 1959. *CAF:* 1959. *National stadium:* Nigeria National Stadium, Lagos (50,000); *largest stadium:* Nigeria National Stadium. *Colors:* Green jerseys with white trim, white shorts. *Season:* January to December.

Honors: African Champions (1980), runners-up (1984, 1988, 1990); World 16-Under Champion (1985) runner-up (1987).

Shortly after independence in 1960, Nigeria emerged as a major soccer power in Africa by virtue of its size. It is the most populous country on the continent but its exceedingly fragmented population has created a certain lack of cohesion at the national level.

Consequently, Nigeria was initially more successful in African club competitions than World Cup qualifying rounds or the African Nations' Cup, but that changed with the 1980s.

The big Nigerian cities of Lagos, Ibadan, and Enugu spawn some of Africa's leading clubs. Increasingly, Nigeria's national team, the "Green Eagles," can be counted on to place well in international competition, though a place in the World Cup finals is still to be attained.

British missionaries were more influential in importing soccer to Nigeria than commercial or military colonists, but the greatest exposure to the game was seen during World War II when the country was inundated by British troops. The Nigeria Football Association was set up in 1945 as a result and became affiliated with The Football Association in London.

Its first unofficial international was played in 1950 against archrival Gold Coast (now Ghana) at Accra, and it was won 1-0 by the Gold Coast.

After learning basic elements of the game, the level of play among Nigerians remained fairly static until the early 1960s. European coaches were hired in ever increasing numbers, and a great surge of public interest in soccer—identified strongly with the new spirit of independence—swept through Nigerian cities.

The "Green Eagles" first entered World Cup qualification rounds for 1962 and qualified for the final rounds of the African Nations' Cup as early as 1963, ultimately facing elimination by the vastly more experienced Egypt and Sudan.

Shortly thereafter, a turning point in Nigerian soccer occurred with "Green Eagles" tours in the north of England (Blackpool and Sheffield Wednesday), the U.S.S.R. (Dinamo Moscow), and Egypt.

But it was not until 1968, after further poor showings in World Cup and African Nations' Cup qualification rounds, that Nigeria appeared on the world scene at the Olympic Games in Mexico City.

In the first round, the "Green Eagles" lost decisively to Japan and the Spanish amateurs, but the team went home with some satisfaction in holding the Brazilian amateurs to a 3-3 draw.

In 1969 Nigeria narrowly missed qualification for the 1970 World Cup when Morocco grabbed the first African berth in modern times by a toss of the coin. Meanwhile, the African Nations' Cup continued to elude the Nigerians, and they bowed out of the 1974 World Cup to Ghana in the third qualifying round.

Nigeria finally gained its rightful place among African powers with a third place finish in the Nations' Cup of 1976 by defeating Zaire and Sudan in the first round and Egypt in the final pool. That foreshadowed the African Champi onship victory of 1980 and three runner-up places in the next ten years.

In 1985 Nigeria won its first major international honor when its 16-Under team defeated West Germany in the final of the first FIFA World 16-Under Championship held in China. Two years later it unluckily lost the title to the U.S.S.R., losing the final on penalty kicks although many thought Nigeria's team the most exciting in the event staged in Canada.

On the club level, Shooting Stars won the second edition of the African Cup Winners Cup in 1976 and Rangers Enugu made it two straight Nigerian triumphs a year later. BCC Lions won the same trophy in 1990 but the African Champions Cup has eluded Nigerian sides.

NORWAY

Address: Norges Fotballforbund, Ullevål Hageby, Postboks 3283, 0805 Oslo. *Founded:* 1902. *FIFA:* 1908. *UEFA:* 1954. *National stadium:* Ullevål Stadion, Oslo (24,500); *largest stadium:* Lerkendal Stadion, Trondheim (30,000). *Colors:* Red jerseys, white shorts. *Season:* April to November. *Honors:* Olympic Games third place (1936).

Though Norway has made less of an impact on international soccer than either Sweden or Denmark, it has made great improvement in the 1980s. In a nation that is buried under ice and snow in winter and is bounded by the world's rockiest coastline, the Norwegian F.A. has successfully included all parts of the country in a sophisticated network of leagues and cup competitions.

Fotball is the major summertime sport in Norway, as it is in the rest of Scandinavia, and Norwegians are second to none in their love for the game. Indeed, when their own leagues and cup are dormant for the winter, thousands of fans follow the English and Scottish game with equal interest through television.

Soccer was introduced in Norway by students in Oslo during the 1880s, and it caught on rapidly, especially in the coastal cities between Oslo and Bergen. The Norges Fotballforbund (NFF) was founded in 1902, and in its first year launched the Norgesmesterskapet (Norwegian Cup) that in many respects is still the most important competition in the country. In 1908, three years after Norway's independence from Sweden, the NFF became one of the early members of FIFA.

The Norwegian Cup was initially won by the Arendal club IK Grane, which was founded only weeks before the competition started. But the first decade was dominated in the main by Odds Skien, whose 11 wins still top the roster of Cup achievement even though the club is no longer a First Division side. Fredrikstad FK, with nine titles, and Viking, from Stavanger (eight), have the most league wins since a championship started in 1938.

Norway's first full internationals were played against Sweden between 1908 and 1912, and it lost all four games by an aggregate of 5-21. Its first international victories finally occurred in 1918 (back-to-back against Denmark and Sweden in Oslo), and its first significant win came in 1923, a 2-0 shutout of France in Paris.

Most of Norway's victories in the 1920s were at the expense of Finland. Numerous wins over its Scandinavian opponents were reinforced in 1930 and 1931 by two draws with Germany and victories over Holland and Switzerland.

Norway proved to be a nemesis for Germany throughout the 1930s. It drew again with Germany in 1933 and 1935, and at the 1936 Olympic Games in Berlin achieved the biggest upset in its history by knocking Germany out of the competition before a huge crowd that included Hitler himself; the score was 2-0.

In the semifinals at Berlin, it lost as expected to Italy, but not until it had taken the Italian amateurs into overtime. A few days later Norway defeated Poland to win a much deserved bronze medal and its greatest honor to date.

The following year, Norway attempted to qualify for the World Cup for the first time, eliminating the Republic of Ireland in the process, and at the games in France in 1938 met the full Italian international team and forced the world champions to an identical overtime result (a 2-1 loss) that had shocked the Italian amateurs in 1936.

Though eliminated in the first round, the Norwegians returned home heroes once again. During the Nazi occupation, in an act of revenge, coach Halvorsen of the 1936 Olympic team was tortured to death by the Gestapo for refusing to allow the national team to play under German sponsorship. Halvorsen had played organized soccer in Hamburg as a student.

In the postwar years, Norway resumed its former rate of success and, from 1952, Norway began to participate regularly in World Cup and Olympic qualification tournaments.

The 1994 qualifying tournament for the World Cup shows signs of possibly being history-making; even if Norway don't reach the finals it has at least demonstrated that they are no longer a minor player on the European stage.

OMAN

Address: P.O. Box 6462, Ruwi-Muscta. *Founded:* 1978.

This sandy sultanate on the Arabian peninsula was not affiliated with either FIFA or the Asian Football Confederation until 15 years ago, but soccer is beginning to be organized there.

Oman entered the 1986 World Cup qualifying but then withdrew, so its first actual World Cup matches came in 1990 when draws with Qatar and Iraq indicated some potential for growth.

PAKISTAN

Address: Pakistan Football Federation, General Secretary, 43 Rettigon Road, Lahore. *Founded:* 1948. *FIFA:* 1948. *National stadium:* Karachi Stadium, Karachi (35,000); *largest stadium:* Karachi Stadium. *Colors:* Green jerseys, white shorts. *Season:* March to October.

The growth of soccer in Pakistan occurred while the country was still a province of British India. At the time of its independence in 1947, Pakistan showed promise as a future power in Asian soccer, having jumped to a head start over its non-British rivals by several years.

Though it has continued to prosper as the sport of the masses and in numerical terms, it has not equaled the traditional national sports of field hockey and cricket in interest. Pakistan has made little impact on international competition. Its 1990 World Cup qualifying participation, when it lost to the UAE and Kuwait, confirmed its relative regional weakness.

Pakistan's lack of progress in international competition since the 1950s has also been caused by the rapid growth of the game in other parts of Asia. As a result of political disorders, Pakistan was rarely been seen in important Asian tournaments such as the Asian Games, the Asian Cup, and qualifying rounds for the Olympic Games and World Cup until recent years.

PANAMA

Address: Federación Nacional de Fútbol de Panamá, Apartado Postal 1436, Balboa Ancon, Panama 1. *Founded:* 1937. *FIFA:* 1938. *Colors:* Red, blue, and white jerseys; blue shorts.

The strong American presence in Panama since the turn of the century dampened the possibility that soccer would find an early home there, but the game eventually seeped into the country by social osmosis from neighboring states.

Panama has traditionally been the second weakest Central American country on the soccer field after Nicaragua. Baseball is still prominent, but soccer has made small gains.

A 1992 victory over Costa Rica in a World Cup qualifying match, followed by qualification for the 1993 CONCACAF Gold Cup are indications of progress.

In the 1930s, there had been a small boom in soccer activities, and the Federación Nacional de Fútbol was founded in 1937. The new federation wasted little time in affiliating with FIFA, and it immediately set out to participate in regional soccer activities.

The Central American and Caribbean Games, held in Panama in 1938, provided its first opportunity, and Panama made its international debut in the soccer tournament of that competition. Its only major trophy to date came in 1951 in a precursor to the current CONCACAF Gold Cup.

PAPUA-NEW GUINEA

Address: Papua-New Guinea Football Association, P.O. Box 1716, Boroko. *Founded:* 1962. *FIFA:* 1963. *OFC:* 1966. *National stadium:* Port Moresby Stadium, Port Moresby (22,000); *largest stadium:* Port Moresby Stadium. *Colors:* Green jerseys with white trim, white shorts. *Season:* February to November.

Soccer was played by British soldiers and technicians at Port Moresby before the turn of the century and in Rabaul and other settlements by the British and Australians during World War II, but Papuans themselves received little exposure to the game until the 1950s. Australians were mainly responsible for teaching it to townspeople and helped local administrators to set up a governing body with permission from FIFA.

Papua-New Guinea, largely through its strong Australian connection, was active in the formation of the Oceania Football Confederation in 1966. It has participated regularly in the soccer tournament of the South Pacific Games and placed second to Fiji in the 1969 edition.

The Papua-New Guinea Football Association, which was founded in 1962 and affiliated with FIFA one year later, did not enter the 1994 World Cup.

PARAGUAY

Address: Liga Paraguaya de Fútbol, Estadio de Sajonia, Calles Mayor, Martínez y Alejo García, Asunción. *Founded:* 1906. *FIFA:* 1921. *CONMEBOL:* 1921. *National stadium:* Estadio de la Liga Paraguaya de Fútbol, Asunción (50,000); *largest stadium:* Estadio de la Liga Paraguaya. *Colors:* Red-and-white striped jerseys, blue shorts. *Season:* May to December. *Honors:* South American Championship winner (1953, 1979), runner-up (1929, 1949, 1963).

Paraguayan soccer has a long and venerable history. Its wide experience has yielded a fair share of successes in international competition, especially when one considers its small population. In overall South American ratings, Paraguay usually ranks fourth, although Colombia has mounted a serious recent challenge to that claim.

The national league, centered in Asunción, was founded in 1906, and it is one of the oldest in Latin America. The usual separation of league and national association did not take place when Paraguayan soccer was first organized, and thus the founding date of the governing body and the league are the same.

The early years of league competition were dominated by some of the same clubs which still figure prominently in the first division: Guarani, Cerro Porteño and Olímpia, who continue to head the honors list. Olímpia has won 33 titles and Cerro Porteño has captured 21, and they often represent Paraguay internationally in the Copa Libertadores. Olímpia has won that competition twice and been runner-up on three occasions.

In 1921 the Liga Paraguaya de Fútbol (LPF) joined FIFA and CONMEBOL, and the national team participated in the South American Championship for the first time, placing fourth in a field of four. Its first international victory was won in this competition with a 2-1 result over Uruguay.

The upward momentum of Paraguayan soccer was thwarted by war with Bolivia between 1929 and 1935 and by the confusion that resulted from the adoption of professionalism in 1931. The league suspended competition for three years, and the national team missed the thirteenth edition of the South American Championship (1935) after being one of that series' most consistent participants.

During this period, Paraguay produced its greatest player, Arsenio Erico, who unfortunately never played for a major club in his native country. He was, instead, the hero of Independiente in Argentina and led his adopted club to successive honors in the late 1930s.

The expansion of professionalism in South America during the 1930s helped to raise the standard of play in Paraguay, but it also marked the beginning of a continuing player exodus to wealthier leagues in Argentina, Brazil, Spain, and Italy.

The immediate postwar years were an age of growth and enthusiasm in Paraguayan soccer.

Several clubs emerged as champions of the first division, holding Olímpia and Cerro to a pair of titles each, and the LPF built a grand new stadium in Asunción during the early 1950s.

Fleitas Solich was hired to manage the national team, which had already achieved an unprecedented pair of back-to-back second place results in the 1947 and 1949 South American Championship, and under him Paraguay raced undefeated to the 1953 title in Lima.

A noteworthy triumph in many respects, this win was charged with historical import and controversy. Paraguay appeared to win the competition outright with a two-point margin over World Cup runners-up Brazil, but its 3-0 win over Chile was rescinded because of a substitution violation. This put Paraguay and Brazil level on points and the Liga Paraguaya de Fútbol organized a play-off, which the Paraguayans won 3-2. The result, however, is still not officially acknowledged by Brazil.

Paraguay's performance in the 1950 World Cup, meanwhile, had done little to capture world attention, as Sweden easily coasted to a 2-2 draw, and the weakest Italian team in decades assured Paraguay's elimination with a 2-0 shutout. Paraguay qualified for the World Cup again in 1958 after stunning Uruguay in the qualification round by a 7-0 aggregate score, but it was no match for the seven goals scored by France in the first round at Norköpping.

Paraguay did, however, manage to hold the strong Yugoslavian team to a draw, and Scotland went down to an expected 3-2 defeat. These generally favorable results punctuated Paraguay's most successful decade in international competition. Paraguay did not qualify for the World Cup finals again until 1986 when it was eliminated by England in the second round. In 1990 a surprising loss to Ecuador cost them

dearly in a group won by Colombia, an eventual finalist in Italy.

The Liga Paraguaya de Fútbol consists of a first division, lower divisions, and regional leagues. The national champion is the winner of the first division. After the first division championship ends, the top six finishers in the first division play against the major provincial champions in a second competition.

The winner of this series plays the runner-up of the already completed first division for the second berth in next year's Copa Libertadores.

PERU

Address: Federación Peruana de Fútbol, Estadio Nacional-Puerta No. 4, Calle José Diaz, Lima. *Founded:* 1922. *FIFA:* 1924. *CONMEBOL:* 1926. *National stadium:* Estadio Nacional, Lima (45,000); *largest stadium:* Estadio Universidad de San Marcos, Lima (60,000). *Colors:* White jerseys with red diagonal stripe, white shorts. *Season:* April to December. *Honors:* South American Championship winner (1939, 1975).

Peru has slipped recently in South American soccer but has been the spawning ground of several dazzling players of world caliber, including the incomparable Teofilo Cubillas, perhaps the most gifted non-Brazilian ball artist to have come from South America in the last 30 years.

The Peruvian style of play in the upper ranks is fluid and pleasing to the eye. When good Peruvian teams are in top form, they can challenge the best of both Europe and South America, as shown by their performances in the 1970 World Cup.

The national team has suffered greatly in recent years by the exodus of top players to Europe and Mexico, and few stars emerged to take the place of its great players of the 1970s. The problems of making an impact internationally are still being felt.

Soccer was introduced to Peru according to the familiar pattern in Latin America. British advisors, engineers, and other technicians played the game among themselves in Callao and other commercial centers during the last decades of the nineteenth century, and the game eventually found its way to the local population.

A league was established in Lima as early as 1912, with Peruvian-based clubs among its membership, but this was not a direct ancestor of the present national federation.

In the early 1920s (a period of tremendous growth in South American soccer), efforts were made to organize Peruvian soccer fully. The Federación Peruana de Fútbol (FPF) was founded in 1922—the first of five national associations founded in the northern part of South America around this time—and while it gained membership in FIFA two years later, administrative difficulties caused a reorganization in 1925.

This led to the introduction of the Liga Nacional de Football in 1926, with clubs from Lima and Callao. The first champion was Club Sport Progreso, but Club Alianza Lima, which became strongly identified with black and poor mestizo neighborhoods in the capital, and Club Universitario de Deportes, founded by Spanish students in 1924, eventually took control of the league.

Alianza Lima has won 16 championships to Universaitario's 19, but it must be remembered that the Alianza club was decimated by a tragic plane crash in 1987 that destroyed the team's corps of experienced players and officials.

Peru's international debut was made in 1927 as host of the eleventh South American Championship. Argentina and Uruguay, both major world powers during the 1920s, defeated the fledgling home team decisively (5-1 and 4-0), but Bolivia, the fourth participant, lost 3-2, and Peru took third place.

In the next three editions of the competition, Peru took last or next to last place each time, but in 1939, when the championship was staged again in Lima, the home side advantage helped Peru win its first South American Championship and international victory. Peru was undefeated in four games against Uruguay, Paraguay, Chile, and Ecuador, but, without either Argentina or Brazil participating, some of the significance of this win was surely compromised.

The Peruvian federation's early interest in international tournaments was further reflected by its entrance in the first World Cup in 1930 at Montevideo, but this proved to be the beginning of a stormy decade in global competition. A brutal 3-1 loss to Rumania, in which the Peruvian captain was sent off and another Peruvian's leg was broken, was followed by a bitter 1-0 loss to the eventual world champion, Uruguay, and both games suffered from poor refereeing. Peru was duly eliminated in the first round.

Though professionalism was adopted in 1931, the FPF was still able to send many of its best players to take part in the 1936 Olympics in Berlin. Since this was Peru's first major sporting effort in Europe, a small but volatile group of Peruvian fans gathered in Berlin to lend support. In the first round, the Finnish amateurs were easy prey for Peru's skilled forwards, but against Austria in the second round extra time was required.

Peruvian supporters rioted in the second overtime period, and after Peru scored two goals in all the confusion, Austria protested. The game was disallowed and a replay was ordered. Peru refused to show up for the replay, Austria was awarded the two points, and Peru went home in disgust. This incident erased the good will and respect achieved in 1933 by Universitario's 30-game tour of Europe, which lasted six months and in some respects marked a turning point in the advancement of Peruvian soccer.

Throughout the 1940s and 1950s, Peru continued to participate in most editions of the South American Championship, usually finishing in the middle of the standings. It narrowly lost to Brazil in 1958 World Cup qualifications rounds, and in 1959 (under Hungarian manager and former great György Orth) it defeated England 4-1 in Lima. In 1970 it finally qualified again for the World Cup.

Managed by the Brazilian star Didi, Peru was the surprise of the 1970 competition, showing flair and a high level of skill. Its 20-year-old inside forward Teofilo Cubillas became the most highly touted South American player since Pelé. After winning elegantly over Bulgaria and Morocco, the same good form was shown in losing to West Germany (on a hat trick by Gerd Müller) and, in the quarterfinals, to Brazil.

By now, Peru was clearly producing players of international caliber, and it was fitting that a Brazilian had been chosen to bring them together and create an atmosphere in which they could fully display their great skills.

Surprisingly, however, Peru could not build on that achievement. After failing to qualify for the 1974 finals, the 1978 team suffered a humiliating defeat against Argentina in the second round, a 6-0 loss which put the home team through to the final and left the Brazilians complaining that Peru had not played to its potential.

Peru's depth of talent, however, was demonstrated in 1975, when it played the same brand of fluid, improvisational soccer and, with more than its fair share of luck, managed to win its second South American Championship.

Having eliminated Chile and Bolivia in the first round, Peru was fortunate to play a provincial Brazilian selection in the semifinals and then advance to the final by lot after the two countries played to an even goal aggregate. In the final, Peru faced traditionally weak Colombia and, on the basis of the tournament's point system, was forced to a third and deciding match in neutral Caracas before finally winning the title.

Peru went on to qualify for that 1978 World Cup in Argentina with nagging managerial disputes threatening it potential effectiveness. In the first round, however, it landed on top of its group after a 3-1 upset of Scotland and a scoreless draw with Holland.

Sadly, this talented team of World Cup veterans failed to score in losses to Brazil, Poland, and Argentina in the semifinals, and went home in disgrace.

The 1982 World Cup proved equally unsatisfactory, with Peru crashing out 5-1 to Poland after uninspiring draws with Italy and Cameroon in which no goals were scored. By then there was little sign of the old Peruvian flair and the next two World Cup finals were missed altogether.

As political unrest troubled the nation into the 1990s, there was little optimism that the 1994 entry would fare any better in qualifying.

In the Copa Libertadores, the South American club championship, Universitario (known as "U") reached the 1972 final, but no Peruvian team has won the trophy.

PHILIPPINES

Address: Philippine Football Association, Room 207, Administration Building, Rizal Memorial Sports Complex, Vito Cruz, Metro Manila. *Founded:* 1907. *FIFA:* 1928. *AFC:* 1954. *National stadium:* Rizal Memorial Football Stadium, Manila (30,000); *largest stadium:* Rizal Memorial Football Stadium. *Colors:* Blue-and-red jerseys, blue shorts. *Season:* July to April.

The Republic of the Philippines, once an American territory, was the principal instigator and organizer of soccer and other sports in the Far East region immediately after the turn of the century. Its importance in this regard is unchallenged. After the 1920s, however, it failed to make any impact at all in international soccer.

The Philippines has since disappeared entirely from the mainstream of the Asian game due to the rising influence of American sports such as baseball and basketball after World War I. In the postwar era, the Philippines have rarely been seen in major international soccer competitions, and in recent years have not even entered World Cup qualifying rounds.

POLAND

Address: Polski Zwiazek Pilki Noznej (Polish Football Association), Al Ujazdowskie 22, 00-478 Warszawa. *Founded:* 1919. *FIFA:* 1923. *UEFA:* 1955. *National stadium:* Tenth Anniversary Stadium, Warsaw (87,000); *largest stadium:* Slaski Stadium, Chorzów (93,000). *Colors:* White jerseys, red shorts. *Season:* August to November, March to June. *Honors:* World Cup third place (1974, 1982), Olympic Games winner (1972), runner-up (1976, 1992).

For 80 years Polish soccer suffered the consequences of political division, a long search for identity, and what seemed to be an incurable inferiority complex. Surrounded geographically by traditional soccer powers, it faced a rare challenge.

In 1970 Polish soccer came of age, and the national team gained and maintained a place among the top half dozen countries in Europe stretching into the middle 1980s. Today it is rebuilding around a successful 1992 Olympic team as an earlier generation of international stars has faded from the scene.

From the beginning, each turning point in Polish soccer has coincided closely with political changes in the country as a whole. The game was first played in Poland by British engineers in Lodz around 1890, but Czarist administrators in central Poland—then part of Russia—suppressed the formation of clubs and leagues, because they were thought to represent the threat of revolutionary activity.

On the other hand, the game flourished in those areas of the modern Polish state that were part of Germany or Austria. In German Poland, several clubs were founded before the turn of the century.

In Austrian Poland (Galicia), the university city of Kraków spawned the first club in the southeastern region—Cracovia Football Club—founded in 1906. Other Galician clubs followed, and in 1911, as befitting Cracovia's cosmopolitan reputation, organizers in Kraków introduced international competition in Poland by inviting Aberdeen F.C. for a two-game series against a local representative team. The Scots won, 11-1 and 8-1, but before World War I this was to be expected when any British team visited the continent.

Efforts to start regional governing bodies in Prussia, Pomerania, Silesia, and Galicia met with some success between 1900 and 1914, but Czarist bureaucrats thwarted a prewar attempt to launch a Polish soccer federation that included Russian Poland. Therefor, when FIFA received an application for membership from Polish soccer administrators, it was turned down. In Czarist Poland, meanwhile, there were barely any clubs to be found.

Poland's self-proclaimed independence in 1918 opened a Pandora's box. In 1919, only six months after the ratification of Polish independence at the Treaty of Versailles, the Polski Zwiazek Pilki Noznej (PZPN) was formed, end all aspects of Polish soccer grew by leaps and bounds. Clubs sprang up everywhere, especially in the industrial regions of Silesia and Galicia.

When the PZPN gained membership in FIFA in 1923, there were hundreds of clubs and more than 15,000 players registered, though Warsaw and other former Russian-held regions were slower to develop. Two leagues—one in the north and one in the south—were introduced in 1920, and the first Polish champion (Cracovia) was crowned after a play–off between the two league leaders. In 1927 this burgeoning activity led to the formation of a national league.

Having just missed in its attempt to enter the 1920 Olympics in Antwerp, Poland made its international debut one year later with a friendly against Hungary in Budapest (lost 1-0), and in 1922 won its first international matches—both away—against Sweden and Yugoslavia. The rise of professionalism in Central Europe, however, soon advanced the level of play in Austria, Hungary, and Czechoslovakia beyond the capabilities of late-blooming Poland.

Balkan, Scandinavian, and Baltic opponents were the only consistently weaker teams during the 1920s and 1930s. A 5-0 loss to Hungary at the 1924 Olympics, Poland's first official international competition, set the tone for many results that were to follow against the rising Magyar tide.

In its first attempt to qualify for the World Cup in 1933, the Poles indicated a marked improvement by holding Czechoslovakia to a 2-1 win in Warsaw. In 1935 it defeated Austria in a friendly, and despite a discouraging loss to Norway at the 1936 Olympic Games, Poland's first crop of truly excellent players came to the fore.

Led by inside forward Ernest Wilimowski, Poland qualified for the 1938 World Cup by eliminating Yugoslavia, but then had the misfortune of drawing Brazil in the first round of the final stages. This match became one of the great scoring bonanzas in World Cup history with Wilimowski and Brazil's Leônidas scoring four goals each in a 6-5 Brazilian win. For the first time the world took notice of Polish soccer.

It was a short-lived day in the sun, however, and after several more losses in 1938 and 1939, the Nazi devastation ended Poland's rise as a budding soccer power.

During the Stalinist years from 1945 to 1953, Poland became easy prey for all Eastern Europe, but a turning point in Polish soccer was reached with the changes in the Polish government that came about in 1956. The end of the Stalinist era signaled the reentry of Poland into European and worldwide competition.

Poland attempted to qualify for the 1958 World Cup, but the Soviets were emerging as an international power at the time and won Poland's qualification round group. And Poland met with successive failures in Olympic and World Cup qualification rounds and European Nations' Cups throughout the 1960s.

The seeds of a renaissance, however, were sown with the rise of Poland's greatest club, Klub Sportowy Górnik, in the late 1950s. Górnik Zabrze won its first championship in 1957, and behind deep-lying forward Ernest Pol it began to dominate league and cup competition in the early 1960s.

With the appearance of inside forward Wlodzimierz Lubanski in 1963, Górnik began an amazing run of titles that included five championships in a row from 1963 to 1967, and five successive cup victories from 1968 to 1972. Their 14 titles through 1992 are still one more than Ruch Chorzow, but Legia Warsaw tops the Polish Cup winners table with nine triumphs.

In 1970, when the political climate in Poland was relaxed again with a change in regimes, Górnik reached the final of the European Cup Winners' Cup, and Kazimierz Gorski became manager of the national team.

The impetus provided by Górnik's success and the combined genius of Lubanski, Gorski, and Legia's extraordinary midfielder Kazimierz Deyna transformed the Polish national team.

Poland captured the gold medal at the 1972 Olympic Games, with Deyna winning the scoring title, and, based on Górnik and Legia players, qualified handily for the 1974 World Cup by eliminating England and Wales.

When Lubanski was seriously injured in 1973, putting his international career into a five-year hiatus, Górnik center forward Andrzej Szarmach was brought in by Gorski, and the Polish manager also picked Stal Mielec forward Grzegorz Lato to play on the right wing, Legia left wing Robert Gadocha, and Stal Mielec midfielder Henryk Kasperczak.

This lineup became the basis for what many believed to be the finest team in the 1974 World Cup. It disposed of Argentina, Italy, and Haiti in the first round and Sweden and Yugoslavia in the second before losing to the home team and eventual world champions West Germany by a mere 1-0. In the third place game, it outplayed Brazil, and Lato, high scorer in the tournament, drove home the winning goal. Playing fluid, crisp soccer on the order of Holland's and West Germany's "total football," Poland had come from nowhere in the space of five years to win the Olympic gold medal and third place in the World Cup.

After a slump in 1975, Poland returned to form and took the silver medal at the 1976 Olympics and went on to qualify for the 1978 World Cup with many of its 1974 stars intact. The attractive Polish style remained, though doubts arose that it could be translated into winning goals in the harsh atmosphere of Argentina.

But in Buenos Aires and Rosario, Poland won its first round group from the world champion West Germans, and despite lackluster performances in the semifinals against Argentina and Brazil— Deyna's decline in form was especially noticeable—it bowed out of the World Cup with its international reputation only slightly tarnished. Another strong side finished third in Spain in 1982, with Zbigniew Boniek emerging as still another Polish international star, while the 1986 team as qualified for the finals but heavily to Brazil, losing 4-0 in the second round after an indifferent opening round performance.

The first division of the Polish league was increased from 14 to 16 clubs in 1973 as a result of interest generated at home by the Olympic success. It is now supported by an 18-team league with a second division of two sections.

PORTUGAL

Address: Federaço Portuguêse de Futebol, Praça de Alegria No. 25, Apartado 21.100, P-1128 Lisboa. *Founded:* 1914. *FIFA:* 1926. *UEFA:* 1954. *National stadium:* Estádio Nacional, Lisbon (51,000); *largest stadium:* Estádio da Luz, Lisbon (70,000). *Colors:* Red jerseys, blue shorts. *Season:* September to July. *Honors:* World Cup third place (1966), World Youth Championship (1989, 1991).

Portugal's game has progressed consistently over the decades after a later start than much of the rest of Europe. Its political isolation became an advantage during World War II, because it was able to play against other neutral countries, such as Spain and Switzerland, and improve its level of play substantially.

Behind the incomparable brilliance of Mozambiquan striker Eusebio, Portugal and its leading club Benfica came of age during the 1960s and played some of the best soccer seen anywhere. Benfica shared dominance over Europe with the defensive-minded Italian clubs, and, indeed, it would have been fitting if the Portuguese national team had emerged victorious in the 1966 World Cup.

Portugal's international standing has declined following the departure of Eusebio and his teammates and Portugal's loss of its African reservoir of good players has caused an uncertain future for Portuguese soccer. A strong youth program, however, has rekindled hopes in the 1990s, Portugal having twice won the FIFA 20-and-under World Youth Cup.

Soccer was first played in Portugal in 1866 by British university students in Lisbon. During the 1870s it was still played by Britons only, but Lisbon Football Club, probably the first club in Portugal, was established in 1875. The first public game took place in the Campo da Parada, Cascais, in 1888.

The 1890s saw widespread acceptance of the game by the Portuguese themselves, as Portuguese boys returned from school in England. Most of the major clubs that were to distinguish themselves in later years were formed around the turn of the century: Clube Internacional de Futebol (1903), Sport Lisboa e Benfica (1904), and Sporting Clube de Portugal (1906).

The Liga de Futebol was founded in 1909 in Lisbon by Carcavelos, Benfica, Lisbon Cricket Club, and Internacional. In 1910 the Associaçao de Futebol de Lisboa (Lisbon) was founded.

Four years later the Lisbon association merged with the Unio Portuguêsa de Futebol (Porto and Portalegre) to form the Federaço Portuguêsa de Futebol and 26 district associations were set up.

World War I delayed Portugal's international debut until 1921. Its first four internationals were played against Spain between 1921 and 1925 without a win, but in 1925 it managed to slip by Italy 1-0 in Lisbon. Its first significant victory took place in Porto in 1928, and again it was Italy that fell.

In 1928 Portugal entered the Olympic Games in Amsterdam, where it defeated the tired Chileans and a disorganized Yugoslavia before losing to Egypt. Spain continued to be the focus of its international activity, though friendlies were arranged with France, Belgium, Yugoslavia, Czechoslovakia, and Hungary during the early 1930s.

Portugal's long-standing reputation for losing away games stems from this period. Indeed, a number of European opponents were not defeated on their home grounds by Portugal until the 1960s. Portugal did not defeat Spain on Spanish soil until 1947. Its first away win, other than the Olympic Games of 1924, was against the Republic of Ireland in 1947 (2-0).

Portugal has entered each World Cup since 1934, and all editions of the European Football Championship, the latter unsuccessfully until 1984, when it shared third with Denmark. It was eliminated from the 1934 World Cup in the qualifying round by Spain and was knocked out by Switzerland in the qualifying round of 1938.

Spain once again eliminated Portugal in 1950, and four years later the fine postwar Austrian national team led by Ernst Ocwirk mounted a 9-1 thrashing in Vienna that knocked Portugal out of the 1954 edition.

Northern Ireland proved to be the surprise winner of Portugal's 1958 qualifying group, but Italy split its results in that group with the rising Portuguese team in 3-0 and 0-3 home and away legs. In its 1962 qualifying group Portugal lost its away leg to Luxembourg 4-2 in one of the great upsets of the postwar era.

Portugal's participation in the 1966 edition in England remains its high point in World Cup ventures. In the end, it was a remarkable performance. Portugal wore down the fine Hungarian team led by Bene and Albert and easily overwhelmed Bulgaria.

As if that were not enough, it effectively ended Brazil's dominance over the world game by winning 3-1. True, Pelé was injured and the Brazilian team as a whole had not been performing well in previous games, but the depth of Brazil's bench—much used in this game—was itself thought to be capable of neutralizing Portugal.

As it turned out, the Brazilian manager's rejection of Garrincha, Gilmar, and Jairzinho, and the heavily bandaged knee of Pelé, mattered after all, and Brazil could not regroup after giving up two goals early in the first half.

In the quarterfinals, Eusebio single-handedly saved Portugal from the upset of the decade by scoring four goals against the Cinderella team from North Korea after losing 3-0 early in the game. The final score was 5-3 in Portugal's favor. Two of Eusebio's goals were from the penalty spot after some hard tackles by determined Korean defenders.

The sting of North Korea's surprise must have been felt in the semifinal match against England, and the stalwart backfield of Cohen, Moore, and Jackie Charlton won the game for the soon-to-be world champions. It was a noteworthy match for the sportsmanlike conduct of all players involved, but ultimately it was won by two skillful goals by Bobby Charlton.

Portugal's 2-1 third place win over the U.S.S.R. was not decided until the last two minutes with a goal by Torres, yet Portugal had played more skillfully than the defense-minded Russians all along. Having nearly reached the pinnacle of world soccer, the tired Portuguese team returned home, drained by the Koreans and numbed by the English, with the knowledge that this was Portugal's finest hour.

Portugal did not reach the finals again for 20 years, an appearance that ended in great disappointed as disputes clouded the entire participation and eventually led to great changes in the national team. A stunning loss to Morocco, following defeat by Poland, negated the value of an impressive opening game victory over England and sent Portugal home after the first round. The rise of Portuguese clubs to the forefront of European soccer corresponded with the successes of the national team, and was made possible by the same personnel: Eusebio, Coluña, and others.

The first Portuguese national championship, centered at the time in Lisbon and Oporto, had been launched in 1922. Its first winner was FC Porto, but it was played on a knockout basis, and is now considered to be the forerunner of the Portuguese cup rather than the league.

The national league was introduced in 1934-35, again with FC Porto the first winner, and a second division was added in 1938-39, followed by a third division in 1947-48.

Benfica has 29 league titles and 21 cup wins; Sporting has 16 league titles and 11 cup wins; but FC Porto, the strongest side recently, has closed the gap on that pair, winning 12 championships and adding seven Portuguese Cups to its collection.

Benfica's greatest era, however, stands out for the quality of its team and for the 11 championships it won between 1960 and 1973. In addition, Benfica won the European Cup in 1961 and 1962, the latter by defeating mighty Real Madrid in the final, and it was a finalist in 1963, 1965, 1968, 1988, and 1990. Sporting Lisbon, meanwhile, won the European Cup Winners' Cup in 1964 while FC Porto captured a European Cup in 1987.

PUERTO RICO

Address: Federación Puertorriqueña de Fútbol, Coliseo Roberto Clemente, Apartado 4355, Hato Rey 00919-4355. *Founded:* 1940. *FIFA:* 1960. *CONCACAF:* 1962. *National stadium:* Country Club, Urbanzación Country Club (8,000); *largest stadium:* Country Club. *Colors:* Red-and-white striped jerseys, blue shorts. *Season:* March to June.

The Commonwealth of Puerto Rico, which has maintained a confusing state of political semi-autonomy from the United States since 1952, presents an unusual story among soccer nations. The game was introduced to the island during the 1890s by Spanish colonists, probably before the American takeover in 1898.

In 1960 the national association joined FIFA, and it became an early member of CONCACAF in 1962. Unfortunately, Puerto Rican clubs have rarely been seen in regional club championships, but there is a reasonably active league structure in spite of formidable opposition from baseball, the island's leading sport.

The 1994 World Cup qualifying attempt produced controversy when American passport holders, who were non-Puerto Rican in origin, were included in the team that eliminated the Dominican Republic in the opening round. Because Puerto Ricans are American citizens, FIFA disallowed the Dominican protest, but it would seem that the issue of eligibility for the national team will need clarification in the future.

QATAR

Address: Quatar Football Association, P.O. Box 5333, Doha. *Founded:* 1960. *FIFA:* 1970. *AFC:* 1972. *National stadium:* Doha Athletic Stadium, Doha (8,000); *largest stadium:* Doha Athletic Stadium. *Colors:* Maroon-and-white jerseys, white shorts. *Season:* October to May.

The Sheikdom of Qatar was introduced soccer by British soldiers who were stationed on the peninsula during its period as a military protectorate from 1916 to 1971, but the local population did not become active participants until well after World War II. The organizing of domestic competition preceded Qatar's international debut by more than ten years with the founding of the Qatar Football Association (QFA) in 1960.

The standard of play in Qatar is growing as evidence by success at FIFA Youth tournaments, but a place in the World Cup finals has not been achieved. A growing national league and a strong youth program clearly indicate

Qatari desire to become a regional force at the very least and an international one if possible.

RUMANIA

Address: Federatia Romana de Fotbal, 16, Ne Vasile Conta, Bucurest 70130. *Founded:* 1908. *FIFA:* 1930. *UEFA:* 1955. *National stadium:* 23 August Stadium, Bucharest (95,000); *largest stadium:* 23 August Stadium. *Colors:* Yellow jerseys, blue shorts. *Season:* August to July.

For decades Rumania has showed great promise of becoming a major soccer power, but it has not yet accomplished a major breakthrough internationally except for Steaua Bucharest's 1986 European Cup triumph.

Overall, Rumania has been among the least successful Eastern European country in international competition, though vast enthusiasm and support for the game exists within its borders.

There is neither the overall winning record of Hungary, Yugoslavia, Czechoslovakia, or the former Soviet Union, nor the persistent threat of a winning era. Rumania has consistently managed to promise more than it has yet delivered.

The early history of Rumania's game engendered considerable hope. British engineers in the oil fields near Ploiesti introduced soccer during the late 1890s, and in 1899 the first competitions were started in Bucharest and Arad.

The game's adoption by the Rumanian populace received its first real impetus from Prince Carol, an inveterate fan, and largely through his aggressive support the Associata Cluburilor Romane de Football, the first national association, was founded in 1908. Two years later, Carol himself formed the Federation Societatilor de Sport din Romania, an umbrella body for all Rumanian sports, and became its first general secretary. The soccer association became a section within the federation.

In 1922, Rumania made its international debut in Belgrade against Yugoslavia, a new country still disorganized after a mere three years in existence, and won, 2-1. A great majority of Rumania's prewar contests were played against other Balkan states, mostly in connection with the Balkan Cup.

Rumania won three editions of the Balkan Cup before World War II, the first edition played on a home and away basis (1929-31), the third in Bucharest (1933), and the sixth in Sofia (1936). None of the Balkan states at this time, however, was a major force in Europe.

At the personal instigation of King Carol, Rumania became one of the small handful of European nations to make the long journey to Montevideo for the first World Cup in 1930. The team was picked by the king himself.

Its first round match against Peru was compromised by unfortunate circumstances: Rumania's right back broke his leg in a melee of hard tackling, and Peru's captain was sent off, leaving Peru severely weakened. Nevertheless, Rumania emerged victorious by 3-1. Against the great Uruguayan team (winner of the 1924 and 1928 Olympic tournaments and eventual winner in this first World Cup), Rumania met with its first world-class opposition and was lucky to lose by only 4-0.

In the 1934 World Cup, Rumania was eliminated in the first round by Czechoslovakia, one of Europe's leading teams at the time. In 1938, defeat came at the hands of unknown Cuba, which had qualified only after Mexico withdrew. The first match with Cuba, a 3-3 draw after extra time, was one of the best contests in the 1938 competition. Equalizers were scored moments before the end of regulation time and extra time.

In the replay, however, despite the benching of Cuba's impressive goalkeeper, Carvajales, the Cubans dominated the veteran Rumanian team and won 2-1 on second-half goals, including one that was thought by many to be from an offside position.

Rumania was then out of the World Cup until 1970, when a 2-1 victory over Czechoslovakia was their only win. They did not qualify for finals again until 1990 when they advanced to the second round but then lost a penalty-kick tie-breaker to Ireland after a 0-0 draw in Genoa.

Rumania has never finished in the top four in European Football Championship, either. In domestic competition, the league has been dominated by Steaua Bucharest and Dinamo Bucharest, both with 14 titles. During the notorious Ceaucescu regime Steaua was often favored, and it is difficult to assess their true place in Europe even allowing for that European Cup win.

RUSSIA
(Formerly part of the U.S.S.R.)

Address: Football Union of Russia, Luzhnetskaya Noberechnaja 8, 119270 Moscow. *Founded:* 1991. *FIFA:* 1946. *UEFA:* 1954. *National stadium:* Lenin Stadium, Moscow (104,000); *largest stadium:* Lenin Stadium. *Colors:* Red jerseys, white shorts. *Season:* February to November.

Honors: Olympic Games winner (1956, 1988), third place (1972, 1976, 1980); European Football Championship winner (1960), runner-up (1964, 1972, 1988).

The Soviet Union was a potential giant in world soccer, but it never quite reached the top. It was blessed with great organizational capabilities,

high motivation, a vast reservoir of players, and several stars of world-class caliber.

After a late arrival on the international scene, the U.S.S.R. moved with astounding speed to the front ranks of European soccer, though its only really significant international honors were a second-place finish in the 1972 and 1988 European Football Championship. It is a legacy Russia inherits in the post-Soviet age.

Russian (or Soviet) soccer will always be faced by two natural obstacles. The first is the long and ferocious winter that most of the country endures, causing ceaseless disorders in schedules and training programs. Second is its distant location from the major soccer centers of Europe and the vastness of its land.

Nevertheless, despite the love of gymnastics, track and field, ice hockey, skating in pairs, the Russians have long loved soccer. Even the personal preferences of the Soviet leadership were leaked out of the Kremlin. Nikita Khrushchev, a soccer player in his youth, was a Dinamo Kiev fan; Leonid Brezhnev was a supporter of CSKA Moscow, the Red Army club; Alexei Kosygin follows Dinamo Moscow; and Nikolai Podgorny is a keen Spartak Moscow fan.

It is a matter of policy that the first nonessential structure planned for each new industrial city is the local soccer stadium-capacity never less than 50,000. The U.S.S.R. Football Federation had more registered players in senior competition than any country in the world. But the strongest soccer-playing region was the Ukraine, now an independent soccer body on its own.

Soccer was introduced in Czarist Russia in 1887 by Britons Clement and Harry Charnock, whose family managed the Morozov Cotton Mills in Orekhovo Zuyevo, an industrial town in Moscow Province about 50 miles east of the city of Moscow.

Clement Charnock gathered together a dozen clerks at the mill and formed a team. He supplied the soccer balls, had blue-and-white uniforms made up in the colors of his favorite club, Blackburn Rovers, and paid all the expenses for one year.

The Clements' uncle took over the team for a time, and around 1890 Harry Charnock developed the club further, even recruiting soccer-playing textile mill workers in the British press.

Despite the influence of the Morozov club and the eventual formation of other Muscovite clubs, the game caught on more rapidly in St. Petersburg. In 1897, the Amateur Sports Club of St. Petersburg formed a team, and others in the capital quickly sprang up in workers' settlements and the industrial suburbs.

Clubs were also formed, however, by middle- and upper-middle-class students at military and secondary schools, and when a St. Petersburg Football League was started before the turn of the century, the entrance fees were set so high that working-class clubs and players were not able to join. This was a pattern that had already been established in Moscow.

The first recorded game in the city of Moscow took place in 1901 on the site of the present Spartak stadium. A Moscow league was founded shortly after the turn of the century, and the winner for five consecutive seasons was the popular Morozovtsi (as the popular Morozov club came to be called). The Moscow league, composed mainly of factory teams, attracted 10,000-15,000 fans per game.

In 1906, Morozovtsi was renamed Orekhovo Klub Sport (OKS), and in later years was relocated to Moscow. (It was adopted by the Soviet Electrical Trades Union in 1923 and became the famous Dinamo Moscow.) With leagues already established in St. Petersburg and Moscow, regional leagues were also started in Kiev,

Odessa, Kharkov, Rostov, Kazan, Baku, Tiflis, Omsk, Irkutsk, and even Vladivostok. In the Baltic region, the Germans founded SV Prussia at Konigsberg in 1904, and established a regional governing body, the Baltenverband, at about the same time.

The game found little opposition among Czarist officials. Indeed, it was given tacit support as a way to mitigate revolutionary fervor (the opposite view taken by Ottoman rulers in Turkey). In keeping with the government's effort to Europeanize the cultural life of the empire, Russian sports federations were soon established, and in 1912 the Vserossyski Fútbollnnyi Sojuz (All Russian Football Union) was founded to regulate Russian soccer.

A national championship for teams representing their respective cities was introduced in that same year, and the Football Union joined FIFA in time to send a national team to the 1912 Olympic Games in Stockholm.

Russia's debut in the Swedish capital resulted in a 2-1 loss to Finland. Two days later in the unofficial consolation tournament for losing teams, Russia was trounced by Germany 16-0, a score that established a co-record for the biggest international win in soccer history.

Before World War I, Russia played in six more unofficial internationals. In 1912, Hungary defeated the Russians twice in Moscow by an aggregate of 21-0. Losing to Sweden 4-1 and drawing with Norway at Moscow in 1913, the Russian team returned these visits in 1914 by drawing games in both Stockholm and Oslo.

The war and the revolution caused a ten-year hiatus in international competition, but in 1924 the newly formed Committee of Physical Culture and Sport of the new Soviet Russia invited the inexperienced Turks to Moscow, where the national team won for the first time by a comfortable 3-0 margin.

In 1925, the Soviets traveled to Ankara and won again. Aside from one obscure match with Estonia, these two wins represented the Soviet Union's complete official international record before Stalin came to power and withdrew his country from all official international competition. A Soviet team was not to surface again in the West until 1945, and a Soviet national team was not to engage in an official competition until 1952.

Club soccer in Soviet Russia was a different story. The famous Dinamo Moscow tour of 1945 was a startling and bewildering experience for all concerned. After brushing aside the Swedish champions IFK Norrkoping 5-0, Dinamo descended on Britain amid unparalleled publicity and gained draws at Chelsea and Glasgow Rangers before defeating Cardiff City 10-1 and Arsenal 4-3 (in dense fog). Local attendance records were set, and before anyone knew it, Dinamo was on its way home.

Aside from the phantomlike quality of Dinamo's appearance (a Soviet team was not to play again in Western Europe until 1952), British players and fans were stunned by the seriousness of Dinamo's effort. Training sessions were conducted with match-day intensity, and in the games themselves Dinamo's fluid teamwork and *en bloc* defensive retreats demonstrated an overbearing will to win.

Despite a tendency toward harsh and physical play, Dinamo succeeded largely due to a surprisingly high level of individual skills and great speed. From an international perspective, Dinamo's tour was the turning point for Soviet soccer.

The All-Russian Football Union having ceased to exist in 1917, the reconstituted Soviet governing body became separately affiliated with FIFA in 1946. Its name was the Football Section of the Committee of Physical Culture and Sport under the Council of Ministers of the U.S.S.R., later to be renamed the U.S.S.R. Football Federation.

Domestic competition in the immediate postwar years was dominated by CSKA Moscow, many of whose players had continued to play throughout the war years. The postwar CSKA team is still thought by some to have been the greatest Soviet team of all time. Although the Dynamo Kiev club of 1970-90 must be its equal.

When a Soviet national side surfaced to participate in the 1952 Olympic Games at Helsinki, all but one of its members were Central Army Club players. Throughout the 1950s, the league and cup continued to be dominated by the big Moscow clubs, especially Dinamo and Spartak, the latter reaching its peak during the last years of the decade when it supplied the bulk of the national team.

The Soviet reentry into official international competition at the 1952 Olympic Games was ended in the first round by the talented Yugoslavs, but in the 1956 Melbourne games, after three unconvincing rounds against marginal opposition, the Soviet Union won the gold medal with a narrow defeat of Yugoslavia in the final.

Its goalkeeper at Melbourne was the youthful Lev Yashin, who—in the 1958 World Cup—was to become the U.S.S.R.'s first international idol and ultimately the most respected goalkeeper in the history of the game.

Some of the Soviet Union's results before 1956, however, were more significant than its Olympic triumph. It defeated world champion West Germany twice, at home in 1955 and in Hanover one year later, and after defeating Sweden twice by an aggregate of 13-0, it played Hungary in Budapest and held the "Magnificent Magyars" to a 1-1 draw. After the Melbourne Olympics, there were several wins over weaker Eastern European teams, and in 1957 the U.S.S.R.

squeaked by Poland to qualify for its first World Cup.

It was a marvelously gifted Soviet team that prepared for the 1958 World Cup in Sweden by holding England to a 1-1 draw in Moscow. The Spartak-dominated World Cup squad included Yashin in goal, captain Igor Netto at left half, and Armenian Nikita Simonian at center forward, and after the heartening results of the past three years much was expected from them.

The U.S.S.R. was grouped with England, Brazil, and Austria in the opening round, and the first matches were difficult. Against Brazil, Vava's two goals and Pelé's excellence—it was his World Cup debut—dealt the U.S.S.R. its only loss of the round, but another draw with England forced a play-off (its third match in one month against the English), which it barely managed to win on a goal by Ilyin. Exhausted by the high quality of the first round opposition, the Soviets finally succumbed in the quarter-finals to Sweden.

Having tasted the exalted heights of World Cup competition, Soviet soccer authorities began to deemphasize Olympic competition in favor of the more elite World Championship and the newly inaugurated European Nations' Cup. Though the latter was not to gain its present stature until 1966-68, the U.S.S.R. led a large Eastern European contingent into the first edition in 1958-60.

As it turned out, all of its opponents in the series were part of that contingent. It defeated Hungary in the first round, and after Spain refused for political reasons to play the Soviet team in the quarter-finals, the U.S.S.R. eased past Czechoslovakia in the semi-finals, then won the championship with a narrow victory over Yugoslavia in the final. Doubts remained, however, about the Soviets' ability to compete consistently well against the world's top teams.

TASS from Sovfoto

Lev Yashin

The doubts remained two years later when the Soviet team stumbled at the 1962 World Cup in Chile. In the first round, the U.S.S.R. defeated Yugoslavia in a brutal grudge match, and defeated Uruguay. Unknown and weak Colombia, however, pulled back from a 3-1 deficit at the half to force a 4-4 draw, and it thus handed the U.S.S.R. its biggest upset ever.

After a poorly played loss to Chile in the quarter-finals, the Soviet team was eliminated and dejected, and critics pointed to all the mistakes Yashin had made tending goal. The results were all the more disappointing because the team had made a very successful tour of South America just before the competition.

At the 1966 World Cup in England, the U.S.S.R. won its first round group against Italy, Korea DPR, and Chile without a defeat, and in the quarter-finals upset one of the favorites, Hungary, with superior physical strength. The semi-finals, however, produced a bruising loss to West Germany, and the Soviets' reputation for hard play was clearly manifested.

In the third place match, the deft skills of Portugal proved superior to the Soviets' more combative skills, and the U.S.S.R. took fourth place in the tournament. It was the Soviet team's highest finish in World Cup competition, and while the team had not been as impressive as it was in 1958, the result was in keeping with its newly found place among the top echelons of world soccer.

The U.S.S.R.'s growing list of successes was also lengthened by a commendable second place finish in the 1962-64 European Nations' Cup in which it lost the final to Spain and neutralized Italy's durable *catenaccio*. Four years later, in the semi-finals of the 1966-68 Nations' Cup, the Soviets and Italians met once again and battled to a scoreless draw, but Italy gained a vengeance of sorts by winning the toss. Still led by Yashin in goal, the Soviets lost the third place match to world champion England.

In 1970, the U.S.S.R. qualified for its fourth consecutive World Cup and was undefeated in its first round group against Mexico, Belgium, and El Salvador. Lacking Yashin in goal, this was a less spirited Soviet team, and it was rumored to be demoralized by broken promises over bonus payments. Whatever the frustrations may have been, its morale was not lifted when it lost the quarter-final to Uruguay by 1-0 on a highly suspect goal.

In the 1970-72 European Football Championship, however, the Soviet team disposed of Spain, Yugoslavia, and Hungary—all stalwart opponents—and gained its third final in four editions of Europe's most elite tournament. In the final against West Germany, the Soviets acquitted themselves as well as could be expected, but the flowing, skillful West German game reached its peak and subdued the Soviets.

In 1973, the U.S.S.R. refused to play Chile on the grounds of the National Stadium in Santiago (citing the stadium's earlier use as a detention center for political prisoners), and FIFA ruled the Soviet Union out of the 1974 World Cup. The U.S.S.R. failed to qualify in 1978 after losses to Greece and Hungary, and it was eliminated in the quarter-finals of the 1974-76 European Football Championship by a resurgent Czechoslovakia.

In less than 20 years, however, the U.S.S.R. had amassed the best international record of any country in Europe, advanced beyond the first round in four consecutive World Championships, and appeared in three Nations' Cup finals. Its teams were technically proficient, as were so many of its individual players, but ultimately the style it came to be associated with relied on a uniquely Russian combination of skill and hard physical play.

The quality of U.S.S.R. soccer as a consistent, if never quite overpowering machine, was never better seen than during the closing decade of the country's existence. Present in every World Cup, runners-up in the 1988 European Championship and always very close to breaking through to the very top level, the best Soviet teams, based on Lobanovsky's Dynamo Kiev side, never seemed quite able to mix their undoubted collective talents with the necessary flair to win a major trophy.

The Soviets returned to Spain after the self-enforced absence from West Germany in 1974 and subsequent surprise elimination from the 1978 event. After an opening round loss to the fancied Brazilians, the Soviets moved into the second round by blanking New Zealand and getting a 2-2 draw with Scotland. The second round exposed their lack of invention, however. After slipping past Belgium 1-0 they could do no better than a 0-0 draw against Poland and went out of the tournament on goal difference.

In 1986 the squad in Mexico showed flashes of brilliance and remarkable self-control but it still added up to a relatively early exit. An opening 6-0 rout of Hungary, which included some wonderful midfield work, fast counterattacks and a seemingly tireless collection of interchangeable parts in the best "total soccer" tradition, stamped the Soviets as a serious threat, but that potential was never realized. In the knockout phase they were somewhat unfortunate to go out to Belgium on penalty kicks after a hint of offside about the game's equalizing goal, but it was another case of a Soviet side that did less than it might have.

The 1988 European Championship entry, however, may have exceeded the sum of its parts, reaching the final with a 2-0 victory over Italy only to lose the last match to Holland by a similar score. It wasn't quite that simple, however, because the final was a game that saw the Soviets squander chances, including a penalty kick, thus a frustrating series of "might-have-beens" seemed to encapsulate the history of Lobanovsky's national teams.

They were back in the World Cup in 1990 but now as only a shadow side. Golden chances were missed in the opening match against Rumania that ended in defeat. A Diego Maradona hand ball overlooked by an indulgent referee helped Argentina to another victory, and the fact that the Soviets hammered Cameroon—the only side to make the Africans look ordinary—offered little solace.

The truth was that the team had passed its peak, and the deteriorating political union at home obviously contributed to the sense of players on a hiding to nothing. Instead of being buoyed by playing together for perhaps the last time the squad seemed to be fragmented by the growing uncertainty.

The first Soviet club to do well in European competition was Dinamo Moscow, but it was the rise of Dinamo Kiev to the front ranks that made the most history. Always a first division club (an honor shared only with Spartak and Dinamo Moscow), Kiev did not achieve consistent championship results until the late 1960s.

Turning its back on the bearlike qualities of postwar Soviet soccer, Dinamo Kiev sought to adopt elements of the Dutch-German approach (flowing teamwork with a license to opt for highly skilled individual performances), and in 1974-75 it won the European Cup Winners' Cup after Oleg Blokhin, probably the most gifted forward the Soviets have ever produced, won the European Footballer of the Year award.

In keeping with administrative tradition, the U.S.S.R. national team during the mid-1970s was based entirely on the Kiev team, but the heightened international schedule of the 1970s drained the players of their stamina, and results on the national level were disappointing.

Valery Lobanovsky, the Kiev coach, went on to lead U.S.S.R. teams into World Cups through 1990, just before the dissolution of the country. His Kiev team won another Cup Winners' Cup in 1986. Dinamo Tbilisi was the only other Soviet team to achieve such a triumph, claiming the same trophy in 1981.

RWANDA

Address: Rwanda Amateur Football Federation, BP 2000, Kigali.

Rwanda ranks with neighboring Burundi as one of the poorest countries in the world, but unlike its neighbor to the south it has not yet found a way to finance continuous international competition and affiliation with external governing bodies.

St. Kitts and Nevis

Address: St. Kitts and Nevis Football Association, P.O. Box 465, Basseterre, St. Kitts, West Indies. *Founded:* 1991.

Having just organized, St. Kitts and Nevis, one of the small West Indies islands, did not participate in the 1994 World Cup competition.

St. Lucia

Address: St. Lucia National Football Union, P.O. Box 255, Castries. *Founded:* 1988. *Colors:* Blue, white, and black.

This West Indian island, known already in the international sports world for its interest in cricket, made its World Cup debut in the 1994 competition, losing in the first round to St. Vincent and the Grenadines. It is expected that St. Lucia will also take part in the Caribbean regional competitions.

St. Vincent and the Grenadines

Address: St. Vincent and the Grenadines Football Federation, P.O. Box 1278, St. Vincent, West Indies. *Colors:* Yellow and white. *Founded:* 1988.

A new CONCACAF and FIFA entry in regional competition, St. Vincent and the Grenadines created one of the romantic stories of 1994 World Cup qualifying, but the final chapters deflated the bubble.

Organized in time to participate in the competition, St. Vincent overcame St. Lucia's prelimi

nary round opposition and then scored a surprising first round triumph over the more experienced Surinam to reach the CONCACAF round of eight.

Drawn against Costa Rica, Honduras, and Mexico, the tiny Caribbean nation with only about 5,000 players converted the local cricket stadium for the matches against their prestigious opponents, attracting enthusiastic, capacity crowds for the matches.

The games were played in a somewhat surreal atmosphere, however, as the field was in the middle of the larger cricket ground and the spectators were far removed from the play. In addition, one of the games was contested in torrential rain that made ball control almost impossible.

At home, St. Vincent and the Grenadines was beaten 4-0 by both Mexico and Honduras and 1-0 by Costa Rica, but the return match with the Mexicans produced an 11-0 rout and clearly showed the difficulty of tiny countries with limited resources trying to compete against fully-professional opposition.

San Marino

Address: Federazione Sanmarinese Giuoco Calcio, Palazzo CONS, Via Del Bando 28, 47031 Borgo Maggiore. *Founded:* 1931.

The Principality of San Marino has just become affiliated with FIFA and UEFA, taking part in qualification for the 1992 European Championship and the 1994 World Cup to make its international debut. A tiny state with no professionals except those who play in Italy's leagues, San Marino was defeated 10-0 by Norway in its World Cup debut match, but rebounded to capture its first point on March 10, 1993, holding Turkey to a 0-0 draw.

Saudi Arabia

Address: Saudi Arabian Football Federation, North Al-Morabbaa Quarter, P.O. Box 5844, Riyadh 11432. *Founded:* 1959. *FIFA:* 1959. *AFC:* 1972. *National stadium:* Fahd Stadium, Riyadh (70,000); *largest stadium:* Fahd Stadium. *Colors:* Green jerseys with white trim, white shorts. *Season:* September to May. *Honors:* World 16-Under Champion (1989); Asian Cup runner-up (1992).

The game was slow to establish itself among the Saudis, whose religious and cultural beliefs prohibited the adoption of Western games until the recent postwar years. Lacking much exposure to European colonists, Saudi adoption of the game was left to a process of slow infiltration from the growing number of western engineers and workers who came to develop the oil industry after World War II.

Currently, though, Saudi Arabia has begun to make a strong impact on the Asian game, attracting European and Brazilian coaches and inviting as many leading teams as possible to play exhibition games with native players.

Although its national association was founded in 1959 and membership in FIFA was granted the same year, Saudi Arabia's regular participation in international competition did not start until the early to mid-1970s.

In its first attempt to qualify for the World Cup in 1976-77, Saudi Arabia split home and away legs with Syria (2-0 and 1-2) but lost to Iran (0-3 and 0-2) and was eliminated.

Since then the Saudi team has competed effectively but without getting to the final round. It did win the 1989 World 16-Under title, was runner up in the 1992 Asian Cup, and hosted the 1989 World Youth Cup, evidence of Saudi Arabia's growing interest in the game. The team also took the 1992 Fahd Cup championship for Africa, Asia, CONCACAF and South America.

Scotland

Address: Scottish Football Association Ltd., 6 Park Gardens, Glasgow, G3 7YE. *Founded:* 1873. *FIFA:* 1910-20; 1924-28; 1946. *UEFA:* 1954. *National stadium:* Hampden Park, Glasgow (54,580); *largest stadium:* Hampden Park. *Colors:* Dark blue jerseys with white trim, white shorts. *Season:* August to June. *Honors:* World 16-Under Championship runner-up (1989).

The former Kingdom of Scotland has been politically united with England since 1707, but an unbroken tradition of independence still exists. The separation of the four British soccer associations—England, Scotland, Wales, and Northern Ireland—has continued because of this historical precedent; thus, the first meeting of representative English and Scottish teams in 1870 is regarded as the birth of international soccer. From the start the Scottish game took on its own unique characteristics.

Though England was the birthplace of soccer as we know it, Scotland was involved from the beginning, and, in fact, may be called the world's first great international power, since it dominated England decisively during the 1870s and 1880s. Scottish teams made the game's first tactical advances during those years, and for many decades remained the strongest influence on changing styles and techniques.

The two great Glasgow clubs, Celtic and Rangers, are world famous. Celtic has won the European Champions' Cup and Rangers has won the European Cup Winners' Cup, and both are perennial contenders in international club championships. These titanic crosstown rivals have dominated Scottish league and cup competition

Hampden Park, Glasgow

since 1891, and between them over 75 percent of league championships and 50 percent of Scottish cups.

Celtic has won 35 league titles and 27 Scottish Cups and is the only Scottish club to have lifted the European Cup. The Rangers team has 43 league crowns and 25 Scottish Cups plus one European Cup Winners Cup. Aberdeen has also won a major European honors, taking the 1983 Cup Winners Cup, but no Scottish clubs can really compare with the Glasgow giants.

Scotland was uniquely qualified as England's competitor in the early history of the game. The newly codified "association football" originated on English playing fields and spread to Scotland during the 1860s. The first Scottish club, Queen's Park Football Club, was formed on the south side of Glasgow in 1867 by members of the Y.M.C.A. who had gathered regularly in Queen's Park to play pickup games. At the beginning, its rules allowed some use of hands, touchdowns, and 15-20 players on each side, but the club tried diligently to conform to new association rules and soon other "association" clubs began to appear.

Several other clubs were founded in Glasgow and its suburbs, and in 1869, the first outlying club, Kilmarnock F.C., was founded in Ayrshire. After Glasgow and the coal fields of Lanarkshire, the second major spawning ground for clubs during the early years was the Vale of Leven (Renton, Dumbarton, and Vale of Leven), and in 1870, Stranraer F.C. was founded in the small port of that name in the extreme south (only 40 miles from the Irish port city of Belfast). In 1873 Rangers F.C. was formed by three outspoken Protestant families in Glasgow who were members of the Football Association (London).

Edinburgh, the intellectual and political capital of Scotland, had strongly favored the rugby game since the formation a of local football association in 1863, because the city had such a small working class population. Soccer was poorly regarded by both the educated establishment and the influential upper class students who came from England to attend school.

In 1874, one of the capital's two great clubs of the future, Heart of Midlothian, (originally known as White Star F.C.), was founded at the Meadows, near the city's center. Hearts played association rules exclusively, and eventually rose to the forefront of Scottish soccer. In 1875, Edinburgh Hibernians (later Hibernian) was founded by Irishmen, entered official competitions and developed into Hearts' archrival a relationship which still exists.

The number of Scottish clubs increased dramatically during the 1870s and 1880s. The big names during this period—Queen's Park, Third Lanark, Rangers, Renton, Vale of Leven, and Dumbarron—compared favorably with their counterparts in England, and the first internationals between England and Scotland demonstrated the Scots' greater sophistication.

Between 1870 and 1872, representative teams of England and Scotland met in five unofficial internationals, each played in London, with England winning three and the other two drawn. But nearly all players on these Scottish teams were London residents and members of London teams.

Beginning with the first official international in 1872 (a goal-less draw played at Patrick, Glasgow), Scottish teams consisted entirely of players living in Scotland. The first such team was an all-Queen's Park team. The trend in England's favor reversed completely. Of the 16 meetings between England and Scotland from 1872-87, Scotland won ten and lost two.

Also during the 1870s and 1880s, Scottish players were great exporters of the game to other countries, ranking second only to England in this respect, and many Scottish coaches went abroad as well.

Scots were responsible for introducing soccer to Ireland in 1878, with an exhibition match in Belfast between Queen's Park and Caledonian. Many of Belfast's important early clubs were manned with Scottish players. Scots were influential in introducing soccer to Canada, and they also had an important hand in spreading the game in the United States and Australia.

In 1890-91, the Scottish Football League was introduced. The charter members were: Celtic, Rangers, Heart of Midlothian, Dumbarton, St. Mirren, Third Lanark, Abercorn, Cowlairs, Cambuslang, Renton, and Vale of Leven—the last six no longer in existence.

Celtic F.C., founded in Glasgow in 1888 by Irish Catholics, rose immediately to the top of Scottish soccer and became the first Scottish club run as an efficient business concern. Its staunch Catholicism led to the great archrivalry with Protestant Rangers. Celtic and Rangers dominated the league almost from the beginning.

One of the SFA's major interests at this time was in finding a stadium to accommodate the huge crowds at matches. In 1894, the new Celtic Park opened with a capacity of 50,000 (then the largest in the world), and in 1900 it was increased to 60,000. This, in addition to Celtic's sophisticated security arrangements, appeared to solidify the club's role as the host of Scottish internationals.

Queen's Park, openly jealous of Celtic's exalted position, built a third Hampden Park in 1903 with a capacity equal to that of Celtic Park, and, with the sentimental edge already in its favor, became the home of all major internationals and

Scottish Cup finals after 1904. In 1920, Queen's Park's famous stadium was enlarged to accommodate more than 120,000, and in subsequent years it became the frequent site of world record attendance figures. Its status as the world's largest stadium was finally surpassed in 1950 with the opening of the Maracana in Rio de Janeiro. Today it is undergoing complete renovation to make it an all-seated, modern stadium.

In the 1920s, Scotland passed through its greatest era in international competition, and perhaps in production of great players as well. It won seven British Championships between 1920-29 (Wales won the other three), and in 1928, ironically one of the years Wales won the title, the Scots buried hapless England (at Wembley) 5-1.

The "Wembley Wizards," as this famous 1928 Scottish team was called, included an illustrious forward line: Jackson, Dunn, Gallacher, James, and Morton. Scotland's great victory prompted an ever increasing list of invitations to play in Europe, and in the summer of 1929 Scotland traveled outside the United Kingdom for its first non-British internationals. After two wins over Norway (their official status is in dispute), the first full-level match on this tour, against Germany in Berlin, ended in a 1-1 draw, and the second, against the Netherlands in Amsterdam, was won 2-0.

After these encouraging results, Scotland defeated France in Paris the next year, but in 1931 got its first taste of top-flight European soccer with a 5-0 loss to Austria (without the benefit of many of its top players), and a 3-0 loss to Italy.

Scotland's prewar potential never materialized, though its international schedule increased substantially. The Scots qualified for the 1954 and 1958 editions of the World Cup, after declining their rightful berth in 1950, but failed to win a single one of their five matches in the final rounds. The extraordinary run has continued. Between 1974 and 1990 Scotland qualified for

every World Cup final but never reached the second round in any of them.

Still, Scotland's overall record in international competition remains very good, especially for a small country. The country continues to produce world-class players, many of whom have gained fame with the leading English clubs.

Scottish clubs have occasionally done well in European club championships and are usually not welcomed as opposition by continental teams because of their reputations for hard work and for persevering against great odds. The Aberdeen, Celtic, and Rangers are considered formidable competitors, while Dundee United had a golden spell in the 1980s, reaching a UEFA Cup final and a European Cup semifinal.

SENEGAL

Address: Federation Senegalaise de Football, Stade de L'Amitie, Route de L'Aeroport de Yoff, Dakar. *Founded:* 1960. *FIFA:* 1964. *CAF:* 1963. *National stadium:* Dakar (40,000); *largest stadium:* Dakar. *Colors:* Green jerseys, yellow shorts. *Season:* October to July.

It was appropriate that Senegal should become one of the first countries from the former French West Africa to qualify for the final rounds of the African Nations' Cup in 1965.

French colonists had established the French West African League in Dakar immediately after World War II, with 45 clubs and 3,000 players registered, and this remained the only governing body of its kind in the entire region until independence was achieved.

Dakar was thus given a head start on the other French West African colonies, and as early as 1956 France (Amateur) visited Dakar and defeated a Senegalese representative team 9-2.

In 1960, two years after independence, Senegal's own Federation Senegalaise de Football was founded, and for a few brief months its jurisdiction included Mali as well as Senegal, as the two countries attempted a political merger. Affiliation with FIFA and the African Football Confederation followed in that order.

Senegal finished fourth in the 1990 African Nations' Cup and hosted the event in 1992. To date, the national team has not qualified for a World Cup finals appearance, but it had reached the African zone final round in competition for a 1994 place.

SEYCHELLES

Address: P.O. Box 580, Mont Fleuri, Victoria. *Founded:* 1986. *Colors:* Green shirts, yellow shorts, red socks.

The game in this tropical Indian Ocean country is still getting organized.

SIERRA LEONE

Address: Sierra Leone Amateur Football Association, S. Stevens Stadium, Brookfields, P.O. Box 672, Freetown. *Founded:* 1967. *FIFA:* 1967. *CAF:* 1967. *National stadium:* Brookfields Stadium, Freetown (15,000); *largest stadium:* Brookfields Stadium. *Colors:* Green, white, and blue jerseys, white shorts. *Season:* May to December.

Among the former British colonies in West Africa, Sierra Leone is culturally more British in character than all the others, yet on the soccer field it has built a meager existence at best. In international competition, it ranks near the bottom of the African list.

Sierra Leone's attempts to qualify for the all-amateur African Games, the Olympics, and the World Cup have met with failure, and, after losing to much stronger Algeria and Morocco in 1982 and 1986 qualifying games, Sierra Leone has not entered the last two competitions, including the 1994 event.

SINGAPORE

Address: Football Association of Singapore, Jalan Besar Stadium, Tyrwhitt Road, Singapore 0820. *Founded:* 1892. *FIFA:* 1952. *AFC:* 1954. *National stadium:* Jalan Besar Stadium, Singapore 8 (20,000); *largest stadium:* Jalan Besar Stadium. *Colors:* Sky blue jerseys, sky blue shorts. *Season:* March to December.

Singapore is a middle-level Asian soccer power where the game has had little difficulty in capturing the attention of a predominantly Chinese population.

With an immensely strong British presence there since the early nineteenth century, it is little wonder that the Singapore Amateur Football Association, founded in 1892, was also the first governing body for soccer in the Far East, predating its Malaysian counterpart by 40 years.

The British were the only players around for some time, but gradually local residents—especially the Chinese—took up the game. It was not until after World War II that Singapore teams became actively involved in international competition.

This delay was caused in part by the island's political connections with Malaya to the north, and was ended when the enormous influx of British soldiers during World War II revitalized Singapore's game.

In 1951, Indonesia defeated Singapore 4-1 in Singapore, and in 1952 the Singapore Amateur Football Association became affiliated with FIFA. Singapore has recorded some wins in the qualifying rounds for the World Cup but has never reached the finals.

SLOVENIA

Address: Tabor 14, pp 47, 61004 Ljublianam. *Founded:* 1991. *FIFA:* 1993 (provisional). *UEFA:* 1992. *Colors:* Blue and white.

When the former Yugoslavia burst apart in a bloody civil war, Slovenia was one of the first areas to declare its independence, and it gained almost immediate UEFA and FIFA recognition.

Although not able to enter the 1994 World Cup qualifying, Slovenian teams did take part in European competition in 1992-93 with entry into both the European Cup and the Cup Winners Cup. A 20-team First Division operated in 1991-92 with Olimpia of Ljubliana the first champion. Maribor Branik won the initial Slovenian Cup.

SOLOMON ISLANDS

Address: Soloman Island Football Federation, P.O. Box 532, Honiara. *Founded:* 1988.

This former British protectorate gained independence in 1977 and entered the World Cup for the first time in 1994. An honorable 1-1 draw with Tahiti and a narrow 2-1 home loss to Australia in that competition helped soften a last-place finish in the Oceania preliminary round section.

SOMALIA

Address: Somalia Football Federation, Ministry of Sports, C.P. 247, Mogadishu. *Founded:* 1951. *FIFA:* 1961. *CAF:* 1968. *National stadium:* C.O.N.I. Stadium, Mogadishu (15,000); *largest stadium:* C.O.N.I. Stadium. *Colors:* Sky blue jerseys, white shorts. *Season:* September to February.

In 1961, a year after the birth of the Somali Republic, the FSGC joined FIFA and seven years later Somalia became affiliated with the African Football Confederation (CAF). Somalia's late affiliation date with the CAF automatically relegated it to the lower depths of African soccer where it has remained.

Somalia was one of only four countries in Africa that has sanctioned open professionalism for its eight first division clubs, but the civil war and widespread famine that has ravaged the region for a decade has made progress in the sport virtually impossible.

SOUTH AFRICA

Address: South Africa Football Federation, First National Bank Stadium, P.O. Box 910, Johannesburg 2000. *FIFA:* Readmitted in 1992.

Soccer in South Africa has inevitably been dominated by the issue of racial separation. The sport has a long history in this part of Africa, and, aside from emotional and moral aspects, the practice and policy of racial division has seriously hindered the advance of South African soccer from a pragmatic standpoint.

If the 80 percent of the population that is "non-white" had been allowed to participate fully in

South Africa's long association with soccer, there is little doubt that South Africa would be the dominant power on African playing fields today.

But as soccer emerged as the most popular sport in black Africa, South Africa found itself ostracized from the boom. It was never allowed to join the African Football Confederation, and finally in 1976 South Africa was expelled from FIFA, ending any possibility of significant growth through international exposure.

The potential of South African players is undoubtedly high. Whites, although active in soccer from the beginning, have traditionally preferred rugby. Blacks and other non-whites, however, have enthusiastically embraced soccer as their game, and non-white clubs are fervently supported.

Soccer has a long history, having been first played on the continent of Africa in Port Elizabeth, Cape Province, in the 1860s by British settlers. Whether association or rugby rules predominated at this early date is unclear, but the association game was certainly played, and it was quickly introduced in other British settlements in Cape Province and Natal. The Dutch republics of Transvaal and Orange Free State were exposed to the game several years later.

The first South African club, Pietermaritzburg County, was founded in the Natal city of that name in 1879. Despite the more obvious popularity of rugby, there was enough interest for a Natal Football Association to be founded in 1882 with five charter-member clubs.

The Natal association and the New South Wales F.A. that was founded in Australia at the same time were the first governing bodies for soccer outside the United Kingdom. A Cape Province association followed, and the first league was established in Cape Town in 1891.

In 1892, the Natal, Cape Province, and other governing bodies formed the South African Football Association (SAFA), forerunner of the present association, and the SAFA soon became affiliated with the Football Association in London.

Organized soccer in Transvaal and the Orange Free State were not under the jurisdiction of the SAFA until after the Union of South Africa was created in 1910. The first official competition, the Currie Cup, was introduced in 1892, and the O'Reilly Cup was introduced in Cape Town the following year.

South Africa's international record has been sparse and decidedly unsuccessful. Only two full international teams had visited South Africa to play in officially recognized matches before Cameroon came in 1992 to mark the end of the long FIFA ban. Back in 1950, Australia had played a series of four games in Johannesburg and Cape Town, winning once and losing once, and Israel won a single match by 3-1 in 1954.

Blacks in South Africa began playing the game around 1900, and after World War II embraced it wholeheartedly, adopting FIFA standards by 1960. The 1950s saw great changes in South African soccer. The SAFA became a member of FIFA in 1952, but it was during this period that apartheid developed as an official policy in all areas of South African life, including sports.

In 1956, South Africa attempted to join Egypt, Sudan, and Ethiopia in founding the African Football Confederation, but when it became clear that the SAFA intended to field an all-white team and a non-white team in the first African Nations' Cup, the other three participants blocked South Africa's membership.

The Football Association of South Africa (FASA), as the SAFA was called in the 1960s, was suspended from FIFA in 1964 for violating antidiscrimination codes in the FIFA charter (specifically Article 2, paragraph 4.5). In 1970, South Africa was expelled from the International Olympic Committee, and pressure on South African authorities to change their policies intensified.

With the birth of the non-white NPSL came the formation of a separate governing body for non-whites, the South African Soccer Federation (SASF), whose officers included some non-whites.

This was seen clearly as a way to accommodate growing non-white interests in the game without having to include them directly in white policy-making bodies.

Citing Article 2, paragraph 4.5 once again, FIFA expelled South Africa in 1976 by a vote of 78-9, with 13 abstentions. A few weeks later, the South African Sports Council decided to allow three players of a non-white race on each white and non-white club. Eleven white clubs in the NFL agreed to participate.

This concept of so-called "multinational sport" was extended in September 1976 to allow white and non-white teams to play each other for the first time. The first such game was played in April of 1977 at Rand Stadium, Johannesburg, in which Cape Town City of the NFL defeated Vaal Professionals, a leading black club, 3-0.

Ceaseless international pressure finally resulted in change. Although soccer has not garnered the same interest among whites as cricket and rugby, international bans were seen as effective forces in finally dismantling apartheid.

Thus, when Cameroon visited in July of 1992, and South Africa was allowed into the 1994 World Cup, there was hope that a truly new era had begun.

SPAIN

Address: Real Federacion Espanola de Fútbol, Calle Alberto Bosch, 13, Apartado postal 347, Madrid E-28014. *Founded:* 1905. *FIFA:* 1913. *UEFA:* 1954. *Largest stadium:* Estadio Santiago Bernabeu, Madrid (101,663). *Colors:* Red jerseys, blue shorts. *Season:* September to June. *Honors:* Olympic Games champion (1992), runner-up, (1920); European Nations' Cup winner (1964), runner-up (1984).

Spanish soccer has found unparalleled success in club competitions at the international level. Its most famous club, Real Madrid, is virtually a bench mark in this respect, and four other Spanish clubs have won major European championships. Barcelona is one of only three teams to have won all of Europe's major club trophies.

Yet many of these accomplishments have been generated by the presence of foreign players who have come to Spanish clubs from almost every country in Europe and South America because wealthy Spanish clubs rank with their big Italian counterparts as the richest in Europe.

Spanish national teams, on the other hand, have little to match the clubs in the way of trophies, although there have been several Spanish-born players of genuine world class caliber—Zamora, Suarez, Gento, Amancio, and Butragueno. The average Spanish players have been overshadowed by foreign talent that has come to Spain since the early 1950s in an unending stream.

Like Italy, Spain did not evolve into an important soccer-playing country until after World War I. Soccer was brought to Spain through the Basque provinces by British mining engineers during the 1890s, a relatively late date by European standards, though it had been played elsewhere on the Iberian peninsula (Gibraltar and Portugal) many years earlier.

British military personnel and residents also introduced the game before the turn of the century in Madrid, Barcelona, and Valencia, and these four locations spawned the first important clubs.

The oldest club is the flagship of Basque nationalism, Athletic Club de Bilbao, founded in the Basque capital in 1898 as Athletic Club. In the same year Madrid Football Club, later Real ("Royal") Madrid, was formed in the national capital by students. Hans Gamper, a naturalized Swiss, introduced soccer in the Catalan capital of Barcelona and founded Football Club Barcelona in 1899.

Real Madrid (25 titles) and Barcelona (12 titles) have dominated the league since it was formally organized in 1945, but Athletic Club de Bilbao still has the most Spanish Cup wins with 23. Barcelona (with 22 wins) is right behind in this much older competition, begun in 1902, while Real Madrid has been victorious 16 times.

The first recorded match in Spain took place in 1894 at Bilbao between a team of British residents and Basques, the British winning 5-0, but matches were probably played as early as 1894 in Madrid as well. To celebrate the coronation of Alfonso XIII in 1902, a knockout tournament was organized in Madrid with four participants: Biscaya (a joint team of Athletic Club and the new Bilbao F.C.), Madrid F.C., Barcelona, and Espanol (a second Barcelona club).

Biscaya defeated all three opponents, and the competition was turned into an annual event that eventually became the Spanish national cup competition. The Spanish cup originally determined the national champion.

A governing body, the Asociación Madrilena de Clubs de Foot-Ball, was founded in Madrid in 1900, but it included only Madrid clubs, and in 1905 it was superseded by the new Federacion Espanola de Fútbol, which soon received its royal designation Real.

No attempts were made to form a properly authorized national team, but the Real Federacion Espanola de Fútbol (FEF) joined FIFA in 1913 with the obvious intent of entering international competition. But World War I intervened, and Spain's debut was delayed until 1920.

Spain finally made its first appearance in international competition at the Olympic Games of 1920 in Antwerp, and it was a great success. Spain's debut was actually staged in Brussels— a 1-0 win over Denmark—but in the second round it lost to Belgium and faced elimination from the tournament.

When Czechoslovakia walked off the field in the middle of the final and the gold medal was awarded to Belgium, a play-off series was quickly organized to determine second and third place.

Spain was given a second chance and proceeded to defeat Sweden and Italy in successive games for the right to meet Holland in the "second and third place game." The Spaniards won, and in their very first international competition went home with silver medals.

Ricardo Zamora, one of Europe's greatest goalkeepers between the world wars, made his first appearance for Spain during this competition. Zamora went on to play in 46 of Spain's 57 full internationals between 1920 and 1936.

Following the Olympics of 1920 Spain won five friendlies in a row against Belgium, Portugal (twice), and France (twice), and its overall record during the 1920s was one of the best in Europe. Led by Zamora, Spain won more than once over Austria, Hungary, and Switzerland as well as its more frequent opponents France and Portugal,

Werek

Estadio Santiago Bernabeu, Madrid

and several of these were away matches. One of its few losses, unfortunately, was to Italy in the preliminary round of the 1924 Olympics in Paris.

At the 1928 games in Amsterdam, Mexico was easily brushed aside, but in the second round a 1-1 draw with Italy forced a replay that the budding Italians won by a huge 7-1 margin. Spain had prepared for its first World Cup by demolishing Bulgaria 13-0 in Madrid in 1933 and eliminating Portugal 9-0 and 2-1 to qualify. In the first round, the confident Spaniards held talented but disorganized Brazil in check, winning 3-1, and Zamora, now one of the great stars of Europe, emerged as perhaps, the most popular player in the competition.

Spain's opponent in the second round was the home team, Italy, which goalkeeper Zamora held to a 1-1 draw, forcing a replay. Only four

players from the first match against Italy returned for the replay—the injured Zamora was not one of them—and Meazza's goal was all the Italians needed to win the game.

This was another rare and untimely loss, but other major victories followed in 1935; it was not until the bleak civil war of 1936 that Spain lost as many as three games in succession. International competition and a new national league that had started in 1928-29, along with the Spanish Cup, were suspended during the 1936-39 civil war but resumed briefly in 1941 with matches against neutral Portugal and Switzerland, and in 1945 when a pair of games with Portugal opened the postwar era.

Spain did not qualify for either the 1954 or 1958 World Championships, but the story of Spanish soccer from 1953 to 1966 had little to do with the national team in any case. At Real Madrid,

Santiago Bernabeu took over as president in 1943, and troubled by losing repeated trophies to Barcelona, the ancient enemy, he began to build an extraordinary team based on attentive worldwide scouting.

In 1953, he signed Alfredo Di Stefano, Francisco Gento, and Hector Rial all in one year, and Real Madrid was instantly transformed. Real's Spanish championship of 1955 put Bernabeu's team in the inaugural edition of the European Cup, and in 1956 Real won its first of five European Cup titles in succession, still the greatest feat in the history of international club competition.

Barcelona, in the meantime, had won several Spanish championships and cups and was now poised to enter another decade of bitter rivalry with Real over the leadership of Spanish soccer.

The bloodless war between Real and Barcelona, one club representing the Castilian establishment in Madrid, the other a personification of Catalan nationalism, was waged on all fronts. In the international transfer market, Real and Barcelona vied with the big Italian clubs for world class stars, and each alternated in outspending the other.

Hungary's Sandor Kocsis and Zoltan Czibor went to Barcelona, joining the Spanish idol Luis Suilrez. Raymond Kopa and Ferenc Puskas joined Di Stefano and another Spanish idol, Francisco Gento, at Real.

As Real busied itself with its five European Cups victories, Barcelona won two successive Fairs Cups (1958 and 1960). The hatred and bitterness peaked in 1960. Real and Barcelona met head-to-head in the semi-finals of the 1959-60 European Cup, and Real won both legs by an identical 3-1 score; in the first round of the 1960-61 edition, however, Barcelona eliminated Real

from the competition it had dominated for five years by an aggregate score of 4-3. Real's long-running superiority in the rivalry had finally been put to an end.

But Madrid and Barcelona were not the only Spanish cities to produce European championship clubs. In the 1961-62 Fairs Cup, Valencia defeated none other than Barcelona in an all-Spanish final—winning the Valencia leg by 6-2—and won the 1962-63 Fairs Cup as well with wins over Dinamo Zagreb in the final.

Spain's incredible domination over European club competitions continued the next year when Real Zaragoza, the popular standard-bearer of soccer in Aragon, advanced to the final of the Fairs Cup, there confronting two-time winner Valencia in another all-Spanish affair, winning its first and only European title.

In 1965-66, a third all-Spanish Fairs Cup final took place with Barcelona defeating Zaragoza in extra time.

In the European Cup, meanwhile, Real reached the final again in 1961-62 and 1963-64, losing both times, and in 1965-66 won the cup for the sixth time with a new generation of players.

Atletico Madrid, not to be left out of the European picture, won the European Cup Winners' Cup in 1961-62 with its own roster of foreign imports and reached the final again the following year, losing to Tottenham Hotspur.

All told, Spanish clubs won a total of 13 European club championships from 1955-66, a record unequaled, with trophies spread around the board rooms of five different Spanish clubs.

These successes managed to spill over into the national team's endeavors briefly in the early 1960s. After reaching the final rounds of the

1962 World Cup and quickly bowing out with mediocre performances, Spain was partly compensated with a distinguished win in the 1962-64 European Football Championship.

While its opposition in early rounds was not the most difficult—Rumania, Northern Ireland, Republic of Ireland, and Hungary—its opponent in the final was the defensive-minded Soviet Union with Lev Yashin in goal, and it took the genius of Suarez to guide Spain to a 2-1 win. The winning goal was scored by Zaragoza's center forward Marcelino. This team also included Real's star right winger Amancio and early international appearances of the Basque goalkeeper from Athletic Bilbao, lribar, who was to keep goal for Spain until 1977.

Spain qualified for the World Cup again in 1966 with a narrow play-off victory over its frequent if unlikely opponent, the Republic of Ireland. In the final rounds, Argentina hacked the Spanish stars Suarez and Amancio into submission and won 2-1 while Switzerland proved a surprisingly worthy opponent in losing by the same score. In its third match of the group, Spain and West Germany fought a close contest, but a goal by Uwe Seeler gave the game to the Germans, and as expected, Spain left the tournament after the first round.

After failing to qualify for the World Cup in 1970 and 1974, a tactically sophisticated team led by Real's captain Pirri staggered into the 1978 World Cup finals after a bruising qualification series with Rumania, but its chances for advancing beyond the first round were dashed by Austria and Brazil.

Greater disappointment was to come in 1982 when, as World Cup hosts, Spain failed to put together a powerful team. Beaten in the first round by Northern Ireland and held to a draw by the largely unknown Hondurans, Spain owed its place in the second round to one good performance, a 2-1 win over Yugoslavia. But defeat by West Germany and a sterile 0-0 draw against England sent the hosts to the sidelines before the semifinal.

Ironically, better Spanish teams performed well in both 1986 and 1990, but had little good luck. Butragueno emerged as a star from Mexico, where Spain reached the quarter-finals before suffering an agonizing penalty-kick loss to Belgium. In 1990, the Italian adventure also ended badly in an extra-time loss to Yugoslavia in the searing heat of Verona. An attacking Spanish team had failed to capitalize on more than an hour's domination, ultimately losing 2-1.

SRI LANKA

Address: Football Federation of Sri Lanka, No. 2 Old Grand Stand, Race Course, Reid Avenue, Colombo 7. *Founded:* 1939. *FIFA:* 1950. *AFC:* 1958. *National stadium:* Sugathadasa Stadium (25,000); *largest stadium:* Sugathadasa Stadium. *Colors:* Maroon-and-gold jerseys, white shorts. *Season:* September to March.

Throughout the years, the resources of the Football Federation of Sri Lanka have been weighted heavily in favor of the domestic game at the expense of international competition. Soccer in the former British colony of Ceylon has had an active and diverse internal structure since the immediate prewar years. The Ceylon Football Association was founded in 1939. During the war years it became defunct, but it was revived in 1946; by the early 1950s, Ceylon was beginning to feel its way into international competition.

In 1952, it played host to India and Pakistan in friendlies at Colombo, losing both games by 3-0 and 2-0, respectively. One year later, in Rangoon, Ceylon participated in the International Quadrangular Tournament with its three closest neighbors, but it proved to be the weakest team in the field. Though Sri Lanka's international experience has been limited, it has continued to enter competitions, including the 1994 World Cup.

SUDAN

Address: Sudan Football Association, P.O. Box 437, Khartoum. *Founded:* 1936. *FIFA:* 1948. *CAF:* 1956. *National stadium:* Khartoum Stadium, Khartoum (30,000); *largest stadium:* Mereikh Stadium, Omdurman (60,000). *Colors:* White jerseys, white shorts. *Season:* July to June. *Honors:* African Nations' Cup winner (1970), runner-up (1957, 1959, 1963).

Sudan, a pioneer in African soccer, shared domination over the continent with Egypt during the late 1950s and early 1960s, and it finally won Africa's most coveted prize in 1970.

Sudanese independence in 1956 was the catalyst for the formation of the African Football Confederation, of which Sudan was a founding member, and for many years Sudanese officials played a leading role in its administration. Sudanese clubs have not had the success of their national team in African competition, but Al-Merrekh did win the 1989 African Cup Winners Cup.

In 1936, the British helped the Sudanese set up the Sudan Football Association (SFA), and after World War II interest in the game increased substantially. The SFA joined FIFA in 1948. In 1950-51, the Sudan Cup Competition was introduced with 16 clubs playing under a knockout format.

By this time, there were over 200 clubs and 5,500 registered players, all but a few being Sudanese nationals, and seven stadiums with a capacity of 5000 or more. The first recorded international involving Sudan was an unofficial

8-0 loss to France (Amateur) in 1956 at a multinational invitational tournament in Bamako, Mali.

In 1956, when Sudan was still one of only three countries in the region affiliated with FIFA, the Egyptian F.A. seized upon the new political climate created by Sudan's recently enacted independence and invited Sudan and Ethiopia to join in forming the African Football Confederation (CAF).

To celebrate Sudan's independence, Khartoum was selected as the site for the first CAF congress and the first African Nations' Cup competition in 1957. Sudan's 2-1 loss to Egypt in this two-day tournament represents its official debut in international competition. On the basis of this narrow score, Sudan was declared the runner-up because Ethiopia lost to Egypt 4-0. Sudan and Ethiopia did not play one another.

Sudan took second place again in 1959 when it defeated Ethiopia and 'lost to Egypt. Political instabilities at home kept Sudan out of the 1962 edition, but in 1963 Sudan entered once again and gained second place for the third time in a row.

The Sudanese won their first round group with a 4-0 defeat of Nigeria and a 2-2 draw with Egypt. In the final, the mighty Ghanaians, trailblazers of black African soccer, defeated them 3-0 on a pair of goals by the redoubtable Wilberforce Mfum.

Sudan failed to qualify in 1965 and 1968, but in 1970, with political calm restored at home, Sudan played host to the tournament and qualified automatically. Its aging and unexciting team was buoyed greatly by the fanaticism of its fans, and in the first round it managed to defeat Ethiopia and Cameroon, providing passage to the semi-finals. In the semi-final, Sudan defeated its archrival, Egypt, by 2-1, and entered the final against Ghana in Khartoum.

The Sudanese fans were now demanding a Nations' Cup victory after so many second-place finishes, and when Sudan's second goal was disallowed by the referee with the score 1-0, fans rioted. Ghanaian players were attacked on the field, a melee broke out, and the police were called in.

At the final whistle, the score stood at 1-0 in Sudan's favor, and the disgusted Ghanaians left the stadium without accepting the runner-up trophy. Government leader Colonel Ga'afer Mohamed Nimeri, acting on behalf of his people's sentiments at the time, ordered the Ghanaian team out of the country that night.

In 1972, Sudan attained a second great international plateau by qualifying for the Olympic Games in Munich. Its opposition in the first round was formidable. It lost successive matches to Mexico's amateurs (1-0), the Soviet Union's full international team (2-1), and Burma's full international team (2-0), placing last in its group. Its low scoring result against the Russians, however, was considered tantamount to an upset.

Bleak days were ahead for Sudanese soccer. In 1972, Sudan played poorly in the final rounds of the African Nations' Cup, and in 1974 did not even qualify. In the 1976 final rounds, it failed to win a single game because of a sweeping reordering of political priorities at home. It has not been a force in African Championship soccer since and did not even compete in the 1994 World Cup despite the fact that club soccer continues to be popular and Sudanese teams take part in African club competitions.

SURINAM

Address: Surinaamse Voetbal Bond, Cultuurtuinlaan 7, P.O. Box 1223, Paramaribo. *Founded:* 1920. *FIFA:* 1929. *National stadium:* Surinam Stadion, Paramaribo (20,000); *largest stadium:* Surinam Stadion. *Colors:* Green-and-white jerseys, white shorts. *Season:* March to December.

The story of soccer in former Dutch Guiana closely parallels that of the Netherlands Antilles, the other former Dutch colony in the Caribbean region, except that Surinam has been considerably less adventurous in international competition.

The Surinaamse Voetbal Bond (Surinam Football Association) was founded in 1920, one year before the Curacao association in the Netherlands Antilles, and a championship was introduced in 1923-24.

The Surinaamse Voetbal Bond (SVB) joined FIFA in 1929, having secured permission from the Netherlands, and Surinam made its international debut in 1934 against Curacao met nine times before World War II. Surinam won two of these and lost six.

In 1934, the Surinam selection visited Port of Spain and held Trinidad to a 3-3 draw. Unlike Curacao, however, Surinam did not participate in either the Central American and Caribbean Games or the Championship of the Central American and Caribbean Confederation that was introduced in 1941.

Surinam did not become a member of the confederation until the early 1950s, and it was only then that it began to participate in the regional championship. Its interest in regional competition continued when the Championship of CONCACAF was introduced in 1963.

Surinam has entered the last several World Cup qualifying rounds but has not yet been strong enough to win through the finals against larger rivals.

SWEDEN

Address: Svenska Fotbollforbundet, Box 1216, S-17123 Stockhom. *Founded:* 1904. *FIFA:* 1904. *UEFA:* 1954. *National stadium:* Fotbollstadion, Stockholm (52,000); *stadium of equal size:* Ullevi, Goteborg (52,000). *Colors:* Yellow jerseys, blue shorts. *Season:* April to October. *Honors:* World Cup runner-up (1958), third place (1950); Olympic Games winner (1948), third place (1924, 1952).

Sweden ranks as one of the world's most successful soccer-playing countries in proportion to its size. It has won a host of trophies and in playing an unusually full schedule within a short season has produced several outstanding players of world-class caliber.

Between the world wars, Sweden took over the lead in Scandinavian soccer from Denmark, and in the postwar era has defeated every world power in its schedule at least once, including Brazil, England, West Germany, Hungary, and Uruguay. This has largely been accomplished without the benefit of full-time professionalism and in spite of the ceaseless poaching of its best players by wealthy clubs in Europe.

Sweden's ability to rejuvenate its international strength with each new generation of players has been little short of awesome. The exodus of players to the continent, however, thwarted Swedish clubs in their quest for European honors until IFK Goteborg won the UEFA Cup in 1982 and repeated again 1986. In 1992-93 the same team played in the European Champions League.

The details of the birth of Swedish soccer are hazy, but it is certain that the game was played in Goteborg and Stockholm as early as the 1870s. British embassy personnel in Stockholm and Scottish textile workers in Gothenburg are credited with introducing both soccer and rugby,

but until 1891 it is difficult to separate the development of the two games. The first soccer club was probably Orgryte IS from Goteborg, still the leading team with 14 championship wins, although 13 came before 1928.

The present SFF was actually formed in 1904, prompted by the founding of FIFA earlier in the year, but took four years to mount a national team for international competition; the spark that caused this move was the official inclusion of soccer in the 1908 Olympics. To prepare for the Olympics Sweden met Norway in Gothenburg, where the only decent playing fields in the region were located. The result was a resounding 11-3 victory in Sweden's favor.

At the 1908 Olympics, however, Sweden had the misfortune of facing Great Britain's amateur team in the first round and lost 12-1. In the third place game, the Swedes lost to Holland by a respectable 2-1, and placed fourth overall in a field of six.

Between the London games in 1908 and the next Olympics in 1912 (which took place in Stockholm), Sweden played as busy an international schedule as other developing powers of the time—10 matches in all—and of these won six. The Dutch put Sweden out of the Olympic tournament in 1912 before a disappointed home crowd, and in the consolation series Italy defeated Sweden, 1-0.

Like Denmark and Norway, Sweden continued its international activity throughout World War I, which included at least one uncommon non-European opponent, the United States, in a 3-2 loss at Stockholm in 1916. Its long rivalry with Denmark began in 1913.

With only Estonia and Lithuania to overcome in the qualification rounds, Sweden entered its first World Cup in 1934. Little was expected of Sweden, but Argentina, now depleted of its great players from the 1930 championship, was not able to unravel the Swedes' effective team-work, and Sweden's left wing Knut Kroon scored the winning goal late in the second half. In the second round, Sweden lost one of its players through injury, but the result had already been decided as Germany took a 2-1 win.

Sweden left Italy with its first taste of World Cup success and began its work on the development of more skillful players to add to its inclination for solid teamwork. This, however, was to come several years in the future. Sweden's first jolting disappointment in world competition came in the 1936 Olympics in Berlin with a 3-2 loss to Japan, a previously unknown force from the far reaches of Asian soccer.

In the 1938 World Cup, which Sweden reached after eliminating Finland and Estonia in qualifying rounds, more predictable losses were suffered at the hands of Hungary and Brazil, both budding world powers, but not before Norrkoping's Gustav Wetterstrom had scored four goals in a colossal 8-0 win over Cuba in early rounds. This drew international attention to Sweden and the possibility that Sweden was indeed able to turn out excellent individual players.

The win over Cuba put Sweden in the semifinals against Hungary, but according to a popular tale, Zsengeller, Dr. Sarosi, and other Hungarian forwards so dominated this match that a large bird landed in the Hungarian part of the field and was left undisturbed for most of the second half. The final score was 5-1 in Hungary's favor, but it might well have been higher.

In the third-place game, Sweden performed admirably against Brazil, but the incomparable Leônidas and the other Brazilian ball artists were more than Sweden could contain. In losing 4-2, Sweden, dubbed "the team of steel" by the press, settled willfully for a fourth place finish in the World Championship. It was a remarkable feat, undiminished by Sweden's losses to Hungary and Brazil.

In 1948, Sweden's national team was taken over by the Englishman George Raynor, who instituted coaching clinics and coalesced Swedish soccer interests in support of his team. At the 1948 Olympics, Sweden not only entered with the best team in the competition, but looked the equal of any professionally based team in Europe. Sweden's success in this tournament was achieved at a time when the state-paid "amateur" countries of Eastern Europe had yet to initiate their domination of postwar Olympiads.

The best players in England, Italy and other big power countries had long since turned professional, but no one doubted Sweden's ability to hold its own with the best of them, Hungary being the lone exception. In London, Austria, Korea, and Denmark went down in quick succession by an aggregate score of 19-2, and in the final Sweden defeated the superlative "A" team of Yugoslavia, 3-1, to win the gold medal.

Never before or since has Sweden produced such a fine collection of players. The team included the three Nordahl brothers, center forward Gunnar, center half Bertil, and right back Knut, (all of whom played for IFK Norrkoping), and featured inside right Gunnar Gren and left wing Nils Liedholm.

The Gren-Nordahl-Liedholm combination on the forward line eventually became known fondly as "Grenoli," and dazzled crowds, as well as Italian and Spanish scouts, in the postwar era's first outstanding series of international performances.

Their skills were so highly touted that all three Nordahls, Gren, Liedholm, and right wing Kjell Rosen were immediately signed by wealthy Italian clubs. AC Milan, in fact, secured the entire "Grenoli" trio, and Gunnar Nordahl went on to shatter Italian league goal-scoring records. Liedholm long remained in Italy working as a manager after his playing career ended. Inside left Garvis Carlsson, meanwhile, went to Atletico Madrid.

Only Knut Nordahl and left back Erik Nilsson of the 1948 team were able to join the Swedish squad that qualified for the 1950 World Cup in Brazil. But George Raynor, disciplined and popular as ever with his players, had discovered inside right Kalle Palmer and a counterpart, "Nacka" Skoglund, on the left side.

In Brazil, Sweden defeated Italy 3-2 (eight members of this Swedish team were eventually signed by Italian clubs), and drew with Paraguay before entering the final pool of four teams.

But Brazil's extraordinary talents were too strong and skillful for what was virtually a "B" Swedish team, and Brazil routed the Swedes 7-1. This was followed by Sweden's 3-2 loss to Uruguay, eventual winner of the competition, and the series was closed with Sweden's fine 3-1 win over Spain. That win sealed third place in the World Championship, an extraordinary accomplishment for a country that was, after all, depleted of its best players.

Raynor's next task was to retain Sweden's Olympic gold medal in the 1952 games at Helsinki. This proved to be a more competitive Olympic tournament than the last, and no team in the world could have stopped Hungary from winning a deserved first place.

Had it not been for an unlucky draw of opponents in the semi-finals, however, Sweden would likely have won the silver. As it happened, Sweden met Hungary in the semifinals and crashed by six unanswered goals. Sweden settled instead for a respectable third place and a bronze medal after brushing aside West Germany in the third place game.

In the space of five years, Sweden had won Olympic gold and bronze medals and took third place in the World Championship with virtually two separate teams. The price they paid for victory was high, however, as Swedish clubs lost all their major stars to outside leagues as a result of their exposure to the outside world.

The 1950 and 1952 teams played without the stars of 1948 because the SFF refused to allow professionals of any kind on the national team. This rule was rescinded before the 1958 World Cup-held in Sweden, and it paved the way for Sweden's greatest triumph of all and the homecoming of Nils Liedholm, now an inside left.

It also marked the return to international competition of Gunnar Gren, now playing once again for a Swedish club. They were joined by right wing Kurt Hamrin, from Padova in Italy, and the entire country was delighted by a nostalgic return to the glory days of 1948. Even George Raynor was at the helm after coaching in Italy and England.

It is unlikely that Swedish nationalism has ever surfaced quite so fervently as it did in the 1958 World Cup. In the first round, Sweden disposed of Mexico 3-0, and defeated the Hungarians on two deft goals by Hamrin.

Though Wales held Sweden to a goalless draw, Sweden won its group without a defeat in three matches. In the quarter-finals, Hamrin led Sweden to a 2-0 shutout over the Russians, and Swedish fans shifted proudly into overdrive.

The semi-final against West Germany took place in Sweden's soccer capital, Gothenburg, accounting, no doubt, for the noisiness of the crowd, but the game's intensity also rose because it was uncharacteristically violent: One German player was sent off, and West Germany's star player, Fritz Walter, was injured and had to hobble through the rest of the game.

Nonetheless, late in the second half Gren scored Sweden's third and clinching goal in a 3-1 win. Skeptical Swedes could hardly believe it, but Raynor's veterans had advanced to the final of the World Cup.

Unfortunately, Sweden's opponent in Stockholm had everything the Swedes lacked—speed, a host of sublime ball artists, and youth—these in addition to soccer's new sensation, Pelé. Brazil had been turning international soccer upside down with its brilliant displays in earlier rounds, unleashing not only Pelé but "the Little Bird," Garrincha, perhaps the greatest dribbler anyone had ever seen. There was no reason for Brazil to break this momentum, even for the much-respected Swedes.

In the final, Hamrin and Skoglund were neutralized by Djalma Santos and Nilton Santos, yet Liedholm scored after only four minutes. It was an elusive early goal. Vava scored twice in the first half, and with Pelé's first goal in the second half the game was virtually over.

Mario Zagalo scored a fourth Brazilian goal, and Pelé scored his second to make it five, and though center forward Agne Simonsson gave Sweden its second goal, the final score of 5-2 was only partially indicative of just how much this scintillating Brazilian team deserved to win the World Cup.

Fine Swedish teams were seen in the years ahead—rarely have they been poor—but the era of 1948-58 has yet to be duplicated. Gren, G. Nordahl, Nils Liedholm, and Kurt Hamrin remain the greatest Swedish forwards of all time, and during their heyday they were among the finest in the world.

In 1962, Raynor barely missed taking Sweden to the World Cup again when a replay in Berlin was lost to the team of another veteran national manager, Karl Rappan's Switzerland.

Success was not forthcoming in other competitions either. Sweden has not done well in the European Football Championship, and its ability to field "A" teams for the Olympic Games was diffused by the exodus of players during the 1950s.

In the Swedish league, which changed from a winter to a summer schedule in 1958-59, the postwar era has brought about numerous shifts of power.

IFK Norrkoping, the club of the Nordahls and Nils Liedholm, dominated the 1940s and 1950s, but Malmo FF emerged after World War II and is now one championship short of tying Orgryte's ancient record for most league titles. IFK Goteborg has also now won 13 championships and IFK Norrkoping has 12.

Sweden made an inauspicious return to the World Cup in 1970 when a 1-1 draw with Israel ruined its chances for advancing to the second round. This was a good national team, but it lacked finishing power even with the presence of Feyenoord's European Cup hero Ove Kindvall.

In 1974, Sweden returned to the World Championship again with a slow and unspectacular team that nevertheless held mighty Holland to a scoreless draw in the first round and advanced to the second round without a defeat.

West Germany and Poland were vastly superior in second-round wins, but Sweden did manage to defeat bewildered Yugoslavia. In Ronnie Hellstrom, Sweden had the finest goalkeeper in its history.

With Hellstrom in the nets, Sweden again qualified for the 1978 World Cup, its seventh in ten attempts, but in Argentina it failed to score in losses to Spain and Austria, and finished last in its first-round group. Two World Cups were missed and an appearance in the 1990 finals was starkly disappointing as the side lost all three games, including one to the unknowns from Costa Rica. However a place in the 1992 European Championship semifinal revived hopes for the 1994 qualification attempt.

SWITZERLAND

Address: Schweizerischer Fussball-Verband/Association Suisse de Football, Laubeggstrasse 70 B.P., CH-3000 Bern 32. *Founded:* 1895. *FIFA:* 1904. *UEFA:* 1954. *National stadium:* Wankdorfstadion, Berne (60,000); *stadium of equal size:* St. Jakobs-Stadion, Basle (60,000). *Colors:* Red jerseys, white shorts. *Season:* August to June. *Honors:* Olympic Games runner-up (1924).

Switzerland's importance in world soccer is derived from its historical role as the home of FIFA and its significant contribution to the founding and growth of that body. Switzerland is also the home of UEFA, and it has participated actively in the organization of European soccer.

In addition, the Swiss were among the early pioneers of the game. From the beginning, Switzerland has been a fulcrum of stability on which Central and western European soccer could depend, and its reputation for fairness and sportsmanship over the years has augmented this role.

On the playing field, however, Switzerland is another matter. Surrounded by several major world powers, and having aligned itself in competition with four giants of European soccer— Austria, Hungary, Czechoslovakia, and Italy— Switzerland's international record is both poor and understandable.

Bright spots have been rare and brief except on its home grounds, where the best teams in the world are liable to go under at any given time.

English football in its various forms was probably first played on the European continent by English exchange students in Switzerland around 1855. The earliest documented date is 1869, when English students at La Chatelaine College in Geneva, near the present site of Servette FC, played under "association" rules.

A handful of small clubs sprang up over the next decade in academic towns around the country, and in 1879 Fussball-Club St. Gallen, the oldest club in existence today, was founded in the German-speaking northeast.

Grasshopper Club, the most successful club in Swiss soccer, was formed in Zurich by English students in 1886, and Servette Football-Club, the second most successful club, was founded in Geneva in 1890.

Many important Swiss clubs in both German and French parts of the country appeared during the 1890s: Fussball-Club Basel (1893); Football Club La Chaux-deFonds (1894); Fussball-Club Biel, Fussball-Club Zurich, Lausanne-Sports, and Fussball-Club Winterthur (all in 1896); and Berner Sportclub Young Boys (1898). Grasshoppers' 22 titles lead the honors list, with Servette next with 15. Grasshoppers have also dominated in the Swiss Cup, winning 17 times.

The strong British influence on Swiss soccer is evident by many club names, but the Swiss themselves were very active by the 1880s and 1890s. In 1895, the Schweizerische Football Association (SFA) was founded at Olten, in the German-speaking north, by seven charter clubs. (The present German-French name of the federation was adopted later.)

A league was introduced in 1897, and in 1898, Switzerland played in its first unofficial international, a match in Basle with representative teams from the country at large and southern Germany.

In 1904, the SFA was one of the first governing bodies to be approached by France and Belgium to help with the founding of FIFA, and Switzerland duly became one of seven charter members at the inaugural meeting in Paris. FIFA headquarters was located in Zurich where it has remained ever since. The following year, Switzerland played in its first full international against France in Paris, France winning 1-0.

Switzerland's first official competition was the 1924 Olympic Games in Paris, and in the wake of its postwar momentum this turned out to be Switzerland's finest hour. The Swiss buried Lithuania 9-0 in the preliminary round, escaped from a reply with Czechoslovakia in the first round, upset Italy in the second round, and gained the Olympic final with a win over Sweden in the semi-finals.

In the final, Switzerland's first encounter with a non-European team, the mighty Uruguayans were far too skilled and sophisticated and had little trouble in shutting out the Swiss 3-0. Still, Switzerland's silver medal from the Paris Olympics remains to this day its highest achievement.

The Swiss were eliminated from the 1928 Olympics by Germany in the first round and narrowly qualified for the 1934 World Cup at the expense of Yugoslavia and Rumania. Their luck continued in 1934 with a first round upset win over Holland on a fluke goal, but in the second round Czechoslovakia won on superior skill and conditioning. Switzerland entered the 1938 World Cup after eliminating lowly Portugal, and here the Swiss made a memorable showing.

Two events that occurred before the 1938 World Cup gave Switzerland a big boost: the defeat of all-powerful England by a score of 2-1 in Zurich, and the hiring of Austrian Karl Rappan as manager of the national team the year before. Switzerland's victory over England two weeks before the start of the competition was its greatest win of the pre-World War II era, and Rappan,

the sometime manager of the Grasshoppers and Servette, became one of the most respected strategists in European soccer. In four different stints as national team manager between 1937-62, he brought prestige and some degree of success to his adopted country.

In the 1938 World Cup, Rappan's Switzerland held a German team, swelled with Austrians and others from conquered lands, to a 1-1 draw in the first round, and in the replay defeated Germany 4-2 after trailing 2-0. The Swiss goal-scoring hero was Trello Abegglen, but it was the system itself and Rappan's leadership that paved the way.

In the second round, Hungary's goal-scoring ace Zsengeller scored two unanswered goals, and Switzerland bowed out of the competition. Rappan's team was able to notch further wins over major powers such as Italy and Hungary before the outbreak of World War II, and during the war itself it played several games against politically neutral Sweden and Portugal.

Under Rappan, Switzerland again qualified for the World Cup in 1950, but the great master did not join his team in the final rounds in Brazil. After losing as expected to Yugoslavia, the Swiss met Brazil in Sao Paulo—a weakened Brazil to be sure—and once again contained its most skilled forwards. The Swiss counterattack was potent enough to equalize near the end of the game, and Switzerland walked away with a 2-2 draw. But even after a win over Mexico, Switzerland still lacked the necessary points to advance to the next round.

Rappan again took over the national team in 1953 to prepare for the next World Cup—to be held in Switzerland. The Swiss reached the quarter-finals of the World Championship before home crowds and for the first and only time in their history. In the first round they defeated Italy 2-1, a major accomplishment even if it was a low period for Italian soccer, and lost to

England 2-0. A replay with Italy was forced to determine which team would join England in the next round, and this was won convincingly by the Swiss 4-1.

This game was one of Switzerland's proudest accomplishments, matched only by its qualification for the 1962 World Cup eight years later. Swiss euphoria came to a horrifying end in the second round, however, when Austria, led by the magnificent Ernst Ocwirk, scored five goals in a record seven minutes to win 7-5. The complete breakdown of Rappan's defensive system, as it happened, was not the result of tactical errors but of a chink in the armor.

Swiss captain and center half Roger Bocquet was at the time suffering from a serious tumor, and against Rappan's suggestion insisted on starting the game. On the field he was mesmerized by the heat and was ultimately responsible for letting in several goals.

Bocquet was the most popular player in Switzerland, and the agonizing question of whether to remove him from the field or switch him to another position was partly decided by Bocquet himself—he refused to leave the field—and partly by the game's strict stoppage laws. At any rate, Switzerland lost the game at its potentially finest hour. (Bocquet's subsequent operation to remove his tumor was successful.)

Spain and Scotland eliminated the Swiss in 1958 World Cup in qualifying rounds, but in 1962 Switzerland again gained the finals by eliminating Belgium and Sweden in a remarkable series of victories (including a play-off with Sweden in neutral Berlin). This was regarded as a startling triumph, and once again Karl Rappan, who had taken over the team for a fourth time in 1960, was at the helm.

In Chile, however, West Germany, Italy, and Chile each won first round games over a Swiss team lacking some of the skills it had displayed in 1938 and 1954. Rappan again stepped down from his post, but he retired as a national sports hero.

Swiss fortunes in international competition have further declined since the early 1960s. Switzerland qualified again for the World Cup in 1966, but was virtually knocked out of the running by West Germany in the first game.

It has not advanced beyond the first round in the European Football Championship in four attempts, and has not qualified for the World Cup final rounds since 1966, although the 1994 team was on course to end that long drought halfway through European qualification play.

SYRIA

Address: Federation Arabe Syrienne de Football, General Sport Bldg., October Stadium, Damascus-Barente. *Founded:* 1936. *FIFA:* 1937. *AFC:* 1970. *National stadium:* Stade Al-Abbassiyne, Damascus (45,000); *largest stadium:* Stade Al-Abbassiyne. *Colors:* White jerseys, white shorts.

With the exception of Jordan, North Yemen, and Oman, Syria has been the least conspicuous of Arab countries on the soccer field. Under the French mandate, the game was not promoted as aggressively in Syria as it was in British mandated countries of the Middle East. In later years, without the benefit of extensive oil reserves, Syria was less exposed to Western European workers and technicians who ultimately helped to establish the game in other Arab states.

Nevertheless, the Federation Syrienne de Football was founded in 1936 and became affiliated with FIFA in 1937. ("Arabe" was added to the name in the early 1970s.) A system of regional committees was developed after World War II to administer local competitions.

Syria's first full international was played in 1949 in a World Cup qualification match against Turkey at Ankara. The Turks won, 7-0. Five days later the same team traveled to Athens and lost a friendly to Greece, this time by a mere 2-0.

In 1951, Syria entered the sparsely attended football tournament of the first Mediterranean Games at Alexandria, in which only three countries participated. Though its presence there was surprising and encouraging for the future of Syrian soccer, the team suffered two lopsided defeats, 4-0 against Greece and 8-0 against Egypt.

From there, Syria's participation in international competition virtually ceased until the qualification rounds of the 1974 World Cup. Syria's reemergence coincided with the rise of soccer in the Middle East generally and appeared to indicate a turning point in Syria's desire to enter the mainstream of the Asian game.

Grouped with Syria in the 1974 World Cup qualification rounds were Iran, Korea DPR, and Kuwait, the Syrians managed to win over Kuwait twice and Iran once, surely the best results in their history, but were not able to compete with Iran before the latter's home crowds in Tehran. Syria's second-place finish, however, was encouraging, especially given such formidable opposition.

In the qualification rounds for the 1978 World Cup, Syria again achieved good results by splitting home and away matches with the determined Saudis, but lost to Iran in Tehran and forfeited the return leg, ending all hope of further success in its third World Cup attempt. Saudi Arabia (1982, 1990) and Iraq (1986) proved too strong in the next three tries, but

Syria's progress has been unmistakable. In 1994 qualifying, they will co-host a four-team group along with Iran.

TAHITI

Address: Federation Tahitienne de Football, Attn. Napoleon Spitz, BP 650, Papeete. *Founded:* 1990. *Colors:* Red and white.

Tahiti's first appearance in Oceania World Cup qualifying produced the expected, a second place finish to strong Australia in a three-team first round group, but the new members did pick up a victory over the Solomon Islands and were by no means outclassed by the Australians in those two matches.

TANZANIA

Address: Football Association of Tanzania, P.O. Box 1574, Dar es Salaam. *Founded:* 1930. *FIFA:* 1964. *CAF:* 1960. *National stadium:* National Stadium, Dar es Salaam (3,000); *largest stadium:* National Stadium. *Colors:* Green jerseys with yellow sleeves, black shorts. *Season:* September to August.

Soccer in Tanzania has been slower to develop than in other major countries of Africa. The population of Tanganyika, the bulky mainland portion of the United Republic of Tanzania, is so sparsely and widely distributed that the use of recreational time was difficult to organize.

Zanzibar, more compact and orderly, has too small a population to make a large difference in the state of the national game, and its semiautonomous politics were not helpful in unifying Tanzania's soccer interests. The change from German to British colonization also damaged the game's growth.

The Football Association of Tanganyika was founded in 1930 and soon became affiliated with The Football Association in London, yet by this time, the smaller but older Sports Association of Zanzibar was already affiliated. A merger of the two associations resulted from the unification of the two countries in 1964, but their special relationship calls for a certain degree of autonomy. In the African Nations' Cup, as well as World Cup and Olympic qualification rounds, the Tanzanian national team represents both Tanganyika and Zanzibar.

Tanzania has not yet qualified for any final rounds of the African Nations' Cup. Its lack of success in international competition has also extended to club tournaments. Its World Cup team tried to qualify from 1974 to 1986 without success but did not enter in 1990 and withdrew before playing a 1994 match.

THAILAND

Address: Football Association of Thailand, c/o National Stadium, Rama 1 Road, Bangkok. *Founded:* 1916. *FIFA:* 1925. *AFC:* 1957. *National stadium:* Suphachalasai Stadium, Bangkok (39,924); *largest stadium:* Suphachalasai Stadium. *Colors:* Crimson red jerseys, white shorts.

Thailand, the only country in Southeast Asia that was not colonized by a European power, was nevertheless introduced to soccer by British tradesmen and technicians around the turn of the century or before, and in 1916 foreigners established the Football Association of Siam to regulate local competitions.

As an independent country, Siam was able to join FIFA in 1925—early by Asian standards— but little was seen of any Siamese teams in international competition until well after World War II.

Among East and Southeast Asian countries, Thailand still ranks below the middle level on the basis of official results, but it has been very active on several levels of international competition and it is a respected organizer of tournaments. The Asian Games have been held twice in Bangkok, and in 1968 the Football Association of Thailand introduced the King's Cup Football Tournament, one of the region's major competitions for national teams.

TOGO

Address: Federation Togolaise de Football, C.P. 5, Lome. *Founded:* 1960. *FIFA:* 1962. *CAF:* 1963. *National stadium:* Stade General Etienne Eyadema, Lome (20,000); *largest stadium:* Stade General Btienne Eyadema. *Colors:* Red jerseys with yellow and green stripes, white shorts.

Togo, like many small nations on the international soccer horizon, have shown how difficult it is to promote a successful national team and a vital league at the same time. For example, in 1971-72, the Togo Football Federation made the decision to support the national team's effort in the African Nations' Cup to such an extent that the clubs at home were nearly abandoned in the process.

For the first and only time in the Nations' Cup history, Togo went through to the final rounds, where it managed to draw with the eventual finalist, Mali, as well as with Kenya before losing to powerful Cameroon by 2-0. Togo's success was the surprise of the tournament.

Between 1972-74, however, Togo's national team did not engage in international play, as the strain of the Nations' Cup run had seriously jeopardized the state of domestic competition. All resources now had to be redirected to save the league from irretrievable harm.

Subsequent World Cup qualifying attempts were unsuccessful, although Senegal was beaten in the 1978 tournament before Togo fell to Guinea. In both 1986 and 1990, Togo withdrew before playing a match, but it did fulfill its 1994 schedule, losing all 5 matches against Angola, Egypt, and Zimbabwe.

The Federation Togolaise de Football was founded immediately after Togo achieved independence in 1960. The association supports a national championship and an annual national cup competition, but the country is too small in size to organize any regional competitions.

TRINIDAD AND TOBAGO

Address: Trinidad and Tobago Football Association, Duke and Scott-Bushe Street, P.O. Box 400, Port of Spain. *Founded:* 1906. *FIFA:* 1963. *CONCACAF:* 1964. *National stadium:* Queen's Park Oval, Port of Spain (20,000); *largest stadium:* Queen's Park Oval. *Colors:* Red jerseys, black shorts.

The Trinidad Amateur Football Association is the second-oldest British-instituted association in the Caribbean region, and was the first to become directly affiliated with The Football Association in London, in 1906.

The population of Trinidad, however, was so small and the distance from many potential Caribbean opponents so great that Port of Prince was never included on the main soccer-playing routes. The earliest record of a Trinidad international, though it was less than a full international, is a 3-3 draw with Surinam in 1934 at Port of Spain.

In 1963, one year after independence, the new Trinidad Football Association joined FIFA as a full member and proceeded to enter as many competitions as it could. The major clubs,

Malvern, Maple Club, and Palo Seco, were seen in the CONCACAF club championship, and Trinidad became a regular participant in the Championship of CONCACAF.

Its highest achievement to date came in the 1990 World Cup qualifying tournament. A team with attacking flair stood one step away from the finals in Italy, only to lose 1-0 to the United States in the last match. A capacity crowd that had come to celebrate in Port of Spain instead stayed to cheer its heroes' efforts, the support boosting interest in soccer to its highest level.

The 1994 team, however, failed to get past rival Jamaica in the CONCACAF first round, so it is difficult to know if the soccer momentum can be maintained in a region where cricket is still the most popular sport.

TUNISIA

Address: Federation Tunisienne de Football, 28 rue Bilal, El-Menzah VI, Tunis 1004. *Founded:* c. 1956. *FIFA:* 1960. *CAF:* 1960. *National stadium:* Stade Olympique, Tunis (50,000); *largest stadium:* Stade Olympique. *Colors:* Red jerseys, white shorts. *Season:* September to June. *Honors:* African Nations' Cup runner-up (1965).

Tunisia ranks with Algeria and Morocco as major soccer-playing countries in former French North Africa. It was the first African nation other than Egypt to gain the final rounds of the Olympic Games, and it was an early participant in the African Nations' Cup.

Tunisian clubs are among the strongest on the continent, but only two have won continental trophies. Club Africain won the African Champions Cup in 1991, while CA Bizerte took the Cup Winners Cup in 1985. Tunisia's national team has qualified for one World Cup finals in 1978.

Although French colonists began playing soccer in Tunis around the turn of the century, the rapid growth of Tunisian soccer began, as it did in France itself, immediately after World War I. The Ligue de Tunisie de Football was founded in 1921 and became affiliated with the French Football Federation.

Two club competitions were started immediately—a league called the Division d'Honneur in 1921 and a cup competition, the Coupe de Tunis, in 1922. Tunis selections began to compete with their opposite numbers from Algiers, Oran, and Constantine on an annual basis in the 1930s and with Morocco in 1948.

Tunisian soccer expanded again after World War II, and in the mid-1950s the Tunisian league finally broke ties with France to form the Federation Tunisienne de Football. In 1960, Tunisia blazed an African trail into the final rounds of the Olympic Games but was thwarted in its first bid for world honors by three first round losses to Denmark and Poland, full international teams, and Argentina.

In 1962, Tunisia became the first French-speaking North African country to enter the African Nations' Cup; in 1965 it served as host of the competition. Tunisia won its first round group-on goal average over Senegal-and moved into the final against Ghana, losing 3-2.

The outstanding player in this game was Tunisia's captain and playmaker, Majid Chetali, who in 1978 coached the national team in its successful run for the final rounds of the World Cup. This was Tunisia's best African Championship finish.

Tunisia's interest in the World Cup, like that of its archrival Morocco, has always been keen. The French-speaking North African countries are closer to the mainstream of European soccer than the rest of Africa, and Europe's World Cup fever spills easily across the Mediterranean.

Morocco having been the first African country in 36 years to qualify for the World Cup final rounds—in 1970—Tunisia put together an impressive effort for the 1978 edition to equal its rival's accomplishment, defeating four big African powers in qualifying rounds—Morocco, Guinea, Nigeria, and Egypt—a tough list of opponents.

In the first round of the World Cup finals in Argentina, the Tunisian team surpassed even optimistic expectations, defeating Mexico 3-1, losing to mighty Poland by a mere 1-0, and, best of all, holding West Germany to a goalless draw.

Though it failed to advance beyond the first round, Tunisia emerged as the Cinderella team of 1978, and following the competition virtually the whole team received lucrative contracts from wealthy Saudi Arabian clubs. But it did not signal Tunisian dominance in Africa. Instead, Algeria and Cameroon stole the show in 1982, and Tunisia has not gotten back to the finals since.

In the first division of the Tunisian league, Club Africain, Esperance, and Stade Tunisien are among the leading clubs in the capital. Of late, teams from Sfax have also become a production center for many top players.

TURKEY

Address: Turkiye Fútbol Federation, Konur Sokkak No. 10, Ankara, Kizilay. *Founded:* 1923. *FIFA:* 1923. *UEFA:* 1962. *National stadium:* 19 Mayis Stadi, Ankara (35,000); *largest stadium:* Atatiirk Stadi, Izmir (70,000). *Colors:* White jerseys, white shorts. *Season:* September to June.

The history of Turkish soccer is an unusually accurate reflection of the modernization Turkey has experienced in its overall cultural life. Growth of the sport falls squarely into two distinct periods: the Ottoman Empire and the republic. Turkey has been surprisingly active in international competition, especially since World War II, and since its official induction into the European soccer community in the early 1960s it has been every bit as active as the other minor soccer-playing countries of Europe.

Turkish teams have occasionally broken through in major international competitions, but they have yet to progress beyond the middle rank despite a hefty domestic league that has helped to spread the power in Turkish soccer to population centers other than Istanbul.

The game was first played in Turkey by British residents and Greek students in Smyrna (Izmir), the Aegean port city, in 1895 or 1896. From the beginning, Ottoman authorities were fearful that soccer was linked with insurrectional instincts, and in the volatile atmosphere of the Ottoman Empire in its last years, the game alone was cause enough to warrant swift retaliatory measures.

To make matters worse, the game immediately became associated in the minds of the police with Armenians, Greeks, Bulgarians and other potential "enemies" of the state. When a group of Galatasaray High School students in Constantinople attempted to form a team around 1899, the effort was suppressed.

In 1905, another brave band of Galatasaray students formed a team, and this was to be the proud forerunner of the present Galatasaray club, the oldest in the country, and the most prominent Turkish cup side with nine victories. At about this time, an Istanbul Sunday Amateur League was introduced, and in 1907, Fenerbahce Spor Kulubu, the most successful of all Turkish clubs, with 12 titles, was founded in the Beyoglu section of Constantinople, not far from the Galatasary High School.

The turning point was the fall of the Turkish Empire after World War I. The Turk Spor Kurumu (Turkish Sports Committee) was established in 1920, and Turks began playing in ever-increasing numbers.

In 1923, the founding date of the republic, the Turkiye Fútbol Federasyonu (TFF) was established in the new capital city of Ankara, and plans were made to introduce a national championship for the 1923-24 season. From that date until 1951, Turkish champions were determined by a knockout competition between the winners of each district league.

The first winner in 1924 was Harbuje, another Beyoglu district club in Istanbul. During the next seven years, the championship was completed only once, and between 1922 and 1935 it reappeared, with three Istanbul clubs taking away the honors. The league was nearly dormant throughout the late 1930s but was revived with some regularity from 1940-50.

Turkey made its international debut only months after the founding of the Turkish F.A. in 1923 against Rumania in Istanbul, resulting in a 2-2 draw. One year later, the TFF ambitiously entered the Olympic Games in Paris, but was unfortunate to be drawn against Czechoslovakia (at that time one of Europe's finest teams), and the result was a predictable 5-2 loss.

After 1950, modernization progressed still further, and the outmoded national championship was changed in 1951 with the introduction of professionalism. The rise of professionalism spawned Turkey's finest era in international competition. Between 1948 and 1955, the national team won 13 games, including a 2-1 triumph over Germany FR in West Berlin and the surprising elimination of Spain in qualification rounds for the 1954 World Cup.

Turkey reached its first World Cup in 1954, and promptly defeated hapless Korea. Turkey then succumbed twice (the second was a replay under old World Cup rules) to the eventual world champion, West Germany, by an aggregate of 11-3 and was eliminated.

There have been no further World Cup qualifications for Turkey, and since 1956, it has returned almost exactly to its pre-World War I level of success, some fine wins serving more to deceive than indicate a true breakthrough to a higher level. Turkish clubs have been eager participants in all three European club competitions, but none have yet reached a final, despite some strong performances by Galatasaray in particular.

The Turkish first division comprises 16 clubs and is both competitive and well supported. Since the introduction of the national league in 1958, however, the big Istanbul clubs, Fenerbahce (12 titles), Galatasaray (8 titles), and Besiktas (9 titles) have dominated league honors.

UGANDA

Address: Federation of Uganda Football Associations, P.O. Box 10475, Kampala. *Founded:* 1924. *FIFA:* 1959. *CAF:* 1959. *National stadium:* Nakivubo Stadium, Kampala (50,000); *largest stadium:* Nakivubo Stadium. *Colors:* Yellow jerseys, black shorts. *Season:* January to November.

Uganda is a middle-level soccer power in Africa with a misleading international record that makes its real strength difficult to pin down. Only three other black African states have qualified more times than Uganda for the final rounds of the African Nations' Cup. But Uganda's overall record in the final rounds is poor, with second place in 1978 being its best finish. World Cup

qualifying is no better with quick exits the rule in qualifying. Political upheavals in recent years have further contributed to the difficulties.

British colonists and workers played soccer in Kampala before the turn of the century, and in 1915 the first club—Nsambya F.C.—was founded. The mini-boom in African soccer after World War I produced the first Ugandan governing body in 1921, and this became affiliated with The Football Association in London shortly thereafter.

Clubs and local leagues, especially in Kampala, were founded in large numbers between the world wars, and with greater intensity after World War II. In 1959, the Federation of Uganda Football Associations (FUFA) joined FIFA. Uganda became one of the first black African states to join the African Football Confederation in 1959.

UKRAINE
(Formerly part of the U.S.S.R.)

Address: Football Federation of the Ukraine, 42 Esplanada, 252 023 Kiev. *Founded:* 1991. *FIFA:* 1993 (provisional). *UEFA:* 1992. *Colors:* Yellow, blue, and red.

Followers of world soccer will have no difficulty believing that the first real international power to emerge from the former Soviet Union is as likely to be the Ukraine as Russia.

Russia had the advantage of being able to enter the 1994 World Cup under its old FIFA membership as the U.S.S.R. and could even use non-Russian players—Ukrainian Sergei Youran for one—but the long-range prospect made it seem as likely that the Ukraine will be able to equal its larger neighbor and make an impression as an Eastern European power in its own right.

In part the old Soviet system will be able to take some credit if that happens because Ukrainian soccer received a major boost back in the 1970's when the Soviet champ, Dynamo Kiev, was turned en masse into the Soviet national team. That was not only because Dynamo Kiev had Oleg Blokhin and a fine supporting cast but also because the Ukraine boasted some of the top coaches in the land. Longtime U.S.S.R. national team manager Valery Lobanovsky doubled as Dynamo Kiev coach right to the end of the Soviet Union.

The new Ukraine staged its first championship in 1991-92 but did not achieve FIFA membership in time to participate in the 1994 World Cup. The league champion, Tavrija Simferopol, also won the first Ukraine Cup, defeating Dynamo Kiev to capture all of the honors in the first season.

UNITED ARAB EMIRATES

Address: United Arab Emirates Football Association, P.O. Box 5458, Dubai. *Founded:* 1971. *FIFA:* 1972. *National Stadium:* Dubai (50,000). *Colors:* Red jerseys, red shorts.

The United Arab Emirates (U.A.E.) is a confederation of six emirates on the Persian Gulf. Its interest in soccer is enthusiastic despite an exceptionally late start in organizing the game. Clubs in the U.A.E. are divided among the emirates as follows: Dubai, Abu Dhabi, Sharja, Ajman, Fujaira, and Umm Al Quwaim. Of the 25 playing fields located throughout the federation, more than half are in Dubai and Abu Dhabi.

International competition with its Arabian peninsula rivals increased markedly after affiliation with FIFA in 1972 and were fully rewarded with a surprise berth in the 1990 World Cup finals. Although beaten decisively by Germany and returning home without a point, the U.A.E. had no complaints as its development program was ahead of schedule.

UNITED STATES OF AMERICA

Address: United States Soccer Federation, U.S. Soccer House, 1801-1811 S. Prairie Ave., Chicago, Illinois. *Founded:* 1913. *FIFA:* 1913. *CONCACAF:* 1961. *Largest stadium:* Rose Bowl, Pasadena, CA (106,000). *Colors:* Red jerseys with white trim, red shorts. *Season:* April to August. *Honors:* CONCACAF Gold Cup (1991).

The history of soccer in the United States is certainly unique. American soccer was long characterized by domestic disorganization and isolation from the international mainstream. By the 1990s, however, it appeared that the United States had its first chance to nurse genuine development of its vast resources as host for the 1994 World Cup.

In the seventeenth century, the American colonies were the first overseas territory of the British Empire to play football-like games, and two centuries later the United States was the first sovereign country outside Great Britain to establish a soccer club and one of the first to form a national governing body. However, the U.S. national team, as late as 1948, lost to lowly Norway by the score of 11-0, and as late as 1975 lost to Italy by 10-0, not to mention a 2-1 defeat at the same time to the reserve squad of the Italian second division club Pescara.

Such embarrassments were eased by two high spots in American soccer annals: the United States' advance to the semi-finals of the first World Cup in 1930, and its shock upset of England in the 1950 World Cup. Towering achievements though these were, they are remembered elsewhere as aberrations that resulted from extraordinary circumstances, and they had no impact at home.

The first descriptions of the game in the United States were written by the students and alumni of the great colleges of the northeast. Freshman and sophomore classes at Harvard initiated an annual football contest in 1827. It was played on the first Monday of the new school year, and entailed such rough play that the annual date became known as "Bloody Monday."

The Harvard faculty banned this event in 1860, but similar games continued to be played less formally. Princeton students played "ballown," in which the ball was hit with the fist, as well as other parts of the body, and by 1840 their form of the game was organized into intramural tournaments. At Yale, "roughhouse football" was played as early as 1840, and became ritualized as the "annual rush" between freshmen and sophomores in 1851.

Various forms of football were also being played during this period at Amherst and Brown. The round, rubber ball was introduced in the 1850s, at which time dribbling and passing skills associated with modern soccer were learned.

Games resembling soccer, rather than rugby, continued to predominate until the mid-1870s. During the Civil War, the prep schools of the Northeast, especially in New England had kept the game alive.

Meanwhile, British immigrants in the large cities were beginning to introduce soccer to the general public. In 1862, three years after the formation of the first "dribbling" club in England, the Oneida Football Club was founded in Boston by Gerritt Smith Miller.

Oneida F.C. was not only the first "dribbling" club in the United States but also the first known club established anywhere outside England.

AP/Wide World Photos

U.S. center forward Larry Gaetjens is carried off the field after scoring the only goal in a stunning U.S. upset victory over England in 1950 World Cup competition.

It preceded the first Scottish club by five years, the first Welsh club by 11 years, and the first Irish club by 17 years. Oneida F.C. played on the Boston Common against scratch teams from 1862 to 1865 without conceding a game or a single goal. These were the first public games played with a round ball in the United States. All 17 members of the club are thought to have been English by birth or heritage.

Immediately after the Civil War, collegiate play was resumed. In 1866, Beadle & Co. of New York published the new rules of both association football (soccer) and the "handling" game (rugby), the latter having been virtually unknown in the United States.

In 1867, Princeton and Rutgers drew up their own sets of rules that adhered to the soccer code. At Princeton, where the rules called for 25 players on each side, an intramural game under the new association rules was played that same year against Princeton Theological Seminary.

The first intercollegiate game under rules approximating soccer was played on November 6, 1869, at New Brunswick, New Jersey, between Princeton and Rutgers. After Rutgers won 6-4, a return match was played at Princeton a week later and was won by Princeton 8-0. A third match was canceled by faculty members worried about roughhousing.

These historic games were played under the rules of the home team, both of which were based on the London Football Association "Laws of the Game" (1863), the official soccer code. Common to both games were the following rules: a maximum of 25 players allowed on either team; a field measuring 110 meters (360 feet) by 70 meters (225 feet) wide; a goal measuring seven meters (24 feet) wide; six points to win; a round ball made of inflated rubber; movement of the ball with all parts of the body, including

hands (the ball could not be carried or thrown while the player was in motion); and restrictions against tripping and holding. In another oddity of U.S. soccer history, these games are often recalled as the antecedent to American college football, not soccer.

The dribbling game with a round ball was adopted at Yale, Columbia, and Cornell, and at Harvard it was taken up again in 1871 in a hybrid form known as the Boston Game, in which the soccer code was combined with the rugby characteristic of picking the ball up and running with it (carrying).

In 1873, Princeton, Yale, Columbia, and Rutgers met in New York to draw up a uniform set of rules that were based on the London Football Association laws of 1863. They settled on the following: 20 players to a team; a field measuring 400 feet by 250 feet; a goal measuring 25 feet wide; six goals to win; and, a point scored by passing the ball between the goal posts. Carrying the ball was prohibited.

In the fall of 1873, Yale defeated Princeton 3-0 under soccer rules, thus initiating the longest continuous rivalry in collegiate sports. (Soon, however, it was to become a gridiron football rather than soccer rivalry.) Within weeks, a team of Englishmen calling itself Eton Players—its captain and other members were Old Etonians— traveled to New Haven to play against Yale in the first Anglo-American international match.

For this occasion, Yale was persuaded to adopt the English custom of 11 players to a team, and the idea was so well received that it was permanently incorporated into the Yale game.

The English method of scoring (one-point goals) was also adopted, and Yale won the match by 2-1. In subsequent years, Yale argued for universal adoption of the 11-player rule among its collegiate opponents. The principle was accepted generally in 1880, and was eventually incorporated into American gridiron football. Harvard, meanwhile, became more interested in the rugby code, and sought competition with like-minded teams. McGill University of Montreal had also adopted rugby, and in 1874, three years after the formation of the Rugby Football Union in England, a two-game series between the two rugby adherents was played in Cambridge.

The second of these matches was played with an oval ball under Rugby Union rules and marks the beginning of American gridiron football. It also spelled doom for the future of soccer in the United States.

In November 1875, Harvard played Yale in a game held under "concessionary rules," which included many rugby characteristics, such as scoring by tries (touchdowns), as well as one-point goals, and a 15-player team instead of the 11-player team preferred by Yale.

Harvard won by four goals and four tries to none, and Yale, after becoming one of the earliest advocates of the soccer code, reassessed its position and took to the rugby rules as played at Harvard. The Princeton observers present at the Harvard-Yale match were also favorably impressed by the rugby rules and returned to New Jersey to report their change of mind.

In 1876, Harvard, Princeton, and Columbia met to form the Intercollegiate Football Association and adopt a code of Rugby Union rules. With this agreement, the soccer code was delivered a death blow that changed forever the acceptance of the dribbling game in the United States. Stevens, Wesleyan, and Pennsylvania Colleges, all of which were playing soccer-like games, were also won over by the rugby code.

At Lexington, Virginia, the Virginia Military Institute and Washington and Lee, both of which played soccer from 1873, switched to rugby in 1876, and the transformation spread to all geographical areas. Colleges and universities that introduced football programs after this period adopted the rugby game to the exclusion of soccer.

After the demise of collegiate soccer in 1876, the game was kept alive by its adherents away from the college campus. The rise of the "ethnic game" during this period signified a second important transformation in early American soccer and one that put its mark permanently on the American game. In the British Isles, as elsewhere in Europe, the working classes were rapidly taking to soccer as their chosen pastime, rugby increasingly being adopted as the sport of the upper classes.

Simultaneously in the United States, as millions of immigrants flooded the major urban centers of the East and Midwest, they brought with them fragments of their culture. Soccer, ever more distinct from the rugby code in Europe, became a major recreational bridge between the old country and the new.

As assimilation into American society took on greater importance, however, immigrants turned increasingly to baseball and American gridiron football. Thus, the number of soccer adherents arriving in the United States was canceled out by the growing number of those who sought "Americanization."

The unwritten social code of the day stipulated that Americans played gridiron football and baseball; foreigners played soccer. This pattern has remained predominant even in an era when native American youth is as likely to choose soccer as football for a recreational game.

The first regions to become ethnic soccer hotbeds were the West Hudson section of New Jersey, New York City, and Philadelphia. The industrial towns of New England soon followed, and by the end of the 1870s factory towns such as Fall River, Massachusetts were primarily soccer-playing communities.

At first the game was played in pick-up fashion or by loosely organized groups of teams, but in time the corporations that employed largely immigrant workers began to sponsor factory clubs and lend financial assistance to local and regional leagues. Similar developments were seen in the industrial centers of the Midwest.

Many British immigrants who were not necessarily employed by factories also sought to organize the game, and in 1884, a group of British-born soccer enthusiasts met in Newark, New Jersey to discuss their future.

The eventual outgrowth of this meeting was the founding of the American Football Association (AFA), the first governing body of soccer in the United States and the third to be formed outside the British Isles.

On November 28, 1885, the United States made its unofficial international debut against Canada in Newark. Canada won 1-0 over an American team selected by the AFA from clubs of the West Hudson region.

This important game predates the first continental European international by 17 years and the first South American international by 20 years, though its status with FIFA remains unrecognized.

In 1886, a second Canadian-American international was played in Newark and the United States won 3-2 with two goals scored near the end of the game (some accounts exist of a three-game series played in Canada in 1886 and a three-game return series played in Newark in 1887 that resulted in two won, two drawn, and two lost, but these series remain unverified).

Once again, however, the growth of American soccer lost its momentum. The inability of administrators to hold together a representative national association precluded the United States from engaging in any further international competition for a period of 30 years, which coincided with the phenomenal development of the game in Europe and Latin America.

Nevertheless, clubs and regional associations were beginning to form in many parts of the country. The Pullman Railroad Car Company of Chicago supported an active team with its own grounds from 1883. The St. Louis Football Association was founded in 1886, and the Bristol County Soccer League was established the same year, reflecting the strength of the game in and around Fall River.

In 1887, the New England Association Football League was established, and the New England Football Association was founded as a regulatory body. Upstate New York and Eastern Pennsylvania also became important soccer centers.

At the same time, the Pennsylvania Football Union was formed, and in 1892 the Denver Association Football Club was founded, the first known soccer organization in the far west.

In Cincinnati, where German immigrants had dominated the sports scene since the mid-nineteenth century, the Irish-based Shamrock Association Football Club was established in 1898.

By 1902, the California Association Football Union had been formed in San Francisco, and in 1906 the Cleveland Soccer Football League was founded in Ohio.

In 1924, the United States embarked on a relatively successful ten-year period in international competition. At the Olympic Games of 1924 in

Paris, it defeated little Estonia 1-0 and managed to hold mighty Uruguay, the eventual gold medalist, to a 3-0 win.

After the Olympic Games, the same U.S. team visited Warsaw and Dublin before returning home. The American amateurs defeated Poland 3-2 (on an own goal), but their luck ran out six days later with a 3-1 loss to the Irish Free State.

After two wins and a loss against Canada in the mid-1920s, the USA again made its way to the Olympic Games in 1928 at Amsterdam and received an 11-2 first round drubbing from Argentina, then ranked with Uruguay as one of the world's leading teams. This was followed by a friendly in Warsaw that resulted in a 3-3 draw.

The first real high point in American soccer was the USA's participation in the first World Cup in 1930, though the event went virtually unnoticed in the United States. For the first time the American game was thrust into the international limelight.

The refusal by most of Europe to make the long journey to Montevideo severely weakened the opposition, leaving only 13 countries to participate, and four pools were set up in the absence of the number required to organize a knockout competition.

The American team was managed by the Brooklyn Wanderers' Jack Croll, and was made up of five former Scottish professionals and one Englishman. Nicknamed the "shot-putters" by the French, the American players were large in size and strong on defense and running attacks.

Performing well, they defeated both Belgium and Paraguay by 3-0 scores and emerged winners of their group. Center forward Bert Patenaude of Fall River F.C. scored three of the American goals, and the Scottish-born left wing Bart McGhee scored two. These were the USA's

first major victories in international competition.

Misfortune struck in the semi-finals against powerful Argentina, whose stars Monti and Stabile were world class in stature. American center half Raphael Tracy of Ben Millers S.C. had his leg broken at ten minutes, reducing the team to ten players, and goalkeeper Jim Douglas of the New York Nationals was virtually crippled by the end of the first half (not to mention left half Andy Auld of Providence, who played most of the game with his mouth stuffed full of gauze after a kick in the face).

Argentina scored five goals in the second half and went on to win, 6-1. On its way home the American team stopped off to play Brazil in Rio and lost by 4-3 after two goals from Patenaude.

It is difficult to determine what would have happened if the USFA had been able to maintain the positive momentum that resulted from the USA's respectable showing in 1930, because, once again, the United States did not seriously attempt to enter the mainstream of world soccer in the years that followed.

Other than its 1-0 loss to the Italian amateurs at the 1936 Olympic Games in Berlin, the USA's only official foray into international competition during the 1930s was at the 1934 World Cup in Italy.

After winning an awkward qualification match against Mexico in Rome, an Italian team inflated with talent and the political climate of Mussolini's capital city buried the American contingent in the opening round 7-1. Soundly beaten, the USA opted out of international competition until 1947.

On the domestic front, the formation of the German-American Football Association (GAFA) in 1923 and the American Soccer

League (ASL) in 1933 further fragmented the game. The GAFA not only became the bastion of ethnic soccer in the New York area but also a model for all other ethnic leagues across the country.

In 1945, the USFA changed its name to the United States Soccer Football Association (USSFA). With two berths allocated to the North-Central American and Caribbean region at the 1950 World Cup in Brazil, the USA team qualified for the final rounds by virtue of its second-place finish in the North American Confederation championship in 1949.

The team was managed by Pennsylvania State University's Bill Jeffrey (a Scot whose record over a period of 30 years was unparalleled in collegiate soccer) and included only three foreign-born Americans: captain Eddie McIlvenny, who later played for Manchester United and coached the Irish club Waterford; Larry Gaetjens, the Haitian center forward who was to end his career as a professional with Rácing Club de Paris and Ales in Southern France before disappearing mysteriously in Haiti around 1970; and Joe Maca, the left back from Belgium.

In the first round, the USA was grouped with Spain, England, and Chile at Curtiba. Against Spain, the Americans maintained a 1-0 lead until ten minutes from time and impressed the opposition with their durable play. But the stalwart American defense, led by Maca and spurred by J. Souza's goal in the 17th minute, finally collapsed and allowed three quick goals.

The final score was 3-1 in Spain's favor. Four days later, however, at Belo Horizonte, the United States cast itself as David to England's Goliath and perpetrated the greatest upset in the history of modern soccer: USA 1, England 0.

Many English apologists over the years have demeaned the accomplishments of the USA on this day, but by the same token, too many American observers have claimed that world soccer was turned upside down in a single stroke.

Neither of these biases is accurate: England suffered from missed opportunities which were caused by a lack of competitive edge after decades of self-exile from organized world competition, and it revealed an inability to adjust to tactical and personnel conflicts arising from the recent appointment of England's first permanent manager-selector, Walter Winterbottom.

The USA, on the other hand, played well above its accepted standard. Tragically, the American public never heard of its team's achievement, and once again American soccer lost a chance to emerge from obscurity.

Even today the average American sports enthusiast would never include this result among the great upsets in United States sporting history nor list it among the top American sporting achievements. Indeed, few would even know about it.

The American goal against England was not convincing: in the 37th minute, left half Walter Bahr—later a successful college coach at Penn State—crossed the ball to the goal. English goalkeeper Bert Williams failed to gather it cleanly, and oncoming center forward Gaetjens deflected the ball into the net with his head, some would say unwittingly.

England, having thus far failed to convert with every conceivable type of shot, did not rise to the occasion, and the American defense was opportunistic in its clearing and distributing. After the final whistle, thousands of Brazilian fans rushed onto the field and carried the giant-killers around the stadium on their shoulders.

The USA, unable to ride the crest of stunned euphoria, fell decisively to Chile 5-2 in its third first round match, and Spain advanced from its group. Jeffrey's team, perhaps the greatest spoilers in World Cup history, returned home to muted adulation in some ethnic quarters and then oblivion.

It is difficult to explain to outsiders why American soccer did not grow from its 1950 World Cup success, needing, in fact, 40 years before a national team good enough to reach the finals could be assembled. Along the way there was the dramatic collapse of the North American Soccer League and the remarkable growth at the collegiate level.

On the one hand, the existence of the NASL produced role models and television coverage of soccer so that young American players did have something to emulate; on the other the college game continued to be played with alien rules, including free substitution, which meant that the traditional proving ground for American athletes was teaching a sport very different from the one the rest of the world played.

Critics said that Americans could not learn to pace themselves or develop the ability necessary to operate in midfield. The evidence showed that the lack of understanding of the international playing environment was often at the root of American failure: inexperienced players being cast into settings that were frequently beyond them.

U.S. teams found that it was no fun playing in front of passionate Central American crowds or contending with the high altitudes and professional mentality of the experienced Mexicans. As a result, American World Cup efforts usually met with harsh, quick failure.

In the 1990 tournament, though, Mexico was not present, FIFA having banned the country because of a violation in a youth qualifying tournament that involved over-age players. So the road was apparently wide open when the United States embarked on what can only be called an agonizing trip to Italy.

Results in some regional play, notably the Pan-American Games, may have led Americans to think that defeating Costa Rica, El Salvador, Guatemala, Honduras and Trinidad & Tobago would be a mere formality, but it turned out to be anything but. Qualification for Italy was not clinched until Paul Caligiuri's goal in Port-of-Spain in November of 1992 finally beat Trinidad & Tobago and allowed the Americans to accompany Costa Rica to Italy. It turned out to be a poisoned pawn.

The United States Soccer Federation had built its improved team around its youth program, a policy that was bringing increased rewards in both regional and international achievement. There was no doubt that American teenagers had improved radically and could compete at world level; but the USSF had no such yardstick to evaluate its national team.

Electing to use primarily young players and to prepare them with a series of matches against world teams that were not of the highest calibre, the USSF made a fundamental gamble that failed dramatically. When Bob Gansler's team opened the World Cup in Florence they looked unprepared for the pressure and emotion of the occasion, to say nothing of the outright pace of the play. They were beaten 5-1.

To Gansler and his squad's credit, the rest of the tournament was better. Italy had been expected to crush the USA but was somewhat lucky to get a 1-0 victory in Rome. There was no rout; instead the Italians could thank fortune that a late-game Bruce Murray free kick was saved on the goal line, thus preventing a draw.

The final game against Austria was an untidy, 2-1 defeat in Florence before a small crowd that was paying more attention to Italy's simultaneous game with Czechoslovakia than to the action in front of them. The Austrian fans, too, had little interest since their side had all but been eliminated hours before the kickoff because of the result from Milan, where Colombia drew with West Germany.

On balance the American achievement in just getting to the 1990 finals was positive, particularly in light of having the host role for the 1994 tournament. But the fallout from the World Cup was far more dramatic than anything that happened on the field.

Under FIFA urging, the American organizational structure was shaken up completely with the election of Alan Rothenberg as new USSF President, and Gansler barely survived into 1991 before Bora Milutinovic, the successful coach of upstart Costa Rica, was brought into to re-tool the national team.

Eschewing the old policy of overlooking older players, Milutinovic also scoured the globe for players with American citizenship qualifications and produced a team capable of winning the 1991 CONCACAF Gold Cup. How far he could take the side, still fragile defensively and obviously lacking in depth, was a question that would have to wait for 1994's answer.

URUGUAY

Address: Asociación Uruguaya de Fútbol, Guayabo 1531, Montevideo. *Founded:* 1900. *FIFA:* 1923. *CONMEBOL:* 1916. *National stadium:* Estadio Centenario, Montevideo (75,000); *largest stadium:* Estadio Centenario. *Colors:* Sky blue jerseys with white trim, black shorts. *Season:* March to December. *Honors:* World Cup winner (1930 and 1950); Olympic Games winner (1924 and 1928); South American Championship winner (1916, 1917, 1920, 1923, 1924, 1926, 1935, 1942, 1956, 1959, 1967, 1983, and 1987), runner-up (1919, 1927, 1939, 1941, and 1989).

With a population of only three million, Uruguay may justly claim to be the world's most disproportionately successful soccer country. It is certainly high on anyone's list of the world's top ten, and a strong case can be made for its being the world's leading exporter of good players, too, although its greatest successes are now nearly a half-century ago.

Uruguay dominated world soccer decisively between 1924 and 1930 with two Olympic gold medals and a World Cup victory, and in 1950 it won the World Cup a second time. In 1954 and 1970, Uruguay advanced to the semi-finals of the World Cup, and in the South American Championship, its record over the years is second only to that of Argentina, its fierce rival across the Rio de la Plata.

The legendary Uruguayan clubs, Penarol (five Copa Libertadores wins) and Nacional (three Copa wins), have been dominant forces in South America ever since international club competitions were organized. Indeed, it is possible that more players of world stature have donned the uniforms of Penarol and Nacional than any other clubs in the world. Sadly, they and the national team have declined in the last 20 years, although Nacional won the Copa in 1988.

Soccer was introduced in Uruguay during the 1870s by British residents and workers. In 1882, an English professor at the University of Montevideo formed the first club, composed entirely of British students, and other clubs were soon established. The first regularly scheduled series of games was played in 1886 at Punta Carretas, Montevideo, the site of the present Estadio Luis Franzini, home of CA Defensor.

In 1891, the Central Uruguay Railway Cricket Club was founded by British employees of the Ferrocarril Central in Montevideo, and a soccer section was established the following a year. Its first match was against the British School in

1892. In 1899, the first native Uruguayan club, Nacional, was founded, and one year later the Uruguayan Football Association was established by Central Uruguay Railway, Albion, another all-British club, and the Deutscher Fussballklub, a German-based club, all of Montevideo.

The first season of the new Uruguayan league was played in 1900 by these three clubs and Uruguay F.C., another British team, and was won by Penarol, the informal name already given to the railway company team and adopted officially in 1914 after it won five championships in 13 years.

In 1901, Nacional joined the league, and from the outset Penarol (38 titles) and Nacional (35 titles) dominated the competition. From 1932 through 1976, no one else won the Uruguan championship.

The founding of the Uruguayan F.A. anticipated the formation of a national team, and on August 15, 1905, the first international in South America was played between Uruguay and Argentina in Buenos Aires, ending in a scoreless draw. This match also inaugurated the Lipton Cup, which along with the Newton Cup (1906) became the basis for the great Uruguay-Argentina rivalry, one of the oldest in the world.

In 1916, Uruguay met Brazil for the first time in the first edition of the South American Championship in Buenos Aires; Uruguay won 2-1 and a second great South American rivalry was born. These were formative years for Uruguay in international competition, foreshadowing the great period to come.

Uruguay began to make its mark on international competition in the South American Championship before 1920. In the first ten editions (1916-26), Uruguay won the title six times and finished runner-up once. Of the other three, one was lost in a special play-off after accumulating an equal number of points with Brazil (1919),

one was played without Uruguay's participation (1925), and the other was undone when Uruguay withdrew in protest after accumulating an equal number of points with Brazil and Paraguay (1922). Uruguay won or shared each Lipton Cup between 1919 and 1929, all Newton Cups (except one) between 1917 and 1924, and lost only one encounter with Brazil between 1916 and 1930.

At the 1924 Olympic Games in Paris, Uruguay launched its golden era of world dominance, and introduced the famous midfield line known widely as *la costilla metallica* ("the iron curtain"), which was made up of world-class right half Jose Andrade, attacking center half Lorenzo Fernandez, and left half Alvaro Gestido.

On the forward line were the legendary inside right Hector Scarone, inside left Pedro Cea, and center forward Pedro Petrone, each a prolific goal scorer who excelled in the various South American Championships of the 1920s.

At Paris in 1924, Uruguay became the first non-European country to win the Olympic soccer tournament with defeats of Yugoslavia (7-0), USA (3-0), France (5-1), the Netherlands (2-1), and, in the final, Switzerland (3-0).

The victory made world stars of many Uruguayan players, and at the 1928 Olympic Games in Amsterdam, Uruguay entered as the odds-on favorite. In Amsterdam, Uruguay prevailed over strong opposition, defeating the Netherlands (2-0), Germany (4-1), Italy (3-2), and mighty Argentina in the final (2-1 in a replay after drawing 1-1).

Uruguay's successes in the Olympic Games of 1924 and 1928, achieved before South America and most of Europe had turned professional, carried further significance in establishing South America as a coequal center of the world game; Uruguay had won its Olympic honors in distant Europe and the seriousness with which it took the game made a deep impression on European observers.

It was appropriate, therefore, that the staging of the first World Cup (1930) was awarded to little Uruguay. The Asociación Uruguaya de Football (AUF), as the national association was now called, promised FIFA that it would build a great new stadium in Montevideo as a worthy location for the first world championship. But a protest by European associations over the staging of the tournament in so remote a place as Uruguay was loud and, at times, offensive, and Uruguayan administrators were piqued by the outcry.

Sadly, most of the leading soccer nations of Europe stayed away. France, Belgium, and Yugoslavia finally agreed to participate, while Rumania entered willingly at the behest of King Carol himself, an avid fan. In the end, the most formidable opposition to Uruguay was its bitter rival Argentina.

Though the grand Estadio Centenario was not completed in time for the first matches, it was eventually opened ceremoniously before Uruguay's encounter with Peru, won sluggishly by the home side 1-0.

Uruguay played only four matches to win this first world championship, but with two Olympic wins to its credit, few ventured to say it was undeserved. There were easy victories over Rumania (4-0) and Yugoslavia (6-1), and in the final the Olympic champions defeated star-studded Argentina 4-2 on goals from Dorado, Cea, Iriarte, and Castro.

England and the powerful Central European teams were sorely missed, and the satisfaction of Uruguay's victory was tarnished by the impact of Europe's snub. When the time came to register for the 1934 World Cup in Italy, the hurt had not lessened and Uruguay declined to participate, the only time in the history of the World Cup a holder has failed to return.

Professionalism was adopted in Uruguay in 1933 by the leading clubs, Penarol and Nacional, about the same time as other important South American powers did likewise.

Uruguay's international experience since 1930 has been fraught with anomalies and uncertainties. The AUF again declined to enter the 1938 World Cup, due in part to a residue of hurt pride from 1930 but also resulting from confusion at home over the question of professionalism. In 1950, however, in only its second attempt, Uruguay won the world championship again, this time upsetting the home favorite, Brazil.

The 1950 Uruguayan team, seven of whom played with Peniarol, included a second generation of world-famous names—left half Rodriguez Andrade (the nephew of 1930 star Jose Andrade), right wing Chico Ghiggia, and the extraordinary inside left Juan Schiaffino, but the genius of the earlier 1924-30 squad was not evident.

In addition, Hungary, whose golden era of Puskas & Co. had already begun, was not in the tournament, nor was Argentina, and England entered without any tactical cohesion or competitive experience after decades of self-exile from world competition.

Uruguay advanced to the final pool after only one match—an 8-0 trouncing of Bolivia on four goals by Schiaffino—and faced the decisive match with Brazil after drawing with Spain 2-2 and slipping past the strong Swedish team 3-2.

Uruguay's 2-1 win over Brazil in what amounted to a "final" was an upset, and will be further remembered as the game that set the world record attendance figure (199,850) that still stands today. Uruguay was once again at the apex of world soccer.

In its fourth place finish in the 1954 World Cup in Switzerland, Uruguay met virtually all the world's leading national teams, and the results on this basis alone are noteworthy: Czechoslovakia (2-0), Scotland (7-0), England (4-2), Hungary (2-4), and Austria (1-3). Seldom has a World Cup participant had to take on such formidable opposition.

Having failed to qualify for the 1958 World Cup, Uruguay fared poorly in 1962 in Chile, placing third in its first round group after the Soviet Union and Yugoslavia. In 1966, a skillful Uruguayan squad entered the final rounds in England, but its defensive posture was no match for the highly motivated English and West Germans, and Uruguay was lucky to advance to the quarter-finals.

In 1970, Uruguay qualified once again. It finished second in its first round group on goal difference after a win over Israel, a scoreless draw with Italy, and a loss to Sweden. Though not among the favorites to win the 1970 Cup, Uruguay advanced to the quarter-final round where it was fortunate not to play against Italy, West Germany, or Brazil. Instead, Uruguay faced the floundering U.S.S.R. and squeaked through by 1-0 after extra time and a disallowed, questionable goal.

In the semifinals Brazil played at the peak of its form against Uruguay, with Pelé, Jairzinho, and Rivelino skillfully taking advantage of all opportunities. Uruguay became defensive and rough in its tackling, eventually losing 3-1, and finished a surprisingly high fourth place in the competition after dropping the third place game to West Germany.

Uruguayan goalkeeper Ladislao Mazurkiewicz drew much praise from observers and was touted as one of the world's best custodians. But by 1974, Uruguay had slipped into its current decline, and at the World Cup in West Germany, its performance was the worst anyone could remember. Decisive losses to the Netherlands and Sweden were followed by a 1-1 draw with

Bulgaria, and Uruguay finished last in its group of four with only one goal to its credit.

Then followed the bitter disappointment of failing to qualify in 1978, when next-door Argentina was host, and in 1982. Uruguay was back in the finals in 1986 but a humiliating 6-1 loss to Denmark in the first round was followed by second round elimination by Argentina. In 1990 an improved side needed a fortunate last-minute goal to defeat South Korea for passage to the second round, where host Italy administered the 2-0 exit blow. It seemed a long time back to 1950 and the glory years.

After the golden era of 1924-30, Uruguay's success in the South American Championship was not as frequent as that of Argentina, whose prestige rose after 1928, but its record still exceeds that of Brazil, the third-ranking country in the competition. After 1930, Uruguay won the South American title seven times and placed second three, compared to Argentina's winning of the championship nine times during the same period and finishing second on four other occasions.

For Penarol and Nacional, a new international challenge opened up in 1960 with the introduction of the Copa Libertadores, the South American club championship. Both were already well experienced in international competition. Since the 1920s, they had made extensive and frequent tours abroad to help defray the high cost of monopolizing Uruguayan soccer and could often be seen paying visits to Europe and even Africa, as well as the rest of Latin America.

The most famous of these international tours was made by Nacional in 1925 when it spent five months in Europe and played 38 games in nine countries. Led by the goal-scoring artistry of Hector Scarone, Nacional won 26 of these matches, scoring 130 goals and allowing only 30 goals. Thus the two clubs were at home in

1960 when the new continental championship was launched, and Uruguayan clubs completed the first decade with more honors than any others in South America.

Penarol was the first of the Montevideo giants to excel in this series. It won the title in 1960, 1961, and 1966, and placed second in 1962, 1965, and 1970. Nacional won the championship in 1971, and finished runner-up in 1964, 1967, and 1969. Argentine clubs dominated in the 1970's, but Penarol won again in 1982 and 1987 and was losing finalist in 1983. Nacional took the trophy in 1988.

In the Intercontinental Cup (the unofficial transatlantic competition played between the winners of the Copa Libertadores and the European Champions' Cup), both Penarol and Nacional have extended their fame worldwide. In 1961, Penarol buried Portugal's Benfica by winning its home leg 5-0, and in 1966 a reorganized Real Madrid suffered 2-0 defeats to Penarol both home and away.

Alberto Spencer, Penarol's Ecuadorean center forward, and Pedro Rocha, the elegant inside forward, led Penarol's attack in these great international victories and helped to establish Penarol as one of the world's two or three leading clubs of the decade.

Nacional's Intercontinental Cup win in 1971, on the other hand, was marred by Ajax's refusal to participate for fear of its physical safety in Montevideo, and Nacional had to settle for European Cup runner-up Panathinaikos of Athens, which succumbed to the Uruguayans by an aggregate score of 3-2.

Nacional won again in 1980, defeating Nottingham Forest, and in 1988, at the expense of PSV Eindhoven (on penalty kicks). Penarol added the 1982 cup to its tally with a 2-0 win over Aston Villa.

A financial crisis in recent years has hurt the game, but the legacy of the sport in Uruguay is extraordinary enough to remain indelible.

VENEZUELA

Address: Federacion Venezolana de Fútbol, Av. Este Estadio Nacional, El Paraiso, Apado, Postal 14160, Candelaria, Caracas. *Founded:* 1926. *FIFA:* 1952. *CONMEBOL:* 1952. *Largest stadium:* Estadio Olimpico Ciudad Universitaria, Caracas (25,000). *Colors:* Dark red jerseys, black shorts.

Venezuela is the least successful of all South American countries in international competition and is widely accepted as having the poorest standard of play as well. This has been due largely to the great popularity of baseball, the national sport, from the early years of this century—a phenomenon whose roots are in the economic ties Venezuela has with the United States. Venezuelan soccer still has little to show for itself, and remains a virtual outsider in South America as a whole.

The early history of Venezuelan soccer is more properly regarded in the context of Central America and the Caribbean rather than South America. The Federacion Venezolana de Fútbol (FVF) was founded in 1926, but in 1929 a second group of clubs established the Asociación Venezolana (AV) and organized a rival league.

A merger was achieved in 1930, and two years later a true national league, the Liga Venezolana, was introduced by the reconstituted federation, now given the name Asociación Nacional de Football. The original name of the association, Federacion Venezolana de Fútbol, was reinstated in the mid-1950s.

The major characteristic of Venezuelan soccer, indeed one of the many facets that resemble the game in the United States, has been the importance of ethnic groups in forming clubs. Spanish, Portuguese, and Italian immigrants to Venezuela stuck closely together as they attempted to advance the game in a nation devoted to baseball.

The names of Venezuelan clubs down through the decades reflect the state of soccer in Venezuela as an ethnic game: Deportivo Portugues (Caracas), Portuguesa (Acarigua), Deportivo Italia (Caracas), Deportivo Galicia (Caracas), and Union Deportivo Canarias (Caracas). Venezuela has never been a factor in the South American Championship or regional World Cup qualifying, nor has a Venezuelan club claimed a major trophy.

VIETNAM

Address: Association de Football de la Republique du Viet-nam, 36, rue Tran-Phu, Hanoi. *Founded:* 1962. *FIFA:* 1964. *National stadium:* Stade Hang Day, Hanoi (40,000); *largest stadium:* Stade Hang Day. *Colors:* Red jerseys, white shorts. *Season:* November to May.

Northern Vietnam was traditionally less developed in soccer than the South, where French cultural and commercial influences were stronger. Northern representative teams competed in Vietnamese cup competitions before the partition in 1954, but seldom won any trophies.

The Football Association of the former Democratic Republic of Vietnam was not founded until 1962, and though it became affiliated with FIFA two years later it did not join the Asian Football Confederation because of the AFC's prior acceptance of South Vietnam. With political unification in 1975, the path cleared for affiliation with the AFC.

Soccer was established in the south earlier than in the rest of Indochina, and before the creation of two Vietnams in 1954, Vietnam as a whole was as active as any colony in Southeast Asia. The former South Vietnam was a major participant in Southeast Asian soccer from 1956-74, winning several minor tournaments and appearing early in official Asian competitions. After the fall of Saigon in 1975, the Tong-Cuoc Bong Tron (Vietnam Football Federation) ceased to function as a national governing body.

The game was introduced in Indochina via Saigon before World War I, and the great influx of French military personnel and engineers during and after the war permanently established the game. The Federation Cochinchinoise de Football, the first governing body on the Indochina peninsula, was founded in Saigon in 1923 and became affiliated with the French federation in 1934.

Much of Vietnam's pre-World War II soccer activity was centered around French colonists and was fairly restricted to southern Vietnam (Cochinchina) and Hanoi. Activity heightened considerably under the Vichy administration during the war, and by 1948 the Cochinchinese federation had assumed direct control of soccer throughout the colony. In 1949, France traveled to Saigon and defeated a Cochinchina selection 4-1 and a Vietnam selection 2-1.

South Vietnam won the soccer tournament of the first Southeast Asian Peninsula Games in 1959 at Bangkok, the 1966 edition of the Merdeka Anniversary Tournament in Malaysia, and was co-winner of the 1971 Pesta Sukan Tournament in Singapore.

It was also active in Olympic qualifying rounds and the Asian games. The unified VietNam did not enter World Cup competition until 1993, when it attempted qualification unsuccessfully in a group including the stronger North Korean and Quatari entries.

WALES

Address: Football Association of Wales, Ltd., 3 Fairy Road, Wrexham, Denbighshire LL13 7PS. *Founded:* 1876. *FIFA:* 1910-20; 1924-28; 1946. *UEFA:* 1954. *National stadium:* Ninian Park, Cardiff (58,000); *largest stadium:* Ninian Park. *Colors:* Red jerseys, white shorts. *Season:* August to May.

The Principality of Wales, while making little impact on the world game in modern times, was a pioneer in the development of association football, and by virtue of its permanent place on the International Football Association Board has wielded considerable influence on the administration of the game off the playing field.

Wales's ability to produce high quality players is disproportionate to its small population: Billy Meredith, Ivor Allchurch, Trevor Ford, John Charles, and Ian Rush are examples of Welsh world-class players.

Wales's accomplishments have been achieved in spite of enormous competition at home from rugby, the principality's favorite sport, and the pervasive drain of Wales's best players to the Football League in England.

Like Scotland and Northern Ireland, Wales's administrative privileges (and absence of privileges) in international competition are peculiar to the United Kingdom. Though the winner of the Welsh Cup is allotted a berth in the European Cup Winners' Cup, the champion club of the Welsh League is excluded from participating in the European Champions' Cup, because Wales's leading clubs are members of The Football League in England.

This ruling by the Union of European Football Associations (UEFA) also precludes Welsh clubs from participating in the UEFA Cup, Europe's third major club competition. Thus, to a greater degree than either Scotland or Northern Ireland, Wales remains an anomaly in European soccer.

Welsh culture, particularly in the lifestyle of the huge mining population and the rugged, damp terrain of the Welsh counties, led to the rapid growth of rugby at the expense of soccer in the late nineteenth century. This was especially true in the southern counties; in the north, the economic and social links with industrial Cheshire and Lancashire in England gave rise to a more rapid growth of soccer and it is here that the roots of modern Welsh soccer are found.

In 1876, the Football Association of Wales was founded at Wrexham, in the north, by a group of Welshmen trying to organize an international match with Scotland. This match, the first international ever played after the start of the England-Scotland rivalry four years earlier, took place in March of that year at Glasgow, resulting in a 4-0 win for the Scots.

But a controversy arose when players from South Wales protested that the Welsh team did not include any representatives from the southern counties. In fact, the charge was true, and many years passed before either the Welsh F.A. or the national team included representatives from South Wales. In addition, most Welsh internationals before World War I continued to be played at Wrexham, rather than Cardiff or Swansea in the South.

The Welsh Cup, the world's third-oldest cup competition, was introduced in 1877. The Welsh Cup is open to all Welsh clubs regardless of league affiliation and to clubs from nearby English counties. The Welsh Football League, on the other hand, was introduced in 1902, and has experienced difficulties from the beginning, as the important Welsh clubs sought to play in higher levels of competition in England. The issue is still a thorny one today.

A major factor in the growth of Welsh soccer in the early days was the presence of Billy Meredith, the legendary right wing from the town of Chirk (in the north) whose skills and goal-scoring genius spanned some 38 years between 1893 and 1924. His importance to Welsh soccer is analogous to that of Artur Friedenreich of Brazil in the level of expertise he brought to his country's game.

Meredith made over 1,100 appearances in top-level competition and appeared in approximately 50 Welsh internationals, most of them while playing for Manchester City and Manchester United in England.

His influence on Welsh soccer resulted from the emphasis he placed on developing new ball control skills that he ceaselessly promoted during an era when preoccupation with tactical innovations was on the rise.

Meredith also anticipated the difficulties that Wales was to experience in securing the release of Welsh players from English clubs for Welsh internationals. Seldom has one player had such a significant impact on the development of the game on a national basis.

The Welsh F.A., like the other British associations, had withdrawn from FIFA between 1920 and 1924 and from 1928 to 1946, and so the World Cup of 1950 provided Wales its first opportunity to qualify for the world championship. This effort was thwarted by England and Scotland, whose wins in the Home International Championship of 1949 doubled as World Cup elimination contests.

The same situation occurred in 1953 when England and Scotland prevented Wales from enter-ing the final rounds of the 1954 World Cup. In 1958, however, all four British countries advanced to the final rounds of the World Cup in Sweden, although Wales's route was among the most indirect ever taken.

In its 1958 qualifying round, Wales placed second to Czechoslovakia. In the Africa-Asia-Oceania qualifying rounds, however, the African states, as well as Indonesia and Turkey, refused to play Israel for political reasons, causing one forfeit after another.

Israel thus advanced to the World Cup final rounds without having to play a single match. FIFA, astonished at the thought of such a development, invited Wales to play Israel in a home and away series to determine that World Cup berth, and the Israelis succumbed in both games by 2-0.

To the surprise of everyone but loyal Welsh fans, FIFA's gift resulted in Wales' greatest international achievement. In its first round group, it drew 1-1 with Hungary, 1-1 with Mexico, and 0-0 with Sweden. In the playoff with Hungary, Wales emerged victorious by 2-1 on goals by Allchurch and Medwin, advancing to the quarter-final round to play against Brazil.

Wales's most memorable achievement in that World Cup, perhaps in all Welsh soccer history, was in holding the legendary Brazilians to a scoreless draw for much of that game. Brazil's game-winning, and only goal, on an opportunistic rebound shot by the 17-year-old Pelé, was a miraculous individual effort, and Wales was given due credit for successfully challenging Brazil's superiority.

Wales has not qualified for any world championship since. Aside from World Cup qualifying rounds, Wales' activity outside the United Kingdom has mainly been in connection with the European Championship, but they have no honors at this level.

Yemen, Republic of

Address: Yemen Football Association, P.O. Box 908, Sana'a. *Founded:* 1940. *FIFA:* 1967. *National stadium:* Stadium of the Martyr Al-Habashie, Crater-Aden (4,500); *largest stadium:* Al-Habashie Stadium. *Colors:* Light blue jerseys, white shorts.

The Aden Sports Association became affiliated with FIFA in 1967 at the time of Aden's independence from Britain. For the next three years, the new South Arabian Federation continued to be known by FIFA as Aden.

The present name, Yemen Football Association, was adopted later. A small nation once divided between communist and non-communist sections, Yemen has only recently unified. The new nation has entered the 1994 World Cup, marking the first Yemeni presence in the competition.

Yugoslavia

Address: Fudbalski Savez Jugoslavije (Yugoslav Football Association), P.O. Box 263, Terazije 35-11000, Belgrade. *Founded:* 1919. *FIFA:* 1919 (currently suspended from international play). *UEFA:* 1955. *Largest stadium:* Crvena Zvezda Stadium, Belgrade (95,000). *Colors:* Blue jerseys, white shorts. *Season:* September to June. *Honors:* Olympic Games winner (1960), runner-up (1948, 1952, 1956), third-place (1984); European Championship runner-up (1960, 1968); FIFA Youth World Champion (1987).

While it has always had a reputation for producing an unusually high number of excellent players, Yugoslavia presents a unique set of circumstances among Eastern European countries. In international competition, Yugoslavia has excelled both in Europe and worldwide, but its record is fraught with peculiarities. Like Denmark and Uruguay, Yugoslavia has suffered the loss of many players to other countries as a result of liberal transfer policies; yet, new players of great skill and natural ability appear from a seemingly endless reservoir.

In the postwar years, Yugoslavia had one of the half-dozen best international records in Europe, but the future has been called sharply into question by the Civil War and the United Nations sanctions imposed on the country. As a result, Yugoslavia entered 1993 banned from international play, and its clubs were also prohibited from taking part in European tournaments.

Soccer was introduced in Yugoslavia via Belgrade in the early 1890s by British residents and workers, though whether or not any local citizens became involved at that time is less certain. In the succeeding 20 years, the game spread to other major industrial centers of the area, and in 1911, Hajduk, the oldest Yugoslav club, was formed in Split on the Dalmatian coast. Now in Croatia, Hajduk Split was one of Yugoslavia's leading clubs until the break up of the Republic.

A national association, the Jugoslavenski Nogometni Savez, was founded immediately after the formation of a South Slavic state in 1919. (It acquired its present name in 1948.) Yugoslavia's first international was played against another new state, Czechoslovakia, at the 1920 Olympic Games in Antwerp, and ended in a 7-0 triumph for the vastly more experienced Czechs.

Yugoslavia's first significant international success was its defeat of Brazil and Bolivia in the first World Cup in 1930 at Montevideo. While Brazil was not yet an international power, Yugoslavia's 2-1 victory reflected well on the growing skill of Yugoslav players. Olympic champion and host team Uruguay, however, leveled Yugoslavia's optimism with a 6-1 victory, and in 1934 and 1938 Yugoslavia failed to qualify altogether.

At home, the national league was introduced in 1922, and its first champion was Gradjanska of Zagreb, now also in Croatia. At the end of World War II, Partizan, a new army club, Dinamo Zagreb, the electrical workers' club, and Red Star Belgrade (Crvena Zvezda), the Belgrade University club, were founded in 1945. From the outset, Yugoslavia's big clubs dominated domestic competition. Red Star Belgrade (19 titles) and Partizan (11 titles) have been the dominant clubs ever since.

Since World War II, Yugoslavia amassed one of the finest international records in the world. Though its highest placing in the World Cup has been fourth (1962), Yugoslavia's Olympic and European Championship records are excellent. In 1950, it was left out of the final pool of the World Cup by a 2-0 loss to Brazil after defeating Switzerland and Mexico, and in 1954 and 1958 it was eliminated from the final rounds altogether.

In 1962, however, a 3-1 win over Uruguay enabled Yugoslavia to advance from its first round group along with the U.S.S.R. In the quarter-finals, against defensive-minded West Germany, the more skillful Yugoslavs prevailed. Its 4-2-4 system, however, was not suitable to penetrating the strong Czech defense in the semi-finals. In the third place match, Yugoslavia was defeated by the home team, Chile, and missed its first World Cup medal.

With characteristic unpredictability, Yugoslavia failed to qualify in 1966 and 1970, but the 1974 World Cup in West Germany, it entered as a possible contender, led by the indomitable left winger Dragan Dzajic. Though Yugoslavia's performances were sometimes disappointing, especially to the fans at home, it finished on top of its first round group after drawing with the fallen idol of Brazil, drawing a second time with the physically tough Scots, and burying hapless Zaire, 9-0.

In the second round, it lost three straight matches to West Germany, Poland, and Sweden. Since then Yugoslavia has returned to finals in 1982 and was beaten in the 1990 quarterfinal on penalty kicks by defending champion Argentina.

Yugoslavia's best results in the European Football Championship were in 1960 and 1968, when it was a runner-up. In the European Champions' Cup, Yugoslavia's highest achievement came in 1991 when Red Star won the trophy on penalty kicks after a disappointing final Marseille. Partizan had been a losing finalist in 1966.

Sadly, Red Star's 1991 triumph was almost immediately followed by the onset of war, and the side quickly broke apart, but not before one last great performance—a 3-0 win over Colo Colo of Chile—made Red Star the 1991 World Club Champion. Red Star was composed of players from all the regions of Yugoslavia that would soon be rent asunder in the violence of the early 1990s.

ZAIRE

Address: Federation Zairoise de Football-Association, P.O. Box 1284, Rue Dima, 10, Kinshasa 1. *Founded:* 1919. *FIFA:* 1964. *CAF:* 1963. *National stadium:* Stade Tata Raphael, Kinshasa (60,000); *largest stadium:* Stade Tata Raphael. *Colors:* Green jerseys, yellow shorts. *Season:* June to March. *Honors:* African Nations' Cup winner (1968, 1974).

Zaire, formerly Congo-Kinshasa, was been one of the early leading soccer powers in Africa but has since slipped. In the international arena, Zaire has won the biannual African Cup of

Nations twice, and its champion clubs have won the African Champions' Cup three times.

In 1974, Zaire captured the attention of a politically embattled continent and became the first black African nation to enter the World Cup.

Though the Zaire government spared no effort to help "The Leopards" make a worthy showing, the strength of Brazil, Yugoslavia, and Scotland was no match for Congolese inexperience, and Africa's hope in the world championship suffered three successive shutouts, including a 9-0 loss to Yugoslavia.

Belgian missionaries introduced soccer in the Belgian Congo via Matadi and Boma near the mouth of the Congo River in 1912. In 1919, the Association Royale Sportive Congolaise (ARSC) was founded in Leopoldville, and a soccer section was established to regulate the league championship that was formed in 1918.

In 1923, the Ligue de Football da Katanga was founded, and the problem of overlapping jurisdiction—so common in the colonial period in Africa—became an issue, even though a full-fledged championship was not introduced in Katanga until 1936. During the 1950s, 11 clubs were members of the Katanga league.

In 1924, at Loopoldville, the Federation de Football Association du Pool was formed as an adjunct of the Union Sportive de Kinshasa, to administer the game around the Stanley Pool, the lake that separates the capital of the Belgian Congo, Loopoldville, from the capital of the French Congo, Brazzaville. That federation became affiliated with the Belgian F.A. in 1928.

The reorganization of Congolese soccer was postponed from 1960, the year of independence, to the end of the Congolese civil war in 1963. The first problem was to give to the national association a name that would distinguish it from that of the French Congo across the river,

so the reconstituted national association was named the Federation Congolaise de Football Association.

The present name was adopted in 1972 when the country became known as Zaire. A national championship was introduced in 1964, and for the first time the major clubs were able to rise above regional competitions.

Zairian clubs have been among Africa's most successful in international competition, especially in the late 1960s. Englebert Lumbumbashi has won the African Champions' Cup twice and placed second twice, while some years later Vita Club also won the Champions' Cup. Englebert is one of Africa's greatest clubs.

Founded in 1936 at Elizabethville (Lumbumbashi), Katanga, its original name was Saint George F.C., and the founders were missionaries whose lives were dedicated primarily to the development of the Boy Scout movement.

In 1944, the name was changed to Saint Paul F.C. When the club again changed its name to Englebert F.C. in 1947, it won the local "native" championship and in the off-season assumed the name Tout-Puissant (All-Powerful) Englebert F.C.

Its rise to the top of Katangan soccer was rocky, but by 1967 it had reached the national championship. Englebert triumphed in the African Champions' Cup in 1967 and 1968, and in 1969 and 1970 it placed second in the cup to Ismaili of Egypt and Kotoko Kumasi of Ghana, respectively, thus establishing a real dominance in African club competition.

Englebert has now relocated to Kinshasa—safe from Katangan civil wars—as T-P Mazembe. They won a trophy again in 1980, this time the Cup Winners Cup, but there have been no further Zaire successes in continental tournaments since.

ZAMBIA

Address: Football Association of Zambia, P.O. Box 34751, Lusaka. *Founded:* 1929. *FIFA:* 1964. *CAF:* 1964. *National stadium:* Independence Stadium, Lusaka (30,000); *largest stadium:* Independence Stadium. *Colors:* Green and copper jerseys, white, green, black, and red shorts. *Season:* March to November. *Honors:* African Nations' Cup runner-up (1974).

In the mid-1970s, Zambia emerged as an important soccer power in Africa, largely as a result of becoming one of only four countries on the continent to adopt open professionalism.

Zambians (or Northern Rhodesians) learned the game from British railroad and mining engineers, who flooded the country after the turn of the century, and possibly from South African whites, who trekked northward during the era of the South Africa Company's rule over the area (1889-1924).

A Northern Rhodesia Football Association was founded in Lusaka in 1929 and was affiliated with the Nyasaland Football Association until the postwar era. (Nyasaland's association in turn was linked directly with The Football Association in London.)

After World War II, British, South African, and Rhodesian whites spread the game widely in both Lusaka and the copperbelt region just north of the capital.

In 1964, the year of Zambia's independence, the Northern Rhodesian association became the Football Association of Zambia and quickly joined FIFA and the African Football Confederation. By 1972, Zambian clubs were participating regularly in the African Champions' Cup, and Zambia was coming closer to gaining entry to the Nations' Cup final rounds.

In the 1970s, Zambia became a prime mover in the formation of the East and Central African Football Federation, whose championship it has won often. In 1974, Zambia's superb assault on the African Nations' Cup ended with an exciting final in which a replay was forced for the first time in the series' history. Zambia had earlier defeated two big continental powers, Ivory Coast and Congo, to reach the final, and it now met its feared rival Zaire. The first game resulted in a 2-2 draw after extra time, but in the replay Zambia lost by a disappointing 2-0.

Zambia made its first major international impact in the 1988 Olympic Games when it stunned a professional Italian team 4-0 in Seoul. That result sent shock waves through the soccer world that were to be reinforced by Africa's 1990 World Cup work.

Zambia, however, didn't make it those finals, unable to turn on its Olympic form in 1990 qualifying. At club level, though, Power Dynamos broke through to capture the 1991 African Cup Winners Cup, claiming Zambia's first such honor on the continent.

ZANZIBAR

See Tanzania

ZIMBABWE
(Formerly Rhodesia)

Address: Zimbabwe Football Association, P.O. Box 8343, Causeway, Harare. *Founded:* 1965. *FIFA:* 1965. *National stadium:* Harare (54,000); *largest stadium:* Harare Stadium. *Colors:* White jerseys, black shorts. *Season:* February to October.

Rhodesia's racial policies and unilateral declaration of independence (UDI) from the United Kingdom in 1965 caused unending problems for the development of soccer before independence arrived for the new nation of Zimbabwe.

The game was brought to the area during the 1890s by British settlers arriving in Fort Salisbury, and for many decades it was played exclusively by white colonists.

After World War II, sports administrators in the colonial government formed a national team, and in 1948 it was entered in South Africa's Currie Cup (amateur), in which provincial representative teams competed for South Africa's national championship.

Rhodesia continued to participate annually in the Currie Cup until the 1960s, winning the competition only once (1959). Attempts were made to join the African Football Confederation (CAF) during the early 1970s, but the CAF was distrustful of Southern Rhodesia's promises of an integrated sports program. Immediately after the unilaterally declared independence in 1965, the Football Association of Rhodesia was reconstituted, and joined FIFA the same year. It was admitted to the CAF for a few short months, but the declared racial policies of the new regime resulted in a quick expulsion.

In 1968, Rhodesia tried to participate in qualifying rounds for the 1970 World Cup, but the black African states refused to play Rhodesia. Instead, FIFA grouped Rhodesia with Australia (in the Oceania sector), Japan, and Korea Republic (both in the Asia sector), but Rhodesia got no further than Australia.

The first two games with Australia were drawn, but Australia won the third and deciding contest for the right to meet Israel. Rhodesia's team in this series was racially mixed (five blacks and six whites), but this was its only venture to date in official international competition.

In 1970, the FIFA Congress voted to suspend Rhodesia from the world body. Rhodesia was thus excluded from participating in any sanctioned international tournaments.

With the creation of Zimbabwe on April 18, 1980, a new era in the country's sport began with immediate entry into the 1982 World Cup qualifying round signalling the debut.

Cameroon proved too strong then as did Egypt in the 1986 event, but Zimbabwe won its first round group in 1994 to take a major step forward toward becoming a serious force in African soccer.

6: Disasters and Tragedies

April 5, 1902: The West Stand at Ibrox Park, Glasgow, collapsed during an international between England and Scotland. Twenty-five spectators were killed and 517 injured. The game was resumed after 30 minutes and resulted in a 1-1 draw. It was subsequently nullified and stricken from official records.

March 9, 1946: Prior to the start of an English F.A. Cup tie between Bolton Wanderers and Stoke City at Burden Park, Bolton, a containing wall fell open in one section of the stands and the spectators were crushed together. Pandemonium broke out, and hundreds of people were pushed and trampled. Thirty-three died, and over 400 were injured.

The entire Turin team was killed when their plane crashed in a fog at Superga Hill, Turin, May 4, 1949.

May 4, 1949: Torino, the Italian champion, was returning home after a game in Lisbon when its plane crashed into the Superga Basilica near Turin. The entire team, including reserves, the manager, trainer, and coach were killed. Within a matter of days, the team would have realized its fifth consecutive Italian championship. A total of 28 people perished.

June 1950: Eight Uruguayans were reported to have died of heart attacks as a result of Uruguay's World Cup victory.

March 22, 1955: Details have remained sketchy, but during the long postwar civil disturbances in Burma, a Karen battalion in Lower Burma invited a group of rival communist insurgents for a friendly game of soccer. When the latter arrived at the designated venue, the Karen hosts murdered the entire visiting team. Number of dead unknown.

November 6, 1955: At the Stadio San Paolo, Naples, the Roman referee who awarded an equalizing penalty to visitors Bologna was attacked by Napoli fans. The referee was near death when police opened fire with carbines and tear gas. Though the riot worsened, the referee's life was saved. There were 152 casualties, including over 50 police and carabinieri.

February 6, 1958: A plane carrying English champion Manchester United home from a European Cup leg in Belgrade crashed at Munich Airport, killing eight players, the club coach, trainer, secretary, and eight journalists. United had just drawn with Red Star Belgrade, 3-3, and advanced to the semi-finals of the competition.

June 30, 1958: Five Brazilians were killed in shootings related to celebrations for Brazil's World Cup victory. Another Brazilian died of a

Popperfoto

Survivors of the Munich air disaster visit scene where eight fellow members of the Manchester United team, its coach, trainer, and eight journalists were killed, February 1958.

heart attack listening to a radio broadcast of the final.

April 3, 1961: A plane carrying the First Division Chilean team Green Cross to Santiago from a game in Osorno crashed into the side of Las Lastimas mountain. The entire team and all passengers aboard were killed.

September 21, 1962: In Libreville, Gabon, a game between the national sides of Congo Brazzaville and Gabon was interrupted when a landslide hit the stadium. Nine spectators died and 30 were injured.

May 24, 1964: The worst disaster in the history of recorded sport occurred in Lima, Peru, when a riot broke out at the National Stadium during an Olympic qualifying match with Argentina.

With two minutes left in the game, Argentina led 1-0. The Uruguayan referee Pazos disallowed a Peruvian goal. Two Peruvian fans ran onto the field and attacked Pazos, who suspended the game. When hundreds more stormed the field, the security force of 40 strong fired tear gas and some shots into the crowd.

Fleeing the police, spectators rushed to the north exit, but they found the gates locked. Because of the stampede, deaths and injuries mounted rapidly. The crowds were finally able to knock down a fence, and the 45,000 spectators began to pour into the streets.

Outside, three buildings and a dozen cars were set on fire by rioters and youth gangs, which had joined the melee. Rioters then marched on the Municipal Palace and the National Palace. At the end of the bleak afternoon, 318 people, including many children, were dead, and over 500 injured.

On May 25, the following day, a national state of emergency was declared, and search and seizure rights were lifted. Students at the university clashed with police, and called for the resignation of the Interior Minister Juan Languasco in protest of police action at the stadium.

Rioters attempted to break into the offices of the Peruvian Sports Federation, and demonstrations near the home of the police commander in charge of stadium security were dispersed by police. On May 26, there were mass funerals for 285 of the dead at Lima's central public cemetery.

June 23, 1968: At River Plate's Estadio Monumental in Buenos Aires, site of the 1978 World Cup final, arch rivals River and Boca Juniors had just completed an intense match in their run for the National Championship, and the spectators moved toward the exits. Jubilant fans threw burning paper from an upper tier, causing thousands to flee. Pressing crowds confronted closed gates and began to stampede. Seventy-four died and over 150 were injured.

June-July 1969: The two-week "Fútbol War" was fought between El Salvador and Honduras during the summer of 1969. Although it is the only full-fledged international military action linked directly with soccer, the sporting contests on the field were not per se the cause of the war. Rather, its origin lay in complex sociopolitical problems that had existed for decades.

Throughout the post-World War II period, the populous Salvadorans had sought work, and in many cases a new life, across the border in Honduras, where good land was available. In 1958, a treaty between the two governments opened the borders, increasing migration and with it the fear among Honduran landowners that the Salvadoran immigrants would agitate for land reform.

The government of Honduras responded with a series of new regulations that culminated in a 1968 law prohibiting Salvadorans from owning land. Adding to the strain was the Central American common market, which hurt the Honduran economy and benefitted that of El Salvador.

Furthermore, treaties written just after the turn of the century to settle old boundary disputes had never been ratified. In 1967, border troops and nearby civilians were seized by both sides, and late in the year diplomatic relations were broken off. U.S. President Lyndon Johnson visited El Salvador in 1968 and helped to restore relations temporarily.

As luck would have it, the two countries faced each other in a World Cup qualifying round in June 1969; the winner would probably represent CONCACAF at the World Cup the following year. Honduras won the first leg at home on June 8, and El Salvador won the second leg at home on June 15, thus necessitating a third and deciding match.

Both games triggered fierce rioting, especially during the return match in San Salvador, and provided the spark that ignited the fire. In Honduras, Salvadoran residents were attacked with a zeal born of years of frustration. Most of the 300,000 migrants began to flee across the border. Reprisals were made against the few Hondurans in El Salvador, and diplomatic relations were again broken off.

On June 24, El Salvador declared a state of siege. Charges of human rights violations and demands for reparations were made by both sides. On June 27, the day El Salvador's national team finally defeated Honduras in neutral Mexico to qualify for the World Cup, Salvadoran settlers in Honduras were accused of having mounted a "massive agricultural invasion." El Salvador defended its nationals' humble intentions. Both parties appealed to the OAS's InterAmerican

Soccer riot at Hampden Park, Glasgow, 1965. Unhappy Glasgow Rangers fans attack members of the Celtic team after they won the Scottish League Cup. One local official said, "My verdict is that they didn't behave at all well."

Commission on Human Rights, and requested a delegation of mediators. As propaganda in the press intensified, so did the level of skirmishes along the frontier. Both sides accused the other of violating air space, and on July 3, a Honduran plane was reported to have attacked Salvadoran border troops.

Mediation proposals made by the Human Rights Commission, as well as by neighboring Costa Rica, Nicaragua, and Guatemala, were approved and promptly broken. By July 11, the military conflict had clearly escalated. Three days later El Salvador's forces invaded Honduras and penetrated more than 40 miles in a single day.

Honduras retaliated by bombing San Salvador and Acajutla. On July 18, after both sides suffered heavy damage and many casualties, the OAS arranged a cease-fire agreement, though Salvadoran troops lingered in Honduras for several weeks. The death toll between the two countries was put at 2,000.

Unfortunately, the dispute, did not end with the cessation of war. In 1970, new skirmishes arose, and a demilitarized zone was agreed upon. Further conflicts flared up again in 1974 and July 1976, the latter lasting a full week. The OAS again stepped in, and in August 1976 a new agreement was reached in which a revised demilitarized zone was drawn up. Today, relations between the two states remain tense.

September 26, 1969: Returning home to La Paz from an out-of-town game, the plane carrying Bolivia's most popular team, The Strongest, crashed in the Andes some 72 miles from the capital. The entire team of 19 players and all club officials were killed.

December 31, 1970: The lower division amateur club Air Liquide of Algeria perished in a plane crash while en route to Spain to play a friendly which had been arranged by club offi-cials as a gesture of gratitude to the players for their loyalty and service to the club.

January 2, 1971: Toward the end of an encounter between Scottish Titans Celtic and Rangers in Glasgow, the crush of spectators leaving Ibrox Park became panic-stricken when a group of Rangers fans attempted to return upon hearing that Rangers had scored an equalizer. A steel barrier collapsed causing 66 deaths and upward of 140 injuries.

September 17, 1971: During a lower division match between Turkish clubs Kayseri and Siwas, a platform collapsed. Forty people were killed and 600 injured.

February 1972: In Cordoba, Argentina, the players of Sportivo Rural assaulted a linesman named Alfredo Basso and kicked him to death.

February 17, 1974: In Cairo, the crowds attempting to enter an important local match broke down barriers, and 49 people were trampled to death. This caused the Egyptian F.A. to publicly discourage fans from attending final round matches of the African Nations' Cup scheduled to begin a few days later in Cairo and Mehalla.

August 19, 1976: Left-wing guerrillas assassinated Retired General Omar Actis, President of the Argentine World Cup Organizing Committee, sending ripples of fear over the fate of the 1978 games. Responsibility for the World Championship was taken over directly by the new military junta of Argentina.

October 31, 1976: When the Gambian referee awarded a penalty kick to Cameroon during a World Cup qualifying match with the Congo in Yaounde, the Congolese goalkeeper attacked him in a rage. A melee broke out, and the President of Cameroon, who had been watching the game on television, sent in paratroopers by helicopter to quash the riot. Two Camerounais bystanders died. The Congo subsequently accused Cameroon of staging the affair, pointing to the latter's swift military reaction.

December 6, 1976: In Port-au-Prince, Cuba equalized in a World Cup qualifying match with Haiti, and a Haitian fan set off a firecracker. Assuming they heard gunfire, spectators behind one of the goals panicked and knocked down a soldier whose machine gun went off, killing a small boy and a girl in the crowd. As the panic heightened, two more people were trampled to death, and one man died jumping over a wall. The soldier made his way out of the stadium and committed suicide. Toll: six dead.

June 1977: Fifteen deaths occurred in Sao Paulo, Brazil, as a result of "celebrations" (eight crimes, five traffic accidents, two heart attacks) after Corinthians Paulista won the Sao Paulo league title, their first in 23 years.

October 1977: In the Colombian second division, Santa Rosa de Cabal left winger Libardo Zuniga was assigned to replace his team's injured goalkeeper for the remaining minutes of an important league contest with a local rival. Zuniga astonished everyone by making one spectacular save after another, but late in the game an opposing striker became so angry with Zuniga's success that he ran up to him and kicked him in the groin with full force. Zuniga died immediately, and the striker was arrested and charged with murder.

June 1978: Several suicides in Argentina and Brazil, deaths by heart attack in Argentina, Brazil, and Mexico, and a murder in France were reported to be the result of fans watching the 1978 World Cup on television.

April 28, 1993: The Zambian national team was killed in an airplane crash off Gabon.

7: FIFA

To any American sports fan, the letter combinations of NFL, NBA, NHL, and NCAA are instantly recognizable—explaining what they are seems as incomprehensible as describing the sports they govern. In recent decades, the International Olympic Committee's IOC has been added to the eye chart of sports organization names.

And while to the rest of the world it may be as common as IBM, in American English the French acronym of FIFA must be followed by a comma and the phrase "the international governing body of soccer"—which of course elicits one of those "Thank you, but I still don't know what is" smiles.

With America's concept of international sports almost exclusively focused on the Olympics, few in the general public understand the role, scope, and power of FIFA, which rivals if not overshadows the IOC in the world of sports competition.

It is difficult for many Americans to comprehend the concept of FIFA because of a somewhat provincial attitude toward sports. With no one else in the world playing football, the national college championship, and National Football League's Super Bowl are the ultimate in the game.

Similarly, the World Series, NBA Finals and Stanley Cup are considered the pinnacle achievements in baseball, basketball and hockey. But the fact that Americans don't recognize other nations' champions in those sports as equals (with the exception of Canadian teams playing in the NHL and Major League Baseball) limits international play to the Olympics or other "amateur" competitions.

International Appeal

With soccer a much more internationally contested sport, FIFA's existence allows for regular competitions among the champions of each country's professional league. It provides for competition among nations. Instead of an exhibition all-star game, all-star teams of each nationality compete for regional and world championships under the auspices of FIFA.

Because of soccer's unmatched stature as the most popular sport in the world, FIFA's power and influence extends from the sporting world to business and even international politics. Starting from its humble beginnings in the back house of the Union Francaise des Sports Athletiques at Rue Saint-Honore 229 in Paris, the Fédération Internationale de Football Association—or in

English the International Federation of Association Football (soccer)—has grown from seven to 178 member countries.

FIFA has six regional affiliates or confederations to help it administer the game. It decides where the World Cup will be held, how many countries each confederation can send to World Cup competition; who is and who isn't eligible for the World Cup, Olympics, and other tournaments; and most importantly, from the pros to the kids, it writes the rules of the game.

Need to Standardize Rules

Beginning with the foundation of the Football Association in England in 1863, there seems to have been a long yearning to have one central authority govern the game. After centuries of play at various forms of the sport, the FA was the first attempt to standardize the game we know today so as to have inter-city, inter-regional, and international play.

Despite the initial English resistance to a non-British authority (much like the American attitude today in several sports), the generally-accepted inventors of the modern game relented in 1905, a year after FIFA was formed. Their joining and inclusion into FIFA rapidly spread the acceptance of the organization as the sport's administrator and arbiter.

With the growth of the World Cup—a FIFA invention—and thus soccer's popularity, FIFA likewise has assumed greater power, which some criticize as being wielded with an almost dictatorial indifference.

The establishment of the Football Association in England was the work of former college players who wished to continue playing soccer after their days at Cambridge, Oxford, and the other British schools.

Within ten years, the FA would begin the first regular tournament, the FA Cup, which further spread the popularity of the game throughout the British Isles. As the Britons extended their colonial empire, soccer went with them, and the game's popularity spread internationally.

While there was a standard set of rules, each region (country) had its own slight modifications. Associations were created in each country to conduct similar functions as the FA in England, including the establishment a single-elimination cup tournament. But they approached changes in the game—which was still in its infancy and still developing—in their own way, irrespective of what other countries were doing.

This created problems when one nation, playing under one set of rules, wanted to play another country, which was under a second set, albeit very similar.

In 1882, the Football Association called for a meeting of the soccer playing nations (in their mind that meant England, Wales, Scotland, and Ireland) to standardize rules so that all would play the same game. The Scots initially didn't want to participate but acquiesced after the English threatened to stop playing them.

The group they formed to standardize the rules was established as the Football Association Board, whereby all four nations agreed to abide by the decisions of the board.

The Birth of FIFA

As soccer grew outside of Britain, the calls for a more universal and inclusive body increased. By 1904, at a match between Belgium and France, the secretaries of the two teams—France's Robert Guerin and Belgium's Louis Muhlinghaus—decided to finally create such an organization.

By May 21, Guerin had invited seven European associations—France, Belgium, Denmark, the Netherlands, Spain, Sweden, and Switzerland—to Paris to form FIFA. The British also were invited, but because they saw no advantage of membership in this new group, they declined.

FIFA's original aim was not to replace the FA Board. In its original articles of foundation, it adopted the Board's rules, but has since become the sole arbitrator of the rules. However, the board itself has changed. When it was formed in 1882, the board had only four members, those of the founding countries. In 1913, FIFA was allowed two members on the board. Today the board has increased to eight, half of them appointed by FIFA.

FIFA's aim was to get everybody playing the same game, which essentially it has accomplished. It took 26 years, but it established the World Cup—its world championship—by 1930.

Since then it has created world championships for men under 17 years of age (the U-17 Championship), men under 20 (the World Youth Championship), women, and five-a-side or indoor soccer.

Its regional affiliates have established continental championships for national and club teams and helps oversee the transfers of players from one club team to another.

To be eligible for the club championships, each professional league must be a member of its national association; in the United States that means the United States Soccer Federation. To play in the World Cup, the national associations must be a member of the regional confederations, which in turn must be a member of FIFA.

By requiring this structured affiliation, FIFA is able to demand compliance with its rules. It can sanction teams or national associations (coun tries) that do not abide by its decisions and, if necessary, threaten sanctions against others who conspire or aid the non-complying entity.

The Structure of FIFA

Headquartered in Zurich, Switzerland, FIFA is ruled by a 22-member executive committee, which has a president, eight vice-presidents, and 13 other members. To handle the day-to-day operations, the Executive Committee appoints a general secretary, which has been likened to a CEO of a corporation.

With the president essentially acting as the chairman of the board, the executive committee handles the most important matters on policy, such as the awarding of the organization of the World Cup, and empowers the general secretariat to implement its decisions.

The president is the only member of the Executive Committee to be elected by the at-large membership. The remaining posts on the board are allotted to the various confederations and national associations.

The six regional or continental confederations: UEFA—the Union of European Football Associations; CONMEBOL—the Confederation of South American Football; CAF—the Confederation of African Football; AFC—the Asian Football Confederation; CONCACAF—the Confederation of North, Central American and Caribbean Football; and OFC—the Oceania (South Pacific) Football Confederation, are allotted representation on the board which are filled by internal regulations.

For example, CONMEBOL elects its representatives at-large while CONCACAF divides its three representatives by region, one from North American, one from Central America and the last from the Caribbean.

The British, by virtue of their historical creation of the game, also are guaranteed representation, irrespective of UEFA's delegation.

Additionally, FIFA has 18 standing committees which operate under the auspices of the Executive Committee. In charge of everything from media and protocol to matters involving medical and legal problems and even referees and the organization overseeing the various world championships sanctioned by FIFA, these panels administer their various functions with final approval required by the Executive Committee.

Among the 18 are the disciplinary, appeals and players status committees, which in 1992 gained some autonomy from the Executive Committee. As CONCACAF General Secretary Chuck Blazer put it, this was done to "depoliticize those aspects of the game which lend themselves to politics."

While the FA Board, today called the International Football Association Board, is a separate entity from FIFA, with four members appointed by the Executive Committee and the other four coming from FIFA-affiliated associations, FIFA virtually controls that too.

The lowest scoring World Cup in history produced a meager 2.21 goals per game in 1990 in Italy. The following year, FIFA, with the approval of the board, experimented with a few rule changes to increase scoring—including the outlawing of goalkeepers from handling passes from their teammates. By the summer of 1992 the backpass rule was adopted by the board, with FIFA's blessing. Although FIFA and the board's authority is incredibly vast, it is not absolute nor complete.

The National Collegiate Athletic Association, the main governing body of college sports in the United States, follows the basic rules of soccer but has several significant distinctions. Instead of allowing only two substitutions per game, the NCAA allows unlimited substitution.

It also does not calculate the accumulation of cautions or "yellow cards" to an individual player beyond the present game. Under FIFA rules, a second yellow card regardless of the time it takes to earn it, or a red card, requires a player to be suspended for one game. But as the NCAA is not a member of the U.S. Soccer Federation, it is not bound by FIFA's regulations or statutes.

Enforcing the Rules

To enforce and administer the game where it can, FIFA utilizes the regional confederations, who have established competitions and tournaments within their own jurisdiction to further increase the popularity of the game.

UEFA has three competitions for club teams: the Champions Cup, the Cup Winners Cup and the UEFA Cup. The Champions Cup takes the champions from each professional league in Europe and holds a single elimination tournament.

The Cup Winners Cup involves the champions of each country's cup tournament, an annual single-elimination event that also includes the amateur and semi-pro teams; and UEFA Cup, which includes the best remaining teams from the professional leagues that didn't qualify for one of the other two.

In South America the tournament is called the Copa Libertatores. It takes the first two teams from each of the 10 South American nations and combines them in an annual competition. The Libertadores and European Champions Cup winners meet in a one-game championship in Tokyo every year called the Toyota Cup.

Furthermore, the regional confederations also stage continental championships for national teams. The European Championship is a quadrennial event while the Copa America, the South American Championship, and the Gold Cup, CONCACAF's championship, are biennial.

The regional confederations are also where nations battle it out for the World Cup. With the World Cup finals limited to 24 teams playing over a one-month period, FIFA must whittle that down from a potential field of 178 countries. To do that, FIFA allots each confederation a certain number of berths based on the past performance of countries from that region in the World Cup.

The host nation and defending champion are guaranteed two of the 24 berths, but everybody else must participate in a qualifying procedure to reach the finals.

For 1994, Europe will get 12 berths (not including defending champion Germany); South America gets three with a possible fourth; Africa gets three; Asia two; CONCACAF one (not including the host United States) with a possible second; and Oceania may get one but is not guaranteed anything.

Each confederation devises its own qualifying procedure, with FIFA's approval, naturally, to determine who will fill its allotted berths.

In CONCACAF, for example, tiny nations such as Surinam and Barbados are required to play in preliminary rounds while larger and more traditional powers such as Mexico and Canada are exempt until later stages.

But the real power still remains with FIFA. By virtue of having created the World Cup, an event watched by an estimated 1.5 billion on television throughout the world in 1990 (that in addition to the 2.5 million in attendance), FIFA has the most prized sporting event on the planet. It also has made soccer the most popular game in the world.

Soccer's popularity can give companies wishing to advertise their products wide exposure, especially at events like the World Cup. The prestige in hosting a World Cup can force nations to make all sorts of guarantees to receive the honor. Because of its control, FIFA can act as arbitrarily as it likes.

FIFA's Critics

One of the most recent incidents in which some criticized FIFA was its battle with the IOC over eligibility requirements for the 1992 Summer Games. Like FIFA's use of regional confederations, the IOC uses individual governing bodies in the various Olympic sports to determine how the events will be run.

Basketball is run by FIBA, the International Basketball Federation; track and field is administered by the IAAF, the International Amateur Athletic Federation; and soccer is run by FIFA. With the acceptance of NBA professionals for the basketball competition of the 1992 Games, the IOC wanted FIFA to adopt similar measures to include professionals in the Olympic soccer tournament.

While the strict rules of amateurism in the Olympics were guarded under the presidency of Avery Brundage, for soccer the rules were slightly relaxed in recent Games and in 1988 any player from outside Europe and South America could play—professional or not—while Europeans could use anyone who had not played in a World Cup.

The idea was to give non-traditional powers a better chance of winning. But as the IOC pushed for all professionals, FIFA balked, citing it did not want a competition to rival the World Cup. FIFA retaliated by creating a third level of youth championship, restricting the Olympics to players under 23 years of age, regardless of contract status or World Cup experience.During the Olympics, attendance was quite poor except for the final, where the host nation Spain beat Poland before 95,000 flag-waving, drum-beating, confetti-throwing Spaniards. FIFA officials charged that IOC officials deliberately restricted promotion of soccer in Barcelona to punish FIFA for its eligibility requirements.

The IOC in turn blamed the under-23 rules for the poor crowds and tersely said that the eligibility requirements for 1996 would be reviewed. The battle of words continued with FIFA saying it felt unwanted and was given the impression the IOC wanted soccer, the first team sport in the Olympics, out of the Games.

The issue has been resolved for the 1996 Games in Atlanta with FIFA maintaining its under-23 age requirement but allowing each nation that qualifies three "wild card" roster spots in which anyone, even a seasoned World Cup veteran like 1986 Argentine hero Diego Maradona, can be used.

FIFA continues to try to expand its influence. Its awarding of the 1994 World Cup to the United States was a clear example. Comments by FIFA General Secretary Joseph "Sepp" Blatter, who has said he wanted American soccer officials to use the World Cup to establish a viable professional league in the United States, illustrate FIFA's desire to have the game spread in North America.

With a viable league, soccer would grow in popularity. With soccer popular in the most lucrative market in the world, FIFA's influence and power would grow exponentially. Additionally, there has been discussion of awarding the 2002 World Cup to Japan, another lucrative market, or China, with over a billion people.

Some have noted that the sellout crowds at the Barcelona Olympics for the basketball competition involving the American "Dream Team" shows a vulnerability of soccer as the world's most popular game and of FIFA's perch among the top of the sports world.

But with 95,000 at the Olympic final and predictions of a sellout of 3.6 million for the 1994 World Cup in the United States, it seems highly unlikely that soccer or FIFA's demise is imminent.

8: U.S. Soccer Organizations

The U.S. Soccer Federation

The United States Soccer Federation (USSF) is the controlling body of soccer in the United States, and, as such, represents American soccer interests in FlFA, the world governing body, and CONCACAF, the NorthCentral American and Caribbean confederation.

The organization was originally founded as the United States Football Association in 1913 after considerable feuding and strong competition from other organizations. The competing powers were the old American Football Association (AFA)—organizers of the American Cup—whose influence was felt primarily in New England, New Jersey, and Philadelphia, and the newer American Amateur Football Association (AAFA), whose control was centered in New York State.

In 1912, representatives of both associations clashed at the FIFA Congress in Stockholm, each arguing their case for international recognition. The AFA, which was affiliated with the Football Association in London, was represented by Sir Frederick Wall, secretary of the F.A., who pointed out that the AAFA did not represent professional players, thereby diminishing its potential authority.

Wall also admonished the Americans that the feud should be settled back in the United States, rather than be brought before the FIFA Congress for arbitration. The AAFA, for its part, was represented by Thomas W. Cahill, secretary of the association and the official representative of the AAFA at the Stockholm Olympic Games then in progress.

FIFA agreed with Wall's admonition and recommended to Cahill that he return to New York and try to organize a mutually acceptable national association that could be brought to FIFA for recognition.

After Cahill returned to New York the two associations appointed committees to find a solution to their difficulties. The AFA committee was made up of Joseph Hughes of Paterson, NJ; John Gundy of Bayonne, NJ; A.N. Beveridge of Kearny, NJ; A. Albert Frost, of Philadelphia; and Andrew M. Brown, of New York City. The AAFA committee was composed of Dr. G. Randolph Manning, William A. Campbell, and Nathan Agar, all of New York.

A series of conferences between the two committees began on October 12, 1912, at the Astor House in New York City, but on December 8, when an agreement appeared imminent, the

AFA voted to discontinue negotiations and dismiss its committee. This unpopular action gained the AAFA much support among local and regional associations.

In March 1913, the Allied American F.A. of Philadelphia and the F.A. of Philadelphia switched their allegiance to the AAFA, and it was this newly found strength from two important Philadelphia associations that gave the AAFA the necessary stimulus to prevail.

On April 5, 1913, representatives from associations across the nation met at the Astor House to formally establish the United States Football Association (USFA), and a committee was appointed to draft a constitution and bylaws.

A second convention was held on June 21, 1913, at the Broadway Central Hotel, and the first election of officers was held: Dr. G. Randolph Manning, president; Oliver Hemingway of the F.A. of Philadelphia, vice-president; Thomas H. McKnight of Chicago, second vice-president; William D. Love of Pawtucket, R.I., third vice-president; Archibald Birse of the Peel Challenge Cup Commission, Chicago, treasurer; and Thomas Cahill, secretary.

The AAFA application to FIFA was withdrawn, and a USFA application submitted. At the FIFA Congress of 1913 in Copenhagen, the pending AFA application was ignored, and the USFA was officially recognized. The AFA, upon hearing the news, voted to join the newly formed national governing body.

The USFA's name was changed in 1945 to the United States Soccer Football Association, and the present name was adopted in 1974. The USSF, a nonprofit corporation registered in New York State, consists of 37 regional associations, the North American Soccer League, the American Soccer League, the Intercollegiate Soccer Association of America, National Soccer Coaches Association of America, and United States Youth Soccer Association.

Via its affiliation with the United States Olympic Committee, it also sponsors the United States Olympic soccer team, and it organizes the National Open Challenge Cup and the National Amateur Cup.

THE N.A.S.L.
(North American Soccer League)

The leading professional soccer league in the United States and Canada during the late 1960s until its demise in the early 1980s was the North American Soccer League (NASL), formed in 1968 by a merger of the United Soccer Association and the National Professional Soccer League.

The NASL was the flagship of big-time soccer in North America, and more closely resembled a true national league than either the American Soccer League or the various ethnic leagues.

Unfortunately, it was regarded abroad with considerable disdain, largely due to its clubs' tendency to poach foreign players on a loan basis, and it suffered from a perilous relationship with FIFA (via the United States Soccer Federation) for its alterations of the time-honored world code.

From the point of view of the average American or Canadian fan, however, the NASL was responsible for the emergence of comparatively high-quality, senior-level soccer on this side of the Atlantic and the Rio Grande. The financial power of its wealthiest clubs, most notably Cosmos of New York, drew instant worldwide attention following the signing of Pelé in 1975.

The league attempted to establish a framework for slowly "Americanizing" its club rosters—in

1978, only 20 percent of its players were born in the United States and Canada—and urged its members to purchase foreign contracts outright and enter the world transfer market.

The NASL season ran from April to August and was one of the shortest in the world. It culminated with an elimination tournament of the top clubs, and ended in a championship final, the Soccer Bowl. Some variation of that format had been in effect since the formation of the league (except in 1969 when there were only five clubs), but each year saw a variety of structural changes to accommodate the fluctuating number of league members.

No NASL champion ever won the title under exactly the same conditions as did the previous year's winner. The only club to win more than one championship was Cosmos. The Atlanta Chiefs were distinctive in winning one championship (1968) and placing second twice (1969 and 1971), but between 1968-78 the title was won four times by new franchises (1970, 1973, 1974, and 1975).

The history of the NASL resembles that of its counterparts in American football, ice hockey, and basketball. It was the televising of the 1966 World Cup final from England (on a 15-minute delay) that proved to be the impetus for a national professional league.

The American Soccer League (ASL) had been in operation since the early 1930s, but, in fact, it was widely perceived as another ethnic league in disguise, and its following was severely limited to a few urban areas in the East. Bill Cox's International Soccer League (ISL), which had imported entire clubs from abroad during the early and mid-1960s had faded from sight. The high television ratings of the 1966 World Cup final, however, caught the imagination of a host of speculators.

Only months after England's world championship triumph, business interests coalesced into no less than two dozen camps, each seeking a franchise in whatever league structure could be worked out. One of the first assumptions to be made was that certain Canadian cities would be welcomed—especially Toronto and Vancouver—as commercially viable prospects because of their large ethnic populations.

The sleepy United States Soccer Football Association (USSFA) and Canadian Soccer Football Association (CSFA) were taken by surprise. Finding themselves in the midst of a "soccer boom," the national bodies meted out franchises for a pittance. So many clubs were formed over the span of a few months that clusters of owners grouped into two separate leagues.

FIFA reminded the USSFA and CSFA that under FIFA regulations they could recognize only one national league per country. The national bodies met and urged the two prospective leagues to merge or be forced to recognize one over the other. The leagues refused, and the USSFA and CSFA gave their blessing to the United Soccer Association (USA) for the 1967 season.

The second league, the National Professional Soccer League (NPSL), ignored FIFA's warnings from Zurich and continued to set up its operation, vowing to bury the USA in the competitive marketplace. The USSFA explained the vagaries of American entrepreneurship to FIFA, and asked the world body to refrain from taking action against the United States and Canada and allow a period of grace until matters could be settled. FIFA reluctantly acquiesced.

The USA plan for success was to borrow Bill Cox's idea of importing clubs wholesale from abroad and assigning them to American franchises. Thus the membership of the United Soccer Association 1967 was comprised entirely of foreign clubs: Boston (alias Shamrock Rovers F.C., Dublin, Ireland); Chicago (Cagliari Calcio, Cagliari, Italy); Cleveland (Stoke City F.C., Stoke-on-Trent, England); Dallas (Dundee United F.C., Dundee, Scotland); Detroit (Glentoran F.C., Belfast, Northern Ireland); Houston (Bangu AC, Rio de Janeiro, Brazil); Los Angeles (Wolverhampton Wanderers F.C., Wolverhampton, England); New York (CA Cerro, Montevideo, Uruguay); San Francisco (ADO, The Hague, Netherlands); Toronto (Hibernian F.C., Edinburgh, Scotland); Vancouver (Sunderland F.C., Sunderland, England); and Washington (Aberdeen F.C., Aberdeen, Scotland).

The United States was divided into eastern and western divisions, and the two divisional winners, the Los Angeles Wolves and the Washington Whips, met in a championship play-off. Los Angeles finally won 6-5 in an overtime goal-scoring bonanza.

Although each of the United Soccer Association teams were members of their respective first divisions in their native countries, there were odd differences in style and noticeable gulfs between their levels of play. The results in the final standings, however, were remarkably consistent. In addition, some temperamental rivalries surfaced to add a "foreign" zest to the competition, e.g., New York (Cerro) vs. Chicago (Cagliari).

The NPSL, on the other hand, took a different approach. Burdened by its renegade status, the NPSL owners were hastily forced to gather what players they could from lowly American ranks and entice either very young or aging veteran players from abroad.

This state of affairs resulted not only in a lower standard of play than the USA, but the players themselves risked suspension by FIFA and their respective national associations. In one remarkable, if unheralded, instance, the St. Louis Stars managed to obtain the incomparable Yugoslav inside forward Dragoslav Sekularac on loan from Karlsruher SC of West Germany.

Ironically, CBS-TV salvaged the league's precarious status by agreeing to broadcast NPSL matches throughout the season. To add to an already self-destructive situation, four NPSL owners in cities where USA franchises also existed (New York, Chicago, Los Angeles, and Toronto) refused to pull out.

In the fall of 1967, when the season was finally over, most of the clubs in both leagues had lost vast sums of money—as much as one million dollars apiece. While the NPSL initiated a lawsuit against FIFA, the leagues commiserated over their collective failure, and in December 1967 they agreed to merge as the North American Soccer League (NASL). The lawsuit was dropped, and the USSFA and CSFA immediately recognized the new league.

In its first season the NASL included nine franchises from the United Soccer Association (Boston Beacons, Chicago Mustangs, Cleveland Stokers, Dallas Tornado, Detroit Cougars, Houston Stars, Los Angeles Wolves, Vancouver Royals, and Washington Whips) and eight from the National Professional Soccer League (Atlanta Chiefs, Baltimore Bays, Kansas City Spurs, New York Generals, Oakland Clippers, St. Louis Stars, San Diego Toros, and Toronto Falcons).

The former USA clubs returned without their foreign teams from the previous year, and started from scratch. Of the former NPSL clubs, two were relocated from other cities to avoid duplication (San Diego from Los Angeles and Kansas City from Chicago). The USA and NPSL franchises that were not included in the new league but found themselves in NASL "markets" received financial compensation.

The 17 clubs of the NASL modeled their building programs on the work of the NPSL and scoured all five continents to fill their rosters. Barely one percent of the NASL player membership in 1968 was American or Canadian. The teams were divided into two conferences (eastern and western) with two divisions in each conference.

The play-off structure featured two conference championships followed by a league championship, each played on a home and away basis. In the championship of that first season, the eastern title holder, Atlanta, defeated the West's San Diego after a 3-0 romp in the Georgia capital.

But the grand experiment failed once again at the box office, and when the league opened for business in 1969, only five clubs remained: Atlanta, Baltimore, Dallas, Kansas City, and St. Louis. To the rescue came former Welsh international Phil Woosnam, player-manager of the Atlanta Chiefs in 1967-68, to take over as executive director of the crippled league.

Woosnam and the league's new director of administration, Clive Toye, (former *London Daily Express* football correspondent and general manager of the Baltimore Bays in 1967-68), set out to learn the ways of American big business, and traveled extensively to attract new speculators from across the nation.

Dividends were slow in coming, but the doldrums of 1969 were eventually put behind, and there was a gradual increase in the number of league clubs in 1970 and 1971.

In 1970 the Baltimore Bays gave up its NASL effort after some strong pressure from the Baltimore Orioles baseball club but the two American Soccer League powerhouses of that year, Rochester and Washington, joined the league and membership was increased to six.

The unpredictability of NASL competition was affirmed when the divisional titles were won by none other than Rochester and Washington, the former emerging as league champion. Modest increases in attendance figures helped to maintain optimism in league offices.

The following year brought three changes in the league structure. Kansas City bowed out, but important new franchises were found in New York (the Cosmos under new head Clive Toye), Toronto (the return of a major ethnic center), and Montreal.

In addition, there were two major innovations in 1971. The first involved an extension of the regular league schedule in which three foreign clubs (Portuguesa of Brazil, Lanerossi-Vicenza of Italy, and Apollo of Greece) were brought in to compete against members of the league in an official cup competition whose results were included in the season standings.

In addition, the play-off schedule was increased to bring in greater box-office revenues: first- and second-place clubs from either division engaged in a best-of-three series to determine the participants in a best-of-three final. Lamar Hunt's Dallas Tornado, the NASL's first Cinderella team, defeated Atlanta for the championship.

In 1972, for the first and only time, the number of league members did not change, but a lack of interest in Washington, D.C., prompted the Darts to relocate to Miami. Also, mounting concern over the absence of American players in the league resulted in the first college draft, and the eight clubs selected 35 collegiate players, of which two eventually made starting lineups.

Additionally, the 1972 season was shorter (each club played the others twice on a home and away basis), and the playoff format of the previous year was retained with one-leg semifinals and a one-leg championship. The New York Cosmos, playing before its home crowds in both the semifinal and the final, won the league title over St. Louis, the latter attempting to vindicate St. Louis's long reputation as the bastion of American soccer.

Philadelphia was the only new club to enter the NASL in 1973, leaving the western part of the United States without a franchise for the fifth year in a row. With the makeup of team rosters changing so dramatically each year, it was not surprising that Philadelphia, the only expansion club of the season, won the championship after winning a one-leg semifinal and final against Toronto and Dallas, respectively.

For the regular season clubs were divided into three divisions of three clubs each, and for the first time a "wild card" team (the idea borrowed from the National Football League) was placed in the playoffs. The major story of the season was the rise to prominence for the first time of two Americans: Philadelphia Atoms coach Al Miller and the first American-born scoring leader and Rookie of the Year, Dallas's Kyle Rote, Jr. Optimists proclaimed a new day for American soccer, but the fact remained that the number of top American or Canadian players in the NASL could be counted on one hand.

The first dramatic breakthrough for Commissioner Woosnam and his struggling league occurred in 1974. Membership jumped from nine to 15 clubs. In the East, Baltimore and Boston returned to the ranks with new owners, and an entire western division was created on the Pacific coast, including two new franchises in

Seattle and San Jose, as well as Los Angeles and Vancouver. Atlanta and Montreal, meanwhile, dropped out, but their places were taken by Denver, a new city to organized soccer, and a new Washington club, the Diplomats.

The league's iconoclastic point system—which until now had awarded six points for a win, three for a draw, none for a loss, and one for every goal scored up to and including three per game—was altered, and draws were eliminated entirely. Matches now ending in drawn scores would be decided by a penalty kick contest (as per FIFA regulations) and called a "draw-win"; the winner would be awarded three points and the loser none. Outright wins and losses would still be awarded six and zero points, respectively.

FIFA had strongly disapproved of the old system to begin with, but the new regulations prompted an even stronger reaction. Yet the world body took no action, and the new point system was instituted. Moreover, the NASL was by now developing a reputation for tampering with the venerable Laws of the Game.

In 1973 the league abolished FIFA's offside rule (written in 1866 and painstakingly revised in 1925) and changed the demarcation from the halfway line to an arbitrary line 35 yards from the opponent's goal, i.e., a player could not be offside until he had crossed the 35-yard line in his opponent's half of the field.

In 1975, the "draw-win" was eliminated, and all matches were either won or lost, if necessary by a penalty kick contest. Six points were awarded for a win and none for a loss. Meanwhile, the league was expanded to 20 clubs. New franchises were awarded to Tampa, Hartford, Chicago, San Antonio, and Portland.

There were no dropouts, but the Toronto Metros merged with a local ethnic power, Croatia, in an attempt to draw some additional support from the stronger semi-professional leagues of the

Toronto area. The four divisions of the 1974 season were retained in their basic configuration, as was the play-off structure of 1974, which included a quarter-final round.

For years, the established policy of the NASL—and the ASL, ISL, and NPSL before it—was to build a commercially viable American game by importing foreign players. Little serious thought had ever been given to the slow, admittedly frustrating policy of developing a native American game from the grass roots, as other countries had done over the decades. This dependence on foreign players reached a feverish peak during the mid-1970s.

When it became apparent around 1974 that the NASL was lifting itself up by the bootstraps and professional soccer on a major scale was making inroads, the possibility of attracting major foreign stars appeared more and more realistic. Hundreds of players were mentioned, and soon the press was dropping a litany of names that read like an international who's who of soccer.

The prospect of a grass roots American game, the public was told, would depend not on many years of laborious planning and hard work, but on one or perhaps two star players from abroad; native American acceptance of the game would follow in turn.

In June 1975, Clive Toye of the New York Cosmos, backed by its high rolling parent company Warner Communications, succeeded in signing Pelé—the world's most celebrated player and recently retired from his famous club Santos. Pelé's arrival in the NASL was, indeed, a watershed.

Worldwide attention immediately focused on America's upstart league. Pelé's multi-million dollar contract reached the front page of the *New York Times* as well as newspapers from Boise to Savannah that had not previously been aware of soccer's advance to American shores. Atten-

dances soared (where the Cosmos played), and Pelé—at once gracious and ingratiating—promised to deliver the world game to the Free World's promised land.

Other international idols whose stars were on the wane—George Best, Jimmy Johnstone, Eusebio, Antonio Simoes, Bobby Moore—soon graced American playing fields, but the league and the press had been searching for someone of Pelé's stature and all others were destined to relative obscurity.

Single-handedly, Pelé could not bring the Cosmos a league championship or even a divisional title, but his club achieved international fame. Florida's expansion team, the Tampa Bay Rowdies, walked away with the 1975 crown. The championship game was renamed the Soccer Bowl—hearkening once again to the National Football League—and CBS-TV again broadcast a handful of games (Pelé's Cosmos vs. whomever).

In 1976, Pelé's first full season, the Baltimore Comets moved to San Diego and Denver relocated to Minneapolis-St. Paul (as the Minnesota Kicks), to give the north country its first NASL franchise. The number of American or Canadian players each club was required to carry was raised to six, and at least one American or Canadian had to be on the field for each team at all times.

The four divisions were again divided into two conferences, the Atlantic and the Pacific, and the playoff schedule was expanded to include the top three finishers from each division. Eusebio was transferred from Boston to Toronto and no one noticed.

In the end, the season proved to be a disappointing anticlimax for most of the NASL's new following, as Toronto, one of the least supported clubs in the league, won the league championship from Minnesota, the best supported club in the league but one that lacked superstars and broad appeal.

The New York Cosmos were runner-up to Tampa Bay in their division, and bowed out of the playoffs to the same Tampa Bay in the divisional championship. The major news items of the season were the record-breaking attendance figures (e.g., 49,572 in Bloomington, Minnesota, for a single game).

By 1977 Pelé and Cosmos had taken a number of worldwide tours and had become, in a sense, the superstars of the NASL without winning a title. Extensive pressure was exerted on the New York club to win the 1977 championship, as befitting the club of Pelé, who would be in his final year as an active player.

To this end, Clive Toye made one last master stroke before leaving Cosmos for greener pastures in Chicago. At the end of the European season, he signed Franz Beckenbauer, captain of Bayern München and the world champion West Germans, and widely regarded as the world's most complete player.

Beckenbauer, still at the peak of his career, transformed Cosmos from a mere oddity into a relatively sophisticated team, introducing contemporary tactical methods that had previously been unattainable with the available talent.

Although Cosmos lost its divisional title to Gordon Banks's Ft. Lauderdale Strikers, it plunged through the playoffs and won the league crown in a much-heralded Soccer Bowl '77. Pelé declared that all he had ever wished for was now achieved, and observers were struck by the relative ease with which Cosmos dominated the play-offs after its ups and downs during the regular season.

Cosmos' championship season had seen four changes in the league alignment. San Diego relocated to Las Vegas; Miami moved up the coast to Ft. Lauderdale; Hartford moved downstate to New Haven and took the name of its state (Connecticut); and San Antonio relocated right off the continent and out of everybody's memories to Honolulu.

The major rule change of the year was the adoption of a new tie-breaking procedure called the "shoot-out," which brought renewed warnings of suspension from FIFA and derisive wonderment from players and seasoned fans. But the league declared that American spectators needed the added excitement of a Matt Dillon-type showdown in front of the nets.

Attendance records fell in quick succession, and in August the all-time high was reached when 77,691 fans at Giants Stadium saw Cosmos bury Ft. Lauderdale by a score of 8-3 in the divisional championship play-offs, outdrawing professional baseball games in New York on the same day.

In 1978, new franchises were awarded to Boston, Denver, Detroit, Philadelphia, Houston and Memphis, to bring the number of NASL members to 24.

Unfortunately, the N.A.S.L. expanded too quickly, attendance in all franchise cities (except New York) fell off, and the costs of operating in a market competing with U.S. baseball, football, basketball, and hockey proved too great a financial burden for teams competing for big-name (and big-dollar) name players, especially when hoped-for television revenues failed to materialize.

The North American Soccer League folded in 1984, but not before it brought soccer to the consciousness of million of American sports fans. It also helped spur the growth of interest in the sport among youth and at the college level, where soccer has taken foothold and established itself as the fastest-growing sport in the United States.

CURRENT LEAGUES AND TEAMS

NOTE:

THIS SECTION COVERS PROFESSIONAL LEAGUES AND
TEAMS, BOTH MINOR AND MAJOR LEAGUE. LEAGUE
ENTRIES ARE ARRANGED ALPHABETICALLY BY NAME;
EACH IS FOLLOWED BY AN ALPHABETICAL LIST OF
ENTRIES FOR TEAMS IN THAT LEAGUE.

A. P. S. L.
American Professional Soccer League

American Professional Soccer League (A.P.S.L.)
10620 Guilford Rd., Ste. 204
Jessup, MD 20794
Phone: (301) 498-4990
Fax: (301) 498-3542

Key Personnel: William C. Sage, Co-Chairman;
Clive Toye, Co-Chairman; Stephen Flamhaft,
General Counsel; Donald S. Burris, General
Counsel; Diane Fritschner, Operations Direc-
tor; Donn Risolo, Media Relations Diredctor.

Founded: 1989.
Publication(s): Media Guide (Annual).

The APSL was formed by the merger of the
American Soccer League (A.S.L.) and Western
Soccer League (W.S.L.). The league is com-
posed of two conferences, the American and the
Western.

Every year, the first- and second-place finishers
from both the American Conference and the
Western Conference qualify for the playoffs. If
a series is tied at one win apiece, a 30-minute
mini-game will be played immediately after the
second game to determine the series winner.

A. P. S. L. Teams

Albany Capitals
5885 State Farm Rd.
Slingerlands, NY 12159
Phone: (518) 456-1015
Fax: (518) 456-5432

Key Personnel: Armand Quadrini, Owner; John
Bramley, General Manager and Head Coach.
Founded: 1988.
Team Colors: Royal blue and white.

The Albany Capitals compete in the American
Conference of the APSL.

Colorado Foxes
6735 Stroh Rd.
Parker, CO 80134
Phone: (303) 840-1111
Fax: (303) 840-1238

Key Personnel: Robert Healy, President; Greg
Tood, General Manager.
Founded: 1990.
Team Colors: Gray and gold.

The Colorado Foxes compete in the Western
Conference of the A.P.S.L.

Ft. Lauderdale Strikers
5620 Yankee Blvd.
Ft. Lauderdale, FL 33309
Phone: (305) 776-1991
Fax: (304) 776-3366

Founded: 1976.
Team Colors: White, red, and navy.

The Ft. Lauderdale Strikers compete in the
American Conference of the A.P.S.L.

Maryland Bays
10620 Guilford Rd., Ste. 202
Jessup, MD 20794
Phone: (301) 880-0047
Fax: (301) 498-3542

Key Personnel: John Liparini, Owner; Paul Marstaller, Asst. General Manager.
Founded: 1987.
Team Colors: Red, white, black, and gold.

The Maryland Bays compete in the Western Conference of the A.P.S.L..

Miami Freedom
1801 Coral Way
Miami, FL 33145
Phone: (305) 858-7477
Fax: (305) 858-7520

Key Personnel: Emily Ballus, Owner and General Manager.
Founded: 1988 (as the Miami Sharks).
Team Colors: Orange and black.

The team became the Miami Freedom in 1989; it competes in the American Conference of the A.P.S.L.

New Jersey Eagles
2 Palmer Terr.
Carlstadt, NJ 07072
Phone: (201) 438-8920
Fax: (201) 438-4620

Key Personnel: Ray Jacobs, Chairman; Doug Jacobs.
Founded: 1988.
Team Colors: Red, white, and blue.

The New Jersey Eagles were on hiatus for the 1991 season, but competed again in 1992.

Penn-Jersey Spirit
808 Roebling Ave.
Trenton, NJ 08611
Phone: (609) 394-2254
Fax: (609) 394-2081

Key Personnel: Hugo Nuziale, Owner; Generale Racz.
Founded: 1989.
Team Colors: Light blue and white.

The Penn-Jersey Spirit competes in the American Conference of the A.P.S.L.

San Francisco Bay Blackhawks
3840 Blackhawk Rd.
Danville, CA 94506
Phone: (415) 736-6801
Fax: (415) 736-0377

Key Personnel: Dan Van Voorhis, President and General Manager; Bonnie England.
Founded: 1988.
Team Colors: Yellow and black.

The San Francisco Bay Blackhawks compete in the Western Conference of the A.P.S.L.

Tampa Bay Rowdies
2225 N. Westshore Blvd.
Tampa, FL 33607
Phone: (813) 877-7800
Fax: (813) 874-3759

Key Personnel: Cornelia Corbett, Owner; Rodney Marsh, General Manager.
Founded: 1975.
Team Colors: Green and white.

The Tampa Bay Rowdies compete in the American Conference of the A.P.S.L.

M.S.L.
Major Soccer League

NOTE:

THE MAJOR SOCCER LEAGUE (M.S.L.) IS A PROFESSIONAL INDOOR SOCCER LEAGUE COMPRISED OF TEAMS THAT COMPETE IN TWO DIVISIONS, EASTERN AND WESTERN. THE LEAGUE WAS FORMERLY KNOWN AS THE MAJOR INDOOR SOCCER LEAGUE (M.I.S.L.). THE LEAGUE SPONSORS AN ANNUAL M.S.L. ALL-STAR GAME AS WELL AS A LEAGUE CHAMPIONSHIP AND IS AFFILIATED WITH THE U. S. SOCCER FEDERATION.

Major Soccer League (M.S.L.)
4500 College Blvd., Ste. 308
Overland Park, KS 66211
Phone: (913) 339-6475

Key Personnel: Earl M. Foreman, Commissioner.
Founded: 1978.
Publication(s): Media guides and rule book.
Program(s)/Project(s): M.S.L. sponsors clinics and seminars, maintains a speakers' bureau and biographical archives, compiles statistics, provides children's services, sponsors competitions, and presents all-star and most valuable player awards.

Teams

Baltimore Blast
1801 S. Clinton St.
Baltimore, MD 21224
Phone: (301) 327-2100
Fax: (301) 327-6410

Key Personnel: John Borozzi, General Manager; Kenny Cooper, Head Coach; Drew Forrester, Public Relations.
Founded: April 1980.
Team Colors: Red, yellow, and white.
Stadium: Baltimore Arena, capacity 12,510.
Training Facilities: Myers Soccer Pavilion.

Ticket Information: (913) 481-6000 or (800) 448-9009.

The Blast competes in the Eastern Division of the M.S.L.

Dallas Sidekicks
Reunion Arena
777 Sports St.
Dallas, TX 75207
Phone: (214) 653-0200

Key Personnel: Ish Haley, General Manager; Gordon Jago, Head Coach.
Founded: 1984.
Team Colors: Green, silver, and white.
Stadium: Reunion Arena, capacity 16,000.
Training facilities: Inwood Soccer Center.
Ticket Information: (214)653-0200.

The Dallas Sidekicks compete in the Western Division of the M.S.L. The Sidekicks won the M.S.L. title in 1987 when they defeated the Tacoma Stars.

St. Louis Storm
St. Louis Arena
5700 Oakland Ave.
St. Louis, MO 63110
Phone: (314) 781-6475
Fax: (314) 781-9727

Key Personnel: Denny Bond, General Manager; Don Popovic, Head Coach; Brian Gravette, Public Relations
Founded: July 1989.
Team Colors: Red, yellow, and blue.
Stadium: St. Louis Arena, capacity 12,884.
Training facilities: Concord Indoor Soccer Club.
Ticket Information: Contact Ron Sadler.

The St. Louis Storm compete in the Western Division of the M.S.L. They became the first non-European team to win a foreign indoor soccer tournament when they won the Zurich International Soccer Tournament in Zurich, Switzerland, in January 1991.

San Diego Sockers
San Diego Sports Arena
3500 Sports Arena Blvd.
San Diego, CA 92110
Phone: (619) 224-4625
Fax: (619) 222-9020

Key Personnel: Randy Bernstein, General Manager; Ron Newman, Head Coach; Jim Morehouse, Public Relations.
Founded: 1980.
Team Colors: Blue and gold.
Stadium: San Diego Sports Arena, capacity 12,884.
Training facilities: San Diego Indoor Soccer Center.
Ticket Information: (619) 278-8497.

Established for outdoor soccer in 1978, the San Diego Sockers switched to indoor soccer in 1980. They compete in the Western Division of the M.S.L. Their former locations and names include: Baltimore Comets (1974-75); San Diego Jaws (1976); and Las Vegas Quicksilvers (1977). They were formerly a member of the now defunct North American Soccer League (N.A.S.L.). The Sockers have won nine of the last ten league championships.

Tacoma Stars
3630 S. Cedar, Ste. G
Tacoma, WA 98409
Phone: (206) 472-7827
Fax: (206)472-8275

Key Personnel: Bob Walz, General Manager; Keith Weller, Head Coach.
Founded: 1983.
Team Colors: Red, white, and blue.
Stadium: Tacoma Dome, capacity 18,000.

Training facilities: Tacoma Sports Center.

The Tacoma Stars compete in the Western Division of the M.S.L.

N. P. S. L.
National Professional Soccer League

NOTE:
THE NATIONAL PROFESSIONAL SOCCER LEAGUE (N.P.S.L.) IS COMPRISED OF TEN TEAMS IN UNITED STATES CITIES. THE TEAMS COMPETE IN TWO DIVISIONS, AMERICAN AND NATIONAL. SIX OF THE TEAMS QUALIFY FOR POST-SEASON PLAY, THE TWO DIVISIONAL CHAMPS AND THE FOUR TEAMS WITH THE BEST WINNING PERCENTAGES, REGARDLESS OF DIVISION. THE LEAGUE PLAYOFFS AND CHAMPIONSHIPS ARE HELD IN APRIL.

National Professional Soccer League
229 3rd St. NW
Canton, OH 44702
Phone: (216)455-4625
Fax: (216)455-3885
Founded: 1984.

Teams

Baltimore Spirit

Buffalo Blizzard

Canton Invaders
1101 Market Ave. N.
Canton, OH 44702
Phone: (216) 455-6060
Fax: (216) 455-9000

Key Personnel: Mike Sanger, General Manager; Timo Liekoski, Head Coach.
Team Colors: Silver and black.
Stadium: Canton Civic Center, capacity 4,200.

The Canton Invaders compete in the American Division of the N.P.S.L.

Chicago Power
10850 Laraway Rd.
Frankfort, IL 60423
Phone: (815) 469-1004
Fax: (815) 469-2469

Key Personnel: Ron Bergstrom, General Manager; Pato Margetic, Head Coach.
Team Colors: Red, white, and black.
Stadium: Rosemont Horizon, capacity 14,618. The Chicago Power compete in the National Division of the N.P.S.L.

Cleveland Crunch
1 Crunch Pl.
34200 Solon Rd.
Solon, OH 44139
Phone: (216) 349-2090
Fax: (216) 349-0653

Key Personnel: Al Miller, General Management; Trevor Dawkins, Head Coach; Scott Hood, Public Relations.
Founded: 1989.
Team Colors: Yellow, red, and black.
Stadium: Richfield Coliseum, capacity 17,213 (for soccer).
Training facilities: Crunch Soccer Center.

Dayton Dynamo
501 E. Wenger Rd.
Englewood, OH 45322
Phone: (513) 832-4625
Fax: (513) 836-0587

Key Personnel: Jerry Butcher, General Manager; Tony Glavin, Head Coach. *Stadium:* Nutter Center, capacity 9,000.

The Dayton Dynamo compete in the National Division of the N.P.S.L.

Detroit Rockers
37361 Laraway Rd.
Livonia, MI 48152
Phone: (313) 473-0440
Fax: (313) 473-0441

Key Personnel: Gus Moffat, General Manager; Brian Tinnion, Head Coach.
Team Colors: Black, white, and silver.
Stadium: Cobo Arena, capacity 9,561.

The Detroit Rockers compete in the American Division of the N.P.S.L.

Harrisburg Heat
P.O. Box 10511
Harrisburg, PA 17105
Phone: 800-242-GOAL

Key Personnel: Pat Flynn, General Manager; Jim Pollihan, Head Coach.
Team Colors: Purple, black, and white.
Stadium: State Farm Show Arena, capacity 7,600.

The Harrisburg Heat competes in the American Division of the N.P.S.L.

Illinois Thunder
4615 E. State St.
Rockford, IL 61108
Phone: (815) 398-4663
Fax: (815) 398-5338

Key Personnel: Mike Kelegian, General Manager; Heinz Wirtz, Head Coach.
Team Colors: Black and gold.
Stadium: MetroCentre, capacity 8,000.

The Illinois Thunder compete in the National Division of the N.P.S.L.

Kansas City Attack
200 W. 14th St.
Kansas City, MO 64105
Phone: (816) 871-3792
Fax: (816) 871-3794

Key Personnel: Keith Tozer, General Manager and Head Coach.
Team Colors: Red, white, and blue.
Stadium: Kansas City Municipal Auditorium, capacity 8,900.

The Kansas City Attack, formerly the Atlanta Attack, compete in the N.P.S.L.

Milwaukee Wave
6310 N. Port Washington Rd.
Milwaukee, WI 53217
Phone: (414) 962-9283
Fax: (414) 962-4837

Key Personnel: Ron Creten, General Manager; Johan Aarnio, Head Coach.

Team Colors: Blue and white.
Stadium: Bradley Center, capacity 17,500.

The Milwaukee Wave compete in the National Division of the N.P.S.L.

St. Louis Ambush

Key Personnel: Vernor Riggs, General Manager; Victor Moreland, Head Coach.
Team Colors: Green, gold, and white.
An expansion team that began as the Tulsa Ambush in 1991.

Wichita Wings
114 S. Broadway
Wichita, KS 67202
Phone: (316) 262-3545
Fax: (316) 263-8531

Key Personnel: Hugh Nicks, General Manager; Roy Turner, Head Coach; David Phillips, Public Relations .
Founded: 1979.
Team Colors: Orange and blue.
Stadium: Kansas Coliseum, capacity 9,686.
Training facilities: Kansas Coliseum.

The Wichita Wings compete in the Eastern Division of the M.S.L. They are the longest-running profession soccer team in the United States.

F.Y.I.

NATIONAL SOCCER HALL OF FAME
(N.S.H.O.F.)

The National Soccer Hall of Fame is sanctioned by F.I.F.A. and the U.S. Soccer Federation. It was designed to promote a better understanding of soccer in America through maintaining a historical record of soccer in the United States, encouraging the involvement of youth in the game, and defining America's role in international soccer.

The N.S.H.O.F. consists of the National Soccer Museum and the 61-acre Wright National Soccer Campus. The Campus has an exhibit hall that houses displays of equipment and memorabilia form soccer's greatest players and teams as well as photos, artifacts, and trophy cases filled with the sport's most sought-after prizes. Clinics and tournaments are scheduled year-round, along with special events, including soccer camps and workshops.

Key Personnel: Albert Colone, Executive Director; Victor J. Porto, Public Relations Director; Lois Emanuelli, Museum Registrar/Curator.

Founded: Although individuals have been inducted into the Hall of Fame since 1950, the Hall was officially established in 1979 and constructed in 1982. *Members:* 191.

Publication(s): National Soccer Hall of Fame News (bimonthly newsletter). $12.50 per year.

9: Women's Soccer

An overview by Michelle Kaufman

Women's Soccer: Then and Now

Women's soccer was a popular spectator sport as early as the eighteenth century, when 10,000 fans showed up annually in Iveresk, Scotland, to watch a celebrated match between married and single women.

Two hundred years later, on November 30, 1991, a worldwide television audience and 60,000 fans watched as the United States defeated Norway 2-1 in the first-ever Women's World Soccer Championship at Tianhe Stadium in Canton, China.

It was a long and frustrating two centuries for female soccer enthusiasts, and they remain far from satisfied. Though 64 countries had a national women's soccer team in 1993 and 20 million women played the game, there were no plans to add the sport to the 1996 Summer Olympics menu.

The international sports world has been hesitant to open the door to women's soccer, a problem that has plagued the sport from its inception. As late as 1952, skeptics were rampant. Dutch psychologist F.J. Buytendijk wrote: "The game of soccer is essentially a demonstration of masculinity.... Women have never been allowed to play soccer." He then added, "Kicking is spe-cifically masculine; whether being kicked is feminine, I prefer not to say."

A Long Tradition

Had Buytendijk known his sports history, he might have altered his words. The first record of women playing a form of soccer dates to sixteenth-century England, the birthplace of men's soccer, or football as it is referred outside the United States. Wives, girlfriends, and daughters watched the men's game from the sidelines and took note.

It was shortly thereafter that loosely organized women's games were played. The violent nature of the game, coupled with the lack of standardized rules, kept most women away from the playing field. Women of the upper classes were more likely to try cricket or golf because soccer was most popular with miners, dock workers, and factory machinists.

There were, however, some brave souls who insisted on trying. Women's games were especially popular at festivals and town gatherings. It was not until the late 1800s that organized women's soccer clubs began mushrooming all over England. Not surprisingly, there was a public outcry.

Unfriendly Public Attitudes

In 1877, Girton Women's College in Cambridge built its first gymnasium. The sports program grew, and soccer gained popularity with the students. Emily Davis, founder of the college, said: "It would certainly shock the world if it were known" that women were kicking a football.

As late as 1891 a women's rugby tour was canceled in New Zealand after a heated protest. Nevertheless, women's teams drew support in industrial towns like Preston, England. A club called Dick Kerr's XI was established in Preston in 1894, and became best-known for its charity work. Kerr, Ltd., was a large electric corporation and used the women's team for promotional purposes.

Dick Kerr's team toured the United States in September and October of 1922 and played exhibition matches against amateur men's teams. They were invited to New York by A. Zelickman of the Brooklyn Football Club. The tour included stops in Paterson, NJ, Pawtucket, RI, New York City, Washington, DC, and New Bedford, MA. Games scheduled in Chicago, Detroit, and Cleveland were dropped for lack of finances.

The women strikers boarded the *SS Scythia* back to England with three wins, two losses, and two ties. Pete Renzulli, the late goalkeeper of the Paterson club and a Hall-of-Famer, once commented: "Here is something. I played against the Dick Kerr's in 1922 as goalie. We were national champions and we had a hell of a job beating them 6-3."

Rejection by the F.A.

Female soccer players in England became so enthusiastic about the game that they asked the Football Association in 1902 to devise a set of rules specifically to govern the women's leagues. The Association ruled that women's clubs were ineligible to join its ranks because it didn't want to be held responsible for injuries that were "bound" to happen to female athletes.

Despite the lack of support from the sport's top brass, women's soccer continued to grow with the suffragist movement in the 1920s. A match between women's teams from France and England in 1920 drew 10,000 spectators.

And the sport was gaining ground in the United States, as well. A 1920 entry in *Spalding's Athletic Library* tells of two American women—Helen Clark and Doris Clark (no relation)—who broke soccer barriers. Doris Clark managed the McKinley Park Football Club in Sacramento, CA, the only woman to hold such a job with a U.S. Football Association team. Helen Clark was a referee for boys' games in Bridgeport, CN.

In a letter published in the *Soccer Guide,* Helen Clark wrote: "After having played, coached and refereed many games, I now consider soccer is the best all-around sport and I hope the women of America will not be afraid to enter in and lead in the game."

Renewed Popularity

Clark's dream took nearly four decades to materialize. Women's soccer was almost dormant during World War II, and it wasn't until the late 1950s that it regained popularity. The West German soccer governing body, the Deutscher Fussball-Bund, declared in 1955 that women's clubs were not welcome.

That did not stop the women from holding an unofficial European Women's Football Championship in West Berlin in 1957. Teams from Austria, England, Germany, and the Netherlands participated. England defeated West Germany 4-0 in the final.

Clubs sprang up all over Eastern Europe during the 1960s, as Communist regimes encouraged women's sporting teams at factories and schools. The state-run sports system produced top-notch athletes. Czechoslovakia became known for its strong, fast, competitive women's soccer squads.

Growth of Organized Play

A Women's Cup was played in France in 1968. That same year a French women's team named the Football Club Feninin Reims was founded, a group of women that would capture the hearts of soccer fans all over Europe. Its founder, Pierre Geofroy, was instrumental in the promotion of women's sports.

The FCF Reims teamed up with the men's club, Stade de Reims, and they toured the world. By 1975 the women's team had been seen by more than 50,000 fans in Haiti, Hungary, Indonesia, Czechoslovakia, and Ireland. Football executives in England took note, and in 1969 reversed their 67-year-old decision not to recognize women's soccer. Wales, Ireland, and Scotland followed suit.

By 1970, there were women's soccer teams from Japan to Algeria to South Africa. As many as 34 countries offered women some type of organized soccer. Most of the teams were either sponsored by the men's clubs or prominent businesses.

The Women's Football Association

The Women's Football Association was founded in England in 1971. Women's soccer was then officially recognized by Italy, Belgium, Switzerland, Iceland, Poland, and Yugoslavia. In 1974, the German National Association established its first national championship for German Women's Football. A professional league was introduced in 1990, and more than 400,000 German women played for clubs at all levels in 1992. Professional women's leagues were also founded in Norway, Sweden, and Italy.

The Asian Football Confederation organized the first Asian Women's Football Tournament in 1975. The tournament, held in Hong Kong, featured teams from Australia, New Zealand, Malaysia, Singapore and Thailand. A Japanese professional league was in the works in 1993.

Soccer in the Americas did not catch on as quickly as it did overseas. In Latin America, the male strangle hold on the sport was most difficult to escape. Paraguay specifically prohibited women from playing soccer, stating in its rule book that the game is "against their natural femininity."

The few South American nations in which women's soccer flourished were Argentina, Brazil, Venezuela, and Guatemala. Mexico was the first Latin American country to allow its women's clubs into the men's organization. The popularity of the sport was never more evident than in 1971, when 100,000 spectators showed up at Aztec Stadium in Mexico City for the unofficial World Championship for Women. Teams came from England, France, Italy, Denmark, Czechoslovakia to participate.

Slow Acceptance in the U.S.

In the United States, sports such as men's American football, basketball, and baseball made it difficult for women's soccer to gain popularity. Women's sports, in general, rarely draw the crowds that are common in Europe and Asia. Case in point: There is no professional women's basketball league in the United States, but the U.S. women playing in the European league are considered superstars.

The American Ladies' Soccer Organization was founded in 1974 in Los Angeles, but it never reached the membership it expected. Other short-lived leagues and organizations sprung up in California and the Northeast, but none with the magnitude of similar clubs in Europe.

American schoolchildren in the 1970s joined youth soccer teams in record numbers, but once those young players reached the college level, they had little incentive to continue. Collegiate soccer in the United States was popular in pockets, but rarely made headlines or television highlights. And there was no place to turn after college except Europe.

It wasn't until 1980 that a women's high school soccer All-America team was named, and the National Collegiate Athletic Association sponsored women's soccer for the first time. Seventy-seven colleges fielded programs.

Expanding Collegiate Competition

Anson Dorrance vowed to change the U.S. attitude toward women's soccer, and would come to be known as the dean of women's college soccer coaches. Dorrance was born in Bombay, India, and lived in Kenya, Ethiopia, Malaysia, Belgium, and Switzerland before landing at the University of North Carolina (UNC) in 1971.

He saw, in all his travels, the possibilities for women's soccer and figured there was no reason he couldn't transfer that excitement to American soil. Dorrance graduated from UNC in 1974 and began coaching the school's men's soccer team in 1977.

Dorrance established a women's program in 1979, and won his first national title two years later. He went on to win 10 of the next 11 national championships. In 14 years, the UNC women's team never lost more than two games a season, compiling a 252-8-9 record.

Because of his success at the college level, *U.S. Soccer* named Dorrance its national women's coach in 1986. He infused youth and speed to the U.S. women's national team, and almost immediately turned Team USA into a world power. Under Dorrance, America's teams won 41 games, lost 15, and tied four en route to the 1991 world title.

The U.S. victory over Norway was historic, and Dorrance said he hoped it set the stage for the future of the sport. Another women's world championship is scheduled for 1995. "When they start listing world champions in women's soccer, the United States is at the top of that list," he said. "That's a thrill."

College programs in the United States numbered more than 300 in 1993, and 82 of those were at the Division I level. Participation is swelling at the high schools, as well. A 1992 survey by the National Federation of State High School Associations revealed that 135,302 girls played soccer in the 1991-92 school year, an increase of 13,580 from the year before. It was the highest increase among all sports.

5.6 Million U.S. Women Players

In all, 5.6 million U.S. females were registered soccer players in 1993. The growth of soccer at the high school and collegiate level pleases Dorrance. "It's the fastest growing NCAA team sport," he said. "Because of the growing popularity of soccer, it definitely has a chance to be the No. 1 women's collegiate sport. There is more investment in scholarships in the sport and more marketing involved. That says something in itself."

The U.S. collegiate programs also attract foreign athletes. "If you are a lady 18-22 years of age, and you want to be a big-time player, then you should be at a college here playing, whether you are Swedish, German, or Italian," Dorrance said.

Despite the strong college system, there are few post-school opportunities in the United States for women who play soccer. Like the top U.S. men, talented American women are forced to take their skills overseas to professional leagues in Germany and Sweden. Michelle Akers-Stahl, the top scorer in U.S. team history and winner of the Golden Boot award at the 1991 world championships, was one of several U.S. players on a European professional roster in 1992.

Entering the 21st century, soccer leaders are optimistic about the future of the women's game on an international level. Though women's soccer will not be a medal sport at the 1996 Olympics in Atlanta, the Fédération Internationale de Football Association (FIFA) pledged a commitment to women's soccer and its future.

Recognition by FIFA

On October 22, 1992, FIFA hosted its first-ever women's football seminar in Zurich, Switzerland. Soccer officials from 39 nations attended the conference. Among the resolutions passed was one to support the participation of women in soccer at the 1996 Olympics.

In his opening remarks, FIFA president Joao Havelange said: "FIFA's first seminar on women's football heralds the dawn of a new era in a branch of our sport which played Cinderella for a little too long. Those of us where were fortunate enough to attend the Women's World Championship in the People's Republic of China last year witnessed sport in every sense of the word." He continued, "Let us hope we will find ways of consolidating the ladies' championship demonstration of blue-blooded football so that less advanced countries may catch up on their sporting sisters without further delay."

According to Poul Hyldgaard, chairman of the FIFA Committee for Women's Football, the stiffest challenge facing women's soccer hasn't changed since the 1800s: Societal differences in views toward women. As long as people around the globe consider physical, aggressive play "inappropriate" for women, soccer will lag behind tennis and gymnastics.

FIFA officials studied the women's game, compared it to the men's game, and came up with several conclusions:

1. Women's soccer tends to be more adventurous and attack oriented, while the men's game is more defensive and calculated. The women's offensive approach is appealing to fans, who prefer action to defense.

2. Women play to win while men play not to lose. Again, the offensive mindset versus the defensive.

3. Women run much more than men during the game, created less dead time. That is good for the fans, but more tiring for referees.

Marketing an Image

The FIFA convention addressed the image of female soccer players and proposed ways to promote the sport. The report read: "In what is uncontestably essentially a male-dominated society, female athletes need to strike a delicate balance in order to be socially acceptable and to project the right sympathetic image to the media.

"To fit this media image," the report concluded, "the modern sportswoman tends to be aesthetically athletic, a media-acceptable figure such as many from the world of tennis, rather than the image projected by many current track athletes and swimmers."

While the statement may seem sexist in itself, marketing expert Keith Cooper added: "If we wish women's football to be socially successful, we must not be surprised if that society requires its players to present a certain pre-supposed, even if prejudiced, personality image."

There were suggestions to play women's games as "curtain raisers" for men's games in order to increase exposure. National soccer associations were urged to send periodic bulletins about women's soccer to newspapers and television stations. FIFA promised to seek sponsors for women's events. In fact, some female players had signed endorsements with sporting goods firms in the early 1990s.

But it is attitudes that are hardest to change. In the United States, members of the men's U.S. national team receive health insurance and are under contract for salaries as high as $75,000. The U.S. women, world champions, have no health insurance and receive only $10 per diem on their road trips.

"I'm real optimistic about the development of the women's game internationally," said Akers-Stahl. "But women still aren't treated the same. Soccer is still seen as a men's game, and that will take many years to change."

Hard as they try, women's soccer leaders realize they might never reach the size audience or international fervor the men's game receives. But that will not stop they from trying. They wouldn't want to disappoint women like Helen Clark.

10: OLYMPIC SOCCER

Soccer and the Olympic Games have been linked in a strange, sometimes stormy, relationship throughout the 20th Century, but there is evidence that they may be on the same wavelength when the new millennium begins.

Although soccer has been an Olympic sport since the Games of 1900 (officially since 1908), it has faced an uncertain status throughout much of its Olympic history. Basically, the ideals of the Olympic movement have not always been in concert with those of the soccer playing nations or the International Soccer Federation (FIFA).

Among the obstacles which have prevented a smooth relationship, four seem most important: 1) The conflict between the Olympics and the World Cup as soccer's championship event; 2) the changing definitions of amateurism as a condition for competing in the Games; 3) the different soccer structures employed by East and West Europe in the four decades immediately after World War II; and 4) the level of competition sought by the Games and the participating nations.

The Olympics didn't have to compete with the World Cup until 1930, but it was the games of 1924 and 1928 which showcased Uruguayan soccer and helped to fuel the creation of a soccer world championship. Today, FIFA has no desire to see the Olympic soccer final approach the World Cup in stature or significance; hence the

International Olympic Committee and the International Soccer Federation continue to search for ways to keep the sport in the Games. Both sides must compromise.

In a similar vein, the disagreement over the definition of an amateur was not a problem early in Olympic history, but soccer's presence as a sport helped to raise the issue as early as the 1920s.

At that time Great Britain withdrew not just from the Games soccer tournament but also from FIFA in a dispute over compensation to competing players. Because soccer had so quickly become professional in much of the world, the Olympic version of the sport was already declining by the 1936 Games, and its future was in question.

Immediately after World War II, the sports world faced the question of East European socialism's sporting definitions. Nowhere was the dichotomy between Western professional and Communist "amateurism" more clearly demonstrated than on Olympic soccer fields.

From 1952 to 1980 every gold medal was captured by an East European nation as the tournament became a showcase for the political ideals of the Communists. By the 1970s the major soccer playing countries of the world disregarded the Games. Many did not bother to enter their amateur teams, which could not hope to compete against entries from the East.

The IOC realized the problem as the soccer gold medal lost its value as a true championship test. In the last two decades of the 20th Century the IOC and FIFA have sought compromise in the definition of allowable participants.

In 1984 there was the first breakthrough as some Western European nations used professional players in qualifying competition and then sent the pros to Los Angeles. France won the gold medal with such a team, a turning point in Olympic history, even though the Eastern Europeans had stayed home to boycott the Los Angeles Olympiad.

In 1988, Seoul hosted the first Olympic soccer tournament open to full-fledged pros, but FIFA imposed certain conditions. The strong soccer-playing countries of the world were not allowed to certify players who had taken part in World Cup play, while emerging soccer nations could choose anyone. Russia won that gold medal against a strong Brazilian side, and the way was paved for continuing change.

The 1992 Games in Barcelona were staged with more limits on the competitors. Again, full-scale pros could take part, but FIFA now moved to make Olympic soccer a part of its worldwide youth-to-World Cup tournament structure.

Having created championships for 17-Under and 20-Under players, FIFA saw the Olympics as a perfect slot for 23-Under players and mandated that age group for the most recent Games. When crowds in Spain fell below expectations, both the IOC and the International Soccer Federation sought further review.

By 1996, in Atlanta, it is expected that Olympic soccer will be open to players 23-Under from across the globe, with the new condition that each nation may add three players of any age to its squad. The IOC hopes that will attract some stars to compete for the gold medal. FIFA seems willing to allow the change, because the teams will still not be full national sides, hence the Olympic final not be a replication of the World Cup championship game.

As part of that compromise, it is also expected that the IOC will allow women's soccer as a gold medal sport in the next American Olympics. That will serve two purposes: first, to extend the range of soccer in the Olympics; second, to afford the United States an opportunity to promote the game in its own country.

One of the paradoxes of soccer development in America is that it is one game in which women have had the greater international success. The United States won the initial FIFA Women's World Championship in China in 1991 and are strong contenders for the gold medal in 1996.

That latest compromise can also be seen as a move on the part of both the Olympics and the world soccer establishment to keep the sport in the forefront of the quadrennial summer games. Despite all of the tribulations, that has never really been a problem.

In fact, soccer's success at attracting spectators to Olympic competitions is one reason why FIFA and the IOC have struggled to keep the sport alive in the Games. Even the 1976 Games in Canada and the 1984 competition in Los Angeles saw soccer matches played to packed stadia in countries where the game has never regularly attracted major audiences.

In part, that success can be easily enough explained: soccer tickets were easy to get in comparison to the higher-profile Olympic events like basketball, gymnastics, and track and field, all of which attract the large North American interest.

But FIFA, certainly, was impressed in particular by crowds of over 100,000 in the Pasadena Rose Bowl during the Los Angeles Games. That attendance is often cited as a reason why the 1996 World Cup was awarded to the United States.

Over the years, Olympic soccer has gone through three distinct eras: The pre-World War II era, dominated initially by Great Britain, eventually served as the platform for South America's emergence as a soccer power and, as a consequence, to the birth of the World Cup; the period from 1951 to 1980, dominated by eastern European Communist nations winning every tournament, while powerful Western European countries like Great Britain and Germany stopped bothering to enter; the modern "professional" Games, starting with Los Angeles and continuing to this day.

The early Olympic era can easily be misunderstood as one when times were simpler and competition more romantic. That may be true of the first four championships (1900 to 1912), when club teams sometimes represented countries and when competitors were likely all gentlemen sportsmen. Great Britain won the gold in 1900, 1908, and 1912, but didn't field a team in 1904 when St. Louis played host to the Games. That tournament featured exhibition club teams from Canada and the United States, with the Canadians winning the title.

By 1920, however, the era of the romantic amateur and soccer-as-diversion was over. The final of those Antwerp Games was the first to be disrupted by dispute, as a Czechoslovakian team walked off the field and allowed Belgium to take the gold medal by default. In 1924 the British, still acknowledged by all as the world soccer leaders, withdrew over another dispute, perhaps slightly devaluing Uruguay's first gold medal.

There was no such question about the 1928 gold, however; the Uruguayans again prevailed with a side that captured the imagination of onlookers

and signalled a new era for the world game. The same country would host—and win—the first World Cup, the tournament which quickly replaced the Olympics as the true world championship of the sport.

The creation of the World Cup—and the fact that America hosted the 1932 Games in far-away Los Angeles—combined to keep soccer out of those Olympics, but they were part of the 1936 Berlin Games, where Italy, not the host, proved the winning Fascist nation.

Hitler's Germans were surprisingly beaten by Norway in the quarterfinal, while Great Britain—back in Olympic soccer—also crashed at that stage, losing to Poland. Although the victorious Italians weren't the same squad that dominated World Cup soccer during the era, they did have the benefit of being led by the legendary Vittorio Pozzo, architect of the world championship side.

The post-War Olympics had one Western European champion—and a glorious one at that—before the Games became the exclusive property of the "state socialist" revolutionaries. Sweden's 1948 winners in London were built around one of the great attacking trios in soccer history, Gunnar Gren, Gunnar Nordahl, and Nils Liedholm, all of who were snapped up by Italian clubs for their professional careers.

Nordahl, whose brothers Bertil and Knut also played with the gold medal Swedes, went from IFK Norkopping to international goal-scoring fame, while Gren was to become a similar hero in Italy. Liedholm has had the longest career in his adopted land, serving as one of Italy's top coaches after the end of his playing career.

After 1948, however, all of the stars were East European. Some of them were brilliant, even if they were winning gold medals considered less valuable than a World Cup trophy. The first great Olympic team was Hungary's 1952 side that contained the heart of the "Magic Magyars," widely regarded as the world's best team in the early 1950s. Goalkeeper Gyula Groscis, the great midfielder Nandor Hidegkuti, defender Jozsef Bozsik, and forwards Sandor Kocsis, Ferenc Puskas, and Zoltan Czibor were all members of the team that won the 1952 final.

The Soviet Union, anchored by their goalkeeping legend Lev Yashin, won the 1956 tournament in Melbourne, and Yugoslavia prevailed in Rome in 1960 before the gold went again to Hungary in 1964 and 1968. By now it was a foregone conclusion that the gold would be won by the Communists because they were entering their full national teams to compete against amateurs from the rest of the world.

Although the number of Olympic entrants was steadily rising—from 25 in 1952 to 68 in 1968—the tournament continued to play second fiddle to the World Cup. It is worth noting that not even the great Hungarians, admittedly the victims of a monumental upset in the 1954 final, won a World Cup during the span when their teams were dominating the Games. Further evidence came in the form of the European Nations Championship, a tournament that had only two East European winners, the Soviet Union (1960) and Czechoslovakia (1976), in an era when Olympic Games medals routinely went East.

To understand what was missing, one needs only look at the great players who never competed in the Olympics. Although Brazil dominated the World Cup with victories in 1958, 1962 and 1970, men like Pelé, Garrincha, Carlos Alberto, and Rivelino were never a part of the Olympic Games.

Similarly, Great Britain became so disturbed by the whole question of amateurism that they eliminated such all designations in their own soccer organizations, even though that meant the end of their historic FA Amateur Cup competition.

Equally important in terms of the direction world soccer was moving, television recognized that Olympic soccer was a pale imitation of the World Cup. At a time when the United States was beginning its infatuation with the Games, Olympic soccer was rarely, if ever, seen on American television screens. That wasn't because the United States failed to qualify. In fact, the Americans were fairly regular participants in Olympic soccer. It was because the Olympics weren't delivering soccer at the same level as the other Games sports.

There was room for one more super side, however, the 1972 Polish gold medalists. The Munich Games served as the "coming out party" for the Poland team that would finish third in the 1974 World Cup and perform well again in Argentina in 1978.

Players like defender Jerzy Gorgon, midfielder Kazimierz Deyna, and strikers Wlodzimierz Lubanski and Robert Gadocha played in the 1972 final. Andrezj Szarmach was the leading Olympic goal-getter in 1976, although East Germany lifted the gold medal that time. A Czech victory in the boycotted 1980 Games completed the era in Moscow.

By then Western Europeans had begun to look at the Games in a slightly different light. True, France had kept its young star Michel Platini an amateur so that he could compete in Montreal in 1976, but by the 1984 Games there was no longer any desire to avoid confrontation over the issue of pros in the soccer tournament. France chose a team that included well-known players from its top league and eventually won the gold. The appearance of acknowledged professionals created no stir in Los Angeles and opened the door for outright professionalism in Seoul.

The fact that the pros—albeit not those with World Cup experience—could represent the top countries meant that the 1988 Games attracted a strong list of entries. But if proof were needed that this wasn't the World Cup one needed to look no further than the opening round. Zambia, unknown outside Africa, created the sensation of the tournament by thrashing Italy 4-0.

The Italians eventually reached the semifinals before losing to the champions from the Soviet Union, a side which had managed to blend promising youngsters with some veterans. Brazil, too, sent a strong side, and the goal-scoring leader of the Games proved to be Romario, now one of the top players in the world game.

That might have been what the IOC wanted, but FIFA is cautious about any tournament that might detract from its money-spinning World Cup. As a result, when FIFA set the rules for 1992 they limited players to 23-and-under, a logical decision in terms of their own world tournament programs, but one which proved unsatisfactory at the final stage.

Spain, a nation where soccer regularly attracts huge crowds, stayed away from the competition, apparently regarding it as nothing more than an age-group event. Fortunately for the organizers the home country progressed all the way to the gold medal, hence the final was played before a capacity Nou Camp Stadium crowd. But there were worries that without the home side the final might have been contested before the empty spaces that had greeted earlier games.

The compromise for 1996, perhaps combining the entry of the expanding-women's game with the presence of some designated over-age stars, may serve to keep Olympic soccer on track, but the Games and soccer have approached a crucial turning point.

That was clearly seen when the 1992 basketball tournament was won by an American "dream team" of National Basketball Association professionals. Having opened the doors, the IOC leaders seem committed to attracting all of the top players for its Games.

FIFA, however, remains jealously protective of its own championship, arguably the only world sporting event which is bigger than the Olympics. The shape of future Games may be determined by the degree to which these two powerful sports organizations are able to manage the creative tension that exists between them.

Appendix A: Soccer Timeline

A Chronology of Important Events

Note:
For a more detailed narrative of the history of the sport, please see Chapter 1

c. 2500 BC

Chinese Emperor Huang-Ti believed to have drawn up the first rules for *tsu chu*.

1700 BC-200 AD

Tsu chu documented in China.

c. 600 BC

a) Documentation of a Greek football game, the forerunner of *episkyros*.
b) The Roman game *harpastum* played.

1st Century BC

Form of indigenous football believed played in Ireland.

1st-5th Century AD

Roman handball and football games spread throughout the empire.

2nd Century

Football believed played in Dalmatia, possibly inspired by Roman games.

217

A Roman army team defeated by a select team of British, though this match is assumed to be mythical.

5th Century

Celtic peoples of Britannia and Gaul may have adopted handball-football as legacy of departed Romans.

6th Century

A pre-Columbian ball game including elements of football depicted by artists in Guatemala.

7th-11th Century

Indigenous football games of Normandy, Brittany, Picardy, Cornwall, Wales, Scotland, Ireland, and English towns develop.

12th Century-c. 1830

Annual Shrovetide celebrations in England include game of football, documented in 1175 by William Fitzstephen.

1154-89

During reign of Henry II *ludus pilae* receives patronage from established classes in England.

c. 1250

A legendary hero, St. Hugh of Lincoln, displays unprecedented ball control skills.

1314

Edward II bans football.

1349

Edward III bans football.

1389

Richard II bans football.

1423

Football in Scotland supported by deposed House of Stewart.

1425

Players paid for the first time (4 pence) by the Prior of Bicester.

1457

James II of Scotland bans football.

1491

James IV of Scotland bans football.

16th Century

a) Interest in football throughout Britain expands rapidly.
b) *Calcio,* the Florentine game, institutionalized and played annually, in the Piazza della Novere.
c) More denunciations by the English crown.

1527

"The great foot balle" supported in Ireland by Statutes of Galway while other sports forbidden.

17th Century

The pre-Columbian ball game becomes extinct with the destruction of Mexican culture.

1609

Football played in the Virginia colony.

c. 1620

Football organized at Trinity and St. John's Colleges, Cambridge.

1654

Oliver Cromwell attends a hurling match.

1681

Charles II sponsors a servants' football match.

1720

a) A Welsh football competition between local teams described by Anna Beynon, a fan.
b) Transfer of players first documented in the poems of Irishman Matthew Concanen.

c. 1750

Football established in Lancashire.

c. 1800

Interest in the game wanes throughout Britain.

1814

Football organized at Harrow.

1823

Pupil at Rugby School breaks school rules and runs with the ball, leading to the beginning of rugby football.

1827

a) Unsportsmanlike conduct in football at Eton is widely publicized, drawing negative reaction to the game.
b) Annual football contest at Harvard begins.

1845

Referees introduced at Eton.

1846

Rugby School Rules drawn up establishing forerunner of modern rugby game.

1848

Cambridge University Rules, precursor of the Football Association Laws of 1863, drawn up.

1857

Sheffield F.C., the first football club, founded and Sheffield Rules written.

1859

Forest Football Club, the first devoted exclusively to the dribbling game and forerunner of Wanderers F.C., founded in northeast London.

1860

Rules approximating the association game introduced in the USA.

1861-67

Clubs spring up throughout England but rules still vary.

c. 1862

Sheffield becomes center of football activity in northern England, London in the south.

1862

a) Rules drawn up for Old Etonians vs. Old Harrovians at Cambridge.
b) Notts County Football Club, oldest club still in the Football League, founded in Nottingham.

1863

The watershed year in soccer history:
a) The Football Association founded in London to promote and regulate the game in England and rules are drawn up.
b) The Blackheath club resigns from the new organization over issues of carrying and hacking, resulting in the split between rugby and soccer.

c. 1865

Game introduced in Africa by Englishmen via Port Elizabeth, South Africa.

1865

Tapes first stretched across goalmouth width eight feet above the ground.

1867

a) Queen's Park Football Club, the oldest Scottish club, founded in Glasgow.

b) Buenos Aires Football Club, the first club in South America, founded in Argentina by British railway workers.

1869

Goal kick introduced to replace kick out.

1870

a) First match between representative teams from England and Scotland.
b) Association rules first played in Germany.
c) Game introduced in Australia by British coal miners.

1871

a) The Football Association Challenge Cup (F.A. Cup) launched.
b) The Rugby Football Union founded, marking the final break between rugby and soccer.

1872

a) First official international between England and Scotland in Glasgow.
b) Wanderers F.C. wins the first F.A. Cup.
c) Game introduced in France by English sailors at Le Havre.
d) Corner kick introduced.
c) Official size of ball fixed.

1873

a) Scottish Football Association founded.
b) Scottish F.A. Cup launched.
c) Wrexham Football Club, the first Welsh club, founded.

1874

Umpires introduced by the Football Association.

1875

First club in Portugal founded in Lisbon by British residents.

1876

a) Crossbars replace tapes across goalmouth.
b) KB Copenhagen, the first Danish club, founded.

1877

The Football Association and the Sheffield Football Association agree on rules.

1878

a) First game under lights played in Sheffield.
b) Whistles used by English referees.
c) Game introduced in Ireland via Belfast.

1879

a) Haarlem Football Club, the first Dutch club, founded.
b) Game introduced in Hungary.

c. 1880

Game introduced in West Africa via the Gold Coast.

1880

a) Shinguards sanctioned by the Football Association.
b) Irish Football Association founded.
c) Irish Cup launched.

1882

a) First Uruguayan club founded at Montevideo University by a British professor.
b) International Football Association Board established.
c) Two-handed throw-in introduced.

d) SK Slavia, Bohemia's first club, founded.

1883

Home International Championship, the world's first full international competition, begins.

1884

American Football Association, first governing body in the United States, founded in Newark, NJ.

1885

a) Professionalism legalized in England.
b) First North American international: United States vs. Canada in Newark.

1886

Caps first awarded in England for international appearances.

1887

a) Game introduced in Russia via Orekhovo by British textile workers.
b) Hamburger SV, the oldest German club still in league competition, founded in Hamburg.

1888

The Football League, world's first national league, founded in England.

1889

a) Royal Netherlands Football Association, the oldest F.A. outside the United Kingdom, founded.
b) Preston North End F.C. wins the first Football League championship and the F.A. Cup for the first "double."
c) Vienna Cricket and Football Club (Cricketer), the influential pioneer club of Austria, founded.

d) A representative eleven from England tours Germany.
e) Valparaiso Football Club, the oldest club in Chile, founded by British residents.

1890

a) Game introduced in Finland by British residents.
b) F.C. Internazionale, the first Italian club, founded in Turin.

1891

a) Referees and linesmen replace umpires in the Football League.
b) Goal nets introduced in the Football League.
c) Game introduced in Greece by British sailors.

1892

a) Division II of the Football League founded.
b) Game introduced in Singapore by the British.

1893

a) Argentine Football Association, the oldest F.A. in South America, founded, and an Argentine championship, South America's first, introduced.
b) First attempt to organize a players' union in England fails.
c) Professionalism legalized in Scotland.

1894

a) Game introduced in Brazil by English ex-schoolboy Charles Miller.
b) Game introduced in Bulgaria.

1895

a) The F.A.'s of Chile, Belgium, and Switzerland founded.
b) CR Flamengo, the oldest club in Brazil, founded in Rio de Janeiro.

1896

a) An unofficial demonstration match is played at the first modern Olympic Games in Athens.
b) Amateur internationals played between some British countries and German, Austrian, and Bohemian selections.
c) Oruro Royal Club, the first club in Bolivia, founded.

1897

a) Concept of "intentional" introduced in the rules.
b) Corinthians Football Club tours South America and South Africa.

1898

a) Promotion and relegation system introduced in the Football League.
b) First players' union organized successfully in England.
c) Italian Football Association founded.
d) Athletic Bilbao, the oldest Spanish club still in competition, founded by British engineers.

1900

The F.A.'s of Germany and Uruguay founded.

1901

a) 110,820 spectators watch F.A. Cup final at Crystal Palace, London.
b) the F.A.'s of Bohemia and Hungary founded.

1902

a) First tragic crowd disaster occurs at Ibrox Park, Glasgow: 25 dead and 500 injured.
b) In Vienna, Austria and Hungary engage in first non-British full international.
c) A Mexican championship, the first in North America, introduced.

1904

a) FIFA founded in Paris by France, Belgium, Denmark, Netherlands, Spain, Sweden, and Switzerland.
b) F.A.'s of Austria and Sweden founded.

1905

Argentina and Uruguay engage in first South American international in Buenos Aires.

1906

a) Laws of the Game substantially rewritten.
b) Cracovia Football Club, the oldest club in Poland, founded in Cracow.
c) Sao Paulo League founded in Brazil.

1908

a) England 'A' team tours outside Home countries for the first time, to Austria, Hungary, and Bohemia.
b) First official Olympic soccer competition.

1910

A Philippine national championship, the first in Asia, introduced.

1912

All-Russian Football Union founded.

1913

a) United States Soccer Football Federation founded.
b) China and the Philippines engage in first Asian international in Manila.

1914

a) First Brazilian international, against Argentina in Buenos Aires.

b) Brazilian Sports Federation founded.

1916

a) South American Football Confederation founded.
b) South American Championship, the first regional competition between nations, launched.

1921

Egyptian Football Association founded.

1923

Wembley Stadium, London, Mecca of world soccer, opens with celebrated "White Horse Final."

1924

a) Uruguay becomes first non-European nation to win Olympic soccer tournament.
b) Scandinavian Championship, the first non-British European regional competition between nations, launched.

1927

a) International Cup, the first regional competition between nations on the continent of Europe, launched.
b) Mitropa Cup, the first international club competition, launched.
c) First radio broadcast of a soccer match: Arsenal vs. Sheffield United.

1928

a) Uruguay wins Olympic soccer tournament a second time.
b) Home countries leave FIFA over issue of part-time payments to amateurs.

1929

Balkan Cup launched.

1930

Uruguay wins first World Cup, in Uruguay.

1931

Argentina becomes first South American country to adopt professionalism.

1932

Substitution first sanctioned for consenting national teams.

1933

Numbers first worn by players in England.

1934

Italy wins second World Cup, in Italy.

1937

a) A world's record 149,547 spectators watch England vs. Scotland at Hampden Park, Glasgow.
b) First television broadcast of a soccer match: Preston North End vs. Sunderland in F.A. Cup final.
c) Official weight of the ball increased from 13-15 oz. to 14-16 oz..

1938

a) Italy wins third World Cup, in France.
b) Laws of the Game rewritten.

1940

Central American Championship launched.

1946

Home countries rejoin FIFA.

1950

a) World's largest stadium, the Maracana, Rio de Janeiro, opened at fourth World Cup.
b) World Cup final at Maracana attracts 199,850 spectators, still a world record for any game.
c) Uruguay wins fourth World Cup, in Brazil.
d) Most famous upset of all time: England loses to the United States 1-0 in Belo Horizonte.

1954

a) West Germany wins fifth World Cup, in Switzerland.
b) Union of European Football Associations and Asian Football Confederation founded.

1955

a) European Cup launched.
b) Fairs Cup launched.

1956

a) Asian Nations' Cup launched.
b) Stanley Matthews elected first European Footballer of the Year.

1957

a) African Football Confederation founded.
b) African Nations' Cup launched.

1958

a) Brazil wins fifth World Cup, in Sweden.
b) European Nations' Cup launched.

1959

Alfredo Di Stefano elected European Footballer of the Year a second time.

1960

a) Copa Libertadores launched.
b) Real Madrid wins fifth consecutive European Cup.
c) The unofficial Intercontinental Cup launched.
d) European Cup Winners' Cup launched.
e) U.S.S.R. wins first European Nations' Cup.

1961

Maximum wage abolished in England.

1962

Brazil wins seventh World Cup, in Chile.

1963

World club attendance record set for Flamengo-Fluminense derby at Maracana, Rio de Janeiro: 177,656.

1964

a) African Champions' Cup launched.
b) Worst soccer disaster in history: 301 killed in riot following Peru vs. Argentina game, in Lima.
c) Spain wins second European Nations' Cup.

1965

The Football League in England sanctions use of one nominated substitute in case of injury.

1966

England wins eighth World Cup, in England.

1967

a) Use of two substitutes sanctioned by FIFA .
b) CONCACAF Champions' Cup launched.
c) Asian Champions' Cup launched.

1968

a) Italy wins third European Nations' Cup.
b) Juventus pays first million-dollar transfer fee to Varese for Pietro Anastasi.
c) Copa Interamericana launched.

1969

a) El Salvador and Honduras wage the Fútbol War.
b) Pelé scores 1000th goal.

1970

a) Brazil wins ninth World Cup, in Mexico, and becomes first nation to win three world titles.
b) Estudiantes wins third Copa Libertadores in succession.

1971

a) Tostao elected first American (Latin American) Footballer of the Year.
b) Use of five substitutes legalized by consenting clubs.
c) North American Soccer League formed.

1972

West Germany wins fourth European Football Championship.

1973

Ajax wins third European Cup in succession.

1974

a) West Germany wins tenth World Cup, in West Germany.
b) Johan Cruyff elected European Footballer of the Year for record third time.

1975

a) African Cup Winners' Cup launched.
b) Independiente wins fourth Copa Libertadores in succession and sixth altogether.
c) Pelé signs contract for record $3.5 million with New York Cosmos.

1976

a) Bayern Munchen wins third European Cup in succession.
b) Czechoslovakia wins fifth European Football Championship.
c) Asian Football Confederation thrown into chaos over China and Israel questions.

1977

World transfer market thrown into chaos by rising American purchasing power.

1978

Argentina wins eleventh World Cup, in Argentina.

1982

Italy wins its third World Cup, defeating West Germany in Spain.

1984

North American Soccer League folds.

1986

Argentina defeats the Netherlands for its second World Cup victory.

1989

East and West Germany unified.

1990

West Germany triumphs over Argentina in Italia '90.

1991

a) U.S. Women's National Team wins first Women's World Championship, in China.
b) U.S.S.R. dissolves, creating numerous nationalistic teams.

1992

a) Yugoslavia dissolves into Serbia, Bosnia, and Croatia.
b) Czechoslovakia separates into Slovinia and the Czech Republic.

1993

Maradona announces his retirement as a soccer player.

1994

World Cup comes to the United States for the first time.

Appendix B: Glossary

A Dictionary of Soccer Terms and Concepts

Advantage Clause

A discretionary decision of the referee, whereby he may refrain from stopping play for an infringement if the offending team would be given an advantage, e.g., when a foul is committed against a team mounting an apparent attack. Application of the advantage clause is irreversible.

Amateur

Ninety-seven percent of all the world's adult registered players are officially amateur in status, and two-thirds of FIFA's national membership remains exclusively amateur. The definition of an amateur, however, has been stretched considerably since the days when it simply meant "one who receives no compensation for playing." The present definition, according to FIFA regulations, is as follows

"Players who have been refunded their actual expenses for travel, necessary maintenance and hotel charges and who, in special cases, have been specifically authorized by their national association to receive expenses for equipment, physical preparation and insurance against accidents during play and whilst travelling [or those] who receive an allowance for wages lost [providing] such allowance ... be an equitable proportion of the actual wages of the player which

have been lost ... are considered to be amateur players.

"Players who receive no compensation whatsoever are still amateur (though FIFA neglects to mention this), as are all players whose compensation is less than that which is outlined in the definition."

Few controversial issues have dogged soccer authorities so mercilessly as that of amateurism. From the 1870s, when the question of professionals was first raised, until the 1920s, when professionalism began to spread in Europe, the issue was primarily confined to Great Britain, especially England and Scotland.

In Victorian England, the amateur ideal was an important element of the sporting gentlemen's mystique, and men from the leisurely classes who had given birth to modern soccer jealously guarded the ideal. In 1885, professionalism was finally sanctioned by the Football Association in London, and the game slowly but steadily became dominated by the working classes whose only hope of full participation in the game depended on professional status.

The amateurs, for the most part upper-class public school graduates and middle-class professionals, retreated into collective self-preservation. Still under the Football Association banner, some amateur clubs organized the F.A.

Amateur Cup in 1893-94, the first exclusively amateur competition in a professional environment.

In 1907, The Football Association ordered all county associations (still bastions of the amateur ideal) to admit professional clubs, but the Surrey and Middlesex associations refused and led a movement to sever amateur soccer interests in England from the Football Association. Thus the Amateur Football Association, the world's first all-amateur body, was formed.

Its split with the F.A. lasted only until 1914, when it agreed to come under the F.A.'s aegis. As an entity, the Amateur Football Association remained intact, changing its name in 1934 to the Amateur Football Alliance, but in 1974 the F.A. Amateur Cup was discontinued when the F.A. decided not to differentiate between amateur and professional status in the future, citing the impossibility of distinguishing one from the other.

After World War I, the question arose on an international scale as professional clubs emerged in the republics of Western and Central Europe. Attention was focused on the Olympics, where the Victorian ideal was further represented by French as well as British administrators. The central issue now was that of "broken-time payments" (compensation for time lost from work).

FIFA coerced the International Olympic Committee into accepting players who had received broken-time payments in the 1924 games, and Great Britain and Denmark boycotted the proceedings in protest.

In 1928, when FIFA persisted, the four British football associations withdrew from FIFA altogether and did not rejoin until 1946. FIFA prevailed, and IOC resistance to broken-time payments for Olympic athletes slowly subsided over the years.

After World War II, the issue still centered on the Olympics, but the geographical focus switched to Eastern Europe, where professionalism was not officially recognized by doctrinaire regimes.

The fact remained, however, that top Eastern European players were "state-sponsored," and devoted as much time to the game as did professionals in other countries.

Furthermore, several Eastern-bloc states fielded virtually the same national teams for both Olympic and World Cup competition, and since 1952 the Olympic gold medal in soccer has been won each time by an East European entrant. The world, especially Western Europe, protested and a solution to the problem has not yet been found.

One step in that direction was taken in 1978, however, when FIFA announced that in the future a player could not participate in both Olympic Games and World Cup during the course of his career.

Appeal

The modern Laws of the Game severely restrict players from approaching the referee and claiming that a foul be recognized or a decision changed. Before 1896, the year referees were given the power to penalize players, a foul was called and a punishment issued only if one of the offended team appealed to the referee to do so; the referee ignored the foul if no appeal was made. From 1896, a player's right to appeal was still guaranteed, but the former significance of the appeal was lost.

Gradually, appeals began to take the form of protests against referees' decisions, creating an increasing number of ugly scenes on the field. In 1924, this situation finally prompted the International Football Association Board to rule that informal inquiries of a referee's decision were allowed, but a player's inherent right to appeal no longer existed and dissent in any form would be regarded as an infringement of the Laws.

In 1935, this concept was incorporated directly into the Laws, and is now found in the form of Law XII's dissent clause.

Aqsaqtuk

An indigenous football game of eskimos in Canada and Alaska, which closely resembles soccer. The exact date of origin is unknown, but *aqsaqtuk* has been played for at least a few hundred years. Contested on snow or ice by two large teams of varying numbers, the object of the game is to keep the ball away from one's own goal.

The size of the two goals vary and are usually spotted many hundreds of yards apart. One Alaskan legend recounts a game played between two villages with goals ten miles from one another. A basically defensive posture seems a necessity over such a large expanse.

Balls are stuffed with moss, grass, or caribou hair. Some smaller balls are filled with sand. Men and women play together, and teams are sometimes divided between married and single people. At other times sides are arbitrarily chosen and games may be played between two villages or groups of villages.

Assist

In the North American Soccer League, a player whose pass to a teammate has immediately

Drawing by Buffin Island artist Tye

The Eskimo football game *Aqsaqtuk*

preceded his teammate's scoring a goal, or who has in some other way assisted directly in his teammate's scoring a goal, is credited with an assist.

According to NASL goalscoring tabulations, which are based on a point system, a player who makes an assist is awarded one point. Assist points are added to the two points awarded for each goal scored to arrive at an individual player's total.

The concept of an "assist" is borrowed from statistical procedures in professional basketball and ice hockey, and is not sanctioned by the International Football Association Board, nor is it found in senior competition outside the United States and Canada.

Association football

The traditional term, now more literary than colloquial, for the game of soccer. It is commonly understood in the United Kingdom, Eire, and the British Commonwealth, but has increasingly fallen out of general usage in recent decades, except in formal designations, e.g., Fédération Internationale de Football Association (FIFA), which translates as International Federation of Association Football.

Originating in the 1860s, the game administered by the Football Association in London came to be known as association football, as distinct from the game based on handling codes, which came to be known as rugby football. The term "soccer" is derived from the second syllable of the word "association."

The only non-British country to acquire the term on a widespread basis has been France.

Association rules

A term used primarily in reference to soccer during the first few decades after 1863—the date of the founding of the Football Association in London—to distinguish it from rugby, or handling, codes.

Attendances

The range of attendances for international matches is illustrated by the qualification rounds of the 1970 World Cup, in which the highest was 183,341 (Maracana Stadium, Rio de Janeiro, for Brazil vs. Paraguay in 1969), and the lowest was 500 (Municipal Stadium, Kansas City, MO, for USA vs. Bermuda in 1968).

World attendance record 199,850 (Brazil vs. Uruguay in World Cup final round, July 16, 1950, Maracana Stadium, Rio de Janeiro).

European attendance record 149,547 (Scotland vs. England in Home International Championship, April 17, 1937, Hampden Park, Glasgow).

World club attendance record 177,656 (Flamengo vs. Fluminense in Rio de Janeiro league match, August 1963, Maracana Stadium, Rio de Janeiro).

European club attendance record 146,433 (Celtic vs. Aberdeen in Scottish Cup final, April 24, 1937, Hampden Park, Glasgow).

North American attendance record 77,691 (Cosmos vs. Ft. Lauderdale in NASL divisional championship play-off, August 14, 1977, Giants Stadium, Meadowlands, NJ).

The unofficial African attendance record of 100,000 has been achieved more than once at both the Nasser Stadium, Cairo, and the Stade Ahmadou-Ahidjo, Yaounde.

The earliest attendance of 100,000 was achieved at the English F.A. Cup final of 1901 at the Crystal Palace ground, London, Tottenham Hotspur vs. Sheffield United. The actual figure was 110,820.

Away

See **Home and away.**

Away-goals rule

A tie-breaking calibration, which is used in certain competitions to determine the relative standing of two teams finishing equal on points in a league table or after home and away legs. There are two variations. A winner may result from 1) scoring a superior number of goals in away legs; or 2) accumulating a superior number of total "goals for" after doubling the number of goals scored in away legs.

Back door

The area adjacent to the goalpost on the opposite side of the goalmouth from which a cross or corner kick is being taken. A ball well placed at the "back door" is often disadvantageous to the goalkeeper.

Back-heel

A kick taken with the heel of the foot in order to move the ball to the rear of the kicker.

Back pass

A pass directed away from the opponent's goal.

Banana kick

A kick that "bends" or curves, as in a free kick around a wall of players. Its curvature is created by striking the ball with the side of the foot to give it a fast spin. In Brazil it's called *folha seca,* or "dry leaf."

Bicycle kick

Also known as **overhead volley.** An overhead kick with a scissors movement of the legs.

Perhaps the most exciting of all individual skills, it was made famous in Europe during the 1940s by Carlo Parola, the great center halfback of Juventus and Italy. In South America, the bicycle kick was perfected by Leonidas, the incomparable "Rubber Man" of Brazil during the 1930s. In Spanish, the kick is known popularly as chileza, in French retourne, in Portuguese bicicleta. *See also* **Overhead kick** and **scissors kick.**

Blind side

The side of a player or group of players that is away from the ball or the play.

Block tackle

See **Front block tackle.**

Box

The penalty area.

Carry

The goalkeeper's holding of the ball in his hands as a result of a save or interception, usually in preparation for a punt or throw. Carrying is unlawful outside the goalkeeper's own penalty area.

Since a 1967 ruling, the goalkeeper has been required to give up possession of the ball after four paces (usually by bouncing the ball on the ground). Previously, he was required only to release the ball from his hands (with a slight toss in the air) at least once every four paces, and before 1931 once every two paces. *See also* **Hands.**

Caution

Also known as **booking.** A referee's official warning to a player who has committed certain serious offenses. To administer a caution the referee must stop play and show the offending player a yellow card. The player is cautioned verbally, and his name is noted in what has become known as "the book."

All cautions must be reported by the referee to the committee under whose aegis the match is being played.

The Laws of the Game require that a player be cautioned for the following 1) entering or leaving the field of play unlawfully; 2) persistently infringing the Laws; 3) dissent from a referee's decision; 4) ungentlemanly conduct.

The yellow card policy was officially introduced by FIFA at the Olympic Games of 1968. *See also* **Send off.**

Center back

A primarily defensive position at the rear of a formation. It differs from that of center halfback because it is always deep-lying and may be one of two such positions on a team.

Center forward

Also known as **No. 9.** The player positioned in the middle of the forward line, whose function is primarily to score goals. This has been the glamour spot on the field since the early days of the game, though some modern formations have supplanted the center forward position with central strikers or inside forwards.

The oddest function of a center forward may be found in the archaic "echelon formation," in which the center forward is positioned at the point of a "V" setup, with both insides and wingers playing closer to the goal.

Center halfback

Also known as **No. 5** and **the pivot.** The middle position among halfbacks or on the midfield line. The center halfback is the most varied of all traditional positions on the field. Its function is pivotal, in that it can be both offensive and defensive, and sometimes encompasses most of the playing area.

Successful center halfbacks tend to possess unusual reserves of stamina, distribute with precision, and tackle with authority. Most formations have now dispensed with the traditional center half in favor of a deep-lying center back on midfield lines of two or four players.

Charge

Running into or leaning on an opponent with the full weight of one's body. Intentional, violent charges, other than a shoulder charge, are unlawful and draw the penalty of a direct free kick. *See also* **Shoulder charge.**

Chip

A delicately lofted kick that is usually placed over the head of a nearby defender. A chip is shorter than a standard lofted kick, and is considerably longer than an arcing flick. It may be either a pass or shot on goal.

Clearance

A kick, throw, or punch by a goalkeeper or a defending player that moves the ball out of his own penalty area or away from his own goal.

Corner kick

A direct free kick taken from within a corner area. It is awarded to an attacking team when the ball passes over the goal line of the defending team, other than into the goal, having last been played by one of the defending team. The kick is taken from that corner nearest to where the ball crossed over the goal line. Opposing players must be 10 yards from the ball when the kick is taken. A player who receives the ball direct from a corner kick cannot be offside.

Corner kicks were introduced in England by the Football Association in 1872. The 10-yard rule was added in 1914. Until 1924, corner kicks were "indirect."

Cross

Also known as **center.** A pass to the center of the field from either the left or right flank.

Crossbar

The horizontal beam that joins the goalposts. The lower edge of the crossbar must be eight feet (2.4 meters) from the ground, and its width and depth cannot exceed five inches (12 cm).

Crossbars were specifically forbidden in the first Laws of the Football Association in 1863. In subsequent years, a tape connecting the posts became prevalent throughout England, especially on public school grounds, but eventually the tapes gave way to crossbars.

The Sheffield Association required crossbars by the early 1870s. In 1875, the Football Association changed its rules to permit their use and in 1882, five years after the two associations merged, crossbars became obligatory for F. A. members.

Cup competition

A knockout tournament or series, in which the winning side is the only team to remain undefeated, as distinct from a league competition, in which the winning side is the team that has accumulated the most points and stands at the top of a table.

In most countries, cup competition allows clubs on all levels to play one another, regardless of divisional standing in the league. A lower division club has the opportunity to knock out a first division club, and it is this possibility that gives a cup competition its dramatic appeal.

Cup competitions are played throughout the course of the soccer season on alternating dates with the league schedule.

Cup competitions are relatively uncommon in most team sports, except in play-off series, but their tradition in soccer is almost as old as the modern game itself. This was the original form of competition devised by English organizers after the founding of the Football Association in 1863.

The first cup competition, the Football Association Challenge Cup (F.A. Cup), was launched in 1871, 17 years before the first English league.

As the game spread across Europe in the last decades of the nineteenth century, the knockout format was adopted more readily than league competition, though it gave way gradually to the rising popularity of leagues by World War I. Its prestige in the British Isles, however, has always remained high.

In England, the F.A. Cup often draws more enthusiastic support than the First Division of the Football League. In Wales, where a national league does not exist, the Welsh Cup takes on a significance all its own.

Central European countries, on the other hand, have seldom given their national cups more than secondary notice, even though the Union of European Football Associations introduced an international competition for all national cup winners, the European Cup Winners' Cup, in 1960. Competition in this tournament rekindled interest in cup competitions in other parts of Europe.

Cup competitions have also been organized in many nations of Africa, and a small number of Asian states have introduced their versions of national cups. In 1975, the African Football Confederation launched the annual African Cup Winners' Cup along the same lines as its European counterpart.

In Latin America, national cup competitions as adjuncts to league competitions are unknown, though some levels of league play are conducted on a knockout basis.

Dangerous ball

A ball that has been put in such a position that an attacking player or team may gain a definite advantage by playing it, or a ball put up for grabs that appears to give a player or team a scoring opportunity.

Dead ball

A ball that is stationary or one that has passed over either the goal line or touch line, and is out of play.

Deep-lying

The positioning of a player behind his normal area of play or to the rear of his team's formation, e.g., a deep-lying center forward or a deep-lying halfback.

Derby

A British term to indicate the games played by two local rivals. The Manchester derby, for example, refers to those matches played each year between Manchester United and Manchester City.

Direct free kick

A free kick from which a goal may be scored. It is awarded to the offended side for the following serious infringements kicking, tripping or throwing, jumping, charging violently, charging from behind other than when obstructed, striking, holding, and pushing. Handling violations also call for a direct free kick. *See also* **Free kick.**

Disallow

A ruling by the referee that nullifies an action on the field. A goal may be disallowed when a player on the attacking side commits an infringement before the ball crosses the goal line.

Distribute

After having gained possession, the act of passing or throwing the ball in an effort to initiate or continue an attacking action.

The term is commonly applied to goalkeepers, who "distribute" the ball to a teammate after making a save, or to halfbacks, who may be described as having well developed "distribution" skills.

Double

In most countries, the winning of the first division championship and the national cup competition in the same year. The term may also be used to indicate the winning of any two major competitions in the same year. A "treble" is the winning of three such honors.

Dribble

The act of moving the ball protectively and skillfully with one's feet, usually to advance the ball up or down the field or to avoid being tackled.

The art of dribbling has flourished and withered at different times throughout the history of the game. Its classical era was surely the 1870s, when English clubs, led by Wanderers F.C. and its influential captain, C.W. Alcock, put their emphasis staunchly on attack and fielded a seven-man forward line.

Dribbling had been primarily a product of the English public schools, from which most of the contemporary players of the day came. Holding onto the ball for as long as possible was encouraged and became a measure of one's skill as a player. Little attempt was made at passing. With only three defenders in Alcock's basic forma

tion, an enterprising forward could often be seen dribbling the ball with cunning down the length of the field to openly challenge a sparse defense.

Among the greatest dribblers were the legendary Robert Vidal, of Westminster and Oxford, and William Kenyon-Slaney, of Eton and Household Brigade.

Inevitably, the preoccupations of dribbling gave way to the virtues of the short pass, which was to become a mainstay of all tactical innovations to come. The prime movers away from the dribbling game were Queen's Park Glasgow, Royal Engineers, and Sheffield, and by the mid-1870s nearly all the important teams had followed their lead.

Since then there have been many skillful dribblers from all parts of the world, but with the adoption of more and more defensive tactics, there are probably fewer now than ever before. The 1930s, 1940s, and 1950s are seen by many observers as a second high plateau in the history of dribbling, as exemplified by the legendary Sir Stanley Matthews.

But the dribbling game of halcyon days will never be duplicated. Its closest equivalent was seen in the freewheeling play of Brazil between the mid-1930s and mid-1950s, prior to its adoption of modern tactical innovations, and only in South America has a consistent reverence for the art of dribbling been maintained. *See also* **Offside.**

Drop ball

Also known as **bouncing.** The referee drops the ball on the ground between two players, one representative from either side, who are positioned face-to-face at a designated spot on the field. The ball must bounce on the ground at least once before being played.

The Laws of the Game require a drop ball for specific infringements a substitute entering the field before securing permission from the referee; intentional tripping or striking another player while both players are outside the touch line or goal line; during a friendly, when the crossbar is broken or displaced causing the game to be temporarily suspended; an offense committed before a previously dropped ball has touched the ground; interference of a shot on a goal by an outside agent, other than at a penalty kick; and, restarting the game after temporary suspension for any reason not mentioned in the Laws.

Fair catch

The fair catch was an integral part of the various football games during the early and mid-nineteenth century, and even found its way into the original Laws of the Game in 1863. It was mentioned in the Harrow Rules (No. 5), Cambridge Rules of 1854-58 (No. 8), and the Laws of the Game (Nos. 8 and 13).

After its removal from the Laws of the Game in 1866, it continued to find expression in one form or another within the structure of Rugby Union and Rugby League.

Defined in its original form, a fair catch is made when a player catches the ball directly from the kick or "knock-on" of an opposing player, before the ball has touched either the ground or a teammate of the catcher.

In most codes, fair catches could not be made from a kick or throw-in from beyond the touch or goal lines. In games where the dribbling code prevailed over the handling code, a free kick or pass was substituted for running with the ball from a fair catch.

Far post

The area adjacent to the goalpost that is farther away from the ball at a given time, especially when an attack on the goal is being made. On a corner kick, for example, the far post is on the opposite side of the goalmouth from the active corner.

Field of play

The size, markings, and characteristics of the playing field are carefully supervised by the International Football Association Board. The evolution of the present field of play, however, was in the making for many decades, as shown by the following chronology of major changes and developments

1863

a) Maximum length of 200 yards and maximum width of 100 yards specified.
b) Corner flags required.
c) Goals defined as two upright posts eight yards apart without any tape or crossbar between them.

1865

Tapes stretched between either goal post eight feet above the ground.

1875

Minimum length of 100 yards and minimum width of 50 yards specified.

1883

a) Crossbars replace tapes.
b) Touch lines added to all sides of the field.

1891

a) Center spot added.
b) Center circle added.
c) Semi-circular lines six yards from either goal post added to designate the goal area.
d) 12-yard line at either end of the field marked off to designate the penalty area.
e) A theoretical 18-yard line sanctioned to indicate the position of a penalty kick.
f) Goal nets sanctioned.

1894

Maximum width of goal posts and crossbars fixed at five inches.

1896

Minimum height of corner flags fixed at five feet.

1897

Dimensions of the field of play altered; for domestic competition, a maximum length of 130 yards, a minimum length of 100 yards, a maximum width of 100 yards, and a minimum width of 50 yards; for international competition, a maximum length of 120 yards, a minimum length of 110 yards, a maximum width of 80 yards, and a minimum width of 70 yards.

1901

A broken line 18 yards from the goal line added to determine the position of penalty kicks.

1902

a) Halfway line added.
b) Present rectangular goal area and penalty area introduced.
c) Penalty mark added 12 yards from the goal line.

1937

Penalty arc added.

1939

Maximum width of touch line and goal line fixed at five inches.

1966

Minimum width and depth of crossbar and goal post fixed at four inches.

The International Board has been reluctant to act on the composition of playing surfaces, but with sophisticated technologies emerging and expanded international competition in differing climates, this is becoming an increasingly important factor in modern soccer.

Grass surfaces abound in most parts of the world, but in Iceland all playing surfaces are gravel. In Malta, Cyprus, and many countries of North Africa and the Middle East, most pitches are composed of dirt or sand.

The advance of artificial surfaces in North America has presented a new set of problems, particularly in regard to their punishing effect on players' legs. The first soccer match ever played on an artificial surface was an exhibition match between Real Madrid and West Ham United at the Astrodome, in Houston, Texas, in 1966. The surface was Monsanto's Astro-Turf.

The first World Cup qualification match to be played on artificial surface was Syria vs. Iraq in 1976 at the Malaz Ground, Riyadh, Saudi Arabia, and it was followed some weeks later by a second match between the same teams. The first European club to announce that it would install an artificial surface was Arsenal F.C. of London, with a completion date set at 1980.

Flick

A very light kick made with a quick, snappy motion, usually in the form of a short pass.

Floodlit soccer

The first match played under lights took place at Bramall Lane, Sheffield, England, on October 14, 1878, and was played between two representative teams of the Sheffield Football Association. Four lights, each projecting the equivalent of 8,000 candles, were mounted on 30-foot high poles, one at each corner of the field. The power was supplied by a pair of Siemens dynamo engines situated separately behind either goal.

The novelty of a match under lights proved to be a great attraction, and nearly 20,000 people crowded into the grounds, far surpassing the record attendance figures of the period. The Football Association, however, did not sanction floodlit games until 1887, and their use did not become widespread in England or elsewhere until the late 1920s.

Flying kick

A kick taken by a player in mid-air.

Forward

A player whose position on the field is on or near the front line of the attack. The five traditional positions on the forward line are outside right, inside right, center forward, inside left, and outside left. One may add the less defined position of striker, though this player sometimes operates from the midfield.

Free kick

An unimpeded kick from a dead ball that is awarded to a team for certain infringements committed by the opposition.

There are two classifications of free kicks a direct free kick, from which a goal may be scored directly; and an indirect free kick, from which a goal may not be scored directly. Certain rules apply to all free kicks

1. Opposing players must be 10 yards from the ball when the kick is taken.
2. The kicker may not play the ball a second time until the ball has been touched by another player.
3. When a free kick is being taken from within the kicker's own penalty area, opposing players must be outside that penalty area, and the ball must be kicked outside the penalty area.
4. A kicker's own goalkeeper may not receive a ball directly from a free kick in order to kick it into play.

See also **Direct free kick** and **indirect free kick.**

Friendly

A game between two teams that is not part of an official league competition, cup competition, or tournament of any kind.

A friendly may be scheduled to prepare for an official tournament or as a testimonial to an outstanding individual, or it may have charitable purposes, such as catastrophe relief or social welfare aid.

A friendly may also be included as part of a specific transfer deal and may have no other motivation than to increase box office receipts.

Front block tackle

Also known as **front tackle** and **block tackle.** A tackle in which the defending player meets the dribbler from the front and blocks movement of the ball by pressing it against the dribbler's foot or ankle. The tackle is completed by the ball spinning off the dribbler's foot into the defender's possession.

Fullback

Also known as **back, No. 2,** and **No. 3.** A defender at the rear of a formation who rarely participates in an attack. The number of fullbacks may vary according to the formation. In the traditional 2-3-5, there are two (right and left), and in the 4-2-4, 4-3-3, and 4-4-2, there are as many as four, though some of these may be overlapping. An important modern adaptation of the fullback position is the sweeper. *See also* **Overlap** and **sweeper.**

Goal [i]

The enclosure into which the ball must pass to score. A goal consists of two vertical goalposts joined by a horizontal crossbar. A net may be attached to the structure and the ground behind it to trap the ball, if it does not interfere with play at the goalmouth. Goalposts must be eight yards (7.32 meters) apart and equidistant from the corner flags.

The lower edge of the crossbar must be eight feet (2.44 meters) from the ground. The width and depth of the goalposts and crossbar must not exceed five inches (12 cm); both must be the same width. The back edges of the goalpost, crossbar, and goal line must be on the same vertical plane.

Goal [ii]

The winning of a point. In order to score, a ball must pass entirely through the imaginary vertical plane that connects the back edges of the goalposts, crossbar, and goal line.

Goal aggregate

The total number of goals scored by a team in a multi-game series, often used in determining the winner of a two-game round in a knockout competition.

Goal average

"Goals for" divided by "goals against." As a tie-breaking calibration, it has been used traditionally to determine the relative standing of two teams that finish equal on points in a league table.

The Football League of England, which adopted it as the official tie-breaking procedure with the league's formation in 1888, was one of the last major loops in the world to drop it in the 1970s in favor of the more equitable "goal difference" procedure.

Goal difference

"Goals for" minus "goals against." A somewhat more equitable tie-breaking calibration than its precursor, "goal average," it has been adopted by most of the world's leading league competitions to determine the relative standing of two teams that finish equal on points in the table.

Goalkeeper

Also known as **goalie, keeper, custodian, between the sticks, stiffie, goalminder,** and **netminder.** The guardian of the goal, and the only player on the field allowed to use his hands (other than for throw-ins).

The goalkeeper's primary function is to gather, punch, or deflect shots on goal. As the last line of defense, the goalkeeper's task demands a unique set of skills, which are among the game's most spectacular to observe when performed with precision.

In the early years of modern soccer, the English rule makers did not acknowledge a separate goaltending position. Revisions in the Sheffield Rules during the 1860s referred to the "goalkeeper" as that player who, for the time being, was closest to his own goal.

In the new Football Association Rules of 1870, goalkeeping became a fixed position for the first time and the goalkeeper's use of hands was sanctioned in the defensive half of the field.

After 1894 a goalkeeper could not be charged except when he was playing the ball or obstructing an opponent. The area in which a goalkeeper could handle the ball was reduced to his own penalty area in 1912, but he was still required to release the ball after every two steps (a flip into the air would suffice).

In 1931, the number of steps was increased to four, and in 1967 he was directed to give up possession of the ball altogether after four steps (usually by bouncing the ball on the ground or by passing to a teammate). Outside his own penalty area, a goalkeeper is confined by the same rules that applied to other players.

The Laws also direct that goalkeepers wear colors to distinguish themselves from other players and the referee. This rule dates back to 1909, when it was determined that goalkeepers in the Football League of England should wear either white, scarlet, or royal blue for the benefit of the referee. In subsequent years, yellow was prescribed for international matches.

Goal kick

An indirect free kick required after the ball has passed over the goal line, other than into the goal, having last been played by the attacking side. The kick is taken within that half of the goal area nearest to where the ball crossed over the goal line and must be kicked beyond the penalty area.

The kicker may not touch the ball again until it has been played by another player. Opposing players must be outside the kicker's penalty area when the kick is taken. A player who receives the ball direct from a goal kick cannot be offside.

Goal kicks were introduced in England by The Football Association in 1869 to replace the kick out. As a result of the 1936 rule that prohibits a goalkeeper from gathering a goal kick with his hands, goalkeepers themselves are usually designated to take goal kicks.

Goal net

Also known as **rigging** and **netting.** A net of hemp, jute, or nylon that may be attached to the goal posts, crossbar, and ground behind the goal to trap the ball. Nets are not required by the Laws, but certain restrictions are placed upon them. Nets must be rigged in such a way that they do not interfere with play at the goalmouth, and nylon netting must be as thick as that of hemp or jute.

Nets were invented in 1890 by J. A Brodie of Liverpool and came into wide use among Football League clubs the following year. The first league-level game in which they appeared was North vs. South at Nottingham in January 1891.

Hack

Kicking the shin of an opponent in order to trip or otherwise impede his mobility. This practice has been prohibited by the Laws of the Game since the first Football Association rules were drawn up in 1863, although it had a place in early nineteenth century football. It is represented in the modern Laws by the phrase "kicking an opponent."

The controversy over hacking became one of the important touchstones marking the break between rugby and soccer during the 1860s. The Rugby School Rules of 1846, which were a hallmark in the development of the rugby game, allowed kicking below the knee.

The Harrow School Rules of c. 1830, the Cambridge University Rules of 1848, and the Sheffield Rules of 1857, each an important step in the growth of modern soccer, specifically banned hacking of any kind.

With the prohibition of hacking in The Football Association Laws of 1863, the break between soccer and rugby became clearly delineated. Hacking apologists gravitated to the rugby camp, as did defenders of the handling game, the second major controversy of the rugby-soccer split.

In the late 1860s, the physical dangers of hacking became a matter of public concern throughout England. Although its use was forbidden by the soccer code, most rugby clubs continued to practice hacking. Finally, at its inaugural meeting in 1871, the new Rugby Football Union abolished hacking and tripping altogether, and the matter was laid to rest.

Halfback

Also known as **No. 4, No. 5,** and **No. 6.** In traditional tactical formations, most notably the 2-3-5, the three positions that link the defense and attack. Their functions may vary, but most commonly halfbacks—right, left, and center—drop back to defend and move up to support the attack as the situation warrants.

The pivotal aspects of the position are most pronounced at center halfback. In some formations, the center halfback may be strictly a defensive player. Right and left halfbacks who confine themselves to corridors on either side of the field may be referred to as wing halfbacks and are rarely assigned to purely defensive tasks.

At the same time, traditional halfbacks are almost never offensive players only. The term "halfback" has fallen out of general use in recent years with the advent of systems that use two, three, or four "midfielders," i.e., the 4-2-4, 4-3-3, and 4-4-2.

Half time

A period of time between the two halves of a game. A half time interval is not specifically required by the Laws, but the players' right to have a period of rest between halves has been asserted by a decision of the International Football Association Board.

The letter of the Laws, however, restricts the interval to five minutes, unless otherwise agreed upon by the referee. In fact, half time periods are customarily longer than five minutes and may vary from country to country. In Great Britain, the interval used to be called Lemon Time, a reminder of the early days of the game when it was common to suck on lemons during the break.

Half volley

A kick taken the instant after the ball has bounced off the ground.

Hands

Also known as **hand ball.** An infringement in which a player other than the goalkeeper intentionally touches the ball with a hand or any part of the arm, except when making a throw-in. The opposing side is awarded a direct free kick.

Handling of the ball has been prohibited since 1866 when the fair catch rule was deleted from the English Laws. Earlier, even after the first break had occurred between rugby and soccer over the issue of hacking, some degree of handling had been permitted.

The Cambridge Rules of 1848 allowed players to stop the ball momentarily with their hands or to catch the ball directly from an opponent's kick, (the latter known as a fair catch), and the Sheffield Rules of 1857 sanctioned similar use of the hands.

Even the Laws of the Football Association, which in 1863 were the rules from which the modern game developed, provided for the fair catch and did not prohibit manual deflection of the ball. The importance of the fair catch rule change of 1866, therefore, cannot be underestimated in a determination of the birth of modern soccer.

Hat trick

The scoring of three goals in one game by the same individual, or the winning of a title three years in succession by the same team.

Traditionally, a hat trick is not credited to a player unless his three goals are uninterrupted by a goal from another player of the same team. The term has its origin in cricket, where a player used to be awarded a new hat for taking three wickets with three balls.

Pelé holds both major world hat trick records most hat tricks in career (92) and most hat tricks in international play (seven), the latter shared with Sandor Kocsis of Hungary. Neither record takes into account the tradition of successive goals.

Head

To pass or shoot the ball with one's head. The art of heading has been perfected by a gallery of great players, perhaps none more so than the inside-right Sandor Kocsis of Honved, Barcelona, and Hungary, whose dazzling work in the air complemented the lethal left-foot shot of his teammate at inside-left, Ferenc Puskás. Kocsis' nickname was the "Golden Head."

Hold

To grip an opponent or his clothing with the hand, an infringement penalized by the awarding of a direct free kick. Holding has been prohibited since the first football rules were drawn up in England during the early decades of the nineteenth century.

Home and away

Also known as **home and home.** A two-legged series with one match played on a given team's home ground and the second match played on the opponent's home ground.

Indirect free kick

A free kick from which a goal may not be scored. It is awarded to the offended side for the following infringements dangerous play, charging unfairly, obstruction, charging the goalkeeper, a goalkeeper's taking more than four steps before releasing the ball from his hands, and a goalkeeper's holding up the game.

In addition, an indirect free kick is awarded to an offended side when the offender is cautioned for persistent infringements of the Laws, dissent, and ungentlemanly conduct. Finally, an indirect free kick is awarded to the opponent to restart the game after play has been stopped by the referee to send off a player, except when a separate offense requiring a more severe penalty has been committed at the same time.

Infringement

A foul or offense against the Laws of the Game.

Injury time

Time allowed at the end of either half to compensate for time lost because of an injury or any other stoppage. The decision to add injury time and how much to add is at the referee's discretion.

In play

A ball is "in play" when it has traveled the distance of its own circumference, unless 1) the referee has not started play; 2) the ball is situated in touch or entirely across the goal line; or 3) otherwise prescribed by the Laws. An example of the third exception is the goal kick, in which the ball must travel beyond the kicker's penalty area to be "in play."

The most significant change in regulations governing "in play" is that relating to throw-ins. The original Laws of the Game (1863) stated that a ball was not "in play" from a throw-in until it touched the ground, whereas, today a ball from a throw-in needs only to cross the touch line.

Inside

Also known as **No. 8,** and **No. 10.** The positions on a five-player forward line that lie between either wing and the center forward the inside right on the right side of the line and the inside left on the left side.

Inside forwards are usually at the vanguard of the attack, but they may also be deep-lying, as in the W-M system and its derivatives. A large number of the game's goalscoring masters have been inside forwards Pelé, Puskas, Kocsis, Law, Sivori, and Kosek, to name a few.

Inswinger

A pass or shot which curves toward the goal, usually in reference to a corner kick. *See also* **Outswinger.**

Intention

A concept in the Laws of the Game that refers to a player's deliberately taking an action.

The Laws became significantly more sophisticated with the introduction of the word "intentional" to the revised Laws of 1897. It specifically referred to the handling rule, but the new term eventually clarified the rules governing most fouls and misconducts, i.e., kicking, tripping, jumping, charging, striking, holding, and pushing, and for this reason its addition holds an important place in the history of the game.

Intercept

To interrupt the course of an opponent's pass.

Interfere

To wrongfully impede an opponent or play on the field, whether by obstruction or other means.

International [i]

A game between two teams sanctioned by the appropriate national governing bodies to represent their countries, i.e., a game between national teams. There are five official levels of international play

1. "A" team, or full international
2. "B" team, or reserve
3. "Under 23" team (Espoirs, Menor de 23, Unter-23)
4. "Amateur" team (Amateur Aficionado, Amateur)
5. "Youth" team, "Under 21" or "Junior" (Junior, Juvenil, Jugend)

In addition, some national associations are able to field national "Veteran" teams, women's teams, and various other youth-level teams. "Veteran" teams are composed of ex-members of the five categories listed above or other retired players of suitable quality, and women's teams have come about only since the late 1960s.

An "A" team is the country's best representative team. The World Cup and all regional nations' cups are contested by "A" teams. Their rosters may include either amateurs or professionals, depending on a given country's policy with regard to professionalism, but the presence of a single professional on a team precludes that team from participating in any "Amateur" competition.

A "B" team is the reserve squad of the full national team, and is usually made up of players from the same club level as "A" team members. In many countries, it has its own separate schedule of games.

A nation's "Under 23" team is made up of the best players aged 21 and 22 who have not been selected for the "A" team. An "Under 23" team maintains its own international schedule, and some regional confederations have tournaments set aside to determine international championships in this category. Many full international players graduate from "Under 23" teams.

The status of various national "Amateur" teams may vary. In countries where professionalism has been adopted, the "Amateur" team comprises non-professional players whose level of play may be lower than that of an "A," "B," or "Under 23" team. It may also have its own separate international schedule.

Some countries, on the other hand, do not recognize professionalism or are simply too small to afford such costs and have been granted permission to be represented by their "A" team in either "A" team competitions or in "Amateur" competitions. In such cases, the "A" team is also the "Amateur" team. The soccer tournament of the Olympic Games is played by "Amateur" national teams, as are the various regional athletic tournaments, such as the Asian Games.

A "Youth" team is the national team for players 20 years old or less. As with the "Under 23" group, an exceptional player who is under 21 years of age may also be selected for the "A" team, in which case he is not likely to play for the lesser "Youth" team. Some regional confederations sponsor international "Youth" tournaments. Most journalistic references to this category use the term "Under 21" or "Junior," e.g., Italy "Under 21" vs. Spain "Under 21."

All internationals, whether friendlies or in conjunction with an official competition, must conform to FIFA regulations. However, responsibility for actually organizing the matches—transportation, accommodations, collection of revenue, selection of neutral referees, and other logistical concerns—rests with the host country.

Making the draw, official observation of the match, and administration of any protests or punitive actions are the duties of either FIFA or the relevant confederation, whichever is sponsoring the contest.

FIFA regulations stipulate that each national association participating in a full international pay a levy to the world body, the amount of which is dependent on gate receipts. The four British associations (England, Scotland, Wales, and Northern Ireland) have been exempt from this rule since 1924, but only with regard to the Home International Championship.

The regulations also require that the FIFA flag be flown at all full internationals to show that the flag be flown at all full internationals to show that the Laws of the Game are being respected.

The first unofficial international contest between representative national teams was held at Kennington Oval, London, on March 5, 1870, between England and Scotland. The result was a 1-1 draw. The match was conceived and organized by C.W. Alcock, honorary secretary of the Football Association in London. The Scottish players were all residents of England and played for English clubs. *See also* **Amateur, non-amateur,** and **professional.**

International [ii]

A player who participates in an international [i].

International appearance

A player who has participated in an official international match on any one of his national teams is said to have made an international appearance, or, been "awarded a cap." International appearances may be credited for any recognized level of play, depending on whether or not the relevant national governing body sponsors such a team.

It is customary that players from Youth level upwards are eligible for A-level, or "full" level, teams. (George Best, for example, was selected to play for Northern Ireland's full international team at age 17.) After reaching the age of 23, however, a player is only eligible for the A-level team, unless there are peculiar domestic regulations stating otherwise, or unless amateurism is a factor.

Until 1971, the FIFA statutes allowed players to play only for their country of birth or for countries in which they had become naturalized citizens. Since then, however, players have been authorized to play also in the country of their father's birth, as well as their own country. The choice is made by the player, though only one country at a time may be chosen.

Under the naturalization rule, two players in soccer history have made international appearances for three different countries Ladislav Kubala (Hungary, Czechoslovakia, and Spain) and Alfredo Di Stefano (Argentina, Colombia, and Spain).

The term "cap," used universally among English-speaking countries outside North America, refers to the time-honored custom of wearing caps as part of the uniform. Caps of different colors were worn to distinguish one team from another as early as 1654 in England, and continued to be seen until the 1880s.

After the custom had fallen out of use, The Football Association in England began awarding caps in 1886 to each player who had made an appearance on the field for England's national team. The tradition, especially the term, remained, and the F.A. now awards caps on an annual basis One cap per year is given to each player who has made an appearance on the field with the name of each of his opposing teams embroidered on it.

Billy Wright holds the world record for most consecutive international appearances with 70 for England between 1951-59.

In touch

A ball is "in touch" when it crosses entirely over a touch line and out of bounds. *See also* **Out of play.**

Jab kick

Also known as **stab kick.** A quick, sudden kick, usually short, in which the leg does not straighten to its full extent.

Jockey

Also known as **shepherd.** A defensive action in which an opponent is closely marked but no attempt is made to tackle him. The purpose is to deprive a player with the ball of a good play. Effective jockeying may force a player wide or into an otherwise difficult circumstance without the defender's having to commit himself. *See also* **Mark.**

Kickoff

A place kick taken from the center spot at the start of a game, at the start of the second half, at the start of extra time periods, and after a goal is scored.

A kickoff must be taken by one of the 22 authorized players on the field, and it must be directed into the opponent's half of the field. At the time of a kickoff all players are required to be in their own halves of the field with those of the opposing team not less than 10 yards away from the center spot.

The kicker may not play the ball a second time until it has been touched by another player. A goal may be scored from a kickoff, but it is the rarest of all conversions in the game. Kickoffs have been the accepted form of starting play at least as far back as the Rules of the Harrow Game c. 1830.

League competition

A series in which the winning side is the team that has accumulated the most points and stands at the top of the standings, as distinct from a cup competition, in which the winning side is the only team to remain undefeated at the end of a knockout series.

Linesmen

See **Referees and linesmen.**

Lofted kick

Any long-distance kick that sails through the air high off the ground.

Mark

Also known as **track.** To guard an opposing player; to defend closely against him. *See also* **Jockey.**

Midfielder

Also known as **linkman.** In modern tactical formations, such as the 4-4-2, 4-3-3, 4-2-4, and their variations, the positions that link the defense and attack. Their function is sometimes equivalent to that of the traditional halfback, but with fewer players on the modern forward line they are an increasingly important part of the attack.

Elsewhere, the term "midfielder" is interchangeable with "halfback," the latter having fallen out of general use in recent years.

Narrow the angle

A defender's advance on a threatening attacker in order to visibly block as much of the goal as possible, thereby lessening the portion of the goal into which the attacker may shoot. The term is usually made in reference to a goalkeeper's "narrowing the angle" of a potential goalscorer.

Near post

The area adjacent to the goalpost that is closer to the ball at a given time, especially when an attack on goal is being made. On a corner kick, for example, the near post is on the same side of the goalmouth as the active corner.

Non-amateur

A player classification recognized by FIFA, which is meant to account for a level of professionalism less than full-time or fully compensatory. A non-amateur may not qualify for amateur competitions that are sponsored by FIFA, affiliated confederations and associations, or the International Olympic Committee.

Thirty-three countries have registered non-amateur players Central Africa, Malawi, Rhodesia, Somalia, Canada, Costa Rica, Guatemala, Honduras, El Salvador, Argentina, Bolivia, Chile, Colombia, Ecuador, Paraguay, Uruguay, Hong Kong, Austria, Belgium, France, West Germany, Greece, Iceland, Republic of Ireland, Italy, Malta, Portugal, Sweden, Switzerland, Turkey, Yugoslavia, Australia, and New Zealand. *See also* **Professional.**

Numbered players

Numbered players were introduced in the English F.A. Cup Final of 1933 and made compulsory by the Football League in 1939. The 1939 numbering system, based on the 2-3-5 formation, became traditional world-wide, though recently it has fallen out of use. It is as follows

1. Goalkeeper
2. Right Back
3. Left Back
4. Right Halfback
5. Center Halfback
6. Left Halfback
7. Outside Right
8. Inside Right
9. Center Forward
10. Inside Left
11. Outside Left

Obstruction

An infringement in which a player intentionally places his body between an opponent and the ball or otherwise impedes an opponent's movement. The opposing team is awarded an indirect free kick. Goalkeepers are exempt from the obstruction rule in most situations.

Although a similar rule was included in the Harrow Rules (1830s), it was not incorporated into the Laws of 1863. By the end of the nineteenth century, however, it was widely accepted.

In Latin America, it was not entirely respected until more frequent international exposure during the 1950s resulted in uniform adherence to the FIFA law.

Offside

The offside rule, which on the surface appears to be elusive and confusing, is actually based on a simple concept it is unfair for an attacking player to gain an undue advantage over his defenders. If this precept is kept in mind, the details of the law follow logically and in good order.

The rule is basically designed for offside infringements that result from a forward pass—by far the most common situation in which the foul is committed. The Laws of the Game stipulate that a player is "offside," that is, "out of play," if he is nearer his opponent's goal line than the ball at the moment the ball is played to him, unless any of the following apply:

1. He is in his own half of the field, or, in the North American Soccer League, behind his opponent's 35-yard line.

2. There are two of his opponents nearer their own goal line than he is.

3. the ball was last touched by an opponent or by him.

4. he receives the ball direct from a goal kick, corner kick, throw-in, or drop ball.

A player who is not in an offside position when the pass is initiated but moves forward into what appears to be an offside position to receive the ball (i.e., advances during the flight of the ball) is not offside.

In further applying the concept of "unfair advantage," however, the Laws add that a player may be judged offside if he is merely located in an offside position, and, though not actually receiving the ball, is interfering with the play or with an opponent, or affects the play by advancing toward the ball or an opponent. This sort of offside infringement is less specific and is rarely called.

An offside infringement is penalized by the awarding of an indirect free kick to the opposing team from the spot where the infringement took place.

The roots of the offside law are found in the various football games of the English public schools in the late eighteenth and early nineteenth centuries. By the time Harrow's rules were written during the 1810s or 1820s, the offside rule had been given the shape it was to keep until 1866.

The Harrow rule stipulated that to receive the ball from any forward pass whatsoever was unlawful. A Harrow player was offside simply by being "nearer the line of the opponent's base [goal line] than the kicker"—an unfair advantage.

This stringent regulation, which bears a closer resemblance to rugby than soccer, meant that for many decades the only way to advance the ball up the field (in games using a round ball) was to dribble.

Thus a vertical or diagonal line of players, rather than a horizontal forward line as in modern soccer, became the chief tactical formation of the era, and the ball was passed backwards along the line from dribbler to dribbler, like a pass in rugby or lateral in American football.

The earliest break with the original offside concept as laid down at Harrow was made in the

Cambridge University Rules of 1848, the first rules to resemble modern soccer, which permitted a player to receive a forward pass if more than three opponents were between him and the goal line. Cambridge players were still reminded not to "loiter between the ball and the adversaries' goal."

This progressive change was not adopted in the Sheffield Rules of 1857, the second important set of rules that anticipated modern soccer, nor in the Football Association Laws of the Game in 1863, soccer's first official code. Accordingly, the "dribbling (vertical) game" continued to prosper until well into the 1860s.

In 1866, however, the Football Association in London adopted a three-opponent offside rule, in which at least three opponents were required between a player and his opponent's goal line. Adjustment to the revolutionary three-opponent concept was not fully realized until the mid-1870s, when the golden era of sophisticated dribbling finally gave way to the "passing game," as promoted by Queen's Park Glasgow and other Scottish teams.

In 1873, the Laws first spelled out that the offside rule applied only at "the moment of kicking" (i.e., the moment the ball is played). Goal kicks, meanwhile, had been exempted from the offside rule from the beginning. The clause specifying "last played by an opponent" was added in 1880. Corner kicks were exempted in 1881-82. Offside was limited to the opponent's half of the field in 1907, and throw-ins were exempted in 1921.

Despite these alterations, the three-opponent rule remained basically unchanged until 1925, a watershed year in which the International Football Association Board accepted a proposal of the Scottish Football Association that reduced the required number of opponents to two. The 1925 rule is still in force, except that it was remodeled with the rest of the Laws in 1938.

But the change in one word—from "three" to "two"—was so far-reaching that it brought about a second tactical revolution, beginning with the introduction of Arsenal's famous W-M system. All tactical innovations since 1925 have revolved around the two-opponent offside rule. Indeed, the whole history of the game would have been vastly different if the concept of offside were not at its core. *See also* **Tactics, offside trap, thirty-five yard line.**

Offside trap

A defensive tactic, in which a defender purposely moves forward to put an attacking player offside.

Although the offside trap is still seen on occasion, the offside rule change of 1925 nearly spelled its doom. During the 60-year period from 1866-1925 when the three-opponent offside rule was in effect, its use in England had gradually increased to a point where it had become a menace to the game. In the years immediately before and after World War I, an alarming number of offside infringements were called, which caused the delay of countless games and much protest from the press and public.

The "no-back game," a tactic in which fullbacks moved forward to blend with halfbacks, was at its height. Newcastle United F.C., and in particular its skillful fullback Billy McCracken, was the first important club to exploit the trap as a matter of strategy, and other clubs soon followed.

By 1925, its unpopularity became so acute that the International Football Association Board, the body responsible for changes in the Laws of the Game, was compelled to adopt the two-opponent offside rule. Although the change forced radical innovations in team tactics, the heyday of the offside trap was effectively put to an end. Today it remains a ploy that is regarded with some derision.

Off the ball

Not having possession of the ball. "Running off the ball" is attempting to play usefully while not in possession, or, to move into an advantageous position on the field while not in possession; for example, to receive a pass.

Out of play

A ball is "out of play" when it crosses entirely over the goal line or the touch line, or when the referee stops play for any reason.

Outside

Also known as **winger, wing, flank, No. 7,** and **No. 11.** The positions at either extremity of a five-player forward line, the outside right on the right side of the line and the outside left on the left side. The two outer positions on a four-player forward line may also be known as outsides, or wings, depending on whether or not they fulfill the traditional functions of an outside.

With the advance in recent years of 4-3-3, 4-4-2, and 4-2-4 formations, their historical place in team strategies has diminished, though the increasingly rare talents of a natural outsides such as Deyna, Jairzinho, and Dzajic, are generally exploited by coaches whenever they are discovered.

Outswinger

A pass or shot which curves away from the goal, usually in reference to a corner kick. *See also* **Inswinger.**

Overhead kick

A kick in which the ball is propelled over the kicker's own head. *See also* **Bicycle kick.**

Overlap

The action of a fullback, center halfback, or other defender in coming forward to aid in an attack, though the player's primary function is defensive.

Over-the-ball tackle

An often-unlawful tackle in which the defending player jumps over the ball and plays the legs of the dribbler. It is referred to in the laws as "jumping at the opponent," and draws a direct free kick by the offended side.

Own goal

Also known as **self-goal.** A goal scored by a player against his own team.

An own goal has decided the outcome of important international competitions on four occasions. Hungary won the 1964 Olympic gold medal after an own goal by Czechoslovakia's Vojta. In 1961, Benfica won the European Cup when Barcelona's goalkeeper Ramallets nudged a poor clearance by a teammate into his own goal.

Two editions of the European Cup Winners' Cup have been decided by own goals. In 1964, MTK's Dansky scored an own goal that allowed Sporting Lisbon to equalize and force a replay; Sporting eventually won the replay and the trophy. In 1966, Borussia Dortmund won the cup on an own goal by Liverpool's Yeats.

An own goal figured prominently in the 1975 edition of the South American Championship. In the final Columbia won the first leg, and in the second leg was losing by one when Zarate scored an own goal to give Peru a 2-0 win, forcing a play-off, which was won by Peru. Ultimately it was to be Zarate's own goal that put Colombia's first major international honor out of reach.

Pass

The lawful movement of the ball from one player to another, as distinct from a shot on goal. *See also* **Back pass, cross, square ball, through ball, throw-in,** and **wall pass.**

Penalty decision

In 1970, the International Football Association Board accepted a proposal that provided for a penalty kick contest to replace the practice of choosing lots to decide the result of a drawn game.

The penalty kick contest is put into effect only if extra time has not produced a winner, and it is restricted exclusively to knockout competitions, such as national cups and international championships.

The rules and conditions of the procedure, whose official name is "taking of kicks from the penalty mark," are as follows

1. The goal at which all the kicks are taken is chosen by the referee.
2. A coin toss by the referee determines which team kicks first.
3. Each team is entitled to at least five kicks, which are taken alternately, first by one team then the other.

4. If, before five kicks are completed, one player fails to score and his opposite number scores, the taking of kicks is ended by the referee.
5. If, after five kicks are completed, both teams have scored the same number of goals, the procedure continues until one team has scored more than the other after both have taken an equal number of kicks.
6. The team that scores the greater number of goals is declared the winner of the contest, but the game is recorded as a draw with an additional notation that the winner was decided on penalty kicks.
7. If the goalkeeper is injured during the contest, he may be replaced by a teammate who is already on the field or by a substitute, the latter provided his team has not already made use of the maximum number of substitutes permitted by the rules.
8. Only players who are on the field at the end of the match may qualify to take kicks.
9. No player may take a second kick until all eligible teammates have had their turn.
10. Other than the kicker and goalkeeper, all players must remain within the center circle while the kick is in progress.
11. The goalkeeper who is waiting for his turn to defend must remain in the field of play but outside the penalty area at least 10 yards from the penalty spot and further than 18 yards from the goal line.
12. Unless superseded expressly by the rules above, all Laws of the Game apply throughout the contest.

Penalty kick

Also known as **spot kick.** A direct free kick from the penalty spot, which is awarded to an offended team for any serious foul committed in the opponent's penalty area. It consists of an unimpeded shot on goal and the attempt to save it by the opposing goalkeeper.

There are numerous regulations governing the penalty kick

1. The goalkeeper must stand on the goal line without moving until the ball is kicked.
2. All players other than the two principals must be within the field of play but outside the penalty area and ten yards from the penalty spot, i.e., outside the penalty arc.
3. The kick itself must be made in the direction of the goal.
4. The kicker may not play the ball a second time until it has been touched by another player.
5. The referee must always ensure that a penalty kick is taken even if time has run out.

If any regulation is broken by one of the defending team, the penalty kick must be retaken if a score did not result. If any regulation is broken by the team taking the penalty kick, the goal, if scored, is disallowed, and the kick must be taken over. If the penalty kicker commits a foul after the kick is taken, the opposing side is awarded an indirect free kick.

The penalty kick was introduced by the Irish Football Association during the 1890-91 season. The first goal from a penalty kick was made by an American named Jeffrey of the Pawtucket club of Rhode Island during a match between Linfield F.C. and a combined USA-Canada team at Belfast in 1891. England adopted the penalty kick for the 1891-92 season.

Pivot kick

A kick in which the player swerves, or pivots, at the moment of impact, projecting the ball in the direction of his turn.

Place kick

Any kick taken with the ball in a stationary position; for example, a goal kick or kickoff.

Point system

The universal point system, which is employed in nearly every league in the world and in all international competitions where a league system is followed, awards two points per game two for a win, one to both teams for a draw, and none for a defeat.

The French point system, used in favor of the universal system in France and some French territories until 1976, awards a bonus point to a team that wins by two or more goals. In French-speaking North Africa and a handful of small countries elsewhere, three points are awarded for a win, two for a draw, and one for a loss (i.e., completing a game).

The North American Soccer League, in which drawn games are not allowed, has developed a unique system whereby six points are awarded for a win, none for a loss, and one additional point for every goal scored up to and including three per game. In the American Soccer League, five points are awarded for a win, two for a draw, none for a loss, and one bonus point for every goal scored up to and including three per game.

Post

See **Far post** and **near post**.

Professional

The checkered history of professionalism in soccer has yielded the following definition of the term according to *FIFA Statutes, Regulations, and Standing Orders*

"Players who receive regular wages, payments for playing, bonuses, salaries deferred payments, or any other allowances' other than [actual expenses for travel, necessary maintenance and hotel charges or expenses for equipment, physical preparation and insurance against accidents during play and whilst travelling], or who have only an apparent, fictitious or sham employment or profession, are considered to be professionals or non-amateurs."

This definition is expressly for the use of FIFA in determining the eligibility of players for international competitions under its administration. FIFA points out, however, that in domestic competition this may be superseded by another definition authorized by the relevant national association.

The countries in which professionalism is officially recognized are Malawi, Somalia, South Africa, Zambia, Canada, El Salvador, Mexico, USA, Argentina, Brazil, Chile, Colombia, Ecuador, Peru, Uruguay, Venezuela, Hong Kong, Austria, Belgium, Denmark, England, France, Germany FR, Ireland Northern, Ireland Republic, Italy, Malta, Netherlands, Portugal, Scotland, Spain, Turkey, Wales, Yugoslavia, and New Zealand. Czechoslovakia and Hungary sanctioned professionalism during the 1920s and 1930s, and Cuba did so from 1949-59.

There are certain regulations governing the activities of professionals and non-amateurs, as stipulated by FIFA 1) all professionals and non-amateurs must be registered as such by the national association concerned; 2) they may not participate in any international tournaments that are officially designated as amateur; and 3) they may, if they wish, be reinstated as amateurs by their respective national associations, but cannot, under any circumstances, again participate in officially designated amateur international tournaments.

Professionalism in soccer was introduced in England between 1876-85, and was one of the major features of the growth of the game among working-class people in the northern and Midlands counties.

Until the mid-1880s, payments to players were made secretly. The impetus for professionalism was the desire of struggling clubs to attract good players from other parts of the country by offering a wage, a job, and perhaps new lodgings in an unfamiliar town.

Many English clubs sought to attract Scottish players during the 1870s and 1880s, because it was generally accepted that Scottish tactics and techniques were more advanced.

The Football Association, which was still dominated at this time by well-heeled upper- and middle-class sportsmen with university backgrounds, fought hard against the adoption of professionalism throughout the early 1880s, citing the practice as disreputable, corrupt, and ultimately evil.

In 1885, professionalism was finally legalized after Preston North End F.C. openly admitted to paying its players, but only clubs in the north and Midlands indulged in it for many years to come. The first London club to accept professionalism, Arsenal in 1891, was at first dropped from the schedules of other southern clubs as a protest, but by the turn of the century the disgruntled London clubs had also begun to sign some professionals.

The adoption of professionalism in England, as elsewhere in subsequent decades, led to greater participation in top flight competition, more advanced coaching, a rise in the standard of play, and the birth of the league competition. *See also* **Amateur** and **non-amateur.**

Promotion and relegation

The system of advancing or demoting teams between upper and lower divisions (major and minor leagues) after the end of each season.

The USA and Canada are among the only soccer-playing countries in the world that have not adopted this procedure. In most countries, a "league" is made up of a number of "divisions," the "first division" being the most advanced.

At season's end, a prescribed number of teams at the top of each division is promoted to the next highest division, and a prescribed number of teams at the bottom of each division is relegated to the next lowest division.

Those teams that finish at the bottom of the lowest division in a league are usually required to seek reelection to the league for the following year, or to undergo some other kind of test, such as a play-off, to retain their place.

Some countries, e.g., Argentina and Brazil, hold an additional competition after the close of the regular league season to determine the national champion. In most cases, however, the winner of the first division is regarded as the national champion.

The concept of promotion and relegation arose from the sporting traditions of England during the nineteenth century, and was introduced in the Football League at the end of the 1892-93 season, the first year of the new English second division. Until 1895-96, test matches, or play-offs, were held to determine promotions and relegations.

The first clubs to gain promotion from the second to the first division in 1893 were Small Heath (now Birmingham City) and Darwen (now playing in the non-professional Lancashire Football Combination). Relegated to take their places in the second division were Notts Co. and Accrington Stanley.

Automatic promotion and relegation based on standings in the division tables was introduced at the end of the 1898-99 season, when Manchester City and Glossop were promoted at the expense of Sheffield Wednesday and Bolton Wanderers. Although a Division II was formed in the Scottish League as far back as 1893, automatic promotion and relegation in Scotland was not adopted until after the 1921-22 season.

In subsequent years, countries in Europe, Latin America, Africa, and Asia borrowed the promotion and relegation system, as the growth of the game demanded the formation of multi-divisional leagues. Other than the USA and Canada, only those countries too small to support more than one division have not yet adopted some variation of the promotion and relegation idea.

Punt

A British term referring to any kick that is not a long "boom" down the field.

Referees and linesmen

A referee is the official in charge of a match with respect to all aspects of the Laws and facts of the game. His decisions are final. He is supported in his effort by two linesmen, whose task is to assist in administering the Laws.

Save

The gathering, deflecting, or punching of a shot to prevent it from scoring. This is the chief function of a goalkeeper.

Scissors kick

A kick taken in the air by meeting the ball with one foot while the other foot moves rapidly in the opposite direction to provide leverage, as in the snapping motion of scissors. *See also* **Bicycle kick.**

Screen

Protecting the ball from a defender with the body, usually during the act of dribbling.

Selection

A national, regional, or otherwise specially chosen representative team, which usually indicates unofficial or less than "full international" status. The Spanish language term *seleccion,* however, is a standard reference to any national or representative team.

Self-goal

See **Own goal.**

Sell a dummy

Any number of body feints, fake moves, or outmaneuverings by a dribbler that lead a defender to believe that the movement of the ball will be in one direction, whereas it is actually moved in another. In its strictest meaning, it is the act of showing the ball to one player but passing it to a second or playing it oneself. "Dummy" refers to the imaginary placement of the ball that nonpluses a defender.

The idea of "selling a dummy" is as old as the ball games of ancient Greece and Rome. Historians have described a position in both *episkyros* and *harpastum,* known as the "in-between man" on the field, whose duties remain unclear, but among them was the act of showing the ball to one player and passing it elsewhere.

He appears to be one of the central figures on the field, and his hoodwink was undoubtedly a common tactic. H.A. Harris describes Pollux's definition of the widely used term *phaininda* in the context of *episkyros.* This is used when a player shows the ball to one man and throws it to another.

Dummies in soccer may also be sold to goalkeepers, as when Pelé almost scored against Mazurkiewicz of Uruguay in Brazil's semifinal win during the 1970 World Cup.

Send off

The ejection of a player from the field of play by the referee. A player who is sent off may not be replaced. To administer a send off the referee must stop play and signify the action by showing the offending player a red card. The player is then ordered off the field verbally.

All send offs must be reported by the referee to the committee under whose aegis the match is being played. By the rules of most governing bodies, a player who is sent off may also be suspended from playing for a specified number of games in the future.

In inter-national competition, ejected players are automatically suspended by FIFA for succeeding international matches.

The Laws of the Game require that a player be sent off for the following

1. Violent conduct or serious foul play.
2. Foul or abusive language.
3. Persistent misconduct after receiving a caution.

The red card policy was officially introduced by FIEA at the Olympic Games of 1968.

Shinguard

A protective pad worn between a player's sock and the lower front half of his leg. Shinguards help thwart bruises, sprains, and fractures that may result from a hard tackle or kick.

They were invented and patented in 1874 by Samuel W. Widdowson, a lace manufacturer who was an agile center forward with Nottingham Forest from 1866 to the mid-1880s. (Widdowson also played once for England in 1880, and was known to be one of the great hurdlers and sprinters of his day, as well as a cricketer.

He later became chairman of Nottingham Forest and a member of The Football Association Committee.)

Shinguards were worn by some players from the date of their invention, but they were not mentioned in the Laws until 1880. From that date, their use has been expressly permitted, but the current Laws make no specific reference to them.

Shoot-out

The tie-breaking procedure of the North American Soccer League (NASL), in which players from both teams challenge the opposing goalkeeper, one-on-one, and attempt to score against him.

The rules and conditions of the procedure are as follows

1. The visiting (away) team kicks first.
2. Each team is entitled to at least five kicks, which are taken alternately, first by one team then the other.
3. If, before five kicks are completed, one team has accumulated an insurmountable number of goals (e.g., one team scores its first three while the other team misses its first three), the shootout is ended by the referee.

4. If the number of goals scored by both teams is equal after five attempts, the procedure continues until one team has scored more than the other after both have taken an equal number of kicks.
5. Each kicker starts with the ball on his opponent's 35-yard line, and must take his shot within five seconds after the referee's signal is given.
6. The kicker and goalkeeper are not restricted in their movement during the five-second period.
7. Only players who are on the field at the end of the match may qualify to take kicks.
8. No player may take a second kick until all eligible teammates have had their turn.
9. The order of a team's rotation may vary in each round of kicks.

Initiated in 1977, the shoot-out is essentially a modification of the penalty decision, but, unlike the penalty decision, was implemented in any NASL game in which a win had not resulted from extra time, including league games as well as knockout competitions. All games in the NASL were required to be won or lost; draws had not been allowed since 1975.

As a result of this regulation, the league felt motivated to devise a tie-breaking procedure that would provide a high level of excitement for the North American fan. The experiment has thus far been confined to North America, and, with respect to professional soccer, appears destined to remain that way.

Shoulder charge

A lawful body contact between two players when only the shoulders touch and the arms remain motionless. The ball must be within "playing distance," as determined by the referee. In most countries, the goalkeeper may not be shoulder charged. *See also* **Charge.**

Show the ball

The commitment of a player in possession to dribble or otherwise move the ball in a given direction, whether actually intended or in order to sell a dummy. *See also* **Sell a dummy.**

Sideline

The touchline.

Signing-on fee

The portion of a transfer fee that is earmarked for the player himself rather than his club.

Until recently, the accepted procedure was to put aside five percent of the transfer fee for this purpose, but percentages now fluctuate more widely, and are always higher when top stars are involved. Signing-on fees stem from the transfer system employed in most countries of Western Europe.

This differs slightly from the system of bonuses that is common to the United States and Canada, in which there is no direct connection between the amount of the bonus and the amount of money that passes between clubs. *See also* **Transfer.**

Sixth forward

A midfielder or back, usually a center halfback, who supports the forward line in an attacking position. The term is applicable only with regard to variations of the traditional 2-3-5 formation. The so-called "Central European system," for example, employs a "pivot" who lies just behind the five forwards, and serves both as a supporting attacker and a link between the front line and the defense (two halfbacks and two backs). *See also* **Tactics.**

Sliding tackle

Also known as **split tackle.** A tackle in which the defender skims across the ground to take the ball from a player, sometimes appearing to jump at the ball from some distance. When the tackler is able to combine this with a front-block tackle, his action is known as a sliding-block tackle.

Snap shot

A quick, impulsive shot on goal that is taken from a deflection, usually in the form of a volley or half-volley at or near the goalmouth.

Square ball

A cross-field or lateral pass.

Stoppage

The temporary or permanent cessation of play by the referee.

The referee's discretionary power to stop a game extends from his normal duties of citing a foul to include the termination of a game for bad weather, spectator interference, or any other reason he deems necessary. In most countries, a whistle is blown to stop play on the field but is not used to restart the game, especially after a foul.

Stopper

A deep back whose duties are exclusively defensive.

In the third-back game, it is usually the center halfback, and with four-back systems, the stopper is likely to be one of the center backs. His function is primarily to plug the area in front of the goalkeeper but is seldom as free in his movement as the modern sweeper.

Striker

Any forward whose function is primarily to score goals. The number on a given team may vary from one to four. The term has come about only since the demise of the traditional five-player forward line.

Substitution

Substitutions in soccer have traditionally been a highly restrictive undertaking. One of the early axioms of football games in the nineteenth century was that if a team suffered the loss of an injured player, it was just bad luck and had to be endured. The notion of substituting one player for another as a tactical maneuver was thought to be unfair.

The present rule, as delineated by a decision of the International Football Association Board and governing all levels of competition throughout the world, allows five substitutions per game, providing the names of prospective substitutes are made known to the referee before the kick-off.

The actual Laws of the Game, however, restrict the number of substitutions per game to two. The five-substitution decision is meant to give local authorities a parameter within which to formulate their own policies regarding substitutions. The two-substitute rule is enforced in all competitions that come under the direct supervision of FIFA.

Most of the world's leading soccer nations have retained the two-substitution rule, and it is this rule which is most commonly observed in first-class competition. In the North American Soccer League, four substitutes per game are al-

lowed. American collegiate rules allow five substitutes and unlimited resubstitution, which is in violation of the Laws.

Unauthorized substitutions, however, are not new. The first substitution in international competition was that of Welsh goalkeeper A. Pugh, who came on for the injured S. G. Gillam against Scotland in 1889.

Laws permitting substitution are a recent development. A decision of the International Board in 1932 first mentioned it by allowing limited substitution in international matches if mutually agreed upon by both teams.

In 1956, the International Board authorized incapacitated goalkeepers to be replaced at any time during the game and one other incapacitated player at any time before the end of the first half, but this rule was restricted exclusively to youth tournaments under FIFA auspices.

Two years later, the 1956 rule was extended to include all levels of competition and for the first time substitution was not specifically forbidden in the upper reaches of the game. The total number of substitutions, however, was restricted to two, and the names of two nominated substitutes were required to be given to the referee in advance of the game.

In 1965, the number of nominated players was increased to five, but actual substitutions remained at two. A major change occurred in 1967, when FIFA authorized two substitutes per game for any reason, injury or otherwise, but the ruling was restricted to friendlies and qualification rounds for the 1968 Olympic Games and the 1970 World Cup.

When the rule was eventually adopted for the final rounds of these competitions, the two-substitution rule came into common use as an integral part of the Laws. The five-substitution decision of the International Board was adopted in 1971, and remains restricted to those competitions or leagues whose governing authorities have themselves sanctioned the rule.

Indeed, national associations have the legal authority to restrict substitutions as they see fit, providing the parameters of the Laws and decisions are not exceeded.

There are additional rules that govern the substitution of players 1) a player who is sent off may not be replaced; and 2) a substitute may not enter the field of play except at stoppages and after the referee has beckoned him to do so, nor may he enter the field of play until the player he is replacing has left the field of play.

Summer tournaments

The summer off-season in Europe has customarily been a period for friendly club competition of all kinds, often involving visits abroad or at least across the nearest border.

In Spain, the European capital of summer tournaments, leading clubs from all over the world are invited to compete in small competitions lasting two weeks or less, maintaining a Spanish tradition that was begun in the early 1950s. Dozens of cities on the Iberian peninsula play host to these tournaments, and the pleasing summer climate of the region provides a suitable backdrop.

The tournaments give clubs a chance to regroup after the previous season, test new players, meet famous clubs from other countries, and, above all, gain additional revenue. Many of the greatest clubs of Europe and South America take part on a regular basis.

To cite just one example of the breadth and scope of the Spanish summer tournaments, the participants in the Trofeo Carranza in Cadiz, since its introduction in 1955, have included the following giants of international competition: Penarol, Nacional, Benfica, Torino, Inter, AC Milan, Rácing Club de Paris, Stade de Reims, Ajax, Flamengo, Botafogo, Corinthians Paulista, Vasco de Gama, Palmeiras, Bayern Munchen, Eintracht Frankfurt, Boca Juniors, Independiente, Estudiantes, Standard Liege, Atletico Madrid, Barcelona, and Real Madrid.

Sunday shot

A colloquial term to indicate a very long or otherwise almost impossible shot on goal, which in fact results in a goal. It is that kind of shot a player might try hundreds of times practice sessions without success, and the one time it is attempted during a league match on Sunday the ball goes in.

Sweeper

A deep-lying defender who marks oncoming attackers by roaming over the entire width of the defensive area, either behind or in front of the defensive line and sometimes both. The most sophisticated sweepers have capitalized on their freedom to move where they please by bringing the ball forward and initiating the attack themselves.

Tackle

To lawfully take the ball away from a player in possession by using one's feet. *See also* **Front-block tackle, over-the-ball tackle,** and **sliding tackle.**

Third back

A nominal halfback, usually the center half, who adopts a defensive position in conjunction with the backs, forming in effect a threeback line, e.g., the W-M system. *See also* **Tactics.**

Thirty-five yard line

In the North American Soccer League, two lateral lines on the field of play that run from sideline to sideline and are 35 yards from each goal line.

In 1973, the NASL introduced the 35-yard line concept in order to modify clause "a" of the offside rule in the Laws of the Game. The official offside rule states that a player cannot be offside if he is in his own half of the field.

Under the 35-yard line rule, an attacking player cannot be offside until he is within 35 yards of his opponent's goal. The intent of the new rule is to effectively pull back a given defense, and allow for a more uninhibited attack.

The 35-yard line concept has not spread beyond the North American Soccer League, and FIFA has refused to sanction it.

Through ball

A pass that is played forward and penetrates the opponent's defense, especially to a waiting attacker or to one who then runs onto the ball.

Throw-in

The action taken in returning the ball to play when it has crossed a touchline. The rules and conditions of a throw-in are as follows

1. The throw is taken from the point where the ball crossed the touchline.
2. Both feet of the thrower must either be on the touchline or on the ground inside the touchline.
3. The throw is delivered with both hands from behind and over the head.
4. The thrower may not play the ball again until it has been touched by another player.
5. A goal cannot be scored from a throw-in.
6. Defending players may not intentionally distract or impede the thrower.
7. In taking a throw-in, some part of the player's body must face the field of play.
8. A player who receives the ball direct from a throw-in cannot be offside.

Throw-ins have been part of the game since the first modern rules were established in the early nineteenth century. The Harrow Rules of c. 1835 required a throw-in when the ball passed over either the touchline or the goal line, and could be delivered in any direction the player chose.

Beginning with the Cambridge University Rules of 1848, however, throw-ins were restricted to balls that crossed the touchline only. This innovation extended to all subsequent codes. The Cambridge Rules, as well as the Sheffield Rules of 1857, specified that the throw-in must be delivered in a perpendicular direction from the touchline.

The freedom to throw in any direction a player chooses was reintroduced in The Football Association Laws of the Game in 1863. The one-handed throw was lawful under all these early codes. Scottish teams, however, developed a two-handed throw-in and adopted it into their rules, but in England, the two-hand throw-in was resisted until the mid-1870s.

Finally, in 1882, The Football Association agreed to adopt the two-hand rule in an effort to lessen tension that had built up between the English and Scottish associations. Since then, the throw-in as we now know it has remained largely unchanged.

Touch

The area of the playing field that is outside the two touchlines. Hence, a ball "in touch" has crossed over a sideline and is out-of-bounds.

The term has survived from the eighteenth and early nineteenth centuries when in most types of football, the ball was touched down out-of-bounds to register a score. As early as the Harrow Rules of c. 1835, English rulemakers differentiated between a ball "in touch" and one "behind." A throw-in was required for a "touch" ball or one that crossed over the opponent's goal line, and a kickout was specified when the ball went "behind" one's own goal line.

In the Cambridge University Rules of 1848, all balls "in touch" were thrown in, and all balls "behind" were kicked out. The Cambridge rule, which distinguishes between the two out-of-bound areas, remains in modern Laws XV and XVI.

Transfer

The movement of a player from one club to another. *See also* **Signing-on fee.**

Trap

To interrupt the line of flight of a ball, and gain possession by any lawful use of the body. There are numerous ways to trap a ball, among them the inside-of-the-foot trap, outside-of-the-foot trap, chest trap, thigh trap, stomach trap, and sole trap (with the bottom of the foot), as well as those that use the head or lower part of the leg.

Trip

To intentionally throw an opponent with the feet or legs, causing him to stumble or lose balance; or to intentionally stoop in front of or behind an opponent, causing him to be thrown. The offended side is awarded a direct free kick. An attempt to trip is also penalized by a direct free kick.

Tripping has been prohibited by all football codes since the first rules were drawn up in the early nineteenth century, i.e., Harrow Rules, Cambridge Rules, Sheffield Rules, and Football Association Laws of the Game. *See also* **Hack.**

Tsu chu

The ancient Chinese game of football, *tsu chu,* was first played during the reign of Emperor Huang-Ti (c. 2500 B.C. Historians believe this is the earliest date ever associated with a football game of any kind. During the Ts'in Dynasty (255-206) B.C., and possibly as early as the period of the contending states in the fourth century B.C., some form of the game is known to have been used in training soldiers. Records also show that it was played extensively during the Han Dynasty (206 B.C.-220 A.D.)

"Tsu" translates as "kicking a ball with one's feet"; *"chu"* refers to "a stuffed ball made of animal skin." *Tsu chu,* as well as the Japanese game *kemari,* is in some ways more closely related to modern soccer than the more famous Greek game *episkyros* and Roman *harpastum.* It appears to have been played in front of the emperor's palace in celebration of his birthday. Two elements of play have been reconstructed from Han sources by Chinese scholars. A net, or mesh, was stretched between two 30-foot high bamboo poles, and the players attempted to kick a ball through a gap in the net.

Players dribbled the ball and were allowed to use their chests, backs, and shoulders to keep the ball from the opposing team. Historians have emphasized the importance of the players' ability to dribble.

No evidence of a direct historical link between *tsu chu* and the modern game has been found, though one or two Italian historians have suggested that medieval Italian explorers brought back a forerunner of *calcio* from China around the time of Marco Polo.

Volley

A kick that is taken before the ball touches the ground. Volleys are usually made with either the side or instep of the foot. An overhead volley is any kick taken before the ball touches the ground and is directed over the kicker's own head, whether or not the player has both feet off the ground. *See also* **Half-volley** and **bicycle kick.**

Wall

A closely knit line of defenders, which is usually positioned between the ball and the goal to prevent a direct free kick from scoring. The wall must be at least ten yards from the ball.

Wall pass

The **give-and-go** A player passes to a nearby teammate, and immediately runs to a third position in order to receive his teammate's deflection of the original pass. The teammate is used, in effect, as a rebounding wall.

Wasted ball

A pass or shot on goal that is seriously off its mark, usually one that crosses the touchline or goal line; a very bad kick.

Whistles

It is generally accepted that a whistle was used for the first time by a referee at Nottingham, England in 1878 during a match between Sheffield Norfolk and Nottingham Forest.

APPENDIX C: EARLY RULES

THE HARROW GAME

The English public schools—Harrow, Eton, Charterhouse, Westminster, Shrewsbury and Uppingham—whose indigenous ball games of the early nineteenth century were the forerunners of modern soccer each made a contribution to the development of the game, but among them Harrow stands out for the consistency and longevity of its influence.

At Harrow, the dribbling game was dominant, and running with the ball and passing by hand were banned altogether, as was hacking, another early rugby characteristic. Methods of scoring now associated with rugby, such as "tries" and "touchdowns," were not part of the Harrow game: the only way to score a goal was by sending the ball over the goal line and between the poles. And it is likely that Harrow was the first school to settle on 11 players to a team (as early as 1814), rather than the limitless number found in other school games.

Although football at Harrow had achieved a semblance of organization by 1815, the Rules of the Harrow Game as we now understand them probably date from the 1830s. Their influence is seen to some extent in the formulation of the Cambridge University Rules, which were also central in the drafting of the Laws of the Game.

The Harrow rules were designed to accommodate the peculiarities of playing in fields that lay at the foot of a hill. Drainage was poor, and considerable movement of players, as well as an unusually large ball, were required to keep the game lively.

The goals, called "bases," consisted of two 12-foot-high poles, and Harrow boys initiated another custom for important games: a school uniform that consisted of white pants and, on certain occasions, black gaiters.

The following text is representative of the rules of the Harrow Game from 1830 on:

1. The choice of bases is determined by tossing: the side that wins the toss must have the choice of bases, the side that loses has the right to kick off.

2. The bases must be 18 feet in width, and the distance between them not greater than 150 yards. The width of the ground must not be more than 100 yards.

3. The ball must be kicked off from the middle of the ground, half way between the two bases. A base may not be obtained unless the ball has touched one of the opposite side to the kicker previously to passing between the base poles.

4. When the ball is kicked, anyone on the same side as the kicker is entitled to kick or catch it, provided that at the same time of the delivery of the kick he is not nearer the line of the opponents' base than the kicker. If he is nearer he is "offside," and virtually out of the game till the Ball has been touched by one of the opposite side. Nor may he interfere with anyone of the opposite side, or in any way prevent or obstruct his kicking or catching the ball.

5-9. (These refer to peculiarities of the Harrow game that have little bearing on the laws of the game.)

10. The ball, if kicked beyond the prescribed limits of the ground, must be thrown in again (at least six yards from the thrower) by one of the opposite side to the player who shall have last touched the ball, and his throw may be made in any direction, but may not obtain a base unless the ball has previously touched one of the players. In making the throw, the thrower may not hold the ball by the lace, nor may he touch the ball after the throw, until it has been touched by one of the other players.

11. From behind his own base a player must kick the ball instead of throwing it, the preliminary run not being longer than three running strides from the base line. From behind the opponent's base the throw must be straight in, and may be of any length. In the first case the kicker, and in the second the thrower, must not again touch the ball until it has been touched by another player. (Neither in Rule 10 nor in this rule does Rule 4 apply.)

12. All charging is fair, but no holding, tripping, pushing with hands, shinning, or back-shinning, either of the ball or the players, is allowed.

13. If the ball strike the base pole and goes through, it shall count as a base, but if, in the opinion of the umpires, it shall have passed over the pole, it shall not count as a base.

14. If the ball strikes the base pole and rebounds into the ground play shall continue.

15. No nails or spikes of any sort are allowed in football boots.

16. There must always be two umpires in a house match, and, if possible, in school matches. Their decision shall be final as to matters of fact, but they are at liberty to refer any question of law to the Committee of the Philathletic Club if they feel unable to decide it at the time.

17. It shall be the duty of the umpires in all football matches to take away a base or "yards" ["yards" referring to Rule 6] unfairly obtained; to award them if clearly and undoubtedly obtained, or stopped by unfair means, and in house matches to put out of the game any player wilfully breaking any of the football rules.

18. If it is necessary to replay a house match, the distance between the base poles shall be doubled, the sides tossing again for choice of bases.

19. After a tie each house is at liberty to play with any alterations or substitutions in its team that it may wish.

20. On the second day of a house match, if a draw be the result, the umpires must compel an extra quarter-of-an-hour to be played, changing ends after seven minutes. The same to apply to Champion House Match on the first day's play if it be a draw, at the end of the hour.

Cambridge Rules

Of all the English schools and universities associated with the birth of modern soccer, Cambridge University holds the most important place. The football rules formulated at Cambridge in 1848 more closely resembled and anticipated the first Laws of the Game (1863) than any before them, and the revised Cambridge codes that were written during the 15 years after 1848 proved to be the model on which the Laws themselves were based.

As it happened, most of the students who drafted the first Cambridge rules in 1848 were graduates of public schools where the dribbling game was dominant, and their rules reflected this fact. The text of the 1848 rules has not survived, but a derivative code drawn up between 1854 and 1858 by the University Football Club has been preserved. They included:

2. At the commencement of play, the ball shall be kicked off from the middle of the ground; after every goal there shall be a kickoff in the same way or manner.

3. After a goal, the losing side shall kick off; the sides changing goals unless a previous arrangement be made to the contrary.

4. The ball is out when it has passed the line of the flag-posts on either side of the ground, in which case it shall be thrown in straight.

5. The ball is "behind" when it has passed the goal on either side of it.

6. When the ball is behind, it shall be brought forward at the place where it left the ground not more than ten paces, and kicked off.

7. Goal is when the ball is kicked through the flag-posts and under the string.

8. When a player catches the ball directly from the foot, he may kick it as he can without running with it. In no other case may the ball be touched with the hands, except to stop it.

9. If the ball has passed a player and has come from the direction of his own goal, he may not touch it till the other side have kicked it, unless there are more than three of the other side before him. No player is allowed to loiter between the ball and the adversaries' goals.

10. In no case is holding a player, pushing with the hands, or tripping up allowed. Any player may prevent another from getting to the ball by any means consistent with this rule.

11. Every match shall be decided by a majority of goals.

Although many details are left to doubt, these rules clearly anticipate modern soccer. For example, the offside rule (Rule 9) more closely resembles the modern concept of offside than does the offside rule in the original Laws of the Game. Points are won only by scoring between the flagposts and beneath a connecting horizontal string (Rule 6).

The mention of string (Rule 7) is unique during this period, and predates its incorporation into the Laws of the Game by almost 20 years. No other method of scoring, such as the "tries" of rugby-oriented games, is mentioned (Rule 7).

Handling the ball is strictly limited to the fair catch (Rule 8), a universal characteristic of football games before 1866. Unlike contemporary handling codes, holding, tripping, and the more severe act of "hacking," are forbidden.

All these characteristics combine to form a game whose appearance would not be unfamiliar to modern soccer fans.

Sheffield Rules

These rules were adopted by the world's first football club, Sheffield F.C., in 1857. The game, as laid down in these rules, may not yet be called "association football," or "soccer," but after the Harrow School Rules and the Cambridge University Rules, the Sheffield Rules were one of the last crucial sets of laws drawn up in anticipation of the Football Association's Laws of the Game in 1863.

Their major significance is the introduction of organized football to the north of England, a part of the country that had the most profound effect on the development of modern soccer.

The Sheffield Rules are linked with soccer rather than rugby, because their primary characteristic was the dribbling rather than the handling game, though it is clear that limited handling of the ball was permitted.

Comparative studies of the Sheffield Rules and those of Harrow and Cambridge reveal many common elements between them. Hacking, for example, was forbidden by all three codes, and Sheffield's fair catch rule (Rule 3) bears a strong resemblance to the Cambridge (1854-58) fair catch rule (Rule 8) and Harrow's three-yard rule (Harrow Rule 6).

Handling of the ball is limited to the fair catch and a quick free kick with the ball in the player's hands, and to changing the direction of the ball with one's hands without actually catching the ball. In Sheffield Rule 11 the earliest mention of differing team colors was made.

The Sheffield Rules wielded much influence in northern English counties. They were immediately adopted by Hallam Football Club, also founded in 1857 and Sheffield's first rival, and in 1862 by Notts County Football Club, the oldest club still in English League competition today.

As the influence of the new London-based Football Association of 1863 spread, the competition for recognition by those who supported The Football Association Laws of the Game and those playing by the Sheffield Rules caused England to be divided roughly into two camps. Allegiance was based primarily on geographical location as a matter of convenience.

But in 1877 the Sheffield Football Association (founded 1867) and the Football Association agreed on common rules. The Sheffield Rules' existence as a separate code vanished with that agreement.

The text of those old rules follows:

1. The kick off from the middle must be a place kick.

2. Kick out must not be from more than 25 yards out of goal.

3. Fair catch is a catch from any player provided the ball has not touched the ground or has not been thrown from touch and is entitled to a free kick.

4. Charging is fair in case of a place kick (with the exception of a kick off as soon as the player offers to kick) but he may always draw back unless he has actually touched the ball with his foot.

5. Pushing with hands is allowed but no hacking or tripping up is fair under any circumstances whatever.

6. No player may be held or pulled over.

7. It is not lawful to take the ball off the ground (except in touch) for any purpose whatever.

8. The ball may be pushed on or hit with the hand, but holding the ball except in the case of a free kick is altogether disallowed.

9. A goal must be kicked but not from touch nor by a free kick from a catch.

10. A ball in touch is dead, consequently the side that touches it down must bring it to the edge of the touch and throw it straight out from touch.

11. Each player must provide himself with a red and dark blue flannel cap, one colour to be worn by each side.

Rules of 1863

The text of the Cambridge University Rules of 1863, which appeared only weeks before the original Laws of the Game and influenced them immeasurably, is as follows:

1. The length of the ground shall not be more than 150 yards, and the breadth not more than 100 yards. The ground shall be marked out by posts, and two posts shall be placed on each side-line at distances of 25 yards from each goal-line.

2. The goals shall consist of two upright poles at a distance of 15 feet from each other.

3. The choice of goals and kick-off shall be determined by tossing and the ball shall be kicked off from the middle of the ground.

4. In a match when half the time agreed upon has elapsed, the sides shall change goals when the ball is next out of play. After such change or a goal obtained, the kick-off shall be from the middle of the ground in the same direction as before. The time during which the game shall last and the numbers on each side are to be settled by the heads of the sides.

5. When a player has kicked the ball, anyone of the same side who is nearer to the opponents' goal-line is out of play and may not touch the ball himself nor in any way whatsoever prevent any other player from doing so.

6. When the ball goes out of the ground by crossing the side-lines, it is out of play and shall be kicked straight into the ground from the point where it is first stopped.

7. When a player has kicked the ball beyond the opponents' goal-line, whoever first touches the ball when it is on the ground with his hand, may have a free kick bringing the ball straight out from the goal-line.

8. No player may touch the ball behind his opponents goal-line, who is behind it when the ball is kicked there.

9. If the ball is touched down behind the goal-line and beyond the line of the side-posts, the free kick shall be from the 25-yards post.

10. When a player has a free kick, no one of his own side may be between him and his opponents' goal-line, and no one of the opposite side may stand within 15 yards of him.

11. A free kick may be taken in any manner the player may choose.

12. A goal is obtained when the ball goes out of the ground by passing between the poles or in such a manner that it would have passed between them had they been of sufficient height.

13. The ball, when in play, may be stopped by any part of the body, but may not be held or hit by the hands, arms or shoulders.

14. All charging is fair, but holding, pushing with the hands, tripping up and shinning are forbidden.

The offside rule (Rule 5), the appearance of the goal (Rule 2), and the method of scoring (Rule 12) in these rules were less similar to modern soccer than their counterparts in the Cambridge rules of 1854-58, but handling and hacking were expressly ruled out (Rules 13 and 14), and the spirit and sophistication of the revised Cambridge code ended one era and prefaced another.

There were also other forces in early rules-making, those clubs playing the game outside of school frameworks. They eventually became the first great soccer clubs of England as the game they played diverged from rugby.

Appendix D: Cup Competition

A knockout tournament or series, in which the winning side is the only team to remain undefeated, is distinct from a league competition, in which the winning side is the team that has accumulated the most points and stands at the top of a table.

In most countries cup competition allows clubs on all levels to play one another, regardless of divisional standing in the league. A lower division club has the opportunity to knock out a first division club, and it is this possibility that gives a cup competition its dramatic appeal.

Cup competitions are played throughout the course of the soccer season on alternating dates with the league schedule.

Cup competitions are relatively uncommon in most team sports, except in play-off series, but their tradition in soccer is almost as old as the modern game itself. This was the original form of competition devised by English organizers after the founding of The Football Association in 1863.

The first cup competition, The Football Association Challenge Cup (F.A., Cup), was launched in 1871, 17 years before the first English league. As the game spread across Europe in the last decades of the nineteenth century, the knockout format was adopted more readily than league competition, though it gave way gradually to the rising popularity of leagues by World War I.

Its prestige in the British Isles, however, has always remained high. In England, the F.A. Cup often draws more enthusiastic support than the First Division of the Football League. In Wales, where a national league does not exist, the Welsh Cup takes on a significance all its own.

Central European countries, on the other hand, have seldom given their national cups more than secondary notice, even though the Union of European Football Associations introduced an international competition for all national cup winners, the European Cup Winners' Cup, in 1960. Competition in this tournament rekindled interest in cup competitions in other parts of Europe.

Cup competitions have also been organized in many nations of Africa, and a small number of Asian states have introduced their versions of national cups. In 1975, the African Football Confederation launched the annual African Cup Winners' Cup along the same lines as its European counterpart. In Latin America, national cup competitions as adjuncts to league competitions are unknown, though some levels of league play are conducted on a knockout basis.

MAJOR CUP WINNERS

EUROPEAN CUP CHAMPIONS

AC Milan, Italy (4)

1963, vs. Benfica Lisbon, Portugal, 2-1; 1969, vs. Ajax Amsterdam, Holland, 4-1; 1989, vs. Steaua Bucharest, Romania, 4-0; 1990, vs. Benfica Libson, Portugal, 1-0.

Ajax Amsterdam, Holland (3)

1971, vs. Panathinaikos, Athens, Greece 2-0; 1972, vs. Inter Milan, Italy, 2-0; 1973, vs. Juventus, Turin, Italy, 1-0.

Aston Villa, England(1)

1982, vs. Bayern Munich, West Germany, 1-0.

FC Barcelona, Spain(1)

1992, vs. Sampdoria Genoa, Italy, 1-0 after extra time.

Bayern Munich, West Germany (3)

1974, vs. Atletico Madrid, Spain 4-0 in replay after 1-1 draw; 1975, vs. Leeds United, England, 2-0; 1976, 1-0 vs. St. Etienne, France.

Benfica Lisbon, Portugal (2)

1961, vs. FC Barcelona, Spain 3-2; 1962 vs. Real Madrid, Spain, 5-3.

Celtic, Glasgow, Scotland (1)

1967, vs. Inter Milan, Italy, 2-1.

Feyenoord, Rotterdam, Holland (1)

1970, vs. Glasgow Celtic, Scotland, 2-1 after extra time.

Inter, Milan<Subhead 2>, Italy (2)

1964, vs. Real Madrid, Spain 3-1; 1965, vs. Benfica, Lisbon, Portugal, 1-0.

Juventus, Turin, Italy(1)

1985, vs. Liverpool, England, 1-0.

Liverpool, England (4)

1977 vs. Borussia Moenchengladbach, West Germany, 3-1; 1978, vs. FC Bruges, Belgium, 1-0; 1981, vs. Real Madrid, Spain, 1-0; 1984, vs. AS Roma, Italy, 4-2 on penalties after 1-1 draw.

Manchester United, England (1)

1968, vs. Benfica, Lisbon, Portugal, 4-1 after extra time.

Nottingham Forest, England (2)

1979, vs. Malmo FF, Sweden, 1-0; 1980, vs. SV Hamburg, West Germany, 1-0.

FC Porto, Portugal(1)

1987, vs. Bayern Munich, West Germany, 2-1.

PSV Eindhoven, Holland (1)

1988, vs. Benfica Lisbon, Portugal, 6-5 on penalties after 0-0 draw.

Real Madrid, Spain<Subhead 2> (6)

1956 vs. Stade Reims, France, 4-3; 1957 vs. Fiorentina, Italy, 2-0; 1958, vs AC Milan, Italy, 3-2 after extra time; 1959, vs. Stade Reims, France, 2-0; 1960, vs. Eintracht Frankfurt, West Germany, 7-3; 1966, vs. Partizan-Belgrade, Yugoslavia, 2-1.

Red Star Belgrade, Yugoslavia (1)

1991, vs. Olympique Marseille, France, 5-3 on penalties after 0-0 draw.

Steaua Bucharest, Romania (1)

1986, vs. FC Barcelona, Spain, 2-0 on penalties after 0-0 draw.

SV Hamburg, West Germany (1)

1983, vs. Juventus, Turin, Italy, 1-0.

Aberdeen, Scotland (1)

1983, vs. Real Madrid, Spain, 2-1 after extra time.

AC Milan, Italy (2)

1968, vs. SV Hamburg, West Germany, 2-0; 1973, vs. Leeds United, England, 1-0.

Ajax, Amsterdam, Holland (1)

1987, vs. Lokomotiv Leipzig, East Germany, 1-0.

Anderlecht, Brussels, Belgium (2)

1976, vs. West Ham United, London, England, 4-2; 1978, vs. FK Austria, Vienna 4-0.

Atletico Madrid, Spain (1)

1962, vs. Fiorentina, Florence, Italy, 1-1, 3-0 over two legs.

FC Barcelona, Spain (3)

1979, vs. Fortuna Dusseldorf, West Germany, 4-3 after extra time; 1982, vs. Standard Liege, Belgium, 2-1; 1989, vs. Sampdoria, Genoa, Italy, 2-0.

Bayern Munich, West Germany (1)

1967, vs. Rangers, Glasgow, Scotland, 1-0 after extra time.

Borussia Dortmund, West Germany(1)

1966, vs. Liverpool, England, 2-1 after extra time.

Chelsea, London, England (1)

1971, vs. Real Madrid, 2-1 in replay after extra time after 1-1 draw after extra time.

Everton, Liverpool, England (1)

1985, vs. Rapid Vienna, Austria, 3-1.

Fiorentina, Florence, Italy (1)

1961, vs. Rangers, Glasgow, Scotland, 2-0, 2-1 over two legs.

Juventus, Turin, Italy (1)

1984, vs. FC Porto, Portugal, 2-1.

Dynamo Kiev, Ukraine (2)

1975, vs. Ferencvaros Budapest, Hungary 3-0; 1986, vs. Atletico Madrid, Spain, 3-0. **Note:** When Dynamo Kiev won the Cup their club was a member of the Soviet Union Football Association.

FC Magdeburg, East Germany (1)

1974, 2-0 vs. AC Milan, Italy.

Manchester City, England (1)

1970, vs. Gornik Zabrze, Poland, 2-1.

Manchester United, England (1)

1991, vs. FC Barcelona, Spain, 2-1.

KV Mechelen, Belgium (1)

1988, vs. Ajax Amsterdam, Holland, 1-0.

Rangers, Glasgow, Scotland (1)

1972, vs. Dynamo Moscow, USSR, 3-2.

Sampdoria, Genoa, Italy (1)

1989, vs. Anderlecht, Brussels, Belgium 2-0.

Slovan Bratislava, Czechoslovakia (1)

1969, vs. FC Barcelona, Spain, 3-2.

Sporting Lisbon, Portugal (1)

1964, vs. MTK Budapest, Hungary, 1-0 in replay after 3-3 draw in extra time.

Dynamo Tblissi, Georgia (1)

1981, vs. FC Carl Zeiss Jena, East Germany, 2-1. **Note:** When Dynamo Tblissi won the Cup they were members of the Soviet Union Football Association.

Tottenham Hotspur London, England (1)

1963, vs. Atletico Madrid, Spain, 5-1.

Valencia FC, Spain (1)

1980, vs. Arsenal, London, England 5-4 on penalties after 0-0 extra time draw.

Werder Bremen, West Germany (1)

1992, vs. AS Monaco, France, 2-0.

West Ham United, London, England (1)

1965, vs 1860 Munchen, West Germany, 2-0.

U. E. F. A. Cup Winners

Ajax, Amsterdam, Holland (1)

1992, vs. Torino, Italy 2-2, 0-0.

Anderlecht, Brussels, Belgium (1)

1983 vs. Benfica, Lisbon, 1-0, 1-1.

Arsenal, London, England (1)

1970 vs. Anderlecht, Brussels, Belgium, 1-3, 3-0.

FC Barcelona, Spain (3)

1958, vs. London XI, 2-2, 6-2 ; 1960, vs. Birmingham City, England, 0-0, 4-1; 1966, vs. Real Zaragoza, Spain, 0-1, 4-2.

Eintracht Frankfurt, West Germany (1)

1980, vs. Borussia Moenchengladbach, West Germant, 2-3, 1-0.

Ferencvaros, Budapest, Hungary(1)

1965, vs. Juventus, Turin, Italy, 1-0.

Feyenoord, Rotterdam, Holland (1)

1974 vs. Tottenham Hotspur, England, 2-2, 2-0.

IFK Goteborg, Sweden (2)

1982 vs. SV Hamburg, West Germany 1-0, 3-0; 1987 vs. Dundee United, Scotland, 1-0, 1-1.

Inter Milan, Italy (1)

1991, vs. AS Roma, Italy, 2-0, 0-1.

Ipswich Town, England (1)

1981 vs. AZ67 Alkmaar, Holland, 3-0, 2-4.

Juventus, Turin, Italy (2)

1977, vs. Athletic Bilbao, Spain, 1-0, 1-2; 1990, vs. Fiorentina, Florence, Italy, 3-1, 0-0.

Leeds United, England (2)

1968, vs. Ferencvaros, Budapest, Hungary, 2-2, 1-1; 1971, vs. Juventus, Turin, Italy 2-2, 1-1.

Bayer Leverkusen, West Germany(1)

1988, vs. Espanol, Barcelona, Spain, 3-0, 0-3, 3-2 on penalties.Liverpool, England (2)

1973 vs. Borussia Moenchengladbach, West Germany, 3-0, 2-0; 1976 vs. FC Bruges, Belgium, 3-2, 1-1.

Borussia Moenchengladbach, West Germany (2)

1975 vs. Twente Enschede, Holland 0-0, 5-1; 1979 vs. Red Star, Belgrade, Yugoslavia 1-1, 1-0.

FC Napoli, Italy (1)

1989, vs. VfB Stuttgart, West Germany, 2-1, 3-3.

Newcastle United, England (1)

1969 vs. Ujpest Dozsa, Budapest, Hungary 3-0, 3-2.

PSV Eindhoven, Holland (1)

1978 vs. SEC Bastia, France 0-0, 3-0.

Real Madrid, Spain (2)

1985 vs. Videoton Szekesfehervar, Hungary, 3-0, 0-1; 1986 vs. 1. FC Cologne, West Germany, 5-1, 0-2.

AS Roma, Italy (1)

1961, vs. Birmingham City, England, 2-2, 2-0.

Tottenham Hotspur, London, England (2)

1972 vs. Wolverhampton Wanderers, England, 2-1, 1-1; 1984 vs. Anderlecht, Brussels, Belgium, 1-1, 1-1, 4-3 on penalties.

Valencia, Spain (2)

1962, vs. FC Barcelona, Spain 6-2, 1-1; 1963, vs. Dynamo Zagreb, Yugoslavia, 2-1, 2-0.

Dynamo Zagreb, Yugoslavia(1)

1967, vs. Leeds United, England 2-0, 0-0.

Real Zaragoza, Spain (1)

1964, vs. Valencia, Spain, 2-1.

Copa Libertadores

Argentinos Juniors (1)

1985 vs. America, Cali, Colombia 1-0, 0-0, 1-1, 5-4 on penalties.

Boca Juniors, Argentina (2)

1977, vs. Cruzeiro Belo Horizonte, Brazil 1-0, 0-1, 0-0, 5-4 on penalties; 1978, vs. Deportivo Cali, Colombia, 0-0, 4-0.

Colo Colo, Santiago, Chile (1)

1991 vs. Olimpia Asuncion, Paraguay 0-0, 3-0.

Cruzeiro, Belo Horizonte, Brazil (1)

1976, vs. Ríver Plate, Argentina, 4-1, 1-2, 3-2.

Estudiantes de La Plata, Argentina (3)

1968, vs. Palmeiras, Sao Paulo, Brazil 2-1, 1-3, 2-0; 1969, vs. Nacional Montevideo, Uruguay, 1-0, 2-0; 1970, vs. Penarol Montevideo, Uruguay, 1-0, 0-0.

Flamengo, Rio de Janeiro, Brazil (1)

1981 vs. Cobreloa, Calama, Chile 2-1, 0-1, 2-0.

Gremio Porto Alegre, Brazil (1)

1983 vs. Penarol Montevideo, Uruguay, 1-1, 2-1.

Independiente, Avellaneda, Argentina (7)

1964 vs. Nacional Monteviedo, Uruguay 0-0, 1-0; 1965 vs. Penarol Montevideo, Uruguay 1-0, 1-3, 4-1; 1972, vs. Universitario Lima, Peru 0-0, 2-1; 1973, vs. Colo Colo, Santiago, Chile, 1-1, 0-0, 2-1; 1974 vs. Sao Paulo FC, Brazil, 1-2, 2-0, 1-0; 1975, vs. Union Espanola, Santiago, Chile, 0-1, 3-1, 2-0; 1984, vs. Gremio Porto Alegre, Brazil, 1-0, 0-0.

Nacional-Medellin Colombia (1)

1989 vs. Olimpia Asuncion, Paraguay, 0-2, 2-0, 5-4 on penalties.

Nacional Montevideo, Uruguay (3)

1971, vs. Estudiantes de La Plata, Argentina, 0-1, 1-0, 2-0; 1980, vs. Internacional Porto Alegre, Brazil, 0-0, 1-0; 1988, vs. Newell's Old Boys, Argentina, 0-1, 3-0.

Olimpia, Asuncion, Paraguay (2)

1979 vs. Boca Juniors, Argentina, 2-0, 0-0; 1990, vs. Barcelona, Guayaquil, Ecuador 2-0, 1-1.

Penarol, Montevideo, Uruguay (5)

1960, vs. Olimpia, Asuncion, Paraguay 1-0, 1-1; 1961 vs. Palmeiras, Sao Paulo, Brazil, 1-0, 1-1; 1966 vs. Ríver Plate, Buenos Aires, Argentina, 2-0, 2-3, 4-2 after extra time; 1982 vs. Cobreloa, Calama, Chile, 0-0, 1-0; 1987, vs America Cali, Colombia, 0-2, 2-1, 1-0.

Racing Club, Avellaneda, Argentina (1)

1967, vs. Nacional Montevideo, Uruguay, 0-0, 0-0, 2-1.

Ríver Plate, Argentina (1)

1986 vs. America Cali, Colombia, 2-1, 1-0.

Santos FC, Brazil (2)

1962 vs. Penarol, Montevideo, Uruguay 2-1, 2-3, 3-0; 1963, vs. Boca Juniors, Argentina, 3-2, 2-1.

Sao Paulo FC, Brazil (1)

1992 vs. Newell's Old Boys, Argentina 0-1, 1-0, 3-2 on penalties.

INTERCONTINENTAL CUP FINALS

1960: Real Madrid defeated Penarol 0-0, 5-1.
1961: Penarol defeated Benfica 0-1, 5-0, 2-1.
1962: Santos defeated Benfica 3-2, 5-2.
1963: Santos defeated AC Milan 2-4, 4-2, 1-0.
1964: Inter Milan defeated Independiente, 0-1, 2-0, 1-0.
1965: Inter Milan defeated Independiente, 3-0, 0-0.
1966: Penarol defeated Real Madrid, 2-0, 2-0.
1967: Racing Club defeated Celtic, 0-1, 2-1, 1-0.
1968: Estudiantes defeated Manchester United, 1-0, 1-1.
1969: AC Milan defeated Estudiantes, 3-0, 1-2.
1970: Feyenoord defeated Estudiantes, 2-2, 1-0.
1971: Nacional Montevideo defeated Panathinaikos, Athens 1-1, 2-1.
1972: Ajax defeated Independiente 1-1, 3-0.
1973: Independiente defeated Juventus, 1-0.
1974: Atletico Madrid defeated Independiente, 0-1, 2-0.
1975: Not played.
1976: Bayern Munich defeated Cruzeiro, 2-0, 0-0.
1977: Boca Juniors defeated Borussia Moenchengladbach, 2-2, 3-0.
1978: Not played.
1979: Olimpia defeated Malmo, 1-0, 2-1.
1980: Nacional Montevideo defeated Nottingham Forest, 1-0.
1981: Flamengo defeated Liverpool, 3-0.
1982: Penarol defeated Aston Villa, 2-0.
1983: Gremio defeated SV Hamburg, 2-1 after extra time.
1984: Independiente defeated Liverpool, 1-0.
1985: Juventus defeated Argentinos Juniors, 2-2, 4-2 on penalties.
1986: Ríver Plate defeated Steaua Bucharest, 1-0.
1987: FC Porto defeated Penarol, 2-1 after extra time.
1988: Nacional Montevideo defeated PSV Eindhoven 2-2, 7-6 on penalties.
1989: AC Milan defeated Nacional-Medellin, 1-0 after extra time.
1990: AC Milan defeated Olimpia, 3-0.
1991: Red Star Belgrade defeated Colo Colo, 3-0.
1992: Sao Paulo defeated Barcelona, 2-1.

APPENDIX E: STADIA

Excluding the Indianapolis Motor Speedway, all of the world's largest sports facilities have been built primarily or exclusively for soccer. There are two basic stadium designs. The first, known commonly as the "English" style, is rectangular in shape and is characterized by stands or terraces that hug the field closely on all four sides.

English-styled grounds are known for their intimate atmosphere as a result of the crowd's proximity to action on the field, and, with less than a half-dozen exceptions, are found throughout the British Isles. There are also some examples in the Benelux countries, France, Spain, Italy, Switzerland, and West Germany.

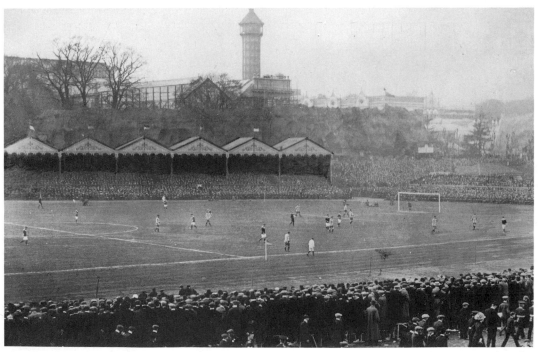

Popperphoto

The Crystal Palace

The second design is the more common oval shape, which generally allows for a diversification of activities, such as track and field and nonsporting events. Most of the world's largest stadiums fall into this category. Of the 23 grounds with a capacity of 100,000 spectators or more, only one resembles the "English" style: Bernabeu.

Seven of the world's 10 largest stadiums are located in Brazil. All are variations of the oval design, and almost all have been built since 1960. The instigation for this surge of great stadium construction was the extraordinary Maracana in Rio, which was built for the 1950 World Cup finals and remains the largest stadium in the world. Its perfectly oval shape and futuristic design has provided the basic concept for many of Brazil's giant futebol facilities.

Nine stadiums with a capacity of 100,000 or more are located in South America; six are in Europe, four in Asia, and two each in Africa and North America.

The first stadium to have a 100,000 capacity was the old Crystal Palace ground in South London (demolished in 1915), which was the site for the F.A. Cup final from 1895-1914.

The first recording of a soccer crowd reaching over 100,000 was at Crystal Palace for the cup final of 1901, when 110,820 fans watched Tottenham Hotspur draw the Sheffield United, 2-2.

The oldest home site for any league club in the world is the Recreation Ground of England's Chesterfield F.C. This location has been in continual use by the Derbyshire club since its founding in 1866. It was originally named the New Recreation Ground, and presently holds 28,500 spectators.

The following is a list of those stadiums whose official capacities are said to be 100,000 or more. Figures in parentheses indicate actual highest recorded attendances if official capacity is exceeded.

—————————————————————————————

1. Mario Filho (Maracana), Rio de Janeiro, Brazil: 220,000
2. Pinheirao, Curtiba, Brazil: 180,000
3. Morumbi, So Paulo, Brazil: *150,000
4. Hampden Park, Glasgow, Scotland (149,547) **134,580
5. Alacid Nunes, Belem, Brazil: 120,000
6. Placido Castelo, Fortaleza, Brazil: 120,000
7. Beira Rio, Porto Alegre, Brazil: 110,000
8. Magalhaes Pinto-Mineirao, Belo Horizonte, Brazil: 110,000
9. Senajan Stadium, Djakarta, Indonesia: 110,000
10. Estadio Azteca, Mexico City, Mexico (110,000): 108,499
11. Lenin Stadium, Moscow, Russia: 104,000
12. Estadio Santiago Bernabeu, Madrid, Spain (134,000): 101,663
13. Stade Ahmadou-Ahidjo, Yaounde, Cameroon: 100,000
14. Aria Mehre, Karadj Auto Band, Iran: 100,000
15. Estadio de la Ciudad Universitaria, Mexico City, Mexico: 100,000
16. Corporation Stadium, Calicut, India: 100,000
17. Eden Garden Stadium, Calcutta, India: 100,000
18. Empire Stadium, Wembley, England (126,047)***: 100,000
19. Kirov Stadium, Leningrad, Russia: 100,000
20. Nasser Stadium, Cairo, Egypt: 100,000
21. Otavio Mangabeira, Salvador, Brazil: 100,000
22. Rei Pelé, Maceid, Brazil: 100,000
23. Zentralstadion, Leipzig, Germany: 100,000

*Cambodian officials list the capacity of the Camplexe Sportif National in Phnom-Penh at 170,000, but this is thought to be the combined figure for all the facilities at this location rather than a single stadium.

**Hampden Park is limited to a capacity of 134,000, but it was actually measured to accommodate 183,570.

***Turnstiles recorded this record figure on opening day in 1923, but it was estimated that as many as 200,000 may have entered the stadium.

WEMBLEY: THE EMPIRE STADIUM

In 1921 the Prince of Wales urged that the showpiece for the newest (and last) British Empire Exhibition (1924) should be "a great national sports ground" that would be the mecca for world soccer and an escape that would "appeal to all Britishers" on grand sporting occasions.

Wembley Stadium became just that, and 55 years after its completion it remains the most famous and hallowed soccer venue in the world. In the late 1970s, its official capacity of 100,000 was reduced slightly for safety reasons, thus ending the era when an automatic 100,000 spectators were expected for F.A. Cup finals and important international matches.

But the true significance of Wembley is in its mystique: the apparent need for the world's most popular sport to have at least one location that serves as a kind of unofficial headquarters or focal point. It is no longer the world's largest stadium—it now ranks about twentieth—but there is seldom a player, whether he has traveled from as far away as Rio de Janeiro or as nearby as the northwest London suburb of Wembley itself, who has not commented on the thrill he experiences when emerging from the tunnel to the deafening chants of a Wembley crowd.

Ground was broken at Wembley by the Duke of York, later King George VI, in January 1922, and within one year the stadium was completed, an astounding rate of construction that has yet to be equaled for a facility of this size. Though its official opening had already taken place, its real inauguration was the first Wembley F.A. Cup final on April 28, 1923, between Bolton Wanderers and West Ham United, the famous "White Horse Final."

Turnstile operators officially let in 126,047 spectators on that day, but at least 150,000 and probably 200,000 people got into the stadium, and another 100,000 hovered just outside. There were so many people that the crowd filled the playing area solidly from goal to goal.

Incredibly, this sea of humanity remained calm, and the occasion was characterized by a total absence of misbehavior or trouble of any kind. Worried officials met to plan a way to disperse the crowd so that the game could get underway, but they decided instead to call the match off.

Before the announcement could be made, Police Constable George Storey—soon to become a legend in English folklore—appeared on the field mounted atop his shining white stallion Billie, and single-handedly nudged and coaxed until everyone was pushed back to the edge of the playing area. The players were called out of the locker rooms, and the game commenced before an undetermined number of people.

Spectators were so tightly packed around the field that one goal was disputed because it was thought that a fan sitting on the goal line had kept the ball in play with his foot. The game ended with a 2-0 win for Bolton, and the next day photographs of Billie and the crowd he gently brought under control were on the front page of every newspaper in the country.

The Empire Stadium is owned by a private corporation and is the regular site for England's home games, the F.A. Cup final, the Football League Cup final, the P.A. Charity Shield, the P.A. Amateur Cup, the F.A. Challenge Vase, the annual University Match (Oxford vs. Cambridge), as well as Rugby league, boxing, track and field meets (it was the principal stadium for the 1948 Olympic Games), hockey, show-jumping, and assorted festivals. Nearby is the Empire Pool, London's major indoor sports arena.

In 1962, the roof at Wembley was extended around the entire seating (and standing) area, and it was built of fiberglass, rather than concrete or metal, to allow in sunlight.

APPENDIX F: WITCHCRAFT

Witchcraft shrouds the sport in some parts of Africa, especially in the East African nations of Kenya, Uganda, and Tanzania. It is reported that in Kenya, 90 percent of all clubs in the upper divisions of the league employ witch doctors. Although African sports officials have sought to stamp out such occult elements, the practitioners of the ancient science have apparently gained a strong foothold in at least these three countries.

The Report of the XIIth General Assembly of the African Football Confederation (1976) specifically mentions the witchcraft problem: "We would like to seize this opportunity to launch an appeal to all African member associations asking them to strive in order to free the African sport from all the evils which obstruct the realization of the noble objectives which we have chosen.

These evils take the form of tribalism, ju-ju and other primitive [forms of magic] which have always been encouraged in our countries and among our people by colonialism in the hope of obliterating the African personality and controlling our people."

In addition, the Kenya Football Association has attempted to impound paraphernalia used by witch doctors, but this effort seems to have been unsuccessful.

The function of the witch doctor is to cast spells on his client's opponent. In return for this, the modern football witch doctor is paid between £5 and £175 per match, depending on the wealth of his club, the importance of a given match, and the stature of the witch doctor. Payment is always made in advance.

To prepare for his wizardry, the witch doctor fasts, concentrates on his mission for a period of time, and eventually performs a variety of chants. Many witch doctors now employ Islamic as well as pagan prayers. The most intense prayer periods occur just before the game in question. Mirrors may be used by the witch doctor to cast a reflection of the opponent so that easier contact can be made. Some spells may be cast on the ball itself.

Several players have described how their game ball has suddenly turned into a snake as they were about to make contact with it on the field. Other spells are said to result in goalkeepers seeing two balls at once when a shot is made. Opposing players of a team known to employ witch doctors often avoid certain areas of the stadium in fear of cast spells.

Potions are also an essential ingredient. They are eaten, worn, or placed around the field prior to a game, and usually consist of herbs, powdered animal and snake skins, roots, or a variety of murky liquids.

Witchcraft in East Africa is the last remaining pagan rite connected with organized soccer, but unlike the deeply seeded ritual of pre-Columbian games, its motivation is primarily monetary rather than spiritual. Though it is likely to linger for years to come, witchcraft in soccer inevitably faces a slow but eventual decline.

AP/Wide World Photos

One of Kenya's soccer witch doctors has words with members of his team at tense moment during a 1964 match.

APPENDIX G: PRE-COLUMBIAN GAMES

The pre-Columbian ball games of Mexico and Central America were among the most advanced football-oriented games outside the direct lineage of modern soccer. Variations were played by the Aztecs *(tlachtli)*, Maya *(pokyah)*, Zapotecs *(táladzi)*, and possibly others, from roughly 600 A.D. to the destruction of the last pre-Columbian civilization in the sixteenth century (though some evidence exists of a similar ball game as early as 500 B.C.).

Archaeological digs from Arizona to Honduras reveal wide geographical dispersion of the games, and their depiction in all forms of pre-Columbian art—particularly ceramics and sculpture—has given us a marvelously clear picture of their characteristics and cultural significance.

In their most common form, the games were played in a recessed court 40 to 50 feet long and shaped like the letter "I." The vertical walls surrounding the playing area were quite high, and in the middle of either wall, along the stem of the "I," a stone or wooden ring was mounted vertically (i.e., at right angles to a basketball hoop). The object was to project a hard rubber ball through one of the rings; only the feet, legs, hips, and elbows could be used.

A player's most important tool was his skill in juggling the ball without the use of hands. Aztec players wore loincloths attached to leather belts and wore leather protection for their hips, groin, thighs, and elbows.

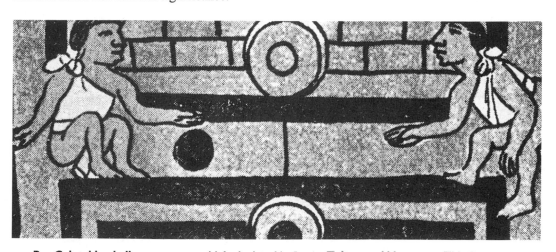

Pre-Columbian ball games were widely depicted in Azetc, Toltec, and Mayan art. This Aztec vase painting shows the games "I"-shaped court, two goals (the two rings), a round ball, and two players.

Mayan garb was similar, but it was embellished by colorful costumes and tall headdresses. In *táladzi,* the "goals" were not vertical rings but two rectangular niches carved out of the wall, one each at the northeastern and southeastern corners of the "I."

These games were not only the most popular sporting activities of the day but also lay at the center of the religious life of the pre-Columbian culture. Players' activities before and after each game were ritualistically supervised by religious leaders, perhaps the king himself, and ball courts were usually built adjacent to the temple.

In *tlachtli,* losing players humbly submitted to sacrifice at the altar.

Though the games probably reached their peak under the Aztecs at Tenochtitlan (the site of Mexico City), the greatest ball court was that at Chichén Itzá, the Mayan ceremonial center in Yucatán.

Perhaps the most important legacy of these games is the invention of rubber balls, which were developed by unknown ancestors of the Aztecs and introduced to Europeans via the Spanish conquistadors.

INDEX

NOTE: PAGE NUMBERS APPEARING IN BOLD TYPE INDICATE MAIN ENTRIES.

Faroe Islands **180**
Fausto **65**
Fédération Internationale de Football Asso-
    ciation
  See FIFA
field of play **36, 370**
FIFA **307–309**, 352
    Committee for Women's Football **333**
    structure of **309**
Fiji **181**
Finland **181–182**
Finney, Thomas **65–66**
flick **372**
floodlit soccer **372**
flying kick **372**
follis **19**
Football Association (FA) **22, 308**
Football Association in London **31**
Football League **349**
Forest Football Club
  See Wanderers F.C.
Forward **372**
4-2-4 System **45**
4-3-3 System **45**
France **182**
free kick **372**
Fried
  See Friedenreich, Artur
Friedenreich, Artur **66**
friendly **372**
front block tackle **373**
fullback **373**
Fútbol War **26**, **303–306**, 357

G

Gabon **186**
Gallacher, Hugh **67**
Galloping Major of Hungary
  See Puskás, Ferenc
Gambia **186**
Garrincha **67–68**
Gascoigne, Paul **68**

Gento Lopez, Francisco **69**
Georgia **186–187**
Germany, Federal Republic of **187**
Ghana **194**
goal **373**
goal aggregate **373**
goal average **373**
goal difference **373**
goal kick **374**
goal net **374**
goalkeeper **374**
Gold Cup **311**
    See also CONCACAF
Goncalves de Andrade, Eduardo
    See Tostao
Goycochea, Sergio **69**
Greece **200**
Guadeloupe **201**
Guatemala **201–202**
Guinea **202**
Guinea-Bissau **203**
Gullit, Ruud **70**
Guyana **203**

H

hack **375**
Haiti **203**
half time **375**
half volley **376**
halfback **375**
Hamburger SV **349**
hands **376**
harpastum **19**, 341
Harrow Game **397–398**
hat trick **376**
head **376**
Henry II **342**
Heysel Riots **27**
Hidegkuti, Nandor **70**
Hillsborough Tragedy **28**
history of soccer **17**
hold **376**
Hogan, Jimmy **119-120, 190**

S

San Marino **255**
Santos, Djalma **93**
Santos, Nilton **93–94**
Sao Paulo League **352**
Saudi Arabia **255**
save **388**
Scarone, Hector **94**
Schiaffino, Juan **94**
Schillaci, Salvatore **95**
Schlosser, Imre **96**
scissors kick **389**
Scotland **255–256**
Scottish Football Association **22, 347**
Scottish passing game **42**
screen **389**
Seeler, Uwe **96–97**
selection **389**
self-goal **389**
sell a dummy **389**
send off **389**
Senegal **258**
Seychelles **259**
Sheffield F.C. **345**
Sheffield Rules **345, 400–401**
Shilton, Peter **98**
shinguard **390**
shoot-out **390**
shoulder charge **391**
show the ball **391**
sideline **391**
Sierra Leone **259**
signing-on fee **391**
Sindelar, Matthias **98**
Singapore **259–260**
Sivori, Enrique Omar **99**
sixth forward **391**
sliding tackle **391**
Slovenia **259**
snap shot **391**
Solomon Islands **260**
Somalia **260**
South Africa **260**
South American Championship **353**

South American Football Confedera-
  tion **353**
Spain **262–264**
square ball **391**
Sri Lanka **266**
St. Kitts and Nevis **253**
St. Lucia **253**
St. Vincent and the Grenadines **254**
Stoichkov, Hristo **99**
stoppage **391**
stopper **392**
strategy **41-47**
striker **392**
Suarez Miramonte, Luis **100**
substitution rules **37–38, 392**
Sudan **266**
summer tournaments **393**
Sunday shot **393**
Surinam **268**
Sweden **268–271**
sweeper **393**
Swiss bolt formation **44**
Switzerland **272–273**
Syria **277**

T

sackle **394**
tactics **41–47**
Tahiti **278**
táladzi **419**
Tanzania **278–279**
Tesoriero, Americo Miguel **100**
Thailand **278–279**
third back **394**
thirty-five-yard line **394**
through ball **394**
throw-in **394**
timeline of soccer events **341-359**
tlachtli **419**
Togo **279**
Tostao **101**
Total Football **10**

Z